CAMP EUROPE BY TRAIN

Lenore Baken

Sixth Edition

Ariel Publications
Bellevue, WA U.S.A.

Suggestions, criticism and information are welcome from travelers. We will pass them along in the next edition. Please take the trouble to write. A questionnaire is provided at the end of the book.

To order this book, send $12.95 plus $3.00 for express postage (3-day service) to Ariel Publications, 14417 S.E. 19th Place, Bellevue WA 98007. Washington State residents please add sales tax. A personal check is acceptable. (206) 641-0518.

To order a Eurailpass, other railpass or Cook's Timetable, call toll free 1-800-FORSYTH and ask for Department CE, or use the order blank.

We would like to gratefully acknowledge the assistance of many fine representatives in the tourist and railroad offices both here and abroad who gave so generously of their time and knowledge.

A thousand thanks go to our readers who have responded with additional information and suggestions, many of which have been incorporated into this book.

Cover photo: Neuschwanstein Castle, West Germany, courtesy of German National Tourist Office.

ISBN 0-917656-06-7 1295
Library of Congress Catalog Card #89-83530

Published by Ariel Publications, 14417 S.E. 19th Place, Bellevue WA 98007, U.S.A. Manufactured in the U.S.A.

CONTENTS

Camping is the way to go! Our trip was wonderful. Many thanks to your book (the cover is now two layers of tape, due to use!). Loved Europe and decided to stay...plan to travel further for two more years.

Leslie Carter, Kent, WA

Camp, Camp, camp! It's the most fun, really! Also inexpensive! We averaged $3.00 a night camping. Met many fine Europeans and Americans. Had a wonderful, wonderful time. Wouldn't have missed it for the world. If I could say to someone thinking of going to Europe. I would only say--DO IT, DO IT, DO IT--it is the experience of a lifetime. Thanks for a great guidebook! It was really all we needed.

Kathy Carlson, Gardena, CA

Thanks for writing such a great guidebook! It always came through for us.

Kris and Ted Bushek, Eugene, OR

A friend and I left last June for our first trip to Europe, and have used your book quite often as our guide. We've found it to be full of the information that nobody else tells us, but that is vital to getting around and keeping our sanity. Your book saved us a lot of time and money, and often we simply could not have found a camp without it. We would use your book again, and will recommend it to our friends.

Frances Packer, Los Altos Hills, CA

Thanks for publishing such a terrific book. It made our trip much more enjoyable and with fewer worries. We enjoyed the trip so much that we plan to take another as soon as possible.

Mr. and Mrs. Robert Cooper, Batavia, IL

Two years ago I used your book during a very enjoyable trip to Europe. It was a big help. This summer I am taking another trip to Europe, this time for the entire summer, and I want to get the latest edition of your book. Thank you very much, and please keep up the good work.

Scott Taylor, Ames, IA

Thank you for opening up a perfect way to travel in Europe. We found early in our journey that your guidebook was the only one needed and we pitched the others.

Jan Dutton, Overland Park, KS

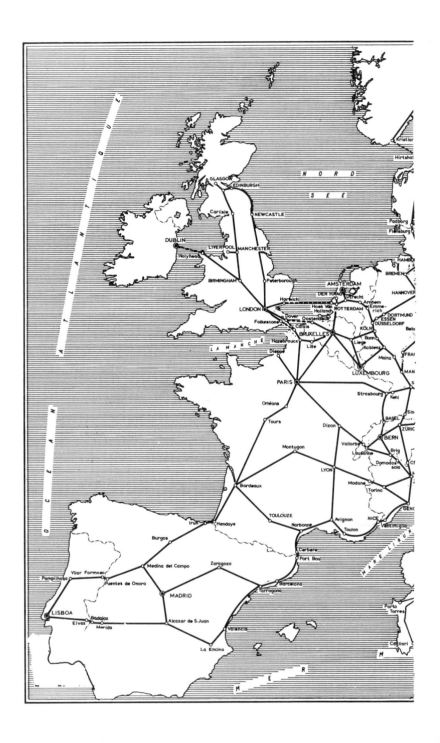

RAIL PASS ORDER BLANK

Name (1st person) _____

Name (2nd person) _____
Address
_____

Daytime Phone
_____

Date of Birth (1st person) _____ (2nd person) _____

Passport No. (1st person) _____ (2nd person) _____

Date of departure from U.S. _____

_____ **Eurailpass** 15 day-$320, 21 day-$398, 1 month-$498, 2 month-$698, 3 month-$860		$_____
_____ **Eurail Youthpass** (through age 25) 1 month-$360, 2 month-$470		$_____
_____ **Eurail Flexipass** - $340 (9 days in 21)		$_____
_____ **Eurail Saverpass** 15 day 1st class $230 each (3 people must travel together)		$_____
_____ **France Railpass** (second class) 4 days in 15 -$99 9 days in 1 month-$160		$_____
_____ **German Tourist Card** (second class) adult 4 days-$81, 9 days-$124, 16 days-$172; **Junior** (through 25) 9 days-$79, 16 days-$99		$_____
_____ **Swiss Pass** (second class) 4 days-$105, 8 days-$125, 15 days-$155, 1 month-$210		$_____
_____ **BritRail Pass** (second class) 8 days-$179, 15 days-$259, 22 days-$339, 1 month-$389; **BritRail Youthpass** (through age 25) 8 days-$149 15 days-$219, 22 days-$289, 1 month-$329		$_____
_____ **BritRail Flexipass** (second class) 4 days in 8-$149, 8 days in 15-$219; **Youthpass** (through age 25) 4 days in 8-$129, 8 days in 15-$189		$_____
_____ **Cook European Timetable** $16.95 plus $3 priority postage		$_____
Please add for Certified Mail and Handling (passes only)		$ 4.25
Total payment enclosed		$_____

Send payment by cashier's check, money order or certified check payable to Forsyth Travel Library Tours. Eurail, French and BritRail passes may be charged to:
_____Mastercard _____Visa _____American Express (not BritRail)

Card No.:_____ Expiration Date _____

Cardholder Name_____

**Please mail to Forsyth Travel Library Tours (CE), PO Box 2975,
Shawnee Mission KS 66201-1375. Toll free 1-800-FORSYTH.**

PREPARING FOR YOUR TRIP

The best kept secret in European travel is that almost all major cities have excellent campgrounds with elaborate facilities that are no more than a 30-minute bus or subway ride from the train station. London costs $2.80 per night, Paris $3.57 and Rome $4.06. For villages, the campground is usually within a 15-minute walk.

This means you can take advantage of the freedom offered by the marvelous European railway system and its unlimited travel Eurailpasses or Eurail Youthpass and keep lodging expenses low by camping. High quality, compact and lightweight backpacks, backpacking tents and down sleeping bags make this possible.

CAMPING EUROPEAN STYLE

European campgrounds are not the rustic, back-to-nature arrangements that come to mind when you think camping. Rather they are facilities set up so Europeans may enjoy the same vacations but at lower cost as people who would be staying in hotels. Many campgrounds occupy some of the most expensive real estate in the city because they are operated by municipal governments on park land. The landscaped sites with carefully tended shrubs and flowers, restrooms with hot showers, laundry rooms with automatic washers and dryers, store, and cooking and dishwashing facilities will bring a measure of convenience to your vacation unobtainable in hotels, pensiones or youth hostels.

Camping also provides an instant community. The friendliness and informality inherent in this unpretentious way of traveling is a major advantage. Camping is worth it alone for all the interesting Europeans, Americans, Australians, South Americans and Canadians that you meet.

2

Because backpackers do not need reservations, camping is the only way to have true flexibility in Europe. It is the rare camp (and we have never found one) that will turn away a camper on foot with a small tent. (The story is different for car or van campers because they can easily go elsewhere.)

Read these descriptions of campgrounds sent by our readers and you will readily see the wonderful opportunity that campgrounds give for low cost touring. *My favorite campground was at Cala Levado, near Tossa de Mar (Costa Brava, Spain). Gorgeous camp--in all different levels on the hill above the coast. Good facilities: very private camp spaces, clean and nice.* (Leslie Carter) *We loved the location of Camp Firenze (Florence, Italy) in an olive grove near Piazaale Michelangelo practically downtown and on a bus line. The view from Camping Reichenau (Innsbruck, Austria) was of the Inn River and the magnificent mountains surrounding Innsbruck. Camping Fontana Bianche (Syracuse, Sicily) was in an almond grove across the street from a beach with some of the most beautiful water I have ever seen.* (Linda Clark)

We stayed at dozens of beautiful campgrounds but we especially liked Le Pylone campground in Biot, France. The grounds were well organized and well taken care of. The van and trailer campers had their area and tent campers had their own area away from the noise of most autos. The sites were pleasingly large and grassy. They were divided by a few small treees on either side. Also, for privacy, each section of sites was divided by waist-high hedges. The campground's location was a great help to us. The train station was only a few blocks away so taking excursions up and down the coast was incredibly easy. (Mr. and Mrs. Robert Cooper)

Camping by train is ideal for the traveler alone, friends, couples or small family. People of all ages, including retired persons and parents with a toddler, have used the previous five editions of this book. The only requirements are being willing to carry a backpack and an adventurous, unpretentious spirit.

THE FANTASTIC EUROPEAN RAILWAY SYSTEM

One of the best things about camping in Europe is that you don't need to have a car. In Europe, lots and lots of people travel by train and they do it all the time. Think of it as a continent-wide rapid transit system. Train travel is frequent and fast between large cities. Paris to Brussels takes two hours and 20 minutes, and Milan to Geneva only four hours. Trains find their way into the smallest hamlet and will take you off the beaten track into the picturesque villages you have come to see.

The railroads provide the most comfortable and stylish mode of travel on the continent. Trains are considerably more relaxing than cars or buses. They are spacious, and allow for reading, conversation and walking around. The plushly upholstered seats invite stretching out to take a nap if you want. When you get there, the station is immediately downtown. A tourist office to assist travelers is inside, and outside is the bus stop for the campground.

The government-subsidized European railroads have made these trains even easier to use by offering unlimited ride train passes. The various kinds of Eurailpasses are valid on trains throughout continental western Europe and (new in 1989) Hungary. Additionally, most countries have their own pass that is valid within its borders. Some countries are simply too small for their pass to be of interest. Other countries price their pass so high that a Eurailpass is the better value.

To determine whether you'll come out ahead with a pass, list the cities you want to see and then calculate the city-to-city fares by referring to the listing in this chapter. If the figures are within $75 of each other, opt for a railpass because its flexibility and time-saving convenience is easily worth at least that. As a general rule, if your plane lands in northern Europe and your plans include Greece, Scandinavia or Rome, a pass is a good buy because the point-to-point fare alone to these destinations represents a substantial portion of the cost of the pass. For instance, second class fare from Amsterdam to Rome is $195 and first class $292.

The passes that are the best buys and most useful are Eurailpasses, and the French and German Railpasses. People over 26 should compare the second class individual country railpasses with the Eurailpass. Second class is perfectly fine in these countries and can represent good savings. If this is your first trip to Europe and have only a month, you would probably come out ahead by combining a second class France railpass with sidetrips over the border to Barcelona in Spain, the Cinque-Terre in Italy, Basel, Switzerland, and Britain. France also borders on Belgium and Germany.

These passes must be purchased before you go. Call toll-free 1-800-FORSYTH, Dept. CE, and charge your pass to national credit cards, or send the order to Forsyth Travel Library (CE), 9154 West 57th St, Shawnee Mission KS 66201. Passport number is required when ordering. See order blank in appendix.

EURAILPASS   Eurailpass is a wallet-sized card that entitles the bearer to unlimited use of first class trains throughout 17 European countries for a specified time period. The 17 countries are Austria, Belgium, Denmark, Finland, France, West Germany, Greece, Hungary, Ireland, Italy, Luxembourg, The Netherlands, Norway, Portugal, Spain, Sweden and Switzerland. A 15-day pass costs $320, 21 days $398, 1 month $498, 2 months $698 and 3 months $860. Children from 4 through 11 pay half these amounts, while those under 4 go free. The price of the pass has gone up about 5 percent at the first of each year in the past. From the day you buy it, you have six months to begin using it.

Here's what you get with Eurailpass. (1) First class travel. First class is more comfortable and less crowded than second class. This is important mainly in Italy and Spain where trains are generally fairly full during July and August. (2) The pass covers all supplements for the fastest and best trains of Europe. (3) Convenience. Except for the initial train ride when the date must be stamped on the Eurailpass to indicate the start date, the pass is used by simply boarding the desired train, finding a seat and showing the pass to the conductor when he checks for tickets sometime during the journey. If you were to purchase each individual ticket within Europe, a half hour could be wasted for each ticket in finding the correct ticket line and then waiting your turn. With Eurailpass you simply hop aboard. The only line waiting to do will be in making reservations, but only one to two, if any, will be needed. (4) Mistake proof. Should you board the wrong train or be in the wrong coach, only time is lost. (5) Bonuses. Some alternative means of transportation are included. The ones worth the most money and most worthwhile are the expensive ferries from Brindisi, Italy, to Greece; Stockholm to Helsinki and France to Ireland. Other bonuses include excursion boats on the Rhine, Mosel and Danube Rivers and on the lakes of Geneva, Zurich and Lucerne. The Romantic and Castle Road Europabuses in Germany are also covered. (6) Some commuter trains within cities. The most important are the S-Bahn trains in German cities. (7) Itinerary flexibility. Since additional miles cost no more, an itinerary can be planned according to the weather rather than on a straight mileage basis.

15-DAY EURAIL SAVERPASS   This is the same as the Eurailpass but is discounted to $230 when three or more people travel together. For travel within October 1 to March 31, only two people need to travel together to qualify. No discount for children, except those under 4 are free. Remember that the "group" must always travel together on the train.

EURAIL FLEXIPASS   This pass is the same as the Eurailpass but can be used only on any 9 days within a 21-day period. The price is $340.

EURAIL YOUTHPASS   This pass can only be bought by those under 26 and its first day of use must occur before the 26th birthday. The cost is $360 for 1 month and $470 for 2 months. It gives unlimited travel in the same countries as Eurailpass but in the second class coaches. New for 1989 is that supplements for the fastest trains are included. The same bonuses apply to Eurail Youthpass as for Eurailpass. You get everything the first class Eurailpass passenger gets but you ride in the second class coaches. This is an excellent value for the itinerary that encompasses Amsterdam, Paris, Madrid, Munich, Rome and Athens.

INTER-RAIL CARD   With proof of prior six months residency in the European country in which you buy it, an Inter-Rail card for one month of rail travel can be bought by anyone under 26 for $260 (subject to currency fluctuations). Buy it at train stations in Europe as it cannot be bought outside of Europe. Try to purchase it a few days before you need it. You get unlimited second class rail travel in 22 countries, except in the country of purchase only a 50 percent reduction is given. It does not include supplements for the faster trains. (In 1989 these have been included in Eurail Youthpass.) A detailed folder comes with the Card. Before you start each journey, the trip must be entered in a log by station personnel and then checked by the conductor as he takes tickets. The Card is valid in Austria, Belgium, Denmark, France, Finland, Greece, Great Britain, Hungary, Italy, Ireland, Luxembourg, Morocco, The Netherlands, Norway, Portugal, Romania, Spain, Sweden, Switzerland, Turkey (European lines only: the route from Athens and Thessaloniki to Istanbul), West Germany and Yugoslavia. Half fare tickets on some private Swiss mountain railways, half fare tickets on Townsend Thoreson between Portsmouth and Le Havre, 30 percent discount on most Sealink shipping services and on Townsend Thoresen between Dover and Ostend, and some ship discounts are included.

The **Inter-Rail + Boat Card** costs about $60 more and includes free travel on the boat to Greece (Adriatica/Hellenic Lines), Irish Continental Line between Le Havre and Cherbourg, France and Ireland, Silja Line between Stockholm and Helsinki and certain others. Not included is travel on sea routes operated by Sealink, Hoverspeed or Townsend Thoreson.

1989 Rail Fares

Amsterdam to:	1st	2nd
Brussels	$ 37	$ 25
Copenhagen	160	115
Florence	263	175
Milan	232	152
Paris	81	56
Rome	292	195

Barcelona to:	1st	2nd
Madrid	$ 66	$ 51
Paris	151	105

Brindisi to:	1st	2nd
Milan	89	63
Rome	62	44
Venice	85	61

Brussels to:	1st	2nd
Amsterdam	$ 37	$ 25
Milan	163	107
Paris	45	31
Rome	223	150

Copenhagen to:	1st	2nd
Helsinki	$146	$ 98

Florence to:	1st	2nd
Amsterdam	$263	$175
Milan	32	23
Paris	168	116
Rome	32	23
Siena	9	7
Venice	26	18

Frankfurt to:	1st	2nd
Milan	$150	$ 98
Paris	102	69
Rome	210	141

Geneva to:	1st	2nd
Milan	$ 72	$ 47
Paris	88	61
Rome	132	90
Venice	98	66

Luxembourg to:	1st	2nd
Milan	$133	$ 88
Rome	193	131

Milan to:	1st	2nd
Amsterdam	$232	$152
Brussels	163	107
Frankfurt	150	98
Munich	78	54
Nice	38	27
Paris	137	93
Zurich	64	42

Munich to:	1st	2nd
Milan	$ 78	$ 54
Rome	113	78
Venice	76	52

Nice to:	1st	2nd
Milan	$ 38	$ 27
Rome	72	51
Venice	64	45

Paris to:	1st	2nd
Amsterdam	$ 81	$ 56
Barcelona	151	105
Brussels	45	31
Florence	168	116
Frankfurt	102	69
Geneva	88	61
Madrid	172	120
Milan	137	93
Rome	173	120
Venice	163	112

Rome to:	1st	2nd
Amsterdam	$292	$195
Athens	210	148
Bari	54	39
Bologna	41	29
Brindisi	62	44
Brussels	223	150
Florence	32	23
Frankfurt	210	141
Geneva	132	90
Genoa	50	35
Luxembourg	193	131
Milan	63	45
Munich	113	78
Naples	22	15
Nice	72	51
Palermo	84	59
Paris	173	120
Venice	57	41
Vienna	136	96
Zurich	127	87

Venice to:	1st	2nd
Brindisi	85	61
Florence	26	18
Geneva	98	66
Milan	27	19
Munich	76	52
Paris	163	112
Rome	57	41
Vienna	82	58
Zurich	90	61

Vienna to:	1st	2nd
Rome	$136	$ 96
Venice	82	58

Zurich to:	1st	2nd
Milan	$ 64	$ 42
Rome	127	87
Venice	90	61

EURAIL TICKET   If you aren't going to buy a rail pass and plan to buy point-to-point tickets instead, the Eurail Ticket is what you get if you buy the tickets here before you go rather then when you get to Europe.   There are certain advantages of doing so, namely a 6-month validity period instead of the 2-month period standard in Europe, and the convenience of prepaying and not having to contend with buying tickets in foreign countries.   Also rates are set at the beginning of each year and the Eurail tariff is used for the entire year despite currency fluctuations.   Of course, you must have your exact itinerary figured when the ticket is bought.   A passenger is allowed to make any stopover enroute with his ticket within the validity period of 6 months.   It is also not necessary to have the tickets validated at any of the stations where the trip is interrupted.   The only thing the traveler has to do is to make sure he keeps the tickets in his possession which have not been used.   The price of the ticket is based on the regular cost of the ticket less any discounts that may apply to that partiuclar journey.

There is also a Eurail tariff for groups which offers a discount of about 30 percent when at least 10 to 24 people travel together.   Also, many European railroads offer a youth group rate which is close to 50 percent less for a minimum of 10 people under 21 years of age, which includes one adult chaperon.   Contact any U.S. office of a European Railroad.

YOUTH RAIL DISCOUNTS WITHIN EUROPE   BIGE and Transalpino point-to-point rail tickets are available from student travel offices within Europe.   When you buy an International Student Identity Card, you are given a booklet listing the discounts available and where to buy them.   Offices are in all major cities, often conveniently by the train station.   In general, the longer the journey, the greater the savings.   Savings are up to 40 percent for longer rail journeys.   As stopovers are permitted within 2 months on these tickets, it's wise to purchase the ticket for the farthest destination.   Anyone under 26, not just students, may buy them.

FRANCE RAILPASS   This pass is sold for both first and second class and is valid for unlimited train travel on a certain number of days within a certain period.   For 4 non-consecutive days travel within 15 days, the cost is $99 second class ($134 first class).   For 9 days within 1 month, you pay $160 for second class ($224 first class).   Children 4 through 11 pay about 65 percent.

GERMAN TOURIST CARD   This card includes unlimited rail travel, Europabus, and KD Line excursion boats on the Rhine River.   Youth under 26 may buy a Junior Card for second class for 9 days ($79) or 16 days ($99).   Adult second class is 4 days ($81), 9 days ($124) and 16 days ($172).

BRITRAIL PASS   For Britain, you're better off not buying a train pass, but buying cheap day-return tickets and savers for trains and buses while you're there.   Buses are cheaper and go more places.   The many special bus and train fares in Britain make Britrail passes seem awfully expensive.

A Britrail Pass for youth 16-25 (economy class) costs $149 for 8 days, $219 for 15 days, $289 for 22 days and $329 for 1 month.   For adults (economy class) the cost is $179 for 8 days, $259 for 15 days, $339 for 22 days and $389 for 1 month.   Children 5-15 pay half.

A Britrail Flexipass for youth 16-25 costs (economy class) $129 for 4 days travel in 8-day period and $189 for 8 days in a 15-day period.   Adults pay $149 and $219 respectively.

HOW MUCH WILL MY TRIP COST?

Excluding airfare and railpasses, anyone can travel for $30 a day to cover all other expenses: campground, food, entrance fees, buses, checking your pack and buying small souvenirs. As a general rule, whatever Frommer's *Europe on $30 a Day* book states a hotel and three meals will cost, the same amount will cover all expenses for a camper. The breakdown is about $4 for a campground, $3 for public transportation, $5 for admission fees, $16 for food and $2 miscellaneous. On days that you're traveling, money is saved on food and admission fees which will pay for the crossing to Britain, having to check your pack occasionally and small souvenirs. Of course, many campers spend much less by cooking or buying picnic supplies and visiting small villages where the campground fee is less and you can walk there from the train station. At the low end, allow $15 a day and save money by taking an occasional overnight train ride, being selective about sights with admission fees and fixing your own food.

Most people spend more the first few days of their trip until they get the hang of it. On some days you will be spending more and on others less. The $15 and $30 figures are averages for the trip. Of course, the more money you have for food the better.

How do costs compare with staying in youth hostels? Generally, assuming two people traveling together, a campground will cost $3-4 each while a youth hostel will cost $9-12 each, if you can get in. Youth hostels are wonderful, the only trouble being that during the summer in the popular places, so much time is spent assuring a bed for the night. At a campground, you just show up; no time is wasted calling to see if there's a bed, looking for other accommodations, or lining up two hours before it opens as happens with youth hostels. Though most people who take camping equipment tend to camp 90 percent of the time, some combine camping with youth hostels. A hostel is handy for rainy days and a tent guarantees a cheap place to sleep.

WHAT SHOULD I WORRY ABOUT?

You don't need to worry about anything.

You don't need to worry about not speaking a foreign language. I don't and I've been writing this guidebook since 1975. Most Europeans speak better English than Americans speak French, German or whatever. Europeans are very polite and never offend us when we improperly speak their language, but the idea that they are flattered by our feeble attempts is much overblown. They would really rather speak their fluent English than have to be patient and listen to us!

You don't need to worry about anything being lost or stolen. It's never happened to me and I hang laundry on the campground lines and leave it up all day and sometimes all night. My expensive tent and down sleeping bags have never been disturbed. Our tent has never been entered even though we leave it unoccupied all day long and merely zipped up without a lock. If you're a woman, you don't need to worry about traveling alone. I've never done this, but I'm sure I will do it sometime in the future. Campgrounds are mainly filled with European families so there's nothing to be afraid of. On the contrary, there will always be helpful people nearby should anything happen. If you're a single parent as I am, you don't need to worry about traveling alone with children. In preparation for the fifth edition, my daughter (17) and son (15) went along and we all had a great time. In large cities, I would go off checking campgrounds while they would go sightseeing with map in hand. Be it Paris, London or Rome, as long as you're old enough to read a map and have common sense for the subways, you can make your way. Last summer, my daughter who was then 18, traveled alone by train and youth hostel and had a wonderful time.

The point I'm trying to make is don't be scared of Europe. The type of traveling available over there is simply not available in the U.S. and once having gone, you will return. I guarantee you will have more exciting experiences by camping by train in Europe for any given time period than you could possibly have anywhere in the United States. Nowhere else except delightful Europe with its diversity of cultures and historical remnants is it possible to travel this way so conveniently and so successfully. You will also have more fun than anyone who either camps by car or stays in hotels, because of the friendliness and sociability of other campers and the interesting people you meet on the trains. Sometimes you may have to initiate the conversation, by smiling and asking a question perhaps, but often the circumstances of putting backpacks up on the luggage rack or doing laundry in the campgrounds result in natural introductions.

FLYING TO EUROPE

Within a matter of hours you'll be there when you fly. Airfare offers the greatest single opportunity to save money. To do so requires some comparison shopping by calling a number of airlines. State at the outset that you want to go the cheapest way possible. After you get a price, ask if it's a special promotion fare and if a ticket has to be bought by a certain time. Also check the Sunday travel section of the newspaper of the largest city near your home. That is where special fares are advertised. If airlines think they may have a hard time filling planes, there may be special promotion fares around February and March. But if the planes begin to fill, then the fare may be yanked. Anyone of any age who can produce a student card, should inquire at the local student travel office for special student rates.

The desirable dates of the start of summer vacation for schools and universities become fully reserved by the end of February. The earlier you make reservations, the more likely you will get your first choice of dates.

RECEIVING MAIL ABROAD

We always buy the minimum amount of American Express travelers checks to show as client identification for their free client mail service and then hold them to the last. American Express offers a free booklet of addresses of their European offices. Allow two weeks for mail to arrive in southern Europe and one and a half weeks for northern Europe. If your plans change, for about $3.00 an American Express office will forward your mail to another of its offices in Europe.

WHAT TO TAKE

If you pack for Europe like you would for a summer vacation spent half in southern California and half in the marine climate of the Pacific Northwest, you can't go wrong. Think of any place south of the Alps as similar to the hot summer climate of southern California. Anywhere else the weather is more like the Pacific Northwest: beautiful warm sunny days, sometimes cool evenings, occasionally cloudiness and rain.

The most you will be carrying your pack at any one time will be about 30 minutes. This might occur when a campground is far from the bus stop or you choose to walk to the campground rather than take a bus. Most times the pack won't be carried for more than 15 minutes at a stretch. Because of these factors, a 30-pound pack is easily managed. Take care not to exceed my suggested amounts of clothing and equipment. The list includes clothing worn and is meant for a summer trip. If your trip extends into spring or fall, bring a warmer jacket or a raincoat. Extra space in the pack should be filled with food which is much cheaper in the U.S. or Canada.

Camping equipment should be selected from the lightweight quality designs featured at specialty backpacking and mountaineering equipment stores. These stores usually have a spring sale of camping equipment and that is a good time to pick up what you need. For instance, REI, PO Box 88125, Seattle, WA 98138-0125, 1-800-426-4840, publishes a free summer catalog in February and a winter catalog in October. Both include two to three pages of sale items that can be ordered by mail. The catalog contains pictures, detailed descriptions and comparisons of equipment. They also ship outside the U.S. The company is organized as a consumer co-operative. You can buy without becoming a member. However, membership costs only $10 per lifetime and returns an annual 8 to 10 percent rebate on purchases.

BACKPACK The pack should be water resistant and made of Cordura or coated nylon pack cloth. The rated capacity should be about 3300-4200 cubic inches. Purchase your sleeping bag and tent before the pack to be certain you get one large enough. It's better to err on the large end. If it's too small, by the end of the trip you may find yourself carrying separate parcels containing extra things you've bought. The best kind are compartmented so belongings do not become all jumbled together. Look for one where the sleeping bag fits into its own zippered area. Built-in padded shoulder straps should be provided. A pack costs from $70.

The three basic types are external frame and internal frame mountaineering packs and internal frame convertible backpack/luggage travel packs. External frame packs have the bag slung onto an outer aluminum framework. Internal frame packs have a smaller amount of aluminum frame fitted inside the pack. External frame packs are the most comfortable to carry because the weight is distributed higher on the frame and there is air space between the pack and your back. These packs are opened from the top. If the sleeping bag must be attached from the outside, make certain the stuffing sack is absolutely waterproof.

An internal frame pack is less bulky but also less comfortable because the weight is carried low on the back and there is no cooling air space at the small of the back. Weight distribution is improved the more compartmented the bag is. Avoid one large undivided bag as everything settles to the bottom making the bag pull awkwardly away from the shoulders.

The best looking but least comfortable of the packs are the convertible travel ones. These packs zip open like a softsided suitcase giving easy access to your belongings. With the backpack straps tucked inside its zippered compartment, the bag looks like a suitcase. Don't get one of this type unless it has a zippered section for your sleeping bag. Otherwise all belongings settle at the bottom making it difficult to walk erect with good posture. The travel pack is the worst offender as far as weight distribution goes. We used this type in 1988 and found it took its toll on posture. You tend to get rounded shoulders in compensating for the way the bag pulls from the shoulder straps.

DAY BAG   This is the bag you take with you when you leave the camp to spend the day sightseeing. It contains money, guidebooks, water bottle, food, sweater, camera, etc. You see all sorts of bags being used: day backpacks, coated nylon oversized bags, airline bags and shoulder bags. Select a waterproof one that does not show soil.

SLEEPING BAG   The requirements of moderate warmth, lightness in weight and compactibility limit the choice to those filled with down. Down is both cooler in warm climates and warmer in cool climates. In southern Europe, we generally slept on top of our sleeping bags. The exception was sleeping on deck on the ferry to Greece when the breeze made us glad they were warm. In northern Europe, we always slept inside the bags, sometimes leaving them unzipped. Down sleeping bags are carried in a stuff sack which makes them very small. In order to restore their insulating properties, they must be well fluffed. Many down bags are designed for mountain use. Be sure to select one meant for lowland camping or you will be too warm unless you plan mostly mountain camping or are going to the Arctic Circle. I take the lightest weight down bag I can find, North Face's Chrysalis bag. The bag measures 83" long with a 60" girth. It contains 17 ounces of down and weighs 35 ounces total. The bag stuffs inside a nylon sack measuring a small 6" by 16". Two of these bags will zip together. There is also a longer 89" version. REI only carries North Face's Blue Kazoo version which is like a mummy bag. You must go to a North Face store itself to find the better and more roomy barrel-shaped Chrysalis style. After Europe, this latter kind will zip open flat to make a nice comforter. The cost is $160. North Face also carries good light weight tents (1-800-888-9991.)

TENT   The styles and designs of lightweight compact backpacking tents are incredible. The tents can be set up in less than five minutes, weigh only 7 to 9 pounds, and are waterproof. For two people traveling together select a tent with a rated capacity for two to three people. If for three people, choose one made for three to four people. You need that extra space to accommodate the backpacks. Choose a tent with an outside framework of aluminum or fiberglass poles. The poles are corded with elastic and simply break down into sections. The tent fabric should be of uncoated nylon. A rainfly is a separate roof which is suspended a few inches over the top of the tent which keeps the tent dry during rain and acts as a sunshade in hotter areas. The rainfly should be of coated nylon and extend to the base of the tent. Avoid any tent whose body fabric itself is of coated nylon. The coating prevents the tent from breathing so condensation forms inside the tent and drips on you. Dome shaped tents are more convenient than A-frame because no cord is required to stake the rainfly. A typical dome tent will pack into a bag 7" by 30". A tent costs from $95. Be sure to follow the directions that come with the tent and thoroughly seal all seams with the waterproofing sealant.

TENT STAKES   Most tents require some staking to keep the floor and sides stretched taut to increase interior roominess. The thin wire kind are easily pushed down by hand in any type of dirt and are lightweight and compact. Pack them in a plastic bag. Don't take any extras because they are easily replaced in Europe.

SMALL LOCK   Purchase a small lock that can be threaded through the holes in the ends of the zippers on the door of the tent after it's closed. Be sure to take an extra key. Campgrounds are on a very effective honor system and even without this lock no one will enter your tent. But we noticed a lot of backpacking Europeans using these small locks so it certainly wouldn't hurt to take one. We have never locked our tent and have never had any theft. We also have never received any report from anybody who has had anything stolen at a campground.

GROUND CLOTH   Take a piece of plastic sheeting or coated nylon cloth that is cut slightly smaller than the outside perimeter of the tent. If the cloth protrudes beyond the edge, rain water collects on the plastic and runs under the tent.

AIR MATTRESS AND AIR PILLOW   The best kind is the old-fashioned nylon air mattress whose tubes are blown up individually. These are quickly inflated and easily deflated. They come in two lengths, regular which is 72" and a shorter backpacking length. The longer length costs $19 and weighs 1 pound 8 ounces. I prefer the shorter length mattress coupled with a separate air mattress pillow. The pillow is 19" by 13-1/2" and costs $4. The advantages are the pillow blows up thicker than the mattress, you can cover it with half a pillow slip and wash the pillow slip with the laundry, and the pillow can be used separately for naps on trains. The Therm-a-Rest style is not as comfortable. It is less thick and after being used once, will never again compress into its original small size. Likewise, the various foam cell pads are too bulky and not thick enough to be comfortable.

FLASHLIGHT   The flashlight is used for lighting in the tent at night after about 9pm when it gets dark, and occasionally for walking to the restrooms. However, the lighting in most camps is adequate for this. Choose a small, lightweight one with a powerful beam. Take along one set of extra batteries.

LAUNDRY SUPPLIES   You will be both hand washing clothing and using an automatic washer and dryer. If an automatic washing machine is available in a campground, either detergent will be included in the price or it will be sold by the small bagful in the camp store. Don't take along any automatic washing machine detergent. In southern Europe, campgrounds tend to have an automatic washing machine but no dryer. Instead lines are provided. We always leave our clothing on the lines all day and sometimes overnight and nothing has ever been stolen. Normally clothes will dry in one day or overnight unless there is morning dew. In northern Europe, both a washer and dryer are usually available. The cost to do a load of clothes averages about $3 to $5. Bring along 2 to 3 small baggies of ivory flakes for doing hand laundry. Additional soap can be bought at the camp store. A 10-foot length of thin cord to tie between two trees by your tent will come in handy when public lines are not provided, as will a few clothespins. Usually clothes can merely be draped over the line and they stay fine, but occasionally wind will blow them off.

CLOTHING   The amount of clothing needed depends on how often you want to wash.   The minimum is two sets, one to wear and another to handwash at the campground, but it's a nuisance to handwash every night. Clothing never gets as clean with hand washing. White synthetics turn gray after a few weeks of this. All-synthetic clothing can be very uncomfortable in the hot weather of southern Europe. Clothing which is at least half cotton is best. Try to bring 4 or 5 sets of skimpy and non-bulky underwear and socks. Don't overload on tops, as the many T-shirts available will tempt you and only cost from $5 to $10. Unless you're model thin, bottoms that fit are harder to buy. Be sure to bring three of these including one pair of long pants or jeans for northern Europe and one pair of shorts (or a skirt) for southern Europe.   Avoid light colors that show soil easily for bottoms. Velcro can be sewn inside the pockets of shorts and slacks making them secure for keeping currency and Eurailpasses handy.

Bring a moderately rainproof thin jacket and a non-bulky cardigan sweater, or a wool blazer that will do for both. The jacket is necessary if it rains. The sweater will provide warmth when needed. Older campers may prefer a less casual garment such as a wool blazer which will provide warmth plus stay warm even if it gets wet. If you plan to head south immediately after your arrival, then you don't need to start with a sweater because a sweatshirt for warmth can easily be bought upon returning to northern Europe. (For example in Munich, Hofbrauhaus sweatshirts cost about $25.)   This will save having to carry the sweater around southern Europe where it's not needed.

Men needn't bring a swim suit as shorts will do just as well. A woman should bring a non-bulky swimsuit if she plans to visit the beaches of southern Europe. Bring nightwear to keep the sleeping bag clean.

Shoes are the most important item that you'll be taking as they affect your comfort the most. Be sure they are not brand new but have been broken in at least three weeks before you leave. Most people take athletic or running shoes. Any shoes are fine as long as the soles are spongy rubber or nylon. This is of the utmost importance for comfort as the terrain varies from cobblestones, pavement, dirt, rocks, wood and stone to hard marble, which can be slippery when wet.

You will feel a lot better if you can wear rubber thongs or sandals into the campground showers. The showers are usually very good and always cleaned at least once a day, but the sheer number of people using them sometimes makes the floor unattractive. Thongs are extremely essential for anyone who easily contracts athlete's foot. The thongs also can double as beach sandals.

TOILETRIES KIT   Bring a durable plastic bag with string or loop attached to hang in the washroom or shower stall. It's better to bring 2 or 3 sample size toiletries rather than one full size. Once a container is used up it can be thrown away. Also, it's easy to forget and leave soap and shampoo in the shower stall and that way you won't lose much. Don't bring more than you will use. All toiletries except dental floss can be easily replaced in camp stores. Bring a small comb rather than a hairbrush. A small separate soft plastic drinking glass is handy to have in your toiletries kit, but you can also use the glass from your picnic supplies. Put soap in a ziplock baggy rather than a soap dish. The baggy doesn't add extra bulk and is waterproof. Bring a thin washcloth and thin towel because they are less bulky and dry faster. The towel should be of small bath towel or large hand towel size. Pack the washcloth in a ziplock baggy. For sunbathing, people use a woven reed mat that all beach resorts sell for $3-4. They roll up easily and can be given away or discarded when done with.

Take along one-third of a roll of toilet paper. Remove the center cardboard, flatten and put in a plastic bag. Some campgrounds do not furnish toilet paper. If this is the case, the camp store will sell it by the roll. What you are bringing is a small supply so you don't get caught without. Put supplies of tissue in 1 to 4 small baggies and tuck into any extra spaces in your pack. If sanitary napkins or tampons will be needed within two weeks, then women should bring along a full supply. If the interval will be longer, only bring what will be needed for the first day as campground stores and pharmacies stock them. All paper goods are more expensive in Europe, so it's well to take a small supply if there's space.

Some campers take along disposable shavers. Others take electric. All campground restrooms have plugs, but both the voltage and socket differ in Europe. On the continent, 220 volts is normally found. Be sure to take a shaver that has dual voltage available. Even so, a round plug will have to be purchased to fit the European round outlets. These are sold in some hardware stores and in travel specialty shops. Britain is a case apart with a variety of voltages and plugs.

PICNIC SUPPLIES   The essential item is a liter or quart-size plastic water container with leakproof top. If you already have one, take it with you. If not, either buy one here or purchase a liter of mineral water in Europe and use the plastic bottle with screw top it comes in. In Greece, a liter bottle of mineral water costs about $.60. Bring along a plastic water glass. If there are two of you, make sure they nest. Standard practice when traveling is to fill the water bottle before getting on board the train so you'll have something to drink enroute. Otherwise, thirst will force the purchase of expensive soft drinks on the train. In hot southern Europe, we always keep our filled water bottle in the day bag and use it constantly.

Other minimum picnic supplies are a spoon and plastic bowl or luncheon-size plate for each person and one pocketknife per group. In France and southern Europe, French bread is handed to you unwrapped. Bring 2 to 3 waxed paper French bread bags and the same number of plastic bags to keep it in. The most common size of French bread sold at campgrounds is baguette size: the long, thin type. Bring 5 to 10 envelopes of the artificially-sweetened juice mixes. These weigh practically nothing and are great for drinks on the train and for picnics.

ODDS AND ENDS   Sunglasses, bandages, safety pins, small scissors, sunburn preventive, medications, writing pens and address list should be brought. If you wear eye glasses, take along a copy of the prescription, but be aware that it can take up to 10 days to have a pair made.

Unless you take photography seriously, a small lightweight and not too expensive camera is less worrisome than a better one. Bring film with you as it's more expensive in Europe. There are one-day developing services in many European cities. A small calculator is handy for figuring out what things cost. Indispensable is some sort of alarm device when an early morning train is to be taken. On one hand, a personal stereo/radio is handy for long train and boat trips and for the tent. On the other hand, it's just one more possession you have to carry around. Batteries are available in Europe, but it's easier to bring along some extras of your own.

Take several manila envelopes to mail back home tourist literature or guidebooks that you want to save. Strapping tape and small scissors are handy. Outside of Britain, paperback books in English are twice what they cost at home. Bring along 2 or 3 to read on long train and boat journeys. After you're through with them, they can be swapped, given away or discarded. Business cards are handy for exchanging with new-found friends. Bring some only if you already have them.

TRAVEL DOCUMENTS AND MONEY   Take along a small cloth pouch that can be either pinned to the inside of the waistband of your slacks or hung around the neck beneath your shirt. Non-replaceable items should be kept in it such as extra cash, airline tickets, Eurailpass receipt and a few travelers checks. A cotton pouch is preferable to nylon because it's cooler. Avoid uncomfortable plastic.

Travelers checks are safe, convenient and easy to use. All brands are readily accepted and refunds are readily given once you find the respective office or bank that's open. Payment of the one percent fee to buy travelers checks can be avoided by calling various savings and loan associations to learn which ones give checks "free" with an account. Denominations in which to buy checks depends on your estimate of daily expenses and length of time spent in any one country. Keep in mind that travelers checks are bulky for a 2-3 month trip and funds ideally should be in the same denomination amount that you plan to cash them. That means $50 and $20 and a few $10. In rural English villages you may have trouble cashing a $50, but not in any size city. American Express sells foreign currency travelers checks for the German deutschmark (DM50, DM100, etc), Swiss franc (SF50, SF100, etc.), British pound and French franc. Dollar travelers checks can be exchanged in Europe for checks of those currencies at American Express offices for a fee. If the dollar is falling rather than rising, buying checks in either deutschmarks or Swiss francs could save some money. (A fee is charged in the U.S. to reconvert foreign travelers check to U.S. currency.) In Europe, aim to exchange travelers checks into local currency only in the amount you anticipate spending in that country as an exchange fee is usually levied with every exchange transaction. However, if you cash deutschmark travelers checks in Germany, or Swiss franc travelers checks in Switzerland no exchange fee is charged.

Travelers checks should be separated and kept in several places. One or two for emergency use should be in the money belt. One supply should be in the day bag. One or two should be tucked deep inside your pack. That way in case some are lost, you've still got funds to use until you can get them replaced. Photocopy the travelers check and Eurailpass receipt and keep one copy in the day bag and one in the backpack. Indicate on the receipts which group of travelers checks are located where.

A passport should be obtained two months in advance of your trip. Passport agencies in large cities and post offices in many smaller cities accept applications for a passport. Take a photocopy along of the identifying pages of your passport and keep it in your pack. Should it be lost (rare), this will simplify obtaining a replacement. Should this happen, contact any U.S. embassy or consulate for a temporary one. Be sure to take along someone who knows you as this person must complete an affidavit swearing to your U.S. citizenship.

A visa is an entry permit that is rubber stamped onto a page in your passport. Most Eastern European countries require one, including Hungary. Write to the respective tourist office or embassy in Washington D.C. for information. For Hungary, write to Embassy of the Hungarian People's Republic, Consular Section, 3910 Shoemaker St., N.W.; Washington, D.C. 20008. No visas are issued at rail frontier points, so it's important to get one before you leave or allow 4 days in Vienna to pick one up. The visa is valid 6 months from date of issue. Two passport photos plus a $15 fee are required. For western Europe, France is the only country that requires a visa, a temporary measure in response to terrorist bombings. Apply to the tourist office for the application and location of the French consulate nearest to you. It's fine to send passports regular mail. Sometimes, a visa can be obtained at the border into France, but it usually means a short delay and wait in line.

Be sure to get The International Student Identity Card (ISIC) if you qualify. Full-time (12 semester hours) college students of any age are eligible to buy the card. Students showing the card receive substantial discounts on many museum entrance fees and other benefits. The cost is $10 plus a handling fee. The card can be bought from any CIEE Council Travel Office, such as the ones at 2511 Channing Way, Berkeley, CA 94704, or 79 South Pleasant Street, Amherst, MA 01002.

Medical insurance is a worthwhile investment. The best kind covers sickness as well as accident as the former is many times more likely to occur than the latter. The first step is to check your present policy to see if its coverage extends to Europe. Most do. Special travelers insurance is available from many firms and any travel agent will sell you some although the premium will be higher than that available from CIEE student offices or the Youth Hostel Association. The latter two will sell insurance to travelers regardless of age and offer the best value. Write to American Youth Hostels, Inc., PO Box 37613, Washington DC 20013-7613.

An International Camping Carnet can be bought in Europe at any campground that requires it, or in advance from the National Campers and Hikers Association, Inc., 4804 Transit Road, Building 2, Depew, NY 14043. The cost is $20 in the U.S. The carnet entitles the bearer to a 10 percent discount on camp fees at numerous camps in Europe. Probably about half the camps you will use will give a discount. I've never bought one because the small discounts hardly cover the cost of the pass. A carnet is required in Denmark and Sweden. If you don't have one you can buy it on the spot for $3 to $4. Those who are camping for three months will probably come out ahead if they purchase a carnet before they go. It also alleviates having to leave a passport at the office until you check out. Of course, there's other ways around this, such as leaving a travelers check for security.

Be sure to bring your Eurailpass or similar, the International Student Identity Card if you qualify, several personal checks and a major charge card if you have them already. Personal checks can be used to pay for a purchase that is being mailed home because the store can hold the merchandise until the check clears. Normally only expensive places take Visa or Mastercharge, but you usually can charge an airline ticket from the continent to Britain with it. Leave all U.S. coins at home, but bring a few $5 bills. It's a great convenience to already have some of the country's currency with you before you get there. It often saves having to pay the high commission that train station banks charge to cash a travelers check.

Bring guidebooks, photocopies of detailed information on museums and archeological sites, the Eurail map that comes with the pass and the free schedule, *Through Europe by Train.*

FOOD SUPPLIES   Food in Europe is much more expensive than at home. If you've extra room in the pack, fill it with nutritious, ready-to-eat snacks. These are convenient to eat on trains during meal time.   The most worthwhile are beef jerky, peanuts, cheese and cracker packets, cans of Vienna sausages and similar.

COOKING EQUIPMENT   If you plan to cook, take a Camping Gaz one-burner stove or buy it in Europe. This stove is the one used by the majority of campers and its disposable fuel cartridges are widely available in campground stores. Be sure your stove is empty when taking it on an airplane. (Fuel is prohibited in planes.) Also bring matches, freeze-dried coffee or tea (both are heavily taxed in Europe) or cocoa, one pan that can be used for both frying and boiling, fork, soup spoon (omit teaspoon), small amounts of any seasonings you use including a meat tenderizer, dishtowel and a scouring pad in a plastic bag. People who plan to cook should take at least a 4,000 cubic inch pack. Stuff it full of any food you would like to cook. Dried noodles, rice, tuna fish, dried soup base, and similar will all come in handy.

Do I cook? No, I don't. I eat a cold breakfast at camp, take off for the day and usually don't return until 8pm or so. Lunch and dinner are frequently grocery-store bought, a sandwich from a cafe, pizza-to-go in Italy, or wurst or rotisseried chicken in Germany and Scandinavia.

CHECK LIST   (includes clothing worn on plane)

Luggage
    Backpack
    Daytime bag

Camping Equipment
    Tent
    Rainfly for tent
    Poles
    Stakes
    Ground cloth
    Lock for tent zipper
    Sleeping bag
    Air mattress
    Inflatable pillow
    Pillow case
    Flashlight plus one extra set batteries

Laundry Supplies
    10-foot length of cord for clothesline

2-3 small baggies of ivory flakes
4-6 tiny clothespins

Clothing

Shoes
Thongs or sandals
4-5 pair underwear and socks
1 cardigan
1 rain jacket
1 pair long pants
1 pair shorts or skirt
Extra pair shorts or long pants
2-3 shirts and tops
Nightwear
Bathing suit for women (optional)

Toiletries

Toiletries bag
Toothbrush
Toothpaste
Dental floss or tape
Plastic drinking glass
Small soap bar in zip-lock bag
Thin washcloth in plastic bag
Thin towel
1/3 roll toilet paper in plastic bag
1-4 small baggies of tissue
Comb
Cosmetics
Deodorant
Sanitary napkins or tampons
Shaving gear

Picnic Supplies

Liter or quart-size water bottle
Pocketknife
Spoon
Plastic bowl or small plate
Plastic glass
3 waxed paper French bread bags
3 plastic French bread bags
5-10 envelopes of artificially-sweetened drink mix

Odds and Ends

5-10 assorted sizes plastic bags
5-10 assorted bandages
Sunburn preventive (small size)
Headache tablets
Medications, if any
Sunglasses
Prescription for eye glasses or spare pair
Small blunt end scissors, sold in baby departments
5-8 safety pins or needle and thread

2 pens
Address list
Small notebook (optional)
Camera and film (optional)
Watch with an alarm
Small calculator (optional)
One-third roll of strapping tape
3 manila envelopes
Personal stereo/radio (optional)
Extra batteries (optional)
2-3 paperback books (optional)
20 business cards (only if you already have them)

Travel Documents and Money
A money pouch that hangs inside clothing
Airline tickets and photocopy
Rail pass, receipt and photocopy of receipt
Passport and photocopy of identifying page
French visa (stamped in passport)
Travelers checks, receipt and photocopy of receipt
International student identity card
4-6 small face photos to use for weekly bus passes
4-5 personal checks if available
Visa or Mastercharge if available
4 $5.00 bills
$50 worth of currency for the first country
$10 worth of currency for the next few countries
Guidebooks
Eurail map and free "Through Europe by Train"
Other travel notes

Food Supplies (optional suggestions)
Coffee, tea or cocoa
Beef jerky
Peanuts
Cheese 'N Crackers
Vienna sausage

Cooking Equipment (optional)
stove
matches
pan
fork
soup spoon (omit teaspoon)
seasonings
meat tenderizer
dish towel
scouring pad in plastic bag

PLANNING AN ITINERARY

An itinerary is best thought of as something you plan for yourself at leisure before you go and use as a basis of departure once you get over there. It is much easier to evaluate touring possibilities here rather than once on vacation when time is at a premium and the sirens beckon. Before you go, do as much reading as possible about the places to see so you will know what you want to see and where. Additionally, understanding their historical significance will make your trip that much more enjoyable and meaningful.

Go with an itinerary in mind, but feel free to tamper with it or throw it out completely once you are abroad. The main advantage of advance planning, besides the fun of it, is that it acquaints you with unfamiliar names, monetary systems and train schedules giving you a headstart once you get there.

CAMPING SEASONS   The middle of July through August is the height of the camping season throughout Europe. This is when schools and universities are closed and Europeans take their vacations. Warm sunny weather usually stretches at either end to include June and September, though temperature and rainfall in these months fluctuates just like at home. Destinations in northern Scandinavia (above the Arctic Circle) should be scheduled for July and August, the warmest period. Northern Europe can be rather cold and/or rainy in May and October. These are fine months for camping in southern Europe, including the south of France, Spain except the northern coast, Portugal, Italy except the Alps, Yugoslavia, Greece, Turkey and Morocco. Winter camping is possible on the island of Sicily in Italy, the Costa del Sol in southern Spain, the Algave in southern Portugal and in Greece, Turkey and Morocco.

Summer weather varies in Europe from year to year just like at home. Some summers may be notably rainy, others have drought conditions. In 1987, northern Europe was unseasonably cold and rainy until about the second week in July when the weather pattern abruptly changed to clear skies and sunshine. Meanwhile, the Balkans which includes Greece, were having a heat wave with 90 degrees in Athens in mid June. In July, the Balkans had another heat wave with record temperatures being recorded. Eurailpasses give you the freedom to change plans according to the week by week weather situation. Even in a rainy year, there is always sunny and warm southern Europe and Greece.

PRICE LEVEL   Food is high throughout Europe. Southern Europe is less than northern Europe. Greece and Portugal are cheaper yet. Oddly enough, camping fees are generally less in northern Europe, except Scandinavia, than southern Europe. France is especially inexpensive for camping. City buses are cheaper in southern Europe than northern Europe.

ITINERARY STRATEGY   For a summer trip, try to leave as early in June as you can. You want to spend as much time in Europe as possible outside of the busy period of the last half of July and the month of August. If possible, find an airline fare where you can arrive in continental Europe and depart from London. This will save both a day of travel crossing the channel and the fare of about $25.

Most people arrive by plane in June somewhere in northern Europe, begin touring, and eventually make their way south, finally visiting Italy and Greece during their hottest and most crowded period in late July and August. The best strategy is to run counter to this pattern and immediately head south. August is the best time to tour northern Europe while northern Europeans are on holiday in southern Europe.

For example, after your plane has arrived, take the train from the airport to the downtown station, check your bags in the station, and spend several hours sightseeing to stretch your legs from the flight. Then if you're including Greece in your itinerary, take an overnight train ride to Venice and spend two to three days there. Venice provides a glorious introduction to Europe. Then take the day train to Brindisi and the evening overnight ferry to Greece. If you're not going to Greece, then continue touring Italy or, if Spain is included in your trip, from northern Europe take an overnight train to Madrid.

If upon arrival in Europe, you feel tired and want to sleep, simply spend a day or two in the city and then head south. On this last trip, we arrived in Amsterdam after an overnight flight and found we weren't tired. We validated our Eurailpasses at the airport, took the train into Amsterdam and checked our bags. Then since we had already started the validity on the passes, we took the train to Leiden to tour the windmill which is a few minutes walk from the station. That evening, we boarded an overnight train to Venice. Enroute we could glimpse the lighted castles along the Rhine River. We virtually had the train to ourselves and stretched out in empty compartments. The repetitive motion of the train lulled us to sleep and helped us adjust to the time change. In the morning we arrived in Verona, Italy; checked our bags at the station, made a quick tour of the Arena, its main sight; ate a wonderful lunch and then continued to Venice.

When planning to include Greece, keep in mind that traveling there takes time. The ferry to Greece takes two days: one on the train to Brindisi, the departure point, and another enroute to Greece. This must be done in both directions. It's worthwhile to investigate what it would cost to extend your flight directly into Athens. Usually, it will only add an extra $100 when it's part of a transatlantic fare anyway. (A flight to Greece from within Europe will cost much more.) That way you can arrive in Greece, visit the islands and take the bus between cities, not starting your Eurailpass until the day of the ferry ride to Italy. Buses are very cheap in Greece and are better than the trains, so using a Eurailpass in Greece is a waste. Starting in Greece also has the advantage of visiting museums in chronological order, starting with Greek civilization, progressing to Etruscan and Roman periods in Italy, and to Medieval in northern Europe.

Every itinerary should include both capital cities and small villages. Keep in mind that the major sightseeing attractions in Rome, Florence, Venice, Paris, Amsterdam, Salzburg and London will have lines in July and August. To avoid frustration, allow at least five days for Paris, Rome and London. The best museums and sightseeing attractions are in large cities, but the most charming part of your vacation will come from time spent in the villages. Try to include these perfectly preserved small ancient towns: Carcassonne in France, Rothenburg in Germany and Bruges in Belgium.

SCENIC TRAIN RIDES   Any train that parallels a coast or passes through the alps or the mountains of Norway will be scenic. Among the most famous of the scenic routes that are included in Eurailpasses are the segment between Oslo and Bergen (mountain scenery), the Golden Pass in Switzerland between Montreux and Spiez (mountain scenery), and the trains following the Rhine River between Coblenz and Bingen (castles along the Rhine). Details on other scenic routes are found in the individual country chapters, especially Switzerland.

SIGHTSEEING STRATEGIES   In planning what you want to accomplish in a day, bear in mind that the two main sightseeing periods available are from about 9:30am until noon and from 1:30-4:30pm. Upon arrival in a region, city, town or museum, do things in priority order. This way what you don't get done will be relatively unimportant to you personally. Try doing the free things first. Most often whether or not admission is charged depends more on whether the state is providing a subsidy rather than on quality. Aim for variety within each day and throughout the trip. Then be sure to quit an activity while you're still ahead. If you stay at a museum until you're famished, it's hard to wait until you discover a reasonably priced restaurant. Try to alternate museums with physical activity.

Be selective. It's only natural to want to do everything and go everywhere but having once discovered camping you will return. Unless you already know that a particular civilization, period or era mesmerizes you, for general cultural purposes be content with only one or two of the best examples of the period. If you are going to Rome, you needn't spend time in museums of antiquity in Germany. The best modern art museums are found in Amsterdam, Paris and Basel, Switzerland. Some civilizations left many more monuments than other equally important periods. Try to see choice morsels from the greatest span of time that you can. Avoid too many three-star duplications from prolific periods. The caves used by prehistoric man are about the earliest in time that you can get in Europe.

CIVILIZATIONS AND PERIODS   To refresh your memory, here's a brief outline of the ancient civilizations and modern historical periods which have left their monuments throughout Europe. After each are listed only a few of the many examples of the period that are found in Europe. Note that the more spectacular the past culture, the better the sightseeing. In modern terms, that means France, Italy, Spain and Greece.

Prehistory
        Caves of Lascaux, France (closed)
        Caves of Les Eyzies, France (open)
        Caves of Altamaira, Santillana del Mar, Spain (open)

Greek Civilization (classical architecture)
Doric Order: Temple of Poseidon, Paestum, Italy
                    Temple of Concord, Agrigento, Sicily, Italy
                    Temple of Segesta, Sicily, Italy
Ionic Order: Temple of Fortuna Virile, Rome, Italy
Corinthian Order: Maison Carree, Nimes, France

Etruscan Civilization (only sculpture remains)
        Etruscan Museum, Rome

Roman Civilization
        Arch of Titus, Coliseum and Pantheon, Rome
        Pompeii, Italy
        Amphitheater, Verona, Italy
        Acqueduct, Segovia, Spain

Byzantine (architectural style originating in Constantinople, then capital of the Eastern Roman Empire)

22

St. Mark's Cathedral, Venice
St. Vitale Cathedral and Basilica of St. Apollinaris, Ravenna, Italy

Romanesque (11th and 12th centuries, medieval style)
Cathedral, Pisa, Italy
Cathedral San Ambroglio, Milan
Autun Cathedral, Autun (Burgundy), France
Madeleine, Vezelay (Languedoc), France
Cathedral, Salamanca, Spain

Gothic (12th to 15th centuries, diagonally ribbed vaulting and flying buttresses; textbook examples are the Cathedral of Chartres, France, and Notre Dame in Paris; other countries had ethnic variations.)
Duomo, Milan
Cathedral, Burgos, Spain
St. Stephens Cathedral, Vienna
Cathedral, Cologne, Germany
Cathedral, Antwerp, Belgium
Salisbury Cathedral, England

Renaissance (15th and 16th centuries, incorporated elements of Greek and Roman architecture into new forms.)
St. Peter's, Rome
Palazzo Vendramin, Venice
Pazzi Chapel, Florence
Chambord, Loire Valley, France
El Escorial, Spain
Antwerp Town Hall, Holland
Heidelberg Castle, Germany

French Classical (17th century)
The Palace of Versailles, France

Baroque (17th and 18th centuries, florid)
Trevi Fountain and St. Agnese Cathedral, Rome
Plaza Mayor, Salamanca, Spain
Belvedere Palace, Vienna, Austria

Neo-Classical (Late 18th and early 19th centuries)
Palais Royal, Paris
Prado, Madrid
Hyde Park Corner Arch, London
Brandenburger Tor, Berlin

SOURCES OF INFORMATION

THE LIBRARY   The richest resource is your public library. Travel guidebooks start in the non-fiction section at Dewey #914. Here is where general travel books about Europe begin. The first volumes cover the entire continent, and then starting with 914.2, books are exclusively about one or another European country or city. Listed are Dewey call numbers.
914.   General travel books about Europe
914.2 Britain, Ireland
914.3 Germany, Holland, Belgium, Luxembourg

914.4   France
914.5   Italy
914.6   Spain, Portugal
914.7   U.S.S.R.
914.8   Scandinavia
914.9   Other European countries

Maps for individual countries are kept in a pamphlet file. Travel books with the emphasis on art and architecture are found in the art section in the 700's.

NATIONAL GOVERNMENT TOURIST OFFICES   These are maintained by the government of each country to encourage people to visit their country. They are literally a goldmine of free material. After you have some idea of where you want to go, send a postcard to the respective tourist office requesting specific information on subjects of interest. There is no charge for the material, and each office has about a hundred different brochures available. Try to request specific subjects, such as a map of a certain city, train schedules, list of campgrounds, cuisine, hiking, children's sightseeing attractions, wine and museums. See Scandinavian National Tourist Office for Finland, Denmark, Sweden and Norway.

Austrian National Tourist Office
3440 Wilshire Blvd, Suite 906; Los Angeles, CA 90010
500 Fifth Avenue, Suite 2009-2022; New York, NY 10110

Belgian National Tourist Office
745 Fifth Avenue, Suite 7104; New York, NY 10151

British Tourist Authority
40 West 57th Street, Third Floor; New York, NY 10019
612 S. Flower Street; Los Angeles, CA 90017

French Government Tourist Office
9401 Wilshire Boulevard; Beverly Hills, CA 90212
610 Fifth Avenue; New York, NY 10020-2452

West German National Tourist Office
444 S. Flower Street; Los Angeles, CA 90017
747 Third Avenue; New York, NY 10017

Greek National Tourist Organization
611 West 6th Street, Suite 1998; Los Angeles, CA 90017
Olympic Tower, 645 Fifth Avenue; New York, NY 10022

Irish Tourist Board
757 Third Avenue; New York, NY 10017

Italian Government Tourist Office
360 Post Street; San Francisco, CA 94108
630 Fifth Ave. #1565; Rockefeller Center; New York, NY 10111

Luxembourg National Tourist Office
801 Second Avenue; New York, NY 10017

Monaco Government Tourist and Convention Bureau
20 East 49th Street; New York, NY 10017

The Netherlands National Tourist Office
681 Market Street; San Francisco, CA 94105
355 Lexington Avenue, 21st Floor; New York, NY 10017

Portuguese National Tourist Office
3440 Wilshire Boulevard, Suite 616; Los Angeles, CA 90010
548 Fifth Avenue; New York, NY 10036

Scandinavian National Tourist Office
3600 Wilshire Boulevard; Los Angeles, CA 90010
655 Third Avenue, 18th Floor; New York, NY 10017

Spanish National Tourist Office
1 Hallidie Plaza; San Francisco, CA 94102
665 Fifth Avenue; New York, NY 10022

Swiss National Tourist Office
250 Stockton Street; San Francisco, CA 94108
608 Fifth Avenue; New York, NY 10020

EUROPEAN NATIONAL RAILROAD OFFICES   The free 156-page booklet of train schedules for major cities, *Through Europe by Train*, is available from offices of the European railroads. Be sure to get it. Use the National Tourist Office address for the Swiss Federal Railways.

French National Railroads
9465 Wilshire Blvd, Suite 713; Beverly Hills CA 90212
610 Fifth Avenue; New York NY 10020
2121 Ponce de Leon Blvd.; Coral Gables FL 33134
11 East Adams Street; Chicago IL 60603
360 Post St. on Union Square, Suite 606; San Francisco CA 94108
150 Stanley Street; Montreal P.Q. H3A 1R3
409 Granville Street, Suite 452; Vancouver, B.C. B6C 1T2

Germanrail
11933 Wilshire Blvd.; Los Angeles CA 90025
747 Third Avenue; New York NY 10017
625 Statler Office Bldg.; Boston MA 02116
442 Post Street; San Francisco CA 94102
9575 W. Higgins Road, Suite 505; Rosemont IL 60018
112 South Ervay Street; Dallas TX 75201
3400 Peachtree Rd. N.E., Lenox Towers #1231; Atlanta GA 30326
1290 Bay Street; Toronto, Ont. M5R 2C3

Italian State Railways
15760 Ventura Blvd., Suite 819; Encino CA 91436
666 Fifth Avenue; New York NY 10103
500 N. Michigan Avenue, Room 1310; Chicago IL 60611
2055 Peel Street; Montreal P.Q. H3A 1V4
13 Balmuto Street; Toronto, Ont. M4Y 1W4

TRAIN SCHEDULES   Each country's railroad publishes a book of local and continent-wide train schedules that is sold at train information offices or magazine kiosks in train stations of the respective country. Each costs about $3-$6. Additionally, free schedules for trains leaving that city are available from train information offices in the stations. Free from a European national railroad office before you go is *Through Europe by Train* containing departure times for major cities. The traveler can get all the schedules he needs without paying anything, but there is one good all-encompassing source which you might consider buying. This is the *Thomas Cook Continental Timetable*, which is 9-1/2" x 6-1/4" x 3/4", contains 480 pages and costs $16.95 plus $3 priority mail. To order, call 1-800-FORSYTH or write to Forsyth Travel Library, Dept. CE, 9154 West 57th Street, PO Box 2975, Shawnee Mission KS 66201-1375. Bankcards accepted. This company also publishes a catalog of guidebooks and maps about Europe and sells Eurailpasses and passes offered by each country.

Cook's timetable is published in London on the first day of each month. The June, July, August and September issues contain the continental summer train schedules. The issues from October to May contain winter schedules. The February to May issues have an advance European summer service supplement to enable users to plan summer itineraries before the complete summer timetable is published. The April and May issues contain winter schedules adjusted to daylight savings time in Europe from the first weekend in April. The May issue also contains summer services in Britain. Each issue contains 8000 tables of rail schedules over every main line railway, grouped according to country. There are separate sections for EuroCity trains and international express routes. Also included are rail maps for each country with the schedule number indicated on the route for quick reference; schedules for passenger ferries on the Rhine, Danube, Gota Canal and Swiss and Italian lakes; ferry schedules including all crossings to Europe such as Stockholm to Finland, Brindisi to Greece, and Britain, Ireland, Scandinavia and throughout the Mediterranean; cross-channel hydrofoil service with connections to and from London and Paris; list of geographical names with corresponding English-language names; list of principal towns not served by rail and their nearest rail gateway; comparative international times in Europe and dates of daylight saving times where adopted; list of Thomas Cook offices; an index listing European towns and page number of their timetables; list of holidays for each country; and inset maps showing the train stations within a city when there is more than one. The timetable does not include schedules for all minor lines such as those taken to some of the chateaux of the Loire, those on the Pelopponese in Greece, and the line to Paestum, Italy. Not all minor rail lines are indicated on the rail maps. It does not give prices. But, all in all, it can be a very valuable aid in planning your trip, and in having up-to-date train schedules at your fingertips while traveling.

OTHER HELPS   *Let's Go Europe* is a bargain. In writing this guidebook, we assume you have it. We therefore try to give more detailed information on campgrounds, train schedules and related information and sightseeing. For language help, the Berlitz, *Pocket Dictionary Plus Menu Reader*, is helpful because it contains phonetic pronunciations. For sightseeing, The Michelin series of tall, slender green guides published by the Michelin Tire Company are excellent.   The books cover museums, monuments, architecture, natural formations, viewpoints, history, art, wine and food, and include maps of the area and town as well as suggested itineraries. Cities and attractions are rated from zero to three stars according to their importance. The guides are easily bought in the country covered.

COMPILING YOUR OWN GUIDEBOOK   Once you've figured out where you want to go and what you want to see, start gathering together historical and cultural information about them.   For instance, because I already have most of the Michelin guidebooks and don't want to have to carry the weight of them with me, I photocopy the pages pertaining to what I'll be seeing.   I read up on an area enroute on the train and discard the material after leaving the city.   This saves money in not having to buy guidebooks over there and has the added advantage of having them on the train to read ahead. Michelin and Baedecker guidebooks are the best for this purpose. They can be easily borrowed from friends or a library.

If I happen to have the Thomas Cook Timetable in advance, I tear out the portions I plan to use, staple each country's schedules together separately and leave two-thirds of the book at home. Anything that can be done to minimize weight and bulk is worth the time it takes. If you're using several guidebooks, only take the pages you need.

TRAVELING IN EUROPE

YOUR ARRIVAL IN EUROPE

After the plane lands, go inside the terminal to the luggage arrival area and wait until your pack appears on the turnstyle. If an airline counter is in the area, this is a good time to take care of reconfirming your return flight. Reconfirmation is a requirement with most airlines. It's easiest to do it immediately and get it accomplished while you're still at the airport. After retrieving your pack, proceed to the customs line marked "nothing to declare." This is usually the green line. The customs inspector will stamp your passport.

The first thing to do after clearing customs is to locate the tourist information office and pick up a map of the city. All airports have clearly marked signs directing visitors to their various services. Usually airport tourist information offices also stock maps and information on other cities of the country and now is a good time to ask for them. If you didn't bring some of the country's currency with you, then find the airport exchange office or bank and cash some travelers checks. Airport banks stay open as long as flights are arriving. Next, follow the airport signs to the bus stop or airport train station. Every airport has swift and inexpensive public transportation available to downtown.

GENERAL OPERATING PROCEDURE

The basic routine goes like this. Whenever you arrive in a new city, first visit the tourist office to pick up a map and verify directions to the campground. Then decide whether to go directly to camp and set up, or to check your pack at the station, spend the day sightseeing and arrive at camp in the evening. In each city, two opportunities arise to save money. The first is to investigate day passes and ticket books to determine which will save the most money in city transportation costs. The other is to find a place to change money at a good rate without paying a high commission.

TOURIST INFORMATION OFFICES

The personnel in these offices speak English and are there to help you enjoy their city. It is helpful to ask specifically for everything you want. Don't discuss a general subject and assume the assistant will volunteer any free maps and literature that will be helpful. Some do, but many don't. Ask "have you a map of the city?". Check to make certain it's a detailed street map, not one that only shows main streets. The map of the public transportation system is usually separate and issued by the bus company but available at the tourist office as well. Be sure to ask for it. Sometimes a small charge is made for the city map, but in all cases the bus map is free and makes a good substitute. Among items these offices stock are road maps, train schedules (unless train information has them), campground brochures, restaurant list, museums brochure, suggested excursions around the city and what's happening in that city during the month or week. Often an office will have maps for other cities in the country. Pick them up ahead of time to study on the train.

If the office has lines, we usually head directly to the campground, verifying with the bus driver that the bus number is still correct. Often campgrounds will have a supply of tourist office maps and literature.

FOREIGN EXCHANGE

Change is the French word for exchanging one country's money for the kind another country uses. On signs, change is usually followed by its Spanish equivalent *cambio* and the German *wechsel*. Whenever those words or *bureau de change, sportello cambio, la oficina de cambio,* or *wechselschalter* appear, you are notified that the establishment will cash travelers checks and change dollars into a foreign currency. A passport is required as identification. Before cashing a travelers check, note the rate of exchange that is displayed and ask the amount of the fee or commission charge for this service. Almost all exchange clerks speak English. Try to avoid cashing travelers checks on weekends because the best places to change them may be closed. In major cities, cashing travelers checks at American Express on a Saturday involves standing in long lines. Always ask for small denomination bills. Otherwise, the clerk will follow standard practice and count out large bills, which can be awkward when paying for small purchases.

Commission charges can be horrendous, sometimes more than five percent when the amount exchanged is small. The fee varies from place to place. Most often it is one set fee regardless of how much is cashed. Sometimes the fee will be one amount for small exchanges and a larger amount for larger exchanges. Sometimes no fee will be charged and the cost for the service is incorporated into the rate. Occasionally, but not very often, a fee is charged based on the number of checks cashed rather than the amount. Sometimes a fee is avoided by changing travelers checks at correspondent banks abroad of the issuing company. Fees are sometimes especially high at airline terminals, railway stations and bus depots. If you find yourself in the situation of having to cash some checks at a train station when the commission is high, check the fee for changing currency because sometimes it will be smaller or nonexistent. One or two countries, such as Italy, impose a tax on each currency transaction. In general, it's best to estimate how much money will be needed for that country and cash sufficient travelers checks up to the amount you feel safe in carrying. Because of fees, too much money is lost by repeatedly cashing small travelers checks. On the other hand, don't change more money than will be needed in that country, because to re-exchange it to another currency often involves another commission. Try to spend loose change in its own country as banks often either won't accept it or will accept it along with bills but fail to convert it.

The rate of exchange is how much foreign currency is given for one dollar before a commission or exchange fee, if any, is deducted. There is both a free market rate that fluctuates daily according to supply and demand, and an official rate that is government set and held. However, most governments float, within set limits, the official rate so it too responds to fluctuations in the money market. The rate for the day is posted in the exchange office. You can shop around for the best exchange rate which will vary among banks and exchange offices within a city. Hotels, shops and restaurants will also change money but usually at poorer rates than available elsewhere. Often, a campground will cash travelers checks at as good a rate as a bank or at a slightly lower rate but without a commission charge, so you often come out ahead. The exchange policy at American Express offices is "there is a cost for this service which is included in the rate of exchange you receive. In some countries there are also government or banking association imposed taxes or handling charges." In general, American Express offices seem to give a rate equal to a bank's but with a lower charge. Some offices will cash their own brand travelers check without a fee, but charge a fee for other brands. Actual policy varies by office.

CAMPING

Most people stay at the many excellent organized campgrounds with all the conveniences provided. However, to save money or secure isolation some people pitch their tent in rural areas without benefit of a campground. This is called freelance camping.

ORGANIZED CAMPGROUNDS   The arbiters of the French language, that group of elite Frenchmen who are official guardians of the virginity of *le francais*, wish the phrase *le camping* would disappear. It is not *(quelle horreur!)* pure French but to them another incidence of that creeping disease termed *franglais*. But a visitor from abroad is grateful that camping remains recognizable regardless of language. The international symbol to denote a campground is the outline of a tent. The number below the tent indicates the distance to the campground in meters.

These signs will lead you to an immense variety of excellent campgrounds in Europe. Many have been placed in breathtaking surroundings and command a view of spectacular mountains, the bright lights of a city, a castle-studded river, or a clear blue lake or sea. In Oslo, Ekeberg Camping spreads on a hillside overlooking the twinkling lights of downtown Oslo. In Paris, the campground nestles between the Seine River and the Bois de Boulogne park. In the Loire Valley of France, campers look up from their island campground, L'lle d'Or, towards floodlit Amboise Castle across the river. In Greece, while everyone else is sweltering in downtown Athens, campers enjoy the cooling winds of the Aegean blowing offshore while viewing the Athenean sunset as it dips slowly into the sea.

When you arrive at the campground, first go into the office to register. The attendant will ask for one passport from your party and record your name and address as required by law regardless of where you stay. Sometimes the passport will be returned then, but more often it will be retained until check out. If you need your passport for changing money in town, the attendant will either let you have it before checking out or ask for a travelers check to keep in its place. Leaving either is perfectly safe.

Occasionally, you pay upon arrival. If you don't know how long you'll be staying only pay for one night and then pay again the next day if staying over. Camping rates are posted in the office. Usually the total camp fee is a composite of separate fees for each adult, child, tent, motorcycle, car, van and hookup. In this case you will be charged per person and per tent. Some camps charge less for a small tent than a large one. Always ask for a lower rate for a small tent, even though one may not be posted, because sometimes there is one. Some camps charge per person and per site. The site fee normally covers both tent and car. Sometimes a reduction will be given on the site fee for a small tent, but often not, especially where units are delineated. Generally, camping costs about $4 to $7 for two people, or about $3 to $5 for one person. In most camps, the registration clerk issues a tag to hang on the tent to show that you've registered. This is returned to the office at the end of your stay when checking out. Campgrounds always issue a receipt after receiving payment.

Most campgrounds are not marked off into sites but some are. In either case, a particular site is rarely assigned. Instead you are free to choose any spot in the camping area which suits you. Usually it's well to camp at the back of the campground to be away from the noise of the road. Often there will be an area where backpacking tents tend to congregate. Some camps have separate areas for tents and trailers. In northern Europe where there's plenty of rainfall, the campground is usually a beautiful green lawn. In more arid southern Europe, you'll find dry grass and hardpacked earth. There are always bushes, trees and dirt or gravel roads. Almost every campground is enclosed by a fence.

If the campground is any size at all, there will be more than one restroom and shower facility. Not all campgrounds provide toilet paper, especially in southern Europe where forests are scarce. In that case, the camp store will stock single rolls of toilet paper. In over half the campgrounds you will be using, the washroom sinks will have hot water in addition to cold water. Almost every campground in Europe has hot showers, but sometimes an extra charge is made. A token is bought from the office and inserted in the meter. The result is about 3 to 8 minutes worth of hot water. (All campgrounds listed in this book have hot showers, unless noted otherwise.) Electrical outlets with the usual voltage of the country and mirrors are provided in washrooms. If uncertain how your razor will react, to avoid burning out the motor, first switch it to the high voltage setting and plug it in. If it runs slowly, switch to low voltage and try again.

Virtually every campground provides separate sinks with at least cold water for hand washing laundry. Often drying lines are available. Some campgrounds have an automatic washing machine for which the charge is about $3-$4 per load. If detergent isn't included in the price, the store will sell it by the bagful. Usually campgrounds in northern Europe will also have a dryer, but only rarely in southern Europe where clothes line-dry quickly. Most campgrounds have a separate set of sinks for dishwashing. It is forbidden to do laundry in dishwashing sinks or dishes in laundry sinks.

Most campgrounds in large cities will have anything from a small store to a mini-supermarket. Fresh bread and rolls are delivered daily early enough for breakfast. You'll also find milk, cheese, sausage, eggs, individual servings of fruit-flavored yoghurt, butter, margarine, fruit juice, cereal, coffee, tea, wine (in southern Europe), canned goods, frozen meats and vegetables, and a limited supply of fresh fruit and vegetables. The store also stocks detergent and dishwashing soap; camping supplies such as Gaz fuel cartridges and plastic plates and utensils; postcards and souvenirs, and miscellaneous items.

In large city campgrounds, usually picnic tables and chairs are outside the store making it easy to cook or eat breakfast in comfort. Some camps have dining facilities such as a snack bar or restaurant.

Most campgrounds provide playground equipment for children, and some have a swimming pool, lake or river for swimming nearby. Some camps have a day room furnished with tables and chairs on a linoleum floor. The day rooms are most often deserted and a good place to have breakfast if tables and chairs are not available by the store. Especially in Scandinavia, hotplates are often available, free or for a small charge. Some campgrounds have a refrigerator campers can use. Sometimes camp personnel will change money, offer free city maps and tourist literature and sell stamps. They all are happy to offer sightseeing advice and explain how to get where by public transportation.

Most campgrounds have rules which you would pretty much expect, like don't pick the flowers or shrubs, turn off the lights, no loud noise after 10pm and don't litter. However, a few are unexpected: don't hang your laundry from the tent lines, but use the drying area provided, and if you arrive after 11pm the car must be left outside the camp and you must walk in.

Campgounds are classified by national governments and organizations issuing campground guides. A government will classify its country's campgrounds to maintain standards and set fees. Campgrounds with more facilities are allowed to charge more. Guidebook compilers rate campgrounds according to criteria important to vacationing Europeans. Since most Europeans go to the beach and stay put for several weeks, guidebooks focus on auxiliary facilities. In effect these two systems give similar ratings. Higher rated camps are not necessarily better than lower rated ones in restroom quality. In general, European campgrounds are very good regardless of classification.

Virtually no campground will turn away a camper on foot even though the camp may be "full." Because of this, we never had any qualms about arriving in a city in the evening and not finding a place to stay. Often a good time to be traveling is in the evening when museums and stores are closed, and you can bring along dinner to eat on the train.

Belongings in your zipped up tent and on the community drying lines will be safe in campgounds in Europe. All campers seem to operate on a strict honor system. We have never experienced, or had reported to us, any campground theft.

FREELANCE CAMPING   In some countries it is legal to pitch a tent outside an organized campground as long as it's not nearby houses or other dwellings and you're careful not to foul the water supply. Those who do this, generally take the train to a small village and start walking along the beach or into forest land until a suitable spot is found.

EUROPEAN TRAINS

In sleek modern coaches of the marvelous European railway network, you will glide from one city center to another in less time than you could fly or drive. The wonder is that this same network finds its way into the most idyllic out-of-the-way hamlet through the most breathtaking scenery in every country in Europe. The railway is the dominant mode of transportation on the continent and is well organized and easy to use.

TO BEGIN USING YOUR EURAILPASS   Before your pass is used the first time, it must be validated at the ticket or information window of any railroad station. The clerk will write the start and end dates on your pass, stamp it, and return it to you. Check to make sure the dates are correct. Keep the validation stub separate from the pass, as it is necessary to show to receive a replacement should the pass become lost.

THE TRAIN STATION   The European train station is an institution in itself. The main station is most always downtown and the main shopping street often begins at its entrance. The bus terminal is normally across the street or within a block or two. Large cities generally have more than one train station. Train schedules indicate the departure station in parenthesis following the city name. Be sure to go to the correct station!

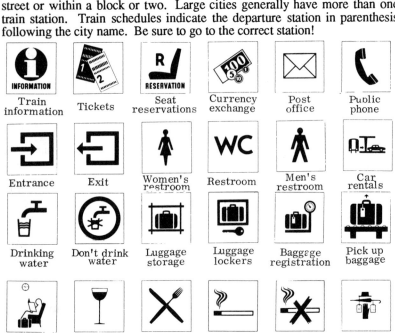

Train information	Tickets	Seat reservations	Currency exchange	Post office	Public phone
Entrance	Exit	Women's restroom	Restroom	Men's restroom	Car rentals
Drinking water	Don't drink water	Luggage storage	Luggage lockers	Baggage registration	Pick up baggage
Waiting room	Snack bar	Restaurant	Smoking permitted	No smoking	Lost and found

The station is always a bustling place with people coming and going at all hours. Some large stations resemble an abbreviated shopping mall. Every capital city station offers multiple services which stay open as long as trains are arriving and departing. You will often find (1) several dining areas ranging from snack buffets, to cafeterias to first class dining rooms; (2) foreign exchange office; (3) train information office for obtaining information on train schedules, picking up free abridged timetables for trains departing and arriving for that city, and sometimes seat reservations; (4) ticket windows for buying tickets and sometimes for reserving seats; (5) sometimes a special window or office solely for seat reservations; (6) a tourist information office; (7) a hotel reservations counter whose assistant will reserve a hotel room for a fee; (8) attended temporary luggage storage facilities; (9) coin-operated temporary luggage storage lockers; (11) restrooms; (12) newstand and candy counter; (13) large readerboard listing train arrivals and departures by track number; and (14) first and second class waiting rooms.

STORING YOUR PACK AT THE STATION   Most stations have two kinds of temporary luggage storage facilties. First, rows of coin-operated lockers in two sizes are scattered throughout the station. Luggage can be left for 24 hours after which it will be removed to the attended baggage check office. Backpacks do not fit in the small size, and it's often difficult to find an empty large size. A large size locker costs about $1-$2. The alternative is to check the pack at the attended baggage check which charges similarly but on a per piece basis, regardless of size. The charge is either per 24-hours or per calendar day. These places are called *deposito bagagli* in Italian, *gepackverwahrung* in German-speaking countries, *depot de bagages* in France and *la oficina de equipajes* in Spain. The checking service is open long hours, but note the posted closing time. Lines sometimes form during the peak demand time of late afternoon.

TRAIN INFORMATION OFFICE   *Bureau de renseignements, auskunftsburo, oficina de informacion and ufficio informazioni* all signify a train information office. The universal symbol is a lower case i. Usually there are lines at the office and it is easier to look up schedule information yourself using the timetables provided. But for personalized service, information assistants will do the work for you and prepare a small itinerary. Free schedules for both local trains and international routes are available from this office, either on racks for the taking or by asking a clerk.

STATION TIMETABLES   Train schedules for arrivals and departures for that particular train station are posted within the station in the lobby and by the tracks. These are large sheets of paper hung on walls or dividers. Departures are printed on yellow paper and arrivals on white. Trains are listed starting with early morning trains and ending with trains arriving or departing near midnight. This makes it easy to arrive at the station and determine what trains are about to leave. Different schedules are generally in effect for "working day trains" which run Monday through Saturday and for trains operating on Sundays and holidays. Times are given using the 24-hour clock which is the same as ours up to noon and then becomes 13:00 for 1pm, 14:00 for 2pm an so forth until 24:00 midnight. Fast trains are printed in red. The train name and number, destination, major intermediate stops and track number are listed. Nearby the schedules, the composition of the most important trains is usually posted. This is useful to determine where first class coaches are positioned. When checking schedules, be sure to note the station from which the train departs. This is given in parenthesis following the name of the city. Most large cities have more than one station and often a train will only stop at one station in the city. It is important to know in advance at what station you want to get off or you might find yourself in the next town. To learn the track number for a connecting train, ask the conductor on board.

GETTING ON BOARD THE RIGHT TRAIN   Consult the large readerboard which is usually suspended from the ceiling or on the wall of every large station. It lists arriving and departing trains, giving the most accurate information including any last minute changes that may have been made.   The right half of the board lists departures by kind of train, originating city, destination, time of departure and track number. Scan the board until you recognize your train.   Make a mental note of the track number.   Track is *quai* in French, *glies* in German, *spoor, spor and spar* in Dutch, Norwegian and Swedish respectively, *perron* in Danish, *voie* in Flemish (Belgium), *binario* in Italian and *anden* in Spanish. Signs point the way to the tracks. The track number is prominently displayed from a post in front of each track. Walk along beside the coaches of your train, noting the markings on the sides of the coaches. Number "1" means the seats are first class. Number "2" indicates second class seats. Sometimes a coach will be half first class and half second class and each end is so designated.   The yellow stripe on the tracks indicate where the first class cars will be stopping.
Each coach has a removable metal nameplate in a slot on the side of the coach by the door. The first line lists the city where the train began its run. The most important intermediate stops are listed on the middle line and the final destination is on the bottom line.

ROMA	ROMA
Firenze - Bologna	Firenze - Bologna
VENEZIA	MILANO

In the example above, the originating point is Rome. Florence and Bologna are the largest city stops enroute though stops are likely elsewhere (look in the schedule for them). Venice is the final destination for the coach with the first nameplate and Milan for the second. What happens is that coaches destined for different cities may be strung together as the train leaves Rome and run together before separating to continue to their final destinations. After the train reaches Bologna, the coaches going to Venice are attached to another engine and each train continues on its way. The important point to remember is that trains can split midway in their journey so be sure to be in the right coach. You can tell when a train is separating because it happens in the switching yard and you can feel the coach being pushed and pulled and another engine being connected. Be sure to check the nameplate in your coach. This is important because people often board one coach and continue down the corridor looking for a vacant compartment.

RESERVATIONS   Generally, in large stations reservations are made at a separate counter from ticket sales. In other stations, a reservation may be made at a ticket window or sometimes in the train information office. The reservation window has the shortest lines monday through thursday mornings. It may be helpful to write the name of the train you want, the date of departure (Europeans write the day BEFORE the month, such as 10-6-88 for June 10, 1988) and the time of departure using the 24-hour clock. You can request a window seat which is handy because of the small table attached to the wall below the window. On trains having airplane-type seating, rather than the usual compartments of 6 persons in first class and 6 to 8 in second, both window seat and side of aisle can be reserved. Also register your preference for either a smoking or non-smoking compartment or section. The reservation fee ranges from about $1.50-$2.00. You will be issued a computer-printed card that indicates coach and seat number. A reservation can also be made at a travel agency for the same fee.

For certain trains a reservation is required by regulations, but for others it depends on your estimate of how crowded it is likely to be. We never made a reservation unless it was mandatory. However, at the least we recommend making a reservation on the train that connects with the ferry in Brindisi, Italy, to and from Greece.

Otherwise, when is a reservation necessary?   This is difficult to answer and the guidelines given here should be refined in Europe by talking with others who have just come from where you're going.   In general, second class is more crowded than first class and might require a reservation upon occasion. Trains are less crowded during the week and when traveling against holiday traffic which travels south on Friday night and Saturday and returns heading north on Sunday evening. Trains are usually busy during the weekend of a national holiday. Trains are more crowded in Italy and Spain. In northern Europe, a reservation usually isn't necessary unless it's mandatory. Throughout Europe, even if a train is full, there are always some people with reservations who are traveling a short distance and their seats will be available after they get off. Another approach if there isn't a seat is to find the refreshment car and order something.

On the train, if a seat is reserved a reservation card will be tucked into the pocket at the side of the seat or in the holder outside the compartment door. The card indicates between which cities the seat is reserved. Other people may occupy the seat either before or after. If there is no card, then the seat isn't reserved.

TYPES OF TRAINS   EuroCity are the best of the international long distance trains. These trains travel through several countries and stop only at main cities. Most EuroCity trains operate wholly during the day. The few that run overnight consist entirely of sleeping accommodations such as couchettes and sleeping cars. As there are no seats, at minimum a passenger must pay for a couchette. EuroCity night trains are often more crowded than a regular overnight train with compartments.

International Express trains make a continuous journey through several countries and always carry both first and second class.

Only a few Trans Europe Express (TEE) trains still exist for most have been converted to InterCity trains. The few in existence offer all-first-class long distance daytime travel.

Train Grande Vitesse (TGV) trains are the fastest trains in Europe and run on their own specially made track. Currently they travel south from Paris to the Riviera and to Geneva and Lausanne in Switzerland. They carry both first and second class. A reservation is mandatory, but can be obtained at the last minute from the machines at the station.

InterCity trains are the best the country has to offer for travel within its boundaries. These trains connect major cities fast and frequently. A reservation is never needed on these in northern Europe unless it's mandatory. In southern Europe, a somewhat equivalent train is the Rapido. A reservation may be needed depending on class and season.

There are other slower trains that stop at smaller cities and commuter trains that serve the suburbs of large cities.

ABOARD THE TRAIN   Two types of coaches are found in Europe. The most fun are the coaches that are separated into compartments of two rows of three or four seats opposite each other. On one end is a window. These compartments offer privacy when you want it or the intimacy of a friendly small group should you desire conversation. A corridor is between the compartment doors and the windows on the other side of the train. Each compartment has a sliding door with an inset window and curtain. The seats are plushly upholstered and very comfortable. There are both armrests and headrests and usually a small pillow attached to the headrest. A small table is between the two seats next to the window. All TGV's and some InterCity trains have airline-type seating with a central aisle having seats on either side. These seats are very spacious with much more legroom than is found on long-distance buses or tourist class in airplanes.

Wire luggage racks are provided above the seats regardless of the type of coach. On a few trains, a luggage storage area is located at either end of the coach.

Compartmented coaches offer comfortable possibililties for sleeping on overnight journeys. In older trains the seats pull forward across from each other to form a sleeping area. In the newer compartments the seats recline but cannot be pulled together. It's possible, though, to stretch across 3 or 4 seats by retracting the armrests between the seats. In this case, three can sleep in one compartment: two on the seats and one on the floor. Taking an occasional overnight journey will save travel time and the money that would otherwise be paid for camping. If the compartment has three or fewer people, everyone can stretch out and get a good night's sleep. Otherwise, the night can be very uncomfortable. Some overnight trains are virtually empty, especially those not on mainline routes and outside of July and August.

On trains that are more than half full, discouraging people from entering your compartment and encouraging them to choose another requires a basic strategy. People generally enter a compartment that won't be disrupted by their entry. Upon finding an empty compartment, go inside and immediately pull the curtain closed across the window on the sliding doors. This will close the compartment off from the outside corridor. Then get out your sleeping bag, stretch across the seats, turn off the lights and go to sleep. People will be reluctant to disturb you. Of course, if the train is full and there are no other seats to be had, you will have to graciously give up your extra ones.

Finding an empty compartment is the most comfortable way to sleep on trains. Barring that, the next most comfortable is a couchette (pronounced koo-SHAY). For about $13, a couchette can be reserved for either first or second class at the reservations counter. It consists of a special coach with compartments containing two rows of three seats facing each other. Each row converts to bunk beds stacked three high. Each side must observe the same bedtime. Usually the compartment will be full because as reservations are made each person is assigned the next available seat. If a border will be crossed, the purser will collect passports in the evening and handle customs formalities allowing passengers to sleep through undisturbed. Without a couchette, the customs official wakens you to check your passport at border crossings.

Restrooms are found at both ends of each coach and are used by both sexes. You can easily tell if one is occupied because locking the latch activates a red sign (ocupado) by the handle on the outside door. Sometimes at each end of the car is a light that turns green or red according to whether or not the restroom is free. In each restroom is a toilet, toilet paper, small sink, paper towels, mirror and electric outlet. The water in the sinks is not drinkable and is meant for washing only. The toilet should not be used when the train is in the station because waste empties directly onto the tracks.

All international trains offer dining facilities, but the price is so high (about $20 and up) that few campers use them. If seating is in compartments, there is usually a dining car. If the train has airplane-style seating, then dinner is served at the seats, complete with fine china, wine goblets and linen. Periodically carts are rolled down the aisle offering a variety of snack food for sale, such as sandwiches, fruit, coffee, soft drinks and milk. Because all food on trains is high priced, the first rule of budget travel is to bring food and water with you. Always fill your water bottle at the station before boarding and have along at least a snack.

When it's time to get off the train, watch out the window for the name of the station as the train is pulling in. You will have a few minutes between seeing the station name and having to get off. Large cities often have more than one station, so you should know in advance which station you want. If you don't know at what stations the train stops, ask the conductor when he checks tickets. Once in the station, find the tourist information office, ask for a map and verify directions to the campground.

FOOD

A last stand for national character is being made in the kitchens of each European nation. Apart from the cross-continent favorite of steak and french fries, the rest of the foods that make up the menu are rooted deep in each nation's history. The tumultuousness of the past has gone a long way in determining current quality of cuisine. By and large, the best eating is in areas where life still revolves around the land. The cooking is not as good in countries most dislocated by industry. The farmhouse tradition of good eating, supported by the intense interest of the French, make France a wonderful mecca for delicious dining. The cuisine is also wonderful in Italy and slightly cheaper.

Food will be your number one expense in Europe, assuming the train fare is prepaid. The camper has the most flexibility of food costs because he can choose among cooking, picnics, takeouts and eating out. Theoretically, one could prepare all one's own meals, but this would mean missing out on the excitement of foreign foods. Greece and Portugal have the cheapest food and restaurants. Other countries are more expensive. For instance, a meal in a taverna in Greece will cost about $5.00. One in a restaurant in Italy or France will run about $10.00. A cafeteria meal in Italy or northern Europe will cost about $6.00.

BREAKFAST   Breakfast is normally purchased from the campground store and brought to the tables and chairs provided for campers.   The opportunity of having a good breakfast is one of the great advantages of camping. A psychologically sound and comfortable approach is to plan to eat for breakfast in Europe similar foods to what you eat at home. If this involves cooking or coffee then bringing along a one-burner Camping Gaz stove is a good idea. It can be set up on the table and the cooking done there. You should also carry some instant, or freeze-dried coffee from home as it is expensive and heavily taxed in Europe. So is tea, except in Britain. If you generally have a cold breakfast of cereal with milk, toast and juice, then the European counterpart would be fresh rolls, cereal (cornflakes, Familia, etc.) with milk and a piece of fruit. Canned fruit juices are very expensive in Europe and fresh fruit is the best substitute. If you're used to orange juice, a juice mix powder could be brought along. Other possibilities for breakfast that are carried by almost every camp store are cheese, sliced luncheon meats, eggs, individual containers of fruit-flavored yoghurt (about $.75), chocolate milk, canned Danish bacon, jellies, jams and Nutella, a delicious chocolate-hazelnut spread.

EATING LUNCH IN A RESTAURANT IN SOUTHERN EUROPE
The best time to eat at a restaurant is for the noon meal when prices are lower. Prices are also lower in restaurants in smaller towns rather than large cities. In France and southern Europe, it is the *table d'hote* lunch that vies for the patronage of the businessman, bureaucrat, shopgirl and officeworker on their lunch hour. This is the daily special which changes each day, incorporates seasonal foods and is served more quickly than anything on the regular menu. It goes by a different name in each country, such as *menu a 52 franc* in France or *el pranzo* in Italy. A weekday is the best time for this lunch. On Sunday, restaurants are geared for the family Sunday outing trade and the selected meal is more expensive as it usually incorporates more costly ingredients. Normally, the meal will have at least three courses. Taxes and service may not be included in the price, but the menu will state this.   If beverage is included, the menu will include that information. Probably you will have your choice of a red or white house wine that varies with the quality of the restaurant, but is always pleasant. Individual carafes are filled from a big barrel in back. Usually, mineral water can be substituted for the wine.

Another menu custom is the government-regulated tourist menu offered in several countries. The rules are uniform within each country and the quoted price is always all-inclusive of beverage, service, cover and taxes. The meal is several courses as stipulated by law. The diner is given a selection for each course and of beverage.

Most every European restaurant posts its a la carte, table d'hote and tourist menu outside near the door and you will quickly get in the habit of menu shopping before deciding to enter. Look for what entree is included and at what price when menu shopping. Whether you find the entree appealing on the table d'hote menu will usually determine if you stay. Normally the locals know the best values. Follow a trail of officeworkers into a restaurant to discover a good value for that particular location. Aim for a 1:00pm lunch in most countries and allow $5 to $13 for this meal.

To help keep costs in line, reserve coffee and other beverages not included in the meal for back at camp where they're cheaper. Do this for dessert too, if it's not included. Water isn't automatically placed on the table like at home and you must ask for it. Make it clearly known that you want tap water as Europeans drink bottled mineral water with wine and food and it hurts the waiter to see you depart from custom. When asking for water use your hands like you're turning on the water faucet so he'll know what you want. Otherwise he will unseal the mineral water bottle before he gets to your table leaving you no choice but to pay for it. A service charge of 12 to 15 percent will be automatically added to your bill if it's not already included in a special menu price such as the tourist menu. Normally the menu will state at the bottom that there is a mandatory service charge. If there isn't one, then a 10 to 15 percent tip is in order. Even when a service charge has been added, you will notice people leaving small change behind. This is not more than five percent of the bill and is a small extra tip.

Much of the cost of the meal will depend upon your selection of entree. Beef is always the most expensive except for shellfish and other exotica. Don't bother with steaks as nothing compares with the best American steakhouses. However, steak and fries are THE continent-wide favorite and the combination is found on most menus. Most times this is a thin filet that has been pounded tender and fried. Chicken and veal are treats; chickens are plump and flavorful and veal is actually less expensive than beef. Fish and especially eel are reasonable and very good. Subtle sauces and fresh herb seasonings are the treats in southern European cooking. Except in an unnervingly expensive haute cuisine-type restaurant where each item is ordered separately and not a morsel is thrown in free, the entree will come garnished with a vegetable or two at least. In a few places in southern Europe, a small sum is charged for each piece of bread eaten from the basket.

LUNCH IN A CAFETERIA OR CAFE IN SOUTHERN EUROPE For something cheaper than a restaurant, go to a cafeteria (self-service) or cafe. Cafeterias are not always like ours with trays and a line. Often there is a central counter where you place your order and then take it to a perimeter counter with stools. In Italy, the food is carefully prepared and very good at these places. They are considerably less expensive than a restaurant, you can see what you're ordering and can order as little or as much as you like. There are also take-out bars where you can pick up a hot slice of pizza or cheese-filled turnover. At the many cafe-bars, ready made cheese and meat sandwiches on a French roll are piled on trays. which make a fine lunch when accompanied by a piece of fruit.

CAFETERIAS IN NORTHERN EUROPE Restaurants are prohibitively expensive in northern Europe, but a cafeteria is more affordable. They are often found in train stations, supermarkets and department stores. Usually, an order can be wrapped "to go" upon request which is handy for train travel.

BUDGET RULES **Omit soft drinks** and canned fruit juices as they are very expensive. Always drink water with cafeteria meals in northern Europe because beverages are generally twice the cost from a grocery store. Coffee drinkers should bring some with them and make it at camp.

Limit ice cream cones ($1-$2 each) to one a day--even when it's hot.

Buy food at the public market whenever possible in France and southern Europe because it costs anywhere from a third to a half less than in the small shops. The public market is generally called the open market in Europe, even though it is sometimes in a building. Large cities have ones in several locations. The main market will be open monday through saturday morning at least. Smaller neighborhood markets may operate only two or three times a week in the morning. In a small town, the market is usually in the central square by the oldest church. The tourist office can tell you when and where the market operates. Anything can be bought in small amounts. Food is sold by gram and kilo rather than ounce and pound, except in Britain. One-half kilo (500 grams) is a little over one pound. One hundred grams is a little less than a quarter pound, or about three ounces. One kilo (1,000 grams) equals 2.2 pounds. Liquids are sold by the liter. One liter is slightly less than a quart. One U.S. gallon equals 3-3/4 liters. The British gallon is larger than ours.

In northern Europe, the best buys are usually found as supermarket specials. Also watch for house brands and plain labeling which are cheaper than brand name similar items. The basement supermarket in the second or third class department store has good values.

Always check the price before buying anything.

Fill up on bread. Fresh, fragrant bread may be the staff of life, but it is the saviour of your budget as well. Most European governments would fall if the price of bread became too high. In France, Italy, Spain, Portugal and Greece, french style bread is sold unwrapped from shelves or baskets according to size and slipped into your shopping bag. When first bought, the bread should be put into a waxed paper bag so that the crust will remain crisp and the moistness of the interior will not migrate into the crust. But bread goes stale quickly, especially after being broken open. At that point, keep the remainder of the loaf in a plastic bag with a twist on it for it to remain fresh. Sliced and wrapped bread is the standard in northern Europe. Each country bakes a variety of bread, but the type eaten by the common man is the cheapest. This means French bread in southern Europe, rye bread in northern Europe and white sliced sandwich bread in Britain.

DAIRY PRODUCTS Milk is a best buy in Europe, and especially in Scandinavia. In small towns of Greece, Portugal and Spain, check for a pasteurization label. Eggs, cheese, yoghurt and refrigerated custard are reasonable in price and a good source of protein. The cheapest cheese is usually a local cheese of mild flavor. It's hard to go wrong when buying it. Cheese is served for breakfast in Scandinavia, Germany and Holland, and as a pre-dessert course in France. Entering a cheese shop is bewildering in the variety of cheese resting behind the counter. If you are unsure of your tastes, the best policy is to buy 100 grams worth. As cheese isn't taken out of the cheese cellar until it is ripe, try to eat it within a few hours or sooner in hot weather. However, hard type cheese keeps longer if the temperature isn't too warm. Cheese is sold in camp stores and supermarkets wrapped in plastic just like you're used to. Dutch and Danish packaged cheeses are distributed throughout Europe.

MEAT, POULTRY AND FISH Chicken is the cheapest of these. The European fowl is a plump, flavorful bird and one of our favorites.

Rotisseried chicken is a popular item that you will see often. These chickens are cooked on a giant rotisserie where about seven rows of birds revolve on long skewers, each row suspended above another row in front of the cooking element. Each newly-to-be-roasted row of chickens is placed on the top rack where their juices baste the birds beneath and so on down to the bottom row. The chickens that are almost done hang on the bottom rack, with a trough beneath to catch juices for basting. To fill an order, a chicken is removed from the spit, hacked in half or kept whole as ordered and slipped into a foil-lined bag. One chicken serves three adults and costs about $6-$8.

Veal is cheaper than beef, particularly in Spain and Italy. Little veal is sold in the U.S. because of high prices and limited production, so Europe is your opportunity to indulge. Beef hamburger costs more but shrinks less because growth-inducing hormones aren't used as much in Europe. Meat cuts differ with the French dividing the carcass according to muscle separation rather than across the grain as we do.

FRUITS AND VEGETABLES   Prices vary according to season and locality. On-the-spot price comparisons will let you know the best buy at the moment. Fruit is somewhat expensive in northern Europe, but you can get your fill in Italy, Spain and especially Greece. The variety of fruit is quite astounding and there are some we've never seen in North America. Europeans commonly eat fruit for dessert. Easily found vegetables are string beans, beets, potatoes, tomatoes, lettuce, green peppers and greens.

BEVERAGES   We drink tap water everywhere in Western Europe without ill effect. Bottled water is available for about $.50-$1 in grocery stores. There are both flat and fizzy types. Two fizzless kinds sold in Italy and France are Evian and Vitelli. If you need a water bottle for the train, use the plastic bottle with screw cap from mineral water. All soft drinks are expensive, which is why the suggested packing list contains envelopes of drink mixes. Expect to be continually thirsty in the hot weather of southern Europe.

Campground stores in Italy stock reasonably priced wines. It is also well-priced in France, Spain and Greece. Belgium, Germany, Holland and Scandinavia are noted beer-drinking countries. The price is less in a grocery store than a cafe, but is taxed in either case.

EUROPEAN CUSTOMS

CITY PUBLIC TRANSPORTATION SYSTEMS   These are well developed, efficient and frequent. Each system has its own deviations, but generally the name on the front of the bus is its destination. Two names indicate both the beginning and end of the run. To make sure you are on the right bus and going in the right direction, as you enter, say the destination you want in a questioning manner and the driver will usually call out your stop when it's time to get off. It's usually cheaper to buy tickets in multiples before you get on a bus. If tickets are sold at all on a bus, they are often more expensive. If you don't see the locals buying tickets, it's because they have weekly or monthly passes which are shown only if an inspector gets aboard.   Some trams and buses operate on the honor system where a machine dispenses your ticket, you cancel it in the machine and show it only if an inspector comes aboard. The subway is always the fastest and least complicated method of getting around, but you miss the scenery.

CROSSING THE STREET   Sometimes in southern Europe, getting across the street is hard. The timid wait for a stout Italian housewife to cross and tag along as she shunts across the street shouting epithets at her countrymen who calculate risks very finely and stop at the last possible moment. Check for underground passageways tunneling beneath main steets carrying traffic swirling around monuments. Towards northern Europe, the frequency of traffic lights seemingly increases in direct proportion to the number of bicycles. Watch out for them. When in Britain, remember to look right before crossing the street as traffic comes from the opposite direction.

DATE AND TIME   Europeans write the date with the day preceding the month, such as 1 June 19880 for June 1, 1988. They write their number 7 with a cross on the stem to avoid confusing it with number 1. Europe uses the 24-hour clock where our 1pm is 13:00, our 2:00pm is 14:00 and so forth until midnight or 24:00.

HIGH ALTITUDE SICKNESS   If you plan any excursions up high mountains in the Alps, there is a slight possibility of experiencing high altitude sickness with symptoms of breathing difficulty, faintness or headache. Sit down until you adjust and then go slow, or take the next lift down.

MANNERS   European manners vary slightly from ours in several respects. It's standard procedure to say *good morning* or *good afternoon* when entering a small shop, bakery, train compartment or other small physical space with few people. Those present return the greeting, but it's not necessarily a prelude to conversation. In France, it's impolite to greet a person with a *good morning* for instance without adding *mademoiselle, madame or monsieur* after it.

During an introduction on a social occasion, a European will shake hands when meeting and usually say his name simultaneously, rather than say *how to do you do*. During a conversation, whereas an American may be more apt to state the literal truth and be very direct, the European tends to avoid this if it might hurt someone's feelings. Europeans tend not to ask personal questions like *what do you do for a living* or *how many children do you have* but are more likely to comment on an item from the newspaper or a sports event. A European appreciates a sincere, favorable comment about his country. In public places, the European tends to keep his voice pitched low and never shouts across open spaces. European children tend to play less exuberantly, not expect quite so much attention from their parents and not run around so freely in public.

Europeans are very friendly once you have indicated your willingness for conversation, but usually you'll have to do the initial ice-breaking. Smiles, questions and compliments always work.

MEDICAL HELP   Competent medical help is never far away. Some campgrounds have a doctor on call, or you can get the name of an English-speaking one from an American consulate 24 hours a day, tourist office or leading hotel. Costs are lower than in the U.S. The American Hospital in

Paris has a walk-in outpatient clinic. French pharmacists prepare prescriptions, but are also trained to dress wounds, treat burns, set bones and give first aid. A pharmacy sells asperin, sanitary napkins, tampons, baby food and diapers. American-trained dentists are reputedly superior to European ones and worth seeking out should the need arise.

OCEAN BEACHES   Apart from pollution, beaches may be unsafe because of tidal action. If a desirable looking beach is little used, there may be a reason so inquire first of the tourist office. Beach conditions are usually posted with green and red pennants on the Atlantic coast.

POLLUTION   Europe has not escaped pollution of its oceans, seas and lakes any more than we. Many sewer systems of coastal towns empty untreated sewage into the sea. Just because you see vacationing Europeans swimming in questionable waters doesn't mean it's safe. Safety is assured in the cold oceanic waters off northern Europe, but swimming in parts of the warm Mediterranean and Adriatic near metropolitan or resort areas, and in the Rhine, Rhone and Po Rivers is risky.

RECEIVING FOREIGN NEWS ABROAD   Major cities have streetside kiosks which stock current English-language newspapers. (The kiosk is, in fact, a small drugstore and has a multitude of minor essentials like writing paper, maps and candy for sale.) *U.S.A. Today* and *The International Herald Tribune* are sold throughout Europe for about $2.

RESTROOMS   Public toilets are found in all the usual places and are not difficult to find until you need one. Museums, train stations, restaurants, department stores and municipal buildings all have facilities. Hot and cold faucets are reversed in Europe. An embossed "C" stands for hot. A red dot indicates hot and a blue dot means cold.

SAFETY OF FOOD AND WATER   Whether or not water is safe depends on its source. In large cities and throughout northern Europe, water comes from a central supply that is watched by authorities. In primitive areas, the source may be a well and might be questionable. However, we drink the water everywhere without ill effect. Egg provides a fertile medium for bacterial growth so be cautious about keeping egg fillings like custards for very long without refrigeration. Avoid shellfish whose beds are in polluted waters such as near Venice and Naples.
     Know in advance what to do if diahrrea should occur. Our doctor recommends drinking only clear liquids for a 24-hour period.

SHOPPING   The best values are generally found in department stores, flea markets, street markets and trade fairs. Avoid small souvenir shops. The lowest prices on souvenirs are in the cheapest department stores.
     A value-added tax is a percentage tax included in the retail price of goods in several countries. Usually the tax is deducted from any purchase mailed out of the country or is reimbursed if the correct forms have been completed.
     Flea markets are fun to browse but hard to find something to buy. They are the place to shop for the whimsical antique item of small size and price. The best time to shop is when weather is terrible and business is slow as in fall or winter. Otherwise, get there when the market opens and preferably on the day new merchandise arrives. Dealers charge what they

think traffic will bear so show no enthusiasm, bargain but be prepared to give up the item or pay the price if the dealer won't come down.

T-shirts are sold throughout Europe for $5 to $15 each. Sweatshirts from the Hofbrauhaus in Munich, Chamonix in France, and other places are widely available in Europe. The cost is about $22-$25.

WRITING HOME   The aerogram is the bargain here. It's a one-page airmail letter that is bought at the post office of the country you're in, written upon, and dropped in the same country's mail box.

PLEASE NOTE

Prices are given for 1989. To use the book in subsequent years, add 10 percent to the campgrounds in southern Europe and 5 percent to those in northern Europe. Always let the registration clerk know you are on foot even when a fee for a small tent is not listed because you may be given a reduction.

Train schedules are given for planning purposes. Departure and arrival times should be checked at the stations. Usually times will vary by about 5 minutes from year to year.

When purchasing transportation arrangements within Europe or entry fees to attractions, always show your student identity card and/or youth hostel card if you have them as unposted reductions are sometimes granted. Often a youth hostel card will net you the same reduction as a student card.

AUSTRIA

That the national anthem is by Mozart is what you would expect from a country where Vienna once stood as the lord of an empire and music reigned supreme. The cultured, graceful and courteous Austrians, the architectural masterpieces from the Hapsburg Empire, and the Alps and small villages combine to make Austria a wonderful country to visit.

CURRENCY   Austrian schilling. One U.S. dollar equals 11.7 schillings. Beware of the large commissions extracted when changing travelers checks at train stations.

WEATHER   June to September is camping season. Prepare for occasional rainfall.

CAMPGROUNDS   Excellent campgrounds are abundant in Austria, a country largely of lakes and mountains and ideal for recreation. Campgrounds cost less outside large cities.   According to regulations, *camping is not restricted to the camping areas, but should one camp on private property, it is first necessary to obtain permission from the owner.*

TRAINS   The Austrian Federal Railways (OBB) are very good and the mountainous routes are particularly scenic though a little slow.   The Transalpin Express, famous for its alpine scenery, goes from Vienna to Basel. The train routes across the Austrian alps into Italy are also good for their alpine views. Trains depart at regular hourly intervals between major cities in Austria. Reservations are not necessary.

Children 6 through 15 pay half fare. Women over 60 and men over 65 pay half price for rail tickets upon presentation of a Half Price Fare Card, purchased for 160AS at the train station. An Austria Ticket is sold giving unlimited rail transportation, but Eurailpasses are more suitable for overseas visitors who are unlikely to fly into Austria and will need transportation to and from the country.

Trains are classified EuroCity, Ex (*expresszug*, international express trains), TS (*triebwagenschnellzug*, long distance express trains, D (general express trains), TE (*triebwageneilzug*, semi fast trains) and E (*eilzug*, general semi fast trains). Corridor trains (*korridorzuge*) pass through Germany or

Italy to reach another part of Austria. It is not possible to get off or on in Germany or Italy on these trains.

Free timetables are available in train information offices. Months are given in Roman numerals. Other abbreviations are:

ab	leaves at	mo	Monday
an	arrives at	di	Tuesday
bis	until, to	mi	Wednesday
und	and	do	Thursday
nur	only	fr	Friday
preis	price	sa	Saturday
von	from	so	Sunday
taglich	daily		

EURAIL BONUSES (1) Puchberg am Schneeberg-Hochschneeberg rack railway. This is reached by train from Vienna's Sudbahnhof to Wiener Neustadt, a town south of Vienna. Then a local train is taken to the transfer point for the cogwheel train that climbs 22 km. to Puchberg am Schneeberg on Schneeberg mountain (6,806 feet). This is the highest peak in lower Austria from which there is a fine view, including sheer rock faces. (2) The rack railway from St. Wolfgang to Schafbergspitze and ferries on Lake Wolfgang. See St. Wolfgang for details. (3) Ferries operated by Erste Donau-Dampfschiffahrts-Gesellschaft between Passau and Vienna. See Vienna for details. (4) Fifty percent reduction on ferry boats operated by steamship companies on Lake Constance (Bodensee). Lake Constance is shared by Austria, Germany and Switzerland. The area has good train access from Innsbruck, Zurich and Stuttgart and many fine campgrounds.

FOOD Mountainous Austria has excellent water. Foodstores are open 7-6:30 on weekdays and close at 2:30pm on Saturday. (In Vienna, small grocery stores in the train stations close about 11pm.) *Feinkost* is a delicatessen. Pastry shops (*kaffeehaus*) have take-out and sit-down service of rolls, pastries, cakes, coffee, tea and hot chocolate served with or without whipped cream (*schlagobers*). Coffee is served in many different combinations of coffee, milk and whipped cream. Cafes are busiest between 3-5pm for *jause* (pronounced YOW-sah). Sitting for a hour over coffee and writing letters or reading a newspaper is perfectly proper. A basement *keller* or *beisel* serves wine or beer. *Seidel* is 3/10th liter and *krugel* is a half liter of draft beer. *Viertel* is a quarter liter of house wine. Austrian white wines are considered better than reds. Drinking age in a bar or restaurant is 16, or 14 if acccompanied by parents. Gasthaus, beisel and keller establishments serve meals as do restaurants. The best clue to figure the establishment's price level is to check the cost of *Weiner schnitzel* (breaded veal cutlet), a mainstay at all eating places. The daily special (*menus*) is often a good buy. Most entrees are served with (*garni*) a vegetable, usually potato. Any dessert may be ordered with whipped cream (*mit schlag*).

Address a waitress as *Fraulein*, a waiter, *Herr Ober*. In general to attract attention politely, hold up your hand with the index finger extended. The waitress may not bring a bill to the table, but figure it when you indicate you're ready to leave.

HIKING Austrian trails are well maintained and well signed. Paths are marked by colored signs on trees and rocks. Alpine huts along the trails provide beds and meals. One can eat at a hut without sleeping there. The Austrian Alpine Club usually has an office in towns such as Innsbruck, which are the hub of hiking activity. Their offices stock trail maps and give good advice. Virtually any Austrian village has trails nearby. *Gruss Gott* (God greets you) is the most commonly heard greeting on the trails.

SALZBURG

If you've seen *The Sound of Music* then you're already acquainted with Salzburg (pronounced ZAHLTS-bork). Much of the film was shot in and around the town. The city of Mozart provides the perfect backdrop for the famous Mozart Festival in late July and August. You'll be able to find space in at least one of the 8 campgrounds around town, but if you're interested in festival events, write 8 months in advance to Kartenburo der Salzburg Festspiele, Hofstallgasse 1, A-5010 Salzburg, Austria.

TRAIN STATION The Hauptbahnhof has a tourist office open daily 8-8, Sparta bank which charges a large commission when changing travelers checks, and post office. From the track area in the station, go downstairs to exit to the front of the station. The station is 12 blocks from Makartplatz, the center of downtown, and within walking distance of the municipal campground. Salzburg's minor train stations are Bahnhof Gnigl and Aigen.

TOURIST OFFICE (*Informationsdienst*) There are several offices, but the most convenient is at the train station. Ask for the town map, bus route map and two-page sightseeing brochure and addenda, *Visiting Hours and Fees for Sights of Salzburg City.*

CITY TRANSPORTATION Single bus tickets cost adult/15AS, but you can save by buying a 5-ride card (*5-Fahrten Karte Erwachsene*) for 50AS. The 5-ride cards must be bought before boarding the bus from a ticket agency or tobacconist with the sign, *Fahrschein Vorvetkauf.* A 24-hour pass costs 40AS, valid on all tram and bus routes, the Fortress Cable-car, Monchsberg Lift and the Lokalbahn (urban railway) as far as Bergheim. The pass is sold at tourist offices, the Lokalbahnhof opposite the train station, at the Fortress Cable-car ticket office, at Monchsberg Lift (from the conductor) and at tobacconists (*Tabak-Trafiken*) that sell bus tickets. The bus driver sells only single tickets. Each person is responsible for cancelling the ticket in the machine inside the door. A bell rings as the ticket is cancelled. Each ticket is good for one ride, including transfers without time limit. A map of bus lines, *Salzburger Stadtwerke Verkehrsbetriebe*, is free from the tourist office.

CAMPGROUNDS **Stadtcamping Fallenegger**, at Bayerhamer Str. 14A several blocks east of the station, is the most conveniently situated. Open May 1-Sep 31; adult/55AS including tent and hot showers. To walk, take the pedestrian overpass at the north end of the station which puts you across from the station on Lastenstrasse. Turn left on Lastenstrasse and walk a half block until the street is intersected (45-degree angle) by Weiserhofstrasse. Turn right on Weiserhofstrasse and then left on Breitenfelderstrasse for one block. Turn right on Bayerhamerstrasse. The longer route to the

48

campground is to walk on Rainerstrasse south from the station to the vehicle underpass. Turn left on Gabelsbergerstrasse and follow the signs. The campground has a store and snack bar.

Stadtcamping Fallenegger

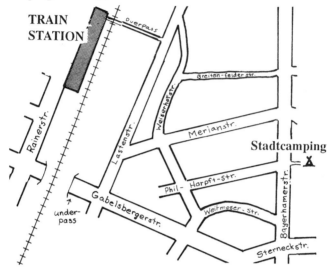

To reach the old town from camp, walk to bus stop *Bayerhamerstr.* on Sterneckstrasse. Take bus 15 in the direction Zentrum/Friedhof (not Kasern). The Rathaus bus stop is the first stop across the river. You can also walk to downtown in about 15 minutes.

Camping Ost-Gnigl, Parscherstrasse 4, is open May 1-Sep 30. Adult/28AS, tent/20AS, store, snack bar. From the main station, local trains leave for Gnigl station only every couple of hours. From Bahnhof Gnigl, walk south for one block to Aglassingerstr. Two blocks farther is Parscherstr. and the camp is on the street near the athletic field. To get there by bus, from the main station take bus 1, 5, 6 or 51 to Mirabellplatz. Transfer to bus 29 to Minnesheimstr. (direction Langwied). To go downtown, walk two blocks north to where Minnesheimstr. intersects with Aglassingerstrasse to the bus stop. Take bus 4 (direction Lieferinger Spitz) which first goes to Makartplatz in the newer part of town before crossing the river to the old town.

FOOD The public markets are at Gruenmarkt on Universitatsplatz in the old town, open M-F 6am-7pm and Sa 6am-1pm, and on Schrannenmarkt, outside Andrakirche, open Thursday morning. Restaurant meals are cheaper in areas outside the central area. You can beat the prices downtown by buying luncheon meat at a *feinkost* and eating in a park. In the old town, not far from the market on Universitatsplatz, is the restaurant complex Sternbrau at Griesgasse 23. The least expensive food is in the self-service section. The tables outside on the terrace can be used for self-service too. This restaurant butchers its own meat and prepares sausages immediately on the premises.

SIGHTSEEING   A walking tour of Salzburg takes at least half a day, and then you should visit Schloss Hellbrunn.

Walking Tour   From Stadtcamping, walk 10 blocks to Schloss Mirabell to explore the grounds, not missing the statues of the funny fat dwarfs featured in *The Sound of Music*. From Schloss Mirabell, walk to Makartplatz, the central square. Cross over Staatsbrucke (bridge) to the old town (innen-stadt) to make the obligatory pilgramage to Mozart's birthplace (Geburtshaus) at Getreidegasse 9. The market is nearby on Universitatsplatz. Continue to Mozartplatz (the center of town) where chimes play at 7am, 11am and 6pm. A tourist office is on Mozartplatz.

Continue past the Cathedral to the base of the funicular ascending to fortress Hohensalzburg, that imposing structure on the hill that lends Salzburg much of its character. The funicular leaves every 10 minutes Apr 9-6, May 8:30-6, Jun 8-8, Jul-Aug 8am-9pm, Sep 8:30am-7pm, Oct-Mar 9-5. Fare is adult/16AS one way, 25AS round trip. The fortress was started in 1077 and continually enlarged until 1681. Forty-minute guided tours through some historically preserved rooms, the castle Museum of Medieval Art and the Rainer Museum are given 9am to 5pm (adult/35AS, student/20AS with tour; adult/10AS, student/5AS without tour.

Schloss Hellbrunn   Completely enchanting are the castle and grounds, termed "manneristic early Baroque style," of Schloss Hellbrunn, located south of Salzburg. Take bus 55 from the main station. Go out to the front of the station, cross the tram tracks and you will see buses beyond. Bus 55 leaves from the far left at 10 and 40 minutes past each hour. Its schedule is posted at the stop. Bus fare is a regular city bus ticket or one ticket from the booklet. The bus also stops at Mirabellplatz and at Makartplatz before proceeding to Schloss Hellbrunn. The trip takes 23 minutes. The bus stops directly in front of the grounds so you don't have to worry about when to get off. On the grounds, follow the signs to the water park. The castle and grounds are open May 9-5, Jun 9-5:30, Jul-Aug 9-6, Sep 9-5, Oct-Apr 9-4:30. Closing time given refers to time the last tour begins. Admission to the castle and 40-minute tour is adult/42AS, student/21AS (German marks accepted). Entry to the grounds is free. The garden is justly famous for its ingenious trick fountains that sprinkle unexpectedly, and as an example of a Baroque ornamental garden incorporating grottoes and a rock theatre. The alpine zoo is adjacent. Some of the castle rooms are unique and cleverly planned. The Folklore Museum is in the Monatsschlosschen, built in 1615. Admission adult/10AS, student/5AS.

Salt Mines   The Salzburgwerke (salt mines) at Bad Durnberg near Hallein are a popular destination, especially for field trips from surrounding elementary schools. The one at Bad Durnberg is tremendously popular, but expect a wait at the mine of at least one hour. The mines themselves are fairly interesting if the tour is in English, but we saw similar things in the Deutsches Museum in Munich without the trouble and expense. But then you don't get the thrill of riding tandem down the steep slides from one mine level to the next. Only go after having visited Schloss Hellbrunn and explored Salzburg. The train for Hallein leaves from the main station, track 3, at 11:15am, 12:41pm, 2:08, 2:37pm, 3:16pm and 4:05pm. The times are from schedules 2 and 22 in the hanging schedule racks at the station. The ride is 30 minutes.

In Hallein, pick up a map of the town at the station ticket window. A bus meets the train arrivals from Salzburg and waits just outside the station on the left. The bus leaves at 7:50am (M-Sa), 8:55am, 9:20am (M-Sa), 11:15am (M-Sa), 12:15pm and 1:05pm (M-Sa). Fare is 16AS one way. The bus goes to the parking lot, and then you must walk uphill for about 3 minutes to the mine entrance. Alternatively, you can walk to the Salzbergbahn lower station in Hallein by walking straight ahead from the station, turning left at the supermarket and continuing through town and across the bridge, where you will begin to see signs to the Salzbergbahn, an aerial cablecar that ascends the mountain. A combination cablecar/mine ticket is sold for 130AS or the cablecar alone is 60AS. The lift leaves every 15 minutes. Save your money if the weather isn't clear. The Saltzbergbahn goes to the top of the mountain and then you must walk back down for 4 minutes to the mine entrance. If you take the cablecar, think about only getting a one way ticket as taking it back down requires walking steeply uphill for 5 minutes from the mine to its terminal. Walking or taking the bus to town is easier and cheaper.

At the mine, pay the 85AS entrance fee (German marks accepted) or exchange the combo ticket at the cashier. The cashier will assign a group number which will be called in turn. Following the tour, the bus from the saltmine to Hallein Station leaves at 10:21am, 11:51am (M-Sa), 12:46pm, 1:41pm (M-Sa), 4:21pm and 5:36pm. Late afternoon trains from Hallein to Salzburg leave from track 4 at 5:48pm, 6pm, 7:08pm and 7:56pm. The last departure continues to Munich.

MEDICAL OUTPATIENT CLINIC Need medical attention? Go to Landeskrankenhaus, the University medical outpatient clinic, for the least complicated approach to medical care at reasonable cost.

To Berchtesgaden, take the train in the direction of Munich and change at Freilassing. The trip is 6 minutes. Trains leave Freilassing at 8:28am, 9:33am, 10:38am, 10:54am, 12:22pm, 1:33pm, 1:58pm, 2:18pm, 3:56pm, 4:49pm, 5:24pm and 6:28pm. One hour or 33 km. Berchtesgaden is much closer to Salzburg than to Munich. Remember your passport!

To Chur and Arosa (Switzerland), leave 10:19am-EuroCity-direction Zurich (ar. Sargans 3:26pm, change trains, lv. Sargans EuroCity 4:19pm-direction Chur, ar. Chur 4:41pm). This is a very scenic route that passes through the Alps into Liechtenstein and then to Switzerland. At Chur, take the small train (included in Eurailpasses) to Arosa and camp there. Trains leave Chur at 4:50pm and 50 minutes past the hour until 10:50pm. The scenic 26 km. takes 62 minutes. For a non EuroCity departure, take the 7:48am non-EuroCity train listed for Lucerne, but stay aboard when you leave Buchs at 2:17pm in the direction of Chur.

To Graz, leave at 7:10am, 9:25am, 9:54am, 11:35am and 3:43pm. 5-1/2 hrs.

To Hallstatt, either take the train to Stainach Irdning (direction Graz), a 2 hour trip, and change for Hallstatt, or preferably go to Attnang-Puchheim (direction Linz), a 45-minute trip, and change for Hallstatt. See departures for Graz or Linz.

To Innsbruck, leave 7:48am, 10:19am EuroCity, 12:14pm EuroCity, 2:19pm EuroCity, 4:19pm, 6:22pm and 8:19pm. Trip is 2 hours.

To Linz, leave at 6:40am and 40 minutes past the hour until 8:40pm. EuroCity departures are 3:40pm, 5:40pm, 7:40pm and 8:40pm. (1 hour, 20 minutes.)

To Lucerne, leave 10:19am EuroCity (change at Zurich, ar. 2:50pm), 12:14pm EuroCity (change at Zurich, ar. 7:50pm), 2:19pm EuroCity (change at Zurich, ar. 9:50pm). A non EuroCity train leaves at 7:48am-direction Innsbruck (ar. Buchs 12:24pm, change trains, lv. Buchs 2:17pm-direction Chur, ar. Sargans 2:34pm, change trains, lv. Sargans 2:49pm-direction Zurich, ar. Zurich 3:50pm, change trains, lv. Zurich 4:01pm-direction Lucerne, ar. Lucerne 4:50pm).

To **Munich**, leave 7:15am, 8:45am, 9:20am EuroCity, 10:38am, 11:56am, 12:34am EuroCity, 1:46pm, 2:47pm, 3:38pm InterCity, 4:13pm, 6:50pm, 7:17pm, 8:47pm and 9:45pm. The ride is 2 hours.

To **St. Wolfgang**, take the train to Attnang-Puchheim and change for a train to Bad Ishl. This is the same train that goes to Hallstatt. See Hallstatt for departure times from Attnang-Puchheim. At Bad Ishl, take the post bus for the 19 km. to St. Wolfgang. One way fare is 28AS. For a more direct route from Salzburg, take the postbus to St. Gilgen, the closest town on St. Wolfgang Lake. Then board the paddle-wheeler boat (free with Eurailpasses) to St. Wolfgang. The bus leaves from the bus area opposite the front of the main train station at 8:15am and 15 minutes past each hour until 7:15pm, then 8:30pm. Between about July 7 and September 9, an express bus leaves at 9:30am and a late nonexpress bus leaves at 11pm. The trip is 50 minutes; the distance is 32 km. and the fare is 52AS one way.

To **Venice**, leave at 8:32am (change at Villach to EuroCity, ar. Venice Mestre only 4:20pm) and 2:09pm (change at Villach, ar. Venice S.L. 10:48pm).

To **Vienna** Westbahnhof, leave 6:40am and 40 minutes past the hour until 8:40pm. EuroCity departures are at 3:40pm, 5:40pm, 7:40pm and 8:40pm. Arrival in Vienna is on the hour, 3 hours and 20 minutes after departure.

SALZKAMMERGUT

Southeast of Salzburg, the Salzkammergut region is noted for limetstone mountains, many lakes and picturesque villages.

Rail lines of the Salzkammergut

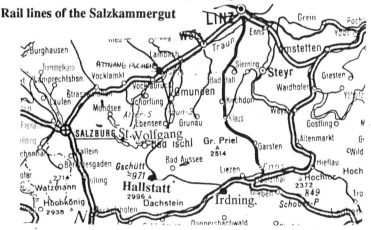

ST. WOLFGANG   Wolfgang See is the best known lake. The beautiful area has many trails giving access to the interior and one that encircles the lake. (Higher than average rainfall in this area though.) Eurailpasses give free use of the boats which connect the towns on Lake Wolfgang and the rack railway from St. Wolfgang to Schafbergspitze, a mountain. (Fare is 168AS roundtrip without Eurailpass.) The summit at 5,850 feet commands a fine view of the many lakes in the area. Allow about 4 hours for the Schafbergspitze trip, including a 2-hour cog-wheel railway ride and sightseeing time at the top. The train departs several times daily; sit on the left for best viewing.

From Salzburg, the 50 km. are most conveniently made by bus. One km. west of St. Wolfgang, is Camping Ried, the best value. Adult/30AS, tent/15AS, tax/3.50AS, store, hot water in sinks, automatic washer. About 1.3 km. east of town is Camping Appesback (adult/39.50AS, tent/25AS), while Camping Berau is slightly farther away towards Stroble.

52

Bus lines of the Salzkammergut

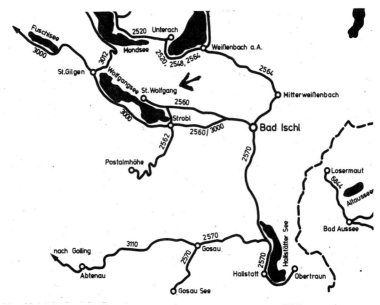

Wolfgangsee

Free Eurail Excursion
to the mountain "Schafberg"
connected with a boat trip
on the lake Wolfgangsee

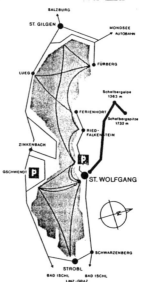

Camping Berau charges adult/36AS, tent/35AS, hot shower/10AS, washing machine/35AS, dryer/35AS. The last bus leaving St. Wolfgang for Camping Appesbach and Berau is 6:20pm from the market square. It arrives at 6:23pm at bus station Appesbach for Camping Appesbach and at 6:27pm at bus station Schwarzenbach for Camping Berau. The closest town served by the railways is Bad Ischl which is 15 km. from St. Wolfgang by bus.

HALLSTATT   Hallstatt is your charming, ever so picturesque Austrian village that eats film. It also has a salt mine without the waiting lines found at the one by Salzburg, is a center of prehistoric finds and the starting point for several trails. To get here, take the train to Obertraun from Attnang Puchheim or Bad Ischl. Get off at Hallstatt Station, the stop after Obertraun. The train is on the line Linz-Attnang Pucheim-Bad Ischl-Bad Aussee-Stainach Irdning. Hallstatt Station and Obertraun are between Bad Ischl and Bad Aussee. Approaching Halstatt from the south, take the train to Bad Ischl from Stainach Irdning. Once off the train, board the connecting ferry (15AS) for the trip across the lake to tiny Hallstatt. Also, frequent postbus connects Hallstatt-Lahn with Obertraun Seilbahn. A tourist office is in Hallstatt village center.

Trains to Hallstatt   Trains from Attnang-Puchheim to Hallstatt leave at 6:20am, 7:22am, 8:57am, 10:30am, 10:48am, 12:20pm, 12:57pm, 1:34pm, 3:40pm, 4:54pm and 6:37pm. Two later trains stop at Obertraun but not Hallstatt. From Obertraun, you can hike around the lake or take a bus or boat to Hallstatt. They leave at 7:34pm and 8:45pm. The trip is 1-1/2 hours.

Trains from Bad Ischl leave at 7:24am, 8:33am, 9:49am, 11:20am, noon, 1:15pm 2:08pm, 2:39pm, 4:46pm, 6:02pm, 6:36pm and 7:33pm. The trip is 25 minutes.

Trains from Stainach Irdning (direction Bad Ischl) leave at 7:47am, 9:46am, 12:41pm, 1:35pm, 3:04pm, 4:05pm, 4:27pm, 5:32pm, 6:44pm and 7:43pm. The trip is 1 hour.

Campingplatz Berta und Franz Hull, Lahnstrasse 6, charges adult/25AS, tent/20AS, tax/3.50AS including hot water. Get off at the dock near Lahn, south of downtown Hallstatt. From the dock with your back to the water, turn left and walk along the road next to the lake for 3 blocks. Turn right, walk one block and turn left onto the main road to Obertraun and Bad Aussee. Follow the signs to camp, one block inland from the main road.

The Hallstatt salt mine is open May 1-Oct 15 daily 9:30am-4:30pm, 85AS. The cogwheel railway to the salt mine costs 70AS round trip. The prehistoric museum (May 1-Oct 31 daily 9:30-6) is 25AS. The Charnel House Museum is free.

To Attnang-Puchheim, leave at 6:51am, 8:46am, 10:47am, 12:33pm, 1:48pm, 2:44pm, 4:07pm, 4:41pm, 5:07pm, 5:32pm and 6:34pm. (1 hour, 15 min.)

To Salzburg, take the train to Attnang-Puchheim and change for Salzburg. Trains to Salzburg leave Attnang-Puchheim at 8:30am EuroCity, 8:46am, 9:30am, 10:14am, 10:33am, 12:35pm, 12:56pm, 1:30pm EuroCity, 2:30pm, 3:30pm, 4:01pm, 4:30am, 5:30pm, 5:38pm, 6:30pm, 6:35pm, 7:30pm, 8:42pm, 9:30pm, 10:30pm, 10:47pm and 1:07am. The trip is one hour.

To Stainach-Irdning, leave at 7:52am, 9:04am, 10:13am, 11:44am, 12:26pm, 1:40pm, 2:37pm, 3:05pm, 5:24pm, 6:27pm and 7:58pm. The trip is one hour.

To Vienna Westbahnhof, through trains leave at 7:47am (ar. 2:46pm) and 4:07pm (ar. 8:38pm). You can also go to Attnang-Puchheim which is on the main rail line and get a train to Vienna from there.

54

Hallstatt

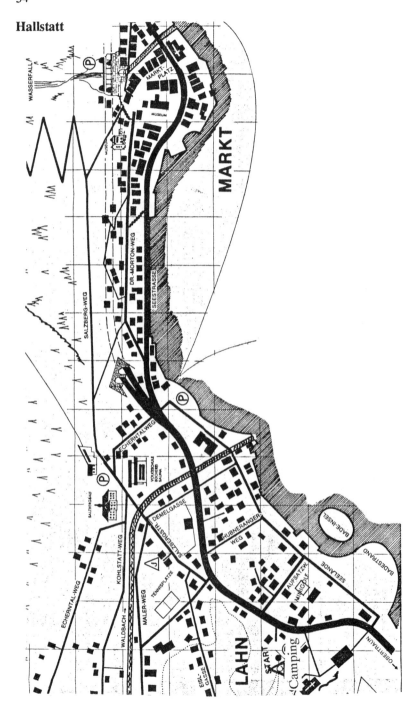

LINZ

Linz is a moderately large city on the main rail line between Vienna and Salzburg. Its historical center has been painstakingly restored. A tourist office is in the train station.

Camping Linz-Pichlingeersee is a very good campingplatz located at Wiener Bundesstrasse 937 on Pichlinger See (lake), 10 km. from Linz. Take the bus to Pichlingersee from outside the train station. The last bus is 10:20pm. Open all year; adult/30AS, tent/30AS. A trail goes around the lake from the campground. The camp itself is grassy and has beach access.

The small lakeside Camping Linz-Pleschingersee, closer to central Linz and next to the Kolmer restaurant, accepts tents only and charges adult/30AS, tent/free. The tourist office reported this camp as new for 1989, transportation available.

Trains to Salzburg leave at 8:54am and 54 minutes past the hour until 10:54pm. EuroCity departures are 8:54am, 10:54am and 12:54am.

Trains to Vienna leave at 8:03am and 3 minutes past the hour until 10:03pm. EuroCity departures are 5:03pm, 7:03pm, 9:03pm and 10:03pm.

KLAGENFURT

Capital of Corinthia, Klagenfurt lies on the east end of the Worthersee, a large lake. Trains from Vienna to Venice pass through Klagenfurt, which lies north of the Yugoslavian border. The tourist office is on bus route A from the train station. The open market is at Benediktiner-Platz, 2 blocks from the tourist office.

Camping Strandbad is an excellent municipal campground south of town in Europa Park (Hobby Land) on the Worthersee (lake). Take bus A (direction Annabichl) which starts in front of the train station and leaves every 10 minutes. The bus travels along Bahnhof Strasse for 7 blocks, turns left on Paradeiser Strasse, passes Neuer Platz, turns right on Dr. Hermanng Strasse, and then you get off in one block at Heiligengeistplatz. Change to bus S which originates at Heiligengeistplatz and leaves twice a hour. It travels on Villacher Strasse for about 20 blocks until it reaches Europa Park and terminates. The park has three bus stops; get off at the one at the beach. Open May 1-Sep 30; adult/40AS, tent/20AS. The grassy camp is part of a large city park with a swimming area, playgrounds, an outdoor chess board, mini-zoo, cultural center, museums, planetarium and the start of a 9-km. trail along Lake Worthersee. The camp has an automatic washing machine, foreign exchange, store and restaurant.

Trains to Venice leave at 12:13pm EuroCity (ar. Venice Mestre 4:20pm and 5:28pm (ar. 10:48pm).

Trains to Vienna Sudbahnhof leave at 7:40am, 9:40am, 11:40am, 1:02pm, 3:40pm 4:35pm EuroCity and 5:40pm. The trip is 4 hours and 20 minutes.

INNSBRUCK

Innsbruck (pronounced EENS-brook), capital of the Tyrol, is a good railway gateway to hiking and climbing country. Its tourist office offers free guided hiking tours, a good way to learn the ropes for European hiking. Here's how it works. Anyone who is staying three days in Innsbruck gets free membership in Club Innsbruck with benefits of free guided hiking tours and discounts for lifts, shops and museums. The hiking tours are offerred daily from June 1 to September 30 and include free bus transportation to and from the start of the hike. Various day hikes are planned, each one having about four to six hours of actual hiking time. Participants must sign up for the tour at the tourist office by 4pm the day before. The next day the group meets in front of the convention center at 8:30am, equipped with raincoat or jacket, hat, sunglasses, food and a canned drink for enroute and some money as hikes involve a cablecar lift to the starting point. On each hike, an Inn is passed where more food may be purchased. Return time is between 4 and 6pm. Bonnie and Doug Robinson report, ...*enjoyed Innsbruck for its Club Innsbruck. Excellent hiking opportunity and great fun with friendly tour guides. We camped there for 3 nights and became eligible. They provide you with rucksacks, hiking boots (well worn) and raincoats if you need them. Our trip consisted of a 45-minute free bus ride into the mountains and inexpensive short chairlift ride. Hiked through incredible scenery that we wouldn't have been able to see otherwise.*

TRAIN STATION   The main station, Hauptbahnhof, is 4 blocks from the main shopping street, Maria Theresien Strasse and five blocks from the old town centering on Herzog Friedrich Str. Buses leave from Sudtiroler Platz in front of the train station. Within the station are a youth information office (*jugendwarteraum*), post office and an exchange office in both the main and departure halls. All international traffic arrives at this station.

The smaller stations, Bahnhof-Hotting and Westbahnhof, serve suburbs, small towns and villages. Local trains can often be used instead of bus or tram to explore Innsbruck's outskirts.

TOURIST OFFICE   Besides the youth information office at the station, Innsbruck's main office is five blocks from the station at Burggraben 3. It may have moved closer to the station by 1989 so check before going there. Their leaflet of Innsbruck contains a map of the town, map of the surrounding area with hiking trails marked, description of 15 marked trails in the area, suggestions for longer mountain hikes, list of cog-wheel railways and cablecars, and weekly program of musical events. Independent hikers should visit the Alpine Auskunft information office, Bozner Platz 7 (2 blocks from the station), to purchase a larger, topographical map.

CITY TRANSPORTATION   Trams and buses cost 14AS per ride or a 10-ride ticket for 90AS.

CAMPGROUNDS   **Camping Reichenau** (Stadt Campingplatz) is on Reichenauer Strasse beside the Inn River. This is the most convenient campground. Open Apr 15-Oct 31; adult/50AS, hot showers extra. Take bus R or O across from the train station. Buses leave at about 10 minute intervals except every 30 minutes after 8:05pm. The bus stops directly at the camp entrance. This is an excellent camp with a view of the Inn River and the magnificent mountains surrounding Innsbruck. The camp provides picnic tables and has an automatic washing machine, store, snack bar and day room.

Camping Innsbruck West (Arala Campingplatz Tirol - Camping Kranebitten) by the Olympic Stadium can be reached by bus LK (Kranebitten) from Bozner Platz. Open Dec 15-Sep 30; adult/50AS, tent/40AS. Another excellent camp, it has hot water in the restroom sinks, automatic washing machines, store, snack bar and day room.

Camping Seewirt by the restaurant of the same name is in suburban Amras. Take bus K from the station. Open Mar 15-Oct 31; adult/45AS including hot showers, tent/35AS. A good campground in beautiful surroundings with hot water in the restroom sinks.

FOOD   The market is in the Markthalle at Marktgraben and Herzog-Sigm.-Ufer. Open M-F 7-6 and Sa 7-1.

SIGHTSEEING   Sightseeing divides into (1) exploring the compact old town with a visit to Hofburg castle and the fine Tyrolean Art Museum, (2) ascending the heights by cogwheel railway and chairlift and (3) hiking. The Tyrolean Folk Art Museum (Tiroler Volkskunst Museum) shows 22 authentic peasant home and inn interiors from several regions of Austria and Germany, and peasant attire.

DAY HIKES   Take tram 1 from Anichstrasse and ride to the last stop, Bergisel, marked by a memorial to Tyrolese killed in battle. There's a good view of Innsbruck and the Nordkette mountain range in the background. The Regimental Museum of the famous Emperor's Riflemen is also here. Bergisel is the staring point for several marked (in blue and white) and numbered hikes. Hike #1 follows Tummelplatzweg to Castle Ambras. It passes the war cemetèry (tummelplatzweg) and leads to the castle. Hiking time is one hour. It is also possible to go from here to Ambras Castle via the Mittelberger railway (line 6) to Igls.   Schloss Ambras was built on a projecting rock and is the dominant landmark for the surrounding valley. The castle is considered one of the finest Renaissance palaces in Austria. Inside a collection of weaponry from the 15th to 18th centuries is displayed. The grounds are fully landscaped with ponds and waterfalls. To return to Innsbruck, take tram 3, bus K or line 6 of the Mittelberger Railway (Mittelgebirgsbahn).
   Hike to Solbad Hall   Hike #2, Bederlungerweg, is an all day hike starting in Bergisel and ending in the interesting town of Solbad Hall from which you can return to Innsbruck by train or bus. The trail parallels hike #1 in the beginning and then branches for an easy ascent to the village of Aldrans and Herzsee (lake). This takes about 2 hours. From the lake, the trail continues to the towns of Jdenstein, Rinn and Tulfes taking another two hours and then reaches Solbad Hall in one more hour.

HIKES IN THE TYROL   Many small towns along the Arlberg Express train route are good starting points for hikes in the valleys and mountains. Always check with the tourist office for trail and weather conditions and have proper maps and gear.
   Kellerjoch Mountain   The trail leaves from the picturesque town of Schwaz, 17 miles from Innsbruck in the direction of Salzburg.   No campground in Schwaz, but there's a camping near the swimming pool in Solbad Hall, on the railway line five miles before Schwaz. The trail to Kellerjoch mountain (7,700 feet) from Schwaz is termed "moderately easy."
   Rattenberg   Seven miles from Jenback, Rattenberg is an interesting old town with a one hour trail to Reintaler lakes for swimming.
   Westendorf   Ten miles before Kitzburhel is Westendorf, where a chairlift to Alpenrosenhaus at 5,250 feet is the start of several trails. In the town of Kitzbuhel, Camping Schwarzsee is a 40-minute walk or take the bus from the station plus a 5-minute walk.

To Munich, leave at 7:58am (ar. 10:12am), 9:48am EuroCity (ar. 11:41am), 12:13pm EuroCity (ar. 2:25pm), 2:06pm (ar. 4:19pm), 6:05pm (ar. 8:12pm) and 6:28pm (ar. 8:34pm).
    To Salzburg, leave at 5:35am and 35 minutes after each odd-numbered hour until 5:35pm. EuroCity trains operate on the 1:35pm, 3:35pm and 5:35pm departures. Trip is 2 hours.
    To Vienna Westbahnhof, leave at the same hours as for Salzburg as it's the same train, except the trip is 5-1/2 hours.
    To Venice, leave at 9:55am and arrive at 4:30pm.

VIENNA (WIEN)

The architecture of Vienna (*Wien* in German) is basically Baroque. The city can be adequately viewed in three days though there's plenty to do if you have more time. If you have come this far, you should consider going a little further to visit close by Budapest in Hungary. Stop at Hungary's embassy at 1 Bankgasse 4-6 early as a visa takes 2 to 3 weekdays to process.
    Vienna is best visualized as a pebble thrown in the water with concentric circles expanding outward. The inner ring is the old quarter with the main sights. Around its perimeter runs Ringstrasse, which refers both to a boulevard and a circular tram route. Pedestrians use underpasses to cross the Ring. Many public buildings, such as the opera, city hall and parliament, are found along the Ring. Beyond is later growth of Vienna with light industry, newer shopping areas and the train stations. Next come the residential areas, and finally the campgrounds and the Vienna Woods are located 7 to 10 km. from the center. The Vienna Woods is a large natural forest threaded by trails and open to the public.

TRAIN STATIONS   The two main ones are Wien-Westbahnhof (west station) and Wien-Sudbahnhof (south station). Westbahnhof serves Scandinavia, Germany, and northern Europe in general, plus the Austrian towns of Salzburg and Innsbruck. A travel agency on the lower level acts as a tourist office and distributes free material (daily 6:15am-11pm). Exchange is open daily 7am-10pm. Sudbahnhof carries traffic from Italy and southern Austria such as Graz and Villach. Its travel agency/tourist office is open daily 6:30am-10pm. A train leaves Vienna on the hour from 6am to midnight from each station to the major Austrian towns it serves. Vienna's third station, Frans-Joseph Bahnhof serves East Germany and Czechoslovakia. Most trains to Budapest leave from Westbahnhof, but one leaves from Sudbahnhof. The train (schnellbahn) can be used from Landstrasse to Schwechat Airport free with Eurailpasses.
    All international trains stop at the suburban station, Hutteldorf-Hacking, which is the start of subway line U4. Get off here if you plan to stay at Campinggrounds Wien West I or II or Wien-Sud Rodaun.

TOURIST OFFICE   The main office has moved to Karntner Strasse 38 in 1989 (open 9-7). It sells *Vienna from A to Z*, a good guide to the sights of Vienna for 30AS and the 72-hour tourist ticket, but not the weekly pass or 8-day ticket.

CITY TRANSPORTATION   Vienna has trams, buses, *schnellbahn* (commuter trains), *stadtbahn* (an elevated/underground train) and underground (U-Bahn or subway). The main interchange point is Karlsplatz, on the Ring. A ticket is good for unlimited transfers on any of the above within the city limits without interruption or backtracking to reach the destination. The tourist office map, *Wiener Stadtwerke, Verkehrsbetriebe,* shows public transportation routes.

The single fare for tram, bus, U-Bahn and schnellbahn is 20AS. A single ticket can be purchased on the tram from the conductor or the ticket machine, but only in the first car; or from the ticket machine in buses or at subway or schnellbahn stations. The cost is reduced to 14AS each if a 4-ticket book is bought for 56AS. Ticket books can be bought in tobacconist ts shops or at Vienna Transport Authorities (Wiener Verkehrsbetriebe) offices. Children under 16 pay 7AS per ride and ride free on Sundays, holidays and during Vienna school vacations (Jul 1-Sep 3). Free for under 7.

A good deal is the new 24-hour ticket(40AS). Still available is the 72-hour Vienna ticket (*72-Stunden-Netzkarte*) for 102AS. For longer stays, a weekly pass valid from monday through the following monday at 9am costs from 116AS depending on number of zones (photo required). If you're traveling with a partner, a good buy is the 8-day Environment Ticket (*8-Tage-Umwelt Streifennetzkarte*) for 220AS that reduces the fare to 28AS per day. The great advantage to this ticket is that each day's use is stamped individually and more than one person can use it as long as one day is stamped for each person. These tickets are valid on all public transport systems: underground, trams, stadtbahn, buses and schnellbahn. The 72-hour ticket is sold at tourist offices, travel agencies in Westbahnhof and Sudbahnhof and at offices of the Vienna transport authorities. Single tickets, 4-ticket books, 24-hour ticket and 8-day Envirionment Ticket are sold by vending machine in the stations. The weekly pass is sold at Vienna Transport offices located in U-Bahn Stations Karlsplatz (M-F 7-6, SaSu 8:30-4), Stephansplatz (M-F 8-6, SaSu 8:30-6) and Praterstern (M-F 10-6, closed SaSu). Between 12:30pm and 4am from Friday to Saturday, Saturday to Sunday, and the night before holidays, 8 buses to all parts of Vienna operate. One ride costs 25AS.

These are the train lines of the Austrian Railways in Vienna, free with Eurailpasses. One line goes north from Franz-Josefs Bahnhof and stops at Heiligenstadt, Nussdorf, Kahlenbergerdorf, Klosterneuburg, Klosterneuburg-Weidling and Klosterneuburg-Kierling on its route to Tulln. Another line goes west from Westbahnhof and stops at Penzing, Hutteldorf-Hacking (change for campground), Hadersdorf-Weidlingau, Weidlingau-Wurzbachtal, Purkersdorf-Sanatorium and Unter-Purkersdorf. Two lines leave from Sudbahnhof. One branch stops at Simmeringer Hauptstrasse, Stadlauer Brucke, Lusthaus, Lobau, Stadlau and then branches north and east. The north branch stops at Kagran, Gerasdorf and continues to Laa a.d. Thaya. The eastern branch stops at Erzherzog Karl-Strasse, Hirschstetten-Aspern and continues to Marchegg. The other line from Sudbahnhof goes to Simmering (Ostbahn), Kledering and towards Bruck a.d. L. Trains from Meidling Station stop at Inzersdorf Ort and Inzersdorf Metzerwerk in the direction of Wiener Neustadt. From Landstrasse Station, trains stop at Rennweg, Simmering (Aspangbahn), Zentralfriedhof, Kl. Schwechat, Gross-Schwechat, Schwechat-Flughafen Wien in the direction of Wolfsthal. There is another line from Sudbahnhof which goes to Meidling Station, but after Meidling, the next three stops, Hetzendorf, Atzgersdorf-Mauer (change for campground) and Liesing (change for campground) are classified as Schnellbahn stops and are not included in Eurailpasses, but the ones after

Vienna Campgrounds

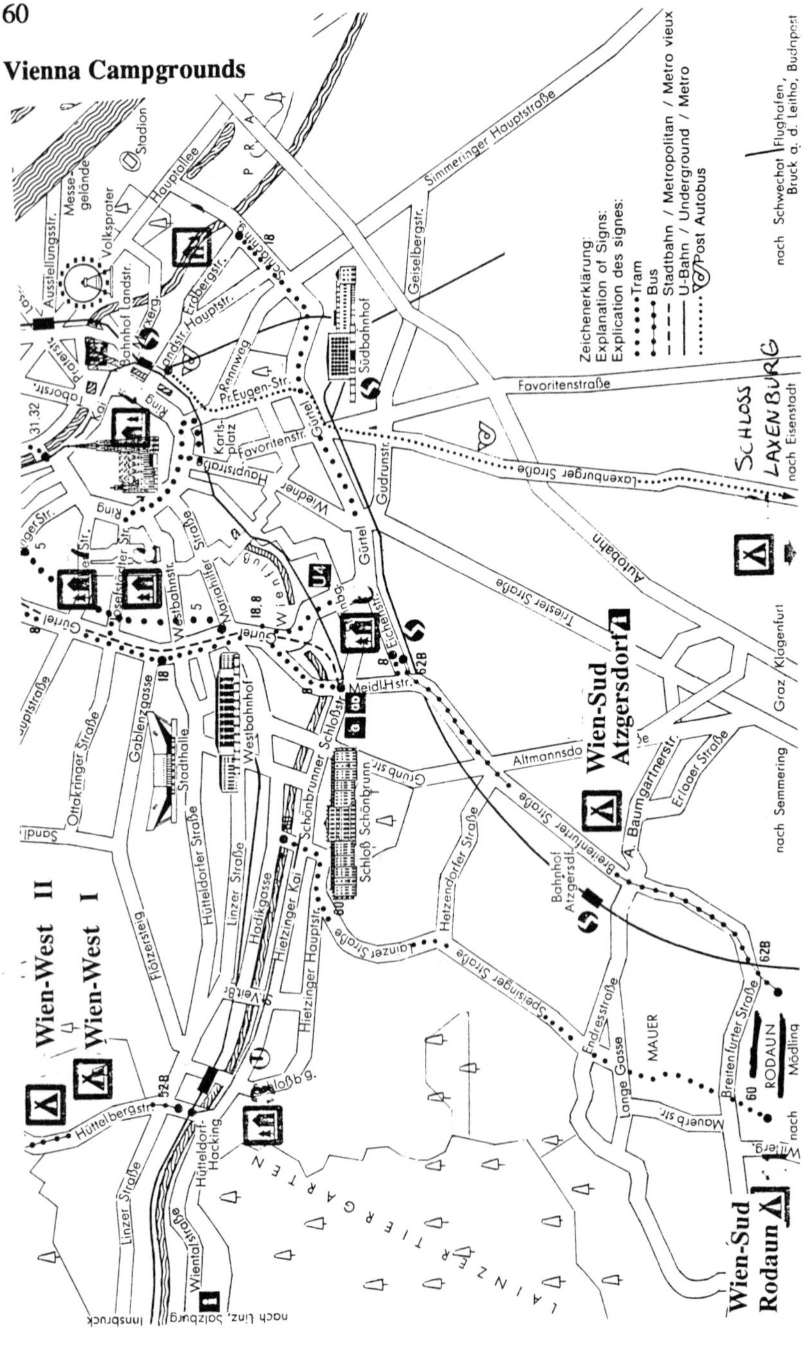

Zeichenerklärung:
Explanation of Signs:
Explication des signes:
- ••• Tram
- ┈┈┈ Bus
- ┄┄┄ Stadtbahn / Metropolitan / Metro vieux
- ───── U-Bahn / Underground / Metro
- Post Autobus

nach Schwechat (Flughafen,
Bruck a. d. Leitha, Budapest

SCHLOSS
LAXENBURG
nach Eisenstadt

Wien-Sud
Atzgersdorf

Wien-West II
Wien-West I

Wien-Sud
Rodaun

Favoritenstraße
Laxenburger Straße
Triester Straße
Simmeringer Hauptstraße
Geiselbergstr.
nach Graz / Klagenfurt
nach Semmering
Südbahnhof
Westbahnhof
Karlsplatz
Pr. Eugen-Str.
Wiedner Hauptstraße
Gürtel
Meidl. H str.
Schönbrunn Schloß
Schloß Schönbrunn
Hütteldorfer Straße
Linzer Straße
Hietzinger Hauptstr.
Hadikgasse
Altmannsdo
Breitenfurter Straße
Erlaaer Straße
Baumgartnerstr.
Bahnhof Atzgersdf.
MAUER
RODAUN
Mödling
nach Wien...
Lange Gasse
Endresstraße
Speisinger Straße
Hetzendorfer Straße
Gainzer Straße
Flötzersteig
Hütteldorf-Hacking
Hütteldorfer Straße
LAINZER TIERGARTEN
nach Linz, Salzburg, Innsbruck
Ottakringer Straße
Stadthalle
Gablenzgasse
Gürtel
Wienfluß
Mariahilfer Straße
Westbahnstr.
Ring
Prater
Hauptallee
Volksprater
Stadion
Messegelände
Ausstellungsstr.
Landstr.
Erdbergstr.
Bahnhof Landstr.
Rennweg
Gudrunstr.
Gürtel
Autobahn

Liesing are Austrian Railways stops again. They are Perchtoldsdorf, Modling, Guntramsdorf and Gumpoldskirchen.

CAMPGROUNDS Of Vienna's five campgrounds, three are accessible by public transportation. Wien-West I and II are the most popular; Rodaun and Atzgersdorf are quieter, less crowded and with fewer facilities.

Camping Wien-West I and Wien-West II are municipal campgrounds located at Huttelbergstrasse 40 and 80, about 6 km. from downtown. Wien-West I is open June 17-Sep 17, while Wien-West II stays open all year. Identical prices at both are adult/50AS and tent/46AS. Coming from western Austria (Salzburg or Innsbruck), all international trains stop at suburban Huttledorf-Hacking Station before entering Westbahnhof. Get off there if possible, and take bus 52B from Hutteldorf-Hacking Station. The last bus 52B leaves at 11:05pm. Get off at the second stop for West I and the third stop for West II. From downtown, take subway line U4 to Hutteldorf and change to bus 52B. The last line U4 subway train leaves from Karlsplatz at 12:30am, but the last U4 that connects with the last 52B bus leaves at 10:49pm. From Sudbahnhof, take streetcar 18 to subway stop Margaretengurtel of line U4, get on the subway and get off at Hutteldorf and change to bus 52B. A slower route from Sudbahnhof is to take streetcar 18, marked Urban Loritz-Platz to the last stop. Transfer to tram 49 (Hutteldorf) to the last stop and change to bus 52B. The last tram 49 from Dr. Karl Renner-Ring to Hutteldorf is at 10:30pm and connects with the last bus 52B. Both camps are very popular and have a store, exchange, post office and washing machines (50AS).

Camping Wien-Sud Rodaun, 10 km. from downtown, is slightly cheaper. Open Mar 17-Nov 16; adult/40AS and tent/47AS. International trains from western Austria (Salzburg and Innsbruck) stop at suburban Hutteldorf-Hacking Station. Get off the train and change to subway line U4. Go until the fourth stop, Hietzing, and change to tram 60. The last tram 60 from Hietzing is at 12:43am. Tram 60 stops at Willergasse and Breitenfurter Str. From there, the camp is a 2 block walk. From Sudbahnhof, take the schnellbahn to Liesing station and change to bus 60A. The last Schnellbahn leaves at 10:42pm, and last bus 60A from Liesing station at 11:03pm. If you're coming by Franz-Josefs Bahn, get off at Heiligenstadt and change to underground U4. Go until the thirteenth stop, Hietzing, and change to tram 60. From downtown at Karlsplatz, the last U4 for Hietzing leaves at 12:30am to connect with the last tram 60. You can also take bus 61A from Liesing Station; the last bus leaves at 8:18pm, or M-F at 10:18pm. The quiet campground has a restaurant, store and free non-heated swimming pool. A *putzerei* with automatic washers and dryers (about 70AS) is at 366 Ketzer Gassse near the campground.

Camping Wien-Sud Atzgersdorf, Breitenfurterstrasse 269, is 7 km. from downtown. Open May 24-Sep 17; adult/50AS and tent/46AS. Take the Schnellbahn from Sudbahnhof to Atzgersdorf-Mauer Station. The last Schnellbahn leaves at 11:12pm. Then take bus 66A (last bus 11:43pm) or bus 60 (last bus 10:48pm) from Atzgersdorf-Mauer Station. These buses stop two blocks from the campground. From Schnellbahn Meidling station, bus 62B (last bus 12:10am) stops at the campground. Store and dayroom.

FOOD   Vienna has 17 public markets scattered throughout the city. Hours are M-F 6am-6pm, Sa 6am-2pm. The largest market is Naschmarkt, located along parallel avenues Linke Wienzeile and Rechte Wienzeile at Getreidemarkt, outside the Ring about seven blocks from the Opera House. Take U4 to Kettenbruckengasse.   On Saturday from 8am-6pm, the flea market is also at the Naschmarkt.

Schwendermarkt, Schwendergasse and Reichsapfelgasse, is on tram lines 52 and 58, and passed as one goes to Camping Wien-West or Wien Sud Rodaun from Westbahnhof. After boarding the tram from in front of the station, get off at the fourth stop and then walk back one block past Holler Strasse to Reichsapfelgasse. Meiselmarkt, Meiselstrasse and Wurmsergasse, is on tram line 49 when taken from Wien-West Camping into town without transferring to bus 52. Get off at John Strasse, a main intersection, and walk forward one block to Wurmsergasse. The market is about 14 blocks from Westbahnhof.

Markets closer to the Ring are Karmelitermarkt, Krummbaumgasse and Im Werd, which is outside the Ring across Salztor-Bridge, then a 3 block walk. Augustinermarkt, Landstrasse Hauptstrasse and Erdbergstrasse, is outside the Ring, one block from Landstrasse Station. Karolinenmarkt, at St. Elisabeth Platz, is by the Cathedral of the same name, 4 or 5 blocks from Sudbahnhof.

Billa and Lowa grocery store chains have the best prices and good quality. All grocery stores are closed from midday Saturday until Monday morning.   Train station stores remain open until 11pm.   Wurst sold at sausage stands is generally priced per 100 grams.

SIGHTSEEING   The **Kunsthistorisches Museum** is Vienna's museum of fine arts, located at 1 Maria Theresien-Platz near the Hofburg. Take U4, U1, stadtbahn, schnellbahn or any tram on the circular route to Karlsplatz. Open Tu-F 10-6, SaSu 9-6, Tuesday and Friday evenings 7-10pm. Adult/45AS, student/20AS.

Beautiful Schonbrunn Palace is in the southwest sector of Vienna far beyond the Ring, but not as far as the campgrounds. From Camp Wien-West, take bus 52B to Hutteldorf-Hacking Station. Then take U4 to Hietzing and change to tram 58 or 10 going downtown for one stop. This puts you in front of the Palace. If you ride U4 to Schonbrunn Station, you have to walk back to the Palace. From Camp Wien-Sud Rodaun, ride tram 60 to the last stop, Hietzing Kennedy bridge. Then take tram 58 or 10 going downtown for one stop, or walk through the grounds to the Palace. Schonbrunn is open daily 9-5, although the grounds don't close until 8pm. The Castle interior is shown by guided tour only. The summer palace of the Hapsburgs, Schonbrunn is a lovely ornate rococo affair done in white and gold and set within formal Baroque gardens. Tour hours are 9-12 and 1-4; adult/50AS, student/25AS.

Belvedere Palace is near Sudbahnhof. From Camping Wien-West I, take bus 52B to Hutteldorf, change to U4 to Margaretengurtel and change to tram 18 to Sudbahnhof/Belvedere. The address is Prinz Eugen Strasse 27. Open Tu-Su 10-4; adult 30AS, student/15AS.

DAY TRIP ON THE DANUBE TO MELK   The Danube River between Krems and Melk, 85 km. from Vienna, is the most scenic part of the river with its castles, terraced vineyards and orchards. Steamers depart from

Danube Ferry Schedule - Eurail bonus

Timetable Vienna – Grein – Vienna 1989

Downriver					Ports of call 1989		Upriver				
L 1189	L 1189	L 1089	L 1089	L 1189			L 1189	L 1189	L 1089	L 1089	L 1189
12.5. to 1.10. daily	21.4. to 29.10. daily	29.4. to 27.5. Thu,Fr,Sa,Su	28.5. to 1.10. daily	12.5. to 1.10. daily			21.4. to 29.10. daily	12.5. to 1.10. daily	29.4. to 27.5. Thu,Fr,Sa,Su	28.5. to 1.10. daily	12.5. to 1.10. daily
🚲 ✕	🚲 ✕	🚲	🚲 ✕	🚲 ✕			🚲 ✕	🚲 ✕	🚲	🚲 ✕	🚲 ✕
			11:45		Grein						9:00
			12:50		Ybbs					19:15	18:15
			13:15		Marbach/M.-Taferl	●				17:55	18:05
			13:30		Pöchlarn					17:20	17:30
10:00	14:00		14:30	15:30	Melk/Donauarm	●	15:05	13:30		17:05	17:00
10:25	14:25		14:55	15:55	Aggsbach Dorf		14:15	12:45		16:10	16:35
10:30	14:30		15:00	16:00	Aggstein	H●	14:05	12:35		15:25	16:00
10:55	14:55		15:25	16:25	Spitz		13:30	12:00		15:15	
11:10	15:10		15:40	16:40	Weißenkirchen	●	13:00	11:05		14:35	
11:25	15:45		15:55	16:55	Dürnstein	●H	12:35	10:30		14:05	
11:45		15:55	16:15	17:15	Krems		12:00			13:40	
		16:15			Tulln				13:40	13:05	
		18:00	18:00		Vienna/Nußdorf				13:05	10:30	
		19:40	19:40		Vienna/DDSG Schiffahrtszentr				10:30	08:25	
		20:00	20:00						08:25	08:00	
									08:00		

Also at Mai 1.15.

On June 24th the trip ends at Ybbs.

🚲 Bicycle transport and/or baggage storage must be arranged in advance. This is especially important for groups in advance. ✕ Restaurant on board. H = Tickets may be purchased on board.
🚲 Bicycle rental at the DDSG station.

Danube Mini Ticket AS 80.–
Valid for only one stop when traveling in either direction between Krems and Linz. Children reduction 50%. No other reduction.

From Vienna into the Wachau

Ship *)	Train 🍴	Train † 🇧	Ports of call	Train daily	Ship *)
15:40	17:30	17:46	Weißenkirchen	09:29	14:05
15:55	17:39	17:53	Dürnstein	09:21	13:40
16:15		18:20	Krems	09:00	13:05
18:00		18:56	Tulln	08:27	10:30
		19:19	Vienna-Heiligenstadt	08:05	08:25
		19:23	Vienna-FJB	08:00	08:00
19:40			Vienna-Nußdorf		
20:00			Vienna-DDSG Schiffz.		

Train/Ship	Adults	Children
Vienna – Tulln – Vienna	170.–	85.–
Vienna – Dürnstein – Vienna	310.–	155.–
Vienna – Weißenkirchen – Vienna	360.–	180.–
Tulln – Dürnstein – Tulln	170.–	85.–

🍴: Weekday †: Sunday/Holiday *) for operation days see timetable, page 4 🇧 Saturday

With train and ship to the 1989 exhibit of "900 years Benedictins in Melk":

Ship *)	Train till 27.5. daily	Train from 28.5.	Ports of call	Train till 27.5. daily	Train from 28.5.	Ship *)
	18:07	18:08	Melk-Railway stat.	10:18	10:03	16:10
14:30	19:04	19:04	Melk-Donauarm			
	19:15	19:15	Vienna-Hütteldorf	09:20	08:56	
19:40			Vienna-Westbhf.			08:25
20:00			Vienna-Nußdorf			08:00
			Vienna-DDSG			

	Adults	Children
	490.–	245.–

Train/Ship, incl. entrance in Melk:
Vienna/Melk by train and Melk/Vienna by ship

64

Praterkai on the Danube in Vienna. A tourist office on the pier. Boats operated by Erste Donau-Dampfschiffahrts-Gesellschaft between Passau and Vienna are free with Eurailpasses. (The Delphin plying between Linz and Vienna is excluded.) For a day trip, ride the 9:20am train to Melk, visit its Baroque Benedictine Abbey (open M-Sa 9-5, Su 9-5, free) the largest monastery north of the Alps and celebrating its 900th anniversay in 1989 with a special exhibition, and sail downstream back to Vienna on the 2:30pm boat (May-Sep), arriving in Vienna at 8pm. Trains leave Westbahnhof for Linz (stopping in Melk on the way) at 7:40am, 8:56am, 9:20am and 12:20pm for the hour trip. To hasten back to Vienna, get off the boat when it arrives at 4:15pm in the interesting village of Krems and get a train.

OPERA AND THEATRE TICKETS Tickets for performances in the state theaters (Burgtheatre, Akademietheater, State Opera and Volksoper) are sold at Bundestheaterkassen 1, Goethegasse 1, open M-Sa 9-5, Su 9-noon. Inexpensive tickets are available in advance or on the evening at the box offices of the Burgtheatre and Akdademietheater for students at 50AS. Almost all other theaters offer about 20 percent off for students. The Vienna State Opera is a different picture. It is often necessary to line up the night before tickets go on sale for the inexpensive standing room tickets.

SHOPPING The flea market adjoins the open market on Naschmarkt, Saturday 7-6. Dorotheum is the national auction house, administered by the government, where reasonably priced goods may sometimes be bought. Located at Dorotheergasse 17, the doors open M-F 10-4, Sa 8:30-12. You must go early in the week to see what there is and then return towards the end of the week to bid as items go on the block. You pay bid plus 10 percent.

To Budapest, leave Westbahnhof at 10:20am Wiener Walzer (ar. 2:10pm), 4:22pm Orient Express (ar. 8:10pm) and 6:05pm Arrabona (ar. 9:40pm). Leave Sudbahnhof at 7:45am Lehar (ar. 10:45am). The Danube hydrofoil, Donaupfeil, makes the run, Vienna-Budapest, in about 6-1/2 hours with the return journey downstream about one hour faster. It leaves daily except Monday from May 1- Sep 20 from Reichsbrucke at 8:10am, arriving in Budapest at 12:50pm. From Budapest (International River Quay Belgrad Rakpart) it leaves at 2:10pm and arrives in Vienna at 7:50pm. Reserve a seat in advance and embarkation is one hour prior to sailing. One way fare is 750AS including beverage and snack, 1,400AS round trip.

To Hallstatt, trains leave Westbahnhof (direction Linz) at 7:35am (ar. 11:44am), 11am EuroCity (change at Attnang-Puchheim, ar. 3:05pm) and 2:40pm (ar. 7:58pm).

To Linz, leave Westbahnhof at 7am EuroCity, 7:35am, 8am, then on the hour until 10pm. EuroCity trains depart 7am, 9am and 11am. Trip is 2 hours.

To Prague, go either from Linz or Vienna. Leave Linz at 12:10pm (ar. 9:42pm). It's 223 km. from the border to Prague. From Vienna Franz-Josefs Bahn, the Vindobona Express leaves at 9:30am and arrives at 3:18pm. From Prague, it returns at 2:42pm, arriving in Vienna at 8:57pm. Eurailpasses are good to the border at Gmund, but a ticket must be bought for the remaining 183 km.. It can be bought in Vienna before you leave.

To Salzburg, Innsbruck, Zurich and Basel The EuroCity Transalpino Express, a scenic train ride which crosses the Alps lengthwise, goes between Vienna, Salzburg, Innsbruck, Zurich and Basel. It leaves Basel at 8:27am and arrives in Vienna at 7pm. It leaves Vienna Westbahnhof at 9am and 11am and arrives in Basel at 7:33pm and 9:33pm. Trains leave for Salzburg at 7:35am, 8am, then on the hour until 9pm. EuroCity departures are 9am and 11am. Salzburg is a 2 hour 20 minute trip. To Innsbruck, trains leave at odd-numbered hours from 7am to 5pm. EuroCity departures are 7am, 9am and 11am. Trip is 5 hours and 20 minutes.

To Venice, leave Sudbahnhof at 8:15am EuroCity (ar. Venice Mestre 4:20pm), 1pm (ar. Venice S.L. 10:48pm), 10:30pm (ar. Venice S. L. 8:32am.)

BELGIUM

In the middle ages, Bruges and Gent rivaled any city in northern Europe with their splendour and wealth. Today, delightful Bruges remains as it was and provides the visitor with the best introduction to Flemish Belgium. The small size of the country and its excellent rail network combine to make the best touring strategy the base city approach. If you only have time for Bruges, then stay there. Otherwise, select Ghent for its excellent campground and interesting sights, or Antwerp for its museums.

CURRENCY Belgian franc. One dollar equals about 33 francs (F). Many banks charge a substantial commission, so be sure to inquire before agreeing to change money.

WEATHER Generally like the Pacific Northwest, expect a few cool nights in summer. Camping in May and September is more wet and cold. High season is July 15-August 15 and any summer weekend on the coast.

CAMPING The Belgian tourist office gives out the brochure, *Camping 1989*, which is only a partial listing of campgrounds as the camps have to pay to be listed. Campgrounds throughout the country are of a high standard. Prices are generally 40-80BF per person and 40-100BF per tent.

TRAINS Belgium National Railways (SNCB) maintain a dense railway network and frequent service. It's usually only 15 minutes to a hour between cities, and trains depart at least every half hour. There are various passes for Belgium and Benelux (Belgium, Luxembourg and The Netherlands), but the territory is still too small to be a good value for the overseas visitor. Those without a Eurailpass might make use of the one day round trip ticket, *Un Beau Jour*, which gives 50 percent off on the return fare. Railway information offices give free time schedules. All stations

66

have coin-operated luggage lockers and large cities have attended baggage checking.

Belgium is a bilingual country and railway signs are posted in Dutch and French.

aankkomst, arrivee	arrival
depart, vertrek	departure
spoor, voie	track

BELGIUM TO BRITAIN   The cheapest way to go from Ostend to London is via Eurolines bus service.   Crossing the channel is slightly less between Calais, France and Dover than between Belgium and Dover.   The discounts students receive on rail travel through a student travel agency brings the rail ticket close to the bus price. Detailed information is included under Ostend.

FOOD   Food is cheapest in the open markets and supermarkets. Belgium's national cuisine is very good and the place to sample it is in the small towns rather than Brussels, Antwerp, Gent or Bruges where prices are higher. Meal hours are noon to 2 and 7-9pm.   The most popular dish among Belgians is a thin steak filet and french fries (*biftek et frites*). Belgians eat more potatoes per family than any other nationality in Europe.   The next most favored vegetable is endive (*witloof or chicorees*) served roasted or as a salad. Brussels sprouts (*choux de Bruxelles*) are often seen.   Good entrees include *waterzooi poulet* (chicken stew), *waterzooi poisson* (fish stew), *poularde Bruxelloise* (chicken), *carbonnades flammandes* (beef stew), *tomates aux crevettes* (shrimp stuffed tomatoes) and *anguilles au vert* (eel). *Lapin* or *lievre aux pruneaux* (rabbit or hare wtih prunes) is commonly eaten in Flanders (Bruges or Gent).   A recurring appetizer is *fondue au fromage* (cheese croquette served with fried parsley).   Beer is the national drink as Belgium has almost no vineyards.   *Biere de table* is light beer.   The strong Orval beer is made by Trappist monks.

HOLIDAYS   Summertime holidays are July 21, Independence Day and August 15, Assumption Day.

MOVIES   In Flemish-speaking regions, movies are shown in the original language with subtitles, whereas dubbing is usual in French-speaking areas.

ANTWERP (ANVERS, ANTWERPEN)

Belgium's biggest port, Antwerp is on the River Schelde, 50 miles from the sea.   Brussels is 25 minutes away by train leaving four times per hour.   In 1989 Antwerp hosts the Biennial Exhibition of Contemporary Sculpture which displays the sculpture throughout the town.

TRAIN STATIONS   The main station, Central Station, is located about 10 blocks from downtown and the riverfront.   The station has foreign exchange (open daily 8-10) and luggage checking.   A tourist office is outside on Koningin Astridplein (open M-F 8:30-8, Sa 9-7, Su 9-5).

Further away from downtown, Berchem Station is on the Brussels train line.   International express and InterCity trains on the route Rotterdam, Antwerp, Brussels and Paris stop only at Berchem Station.   Some of the other trains on this line stop at Central Station only while others stop at both. Trains to Gent stop at both stations and leave at least once an hour.

TOURIST OFFICE   The office on Koningin Astridplein in front of Central Station is open daily. The main office at Grote Markt 15. The tourist office city map for 50BF contains a compendium of helpful sightseeing information. Also available is a free map inside its English-language *Antwerp* brochure.

CITY TRANSPORTATION   A single ticket is 30BF, an 8-ride card is 154BF. A 24-hour pass costs 140BF. This *Toeristenkaart* is sold at the tourist office.

CAMPGROUNDS   Both campgrounds are operated by the city of Antwerp and are the best buys for campgrounds in Belgium. It is easy to base yourself in Antwerp and make day trips from here. The one on Jan Van Rijswijcklaan has hot showers, but De Molen has the more attractive location at the beach.

Stedelijk Kampeerterrein Jan Van Rijswijcklaan, Jan Van Rijswijcklaan 193, is just off that street behind the Building Center. Open Apr 1-Sep 30; adult/115BF, tent/115BF. Take tram 2 from the subway (entrance is in Central Station) or bus 27 in Pelicanstreet next to Central Station. The camp has a capacity of 170 persons, is not crowded, and is basically a flat, grassy field. On site is a modern restroom building; otherwise facilities are minimal. A 15-minute walk from the campground is a suburban mainstreet with shops.

Camping De Molen at St.Ann's Beach (St. Annastrand) on the left river bank is reached by bus 36 from Koningin Astridplein in front of Central Station. Open Apr 1-Sep 30; adult/115BF, tent/115BF. Snack bar, cold showers only, minimal facilities.

FOOD   The public market is on Oude Vaartplaats (off Frankrijklei), Sa 10-4 and Su 9-1. The Grand Bazar department sotre at Gorenplaats and Eiermarkt has a supermarket and cafeteria.

SIGHTSEEING   **Middelheimpark**, Middelheimlaan 59, is a 15-minute walk from the municipal campground on Jan Van Rijswijcklaan or take tram 15 or bus 17, 27 or 32 from Central Station. Daily 10-sunset, free. The permanent collection of pieces by Rodin, Maillot and others is worth seeing.

If you plan to visit more than one of the 27 museums in Antwerp, buy at the first museum a 3-museum card for 100BF. A season ticket to all museums costs 200BF. The **Plantin-Moretus Museum**, 22 Vrijdagmarkt, is a 16th century patrician house with the original printing shop intact. Open daily 10-5, adult/50F, student/20F. Take tram 3, 2 or 15 from Central Station. **Rubens House and Gardens** is the artist's luxurious 1610 villa now open to the public as a museum. Open daily 10-5, adult/50F, student/20F; tram 2 or 15 from Central Station or one km. walk. **Steen Castle** on the waterfront houses the maritime museum, National Scheepvaartmuseum. Open daily 10-5, adult/50F, student/20F; tram 2, 3, 20, 11 or 15 from Central Station.

The **port** itself is the third largest in the world with 3167 acres of docks, 18 dry docks and 6 locks. Flandria Excursion boats offer tours of the port and River Schelde for 170BF to 300BF depending on length of tour.

68

Another Flandria boat goes to Flushing in The Netherlands by motoring on the River Scheldt and across to the island of Walcheren to visit the picturesque towns of Middelburg and Flushing (Vlissingen). All boats leave from Steenplein. St. Anna tunnel, the pedestrian and bicycle underpass beneath the River Scheldt, is one block away on your left as you face the river from Steenplein and leads to a modern district.

Grote Markt, focal point of the old town, is lined with the Town Hall (Stadhuis) and Gothic and Flemish Renaissance Guild Houses. Take tram 2, 3, 10, 11 or 15 from Central Station. The important and enormous Gothic **Our Lady Cathedral** rings with Carillion Concerts on Friday at 11:30am and Monday at 9pm from June-Sept.

Royal Gallery of Fine Arts (*Koninklijk Museum Voor Schone Kunsten*), Leopold de Waelplaats about 10 blocks from Grote Markt, shows an excellent collection of Flemish primitives and 16th and 17th century painters. Contemporary art is also shown and Belgium's foremost modern artist, Ensor, is represented by his reputed best work, *Entry of Christ into Brussels*. Open Tu-Su 10-5, free. **Brouwershuis**, Adriaan Brouwerstraat 20, is the original brewers' house constructed to supply pure water to the breweries and is now a museum showing the original hydraulic works. Open Tu-Su 10-5, adult/50BF, student/20BF. **Mayer Van Den Berg Museum**, Lange Gasthuistraat 19, has a small collection of choice paintings, open Tu-Su 10-5, adult/50F, student/20F. **Volkskundemeseum** (regional ethnology) shows folklore and has a puppet theater, open Tu-Su 10-5, adult/50BF, student/20BF. **Het Vleeshuis Museum** (Butcher's House), Vleeshouwersstrat 38-40, contains musical instruments and weaponry, open Tu-Su 10-5, adult/50BF, student/20BF.

The world famous **zoo** beside Central Station has an aquarium, dolphin tank, museum of natural history, planetarium and reptile house. Open 8:30-5:30, adult/240BF. A diamond exhibition museum at Lange Herentalsentrout 31-33, is open daily 10-5 and gives demonstrations upon request on Saturday from 2-5pm. Free entrance.

DAY TRIP TO BOKRIJK Belgium's outdoor museum of historic rural buildings from the Flemish speaking part of Belgium is in Bokrijk. The farms, stables, thatched roofs and windmills are part of a larger recreation complex including four restaurants or snack bars, trails, arboretum, museum of natural science, lakes, rose garden, deer reserve, playground which has an immense wading pool with water slide, climbing bars, twinned roller coaster slide and swings. Open daily Apr-Oct 10-6, 120BF. Take the train to Hasselt that leaves Central Station at 6:12am and 12 minutes past the hour until 11:12pm. The trip to Hasselt takes 1-1/2 hours. At Hasselt, change to the train to Genk. Trains leave Hasselt at 6:35am and 35 minutes past each hour until 9:35pm. In about 10 minutes, get off at Bokrijk Station which is at the park entrance. The nearest town on the rail line with a campground is Hasselt. Trains return from Bokrijk for Hasselt at 55 minutes past the hour until 9:55pm. Trains leave Hasselt for Antwerp at 53 minutes past the hour until 7:53pm.

To Amsterdam, trains leave Central Station at 6:54am and 54 minutes past the hour until 11:54pm. Trip is 2 hours 15 minutes.
To Brussels, trains leave Central Station at 6:19am and 19 and 49 minutes past the hour until 10:49pm. These trains stop at all three Brussels stations. From

Berchem station, trains leave at 6:23am and 23 and 53 minutes past the hour until 10:53pm. Trip is 30 minutes.

To Gent, Bruges and Ostend, trains leave Central Station at 6:27am and 27 minutes past the hour until 10:27pm. Trip is 45 minutes to Gent, 1 hour 10 minutes to Bruges and 1-1/2 hours to Ostend.

To Paris Nord Station, trains leave Berchem Station at 9:17am (ar. 1pm), 10:59am EuroCity not Sunday (ar. 2:15pm), 1:15pm (ar. 4:55pm) and 6:12pm (ar. 10:06pm).

BRUGES (BRUGGE)

Bruges (pronounced broozh) is a choice medieval, gothic and renaissance town that is very convenient to the main rail routes of Europe. If you can only make one stop in Belgium, this should be it. The city is an hour train ride from Brussels and a 14-minute ride from Ostend on the English Channel. A very rich and important city in the 13th to 15th centuries, the town went into decline when its shipping route filled with silt. Allow a day for this very pleasant and tranquil walking town. The town is crowded during the music festival in late July and first week in August.

TRAIN STATION   The station is a 15-minute walk from the Markt, the central and most impressive square of Bruges. A tourist information desk is in the station and maps of the town are tacked on signposts throughout the medieval city. Exchange is open M-Sa 9-6. Luggage checking is available.

TOURIST OFFICE   Dienst voor Toerisme is on Burg Square, one block east of the Markt. Open Apr-Sep, M-F 9-6:30, SaSu 10-12 & 2-6:30. Their Bruges map for 5BF also describes the sites and outlines 5 walking tours. An equivalent map but without the sightseeing commentary is in the free brochure, *Hotels, Restaurants, Snacks, Campings.* The tourist office will change money on weekends when banks are closed.

CAMPGROUNDS   **St. Michiel Camping**, Tillegemstraat 29, is 3 km. from the station and accessed from the main highway to Gent. Open all year; adult/75BF, tent/90BF. Take bus 7 (St. Michiels) from immediately in front of the station and slightly to the right as you exit. The bus shelter provides seating and a bus map is posted. Bus fare is 29BF one way, or a cheaper strip ticket can be bought in the station. Bus 8 leaves M-F at 5:39am, 6:09am and every 30 minutes to 8:09pm, then 8:39pm and 9:09pm; Sa at 7:29am, 7:59am, 8:29am and every 30 minutes until 8:29pm, then 8:49pm and 9:14pm; and Su from 7:55am to 10:07pm about every 40 minutes. (Bus 66B also goes near the camp. It leaves from the island in front of the station.) After leaving the station, get off at the fifth bus stop. The stop is soon after passing the Dophinarium. After getting off the bus on Rijselstraat, walk to the end of the block in the direction the bus was going. The intersecting street is Pierssensdreef and a sign for the Dolphinarium is across the street. Turn right onto Pierssensdreef and walk on this street past the sidestreet, Tillegemstraat. Pierssensdreef is now renamed Jagerstraat. Walk on this street to the main highway. Cross the highway and walk on sidestreet, Tillegemstraat, to the campground. The camp is well signed from the highway. Tennis courts are across the street. The walk from bus stop to campground is 9 minutes. To walk from the train station, take the back exit and cross to the highway on the other side of the tracks. Then follow signs to the highway to Gent. The camp is well signed from the highway.

Bruges

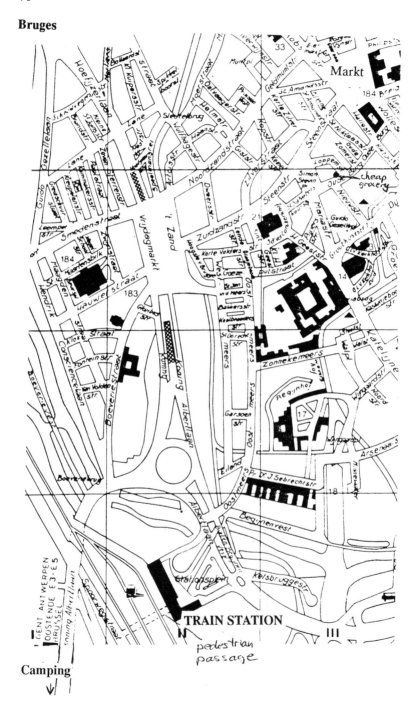

When returning to town, either walk along the highway into Bruges, or return to Rijselstraat and wait at the bus stop across the street. Both bus 7 and 66B go to the station. After stopping at the train station, bus 7 continues to the town center and stops at the theatre, J. Van Ooststraat.

The campground gets a lot of business because of the popularity of Bruges. Upon entering the site, you see lots of permanent trailers, but there is a well kept separate area for tents in the back. The restroom sinks are in individual stalls; 2 automatic washers and 1 dryer are in the laundry room; and a restaurant and store are provided.

Lac Loppem Camping, Lac 10, is on the lake in the village of Zedelgem, farther from Bruges than St. Michiel Camping. Open all year; adult/70BF, tent/70BF. Take bus 66B (Brugge-Roeselare) from the island in front of the station, then walk 300 meters down the road to the right after the bus lets you off. A supermarket is by the bus stop and the camp has 3 automatic washing machines, dryer, store and restaurant. Lac Loppen is rated higher than St. Michiel.

Memling Camping, Veltemweg 109 in the St. Kruis area, is 2 km. from central Bruges, in a wooded and quiet area. Open all year. Take bus 58 (Brugge-Eeklo-Gent) from the station. The last bus leaves at 10:24pm.

Memling Camping

SIGHTSEEING   The **Markt**, focal point of Bruges, is of similar characterization though smaller as the *Grand Place* in Brussels. Its notable Gothic tower, the Belfry, can be climbed for a view of the town. Open Apr-Sept, daily 9:30-12 & 2-6, shorter hours rest of year, adult/50BF. Below the tower is a 14th century market house. Historic guild houses surround the square.

Though the town is a museum in itself and wandering around is sufficient attraction, you may still wish to visit a few museums in Bruges. A central museum ticket, good for entrance into the Groeninge, Arentshuis, Gruuthuse and Memling museums, is 200F and sold at each museum. General museum hours are Apr-Sept, daily 9:30-12 & 2-6. **Groeninge Museum** on Dyver Canal is nearest the square and a fine arts museum. Highlight is the collection of early Flemish masters which are displayed in separate rooms with one important work in each. In the 17th century, every painter in Bruges was required to belong to the Corporation of Painters and Saddlemakers. The museum started when dissidents formed their own

Academy requiring each to donate a painting as dues. In this museum are the most reproduced panels of vanEyck, Memling and Bosch. Adult/80BF. Close by is the **Gruuthuse Museum** which displays period rooms including an interesting kitchen, and silver, lace china and musical instruments within its 15th century mansion. Adult/80F. **St. John's Hospital** has the important **Hans Memling Museum** (80F), including entry to the Old Dispensary.

The **Beguinage**, home of secular nuns, is a tranquil spot, open M-Sa 10-12 & 1:45-6, Su 10:30-12 & 1:45-6. No charge to visit the grounds and the house which costs 40BF to enter is of minor interest. The famous Virgin and Child sculpture of **Michelangelo** may be seen in the south transcept of the Church of Our Lady, open Apr-Sept 10-12 & 2:30-5, closed Sunday mornings. Also of interest are the Van Eyck Square in the old quarter, fish market, Gothic Basilica of the Holy Blood and the lace makers on Walplein. The **Lace Center** on Balstraat is a lace-making school which can be visited daily 10-12 & 2-6 except Sunday.

Boat Trips on the canals last 35 minutes and uniformly cost 110BF. Boats leave from several docks such as the one beside the Town Hall on the Burg. Before buying a ticket make certain that the tour will be in English, and wait for another boat rather than accompany an incredibly noisy boatload of gradeschoolers on a field trip. The canals and historical monuments are floodlit nightly from May to September.

The **Flea Market** is on Dyver on Saturday and Sunday. The Flower Market is on Burg square, Saturday and Wednesday morning. Carillion concerts peal from the Markt, June 15-Sept, M, W, Sa 9-10pm, Su 2:15-3pm; the rest of the year, W, Sa, Su 2:15-3pm.

FOOD   The public market is Saturday morning on the Zand, 7 blocks southwest of the Markt. A very low priced, unimposing looking, small supermarket is Disco Prof on Oude Burg #22, 3 blocks from the Markt. This one is an oasis from the higher prices charged on the main streets. It is marked on the map.

BIKE RENTALS   A good way to get out in the countryside, bikes can be rented at train stations for 150BF (105BF with train ticket or Eurailpass) per day (tandems 250BF) and can be returned to any station in Belgium. For an enjoyable afternoon, rent a bike in Bruges and ride to Zeebruges.

To Brussels, leave at 23 and 50 minutes past each hour until 10:50pm.
To Gent and Antwerp, leave at 6:02am and 2 minutes past the hour to 10:02pm.
To Zeebrugge, leave at 6:56am and 56 minutes past the hour until 9:56pm. The trip is 15 minutes.

BRUSSELS (BRUXELLES, BRUSSEL)

If you haven't time for anything else in Brussels, at least try to stop off to see the illuminated Grand Place at night. This central square is only a few blocks from Central Station.

AIRPORT   In Zaventem, nine miles from downton, the airport has currency exchange, tourist information, restaurant, hotel and daycare (open 7am-10pm daily for children under 12). The airport is connected by train with Central Station in downtown Brussels. Trains leave every 20 minutes and stop midway at Gare du Nord Station. The entire trip takes 18 minutes. Follow signs in the airport to the railroad platform.

TRAIN STATIONS   Brussels has three main stations: Brussel-Noord (*Bruxelles Nord*), the downtown station, Brussel-Centraal (*Gare Centrale*) and Brussel-Zuid (*Bruxelles Midi*). Though all three stations are connected and trains zip through the heart of Brussels underground, International and EuroCity trains do not stop at Central Station, but only at the other two. Local trains stop at all three, so it's always easy to get to Central Station. Midi Station is the largest with the most facilities and bus connections. All stations have luggage checking, and foreign exchange. Reservations can only be made at Nord and Midi Stations, not at Central Station. At the train information office, pick up the brochure on one day rail excursions called, *A beautiful day at..*, for ideas on day trips.

TOURIST INFORMATION   The main office, 61 rue du Marche-aux-herbes, is near the Grand Place. Open Jun-Sept, M-F 9-8, SaSu 9-7; Oct-May daily 9-6. The *General Plan of Brussels and Suburbs* has campgrounds marked. *Plan du Reseau* shows bus, tram and subway routes. Request its excellent brochure on the Grand Place, and *Brussels Guide* which lists museum hours. The office also stocks information on the other cities and towns in Belgium. A branch office is in the town hall at the Grand Place.

CITY TRANSPORTATION   Subway (metro), pre-metro (tram lines which run underground), trams and yellow buses are part of the STIB (Societes des Transports Intercommunaux de Bruxelle) network. There are also orange suburban S.N.C.V. buses. A one day tourist ticket is sold by the tourist office, railway stations, newspaper kiosks in metro stations and from drivers of S.N.C.V. buses (orange buses in Brussels area). Cost is 140BF for one day of unlimited travel on metro, pre-metro, tram, yellow buses and orange buses within the Brussels area. Have the ticket stamped by the automatic machine or collector before starting your day's travels.

Price of a single ticket is 35BF, payable to the driver of a bus or tram, or at the ticket office at a metro entrance. A card valid for 5 rides is 155BF, 10 rides 220BF. Buy them in metro ticket offices and some newspaper kiosks. Punch the card in the machines at metro entrances or near the front door of buses and trams. Transfers are free but you must remember to pick up a transfer ticket by pushing the button marked *transit* at the entrance to metro stations or near the entrance door of trams and buses.

Metro stations are marked by a big M in white on a blue background. Tram and bus stops are indicated by red and white or blue and white signs. Belgian Rail local trains can be used to some extent in the greater Brussels area.

CAMPGROUNDS   **Camping Beersel**, 9 km. south of Brussels at Ukkelsesteenweg 75 in suburb of Beersel, is open all year. Take tram 55 from Nord or Midi Stations (or local train from any station) to Uccle-Calevoet. Change to bus UB outside of Uccle-Calevoet Station to Beersel. Camp is 100 meters from the bus stop. Adult/30BF, tent/20BF, extra charge for hot shower.

Camping Provinciaal Domein, 13 km. south of Brussels at Provinciaal Domein 6 in Huizingen, is open Mar 15-Sep 30. Take a local train to Huizingen Station, 1 km. from camp, or to Buizingen Station, 1.2 km from camp. There is also a bus which stops 200 meters from camp. Restroom sinks have hot water; store and restaurant are 1/2 km away; adult/50BF, tent/50BF.

Camping Grimbergen, 13 km north of Brussels at Veldkantstraat 64 in Grimbergen, is open Apr 11-Oct 31. From Station Nord, take bus G (not bus G with a slash because it goes in the other direction) and get out at the Barcelle Kerk (church) bus stop. Hot water in restroom sinks, one km. to store and restaurant; adult/70BF, tent/100BF.

Camping Paul Rosmant, Warandeberg 52 in Wezembeek-Oppen, 10 km. east of Brussels, is open Apr 1-Sep 30, adult/57BF, tent/57F.

FOOD The market is on Place St. Catherine, about 11 blocks from Central Station (M-Sa 8-6). Department stores offer a noon fixed-price meal. Au Bon Marche, across from Place Rogier on corner of Rue Neuve and Boulevard du Jardin Botanique, 5 blocks south of Nord Station, has a fourth floor cafeteria. Its Self-Service Express offers a set menu between 11am-2:30pm, M-Sa. Cafeteria is also open 11-6 and to 9 pm on Friday. Nopris department store, 32 Rue du Marche aux Poulets, a fairly short seven blocks west of Central Station, has a second floor cafeteria. Sarma department store, 17 Rue Neuve and about 9 blocks northwest of Central Sataion has a cheaper menu, open M-F 11:30-3. Mister G.B. Cafeteria chain has a good branch at Pte de Namur. This large, modern operation is open 8am-10pm.

For snacking, nothing beats the waffles (gaufres) sold in department stores. In the evening, vending carts selling mussels and tiny shish-ka-bobs line Petite Rue au Beurre, near Place de la Bourse.

SIGHTSEEING **Grand Place** is the top attraction and worth a return visit when it's illuminated at night. The most important building in the square is Hotel de Ville (town hall), a most imposing example of Gothic architecture. **Musee de L'Art Ancien**, 3 Rue de la Regence, five blocks south of Central Station, has a good collection of Old Masters, including outstanding works by Breughel and Bosch. Open Tu-Su 10-12 & 1-5. Subway is Parc Royale or bus route, Place Royale. **Royal Central African Museum**, Leuvensesteenweg 13 in Tervuren, has a fine group of African art and departments of zoology, anthropology, etc. which cover every phase of African life and history. Open Tu-Su 9-5:30, free; take tram 44 from Central Station or tram 45 from Midi Station to last stop. **Musee d'art Moderne**, Place Royale, shows mostly 19th and 20th century Belgium paintings and some contemporary French, German, English and Dutch paintings and sculpture. Open Tu-Su 10-12 & 1-5, free. **Atomium** in Heysel, symbol of the Brussels World Fair, can be reached by tram 18 from Porte de Namur. The huge Bois de la Cambre park has trails threading through its pruned woods.

To Amsterdam, leave Central Station at 6:14am and 14 minutes past the hour until 7:14pm, then 8:19pm, 9:14pm and 10:14pm. The trip is 3 hours.
To Antwerp, leave Central Station at 6:14am and 14 and 46 minutes past the hour until 10:14pm, then 10:35pm, 11:14pm and 11:39pm. The trip is 45 minutes.
To Gent, Bruges and Ostend, leave Central Station at 8:21am and 21 and 50 minutes past the hour until 11:50pm.
To Milan leave Midi Station at 7:16am (ar. 7:25pm), 6:15pm (ar. 7:40am) and 10:23pm (ar. 11:50am).
To Paris Nord Station, leave Midi Station at 7:10am EuroCity not Sunday (ar. 9:43am), 8:04 (ar. 10:50am), 10:10am (ar. 1pm), 11:49am EuroCity not Sunday (ar.

2:15pm), 2:07pm (ar. 4:55pm), 4:10pm EuroCity (ar. 6:56pm), 6:38pm EuroCity not Saturday (ar. 9:13pm), 7:12pm (ar. 10:06pm) and 8:41pm (ar. 11:15pm).

GENT (GHENT)

Gent is Belgium's second great medieval museum town. In contrast with Bruges, the old parts of Gent are mixed with the new, thriving city so sightseeing is not as self-contained. Musical performances are given in the great medieval buildings of the town during the Festival of Flanders, from August to October.

TRAIN STATIONS   St. Peter's Station (St. Pietersstation), located at K. Maria-Hendrikaplein (square), is where international trains stop. From the train window, the sign reads Gent-St. Pieter. Buy the 8-ride bus card from the regular ticket window in the station. Europa Bank charges a commission, but the bank on the left doesn't. A regional tourist office (Federatie voor Toerisme in Oost Vlaanderen) is outside the station on the left, across the square. Open M-F 8:30-noon & 1:15-4:45pm. Tram 1 in front of the station goes to Korenmarkt, downtown Gent.

As you exit St. Peter's Station by the front door, the first street on the right, the one that looks like a continuation of the station, is Clementinalaan. The Transalpino student travel office is half a block along it on the right. On the second street on the right, Kon. Astridlaan, a bakery is half a block down on the left side of the street. A half block further on Kon. Astridlaan on the right hand side of the street is small Alpin supermarket which sells lunch meat, cheese, fruits and vegetables, etc.

Dampoort Station (*Dampoortstation*) is closer to downtown, used for local trains and does not have a tourist office.

TOURIST OFFICE   Dienst voor Toerisme is in the Crypt of the Town Hall on Botermarkt. Open Su-Th 9am-8pm, F & Sa 9-9 in summer.

CITY TRANSPORTATION   A single bus or tram ticket is 30BF. A card good for 8 trips (8 rittenkaart) costs 138BF and is the best buy. Purchase it from the regular ticket windows on the left in St. Peter's Station. There is a 24-hour ticket for 105BF.

CAMPGROUNDS   Blaarmeersen Camping, Zuiderlaan 12, was built in 1979 and is rated four stars by the Belgian Tourist Association. It is operated by the city of Gent. Open Mar 1-Oct. 15; adult/75BF, tent/90BF.

From the tracks of St. Peter's Station, go out the front entrance, not the back exit--St. Denislaan. On your way out, stop at the ticket windows on the left and buy an 8-ride bus ticket for 138BF. For 1989, a new bus is taken to the campground. Take bus 6 to Europaburg (the bridge) and there change to bus 38 to the campground. From camp, bus 38 will take you directly downtown to Korenmarkt. The camp is well-signed in the sports complex. From Dampoort Station, take bus 70 to the last stop. From Zuid, bus 70 leaves for the campground at 8:43am, 2:04pm and 4:12pm. From the Korenmarkt, bus 38 leaves for the campground at 9:45am, 11:45am, 12:57pm, 6:33pm and 7:45pm. There are other departures, but they don't go all the way to camp and require a 15-minute walk.

The camp is in a suburban area of high rises, and the modern Georges Nachez Aquatic Stadium is on the same side of the river. The campground office is open 8:15am-12:30pm and 2-5pm. The helpful workers will register you on their Commodore 64 computer. Both single and the 8-ride card ticket can be bought at the office. Check out must be by 3pm. The campground has excellent facilities and is so large that it doesn't get crowded. Tents are assigned to a separate area of their own where the ground is flat and grassy. The showers in the excellent restrooms have a shower stall and an outer dressing area with a bench and mirror. The sinks are compartmented and a hot air hand blow dryer is available. Soft toilet paper in gigantic 12 inch rolls are in the restrooms. The laundry room has 2 automatic washing machines which cost 80BF including detergent, a large dryer costing 40BF, laundry sinks and indoor lines for drying. The camp snack bar is open noon-2 & 6-9pm and sells such items as half a chicken for 85BF, egg roll (loempia) for 60BF and a liter of soup for 55BF. There is also a restaurant serving full meals. A playground across the street from the office has swings, slide, teeter-totter and climbing ropes. All manner of sports are available in the sports complex: ping-pong, tennis, roller skating, canoeing, fishing and swimming.

From the campground to St. Peter's Station, bus 70 leaves across from the office by the playground at 9:04am, 2:24pm and 4:33pm. For the Korenmarkt in downtown Gent, bus 38 leaves from the campground at 10:02am, 12:02pm, 1:14pm, 6:50pm and 8:03pm. It's also possible to take any departure from camp and then transfer to the correct bus at the main road. It takes 17 minutes by bus from camp to St. Peter's Station.

FOOD   The fruit and vegetable market is at Groentemarkt, open M-F, 7-1 and Sa 7am-7pm. Chickens and rabbits are sold at Oude Beestenmarkt on Friday 7-1.

SIGHTSEEING   The **Old Quarter** centers around St. Baafsplein and Korenmarkt.   On St. Baafspelein is St. Baafskathedraal (St. Bavo's Cathedral) with its 15th century tower. Inside is the masterpiece, *The Adoration of the Mystic Lamb*, by the van Eyck brothers. At the other end of the square stands the Belfry and Cloth Hall, a towered building dating from the turn of the 14th century. In the Cloth Hall, an audio-visual show, *The Ghent Experience* is presented in English daily at 10:40am and 3:20pm for 40BF, student 20BF.

From St. Baafsplein, walk to **Botermarkt**, anchored by the Town Hall (15th century Gothic and 17th century Renaissance) with flags flying. In Korenmarkt, oldest of the old, St. Nicholas Church dates from the 13th century. Behind Korenmarkt on Graslei, facing the canal, a row of guild houses with decorated facades and stair-stepped roofs can be seen. Guild House of the Grain Measurers (1698) is the one with wreathlike decoration near the peak of its front. To its right is Guild House of the Free Boatmen (1531). The tiny house of the Toll Collector (1682) flanks its left. Grain Warehouse (1200) is next to it, followed by First Grain Measurer's House. The building with a top looking like candles on a tiered birthday cake is the Mason's Guild House, dating from 1526.

Museum of Folklore, 3 blocks from Korenmarkt, recreates life around 1900 with 18 Flemish houses and lifelike room settings. St. Michael's Church is across St. Michielshelling bridge near St. Nicholas Church. The former was started in 1440 and completed in 1648 and now shows 17th century art. The **Castle of the Counts** (Gravensteen) was built in 1180 by the Count of Flanders, Philip of Alsace, and is located 4 blocks north of Korenmarkt on St. Veerleplein. It now houses an unusual museum of medieval torture apparatus. Daily 9-6, 40BF, student/20BF.

Together are **Citadel Park, Sports Stadium, Museum of Fine Arts and Floralia Palace.** From camp, take bus 38 to Europabrug at the bridge and change to bus 51 or 52 to Heuvelpoort. The Museum of Fine Arts (Museum voor Schone Kunsten), noted for its Flemish School (15th-20th centuries) and Bosch works, *The Bearing of the Cross* and *St. Hieronymus.*

SHOPPING The flea market on Beverhoutplein near St. Jacob's Church is open F 7-1 and Sa 7-6. The flower market, Kouter, operates daily 7-1. The bird market on Prof. Laurentplein and the Pet market on Oude Beestenmarkt are open Su 7-1.

To Antwerp, leave St. Peters Station at 6:28am and 28 minutes past the hour until 10:28pm.

To Bruges and Ostend, leave St. Peters Station at 7:17am and 17 minutes past the hour until 10:17pm and then 11:30pm.

To Brussels, leave St. Peters Station at 6:48am and 15 and 48 minutes past the hour until 9:48pm, then 10:15pm and 11:15pm.

OSTEND (OOSTENDE)

The ports of Ostend and nearby Zeebrugge are used by ferries crossing the channel to Britain. Ships from Ostend cross to Dover, while ships from Zeebrugge cross either to Dover or Felixstowe. Both SeaLink and Townsend Thoresen operate ferries out of Ostend. Inquire of a travel agent upon arrival as to which line has the best fare at the moment. If you are leaving from Zeebrugge, do not take the train to Ostend, but change to the line to Zeebrugge at Bruges.

TOWNSEND THORESON FERRIES Townsend Thoresen charges the same fare for foot passengers regardless of departure or arrival point. If you're looking for an overnight crossing, choose Zeebrugge to Felixstowe. Ferries leave at 11pm or 11:59pm and arrive at 7am the next morning. Don't come to Ostend, but change at Brugge for the train to Zeebrugge. The other crossings are only 3 to 4 hours.

If you're not interested in the overnight sailing, be aware that the crossing from Calais (France) to Dover is slightly cheaper than from Ostend or Zeebrugge on Townsend Thoresen; foot passengers pay 1040BF one way, 1280BF for 60-hour round trip ticket, and 1680BF for a 5-day round trip ticket. Passengers in cars pay 840BF one way or 60-hour round trip and 1280BF for a 5-day round trip. Sailings occur every hour and 45 minutes.

Townsend Thoresen charges a uniform rate from Ostend or Zeebrugge regardless of route of 1220BF for foot passengers for a one way ticket. A round trip ticket valid for 60 hours is 1350BF, whereas a round trip ticket good for 5 days (120 hours) costs 1690BF. (Passengers of vehicles get a better rate, only 840BF single or 60 hour round trip and 1280BF for 5 day round trip to Dover; 1000BF one way or 60 hour round trip, 1440BF for 5 day round trip to Felixstowe. Before buying your ticket, make friends with a driver.) Taking a hydrofoil reduces the crossing to 40 minutes and adds 453BF to the foot passenger fare.

Townsend Thoresen ferries leave from Ostend to Dover at 8am, 11:45am, 1:45pm, 5:45pm and 8pm. Jetfoils leave at 8:30am, 11:55am,

1:45pm, 4:35pm and 7:30pm. Passengers should check in 45 minutes before sailing time if possible.

EUROLINES BUS TO LONDON   Eurolines provides the lowest fare for regular passengers to London. On Port Service 114, the fare is 20 British pounds one way or L32 round trip within 3 months. Students and youth 15 to 26 years of age pay L19 one way or L29 round trip. Sailings from Ostend are at 1am (May 31-Sep 27, ar. 8:55am) and 12:45pm (ar. 7:45pm). Check in at Ostend's RMT terminal.   Sailings from Zeebrugge, Townsend Terminal, are at 6am (ar. 1:45pm) and noon (ar. 7:45pm). The service is operated Apr 1-Sep 30. The last 3 days in September the ships at Zeebrugge depart one hour earlier. Dates vary according to when weekends occur.

Even cheaper is **Eurolines Port Service 115**, which charges 19 British pounds one way (L31 round trip) and L18 one way for students and youth 15 to 26 (L28 round trip). This is a comfortable overnight sailing because it goes to Felixstowe, allowing for a good night's sleep enroute. Check in at 11pm at the Townsend Terminal in **Zeebrugge**, sail at 11:59pm, arrive in Felixstowe at 7am and London at 12:05pm. Operates about Apr 1 to Sep 30. The last 4 days in September the ferry departs 1 hour earlier.

TRAIN STATION   Next to the ferry terminal. The jetfoil departure dock is across the water at Vuurtorenook. The **tourist office** is in the Festival Hall on Wapenplein, a 6-block walk.

CITY TRANSPORTATION   The information office is at Brandariskaai, near the station. Tram 1 travels between Ostend and the nearby resort of Knokke. Tram 2 goes between Ostend and the resort town of DePanne. A private railway connects Ostend to Zeebrugge. Buses cost 27BF. Multi-trip tickets and a one day pass are sold.

CAMPGROUNDS   Four camps are reached by bus 6 (direction Raversijde not Stene) from the train station. The last bus on M-F is at 11:20pm, and SaSu at midnight.   De Kalkaert, Fleriskotstraat 8; Ostend Camping, Nieuwpoortsesteenweg 514; Petit Bruxelles, Duinenstraat 93; and Ramon, Duinenstraat 127, are all resort camps and charge about adult/70BF and tent/100BF.

FOOD   Markets are held starting at 8am on Thursday, Saturday and ts Monday on the Wapenplein, the Groentemarkt and the Mijnplein. An old fashioned picturesque fish market operates on the Visserskaai each morning.

To Amsterdam, Bruges, Gent and Antwerp, leave at 5:48am and 48 minutes past the hour until 9:48pm. To Brugge is 15 minutes, to Gent 35 minutes and Antwerp one hour and 15 minutes. For Amsterdam, change at Roosendaal; total trip is 4 hours.
To London, leave at 8:30am (hydrofoil, ar. 11:05am), 10am (ferry, ar. 3:05pm), 11:55am (hydrofoil, ar. 2:36pm), 1:45pm (hydrofoil, ar. 4:23pm), 1:45pm (ferry, ar. 7:02pm), 4:35pm (hydrofoil, ar. 7:05pm) and 7:30pm (hydrofoil, ar. 10:06pm).

BRITAIN

Shakespeare, the Beatles, parliamentary democracy, the Royal Family, tongue-in-cheek and the Queen's English--this much of Great Britain visitors know.   London dominates its country, more so than you'll find major cities do in the rest of Europe. But Britain is not all London and the beauty of the rural countryside is easily accessible. Just south of London are magnificent Gothic cathedrals and English-style medieval towns that can be visited even as you journey to Dover to board the ferry across the channel.

Remember that cars are driven on the "wrong" or opposite side of the road, which puts the steering wheel on the right. This won't affect your visit if you take care in crossing streets and look for cars coming in the opposite direction. Aside from this, Britain is one of the easiest countries in which to travel because of the lack of a language barrier.

CURRENCY   The pound sterling is divided into 100 new pence. One pound is worth $1.77 U.S.

WEATHER   Much has been written about the English climate. The weather is variable. June days can be sunny or they can be cold, damp and rainy. July and August are more reliably warm and rainfree, but the first time I encountered rain in London was last year and that was in July. It rained only intermittently during the day and our tent withstood the heavier rainfall during the night so we weren't bothered. Much of the sightseeing takes place indoors anyhow.

CAMPING Camping is extremely popular in Britain, but lots of the British tend to use trailers, which they call caravans, rather than tents. Campgrounds generally charge a set fee per site or per person, rather than charge separately for each person and tent. Camping fees average L1.60-L2.40 per person. If requested, some campground managers will reduce the fee for two backpackers with a small tent, because camping rates are set on the assumption of a large tent with four people. In general, campgrounds are considerably nicer on the continent than in Britain.

TRAVELING WITHIN BRITAIN   Eurailpass and Eurail Youthpass are not valid for Great Britain. British Rail offers similar BritRail passes, but they don't offer the value the Eurailpasses do. For public transportation, you're better off waiting until you arrive and then using a combination of special rail and coach (bus) fares offered in London and the various regions. Cheap deals abound: round trip fares for the price of one way or almost one way, and Rover tickets valid for unlimited transportation in a region for a day or a week.

TRAINS   Many types of tickets are offered by British Rail. The most valuable are the **Cheap Day Returns.** For travel after 10am weekdays and anytime weekends, the ticket includes round trip fare on the same day at only slightly more than the one way fare. **Intercity Savers** tickets are discounted (about 30 percent) round trip tickets valid for one month. Rail Rover tickets offer unlimited travel in different regions of Britain for one or two weeks. An **All-Line-Rover** covers the entire British Rail system (England, Scotland and Wales), but is not a good value.

A **Young Persons Railcard** can be purchased by anyone under 24 and by fulltime students of any age for L12. With the card, tickets for travel within Britain can be purchased at a discount. The card is good for one-third off Savers, Day Return (both cheap and standard), single and roundtrip tickets, and rovers (including All-Line-Rover). For trips before 10am on Monday through Friday, outside of July and August, a minimum fare is set of L6 for round trip fares and L3 for Standard Day Returns. No minimum applies in July and August, on weekends and holidays or after 10am on weekdays. The cards may be purchased at British Rail offices. You will need two passport type photos, your passport for proof of age and an ISIC card or a university ID card with your photo. A similar card for L12 is available to women over 60 and men over 65.

The **Rail Europ Family Card**, available within Europe as well, costs L5 and gives discounts on rail travel on the continent. The card covers up to eight people living at the same address. The cardholder who must be an adult pays full fare, while the other adults receive one-third off and children 5-11 get two-thirds off. Purchase at British Rail offices.

LONG DISTANCE BUSES   In Britain, they are called coaches. A bus is a city bus. Coaches cost less than trains and go more places. The major company is National Express. For L3.50, full time students can buy a Student Coach Card that discounts by one third, regular coach fares including one way fares (singles), day return and period return fares. The discount does not apply to Midweek Return Tickets. Children from age 5 to under 17 and people over 60 normally receive about one third off. Children receive a discount on Midweek Return Tickets as well. Traveling by coach is a best buy.

In London, all coaches leave from Victoria Coach Station, two blocks from Victoria Train Station. National Express has two types of journeys. For a Rapide journey, the coach has reclining seats, video, restrooms on board, refreshments available and a hostess on board. On most non-Rapide routes a refreshment/toilet stop is made during the journey. For Rapide and overnight journeys, a free reservation should be made in advance as accommodation is relatively limited.

Midweek Return Ticket   National Express offers a special Midweek Return fare from London that provides a round trip ticket for the price of one way where travel in both directions is on a Tuesday or Wednesday, but travel needn't be on the same day. The price of a Midweek Return, Day Return (round trip ticket valid one day), and simple one way fare is the same. Prices for these tickets from London are: L9 to Bath, L6.50 to Brighton, L7 to Cambridge, L7 to Canterbury, L12 to Cardiff, L12.50 to Chester, L8.50 to Dover, L8.50 to Folkstone, L8 to Hastings, L16 to Llandudno, L10 to Salisbury, L8 to Southampton, L8.50 to Stratford-upon-Avon, L17 to York and L8 to Winchester.

Period Return Ticket   National Express' Period Return ticket is a round trip ticket valid for six months. Sample fares from London are L21 to Llandudno, L17 to Liverpool, L21 to Swansea and L23 to York.

FOOD   The best meal value is fish and chips. Milk, cheese sold in bulk, bread and tea are good values. Milk can be kept for a month without refrigeration if unopened. The date indicates the last day it can be used. Once opened the milk must be used within 24 hours or refrigerated.

LONDON

The heart of Britain is London. London warrants more time than everybody has as its sights are inexhaustible. This is the center of theater, arts, music, education, the fourth estate, sports and cheap day return tickets.

AIRPORTS   The British Airports Authority owns and manages seven airports in the United Kingdom, of which Heathrow, Gatwick and Stansted are in the London area.

Heathrow is the busiest international airport in the world, handling over 23 million passengers each year. Upon arrival from abroad, pass through Immigration and Passport Control. Then go to the Baggage Reclaim area where your luggage is put onto a conveyor belt or revolving table marked with the number of your incoming flight. When going through customs, enter the green line if you've nothing to declare--that is you haven't brought substantial gifts for anyone. This is the fastest line.

An information desk in each terminal is open 7am-10pm and provides free tourist literature. A bank is in each terminal as well, and the Barclays Bank in the arrival terminal (#3) is open daily for 24 hours. For passengers leaving Britain, admittance to the duty free supermarket is given upon presentation of the airline boarding pass or ticket. Each terminal has a temporary baggage storage counter, open 24 hours a day. You may be asked to open your luggage for a security check. In terminals 1 and 2, mothers and children under 9 have available a special room, staffed by a nurse, with a play area and changing and feeding facilities. An unstaffed children's room is in terminal 3, open 8am-8pm, and can be opened at other hours by asking an airline staff member. Porters, whose services are free, and free self-service baggage carts are provided in the terminals. Each terminal has a post office and eating facilities. In the roof gardens of the Queen's Building, you can watch the planes take off and land, and there is a children's playground,

82

all for a small fee. British Airways, Air Canada, Pan Am and TWA have executive lounges in terminal 3.

To get to London from Heathrow, take either bus or subway (Underground). Flightline bus 767 costs L3.00 (1988) and stops at Kensington, Knightsbridge, Victoria Train and Victoria Coach Stations. The trip is one hour. Airbus costs L4.00 (1989) one way and has two routes: A1 goes to Victoria Station (Grosvenor Gardens) and stops at Hyde Park Corner enroute; A2 goes to Euston Station and stops at Holland Park Avenue, Nottinghill Gate, Bayswater Road, Lancaster Gate Station, Marble Arch, Bloomsbury and Russell Square. Cheapest and most convenient is by Underground. One way fare to Central London is L1.90 for the 50-minute trip. For only 40p more you can buy a 1-day Travelcard for L2.30 which gives unlimited underground, BritRail and bus travel for 1 day. Heathrow is the end-underground station on the Picadilly Line. To Liverpool Street for the bus to Hackney Camping requires a change at Holborn and takes 61 minutes. For Abbey Woods Camping, change at Green Park Station to Charing Cross Station where you change to the BritRail train. The Underground trains leave every 4-10 minutes between 5am (5:50am Su) and 11:40pm. (The first arrival from downtown London is 6:30am (7:45 Su) and the last is 1am (12:15am Su).

Gatwick is Britain's second most important airport. Flights from Paris and Amsterdam arrive here. Upon arrival from abroad, go through immigration and passport control and then proceed to the "buffer" lounge where you wait until the television monitors show your flight number. This means your luggage has been unloaded onto the circular tables in the baggage reclaim area. Claim your luggage and then get in the green line for Customs if you've nothing to declare.

In the international arrival hall there is an information desk that stocks free tourist literature. The Barclays Bank, open 24 hours daily in summer, cashes travelers checks at a good rate without commission. The duty-free store is in the international departures lounge beyond the passport control station. An airline boarding card must be shown to make purchases. Temporary luggage storage is available 24 hours a day. **To downtown London from Gatwick**, the cheapest way is via Flightline bus from outside the airport. Fare is L3 one way, or L5 roundtrip. Children 5 to 15 pay half fare. The bus departs at 20 and 50 minutes past the hour to 5:50pm and then 6:50pm, 7:50pm, 8:50pm and 10:15pm. The ride takes 70 minutes to Victoria Coach Station. The more expensive but faster British Rail train costs L4.60 one way or L9.20 roundtrip (valid 3 months) to Victoria Station. If you are going to take another BritRail train or the underground, it's more convenient to purchase the ticket here. For instance if you're going to Liverpool Station to get the bus to Hackney Camping, pay the entire fare at the airport and you will be issued a separate 40p ticket for the underground portion. Trains leave every 15 minutes until 10pm and then every half hour until 12:01am, the last train. The ride takes 35 to 45 minutes. If you plan to stay at Crystal Palace campground, check the schedule in the station and only board a train that stops at Crystal Palace station.

Stansted Airport, 34 miles from London, is used by some flights arriving from the U.S. The terminal has a Barclays Bank which opens to coincide with scheduled arrivals, duty-free shop, free mother's room (nursery), free porters and free self-service luggage carts. Tranportation to

London is not as good as at Heathrow and Gatwick Airports. Normally your airline will have made arrangements for a bus to take its passengers to London; a fare is payable. Otherwise, the airport advises the best way is to take a taxi the four miles to British Rail's Stortford Station and take a train to Liverpool Street Station in London where you can get the subway. There is a Stansted train station, but connections are better from Bishop's Stortford Station.

TRAIN STATIONS   The main train station is **Victoria** which·handles departures to the European continent, except for Holland. Within Britain, trains for South and South East England leave from here. The station's tourist information is open daily 9am-8:30pm (8am-10pm Jul-Aug). A Thomas Cook *Bureau de Change* is open daily 7:45am-10pm. National Travel Ltd. (NBC), open daily 8am-9pm, gives information on long distance buses and sells bus tickets. During summer, long lines form for luggage checking (open 24 hours).

London Buses

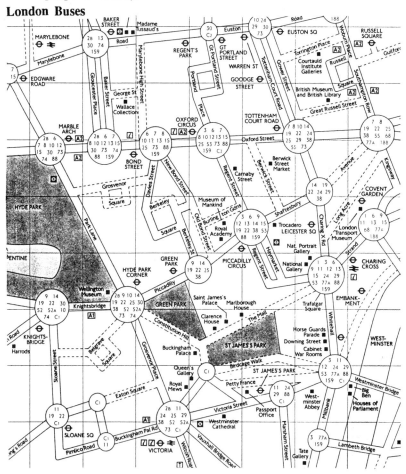

Victoria Station and Victoria Coach Station

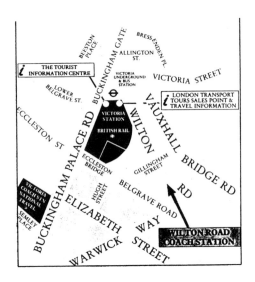

Liverpool Station was remodelled in 1987. The luggage check at this station has no lines, charges L1.15 per backpack and closes at 10pm. There is also foreign exchange without lines. Trains leaving for Amsterdam via the Harwich channel crossing leave from Liverpool Station. Essex and East Anglia within Britain are also served from here.

Many train stations share an underground station. These interchange stations are marked on the underground map with the BritRail symbol. BritRail trains for various parts of Britain leave from certain stations. Trains from Liverpool Street and Fenchurch Street stations go to Essex and East Anglia. Trains from King's Cross station go to West Yorkshire, North East and Scotland. Trains from Euston and St. Pancras stations serve the Midlands, North Wales, North West and Scotland. Trains from Paddington Station go to the West of England, West Midlands and South Wales. Trains from Waterloo, Victoria and Charing Cross Stations go to South and South East England, the area between London and the channel ferries.

VICTORIA COACH STATION   Long distance buses arrive and leave here. The station is about two blocks from Victoria Train Station. A yellow van provides continuous shuttle service between Victoria Train and Coach stations for 36p. If you start walking, you will probably pass the stop for the van. Luggage checking is available at Victoria Coach Station.

FOREIGN EXCHANGE   When cashing travelers checks on a weekend when banks are closed, watch out for the many places that charge 4 to 8 percent commission.   Thomas Cook agents change theirs without commission as does American Express. Banks generally give good rates and cash travelers checks without commission.

TOURIST INFORMATION   A London Information office is in the Victoria Train Station Forecourt, open daily, 9am-8:30pm (8am-10pm Jul-Aug).   Other offices are at Selfridges department store (ground floor), Harrods department store (fourth floor) and The Tower of London (west gate).   The British Travel Center on Regent Street between Piccadilly and Pall Mall, near American Express, will help with information on places outside London.

CITY TRANSPORTATION   It takes time to get around London no matter whether you're riding the subway (called underground or tube), a bus or a BritRail train.

The one thing to remember when changing in the Underground at Liverpool Station, is that trains for more than one destination leave from the same track.   Be sure to watch the sign suspended above the platform to ensure boarding the correct train.   We changed at Liverpool frequently, made this mistake, and subsequently encountered several others who did the same thing.   At other underground stations, all trains leaving from a platform go the same place.

Free bus and underground maps are given at London Transport Offices at Victoria, Piccadilly, Oxford, Euston and King's Cross stations. The London area is divided into zones and fares are according to zone.

Travelcard   A good deal is the **Travelcard** which gives unlimited use of the underground, London buses and BritRail trains within the zones you choose.   In addition, Travelcards that cover zones 3 and 4 or zones 4 and 5 are valid on most London Transport bus services outside Greater London. The cards are valid for one day, 7 days, 1 month or 1 year.

For the **1 day card** only, travel must occur after 9:30am M-F, but anytime on weekends, and it's not valid for night buses.   The 1-day card is good for travel throughout the greater London area (all 5 zones) for L2.30 (80p for under 16).   The 1-day card is an especially good value for those arriving at Heathrow Airport which is in zone 5.   An ordinary one-way ticket to London is L1.90 so for just 40p more you can have transportation for the entire day.

A **7-day Travelcard** for the central zone (blue) only is L6.40 (single ticket is 60p).   For the central zone and the next zone (green), the cost is L8.20 (single ticket is 90p).   Hackney Camping is in the green zone so buy a 2-zone card.   For the Central Zone and the next two zones, the fee is L11.20 for a 3-zone card (single ticket is L1.20).   For Crystal Palace Camping, you need a 3-zone card.   A 4-zone card costs L14 (single ticket is L1.50) and is the one to buy if you're staying at Abbey Woods Campground.   A month Travelcard is about 4 times the cost of a 7-day one less L1.   No restrictions are put on night buses or weekday travel on the 7-day and month Travelcards.   The Airbus to Heathrow is not included in any Travelcard.

The cards can be bought at the ticket counter in any underground station and at some newsstands.   Bring along one passport type photo for the 7-day or 1-month card.   Travelcards can start any day.   A card can be purchased for any number of days between 7 days and 1 month, but you must go to an Underground Station and give them at least 12 hours notice. Also, a 7-day card can be extended any time after noon on the expiration date.

Bus Fares   The same zones apply for bus tickets.   A single bus fare for 1 zone (except central) is 40p; for the Central zone, 60p, and 4 zones,

The Underground

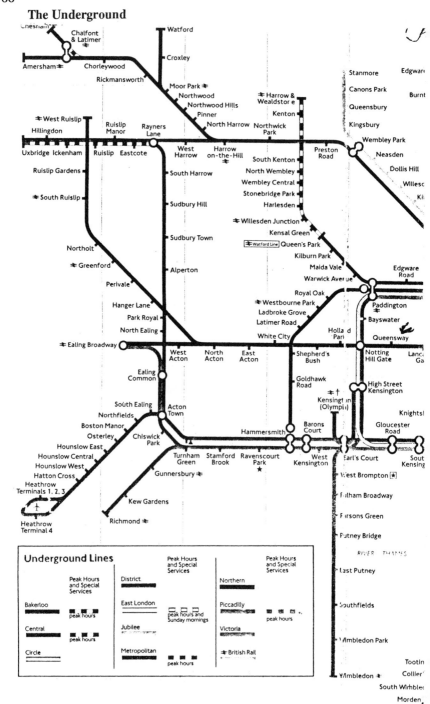

Underground Lines

	Peak Hours and Special Services			Peak Hours and Special Services			Peak Hours and Special Services
Bakerloo	peak hours		District		East London	peak hours and Sunday mornings	Northern
Central	peak hours		Jubilee		Metropolitan	peak hours	Piccadilly
Circle							Victoria
							British Rail

High Barnet
Totteridge & Whetstone
Woodside Park
West Finchley
Finchley Central
East Finchley
Highgate
Archway
Tufnell Park
Kentish Town
Mill Hill East
Cockfosters
Oakwood
Southgate
Arnos Grove
Bounds Green
Wood Green
Turnpike Lane
Manor House
Buckhur
Woodfo
Tottenham Hale
Walthamstow Central
Blackhorse Road
Snaresbro

Oak
Colindale
Hendon Central
Brent Cross
Golders Green
Hampstead
Belsize Park
Chalk Farm
West Hampstead
Finchley Road
Swiss Cottage
St. John's Wood
Marylebone
Great Portland Street
Euston
Euston Square
Warren Street
Goodge Street
Mornington Crescent
Camden Town
Caledonian Road
Holloway Road
King's Cross St. Pancras
Finsbury Park
Arsenal
Seven Sisters
Drayton Park
Highbury & Islington
Essex Road
Old Street
Angel
Farringdon
Russell Square
Barbican
Moorgate
Liverpool Street
Leytonst
Leyt
Stratf
Bethnal Green
Shoreditch

en Green
burn
Baker Street
Edgware Road
Regent's Park
Oxford Circus
Tottenham Court Road
Covent Garden
Chancery Lane
Holborn
St. Paul's
Bank
Marble Arch
Bond Street
Hyde Park Corner
Green Park
Piccadilly Circus
Leicester Square
Aldwych
Cannon Street
Aldgate
Aldgate East
bridge
Sloane Square
St. James's Park
Westminster
Charing Cross
Blackfriars
Mansion House
Monument for Bank
Tower Hill
Fenchurch Street
W
Si
ster
te

Victoria
Embankment
Charing Cross
Temple
Waterloo & City Line
London Bridge
New Cross Gate
Pimlico
Waterloo
Lambeth North
Borough
R
S

Vauxhall
Elephant & Castle
Kennington
Oval
Stockwell
Clapham North
Clapham Common
Clapham South
Balham
Tooting Bec
g Broadway
s Wood
ton
Brixton

Key to symbols

○ Interchange between Underground Lines

⇌ Interchange with British Rail

⇌ Interchange with British Rail within walking distance

☆ Closed Sundays

★ Closed Saturdays and Sundays

Certain stations are closed during public holidays

▲ Served by Piccadilly Line early mornings and late evenings Mondays to Saturdays and all day Sundays

L1.30. Children under 16 pay 20-30p. For example, adult bus fare to Hackney camping is 90p.) A half mile ride in the Central zone is 40p. Tickets are puchased on board.

How to Ride the Buses   On buses, standing is subject to regulations. No standing is allowed on the upper floor of a double decker bus and limited standing on the lower deck. Bus stops are easily identified, but there are two kinds. Every bus stops automatically at a regular stop, but will stop only on request when the bus stop sign has "request" written on it. To "request," ring the bell on the bus or wave your arms at the bus stop.

Red Arrow Buses are downtown shuttle buses with a flat fare of 40p and require exact change. The buses stop only where indicated by special blue plates at the stops. Buses 501, 502, 503, 506, 507, 509 and 513 are Red Arrow Buses. Their routes are as follows. Bus 501: Waterloo Station, Holborn, Bank, London Bridge Station; operates M-F. Bus 502: Waterloo Station, Aldwych, Fleet Street, St. Paul's, London Wall, Liverpool Street Station (M-F). Bus 503: Russell Square to South Kensington (M-Sa shopping hours only). Bus 506: Victoria Station to Paddington Station (M-Sa only). Bus 507: Waterloo Station, Lambeth Bridge, Victoria Station (daily). Bus 509: Liverpool Street to Oxford Circus (M-F shopping hours only). Bus 513: Waterloo Station, Aldwych, Fleet Street, St. Paul's, Cannon Street Station, London Bridge Station (M-F peak hours only).

The Underground   You must have a ticket before boarding the underground trains. In the subway stations are easy to read fare charts indicating what price ticket to buy from the automatic vending machine before boarding the train. There is also a manned ticket booth. Fares range from 40p to L1.90 depending on distance. The minimum fare in Central London is 60p. In the greater London area (within the zones) the maximum fare is L1.90 for 5 zones. Save the ticket to hand to the collector, if necessary, when exiting.

Brit Rail Trains   For British Rail trains, the cheapest fare is called *Day Return* and is a round trip fare in which both directions of travel must be used on the same day. A Day Return must be used after 9:30am on Monday through Friday, but anytime on weekends. *Return* fare is a regular round trip ticket. *Single* is a regular one way ticket. The best buy for travel within the Greater London area is the already-mentioned Travelcard.

Green Line Buses   London County Green Line buses serve suburban London and are the cheapest way to reach Windsor Castle and Hampton Court. Their London terminal is by Victoria Coach Station. Some Green Line buses are included in the 1-day Travelcard, such as to Hampton Court Palace which is in zone 5.

Children's Fares   Children under 16 receive a 50 percent or greater reduced fare on public transportation. Those 14 and 15 must have a child rate photocard, available at post offices, to show when purchasing children's tickets for buses and the underground. Bring a photograph.

CAMPGROUNDS   London has 8 or more campgrounds in the general vicinity. Hackney Camping is the cheapest. Abbey Wood is much better, takes no longer to reach, the ride is more comfortable because it's via train rather than bus, and a grocery and bakery are closer. However the cost is slightly greater for both the campground and the public transportation.

Hackney Camping, Millfields Road, Hackney Marshes, London E5, open Jun 18-Aug 25, 1989, is reserved for overseas visitors. People arriving in the middle of June or the last few days in August should check opening and closing dates with London information before going out for years other than 1989. The phone number is 985-7656. The charge is L2 per adult. The camp is in zone 2, the green zone. Single bus fare is 90p. A 1-day Travelcard is L2.30 and a 7-day Travelcard valid for 2 zones is L8.20. If you plan to return to town after setting up camp, it's worthwhile to purchase a Travelcard at the ticket office in Liverpool Station. If you will be in London for 4 days or more, then you'll come out ahead by buying a 7-day Travelcard.

Hackney Camping

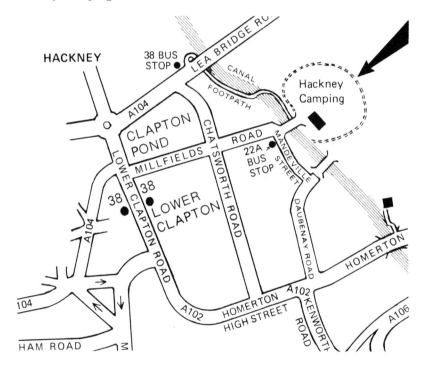

If you're coming from Victoria Train Station, either take bus 11 to the end of the line, Liverpool Station, or Circle line underground to Liverpool Station. From anywhere in London, take the underground to Liverpool Station. Liverpool Station is on Circle, Central and Metropolitan Lines. (Liverpool Station is both an underground and British Rail Station. Trains from Amsterdam via Harwich arrive here. The station has exchange and luggage check without the long lines of Victoria Station.) **Be sure to exit Liverpool Station onto Bishopsgate.** Bishopsgate is a main arterial. Then take bus 22A from slightly to the left of the station entrance as you go out. (Bus 22A also stops at Aldgate Station.) The bus ride is about 25 minutes to the campground. It's best to ask the driver to alert you for the stop. After 20 minutes on the bus, you've arrived in the general neighborhood. In a commercial area, the bus stops in front of a *Dental Surgery* office. This is the closest shopping area to the campground. In about two more blocks, the bus passes a *launderette* on the right. This is the closest one to camp. Then the bus leaves the shopping district and passes by highrise apartment buildings. On the left is the Gly Arms Pub. Get off at the next stop, Mandeville Road. Then, continue to walk in the direction the bus is going, but at the end of the block cross the street and walk over the small bridge to the campground, a 3-minute walk.

There are other ways to get here. Bus 55 originates at Victoria Train Station, stops at Piccadilly circus and Bloomsbury and then takes a slower route to the campground than Bus 22A. Bus 38 leaves from Lower Clapton Road at the stop called Clapton Pond, a 10 minute walk from camp. It stops at Bloomsbury, Piccadilly Circus and ends at Victoria Train Station. The last bus 38 from Victoria leaves at 12:18am. Bus 22A can also be taken from Hackney Central BritRail Station, which shortens the ride considerably.

The camp is a level, grassy lawn, part of a large park. Though it has room for 200 tents, in July we found only about 15 when we were there. Only tents are allowed on the lawn; a parking area is provided for cars and campers. The office in the main building is open 8am to 11:30pm. The facilities are adequate but of average or lower quality. There are free hot showers, some laundry sinks and a clothes drying room. The building is a converted gym locker room. (The other campgrounds in the London area have better restrooms.) The camp is only partially fenced, and campers must remove everything from their tent and check it in the main building before leaving for the day. This is the only camp we have ever encountered that requires this, which is due to the camp not being fenced and open to neighborhood children. The tent itself can be left up. Our tent remained undisturbed and we never saw any neighborhood children. After 11:45pm, the central building is locked and toilets outside must be used. A food kiosk (open 8-noon and 6-11pm), two tables and chairs are under cover outside the building. A few items such as corn flakes by the bowl, hot coffee, bread, milk and cheese are for sale.

Crystal Palace Campground, Crystal Palace Parade, is in Crystal Palace Park in the southern part of London, and beside the Crystal Palace TV transmission tower. Open all year; May 22-Aug 31: adult/L2.10, under 17 yrs/L.1.00, small tent/L1; Sep 1-May 21: adult/L1.75, small tent/L1.00. The camp is the closest to downtown London, easy to get to, crowded in summer, has somewhat gravelly terrain, and mainly RV's. Guidebooks and Travelcards are sold in the office; self-serve laundry is nearby.

The camp is in zone 3. If you will be returning to London, purchase a Travel card for 3 zones. From outside Victoria Train Station, you can take bus 2B (direction Crystal) to the campground. The ride is about 45 minutes. It's faster by local British Rail train from inside Victoria Station, but there's a 15-minute walk from the BritRail Station to camp. Trains leave every 30 minutes and the trip takes 20 minutes. Get off at Crystal Palace Train Station. Turn right as you come out of Crystal Palace Station onto the road. Go to the top of the hill and turn right. The camp is on the right side before the high television tower is reached. From Victoria Coach Station in London, walk on Buckingham Palace Road to Victoria Railway Station and then take either bus 2B or the train as above. From Heathrow Airport, take the underground to Piccadilly and then change to bus 3 on Regents Street to Crystal Palace. From Gatwick Airport, take a British Rail train direct to Crystal Palace Station, without having to go into Victoria Station. Be sure to board only a train that stops at Crystal Palace Station as some don't.

To go downtown from camp, take double-decker bus 3 into Fleet Street or Piccadilly Circus, a 40-minute ride. The route is Crystal Palace, West Dulwich, Herne Hill, Brixton, Kennington, Lambeth Bridge, Westminster, Trafalgar Square, Piccadilly Circus, Oxford Circus, Great Portland Town and Camden Town. Alternatively, from Crystal Palace Station to Victoria Station, British Rail trains leave every 30 minutes.

Abbey Wood Campground, Cooperative Woods Camping and Caravan Site is 4 miles from central London on Federation Road in Abbey Wood, a southeastern section of London. Open all year; adult/L1.90 and tent/L1. The best buy is the 1-day Travelcard for L2.30, or the 7-day Travelcard for L14 for 4 zones. The advantage of the 7-day card is that you can travel before 9:30am M-F. Take a British Rail train from Charing Cross Station to Abbey Wood Station, then a 5-minute walk. During peak hours, trains depart every 10 minutes. Charing Cross to Abbey Wood takes 35 minutes. To get to Charing Cross from Victoria Station, take Circle or District Line underground to third stop, Embankment, and change to Northern line for Charing Cross. Also, bus 177 from Greenwich leaves every 20 minutes and goes near the campground. Bus 180 from Abbey Wood goes to Greenwich every 20 minutes; trip is 15 minutes. When you exit Abbey Wood train station, Kneehill Brampton Road is directly in front of you. Just walk out of the exit and go straight in that direction. It's a slight uphill walk to get there. Turn right at the sign.

Abbey Wood Campground

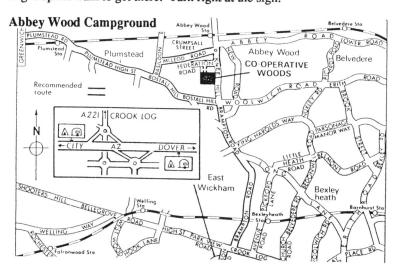

The site is sloping and grassy with trees. Most people have campers. It's a quiet campground, with the area from tents being away from the road which is not heavily traveled. Maximum stay is 14 days. There are three large bathroom/shower facilities, each with 7 sinks with hot water, 8-10 toilets with toilet paper, 4 hot showers and an air hand and hair dryer. An automatic washing machine and dryer are available, but sometimes aren't working. There's a vegetable preparation and dishwashing area with 6 aluminum sinks with hot water and ironing room. The camp store is open daily 8-11am and 4:30-8pm and sells food, pop, yogurt, milk, wine, beer etc. There's a pay phone, maps for the tube and posted bus schedules. A warning sign says to protect food as squirrels are hungry. A small playground has tire swings.

Eastway Camping, Temple Mills Lane, Leyton, E.15. is 4 miles from downtown London. Open Apr 1-Sep 30; adult/L2.50. The camp is in zone 3. From Victoria Station, take Victoria underground to Oxford Circus Station. Change to Central Line underground to Leyton Station. The trip is 20-25 minutes. Upon exiting Leyton Station, turn left onto the main street, Leyton High Road, which goes over (a bridge) the train tracks and puts you on the correct side. Walk until the traffic light, then turn right onto Temple Mills Lane which goes over a bridge over the railroad tracks. Temple Mill then curves right and follow that around and you reach camp. The walk is 15-20 minutes. (There is a shortcut over a fence and up a bank but you need someone to show the way.) Another way is from British Rail Liverpool Station, take British Rail to Stratford Station and then walk 20 minutes. (Stratford Station is also a stop on the underground.) Buses 6, 30, 236 and 299 all pass close by Eastway Camping. Bus 6 stops at Marble Arch, Oxford Circus, Piccadilly Circus, Trafalgar Square, Aldwych St. Paul's, Bank and Liverpool Street Station. Bus 30 stops at Earl's Court, South Kensington, Knightsbridge, Hyde Park Corner and Marble Arch.

The camp is part of a 40-acre park containing a unique bicycle track which has races and rental bikes. The Eastway athletic complex is a few minutes walk from camp. The beautifully landscaped grounds include grass lawns for tents. The modern restrooms of the Cycle buildings are locker room style and contain lockers, hot showers, sinks and toilets and are used by campers. When the building is locked for the night, a separate toilet is available in the campground. The snack bar in the Cycle building is open to campers and milk and bread can also be bought there. Camping is restricted to 60 units. A reservation may be needed in July and August. The camp is part of the Lee Valley Leisure Park group.

Sewardstone Caravan Park, Sewardstone Road, Chingford, London E4 is 12 miles from Central London at the edge of Epping Forest. This is a very nice country site away from the rush of London. It's better than Picketts Lock Centre. Open Apr 1-Oct 31; adult/L2.50. Sewardstone is in zone 5. From Victoria Station, take Victoria Line underground to Walthamstow Central Station, the last station. BritRail trains also go to Walthamstow Central. Then take bus 215 from the station to a half mile from the site. The bus ride is 20 minutes. The park also accepts tents. The lovely grassy site near a river has modern restrooms, store, automatic washing machine and dryer. Winner of a regional 1985 campsite of the year award, the camp is part of the Lee Valley Leisure Park chain.

Picketts Lock Centre, Pickets Lock Lane (off Montague Road), Edmonton, N.9. is 10 miles from central London. Open Mar 1-Sep 30; adult/L2.50. The faster way to get there is to take a British rail train to Lower Edmonton and then bus W8 to the site. Lower Edmonton is in zone 4. Not recommended is to take the bus from London which can take 2 hours to get there. For instance, bus 76 starts at Waterloo Station and stops at Blackfriars, Ludgate Circus, St. Paul's, Mansion House, Bank and near Moorgate tube stations. About 20 minutes beyond Moorgate and just past the 7 Sisters Market you change to bus 279. Then at Edmonton Shopping Center change to bus W8 to the site. Alternatively, you can take the tube to Moorgate and then get the bus. Coming out of Moorgate tube station, take the way out marked "Northbound buses," then take a left and go two blocks until reaching the #76 bus stop. Boarding the bus at Moorgate you still have about one hour and 15 minutes on buses before reaching the site. Bus 76 runs M-Sa, 2 to 4 times each hour.

The site is operated by Lee Valley Park and includes modern restrooms with toilet paper, automatic washers and dryers and small store (luncheon meat, crackers, milk, candy, etc.). The recreation complex includes a restaurant, 9-hole golf course, putting green, tennis courts, football field, swimming pool, sauna, roller skating, squash and badminton.

FOOD   Harrod's All-you-can-eat dessert buffet   The institution of British tea should be experienced, especially when it includes all the desserts you can eat. Dessert and chocolate lovers should run to the afternoon tea buffet in the Trafalgar Bar, on the fourth floor of Harrods Department Store at 3:30pm (closes 5:30pm). For about L6.50, you are served tea at your table and then can make unlimited trips to the dessert table. The table is constantly being replenished with new platters of rich desserts. There's always at least 30 varieties from which to choose. Sacher torte, carrot cake, cheesecake, fruit tartlets, French pastries, buttercream pastries, florentine cookies, strawberry shortcake, and simple buttered bread are a sample of what's available. The dining room itself is elegant and the service quintessentially British. Take the underground to Knightsbridge. Harrod's is across the street from the station.

Expensive, but worth it if you're really hungry and can eat substantially, is lunch at **The Carvery** in the Regent Palace Hotel (Piccadilly underground) or The Cumberland Hotel (Marble Arch underground). For L7.75, The Carvery serves a delicious buffet lunch. First help yourself from the buffet table filled solely with appetizers of every variety. Then go to the entree table where you can carve as much as you like of roast beef, a leg of lamb and roast pork. Next serve yourself the accompaniments of gravies, vegetables, hot Yorkshire pudding (popovers) and side dishes. When you're finished, the waiter or waitress will roll the dessert cart to your table for your selection. (The dessert is not unlimited.) The Carvaries are open for lunch, M-Sa 12:30-2:30 and dinner M-F 5:30-8:30, but for dinner the price rises to L11.75. They are also open Sunday.

SIGHTSEEING   The Michelin green guide for London is excellent for historical and cultural background and what to see. The extremely popular Tower and British Museum are less crowded on weekdays.

The **Tower of London**, open M-Sa 9:30-5 & Su 2-5, Tower Hill underground or bus 42 from Aldgate or 78 from Liverpool Station.

Admission L4. Services at the Chapel Royal are held on Sunday at 9:15am and 11am and weekdays at 5:15pm, except August. For free entry, contact the Yeoman Warder at the main gate about 30 minutes ahead. Free tours of the Tower are given half-hourly and start from the Middle Tower, close to the main entrance. The 700-year old ceremonial locking of the main gate of the Tower occurs nightly by the chief warden and an escort of guards at 9:50pm, but be there before 9:35pm. Free passes can be obtained by writing to The Resident Governor, Queen's House, H.M. Tower of London EC 3, Great Britain. The Changing of the Guard takes place at 11:30am on days when there is a Guard change at Buckingham Palace. Ask at the tourist office. There are Gun Salutes at the Tower of 62 guns at 1pm by the Honorable Artillery Company from Tower Wharf on April 21 (Queen's birthday), June 2 (Coronation Day), June 10 (Prince Philip's birthday) and August 4 (Queen Mother's birthday).

Other 3-star rated Michelin attractions are: **British Museum,** Holborn or Tottenham Court Road Stations or bus 8 or 22 from Liverpool Station, M-Sa 10-5, Su 2:30-6. Free admission. **The City of London. St. Paul's Cathedral,** bus 8 or 22 from Liverpool Station, open M-F 10-4:15, Sa 11-4:15. Free. **Hampton Court Palace and Gardens,** take Green Line Coach 718 from Victoria Station, open M-Sa 9:30-6, Su 11-6, L2.20. **The Science Museum,** Exhibition Road in Kensington, underground South Kensington, open M-Sa 10-6 & Su 2:30-6, admission L2.50, student/L1.50. Free hours are M-F 4:30-6pm, SaSu 5-6pm. Seven acres worth of exhibits such as locks and fire starting, in the basement; mechanical, hot air, gas, oil, electrical energy on ground floor; machines, meterology, astronomy on first floor up; photography on second floor; and optics, acoustics and geophysics on third floor. **Victoria and Albert Museum,** South Kensington Station or bus 14 from Picadilly, M-Sa 10-5:50 & Su 2:30-5:50, free. **Kew Royal Botanic Gardens,** open daily 10-8. **The National Gallery,** M-Sa 10-6 and in June-Sep Tu-Th to 9pm, free. **The Tate Gallery** (includes modern art section), M-Sa 10-6 & Su 2-6, free, Pimlico Station. **The Palace of Westminster,** Sa 10-5 & M,Tu,Thu in Aug (check hours). **Westminster Abbey,** M-F 9-4, Sa 9-2 & 3:45-5:45. **Windsor Castle,** M-Sa 10:30-5, Su 1:30-5, Green Line Coach from Victoria Coach Station. **Greenwich** by boat from Westminster or the Tower for one hour trip to Greenwich Pier, or trains leave from Charing Cross, Waterloo and Cannon Street for the 20-minute trip; buy cheap day return ticket. Buses also go there. In Greenwich see the National Maritime Museum, daily 10-6; Cutty Sark, M-Sa 11-6, Su 2:30-6 and Old Royal Observatory.

THEATER   Hit musicals are sold out months in advance. If you want to go, buy tickets through an agency 3 months before you leave for Europe. In New York, contact The Theatre Office, Number One, Times Square Plaza, New York, NY 10036, 212-944-0290. You have to pay a fee, but you'll have tickets, good as gold come July and August for hit musicals. British Airways will book shows for their passengers. You can also write directly to the theater, enclosing a check or money order, and giving alternative dates. If your trip starts and ends in London, upon arrival purchase tickets directly from theater box offices for dates during your return.

Plays available in summer on the spot are classics, British farces, well-received nonmusicals and less successful productions. For sold out shows some people return tickets to the theaters before the play starts and people form a line one to four hours before the performance starts hoping to purchase one.   Usually only a few are returned and most people simply waste their time. Scalpers hawk tickets outside the theatre just before opening but the prices are high.   The free London *Theatre Guide* is published weekly and available at any theatre. It lists current shows and includes a map locating theaters.

The National Theatre performs classics and hope-to-be classics. If a play is sold out, standing room is sold for L2 on the day of performance (limit two tickets per person). Unsold seats are sold to anyone two hours before the performance starts for L8 (matinee L6). Student standby tickets are available 45 minutes before the performance for L5 (matinee same price). Forty *day seats* are sold for L6.50-L90 (matinee L5.50-L7.50) starting from 10am on the day of performance at the Box Office. Normal ticket prices are L6.50-14 (L5.50-L12 for matinees). The Barbican Centre also sells standby tickets on the day of performance.

Discount theatre tickets   In Leicester Square, a blue temporary looking building sells the more expensive tickets to the less popular shows for half price plus a 80p fee on the day of performance. Available plays are written on the blackboard outside the booth. There are separate lines for matinee and evening performance tickets. Tickets for matinees go on sale from noon to 4 (some matinees don't start until 5pm) and for evening performances from 2:30 to 6:30 or so. If half price tickets are being sold, then the theater box office itself will likley have tickets available. The cheapest ticket purchased directly from a theatre may be about the same as the half price ticket bought at the booth.

NATIONAL EXPRESS COACH SCHEDULES FOR BRITAIN
One-way, Midweek Return and Day Return tickets all cost the same. For prices see introductory comments to Britain. All buses depart from Victoria Coach Station.

To Bath, leave 8am and every two hours until 8pm, arrive two hours later. From Bath, leave 6:05am and every two hours until 6:05pm, arrive two hours later.

To Brighton, leave 9am and every hour until 9pm, arrive 1-3/4 hours later. From Brighton, leave at 6:30am and every hour until 6:30pm, then 8:30pm, arrive 1-3/4 hours later.

To Cambridge, leave 9am and every hour until 8pm, arrive 1 hour and 50 minutes later. From Cambridge, leave at 7:30am and every hour until 5:30pm, then 7:30pm.

To Dover, leave 8am, 10am, 11:30am, 1pm, 2:30pm, 4pm, 5:30pm, 7pm, 8:30pm, 11:30pm, arriving 2-3/4 hours later. From Dover on Pencester Road, leave 6am (M-F), 6:45am (SaSu), 8:15am, 9:45am, 11:15am, 12:45pm, 2:15pm, 3:45pm, 5:15pm, 6:45pm and 8:15pm.

To Gatwick Airport, leave 4:55am, 6:55am, 8:30am and then each hour until 9:30pm, then 11:30pm. From Gatwick, leave 6:35am, 7:20am, 8:35am and then every hour until 8:35pm, then 9:45pm and 11:15pm.   The journey varies in duration depending upon traffic, but takes about one hour and 10 minutes.

To Heathrow Airport, leave 5:50am, 8am, then every 30 minutes until 8:30pm, then 9:30pm, 10:45pm and 11:30pm. From Heathrow, leave 4:15am, 6am, 7am, 8am, 9am, then every 30 minutes until 9pm, then 11:10pm. The trip varies in duration but usually takes about 35 minutes.

To Llandudno, leave 1pm (ar. 7pm) and 5pm (ar. 11pm). From Llandudno, leave 9:10am (ar. 3:25pm) and 1:10pm (ar. 7:25pm). These journeys are all Rapide; reserve a few days in advance to make sure of a seat.

To Oxford, leave 9am (ar. 10:30am).   From Oxford, leave 7:50pm (ar. 9:20pm). This trip operates for a limited period in summer. (Brit Rail's Intercity service has the monopoly on this route.)

To Salisbury (change for Stonehenge at Salisbury), leave 9am, then every 2 hours until 7pm. From Salisbury, leave 6:55am, then every two hours until 4:55pm. Trip is 3 hours and 5 minutes.

To Stratford-Upon-Avon, leave 8:30am, then every two hours until 6:30pm, then 8:30pm (F & Su). Return at 6:20am, then every two hours until 6:20pm. Journey is 3 hours and 10 minutes.

To Winchester, leave 9am, then every 2 hours until 7pm, then 9:30pm, 11:30pm. From Winchester, leave 4:50am, 5:50am, 8:05am, then every two hours until 6:05pm. Two hour trip.

To York, leave 10:30am (ar. 2:50pm), 2:30pm (ar. 6:50pm) and 6:30pm (ar. 10:50pm). From York, leave 8:30am (ar. 12:50pm), 12:30pm (ar. 4:50pm) and 4:30pm (ar. 8:50pm). All are Rapide; reservation may be necessary; train is much faster.

To Ireland by Coach   National Express provides Supabus service to both northern and southern Ireland. Fares are more expensive during the peak period, about July 3 to September 30. From London to Dublin, bus 553 offers the cheapest fare outside of the peak period, of L24 one way or L35 round trip. Peak period fare on this line is L31 one way or L47 round trip. Bus 553 leaves at 9am daily from April 15 to September 30 (ar. 9:20pm), and 9:30pm daily June 18 to August 30 (ar. 10am). During the peak period, the cheapest fare is provided from June 25 to September 14 by bus 851. Peak fare is L29 one way or L45 round trip. The fare on this line is L26 one way and L39 round trip at other times. Bus 851 leaves at 7pm and spends from 1:30am to 6:45am on the ferry, arriving in Dublin at 7:40am. Tickets and departures are from Victoria Coach Station.

TRAIN SCHEDULES WITHIN BRITAIN

To Canterbury, take the train from Victoria Station to Dover and get off at Canterbury East. (See trains to Dover.)

To Dover, trains leave from Victoria, Charing Cross and Waterloo Stations. Trains from Charing Cross, stop at Waterloo East about 3 minutes after leaving Charing Cross, and follow the route London-Ashford-Folkestone-Dover. Trains leave about every half hour on this line, from 7am to 9:25pm (usually at 30 and 55 minutes past the hour) and then 10:25pm and 11:25pm (M-Sa). If you're going to buy a Kent Rover (see Dover), purchase a ticket only as far as Tonbridge, the geographic start of its validity. Trains from Victoria Station follow the route Bromley South, Chatham, Sittingbourne, Faversham, Canterbury and East Dover. Trains leave at 20 and 50 minutes past each hour from 7:50am to 3:50pm and then about twice an hour at irregular times slowing to once an hour until 11:50pm. If buying a Kent Rover, purchase a regular ticket as far as Strood. Trips on either route take about two hours.

To Llandudno, trains leave Euston Station at 8:50am Su (change at Chester), 9:20am M-Sa (change at Chester), 11:30am M-Sa (ar. 3:17 Llandudno Junction), 4:17pm M-Sa (ar. LLandudno Junction 8:02pm) and 5pm Su (ar. Llandudno Junction 9:03pm).

To Rye, take the train from Charing Cross Station, Waterloo East or Victoria in the direction of Ashford. From Charing Cross and Waterloo East the end station on this line is Dover. For trains from Victoria, the line ends at Ashford. On both lines, trains leave about twice an hour. From Charing Cross, trains leave at 30 and 55 minutes past the hour. To Ashford takes 1-1/2 hours. Get off in Ashford and change to the train to Rye and Hastings. From Ashford to Rye, trains leave once an hour, usually at 4 minutes past the hour, for the 24-minute journey. From Rye to Ashford, the last train leaves at 9:28pm.

To York, trains leave from King's Cross Station Monday through Saturday at 8am (The Flying Scotsman, ar. 10:11am), then on the hour until 8pm. On Sunday, trains leave at 8:40am, 9:30am, 11:05am, noon, 12:30pm, 1pm, 1:30pm, 2pm, 3pm, 4pm, 4:30pm, 5:30pm, 6pm, 5:50pm, 7pm and 8pm.

LONDON TO THE CONTINENT

Visting Rye or Sandwich enroute to channel crossings.   Two lovely English medieval towns, Rye and Sandwich are only a few miles from Dover, a major departure point for channel crossings. Trains for Dover leave from Victoria, Waterloo and Charing Cross Stations in London every 30 to 45 minutes for the two hour trip. If you'e going to buy a Day Rover, pay for the train as far as Tonbridge or Strood, depending on which line you're taking, and buy the Rover there. Also, see National Express Coach schedules as buses are less than the train, only L8.50 London to Dover. From Dover, some trains continue on to Sandwich. For Rye, trains leave from Charing Cross or Cannon Street in London and you must change at Ashford. The train trip is 1-1/2 hours.

Fares to the Continent   Airline, train and coach operators are constantly coming up with new fares and promotions, so watch the posters around town to learn of them. If you're flying, make reservations upon arrival as cheap flights sell out. Often train and bus space is available at the last minute, but it doesn't hurt to reserve ahead.

Beware that the youth travel agency, Transalpino, located across Buckingham Palace Road from Victoria Train Station, has long lines in summer. For **plane and train** reservations, bring the student cards and passports of everyone who is going. The Transalpino train fare to Amsterdam for people under 26 is L17.90 one way with a L9.90 supplement due for overnight travel. A berth in a 4-bed compartment is L9. The Transalpino night train leaves at 7:15pm for Amsterdam via the Hook of Harwich ferry crossing. The cheapest bus fare is L19 one way for the Eurolines bus to Amsterdam. Anyone can go for that price and buses leave a few times a day from Victoria Coach Station. The night bus leaves at 6:30pm and arrives in Amsterdam about 9am.

Eurolines buses offer low prices to the continent. Reservations can be made outside Victoria train station, at Victoria Coach Station or through an agent. Buses leave from bay 20, Victoria Coach Station. Youth fare is valid for those under 26, women over 60 and men over 65. The fare to Amsterdam is L22.50 one way, L45 round trip, L20 one way youth, L39 round trip youth. Buses leave at 6:30pm (ar. 8am), 7pm (ar. 8:30am)and 10pm (ar. 11:30am). To Paris the fare for everybody is L25 one way or L44 round trip. The bus to Paris leaves at 9:30am (ar. 6:45pm), 12:30pm (ar. 9:45pm) and 9pm (ar. 7:15am). The cheapest route across the channel is to Dover or Calais for L20 one way, L33 round trip, L19 one way student, L31 round trip student. At Calais, a free Townsend Coach bus goes to and from the ferry terminal and the town center, Place d'Armes, which is near the train station. A round trip ticket valid for a single day is called a day return and sells for L25.50 from London to Calais. It reportedly is a common practice to purchase the day return and sell the return portion in Calais to a traveler bound for London. (This is also practiced at Dover and Ostend, often for only the ferry ride.)

National Express bus service to the continent is called CitySprint service. Students under 26 qualify for the student fare. The fare to Amsterdam is L23.50 one way, L42 rountrip, L21.50 one way student, L38 round trip student; to Paris, L24.50 one way, L41.50 round trip, L22.50 one way student, L39.50 round trip student. The cheapest point to the continent is Calais for L22 one way, L37 round trip, L20 one way student, L35 round trip student. The trip to Amsterdam takes 11 hours, to Paris about 9 hours. Buses depart from bay 20, Victoria Coach Station, several times daily.

Train Schedules to the Continent   For destinations to Switzerland or Italy, see schedules under Milan or Venice.

To Amsterdam, the best train for saving time is the night train because you can get 8 hours of sleep stretched out on a lounge on the ferry. The night train leaves Liverpool Station at 7:50pm, arrives in Harwich at 9pm where you get off the train and onto the ferry. As all passengers are looking for a place to sleep, be quick and "reserve" a spot as soon as you board. (You can also pay for a cabin.) The ferry leaves at 9:45pm and arrives at the Hoek van Holland at 6:30am. At the Hoek, take any train for Amsterdam or wait for the EuroCity that leaves at 7:32am and arrives in Amsterdam at 9:02am. Day trains leave Liverpool Station at 9:20am (Sunday) or 9:40am (M-Sa) and both arrive at 9:32pm. Other trains leave from Victoria Station and take the ferry or hydrofoil at Dover. They leave at 9:15am (change at Roosendaal, ar. 8:38pm) and 11:30am hydrofoil supplement (change at Roosendaal, ar. 8:38pm).

  To Bruges, Belgium, trains leave Victoria Station at 9:15am (ar. 4:48pm) and 1pm (ar. 8:48pm). Trains that connect with a hydrofoil (supplement payable) for the channel crossing leave at 8:15am (ar. 1:48pm), 11:30am (ar. 4:48pm), 1:30pm (ar. 6:48pm) and 4pm (ar. 9:08pm). Passengers must report to the Jetfoil Lounge in Victoria Station, 20 minutes prior to train departure to get a jetfoil boarding card.

  To Milan (change for **Rome**), a through train leaves Victoria station at 1pm, arrives in Lucerne, Switzerland, at 7:28am and Milan at 11:50am. (See Milan for schedules to Italian cities.)

  To Venice, a through train is available from May 31 to September 25, reservation advised. (This is also a good train to take for Berne, Interlaken and Zermatt; change points are indicated.) The train leaves Victoria Station at 2:30pm and arrives at Dover Western Docks at 4:30pm. Change to a Sealink ferry for the channel crossing and arrive at Calais at Gare Maritime at 7:32pm. At Calais, transfer to a train for Paris, arriving at its Gare du Nord at 10:55pm. In Paris the train continues on without the usual practice of passengers having to change train stations in Paris. The train reaches Lausanne (change for Berne) at 6:21am, skirts along the scenic shores of Lac Leman and arrives in Montreux (change for Interlaken) at 6:45am. At this point spectacular mountain scenery begins and crescendos as the train climbs higher into the alps, passing Martigny (change for Chamonix by private railroad) and Visp (change for Zermatt). The train arrives in Brig at 8:05am, enters the Simplon tunnel, passes the border station, Domodossola, at 8:43am, enters Milan at 10:55am, leaves Milan at noon, and reaches Venice Mestre and then Venice Santa Lucia stations at 3:08pm.

SOUTHEAST BRITAIN

The villages and towns of Great Britain are a world apart from London. You haven't really seen Britain unless time has been spent away from the metropolis. The towns between London and the English Channel are rich in history and easy to tour. Rye, a typically English medieval town, is the jewel in this area. Sandwich and Deal attract their share of recommendations, while Canterbury beckons visitors to its magnificent Cathedral. All of these towns are served by both bus and train.

Brit Rail Kent Rover

Various special coach and train tickets are available at train or coach stations in the towns. The most comfortable way to do this is with a **BritRail Kent Rover ticket**. The cost is L4.50 for one day or L16.50 for 7 days on any BritRail train in the designated area. Travel must be taken after 10am M-F, but is good anytime on weekends. Included are Dover, Canterbury, Rye, Deal, Sandwich, Snowdon, and Hastings, to name just a few. (Brighton is just west of Eastbourne, the town on the limit of the ticket's validity.) If coming from London, purchase a ticket only as far as Strood or Tonbridge depending on the route you taken, and then buy the Kent Rover at that station. If in Dover, buy the ticket at Dover, Western Docks Station. If you are going to tour a lot of Britain, remember that by buying a Youth Railcard for L12, you save 30 percent on subsequent rail rover ticket purchases. However, remember that National Express coaches offer similar arrangements at much lower prices. **Bus Ranger tickets** are valid on East Kent, Maidstrone and District, South Downs, and Hampshire buses.

DOVER The main Dover Station is Dover Priory on Folkestone Road. Dover Western Docks Station is by the channel ferries. Some trains from Victoria Station in London proceed directly to Dover's Marine Station at the western docks, the departure point for jetfoil services. Most regular ferries leave from the Eastern Docks. Free buses operated by the ferry lines go between Dover Priory and the docks.

The **Coach Station** is at Pencester Road, but coaches continue to the Eastern Docks after stopping there. The **tourist office** is located on Town Wall Street, open 9-6.

For student discounted **Transalpino** tickets, visit the travel agency, Pickford's, at 10 Worthington Street. Ferries are operated by Sealink or Townsend Thoreson and hydrofoil service is offered by Hovercraft. Both Sealink and Townsend Thoreson offer similar rates. Both company's day return fare (where you go and return on the same day) is only slightly more than the one way fare. (Sometimes you can buy the return portion of a day return ticket from someone arriving on the incoming ferry who bought the day return for the express purpose of reselling the other half.) The Hovercraft fare is reduced for departures at 8am or earlier.

Hawthorne Farm Campground is the closest camp to the channel ferries. Open March through October; adult/L1.75. BritRail's Martin Mill Station is 300 yards from the campground. Martin Mill Station is the station before Dover on the line to and from Margate. If coming from another route, get off at Dover Priory and change. Martin Mill is one station from Dover Priory Station. The 27-acre camp provides a separate area for tents and has a store and automatic washing machine.

The **market** is held Saturday in the Market Place. For a reasonably priced (L3-4) typical English meal of roast beef and yorkshire pudding, visit Jermain's Cafe on Leighton Street. The cafe is open for lunch only from 11:30-2pm. The Tea Caddy, 29 Castle Street, is also reasonable, open daily 8:30-6. For traditional English meals in the splurge category, try Hubert House Restaurant on Castle Hill Road, open M-Sa 8:30-8, Su 8-6, about L7. Dover offers many other restaurants, plenty of inexpensive fish and chips eateries, and grocery stores.

See the Roman Townhouse (Tu-Su 10-5, 80p) and Dover Castle (9:30-6:30 L2), but be sure to leave time for the medieval town of Rye.

100

To Rye from Dover Priory Station, take the train to London that goes via Ashford and change at Ashford. Trains leave M-Sa at 13 and 30 minutes past the hour until 6:30pm and then at 7:32pm, 8:32pm, 9:32pm and 10:02pm. On Sunday, trains leave at 7:30am, 8:30am, 9:30am and every half hour until 7:32pm, then 8:32pm and 9:32pm. Some trains, such as the 1:45pm and 5:54pm trains, meet the ferry and leave from the Western Docks. The ferry companies provide free shuttle buses to and from Dover and the Eastern docks. At Ashford, take the train to Hastings and get off in Rye. From Ashford, trains leave for Rye at 4 minutes past the hour from 7:04am to 8:04pm and then 9:06pm.

To Sandwich from Dover Priory Station, take the train in the direction of Ramsgate or Margate.

To Canterbury, take the train to London Victoria Station and get off at Canterbury East. Don't take any train to London Charing Cross Station because it goes via Ashford rather than Canterbury. Trains leave M-F from Dover Western Docks at 5:45am, 6:47am, 7:25am, 7:50am, 8:30am, 9:02am, 9:47am and at 47 minutes past the hour until 3:45pm, then 4pm, 4:34pm, 5pm, 5:34pm, 6:28pm, 7:28pm, 9:28pm, 10pm and 10:30pm. Trains leave Dover Priory five minutes later. Free shuttle buses connect the Eastern docks with Dover Priory Station. The ride to Canterbury East Station takes 40 minutes.

RYE Extremely picturesque, Rye merits a visit on your way to or from London. The tourist office, 48 Cinque Port Street, is open M-F 8:30-1 & 2-6:30, SaSu 10:30-1 & 2-5:30. Buy *Adam's Guide to Rye Royal* for 75p to equip yourself to explore on your own. Highly rated Silver Sands Caravan Park, Lydd Road, is 3 miles east of Rye in Camber and accessible by bus. Further out is Old Coghurst Farm campground, at Three Oaks near Guestling, and also reached by bus. Winchelsea Caravan Park in Rye does not take tents.

To Brighton from Rye, take the train to Hastings and change for the train to Brighton. The end of the Kent Rover validity is Eastbourne, 22 miles from Brighton. Trains depart once an hour. The bus is also available.

SANDWICH The old world town of Sandwich was one of the medieval cinque ports and, like Rye, has retained its character. Sandwich is the fourth station from Dover Priory when traveling north to Margate. The tourist office sells a guide to Sandwich for 60p. The ramparts are open to strolling. For an Olde English atmospheric lunch for L5, go to the sixteenth-century historic building that is the Teahouse. Address is 9 Cattle Market, across from the Guildhall. The saturday market is near the Guildhall.

Camp at **Sandwich Leisure Park**, Woodnesborough Road, half a mile outside town, and only 10 minutes by foot from the train station. After leaving Sandwich Train Station, cross the main road and take the Rope Walk into Woodnesborough Road. The Campground lies a short distance from the end of Rope Walk over the railway crossing. Open Mar-Oct, the 10-acre quiet, grassy site, accepts 72 RV's and 28 tents, charging L4.75 per tent including 4 people. Store, automatic washing machine and dryer.

DEAL To reach the Sandhills Campsite walk to the beachfront promenade, turn left and continue to its end. On the Golf Road turn right where you will pick up signs for the campground. Tent/L2.25, adult/30p.

CANTERBURY Guided tours are offerred of the historically important medieval Cathedral M-F, each hour from 1:30-2:30, for a fee of L1. St. Martin's Touring Caravan and Camping Site is 1-1/2 miles east of the city center, near the golf course. Open Apr-Oct; L2.20 for small tent and two people. The grassy site has a store and automatic washer and dryer.

Oxford

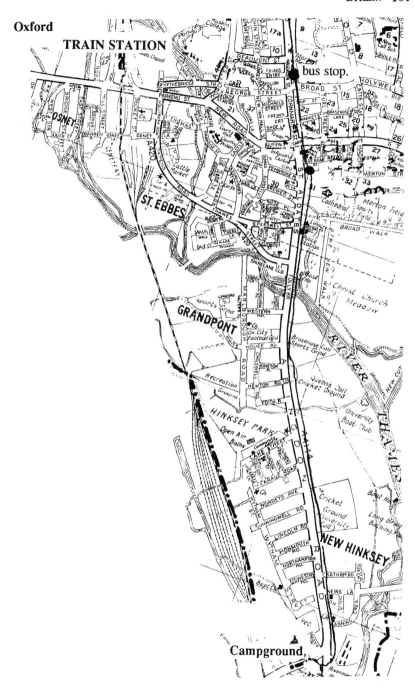

SOUTH BRITAIN

Many of these towns can be seen on day trips from London, or a circular route can be taken. Both train and coach transportation are available in this region.

OXFORD   From London, CityLink 190 leaves every 20 minutes from Victoria Train Station. Journey is 100 minutes. Both round trip and day return tickets offer savings.

   Camping International, 426 Abingdon Road, is across from Redbridge Park and Ride.   Adult/L1.00, small tent/L1.70 including hot shower and hot water in the sinks. There are no buses directly to the camp from either the train or coach station. You must walk from one of these stations to the main road running North and South through the city. From this street buses run every 10 minutes to the Peartree-Redbridge Park and Ride. Both double-decker and minibuses operate this route and they are clearly marked. The nearest stop to the Coach Station is less than a 5-minute walk to Magdalen Street. The stop is next to and on the same side of the street as St. Mary Magdalens Church. The nearest stop to the Train Station is east up Park End Street/New Road/Queen Street to Carfax. Turn right onto St. Aldates and the stop is just beyond the Town Hall on the same side of the street. The walk is 10 minutes. The last bus is 7pm. After that buses leave at 24 and 54 minutes past the hour opposite GPO in St. Aldate's until 11:16pm. It's also possible to walk the 1-1/2 miles to the campsite. Bus fare is 50p for a day return, 30p for single ticket valid 9:30am-7pm M-Sa.

Winchester

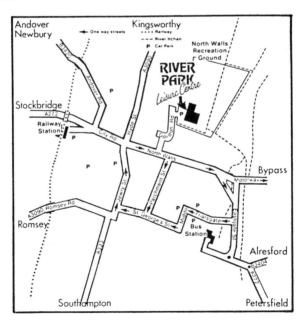

Bath

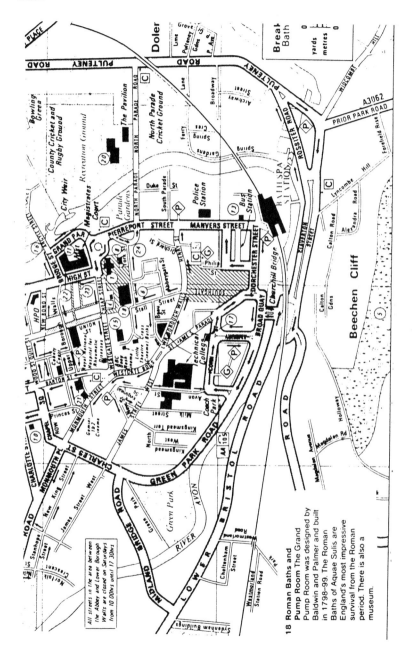

18 Roman Baths and Pump Room The Grand Pump Room was designed by Baldwin and Palmer and built in 1798–99. The Roman Baths of Aquae Sulis are England's most impressive survival from the Roman period. There is also a museum.

WINCHESTER   The medieval town and its famous Cathedral attract visitors, as does the nearby town of Chawton where Jane Austen's home can be toured (open daily). Chawton can be reached by bus from Winchester. Winchester's market is Wednesday, Friday and Saturday.

River Park Leisure Center, operated by the Winchester City Council at Gordon Road north of North Walls, is within walking distance of train and coach stations. Open Jun-Sep, the camp accepts tents only and has room for 60 on a grassy level site. Fee is L2-4 per tent. Heated swimming pools and a Terrace Buffet are part of the Leisure Center.

BRIGHTON   An English seaside resort of *Brighton Beach Memoirs* fame, the town continues to fulfill its destiny. The municipal campground, Sheepcote Valley, is on Wilson Avenue, 1-1/2 miles from town. Take bus 1 which goes directly to camp, or bus 17 or 27 which travels along the waterfront. The camp is open March 1 to October 31 and has a store. For small tents, the fee is L1.20 per person.

SALISBURY   The campground is about one mile out of Salisbury. The bus from Salisbury to Amesbury-Stonehenge goes right by. The bus leaves from the coach station in Salisbury. The Salisbury Youth Hostel allows camping anywhere outside the main building. A level, grassy and shady area large enough for 10 to 15 tents is available. There's no limit on number of tents accommodated. Camping cost is half the Hostel adult price or L1.80. Campers use the hostel facilities. Hot showers, washing machine and dryer, no cooking facilities.

BATH   Bath was in its heyday in the 18th century. Even today its Georgian elegance easily lures visitors.

Newton Mill Touring Centre is 2-1/2 miles from Bath, set in 43 acres of a wooded valley. 1988 fee is adult/L2.75. From the coach or train station, take bus 5 to Newton Road. Then walk downhill to the site. To walk from Bath, follow A36 towards Bristol. Turn left at Twerton under the railway bridge. Walk through the village to Newton Road. The walk takes about 35 minutes. The nicely landscaped camp has modern restrooms, automatic washing machine and dryer, store and restaurant.

NORTH ENGLAND

YORK   Another picturesque town, York is 2-1/2 hours North of London by train. The town makes a good stop enroute to Edinburgh. The tourist office presents a free walking tour. The Market is near King's Square, open M-Sa.

Rawcliffe Manor Caravan Park is at Manor Lane, Shipton Road, on a former RAF bomber airfield 3 miles from York. Lawns and trees have been planted on the level site. 1988 fees are L2.80 for tent and one person, L3.70 for tent and 2 people. Take bus 5 or 5A from the BritRail Station to its terminus at Mitre Public House. Then a 5 minute walk. The campground has an automatic washing machine, dryer and a clubhouse with restaurant, billiards and a dance floor.

NORTH WALES

North Wales abounds in scenic beauty and trails. Its position enroute between Dublin, Ireland, and England or Scotland, makes it easy to visit. To Ireland, the shortest ferry crossing is between Hollyhead in North Wales and Dun Laoghaire, a short distance from Dublin. Within North Wales, there are various special rail and bus tickets from which to choose. Coach tickets are less than train fares.

The **Crosville Bus 7 Day Rover** ticket costs L7 and is valid on all lines in the county of Gwynedd, which includes Snowdonia National Park, Porthmadog, Caernarfon, Bangor, Holyhead, Llandudno and Llandudno Junction, Betws-y-Coed, Chester and more. In addition, the Tourist Board offers a BWS GWYNEDD One Day Rover Ticket for L2 for all buses within Gwynedd. It can be bought on the bus.

The **North Wales Coast Rail Day Ranger**, available Monday to Friday from about May 11 to October 2, gives unlimited rail travel for one day between all stations from Chester to Llandudno Junction, including the spur to the resort of Llandudno, and on to Holyhead. In the westbround direction, the ticket is not valid for travel on or before 9:15am. Eastbound, the ticket is not valid before 10am. The price is L7 or, with railcard, L3.50.

THE CONWY VALLEY AND FFESTINIOG RAILWAY Not part of the above ranger ticket, the Conwy Valley single track rail line begins at sea-level at Llandudno and climbs up through the valley past Betws-y-coed to Blaenau Ffestiniog. From Blaenau Ffestiniog, begins the Ffestiniog Railway which runs through Snowdonia National Park which is laced by trails, to Porthmadog on the Cambrian Coast. Originally built to carry slate from the mines of Blaenau Ffestiniog to the coast, it now does duty as one of the most scenic routes in Wales.

A day return from Llandudno Junction to Blaenau Ffestiniog and then by the Ffestiniog Railway to Porthmadog and return costs L8.50 or, with railcard, L4.25. Holders of the North Wales Coast Day Ranger can purchase the ticket for L4.80, but the ticket must be bought before the journey starts from the station at Llandudno Junction or Llandudno. This ticket is available from about March 28 to October 31, Monday to Saturday only.

The Conwy Valley Day Ranger gives unlimited travel for one day between all stations from Llandudno to Blaenau Ffestiniog, without time restrictions. The cost is adult/L4.50 or, with railcard, L2.25. The Ranger may be bought from Monday to Saturday from about May 11 to October 3. An Evening Ranger is sold Mondays to Saturdays in the same period and gives unlimited travel by train after 5:30pm between rail stations Bangor to Prestatyn and Llandudno to Blaenau Ffestiniog for adult/L1.80, with railcard/90p.

On **Sundays** from about mid-July to the end of August, shuttle charter trains provide the only service on the Conwy Valley and Ffestiniog lines. The line is chartered by the County Council and does not accept British Rail tickets on this day. Tickets must be bought on the train. Members of the Railway Club accompany the train and provide history and leaflets on places to visit. Various Sunday tickets are sold. Ticket 1, Conwy Valley Day Ticket, allows unlimited travel for the Sunday, adult/L3. Ticket 2, Ffestiniog Railway Inclusive Tour, is a round trip from Llandudno to Porthmadog, including a trip on the Ffestiniog narrow gauge railway,

Conwy Valley and Ffestiniog Railway

Llandudno

Deganwy

The Great Orme
Look out for the coastline of North
Wales, Anglesey and Puffin Island.
Conwy Castle stands prominently
above the walled town of Conwy.

Conwy

The spectacular Conwy estuary with
its abundance of wildlife.

Conwy. A walled town with
a fine 13th century castle,
it is considered to be a
perfect example of a
medieval fortification in
Britain. At the end of June
a new station opens in the
town which will allow
easy access to the centre
of this thriving tourist
centre and fishing port.

Glan Conwy

to Holyhead
Tal-y-Cafn bridge replaced a ferry
crossing which existed since Roman
times.

Tal-y-Cafn

The village of Dolgarrog; you can
glimpse the pipes from a dam high in
the mountains supplying hydro-electric
power to the aluminium works in the
valley bottom.

Dolgarrog

Trefriw village with its mineral springs.

Llanrwst

Look out for the miniature steam
railway alongside the Railway Museum
at Betws-y-Coed Station.

Sherpa bus service around Snowdon
Lledr Valley and Wales' 'Little
Switzerland'.

First glimpse of Snowdon.

Betws-y-coed

Superb views into the heart
of Snowdonia National Park.

Dolwyddelan Castle backed by
the 2860' high Moel Siabod.

Pont y Pant

Dolwyddelan

Roman Bridge

**Dolwyddelan/Pont y
Pant/Roman Bridge**
Ideal rural halts from which to
explore riverside and
forests. The 12th Century
Dolwyddelan Castle is reputedly
the birthplace of Llewelyn the
Great, Prince of Wales.

Slate mines

The longest single track
railway tunnel in Britain
(2 miles).

Blaenau Ffestiniog

Blaenau Ffestiniog
Slate mining mountain town at the
head of the beautiful Vale of
Ffestiniog. It is the junction of the
Conwy Valley and Ffestiniog
Railway Lines which share a new
station in the town centre.

Porthmadog

Ffestiniog Railway
The Ffestiniog Narrow Gauge
Railway links Blaenau Ffestiniog
with the Cambrian Coast Line and
Porthmadog. Originally built to
carry slate from the mines to the
coast this line is famous for its
unique steam locomotives and
outstanding scenery.

adult/L6.50. Ticket 3, Llandudno to Betws-y-Coed, gives unlimited travel between Llandudno and Betwy-y-Coed on Sunday, adult/L2. Ticket 4, Liedr Valley, allows unlimited travel between Llanrwst and Blaenau Ffestiniog on Sunday, adult/L1.50.

A **circular day tour** of North Wales via the Ffestiniog Railway costs adult/L18, with railcard/L9. The circle is Chester, Llandudno Junction, Blaenau Ffestiniog, Porthmadog, Machynlleth, Shrewsbury, Wexham, Chester. The tour can be joined at any station. The circular day tour is available Monday through Saturday, from about March 28 to October 31. A day return (round trip in one day) ticket from London for this route costs adult/L36, with railcard/L18. The London day return is only available Mondays to Saturdays from about March 30 to May 2, June 1 to June 27, and September 28 to October 31.

Trains from London Through trains leave Euston Station in London for Holyhead 10 times daily. The route is via Chester and Llandudno Junction. The trip is about 4 hours to Llandudno Junction. Some through trains do not stop at Llandudno Junction, in which case you must get off at Chester and change to one that does. (About 21 non-through trains from London require a change at Crewe, which is about 1 hour and 10 minutes out of London.) For Betws-y-Coed, change trains at Llandudno Junction for the Llandudno-Bl. Ffestiniog-line. Eight trains depart daily; the last train departs from Llandudno Junction at 8:35pm.

BETWS-Y-COED Famed for its beauty, this small village is set in a green valley surrounded by forested hills in the Snowdon Region of North Wales. Betws-y-Coed is a half hour ride from Llandudno Junction on The Conwy Valley rail line. Eight trains run each day on this line.

The tourist office in town has free leaflets and sells a trail guide. **Riverside Caravan Park**, located behind the train station, is only a few minutes walk. Cross over the railway station footbridge. Turn left over the bridge, past the church and through the grounds of the Railway Museum and follow the trail. Mr. Harrison of the Park accepts tents as well as trailers and charges adult/L2.20, including hot showers.

TO IRELAND By train from Llandudno Junction to Holyhead to connect with the boat to Ireland, the best departure M-Sa is at noon. The train arrives in Holyhead at 1:01pm, ample time to board the ferry which doesn't leave until 2:45pm. The boat arrives in Dun Laoghaire at 6:30pm, where a bus meets the ferry to take passengers the remaining distance to Dublin (ar. 7:35pm). On Sunday, the train leaves at 12:15pm from Llandudno Junction.

The **B & I lines offer walk-on specials** between Holyhead and Dublin or Pembroke Dock and Rosslare for (1989) Aug 21-Jul 13 (L15 one way, L27 round trip), Jul 14-Aug 20 (L20 one way, L32 round trip.) Two sailings daily at 5:30am (ar. 9am) and 5:15pm (ar. 8:45pm). May need to reserve for weekends in July and August. Exact sailing times vary according to the tides. Can board 1 hour prior to sailing; check in at least 20 minutes ahead. Other operators have other sailings.

FROM IRELAND From Holyhead to London, trains that connect with the boat from Dun Laoghaire, leave Holyhead M-Sa at 12:45pm (ar. London 4:57pm), and at 1:05pm on Sunday. These trains do not stop at Llandudno Junction. To Llandudno Junction a train leaves M-Sa at 1:28pm and Su at 1:19pm.

108

SCOTLAND

The capital of Scotland is historical Edinburgh. More so than in England, everything closes down on Sunday; this is a good day to be traveling. Buses are the cheapest transportation in the area. A Scottish Travelpass is sold, but it's not a very good value. For L49 during June-Sept (L30 Mar-May & Oct) you can travel for 7 days on the long distance buses, trains and ferries within The Scottish Highlands and Islands. The area includes Glasgow, Edinburgh, Aberdeen and the Highlands and islands. A 14-day pass costs L75 June-Sept (L50 Mar-May & Oct). In Glasgow, the pass may be purchased at Queen Street Train Station or Glasgow Central, in Edinburgh at Waverley Station.

GLASGOW   If you have arrived in Glasgow, move on to Edinburgh immediately as Glasgow is industrial and of little interest. From May to October, a bus runs daily between Prestwick Airport and Edinburgh. From Edinburgh, the bus leaves from St. Andrews Square Bus Station. An airline bus connects with scheduled flight arrivals and departures to and from Anderston Cross bus depot in Glasgow. Cheaper than the airport bus, is a local bus that runs to and from the Airport and Glasgow every half hour. Once in Glasgow, there is hourly bus service to Edinburgh.   At Prestwick Airport, there is a Scottish Tourist Board counter and a Clydesdate Bank (M-F 6am-7pm, SaSu 6am-5pm) on the main concourse. Airport porters carry baggage at no charge and free baggage carts are available.

EDINBURGH   The international Festival of Drama and Music is held annually during three weeks from late August to early September. Besides theater companies and world-famous orchestras, the festival includes art exhibits, film festival, military tattoo and theater productions by student groups playing on the Festival *fringe*. The best procedure is to get the program and subsequently order tickets from the British Tourist Authority in the U.S. Wait until April 1 when the program and tickets become available.
    Waverly Train Station   Foreign exchange closes at midnight and luggage storage is open until 10:50pm. The City of Edinburgh Tourist Information and Accommodation Service is at 3 Princes Street, in the Waverly Market next to Waverly train station.
    Camping Muirhouse, 37 Marine Drive and 4 miles out of town, is on the Firth of Forth bay. April 15 to October 31; tent/L5. The grassy, level site has a store. During the Festival, reserve in advance by writing to the City of Edinburgh Parks and Recreation Department, 27 York Place, Edinburgh EH1 EHP, Britain. From the bus station, take the bus to Silverknowes from nearby York Place and ride to the last stop (Silverknowes). From the train station, walk on Market Street to The Mound (street) and take the bus to Silverknowes going north; get off at the last stop.
    Little France Caravan Park on Old Dalkieth Road is 3 miles from Edinburgh. April to October; tent/L6. Take bus 33 from the North Bridge, 1 block from Waverly Station. Grassy site, laundry room.
    Sightseeing   Top priority is the Royal Mile bridging Edinburgh Castle with Holyrood Palace. The Military Tattoo performed in the Castle courtyard is famous. Bring raincoats.
    To York and London, trains leave M-Sa at 7:25am, 8:35am, 9am, 9:35am and 35 minutes past the hour until 6:35pm. The trip is 2-3/4 hours to York, and 5 hours to London.

DENMARK

There is a lovely land
That proudly spreads her beeches
Beside the Baltic strand,

A land that curves in hill and dale
That men have named old Denmark
And this is Freia's hall.
Danish National Anthem

Though Denmark is one of the smallest countries in the world, it encompasses several hundred islands besides its mainland peninsula, Jutland (pronounced YOO-lan). During the Ice Age, glaciers carried Norway's topsoil south, dumping it on Denmark's chalk foundation and assuring its future as a prosperous agricultural country. Though Copenhagen is its glittering star, Denmark is predominantly farmland and you should try to break out of the city and pass through the villages and neatly tended agricultural lands of Jutland and Fyn. Try to see one of these interesting old villages: Ribe (see Esbjerg), Ebeltoft (see Arhus) or Kerteminde (see Odense). Legoland in Billund is obligatory for families with young children.

CURRENCY A Danish krone is divided into 100 ore. There are 7 kroner (pronounced crown-nur) to $1.00 U.S. Banks and exchange on ferries generally extract a 20 to 30kr commission per transaction. American Express is your best option for lessening the charge. MOMS (pronounced mumps) is the value added tax included in the price of goods and services. The amount is deducted on any item sent out of the country, or on large items refunded upon request if the necessary forms have been completed.

WEATHER June through August is the warmest period, though September can be pleasant too. Brief periods of rain sometimes come amidst sunny skies, but the duration is usually less than half an hour. Evenings are chilly at times. July and August are high season.

CAMPING   Whenever he can, a Dane will take off for the beach or go camping. The 500 approved Danish camping sites require the International Camping Carnet or the Danish Camping Card. The latter can be bought for 28kr at any site requiring it. It's valid for the entire year for the family and carries third party liability insurance. The fee for camping is per person with no extra for tent, car, etc. The fee depends upon camp classification but is generally 33kr. each adult.

TRAINS   The Danish State Railways (DSB) operate the excellent trains. Some routes involve a ferry crossing where the train rolls onto the ferry and passengers can get off to go above deck. Duty-free shops are only available on ferries connecting Denmark to other countries, i.e. Denmark-Germany (Rodby-Puttgarden, Gedser-Warnemunde), and Denmark-Sweden (Helsingor-Helsingborg, Frederikshavn-Goteborg). The smorgasbord (kolde bord) is a wonderful value, but is only served on ships with lengthy crossings, particularly Frederikshavn to Goteborg, Sweden. The fastest and best trains are *Lyntog* (pronounced LUEEN-taw) trains. These travel the route Copenhagen, Odense, Kolding and then the train splits with some cars continuing west to Esbjerg and Struer and the remainder going south to Sonderborg and the German border.

Intercity trains are fast modern trains on the main city to city routes within Denmark. Each second class compartment has six seats rather than the standard eight. Intercity trains leave every hour on the hour between 6am and 9pm from Copenhagen to Arhus, and 15 minutes past each hour between 5:15am and 7;15pm from Arhus to Copenhagen. The trip is five hours. Interity trains also run between Fredericia and Flensborg, Fredericia and Esbjerg, Vejle-Herning-Thisted-Skanderborg-Silkeborg, and Arhus-Alborg-Frederikshavn. Trains serve many other Danish towns as well, and where trains leave off the buses take over.

A seat reservation costs 20kr for Intercity trains and 30kr for Lyntog. They are mandatory on trains crossing the Great Belt. The Great Belt refers to the ferry crossing between the islands of Sjaelland and Fyn. For instance, the Great Belt ferry route is taken when traveling between Copenhagen and Odense.

Train information offices have free schedules covering individual routes, and a free booklet, *Fjerntrafik Udland*, which gives important international European routes. It's not necessary to buy the 1-1/4-inch thick *DSB Koreplan* which lists all train, ferry and bus schedules for Denmark, including fares, maps with train and bus routes indicated and small inset maps showing the relationship of the train to the bus station for some cities.

afgang	departure
ankomst	arrival
banegarden	train station
billetkontoret	ticket office
indgang	entrance
koreplan	timetable
oplysning	information
pladsbestillingen	reservations
perron	track
udgang	exit

EURAIL BONUSES (1) Domestic ferry crossings Arhus to Kalundborg, Knudshoved to Halskov, Nyborg to Korsor, Fynshav to Bojden. (2) Ferry crossing Rodby Faerge to Puttgarden, Germany. (3) Ferry crossings operated by the Danish and Swedish State Railways between Helsingor and Helsingborg (Sweden). (4) Steamers operated by Stena Line, a private steamship company, between Frederikshavn and Goteborg (Sweden). (5) A 50 percent reduction on the Danish Navigation Company *Oresund*, for travel on the hydrofoil between Copenhagen and Malmo. (6) A 20 percent reduction on the normal fares of the Steamship Company DFDS between Esbjerg and Harwich, Newcastle, Faroe Islands, and between Copenhagen and Oslo.

FOOD Food production is a principal industry of Denmark. The main exports are livestock, bacon, meat, butter, eggs, cheese, milk, cereals and lard. Canned meat, condensed milk, sugar and canned fish are processed. Denmark is the largest exporter of pork products in the world.

To control food costs, the best strategy is to buy take-out rotisseried chicken, picnic or cook at camp, and drink plenty of the delicious and reasonably priced milk. Whole milk (*sod maelk*) and skim milk (*skummet maelk*) cost about 5.50kr for one liter. Rye bread is cheaper than white or wheat. In a cafeteria, the daily special (*dagens ret*) is a good value. Danish pastry (*wienerbrod*) and milk by the glass are sold in Danish bakeries, which are also open Sunday morning.

COPENHAGEN (KOPENHAVEN)

Copenhagen means merchant's harbor. Old Copenhagen has lived for 800 years. Some of its original fortified walls and moats can be seen in the city's parks. Be sure to see more of Denmark than the area between Copenhagen's train station and the end of the main shopping street. Nearby small villages with thatched roof cottages and half-timbered houses counter balance the city atmosphere of central Copenhagen and provide a welcome relief.

TRAIN STATION Coming off the tracks, you will find luggage checking, lockers, a waiting room and a Eurailpass center on the right end. Luggage checking is open 6:30am-12:20am, 15kr per backpack. Large lockers cost 10kr; buy the token from luggage checking. (Luggage can be left for free in the Inter-Rail center but it's unguarded.) From the tracks, if you turn left and go out the side door of the station, the bakery across the street has lower prices than the one in the station. The station bank is open 6:45am-10pm. (Banks generally extract 30kr per transaction, but American Express at Amagertorv 18 takes only 10kr.) The small station supermarket stays open 8am to midnight, including Sunday. The post office is inside the station by the main entrance (open M-F 9-9, Sa 9-6, Su 10-4). No tourist office, but the InterRail Center has maps as does the Hotel booking office.

Of the station restaurants, the Bistro serves smorgasbord. Breakfast is served daily from 7-10am for 39.50kr. You can select from tomato juice, orange juice, milk, coffee, canned mixed fruit, corn flakes, granola, yoghurt, toppings, ham slices, pate, sausage slices, cheese slices (such as swiss), wrapped individual portions of cheese, 3 kinds of Danish pastry, 2 types of hard rolls, assorted flatbread and crackers and individually wrapped butter portions. Dinner smorgasbord costs 96.50kr and is served from 11am-

10:30pm. (But if you're going to Finland, wait for the Silja Line's smorgasbord, which is much better and costs less.)

Central Copenhagen

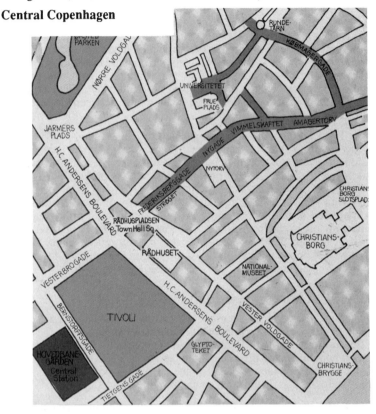

TOURIST OFFICE *Danmarks Turistrad* is at 22 H.C. Andersens Boulevard, by Radhuspladsen (pronounced RAWTH-hoose-PLSH-sehn), and open May-Sep M-F 9-6, Sa 9-2, Su 9-1. Pick up *Copenhagen This Week* for information on the city plus suggested walking tours, hours and prices of museums and a map of the city.

CITY TRANSPORTATION The S-trains (*S-tog*) are part of the Danish State Railway and are included in Eurailpasses. Considerable money can be saved by taking the S-tog to the nearest station and walking from there. The S-tog starts M-Sa at 5am and Su 6am. Trains leave every 10 to 20 minutes with the last trains leaving about 12:30am. Free schedules and maps are available at the stations. The train station, Kobenhavn H at which you arrive in Copenhagen, is the main terminal for the S-tog. Three blocks uptown is Radhuspladsen, Town Hall Square, from which many buses leave. (Go out the front door of the train station, walk forward to the main street, Vesterbrogade, and turn right. Tivoli encompasses the first long block and the bus terminal is in the next block.)

S-Tog

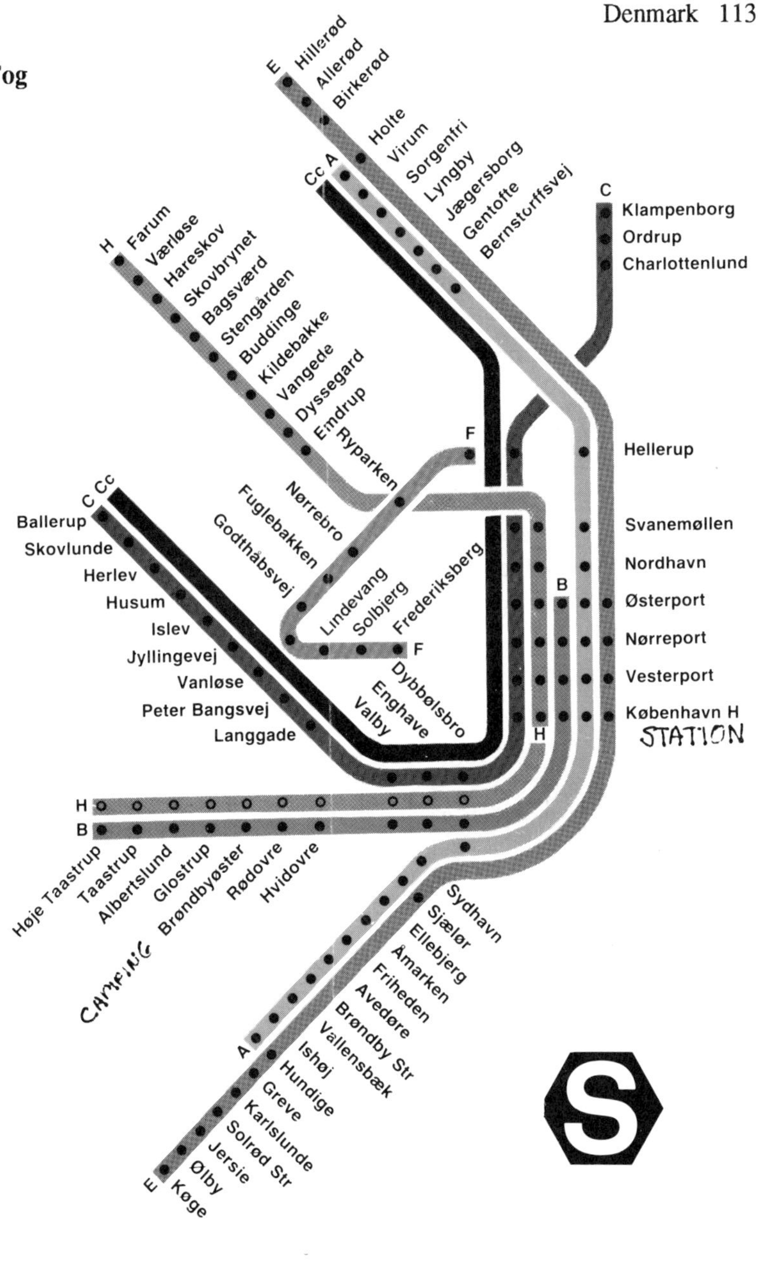

E Hillerød
Hillerød
Allerød
Birkerød
Cc A
Holte
Virum
Sorgenfri
Lyngby
Jægersborg
Gentofte
Bernstorffsvej

C
Klampenborg
Ordrup
Charlottenlund

H Farum
Værløse
Hareskov
Skovbrynet
Bagsværd
Stengården
Buddinge
Kildebakke
Vangede
Dyssegard
Emdrup
Ryparken

F
Hellerup

Nørrebro
Fuglebakken
Godthåbsvej

C Cc
Ballerup
Skovlunde
Herlev
Husum
Islev
Jyllingevej
Vanløse
Peter Bangsvej
Langgade

Lindevang
Solbjerg
Frederiksberg
F
Dybbølsbro
Enghave
Valby

B

Svanemøllen
Nordhavn
Østerport
Nørreport
Vesterport
København H
STATION

H
B
Høje Taastrup
Taastrup
Albertslund
Glostrup
Brøndbyøster
Rødovre
Hvidovre
CAMPING

Sydhavn
Sjælor
Ellebjerg
Åmarken
Friheden
Avedøre
Brøndby Str
Vallensbæk
A
Ishøj
Hundige
Greve
Karlslunde
Solrød Str
Jersie
Ølby
E Køge

S

All buses and trains in North Sealand use the same tickets. The fare
depends on the number of zones entered. Tickets are sold on buses and at S-
tog stations. The cheapest ticket is 3-zones, costs 8kr and is valid one hour.
A 10-ride card (*gule kort*) valid for 3 zones costs 70kr and can be used by
more than one person provided sufficient tickets are cancelled. There are

also multi-ride cards for 6 and unlimited zones. Stamp the tickets in the machine after boarding the bus or before entering the S-tog. A Copenhagen Card is available for unlimited bus and train rides in the metropolitan area and free admission to 51 museums and sights. The card includes all museums and sights mentioned in this guide including the day trips. The cost is 80kr for 1 day, 140kr for 2 days and 180kr for 3 days.

Copenhagen is a good base from which to make day trips. The Coast Line serves towns along the Danish Riviera as far as Helsingor (Elsinore) two times an hour. The Western Line goes to Roskilde 3 to 6 times an hour.

CAMPGROUNDS   Copenhagen is generously supplied with campgrounds. Seven are found within a 25-km. radius of downtown and all are served by public transportation. All are members of the Danish Camping Union and charge the same all-inclusive rate, adult/33kr and child/16kr. Campgrounds are generally open 7am-10pm for new arrivals, but you can always set up later and register in the morning. Absalon Camping is reached via S-tog, free with Eurailpasses. Bellahoj Camping is closest to downtown.

Absalon Camping, Korsdalsvej in the Rodrovre district is 9 km. from the train station. Open all year. From the train station, take S-tog, *linie B* to Brondbyoster Station. Then a 6-block walk. This is a large camp with all facilities: hot water in the sinks, store, washing machine and dryer and dayroom.

Absalom Camping   **Bellajoh Camping**

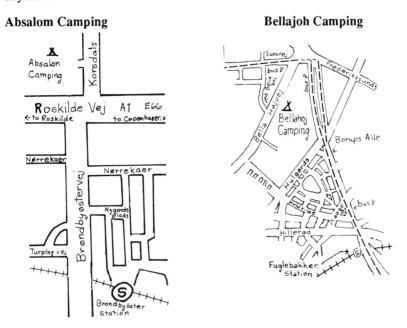

Bellajoh Camping (pronounced BELL-lah-hoy), Hvidkildevej 64 in the Bronshoj district, is 5 km. from downtown. Open Jun 1-Sep 1. From the train station, walk 3 blocks to Radhuspladsen and take bus 8 (direction Tingbjerg) or bus 2 and get off at bus stop, "Camping" and then a 10 to 15 minute walk. The camp is within a cyclone fence. You must walk around it to the entrance. The camp is flat and grassy with a few trees and has a store, snack bar and day room.

Strandmollen Camping, Strandvejen in Klampenborg on the edge of Deer Park (Jaegersborg Woods) which is laced with trails, is 14 km. from Copenhagen. Open May 15-Aug 31. From the train station, take the S-tog leaving from tracks 3 and 4 to Skodsborg. Skodsborg is a stop on local trains to Helsingor. (Fast trains do not stop in Skodsborg.) The camp is for tents only; cars and vans must be parked outside. The camp has a day room, no store.

Naerum Camping, Ravnebakken, is 15 km. north of downtown. Open Apr 11-Sep 13. From the train station, take the S-tog to Jaegersborg Station. Change to a train to Naerum Station, the terminus. Then about a 1 km. walk to camp. Full facilities including store, washing machine and clotheslines.

Hundige Camping, Hundige Strandvery 47 and 72, is 19 km. from downtown. Open Apr 1-Sep 1. From the train station, take the S-tog to Hundige Station and change to bus 121. Get off at Lejrklubben Danmark. This is a large, well organized permanent campsite with space for temporary guests.

Undinegardens Camping is 25 km. from downtown. Open all year. From the train station, take the S-tog to Farum Station and change to bus 332. Get off at Undinevej and walk 10 minutes. The campground is beautifully situated near Lake Bastrup, has access to the lake, and is one portion of a farm operated by owner Ivar Petersen.

Vallo Stifts Camping in Koge 37 km. south of Copenhagen is a good choice if you want to stay in a charming small town and commute 40 minutes by train to Copenhagen. The camp at 102 Strandvejen is only 300 meters from the beach and 1 km. from the S-tog to Copenhagen. HT buses stop at the camp entrance. Windsurfing, minigolf. (Mar 17-Sep 18, adult/32kr). The Koge open market is W & Sa mornings at Koge Torv, the town square.

SIGHTSEEING   **Ny Carlsberg Glyptotek Museum** on Dantes Plads, across from the rear entrance to Tivoli and 3 blocks from the train station, is a private foundation that shows well planned exhibits tracing the development of art from the Egyptians and Mesopotamians through the Romans, and modern French and Danish art. Gauguin and Degas are well represented in the modern art galleries with about 25 paintings and 3 woodcuts by Gauguin, and paintings and a set of 73 bronzes by Degas. May-Aug Tu-Su 10-4; Sep-Apr Tu-Sa 12-3pm, Su 10-4; 15kr, free W & Su.

The Royal Museum of Fine Arts (*Statens Museum for Kunst*), 48-50 Solvgade, contains art from many periods, much of it Danish, and a fairly large group of 20th century French works. Its department of prints and drawings shows 600 years of graphic art. S-tog to Osterport or Norreport. Open Tu-Su 10-5, free.

Christiansborg Palace (pronounced kres-tee-ahnz-borh) opens its Royal reception rooms for guided tours Jun-Aug Tu-Su at 11am, 1 & 3pm; May & Sep Tu-F & Su at noon and 2pm; 17kr. Part of Christiansborg, tours of parliament (*Folketing*) are given Jun-Sep Su-F on the hour 10-4, free.

Tojhusmuseet (Royal Arsenal Museum), 3 Tojhusgade near Christiansborg Palace, contains a huge collection of military items housed in a 16th century armoury. Cannons are on the first floor; guns, swords, armor and artillery on the second; and uniforms on the third. Free checking. Restrooms by the entry room. Open Tu-Sa 1-3, Su 11-4, free.

Rosenborg Castle Collections, Ostervoldgade 4a, was built between 1606 and 1617 as a summer palace for King Christian IV. This small Renaissance style castle now serves as a museum of the history of the Danish kings. The collections comprise arms, family portraits, crown jewels, royal costumes, Venetian glass, silver, furniture, an ivory coronation chair, 3 life-size silver lions and an elaborately decorated Gothic drinking horn made in 1470. A park surrounds the palace. Take the S-tog to Norreport. Open Jun 1-Aug 31 10-3, Oct & May 11-3, 20kr.

Zoological Museum, 15 Universitetsparken, shows Danish imagination in its presentation. It's at the other end of the spectrum from the old-style stuffed birds and animals behind glass exhibits. The Danes have recreated the environment of the spotlighted birds and animals. You can hear the wind blowing in the arctic and the sounds of a swamp, view what goes on underwater or feel musk ox fur over ice to demonstrate its insulation properties. Bus 24 or 84 from Norreport Station. Open Tu-Su 11-5, free.

Frilandsmuseet (open-air museum), 100 Kongevejen, is reached by Lyngby S-tog to Sorgenfri. A collection of original old houses and cottages from different parts of Denmark have been moved to the park. Old-time skills such as lacemaking, pottery, weaving, dyeing and candle making are demonstrated. Open May-Sep 10-5, 10kr.

Frederiksborg Castle, north of Copenhagen, is one of the prettiest castles in Denmark. Open 10-4, 20kr. Take S-tog line E to Hillerod, a 35-minute trip. From Frilandsmuseet, you're already part way there; take the S-tog to Holte and change to line E for Hillerod, then walk 1 km.

The National Museum, Frederiksholm Kanal, has interesting sections on prehistory and Greenland. Take bus 1, 2, 5, 6 or 10. Open Tu-Su 10-4, free. Special interest museums emcompass antiques, working models of motorships, brewing, plants, musical instruments, Oriental handcrafts, film, model theaters, World War II, lightship, Danish art, town history, toys, medicine, mechanical music, minerals, fossils and meteorites, boat models, post office, rose garden with 250 varieties, reptiles, works of Danish sculptor Thorvaldsen and zoo. Information from the tourist office.

Tivoli, one block from the train station, is open Apr 26-Sept 10, admission 27kr. Basically a smaller and more intimate Danish version of a stateside civic entertainment center, Tivoli encompasses much inviting open space around a meandering lake, several small outdoor stages, a modern concert theater, gourmet restaurants and an amusement park. Bring a snack with you as food is expensive--also a sweater for evening. Most of the activity goes on after 7pm, but the gardens and children's supervised playground open at 10am. Children's amusement rides open at 11:30am, and children's theater performances are at 12:30, 1:30 and 2:30 daily except Tuesday from Jun 1-Aug 16, on weekends only the rest of the season. Adult amusement rides open 1:30pm. The Tivoli Guard Band plays at 3:30pm on Saturdays and the Drum Corps marches on Thursdays at 4:45pm. On weekends and holidays, at 5pm is a performance on the outdoor stage and at 6:30pm and 8:30pm a Tivoli Guard Parade. Nightly except Sunday at 7:45pm and 9:45pm are pantomime performances, 8pm Jazz Hall performance and 8pm Folk music hall performance. Nightly except Monday at 10:30pm is a performance on the outdoor stage. Fireworks start at 11:30 or 11:45pm, W, F, Sa. All events free except rides.

For rides, a Tivoli Tour Pass is sold valid on all 25 amusements for 110kr for one day. Individual tickets cost 7kr and rides require one or more tickets. The 25 amusements are The Flying Carpet, Ladybird, 2 ferris wheels, caterpillar, viking ship, motor boats, mini and full size bumper cars, hall of mirrors, 2 carousels, forest troll, veteran cars, traffic, hall of mystery, trolley car, haunted house, junior pilot, odin express, galley ships, tubs ahoy, gondola, roller coaster and fun house playground.

Tuborg Brewery, 54 Standvejen in Hellerup, has free tours M-F 8:30am-2:30pm. Take the S-tog to Hellerup and then a 10 minute walk to a giant replica of a Tuborg bottle which marks the factory. Free beer and soft drinks at the end. **Carlsberg Brewery**, Elephant Gate, Ny Carlsbergvej, is open M-F for free tours at 9am, 11am and 2:30pm. Free beer at the end. Take the S-tog to Enghave Station.

The Royal Porcelain Factory, 45 Smallegade, offers free tours Tu and Th at 9:30am. **Bing and Grondahl**, 149 Vesterbrogade has free tours May 18-Sep 1 M-F at 9:30am, 12:15pm & 1:15pm. Bus service is provided from Bing & Grondahl at Amagertorv, 15 minutes before tour starts.

Holmegard Glasswork in Fensmark has free tours. Take the train to Naestved and then bus 75 to the factory. Open M-F 9am-noon & 12:30-1:30pm, SaSu 11-3. If you have extra time, the town of Naestved has some interesting half timbered houses. In particular, see Boderne where one house is now a crafts museum.

Two-hour **guided walking tours** of Copenhagen cost 15kr and leave from the fountain at Radhuspladsen M, W & Thu at 5:30pm and Su at 4pm from Jun 20-Sep 6. Two examples of **preplanned communities** are Askerod and Hundie (S-tog A to Hundie for both).

Dragor, a taste of "real" Denmark is a quaint old seaport on the southeast tip of Amager Island, 14 km. from downtown. Its old quarter is officially protected and kept as it was when the town flourished as an important fishing port. Take bus 30 or 33 from Radhuspladsen. Also, ferries to Linhamn, Sweden leave from Dragor.

DAY TRIP TO HUMLEBAEK AND HELSINGOR   Trains leave Copenhagen at least twice hourly for the 45-minute trip to Helsingor, north of Copenhagen. Humlebaek is 36 minutes from Copenhagen enroute.

The Louisana Museum (*Louisiana Museet*), Gl. Strandvej 13, is at Humlebaek, a 15 minute walk (or shorter bus ride) from Humlebaek Station. Open daily 10-5, 25kr. This is Denmark's prime museum of modern art. An excellent collection of modern European paintings is shown indoors. Sculpture is mounted outdoors within a park overlooking the sound. The original museum building was the home over a hundred years ago of a Danish nobleman who successively married three times, each time to a woman named Louise. The new contemporary structure is linked with the original manor house by a series of covered walks. The museum shop has a good selection of reproductions and frames for sale.

Kronberg Castle at Helsingor (Elsinore) of Hamlet fame is within walking distance of the ferry dock. Between the town and the ferry dock, a camping sign is posted near the Hamlet Hotel and the camp is within 20 minutes of there. Kronberg Castle is open daily 10-5, 12kr. If you get off at Helsingor Station, take a local bus to the castle. If you get off while the train is stopped before it rolls on the ferry, you can walk to the castle. To Helsingborg, Sweden ferries leave every 15 minutes for the 20-minute crossing. Ferry lines DSB and SJ are included in Eurailpasses, Sundbusser and LB-Faerger are not.

DAY TRIP TO ROSKILDE   Trains leave two to three times an hour for the 30-minute ride to Roskilde, 31 km. west of Copenhagen. One of the largest rock festivals in Northern Europe is held each year in Roskilde. 1989 dates are Jun 30-Jul 2. The tourist office in Roskilde is 7 blocks from the train station. One block from the tourist office is the magnificent medieval Cathedral (Domkirke) where 38 Danish Kings and Queens are buried. Open M-Sa 9:am-5:45pm, Su 12:30pm-5:45pm, 3kr. From the Cathedral, a 15-minute walk will bring you to the **Viking Ship Museum** (*Vikingeskibshallen*) which exhibits five viking ships from 1000 A.D. and shows an English language film on how the ships were recovered and restored. Open daily 9-5, 20kr. The museum is a long walk from the station; take a bus to Hillerod and ask to be let off by the museum.

In Roskilde, **Vigen Strandparks Camping**, at the beach 5 km. north of downtown, can be reached from Roskilde Station by bus 602 (direction of Veddelev) which leaves between 6:07am-8:27am & 2:07pm-5:27pm at 7, 27 and 47 minutes past the hour. At other times bus 602 leaves at 7 and 37 minutes past the hour. The last bus from the station leaves at 12:07am. The bus can also be taken from near the Viking Ship Museum. Fare is 7kr. The camp is one km. from the bus stop. Open Apr 15-Sep 10, adult/31kr.

The public market is held Wednesday and Saturday in Staendertorvet, the town's central square.

If you have time, visit **Oldtidsbyen** (*Lejre Arkaeologisk Forsogscenter*) west of nearby Lejre, a reconstructed prehistoric settlement of houses, well, fences and fields seeded with crops grown during that period. Visitors can grind corn with a stone grinder, log with Iron Age axes and ride in a dugout canoe. Trains leave on the half hour from Roskilde to Lejre. Outside Lejre Station, take connecting bus 233 leaving at 43 minutes past the hour to the site. Open daily 10-5, 31kr.

DAY TRIP TO GILLELEJE   A fishing village 60 minutes from Copenhagen, Gilleleje is a jewel at the extreme northern tip of Sjaelland (the island that Copenhagen is on). Change trains at Helsingor or Hillerod for Gilleleje. Beautiful old half-timbered houses, narrow streets and tiny shops will intrigue you. Try to visit on market days: Jun 26-Aug 7, Th & Sa, 9-1.

SHOPPING   The added value tax, MOMS, is 18.03 percent. The amount can be refunded to you by check or charge card credit for purchases sent or taken out of the country. For major purchases be sure to ask about it.

Bring drapery measurements, reupholstering requirements, dining room table size, etc. as fabrics are outstanding. Some Scandinavian furniture such as safari chairs knock down into small enough packages to be sent regular parcel post. For larger shipments inquire as to shipping costs and brokerage fees in advance. The normal procedure is to pay the transportation costs (as quoted by the firm's shipping agency at the time of purchase) on arrival of the goods in the U.S. port city. By picking up the shipment in the U.S. port city yourself, a brokerage charge can be avoided.

Stroget (pronounced stroy-et) is the famous shopping street prohibited to traffic in downtown Copenhagen. At the Kongens Nytorv end you'll find its most outstanding store, Illums Bolighus, a visual delight in home furnishings. Also good, Den Permanente on Verterbrogade offers jury-screened merchandise of furniture, fabrics, dinnerware, toys and souvenirs. The average Dane shops at Ikea, a large furniture complex in Tastrup, for good quality and reasonable prices. The huge, multi-level store is open M 11-7:30, T-Th 11-5:30, F 11-7:30 & Sa 7-2. Take the S-tog to Tastrup and then a 25-minute walk or bus 199 from outside Tastrup Station.

FERRY CROSSING   To Germany, on the Rodby-Puttgarden crossing, the Danish ships charge 14.50kr to change currency and 30kr to cash a travelers check. On board are a duty-free shop and cafeteria.
  To Amsterdam, leave 9:20am EuroCity (change at Osnabruck and Amersfoort, ar. 8:32pm), 10:10am (ar. 9:32pm), 10:10pm (ar. 9:54am) and 11:40pm (change at Hamburg and Osnabruck, ar. 1:32pm).
  To Arhus, an alternative to the intercity train between Arhus and Copenhagen which requires a mandatory reservation, is the route via Kalundborg which doesn't require a reservation fee be paid as is necessary for the Nyborg-Korsor crossing. Trains leave 3 to 4 times daily. You must get off the train at Kalundborg and walk onto the ferry for the 3 hour ride to Arhus Harbor Station.
  To Frankfurt, leave 7:15am Eurocity (change at Hamburg, ar. 5:36pm), 9:20 EuroCity not Saturday (change at Hamburg, ar. 7:36pm), 10:10am (change at Hamburg, ar. 8:36pm), 5:45pm (change at Hamburg, ar. 6:33am) and 11:40pm not Saturday (change at Hamburg, ar. 11:36am).
  To Hamburg, leave at 7:15am EuroCity (ar. 12:25pm), 9:20am EuroCity (ar. 2:25pm), 10:10am (ar. 3:22pm), 1:10pm not Saturday (ar. 6:30pm), 4:40pm EuroCity (ar. 9:59pm) and 11:40pm (ar. 6:26am).
  To Odense, trains leave on the hour from 7am-8pm for the 3 hour trip.
  To Oslo, trains go via Helsingor and Helsingborg which entails a 15-minute ferry ride. They leave at 7:17am Jun-Aug (ar. 5:05pm), 9:47am (ar. 7:25pm), 12:17pm (ar. 9:40pm) and 9:21pm (ar. 7am).
  To Paris Nord Station, leave 7:15am EuroCity (change at Hamburg, change at Cologne, ar. 10:09pm) and 7:40pm (ar. 11:19am). Other trains can be taken that require changes at Hamburg and Cologne. The best bet is the through night train that leaves at 7:40pm.
  To Stockholm, trains board the ferry at Helsingor for the 15 minute crossing to Helsingborg. Trains leave at 6:47am (ar. 2:46pm), 8:17am (ar. 4:46pm), 10:17am (ar. 6:46pm), 2:17pm (ar. 10:55pm) and 11:21pm Jun-Aug (ar. 7:46am).

ODENSE

On the island of Fyn, Odense (pronounced OH-then-seh) is two hours from Copenhagen on the Lyntog, high speed diesel train. The tourist office is in the Town Hall, 7 blocks from the station. Autocamp Hunderup, Odensevej 102 in the southern part of the city, is reached by bus 1 from outside the train station. The camp is a 5- minute walk from the bus stop. **Autocamp Hunderup** charges adult/29kr and has good facilities including a washing machine and store. The public market, open Wednesday and Saturday mornings, is on Sortebrodre Torv, in the general area of Hans Christian Andersen's home. **The Funen Village** (Den fynske Landsby) at Sejerskovvej is an outdoor museum of peasant houses, farms and workshops showing Danish pastoral life of the 18th and 19th centuries. Take bus 2 from the station, or walk the short distance from the campground.
  Kerteminde, 25 km. from Odense, is an interesting old town with picturesque old houses on Langegade and old general shops, currently functioning as a fishing port and resort. Its most important attraction is at nearby Ladby, an 8 minute bus ride. That is the burial place for an 1100 year old Viking Ship, 72 feet long and 9 feet wide, which has been preserved

along with the Viking Chief, his weapons and belongings including four hunting dogs and 11 horses.

From Odense, buses take three different routes to Kerteminde. If you wish to stop at Ladby on the way, take the bus marked *Odense-Kolstrup-Kerteminde* which leaves from the bus station (rutebilstation) behind the train station several times a day. In Kerteminde, the municipal campground, Kerteminde Camping, is open May-Sep 15. Full facilities including an automatic washer, hot water in the restroom sinks and day room.

From Odense, **trains to Copenhagen** leave at 9 minutes past the hour and involve a mandatory reservation fee as a crossing on the Great Belt is made. The trip is 3 hours. To Arhus, trains leave at 56 minutes past the hour. The ride is 2 hours.

JUTLAND (JYLLAND) PENINSULA

Jutland (pronounced yoo-lan) is the largest land mass in Denmark, the top of the European continent that reaches northwards from Germany. Arhus, Denmark's second city, is here and its recreated old town of tradesmen's shops is exceptional and one of the best outdoor museums in Europe. Children love Jutland for Legoland at Billund. Viking remnants, picturesque small towns and sandy beaches complete the picture. We will start at the southern end and proceed west and north. Trains connect all of these towns with about hourly service.

KOLDING, a main crossroads of the Jutland peninsula, boasts a 20-acre plant conservatory (*Geografisk Have og Rosenhaven*) with 2,000 plants from all over the world, grouped according to origin. Rare specimens include a pigeon tree from Szetschwan province and a water spruce from China. Open daily 9am-sunset, 10kr. Legoland in Billund can be reached in 1 hour by bus from the bus station next to the train station. The bus leaves M-F at 10:30am, 12:10pm, 2:05pm and 3pm; Sa at 9:05am, noon and 5pm, Su at 10:30am, noon and 1:40pm.

The tourist office, Helligkorsgade 18, is about 6 blocks from the train station (M-F 9-5, May-Aug also Sa 9-12). Vonsild Camping & Feriecenter, Vonsildvej 19, is open all year. Take bus 3 (direction Vonsild). The market is Tuesday and Friday, 7am to noon, at Pakhustorvet.

ESBJERG is the largest town on the west coast of the peninsula. The train and bus stations are next to each other downtown. The tourist office, Skolegade 33, is three blocks from the station (M-F 9-5, Sa 9-12).

Standskovens Camping (*Kommunnens Lejrplads ved Strandskoven*), Gl. Vardevej 76 next to the stadium in Idraets Park, is within walking distance of the station or take bus 1, 9, 11, 12 or 31 from the station. The last bus is #9 which leaves at 11:43pm. Bus fare is 7kr. The municipal camp charges adult/27kr and has all facilities including an automatic washer, day room and swimming pool.

The daily catch of Denmark's largest fishing fleet is auctioned at Fish Auction Hall (*Auktionshal*) M-F starting at 7am. The Fishery and Maritime Museum and Aquarium, Tarphagevej, is open daily Jun 10-5, Jul-Aug 10-8, 25kr. Built in 1968, fishing equipment, boat models and examples of small boats are displayed.

RIBE, 31 km. south of Esbjerg, is Denmark's oldest town. It enjoyed its greatest prosperity in the Viking Era and Middle Ages as a trading port and has kept its medieval atmosphere. Ribe is about a 40-minute train ride from Esbjerg via Bramming in the direction of Tonder on the German border. The train and bus station are next to each other on the east side of town. The tourist office, at Overdammen, a street off the main square, Torvet, about six blocks from the station, has a good leaflet giving a building by building description of the old town.   To see are the Cathedral, Sct. Catherines Church and Monastery, the Old Townhall, the Ribe Museum of Art and the Tidal Area Exhibition.

The municipal **campground** *(turistforeningens lejrplads)*, at Farupvej is north of Ribe, 2 km. from the train station. A bus goes from the train station to the intersection of highway A11 and Plantagevej and then you must walk 15 minutes. Open Easter-Sep 15, adult/33kr.

Ribe

VEJLE is on a fjord and the closest gateway town to Legoland in Billund. The bus to Legoland leaves from the bus station (rutebilstation) located next to the train station. In 40 minutes, the bus stops in front of Legoland, the stop before the town of Billund. Bus 912 (Vejle-Grinsted-Varde) leaves at approximately 8:20am, 9:20am, 11:05am, 1:20pm, 2:10pm, 3:20;m, 4:20pm, 5:20pm, 8:20pm and 11:05pm.The tourist office is at Sondergate 14.

The **campground** (*Communens Lejrplads*) is on Hellig-Kildevej, 3 km. from the train station. It is a 40-minute walk or bus 4 from opposite the train station to Norremarken. Get off at the stadium. The bus leaves on the hour and half hour and costs 9kr.   The last bus leaves the bus station at 11:15pm. The large and attractive site has an automatic washer and dryer and charges adult/23kr.

LEGOLAND, BILLUND   Billund is a tiny town with hourly bus service from Vejle, almost hourly service from Kolding and an airport served by SAS.   Danish families flock here to enjoy the utterly charming Legoland amusement park where all rides and dioramas are constructed of gigantic Legos.   Open May 1 to the third Sunday in September, 10am-8pm. Adult/40kr, child/20kr, rides 7kr each. Some rides are charges per car *(pr. voon)* rather than per person. The Safariland ride sends youngsters through the jungle of Lego giraffes and Lego vultures in Lego jeeps. A Lego train, *minibade* (boat ride), goldmine ride and Legoredo, a Scandinavian version of a western town will entertain you. Miniature Lego dioramas throughout the park feature famous Danish castles and manor houses, typical scenery from Dalsland to Norway, a Norwegian town with a stave church, a working harbor, miniature Amsterdam and more. There is a free marionette theater, free doll museum, free cultural exhibits, free bandstand performances and free play equipment. You can bring your own food and eat on picnic tables at the rear of Legoland or buy hot dogs or a restaurant meal. At the far back of the park behind Legeplads are tables and benches under cover with sunken circular baskets of all shapes and sizes of Legos, free for anyone to use. This is where everyone headed during the frequent though short lived spurts of rainfall throughout the otherwise sunny early June afternoon that we were there. The Lego Toyshop sells everything the Lego factory makes at list prices. Postcards mailed in the postal box in the Toyshop receive a special Legoland postmark. Foreign exchange is next to the information office.

Billunds Communes Campingplads, across the street from the entrance to Legoland, is open May-Sept 15, adult/31kr. The excellent site has all facilities including hot water in individual restroom sink cubicles, automatic washer and dryer and day room.

Bus 912 (direction Grindsted-Varde) leaves from the bus station next to the train station in Vejle from 7:20am to 10:20pm at 20 minutes past the hour, and at 11:05pm. The trip is 42 minutes. Bus 406 (direction Billund-Grindsted) leaves the Kolding bus station next to the train station M-F at 8:15am, 10:30am, 12:10pm, 2:05pm, 3pm, 5:10pm and 7:05pm; Sa at 9:05am, 10:30am, 1:40pm and 4:30pm; Su at 9am, noon, 6pm, and 8:10pm.

ARHUS (pronounced aw-hoose) shouldn't be overlooked for here you can visit The Old Town of 65 authentic tradesmen's shops and buildings and the Moesgard Prehistoric Museum. This is Denmark's second largest city.

The main **train station**, Arhus H Station *(hovedbaneg)*, is downtown. It has train information (Open 8-7), luggage check, supermarket (open daily 8am-midnight) and a restaurant. Secondary train stations are Arhus Havnestation serving the ferry docks and Arhus O Station near the waterfront. From Arhus H Station to Arhus Havnestation (ferries to Kalundborg) is about a 5 minute walk. The bus station *(rutebilstation)* is 2 blocks from Arhus H. Station.

The **tourist office** is 2 blocks from Arhus H Station in the Town Hall at the base of the tower. Open Jun 19-Aug 31 daily 9-6, Jul 7-Sep 10 9-7, Sep 12-Jun 18 M-F 9-4:30, Sa 9-12. They offer a walking tour for 20kr, a bus tour, and a 24-hour pass good on all buses in Arhus and the surrounding area. Bus 20 leaves from the tourist office daily Jun 15-Sep 10 at 10am for a 2-1/2 hour guided tour in English for 25kr, including 24 hours of unlimited travel on city buses.

The best camp, **Camping Blommehaven** (Plum Forest) is 6 km. from downtown in a beautiful setting near the sea. From Arhus H. Station, bus 19 leaves from the square in front opposite the station building twice an hour. Fare is 10.50kr. Last bus leaves at 9:40pm. Bus 19 stops in front of the camp, but only operates during high season from May 30-Aug 16. After that, take bus 6 to Horhavevej and then walk. Open Apr 15-Sep 15; adult/31kr. The terraced sites lead to Arhus Bay; automatic washer, dryer and store. The camp is the starting point of a 7 km. trail that parallels the sea, passing Moesgard Beach and then turning inland to Moesgard Forest Mill *(Skovmolle)* Restaurant, next to a 300 year old water mill. The return route is through the woods. The trail is well marked with yellow signs. From the restaurant, it's possible to walk to the Moesgard Prehistoric Museum.

Camping Arhus Nord is 8 km. north of town on A10, beyond Lisbjerg. Open all year; adult/33kr, hot shower/8kr. Take bus 117 or 118 from the bus station, two blocks from the main station. Last bus leaves at 11:40pm. The bus stops directly at the camp. Bus fare is 10.25kr. Facilities include store, swimming pool, day room and automatic washing machine and dryer.

Den Gamle By (The Old Town) entrance is at the intersection of Warmingsvej and Viborgvej. Take bus 3 from Arhus H Station. The Old Town is part of the Botanical Gardens which are open for strolling all day and into the evening, admission free. Picnic tables are available in the Tea Garden. The buildings are open daily 10-5; the admission fee (about 30kr) gives entry to your choice of five buildings. The buildings of the old town have been arranged to recreate a typical Danish market town of 1600-1850. Buildings open for a whole day or most of it are: Mayor's Residence, Textile Collection, Aalborg Mansion, Clock Museum, Apothecary, Holst's Mansion, Customshouse, Post Office (can buy stamps and letters are postmarked, "The Old Town"), Bakery, Potter at work in Mansard Warehouse and Wine Cellar. Other buildings are open only when a tour is scheduled. Two tours detailing the way things used to be made are offered every half-hour. At 10am & 2pm: tour 1 covers the Pinemaker's and Candlemaker's Workshops, Cooper's Workshop and Shoemaker's Workshop; tour 2 does the theater. At 10:30am & 2:30pm: tour 1 visits the Tobacco Factory and Rope Walk; tour 2, the Tannery and Sadler's Workshop. Noon & 4pm: tour 1 sees the Gardener's House and Mill; tour 2, the post office and brewery. At 1:30pm: tour 1 goes to the Distillery, Bakery, Engraver's Workshop, bookbinder's and Basketmaker's; tour 2 to the Printer's Workshop, Wood Engraver's Workshop and Stove Collection.

The **Moesgard Prehistoric Museum** is at Moesgard, 6 km. south of Arhus. Take bus 6 (Moesgard) from Arhus H Station to the last stop at the museum entrance. Open daily 10-5, adult/20kr, student/10kr. The museum is installed in an attractive red brick manor farm of 1784. Well displayed weapons, rune stones and the 4th century body (Grauballe Man) found nicely preserved in a nearby bog are within. In the ethnography section, an Afghanistan exhibit comprises rooms arranged to resemble a souk with winding passageways, sound effects, smells and a characteristic house. On grazing land behind the manor house, a trail leads past a Thai house on stilts and farther along are viking age stones and reconstructions of viking age buildings. Descriptions are in the booklet, Prehistoric Pathway, for sale at the museum entrance, or consult the wall map of the trail.

Other sights in Arhus include the Cathedral dating from 1201, the crypt underneath the Church of Our Lady from 1060 (the church is the oldest vaulted church in Scandinavia), Fire Brigade Museum (largest of its kind in the world), Arhus Art Museum and Natural History Museum.

Ebeltoft, 47 km. from Arhus, is a small interesting town featuring the Frigate, Jylland, moored in its small boat harbor. The man-of-war was used in the Battle of Helgoland in 1864 and can be toured (6kr). Bus 123 leaves the bus station at 10 minutes past each hour between 7:10am and 9:10pm for the 90-minute trip. Returning, bus 123 leaves at 20 or 25 minutes past each hour. With Eurailpass, it's cheaper to take the train (direction Grena) to Morke and then the bus to Ebeltoft, but few departures.

The **market** is Wednesday and Saturday morning at Bispetorv, near the Cathedral, and at Ingerslev Boulevard.

To Hobro, Aalborg and Frederikshavn, leave at 5:04am and 4 minutes past the hour until 10:04pm, except no train goes at 11:04am. The trip is one hour to Hobro, 1-1/2 hours to Aalborg and 2-1/2 hours to Frederikshavn.

To Vejle, leave at 6:15am and 15 minutes past the hour until 10:15pm. The trip is one hour.

To Odense and Copenhagen (reservation mandatory between Odense and Copenhagen), leave at 15 minutes past the hour except 2:15pm. Lyntog service leaves at 5:45pm and arrives in Odense at 7:20pm and Copenhagen at 9:59pm. (Supplement of about 15kr payable for Eurail Youthpass, and reservation fee mandatory for all to Copenhagen.)

To Hamburg, take the train to Fredericia (same departures as for Vejle). Trains to Hamburg leave Fredericia at 8:42am (ar. 12:34pm), 10:42am (ar. 2:24pm), 3:42pm (ar. 7:23pm) and 5:42pm (ar. 9:41pm).

Strandparken campground is on the western outskirts near the fjord and the outdoor swimming pool. Take bus 2 opposite the train station. Open May 15-Sep; adult/27kr. **Lindholm Camping** north of Limfjord is open May 15-Sep; adult/22kr. Take bus 202 from the bus station. The **North Jutland Museum of Art** designed by Aalto, viking burial grounds, an excavated village of 1000 A.D. and the old town with 150-400 year old houses can be seen. The market is W Sa, 7-2, on Aagade near the station.

FREDERIKSHAVN   Frederikshavn is where you take the Stena Line ferry (included in Eurailpasses) to Goteborg, Sweden. The train station is on Skippergade about a 10 minute walk to the ferry dock.   From June 29-August 13, a ferry leaves at 3:30am, 7:30am, 9am, 11:30am, 1:30pm, 3:30pm, 7:30pm and 11:30pm. Otherwise, a ferry leaves at 9am, 12:30pm, 2:30pm, 8:15pm and 10:15pm. The trip is 3 hours and 15 minutes.

The best food values in Scandinavia are found on those international ferries which serve a smorgasbord. (The most often used crossings at Rodby and Helsingor are too short to have any. The savvy traveler routes his trip through Frederikshavn to enjoy a longer crossing and ferry line food.) The cafeteria serves a *middag* for 33kr, but go to the dining room for the buffet. Depending on the time of sailing, it will be either a breakfast *(morgenmad)* or dinner *(koldt bord)* buffet. Dinner will include herring prepared several different ways and some other kind of fish, an assortment of coldcuts *(palaeg)* to put on a variety of breads, butter, several hot dishes, and perhaps cheese and crackers and fruit. The price does not include beverage. Less expensive is the breakfast buffet (38kr) which includes cheese, sausage, Danish pastry, assorted breads, crackers, butter, jams, herring, liverpaste, corn flakes, milk, coffee, hot chocolate, sugar and cream. Beverages are included in the price for breakfast.

Nordstrand Camping, Apholmenvej 40, is one of the best camps in Denmark. The large and modern camp is about a 30 minute walk north of the train station and dock area, or take bus 2 from in front of the station. The bus stops about 10 minutes from camp. Bus 2 leaves at 17 and 47 minutes past the hour; the last bus leaves at 9:47pm; 20-minute ride. Open Apr-Oct 1; Jun 14-Aug 15, adult/33kr, other times 27kr. Outstanding facilities including washers, store, cafeteria, rental bicycles and peddleboats.

Trains **to Aalborg, Hobro and Arhus** leave once an hour. Lyntog service is at 3:06pm.

FINLAND

Though isolated both by language and location in the northeast corner of Europe, any Eurailpass is your free ticket to a luxurious arrival to this unspoiled country. The Silja Line ferries to Helsinki and Turku are no less than floating luxury hotels. The line is so accommodating that it provides a dormitory free for its passengers to use on overnight trips! Try to come before August 31 when many campgrounds close and sightseeing attractions shorten their hours. *Suomi* is the finnish word for their country.

CURRENCY Finnish markka (Fmk) divide into 100 penni. There are 4 marks to a U.S. dollar.

WEATHER In southern Finland, it's warm enough to camp from June through August. In northern Finland camping is best restricted to the last week in June through the first three weeks in August.

FERRIES TO STOCKHOLM Included in Eurailpasses is deck passage on Silja Line ships between Finland and Stockholm. There are no extra taxes or fees. These are wonderful luxury cruise ships with free dormitory accommodations. The overnight sailing allows views of Helsinki or Turku and the Aland Islands from the water when leaving and of the archepelago at the entrance to Stockholm on arrival. You may miss seeing a few islands during the night, but the morning scenery, a free night's sleep, and 8 hours of saved travel time more than compensate. These large 6,000-12,000 ton car ferry/cruise ships offer everything you could possibly want: movies, duty-free shop, cocktail lounge, restaurants, smorgasbord for breakfast, lunch and dinner, evening dancing and floorshows, gambling, cafeteria and many indoor and outdoor lounge areas. For the overnight trip, reservations for the evening smorgasbord are taken starting at 4:30pm at the entrance to the 8th floor restaurant. You are assigned a table to either the 6pm or 8:30pm sitting. The smorgasbord is a bargain at 58Fmk, excluding beverage. Another good buy is the breakfast smorgasbord (26.50Fmk), served from 7-9am in the same restaurant and not requiring a reservation. Additional details are given under Stockholm.

From May 1-Sep 20, from Helsinki, a ferry leaves at 6pm and arrives in Stockholm at 9am. From Turku (Abo), a ferry leaves at 9:30pm and arrives in Stockholm at 7am. From Turku via Mariehamn in the Aland Islands to Stockholm, a ferry leaves Turku at 10am, arrives Mariehamn 3:30pm, leaves Mariehamn at 3:40pm and arrives Stockholm at 8:15pm.

TRAINS The Finnish State Railways (VR) cover a vast portion of this country, extending northward far enough to connect with Swedish trains. It's necessary to change trains at the Swedish-Finnish border as the tracks are of a different width. There are about 6,000 km. of track and where trains don't go, buses do. A nuisance and expense is the mandatory reservation fee of 13Fmk required for certain express trains (*erikoispikajunat* or EP). These trains are marked with the letter R with a box around it on the schedules in the stations. Children under 4 travel free and those between 4 and 11 pay half.

aikataulut	timetable	matkalippujen	reservations
lahto	departure	neuvontatoimist	information
laiturilta	track	odotussali	checkroom
saapuminen	arrival	lippuluukku	ticket office
sisaan	entrance	rautatieasemalle	train station
ulos	exit		

CAMPING   Campgrounds are well-equipped, spacious, in beautiful natural surroundings and in most every town. Normally, a set fee is charged per family up to five members and includes car, tent, trailer and people. A single camper usually pays half the family fee. Always close your tent tightly when leaving for the day as unexpected showers, though brief, are not uncommon. The tourist office has a pamphlet which lists campsites. Many camps are open only during June through August; opening times are listed only if the camp is open differently. Many campgrounds have a sauna (40-50Fmk for 4 persons), and cabins for rent (95-180Fmk for 3 people).

FOOD   The best prices are in the open markets and supermarkets. Lunch is normally eaten from 11am to 2pm and dinner from 5pm to 6pm. Staples of the Finnish diet include milk, butter, potatoes, fish, meat, rye bread and fresh berries in season. Meatballs (*lihapullia*), meat and rice filled crepe (*piirakka*) and fish pie (*kalakukko*) are frequently seen. Lappi, a milk semi-soft white cheese similar to mozzarella in taste and cooking properties is reasonably priced. Finnish smorgasbord (*voileipapoyta*) is a buffet of many different fish dishes, meat and salad specialties. Reasonable prices are found in cafeterias (*baari and grilli*) and fast food establishments (*grilli-kioski and shaslik-grilli*), the latter specializing in grilled meats like shish-ke-bob.

HELSINKI (HELSINGFORS)

Planned on a grand scale, you will find yourself walking down long blocks to get places, but there are plenty of monumental buildings to use as landmarks.

ARRIVING ON SILJA LINE FERRY   The Silja terminal (*Etelasatama*) in Helsinki's South Harbor is within several blocks of Market Square. The terminal itself provides luggage checking (5Fmk), foreign exchange (10 Fmk commission), and tourist information. The information booth sells bus and tram tickets, including the 10-ride strip ticket, Tourist Ticket and Helsinki Card. Also in the terminal are offices of the various ferry lines sailing to the U.S.S.R. You can get prices, buy tickets and make reservations, but to actually make the trip requires a visa which takes from a few days to two weeks to process. The bus and tram terminal is outside on the right. Tram 3T and bus 1A go to Market Square, but walk unless you have a pass. Tram 3B goes to the train station.

LEAVING HELSINKI ON SILJA LINE (free with Eurailpasses) Trams 3B and 1A go to the Silja Terminal (*Etelasatama*). Tram 3B goes in the opposite direction of tram 3T, the tourist route tram. In the Silja Line terminal go straight to the booth marked "check in" to the left of the Silja Line ticket counter where you will be issued a boarding pass if you have a Eurailpass. Upon entering the ferry, the purser will tear off the top part of your boarding pass. You can get on the boat as early as 4:30pm for the 6pm sailing. If you didn't arrive by Silja Line, refer to Stockholm for details.

FOREIGN EXCHANGE   The charge for cashing 1 to 4 travelers checks is 10Fmk. Banking hours are M-F 9:15am-4:15pm. Foreign exchange at the Silja Line terminal is open for arrivals and departures of ferries.

TRAIN STATION   The central terminal was built in 1919 by Saarinen in granite. Inside are foreign exchange (M-Su 11:30am-6pm), cafeteria, and luggage checking (6:15am-11:25pm). The city's Hotel Booking Office, a branch of the tourist office, is nearby at Asema-aukio 3. Open May 16-Sep 15, M-F 9-9, Sa 9-7, Su 10-6. The subway starts from the train station. The shops in the underground arcade keep late hours.

TOURIST OFFICE   The main tourist office (*matkailutoimisto*), Pohjoisesplanadi 19 is near Market Square. Open May 16-Sep 15, M-F 8-6, Sa 8:30-1. Be sure to ask for the booklets, *See Helsinki on Foot* which outlines 6 walking tours, Helsinki Museums, and Holiday in Helsinki.

CITY TRANSPORTATION   Green and yellow or orange and gray trams, dark blue buses and the subway (metro) go everywhere of interest. If you aren't buying a day pass and have arrived via Silja Lines and want to go to Market Square, the distance is only a few blocks and it's well to walk. For other destinations, you'll need to take the bus or tram or be prepared to walk long blocks. A single ticket is 6.50Fmk, a 10-trip strip ticket (*matkan lippu resorsbiljett*) costs 51 Fmk, and a 24-hour Tourist Ticket costs 40Fmk, valid for unlimited rides on any form of public transportation including some short ferry trips. The symbol for the public transporation company is two curved, black arrows on a yellow background. Tickets are good for unlimited rides in any direction for one hour. Transit maps are posted at the shelters.
    The Helsinki Card includes unlimited travel on buses, trams, metro and some ferries including Suomenlinna island and Korkeasaari Zoo, a 1-1/2 hour free city coach tour that visits the most important sights, free admission to over 40 museums and 10 other places of interest including Linnanmaki amusement park and the zoo, and little thank you gifts from department stores for coming there. The coach tour normally costs 50Fmk and departs Jun 1-Aug 31 daily at 1pm from the Hotel Booking Office at Asema-aukio in railway square by the train station.   The tour is operated by Suomen Turistiauto Oy. Commentary is in Finnish, English, Swedish and German.

The card is sold by the tourist offices, the campground, the Hotel Booking Centre, travel agencies, hotels and the Silja Line terminals in Helsinki and Stockholm. The card costs: 1 day 65Fmk, 2 days 85Fmk and 3 days 105Fmk. Typical museum admission is adult/5Fmk and student/3Fmk; a bus ride on the 10-trip ticket is 5.1Fmk. Generally in any given day, at minimum you'll need a ride from camp to the first sightseeing attraction, from there to a second sightseeing attraction and a ride back to camp. On a one day visit without going to the campground, you could walk to Market Square then take the bus to Temppeliaukio Church, a bus to the Sibelius monument, a bus to Seurasaari (open air museum) or to the National Museum and a tram or bus back to the terminal; total 5 rides.

On **trams**, get on at the back and exit in the middle or front. The ticket is self-cancelled in the machine at the back. (If you need to buy a single ticket, the tram driver will sell you one so get on at the front.) Most people just get on because they have longterm passes or are transferring within the hour's validity. Trams are on the honor system with an occasional inspector. On buses, get on at the front and exit in the middle or rear. The ticket is stamped by the passenger in the machine at the front of the bus near the driver. The metro goes from Kamppi to Itakeskus, M-Sa 5:50am-11pm, Su 7am-11pm and stops at the train station.

Tram 3T is both city transportation and a sightseeing tour with commentary in four languages including English. It leaves every 5 to 15 minutes M-Sa from 6am to 12:30am, Su 7am-12;30am. The commentary is provided M-F 10am-3pm and 6-8pm, SaSu 9am-8pm during summer only. The tram follows a figure 8 through the center of Helsinki and takes 45 to 60 minutes for a complete go around. It can be boarded anywhere along its route, such as the Silja Line terminal or train station, but the commentary starts from Market Square (Kauppatori). Regular tram fares apply.

Ferries and motorboats to the various islands off Helsinki's shore depart from Market Square.

CAMPGROUND   **Rastila Camping** is 13 km. east of the city center. Open May 15-Sep 15; family/40Fmk, 1 person/20Fmk. From Silja Line terminal, take tram 3B to the train station, change to the metro to Itakeskus (Itakeskusostra Centrum) and change to bus 96 or 97. (This can all be done on a single ticket.) The excellent site has hot water in restroom sinks, cooking facilities, restaurant, day room, row boats and rental cabins.

SIGHTSEEING   The most unique sight in Helsinki is the striking, modern **Temppeliaukio Church** at Lutherinkatu 3. Open M-Sa 10am-8pm, Su noon-2pm & 5-8pm. The church was hewn out of rock to superbly blend nature with art. (Farther out, the Jean Sibelius Monument is a lovely piece, but for those on a day trip not worth the time it takes to get there. Take bus 18, then walk 10 minutes.)

To **Seurasaari Open-Air Museum**, 5 km. from downtown, take bus 24 from Erottaja next to the Swedish Theatre. Bus 24 leaves twice hourly. Also, M/S Katarina boat leaves Market Sqaure Jun 1-Aug 31 at 1pm and 3pm for the 40 -minute trip. The museum shows actual farmhouses, smoke sauna, barns, church boats and buildings from different areas of Finland. Earliest building is the 17th century Karuna church; 12 groups of 87 buildings total. Jun 1-Aug 31 daily 11:30-5:30, Wed to 7pm. Free entrance with Helsinki Card, otherwise 5Fmk or free on Wed. Free guided tour except

Wednesday in English at 11:30am and 3:30pm from the notice board by the bridge on Seurasaari. On Midsummer night eve starting at 6pm, there is a large celebration with bonfires and dancing for 50Fmk admission fee. Folk dancing is performed Tu-Th and Su at 7pm for 25Fmk. On Thursday at 6pm about twice a month, folk dance rehearsals are held, admission free. The public beach has segregated mens and womens sections with nude sunbathing. Admission fee, open M-Sa 8:15-7, Su 9-7. Across the bridge to Meilahti are a ceramics exhibition, the Helsinki City Art Museum (open W-Su 11-6:30) and Friends of Finnish Handicrafts.

To **Viapori-Sveaborg Fortress** on Suomenlinna Island, take the motorboat from Market Square to the museum, which leaves 1-2 times an hour. Trip lasts 15 minutes. One way ticket is 7Fmk or free with Helsinki Card. The fortress dates from the 18th century and is now a national monument. Free entrance, optional tour in English from the INFO kiosk for 14Fmk at 12:30pm and 2:30pm. The Armfelt Museum, Ehrensvard Museum, Coastal Defence Museum and submarine Vesikko can be seen on the island. The submarine is a 250-ton coastal submarine used during World War II; open May 15-Aug 31 11-5. All 3 have admission charges of 3-5Fmk or free with Helsinki Card. Bring a picnic lunch.

The National Museum, Mannerheimintie 34, shows the history of Finland plus ethnic collections including a good Lapp section. Daily 11-4, Tu also 6-9pm; 5Fmk, free Tu or with Helsinki Card. The **Finnish Design Center**, Kasarmikatu 19, is by Finlandia Mall (M-F 10-5, Sa 10-3, Su 12-4, free). The best in Finnish design in housewares are displayed.

Korkeasaari Zoo is reached by motor boat 1 to 3 times an hour from Market Sqaure and from Hakaniemi. Ride is 10 minutes. Round trip ticket is 20Fmk or boat and entrance are free with Helsinki Card. By land, take bus 16 from Erottaja to Julosaari, then walk 1.5 km. through Mustikkamaa island and across to Korkeasaari. One of the most northerly zoos in the world with such rare animals as the Siberian tiger, snow leopard and lesser panda. Open daily 10-9, admission 10Fmk or free with Helsinki Card.

FOOD   Market Square (*Kauppatori*) is the site of Helsinki's open market. Because it's a big tourist draw, you can also find all manner of Finnish goods, such as weavings, woodwork, crafts and souvenirs made of reindeer toenails. Fruits and vegetables, smoked fish, fresh fish and bread are also sold. The market is an 8 -minute walk from the Silja Lines Terminal. Open M-Sa 7-2, also May 18-Aug 28 M-F 3:30-6. Dried fish is reasonable and ready-to-eat and can be bought at the market or in supermarkets. Finnish smorgasbord (*voileipapoyta*) is served in some Hotel restaurants.

SHOPPING   For major purchases it's worthwhile to ask for a tax-free repayment check, which amounts to 11 to 13 percent of the purchase price. The check can be cashed at the Silja Line Terminal before boarding. Department stores close at 2pm in summer.

VISITING RUSSIA   Helsinki is the perfect entry point for visits to Russia. You can't enter Russia without a visa and you can't get a visa without confirmed reservations. Finnsov Tours, Ltd. at Eerikinkatu 3 in the vicinity of the train station has tours at the some of the lowest prices. They also have counter service at the Silja Line Terminal. It takes anywhere from four days to two weeks to obtain a visa after reservations have been made. Waiting until arrival in Finland to find a tour is less expensive than booking one from outside Europe. The problem is the time it takes to get a visa. Those with Eurailpasses can take advantage of the free dorms on the luxury Silja liner and upon arrival in Stockholm go directly to Helsinki to make arrangements and apply for a visa. Then return to Scandinavia and tour until time to return to pick up the visa and head for the U.S.S.R. In Helsinki, to apply for a visa, go to the Russian embassy which is 3 blocks from the Silja Line terminal. Ask the operator you went through to get your confirmed reservations for the location and hours of the Russian embassy. There is no inexpensive way to tour Russia, but the difference between eastern and western culture is considered to be well worth the price.

Tallin, across from Helsinki on the shore of the Gulf of Finland, has preserved its appearance from the 13th to 15th centuries. For a short trip across the sea to this historic city, the Estonian Shipping Company provides cruiseship service on its MS Georg Ots. The company has counter service at the Silja Lines terminal; their main office is at P. Makaslinikatu 7. Their New York representative is International Cruise Center, 185 Willis Avenue, Mineola, NY 11501. These are the prices if booked in Helsinki. Helsinki to Tallin, midweek prices are valid M-Th and Su, weekend prices on Friday and Saturday. Tallin to Helsinki, midweek prices are valid Tu-Sa, weekend prices Sunday and Monday. Deck passage costs 105Fmk one way midweek or 135Fmk one way weekend; round trip costs 185Fmk midweek, 220Fmk midweek in one direction and weekend in the other, and 250Fmk weekend. If you can get 10 people together, the price drops to 80Fmk one way midweek. Children under 12 years travel free on deck. From April through August, the liner leaves Helsinki daily except Thursday at 10:30am and arrives in Tallin at 3pm. From Tallin, the boat leaves daily except Wednesday at 7:30pm and arrives in Helsinki at 10:30pm.

You can also take the **train to Leningrad** from Finland for about the same amount as the boat to Tallin. You will not be admitted in Russia without a visa, which requires confirmed reservations. The train to Leningrad (reservation may be necessary) leaves Helsinki at 1:10pm and arrives at the border town, Vainikkala, at 4:02pm and in Leningrad at 9pm.

Items that Soviet citizens like and will swap for are chewing gum (can exchange several packs for a Russian army belt), Levis, printed t-shirts and American and European cigarettes.

To Jyvaskyla, leave at 8am, 10am, 1pm not Sa, 2pm and 5:05pm (not Sa after Aug 16). Trip is 4 hours.

To Narvik, Norway, take the 10pm departure (second class only) from Helsinki which arrives in Kemi at 9:12am. Change for the train for Boden that leaves Kemi at 9:35am and arrives at the Finnish border, Tornio at 10:05am Finnish time and at the Swedish border, Haparanda, at 9:12am Swedish time which is an hour earlier. Change trains and depart at 10:30am, arriving Boden 12:45pm. Leave Boden (direction Narvik) at 2:40pm, arrive Galivare at 4:56pm, Kiruna at 6:20pm and Narvik at 9:40pm. The portion between Kiruna and Narvik only runs May 31-Aug 30. It's still plenty light at 9:40pm in Narvik to set up camp.

To Oulu and Rovaniemi, leave at 7am (ar. Oulu 2:02pm, Rovaniemi 5pm), 10am (ar. Oulu 5:33pm, Rovaniemi 8:50pm) and 10pm second class only(ar. Oulu 7:37am, Rovaniemi 10:59am). To go to Boden, Sweden, change trains in Kemi.

To Savonlinna, leave at 7:30am (change at Parikkala, ar. 1:20pm), 1:30pm (reservation mandatory, change at Parikkala, ar. 9:45pm) and 10:10pm (second class only, ar. 6:30am).

To Tampere and Seinajoki, leave at 8am, 9am M-Sa, 10am, 11am, 1pm not Sa, 2pm, 3:30pm, 5:05pm (not Sa after Aug 16). 2 hours to Tampere, 4 to Seinajoki.

To Turku, leave at 7:02am, 9:12am, 12:42pm, 4:02pm, 6:02pm and 9:12pm noy Sa. The 7:02am and 6:02pm departures go to Turku Harbor on days the ship sails.

TURKU (ABO IN SWEDISH)

Turku, Finland's oldest city, is where the ferry arrives via the Aland Islands. In the Aland Islands, the ferry stops at Mariehamn (Maarianhamina), an unspoiled town. In its harbor is the Pommern, a 4-masted barque and now a museum ship. Grona Udden Camping is at Mariehamn.

In Turku, tourist offices are in the Silja Lines terminal, and at Aurakatu 4 (M-F 8:30-7:30, SaSu 8:30-4) and Kasityolaiskatu 3 (M-F 8:30-4). Pick up their leaflet on walking tours. Camping Ruissalo is 10 km. from downtown. From the harbor, take bus 1 to the market place and then bus 8 by the Orthodox Church by the market place. The campground shares the lovely island of Ruissalo which has a Botanical Garden and recreation area. The camp has a sauna (fee), swimming beach and store. Fees are family/50Fmk, 1 person/25Fmk. Bus fare is 7mk or a 24-hour pass is about 15Fmk. The open market at Market Square operates M-Sa 7-2. The covered market (*Kauppahalli*) is open M-F 8-5, Sa 8-2. Important sights are the 12th century Castle near the harbor train station, Handicrafts Museum (*Luostarinmaki*), Museum ship Sigyn, Sibelius Museum and Art Gallery.

To Helsinki at 8:45am, 10:25am M-Sa, 12:15pm, 3:45pm, 5:30pm and 8:46pm. There is a direct connection from the harbor on arrival of most ferries.

To Seinajoki, Oulu, Kemi and Rovaniemi, take the train to Tampere and change. Trains leave for Tampere at 7:55am, 9:10am from Harbor Station or 9:45am from Turku Station, 3:35pm and 7:15pm (not Saturday). For Jyvaskyla, these same trains apply but remain on the train. The 3:35pm departure does not run on Saturday between Tampere and Jyvaskyla. The trip is 4 hours from Turku.

CENTRAL FINLAND

TAMPERE   Finland's second largest city is situated on the isthmus between two lakes. The tourist office (Kaupungin Matkailu) is at Verkatehtaankatu 2 (Jun-Aug M-F 8:30-8, Sa 8:30-6, Su 12-6). **Camping Harmala**, is at Harmala, 5 km. from the station. Take bus 1 from the main street bridge about 300 meters from the train station. Upon leaving the station, walk forward on Hameenkatu for about 5 blocks and the bus stop is before the river. Fare is 5Fmk for a single ticket or 10 tickets are 45Fmk. The bus stops 200 meters from camp and there is a big sign on the right side of the street. The camp is 200 meters on the right. Jun 1-Aug 20, family/50Fmk, 1 person/30Fmk, sauna 50Fmk; day room, store, tourist info. Tampere's open **markets**, Tammelantori and Laukontori, are open M-Sa 7-1. On Hameenkatu, the market hall is open M-F 8-5 and Sa 8-1. The Sarkanniemi Pass covers all sightseeing.

To Helsinki trains leave about once an hour, to **Jyvaskyla** at 10:13am. 12:15pm, 3:05pm, and 8:35pm.

JYVASKYLA   The renowned Finnish architect, Alvar Aalto, spent his adolescence and began his career in Jyvaskyla. Pick up an architectural map from the tourist office for a tour of his many buildings, including the Museum of Central Finland (1960), Alvar Aalto Museum (1973), Police Station (1970), College of Education (1957) and Student Union Building. The tourist office is near the train station at Vapaudenkatu 38 (open M-F 8-7, SaSu 10-7). Walk one block forward from the train station and turn left on Vapaudenkatu. The tourist office is in the first block on the left side of the road. The market is by the bus station and is open M-Sa 7-2.

Tuomiojarvi Camping is about 2 km. from the train station. The easiest way to go there is by foot through the center of town. Otherwise, walk to the bus station and take bus 22, 23, 32, or 34 to the campground. The bus stops outside the camp. The excellent camp has hot water in the restroom sinks, sauna (10Fmk), a large store (open 8am-10pm), canoe rentals and charges family/60Fmk, 1 person/25Fmk.
To Tampere leave at 9am, 11:15am M-F, 2:06pm, 4:50pm and 6:25pm not Sa.

SAVONLINNA   Remnants of its medieval past are Olavinlinna Castle on an island in the lake and the surrounding houses on Linnankatu.   During July, the Opera festival attracts crowds. There are two train stations. The first one (Kauppatorin seisake) is the central station, near the tourist office and the bus stop for the campground. To reach the tourist office walk out to the main arterial, Olavinkatu and turn right, walk across the bridge and the tourist office is across the square at Puistokatu 1 (open 8am-10pm). The main railway station (*rautatieasema*) is about 8 blocks from the other, away from the downtown area. **Camping Vuohimaki** is 7 km. from downtown in the direction of Leirintaalue. Take bus 3 from the main arterial of the town, Olavinkatu, half a block from the central train station. Buses leave twice an hour; last bus 10:55pm. May 26-Aug 20; family/58Fmk, 1 person/29Fmk.
To Helsinki leave at 8am (reservation mandatory, ar. 1:30pm), 10:45am (all second class, ar. 4:30pm), 4:40pm (ar. 10:55pm) and 10:35pm (all second class, ar. 7:05am). Change at Parikkala for all of these trains.

SEINAJOKI   Founded in 1960, Seinajoki is a junction of five railways and famous for its administrative and cultural center designed by Alvar Aalto. The center comprises Lakeuden Risti (church), the symbol of the "City of the Plains," parish center, town hall, library, state office building and theater. The **tourist office** is on Kauppakatu 17, 4 blocks from the train station (open M-F 8-6, SaSu 10-5). **Tornava Camping** is part of Tornava tourist center, a former manor estate. It now comprises museum areas (powder museum in a powder mill, agricultural museum, outdoor museum), an old church, manor house with the park, Tornava Island, summer theater, beach and hotel. The camp is 3.5 km. from the station. Take bus 1 from the bus stop on Ruukintie street just across from the station. The bus leaves at 6:45am, 7:05am, 8:05am, then every full hour until 10pm (4.5Fmk). The camp has hot water in the restroom sinks, automatic washing machine, restaurant, store, fishing and a beach. Family/44Fmk, 1 person/22Fmk. The open market is 3 blocks from the train station and operates M-Sa 7-2.
Trains go south to Tampere, Toijala and Helsinki at 8:05am, 2:20pm 4:45pm and 7:50pm. Change at Toijala for Turku.

OULU   The largest city in northern Finland, Oulo is situated at the mouth of the Oulu River.   The modernity of its university and medical centers contrasts with the nearby village of Ii, reminiscent of the Middle Ages.   The **tourist office** (Kaup. matkailu toimisto) at Torikatu 14 towards the waterfront is 8 blocks from the train station (open M-F 9-7, Sa 9-1).
Nallikari Camping, the most popular camp in Finland, logs in 38,000 visitors a year.   The camp is 4 km. from downtown in a birch grove next to the sea with a sandy beach. Take bus 5 from the bus stop on the one way street, Heikinkatu, 3 blocks from the station to the camp entrance. From outside the station, turn right and walk to Heikinkatu and then turn left. The resort camp has all amenities; family/44Fmk, 1 person/22Fmk.

The **open market**, Kauppahalli, is downtown on the waterfront. Turkansaari, an island outdoor museum of 22 buildings from olden times, includes a church dating from 1694 and an authentic tar pit from the days when northern Finland produced a large amount of the tar needed for 18th and 19th century sailing ships. Open 11am-9pm. Take the boat from the dock near the bridge of Pohjantie which crosses the River Oulu; 3-hour trip. Koskikeskus, designed by Alvar Aalto, includes North Ostrobothnia Museum, Art Museum, modern University Hospital and University of Oulu. Hailuoto, an island with good beaches, is reached by free 20-minute ferry from Oulu.

Ii (Iin Hamina), 37 km. north of Oulu, is a picturesque fishing village with narrow alleys and small wooden dwellings seemingly perched one on top of another above the harbor of what once flourished as a market and trading center during the Middle Ages. A campground is within walking distance. Take the local train from Oulu (direction Kemi).

To Kemi and Rovaniemi, leave at 8am, 10:40am, 2:15pm and 5:55pm. To Helsinki, at 12:40pm and 4:10pm.

LAPLAND

The rail line north from Helsinki ends in Kemijarvi. The one through train leaves Helsinki at 7:05pm, arrives Rovaniemi at 7:35am and Kemijarvi at 9:20am. The only other train that goes from Rovaniemi to Kemijarvi leaves Rovaniemi at 4:15pm daily except Saturday. From Kemijarvi to Rovaniemi, trains leave at 6:20am daily except Sunday, and 7:15pm. The 7:15pm departure is a through train to Helsinki, arriving there at 8:55am. A train leaves Kemi for Kolari at 7:50am (ar. 10:35am). On Fridays at 8:25pm, a through train leaves Helsinki for Kolari, arriving there at 10:35am. This train returns on Saturdays, leaving at 6pm, and arrives in Helsinki at 8:21pm.

ROVANIEMI   In Rovaniemi, the capital of Finnish Lapland, a branch tourist office is at the train station (Jun 1-Aug 31 daily 7:30am-noon & 2:30pm-6pm). The market is M-Sa 7am-4pm, Sa 7am-2pm at Kaupatori.

Ounaskoski Camping, Jaamerentie 1, is 1.5 km. from the station. The distance can be walked, or take bus 6 from the train station. (From the bus station take bus 9 or 10, 5.10Fmk). To walk, with your back to the station, turn right on Ratakatu and walk east for about 5 blocks. The street will lead into the bridge that crosses the river. Cross the river and turn left on the first street. The campground is beautifully situated on the banks of Kemijoki River. Family/50Fmk, 1 person/25Fmk, store and cafeteria.

The Lappia-House, Hallituskatu 11, contains a theater, congress and concert building, designed by Alvar Aalto (free guided tours). **Ounasvaara Hill**, 3 km. from town, affords a panoramic view of the area and the midnight sun. Take bus 12 from town or from the highway by the campground. **Santa Claus Village** at the Arctic Circle 8 km. from Rovaniemi is a workshop village that features high quality Lappish arts and crafts, not to mention the Santa Claus. Jun 1-Aug 31 9am-8pm, Sep 1-May 31 9am-5pm. In June and July, 8am-10pm; Aug-Sep 9am-8pm. Take bus 8 from Tomminsilta near the bus station.

To Kemi (change for Sweden) and Helsinki, tlleave at 9:35am (ar. 9pm), 1:10pm (ar. 11:30pm), 6pm (ar. 8am) and 9:05pm (ar. 8:55am). Arrival times are for Helsinki.

134

Rovaniemi

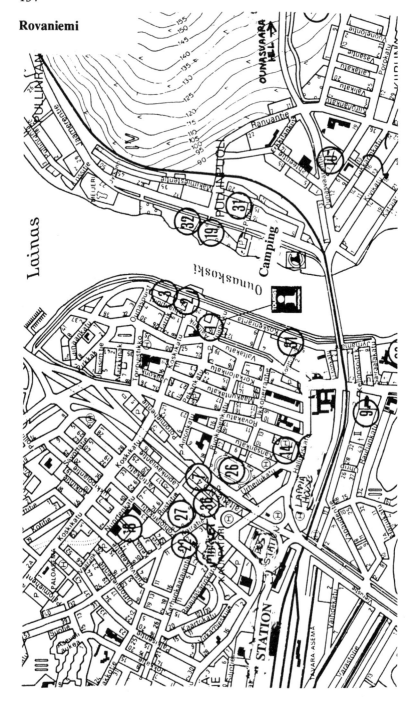

FRANCE

France is the one country in Europe that has both sufficient diversity of sights and reasonably priced unlimited mileage railpasses. From the caves where prehistoric man dwelt, to Roman ruins, medieval villages, Renaissance chateaux and avant garde art, you have only to venture to another French province to see them. Greek civilization is the only major past civilization that France can't show you. If you have only a month or less to spend in Europe, you will come out ahead by buying a France Railpass rather than a Eurailpass. Because France borders on Spain, Germany, Belgium, Switzerland and Italy, it's possible to expand your tour by paying the fare from the border. Plus, **French campgrounds are some of the least expensive in Europe**.

The virtues of France are delicious food, great cheese, good (but expensive) wines, wonderful ancient walled towns in the countryside, magnificent chateaux, gardens and furniture, superb collections of modern art, the French Alps and the animation and *joie de vivre* of the French people. In general, the French seem to be a little more lighthearted on the average than other Europeans which may stem from the French point of view of life that nothing could be so bad that it couldn't be worse. The hallmark of French society is tolerance to let people be themselves. The French are realistic and practical. Individual liberty is given highest priority.

If you must do France once-over-lightly, five days in Paris, one day each in Chenonceaux (chateau of the Loire), Les Eyzies (prehistoric capital), Carcassonne (medieval fortified town), and Chamonix in the French Alps might be considered. Of course, this would miss the Riviera with its medieval villages and modern art collections, the Roman ruins of Arles, Nimes and Orange, many other castles of the Loire, the wine villages of Alsace-Lorraine, and the other French provinces, each one worth visiting.

Michelin guidebooks take many of the wrinkles out of touring. Their series of green-covered regional sightseeing guides are indispensable for understanding what you are seeing. They are available in English editions for Paris, Chateaux of the Loire, Brittany, Normandy and Cote D'Azur (Riviera). For serious gourmets with adequate food budgets, the red *Michelin Guide France* has venerated restaurant ratings, as well as maps of cities and towns of any size. The cheapest Michelin-listed restaurant represents a good value in fine cuisine. Buy all Michelin guides and maps in France as the cost is at least 40 percent below prices abroad.

CURRENCY   The currency is French francs. Each franc is divided into 100 centimes. The rate is 5.6 francs to the U.S. dollar. Foreign exchange is *bureau de change.*

WEATHER   In Paris camping weather is best from June to September. Camping on the Riviera is pleasant from May into October, with September and October being warmer than May. August is the most crowded time in the resort areas of France as this is the month of the great escape for the French people. Try to avoid it, but don't worry if you can't. Just stay put at the beginning (especially the first Friday and Saturday) and end of the month when the French are on the move.

CAMPING   There are 3600 campgrounds in France. The French Tourist Office has regional listings of campgrounds, the map *Go Camping in France* and the brochure *Castels et Camping Caravanning* which lists deluxe camps set on the estate of a chateau. At the French Touring Club's camps, you can obtain free their annual Directory of Campgrounds (*Indicateur du Camping Caravanning*) which lists camps and prices and indicates whether they can be reached by bus or train.
 French campgrounds are a bargain when compared with the rest of Europe. The average nightly campground fee is about 9F per person and 7F per tent. According to law, charges must be posted at the camp entrance. No camping carnet is needed in France except in the State Forests in which you are unlikely to camp. A passport is accepted even when a sign states *license exigee* (camping permit needed). Some French camps do not furnish toilet paper, and some have Turkish type toilets with one conventional.

redevance	charge
auto	car
tente	tent
emplacement	site
caravan	trailer
reduction	discount
par personne	per person
infirmirie	first aid
glacieres	ice chest
plats cuisines	takeout food
taxe de sejour	residence tax
demi-tarif	half price
location	for rent
douche chaude	hot shower
machines a laver	washing machines
piscine chauffee	swimming pool
aucune redevance	no charge
rechauds a gaz	gas stoves
hors saison	out of season
material de camping	equipment
distribution d'eau chaude compris	fee includes hot water

TRAINS   The French National Railroads (SNFC or Societe Nationale des Chemins de Fer Francais) are excellent.   The best railway lines radiate outward from Paris like spokes of a wheel.   Keep this in mind when planning an itinerary as criss-crossing the hinterlands is slower.

FRANCE RAILPASSES   Alone in Europe, the French offer a railpass that is excellent value.   It is available to persons living outside France only. They can be purchased through Forsyth Travel Library, Dept CE, PO Box 2975, Shawnee Mission, KS 66201, toll-free 1-800-Forsyth.

The France Railpass can be bought for either first or second class train travel for a period of 15 days or 1 month.   The pass is valid for unlimited rail travel on only a certain number of days within the validity period.   For any four days of rail travel within a 15-day period, the price is adult/$99 or child/$60 in second class, and adult/$134 or child/$80 in first class.   For any 9 days within a 1-month period, the price is adult/$160 or child/$100 for second class and adult/$224 or child/$130 for first class.   A child is 4 -11 years; under 4 is free.   If a trip begins after 7pm, the next day's date will be used and other trips may be taken during that day.   This does not apply on the last day of the pass.   Second class is fine in France.   The passes include riding the TGV trains without paying a supplement.   Bonuses are a free roundtrip transfer by rail from Orly or Roissy Airports to Paris, a one-day pass for travel on Paris buses and metro (second class) and discounts on car rental and some museum fees.

TYPES OF TRAINS   The world speed record of over 237 mph is held by the French railroads by its **TGV** (train *a grande vitesse*--of great speed) model, introduced in 1981.   The low-slung orange, gray and white "Flying Peacock" makes the 265 mile Paris to Lyon run in two hours, chopping in half the previous time for a TEE.   Developing the new system has cost SNCF over 1.6 billion dollars since 1970.   Each train carries a single unit of eight cars, holding 111 first-class passengers and 275 second-class passengers. The TGV needs 2 miles to stop when going 162 mph, so a special track was built without any track crossings.   The TGV uses about the same amount of fuel as conventional trains and much less than a car or plane on a per passenger basis.   The electric railroads reduce the country's dependence on foreign oil, using instead France's hydroelectric and nuclear energy.

On its commercial runs, the TGV does not exceed 170 mph.   To experience that speed, you need to ride the TGV between Paris and Lyon because on this route the train rides on its own special track.   However, the TGV continues on from Lyon using the regular track on the route Avignon, Nimes, Montpellier, Marseille and Toulon.   You can ride directly to Lausanne on the TGV and will experience its famous speed on the portion between Paris and Dijon.   The same goes for the TGV to Geneva and Grenoble.   Of course the TGV can be taken between intermediate points as well.   Paris to Tours and Nantes and Bordeaux by TGV are planned.

Eurailpass and Eurail Youthpass include travel on the TGV without having to pay the supplement which is normally charged for departures during peak hours and days.   A reservation is required for all TGV departures and costs the same as for a reservation for any other train.   It is preferable to make it at the reservation counter, but there are special TGV Reservation Rapide machines in the station that can be used to make a reservation within 1-1/2 hours of departure providing you already have a

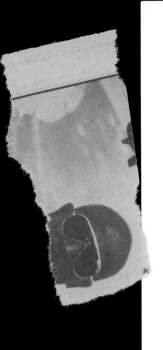

138

ticket, Eurailpass or Eurail Youthpass. Eurailpass and Eurail Youthpass holders are advised to use the reservation counter because only there can you indicate your choice of a window seat and nonsmoking or smoking car. TGV seating is airplane style with two seats on either side of the center aisle in second class, and three seats in the same amount of space in first class. Luggage is placed in an area just inside the door. Formal meals are served at your seat on a TGV, rather than in a separate dining car as on a TEE. A TGV carries a bar car which sells sandwiches and simple fare, but no matter where you are served, food is expensive. A reservation for a formal meal should be made at the same time the TGV reservation is made.

A special first class service, **La Nouvelle Premiere**, connects Paris to Strasbourg and provides a dining car managed by the chef of Paris' Michelin 3-star restaurant, Jasmin. Supplement required for all passes.

Only one or two **TEE** trains remain. They are all first class and included in the first class Eurailpass only. A reservation is required only for a TEE which crosses a border, not for a TEE whose entire run is within France. Because of low ridership, most TEE's have been converted to International InterCity trains and carry both first and second class. Some examples are *Le Capitole* (Paris to Toulouse), Stanislas (Paris to Strasbourg) and Aquitaine and *L'Etendard* (Paris to Bordeaux). A reservation is mandatory for an InterCity (IC) train which crosses a border, but not if it runs solely within France.

Rapides serve France internally, and these fast trains do not charge supplements to anyone. Rapides make limited stops just as the TGV, TEE and IC, carry both first and second class, do not require a reservations, can attain speeds of 125 mph, use Corail and Turbotrains, have the same seating configuration and luggage area as a TGV, are air-conditioned and announce the train's imminent arrival at stations over a public address system. Always remember that an **Express** train is slower than a **Rapide** but stops at many more towns. At the bottom of the hierarchy are the local trains, **Direct** ones don't stop at every station, but **Omnibus** do.

TICKETS For tickets purchased in France, the validity is two months, stopovers are free, and children 4 - 9 pay half. From Paris to destinations within 50 miles, special Sunday one-day excursion tickets and 3-day weekend tickets are discounted 30-50 percent. For senior citizens, a Vermeil Card is sold in France which gives 50 percent reductions for non-peak travel. All tickets purchased in France MUST BE validated before boarding by inserting them into the orange machines *(composteur)* located at the gate to the platform. The machine will stamp the ticket with the date and make a clicking sound. The sign, *compostez votre billet*, translates as "stamp your ticket." Tickets are spot checked on the train and the fine is 20 percent for an unstamped ticket or the cost of a ticket plus fine if the passenger has no ticket. This doesn't apply to tickets purchased outside France or railpasses.

SCHEDULES Free train schedules for individual routes are available in racks in the train stations. SNCF publish the official timetables in ten volumes. Volume A Indicateur Renseignements Generaux gives European-side schedules and is given free when any other schedule A is purchased. The other schedules cost from 20-30 francs at train station newspaper kiosks. They are: #A1 *Horaires du reseau de l'Est* covering eastern France, #A2 *Horaires du reseau du Nord* covering northern France, #A3 *Horaires du* *reseai de l'Ouest* covering western France, #A5 "*Horaires du reseau de Sud-Est* covering southeastern France, #B1 *Horaires de la banlieue de Paris-Est* covering suburban lines east of Paris, #B2 *Horaires de la banlieue de Paris-Nord* covering suburban lines north of Paris, #B3 *Horaires de la banlieue de Paris-Ouest* covering suburban lines west of Paris, and #B4 *Horaires de la banlieue de Paris-Sud* covering suburban lines south of Paris.

THE TRAIN STATION   *Buffets de Gare* are station restaurants which serve very good food and the French go there just like they would to a regular restaurant. Station automatic lockers are 29" deep, 12" wide and 17" high. The large size is twice as wide.

la gare (lah-GAR)	station
quai (quay)	track
banlieue	local train departures
bureau de change	currency exchange office
renseignement	train information office
voiture	coach
non fumeurs	no smoking
fumeurs	smoking allowed
salle d'attente	waiting room
consigne	baggage storage
arret facultatif	stops on signal
a, de	to, from
lundi	monday
mardi	tuesday
mercredi	wednesday
jeudi	thursday
vendredi	friday
samedi	saturday
dimanche	sunday
arrivee	train arrivals
depart	train departures

EURAIL BONUSES   (1) Ferry crossings on the Irish Continental Line between Le Havre or Cherbourg, France to Rosslare, Ireland and Le Havre to Cork, Ireland. Port taxes are extra and must be paid in French francs. Passage is for deck class on these luxurious ships equipped with lounges, discotheque, movies on closed circuit television, snack bar, duty free shop and restaurant. A bed in a 4 or 6-bed cabin costs about $7 to $10. Advance reservation is not necessary for deck class. Passengers must check in not less than one hour before sailing time. The ships in service are St. Patrick and St. Gillian, carrying 1,040 and 1,500 passengers respectively. (2) A discount on car rentals through The French Train + Auto program in over 200 French railroad stations. No drop off allowed. Reservations required at least 8 days in advance.

FOOD   Food is the superlative of French civilization. Here is where gastronomy has reached the status of a fine art. Considering the high quality of cooking, we found restaurant meals to be good value compared to what's available in the U.S., but you'll need to spend at least $8 to discover this. If you do, try to eat the noon meal in a restaurant and settle for a camp meal of perhaps bread, cheese and fruit for dinner. You can never go wrong by patronizing the cheapest Michelin-listed restaurant, and the full meal will cost between 60-90F. Another good approach is to ask the tourist office for its free list of restaurants (every tourist office has one and menu prices are given) and seek out the ones with the cheapest menu, usually about 45-70F. These places usually have a worker clientele and are away from the downtown area, but often not too far from the station in the direction away from the downtown area.

If it's the height of the dining hour (12-2 or 7:30-9:30), a good restaurant should be fairly full. The only problem is a *complet* sign already may be hanging in the window, signifying that no more diners can be accommodated. Avoid restaurants with an employee stationed outside the door. The recommendation of campground personnel, a policeman, store clerk or any local person can be relied upon. A small, family-run restaurant will be better value than a middle class establishment. There may be only two or three menu selections, but each one will be good. Don't judge a restaurant by its exterior but by amount of patronage. If a restaurant lacks a posted outside menu, it's very expensive no matter how it looks. A brasserie sometimes indicates a less expensive restaurant. Avoid shopping mall cafeterias; their food is not up to French standard.

In general, always order the *menu* which is a three or four course meal at a set price, never a la carte. The exception might be if you just want an omelet. The custom in France is for the house specialties, those items on which the restaurant has built its reputation, to be printed on the menu in red. These items are never the cheapest offerings on the menu and usually fall in the higher price ranges but they are always very, very good. On the menu hors d'oeuvres are the the first course. Most common is a combination plate of sliced tomatoes, sliced cucumbers which have been left to drain in *gros sel* (crystal salt), never *sel fin* as that would not *fatiguer* them properly, and lightly dressed potatoes with parsley. If radishes are part of the appetizer, butter will accompany them, and that is the only time you will see butter on the table as it is not served with the French bread. Appetizers are freshly prepared for the noontime meal, whereas sometimes soup is the first course for the evening meal. The entree follows and is normally garnished (garni) with a vegetable. Fruit, ice cream *(glace*--pronounced glass) and caramel custard are usually the dessert choices. If there are four courses, a fish dish or omelet will precede the entree, a salad will follow it, or a cheese platter will be served before dessert. The waiter presents the cheese try with good sized wedges of five or six varieties for your inspection. The custom is to indicate perhaps two from which you would like a slice. Most cheeses are served as a triangular wedge which is correctly eaten by cutting off sequential wedges (like slicing a pie) always starting from the same point. Coffee is served after dessert and the French commonly go elsewhere for it. To ask for the check, say for example, *l'addition, s'il vous plait, mademoiselle.*

Good, basic entrees include *pot au feu* (pot roast), *boeuf bourguignon* (beef stew), *blanquette de veau* (veal stew) and *poulet a la chasseur* (chicken in tomato sauce and shallots). White chicken meat is *blanc de volaille*. The best way to get acquainted with French menu terms is to peruse the two volumes by Julia Child, et al., *Mastering the Art of French Cooking*. The French cook with butter and peanut oil mostly with walnut oil sometimes in salad dressing. Olive oil is incorporated very successfully in the south of

France. The words a la florentine mean with spinach, and a l'alsacienne indicates sauerkraut.

Tap water *(eau nature)* is safe even in small towns but the French feel it lacks joie de vivre and prefer mineral water for its taste, carbonation or special mineral properties. Evian is the standard non-carbonated mineral water. Lemonade is *citron presse*. Whole milk is *lait entiere* and skim milk is *lait ecreme*. Most restaurants stock a house wine *(vin ordinaire)* that comes in either red or white, can be ordered by quarter, half or whole liter and is served in a carafe. *Vin compris* on the menu means a certain portion of house wine is included in the menu price. Some small family restaurants price their meals on the assumption that a beverage will be ordered separately as all French people do, and are distressed if you do not order a beverage because the restaurant's profit margin is lost.

Sunday dinner taken around 1:00pm is the most important meal of the week for the French and will be eaten at as good a restaurant as can be afforded. This is when you will see entire families dining out together.

GROCERY SHOPPING When grocery shopping, sidewalk markets offer the lowest prices. Remember to say Bonjour, Madame and Au Revoir, Mademoiselle as appropriate when shopping at the market and small shops. Bread is baked three times a day and sold according to weight in grams in a boulangerie. The crusty bread with chewy interior is made of soft wheat, yeast and coarse salt and baked in brick ovens. In the food category, it is the best value in France and the only inexpensive snack item.

Meat is expensive. Beef is particularly high and does not cost that much more when served in a restaurant as when bought at the market. Meat is divided according to muscle separation as in Belgium and Switzerland. Listed are approximate French equivalents to U.S. cuts of meat.

Beef	cote premier	prime rib
	entrecote	sirloin steak
	faux-filet	tenderloin
	tenderloin	T-bone
	grumeau	brisket
	tranche carree	bottom round
	flanchet	flank
	hache	hamburger
Pork	cote premiere	loin chop
	filet	loin
	jambon	ham
	lard	bacon
	sous epaule	shoulder

A *charcuterie* sells cooked meats such as pork, ham, chicken, roast beef, meat loaf, veal, *pate* (pah-TAY) and *terrines* (ground meat mixtures) and various side dishes, all delicious. There are always several varieties of pate, each based on a different meat or combination of ingredients. Most expensive is *pate de foie gras* (pah-TAY-duh fwah grah) which is made from diseased liver of geese which have been locked up in the attics under gabled eaves.

A *cremerie* sells a great variety of cheese. *Chevre* are goat milk cheeses, small and round with a natural green-gray covering. *Cabecous*

142

d'Aurie is a dry goat cheese. A *patisserie* sells cakes, croissants, creme puffs and such but no bread. A *confiserie* sells candy and ice cream. An *epicerie* is a small "mom and pop" grocery store. Supermarkets are usually chains, such as Co-op, Monoprix, or Prisunic, and it was in these supermarkets in France where the idea of plain labeling began.

SHOPPING   A droguerie sells household goods like clothespins and detergents not drugs as you might expect. A drugstore is a farmacie and sells prescriptions, baby food, diapers and sanitary napkins. Flea markets are *marches aux puces* and used goods dealers are *brocanteurs*. VAT is the value added tax which reaches 33 percent on luxury items, is lowest on food, ranging from 5.5 to 7 percent and usually is about 18.6 percent on clothing. Visitors can have the VAT refunded for goods taken with you if they total 1200F worth from a single store. When you leave France, you must hand your receipt to French customs who will add its stamp. Customs will return the receipt to the store and the store will send you the amount of the discount through a bank. If you wish to go through this, be sure to ask about it at the store as the necessary papers must be completed. When leaving by train, the paper must be stamped by customs either at the station or by a customs official enroute or at the border station if the train stops long enough.

LE POTPOURRI   The French have high standards of politeness and *monsieur, madame or mademoiselle* is always appended to any short answer or request you give. For instance, say *Bonjour, monsieur, Oui, madame, or Non, mademoiselle*. You will hear yourself addressed this way many times and will be rewarded with friendship and better service if you follow suit. Always say *s'il vous plait, madame* (or *monsieur*) when making any request.
    It's not considered good manners to go in and use the restroom of a small family cafe without buying something. Summertime holidays are July 14, Bastille Day with celebrations in Paris and throughout France, and August 15, Assumption Day. The main floor of a building is *rez-de-chaussee* and marked "RC" in an elevator. The "first floor" is what we would consider the second.
    A French Postoffice (PTT, pronounced pay-tay-tay) provides the least expensive way to call home. Go to the counter window closest to the phone booths, hand the clerk your passport and he'll indicate a booth for you to use. You can then direct dial to your home without worrying about inserting coins. After hanging up, return to the counter, and the clerk will state the charge, collect payment and return your passport. A short call to the U.S. cost 20F in 1988. For calls overseas, dial 19 plus the country code.
    When mailing a package, keep in mind that it must be two kilos or under, except books which may weigh three kilos. Oversized packages may not be accepted. Stamps are also sold in tobacco shops and that's where most people buy them.

PARIS

Paris combines the charm of a village on a grand scale with the attractions of a metropolis. If you are leaving Europe from London, Paris is the ideal city in which to arrive just before the expiration of your Eurailpass. The City of Light requires at least a 5-day stay which will idle your pass if scheduled in the middle of your trip.   Another advantage is that Paris has the cheapest flights to London of any European city.

France's major summer holiday is Bastille Day on July 14.   On that day, a parade is held on the Champs-Elysee, in which the military rolls every kind of armored vehicle imaginable down the broad boulevard while performing air maneuvers overhead.   In the evening, fireworks are held on the Seine and Parisians gather to watch from bridges and river banks.   The bridge, Bir Hakeim, is packed with viewers as are other vantage spots.   The lights on the Eiffel Tower are extinquished.   The preceding evening each neighborhood has its own celebration, with a band, street dancing and street vendors.   For instance, in the market place of Porchefontaine near Versailles Camping, an outdoor dance with a live combo is featured.

FOREIGN EXCHANGE   It's worth asking the fee before committing yourself to changing travelers checks.   American Express charges a 5F fee to cash travelers checks other than their own brand.   The Banque Nicoise de Credit, 101 av. des Champs Elysees, near the tourist office is open long hours and charges no commission.   Some postoffices cash travelers checks without commission.   Generally, the banks at the train stations extract a fee.

TRAIN STATIONS   Paris has 6, each serving a different area of France and Europe.   French trains do not pass through the center of Paris.   Instead they come into their respective station and stop.   This only becomes a problem if you are passing through Paris on your way somewhere else.   Be sure to note the station at which your train arrives and the station from which the connecting train departs.   All stations are connected by metro or bus, but be sure to allow sufficient time to make the connection.   For certain trains, a special bus waits outside the station to whisk passengers to the connecting train at another station.   There is regular inter-station bus service between Austerlitz, Est, Nord and St. Lazare.

Gare du Nord serves Flanders, Artois and Picardie within France and Belgium, The Netherlands, Great Britain, Germany, Scandinavia, Poland and the U.S.S.R.   There is a direct connection to trains going to the Riviera or Spain via Hendaye for certain trains that arrive at Gare du Nord.   A Welcome Information Office is near the International Arrivals platform, open M-Sa 8am-10pm, Su 1-8pm.   The reservation office is open 7am-9pm; exchange daily 6:30am-10pm; luggage 6am to midnight; postoffice M-F 8am-7pm, Sa 8am-noon.

Gare de l'Est serves Champagne, Lorraine, Vosges and Alsace within France, and Switzerland, Italy, Germany, Austria and Eastern Europe.   Its Welcome Information Office is open M-Sa 8-10.   The reservations office is open M-Sa 8am-1pm & 5-10pm; exchange M-F 7:30am-8pm; luggage storage 6am to midnight; postoffice M-F 8am-7pm, Sa 8am-noon.   Bus 65 connects Gare de l'Est with Gare de Lyon.

Gare de Lyon handles trains to Burgundy, Savoy, Dauphine, Provence, Riviera, Corsica, Auvergne and Languedoc, and Switzerland, Italy, Yugoslavia, Greece, Bulgaria, Turkey and Great Britain.   An exchange office is open daily 6:30am-10pm; tourist office M-Sa 8am-1pm & 5-10pm; reservation office daily 8am-9pm; luggage storage never closes; and post office M-f 8am-7pm, Sa 8am-noon.

Gare d'Austerlitz serves the Loire Valley, Auvergne, Atlantic Coast, Basque country, Pyrenees and Languedoc, and the Roussillon provinces of

144

The Metro - northern part

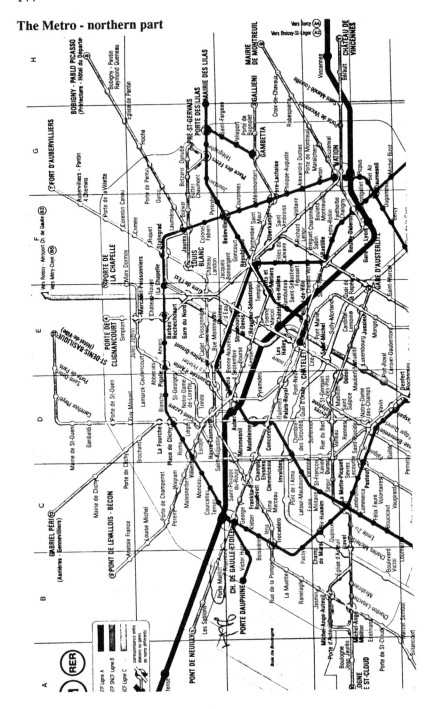

The Metro - southern part

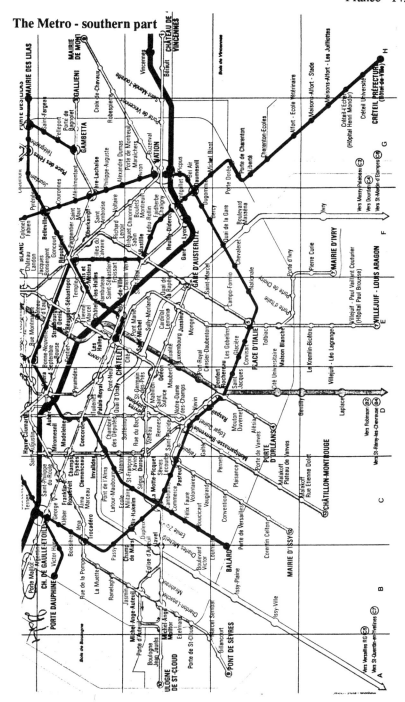

Spain and Portugal. The tourist office is open M-Sa 8am-10pm; exchange M-F 8:45am-5pm; luggage storage 6am-12:30am; and post office M-F 8am-7pm, Sa 8am-noon.

Gare Montparnasse serves the Paris suburbs and the Atlantic Coast. **Gare St. Lazare** serves Normany and Great Britain, and commuter trains.

TOURIST OFFICE Offices are at all train stations. L'Office de Tourisme de Paris, 127 avenue des Champs-Elysees is open M-Sa 9am-10pm, Su 9am-8pm.

CITY TRANSPORTATION Paris can't possibly be navigated without taking the metro (subway). If you have a little extra time for the ride and to determine which bus to take, Paris buses give a good non-subterranean view of the city. The free map that takes over where the tourist office one ends is *Banlieue Bus RER*, available from any ticket office. This map extends even beyond the area where the campgrounds are.

A single metro ticket costs 4.70F, but nobody buys them this way. Most people without a pass of some sort purchase a **carnet** (pronounced CAR-nay) of 10 small yellow tickets for 28.50F. Transfers are not allowed on these tickets. You can ride the metro on one single ticket as long as you never leave the station, but if you want to change to a bus another ticket or two will be required. The RER is priced according to distance traveled. The same yellow tickets are valid for metro, bus or RER, but only the metro charges a flat rate of one ticket. A carnet can be shared among you. Save your ticket until you have exited the area where tickets are required.

The best buy in Paris transportation is the **Orange Card** (*Carte Orange*). It is valid for all buses, metro, RER and *banlieue* (commuter trains) in the greater Paris area. The weekly pass, *Carte Orange Hebdomadaire*, is good from any monday through sunday. A monthly version *(mensuel)* is also available. Greater Paris is divided into zones. The Carte Orange is priced according to the number of zones included. The various campgrounds require from two to five zone cards. Select your campground before purchasing the card. The week pass (second class) costs 46F for zones 1-2; 59F for zones 1-3; 81F for zones 1-4; and 98F for zones 1-5. The month pass (second class) costs 162F for zones 1-2; 208F for zones 1-3; 284F for zones 1-4; and 342F for zones 1-5. The roundtrip week pass costs 19F for zones 1-2; 24F for zones 1-3; and 35F for zones 1-4. This pass is valid for one round trip per day.

Orange Cards are sold wherever tickets are sold, but require a photograph. Any will do, even a tiny face cut from a snapshot. If you don't have one, all the train stations have fotomats. The picture is affixed to the orange card, which you are required to sign, and then placed in a plastic sleeve. In a small pocket on the sleeve, an individual yellow metro ticket is placed. You will be using this same metro ticket for the entire week to insert in the turnstyles which allow passage to the tracks. Be sure to return it to its case each time and not inadvertently throw it away.

A **daily ticket**, Formule 1 (forfait journalier), is sold at any ticket booth for 19F for zones 1-2; 24F for zones 1-3; and 35F for zones 1-4. This is not a very good buy, compared to the week ticket. Most people would be better off using tickets from a carnet. Avoid the Tourist Tickets.

The important point to remember for both bus and metro is that each line is identified by both a number and its terminal point. The metro is marvelously efficient and very simple to use. Each station has a large map of metro lines and each line is a different color. In principal stations the maps are electrified; you have only to push a button indicating your destination and the proper metro line and change points *(correspondances)* will light up. Remember to note the terminus of the line. A map is also provided within each metro car. Tickets are sold by machine or at ticket windows. You stamp your own ticket in the slot as you go through the entry gate. The date and entry number are recorded on the back of the ticket. First class cars, painted yellow and located in the middle of the train, stop at the painted section in the middle of the platform. The rest of the train is second class which is cheaper and perfectly fine, except somewhat crowded during rush hour. Anyone can sit in first class outside of the hours 9am to 5pm. The seats next to the doors that pull down are supposed to be used only when the train isn't crowded, except in the case of the disabled. The mechanical gate to the tracks is timed to the arrival and departure of trains. The gate opens immediately after a train has left and closes again just as another enters the station. Always wait for the next train and never try to squeeze through as a gate is closing. (The gate prevents would-be passengers from rushing through a closing train door.) Each metro station is three minutes apart, including time spent getting on and off. Board quickly and get off immediately. The door handle must be turned for it to open. Exits are well marked with signs directing people topside to each side of the street.

The **RER** has three lines, A, B and C, which are divided into sections and priced according to distance traveled. Inside Paris itself the price is the same as for the metro.

CAMPGROUNDS   One is within Paris and more are in outlying areas but accessible by public transportation.   A good choice for backpackers is Terrain Municipal de Campisme, provided by the town of Versailles.   If you're staying at least five days within a Monday to Sunday period, the best transportation buy is the weekly Carte Orange.   (See city transportation.)   For Versailles Campground, purchase one good for 4 zones at any metro ticket window before taking your first ride.   Camping Bois D'Boulogne requires a 2-zone card for taking bus 244 or a 3- zone card for bus 144. The highest rated camp in the Paris area is Camping Airotel International at Maison Laffitte.

VERSAILLES CAMPGROUND (*Terrain Municipal de Campisme*) is in the Porchefontaine district of Versailles. The campground is open April 15 to October 31. The camp charges a one time registration fee of 10F per tent plus adult/12F and tent/12F per night. Payment is made in advance upon registering. It's probably best to pay for only three or four nights at first and then pay later for the rest of the stay. As in many campgrounds in Europe, a computerized printout of your bill will serve as a receipt. Because payment is collected in advance, leaving a passport at the desk is not required.

To reach the campground, take RER Line C (direction Versailles R.G), get off at Station Porchefontaine, and then walk ten minutes.   From your arrival point in Paris, consult a metro map and select a route to take you to RER Line C.   RER Line C is in red on the metro-RER map; Porchefontaine Station is in the lower left corner. Major metro interchanges between RER Line C and the metro are Invalides and St. Michel. If you arrived at Gare de L'Est, take metro, direction Mairie D'Ivry, to Opera and change to direction Balard to Invalides. From Gare D'Austerlitz, you can board RER Line C directly. From Gare du Nord, take metro, direction Montreuil, to Les Halles and change to direction Montrouge to St. Michel. From Gare St. Lazare, take metro, direction Vanves, to Opera and change to Balard for Invalides.

Camping Versailles

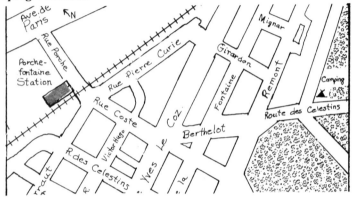

You are now probably at RER Line C at Invalides, St. Michel or Gare D'Austerlitz on the platform waiting for a train in the direction of Versailles R.G. R.G. stands for Rive Gauche (left bank). The important point to remember is that you can't just board any train that arrives like you would at metro stations because some trains go to St. Quentin and not Versailles R.G. Each train has a name. Check the suspended sign above the platform which posts the name of the oncoming train a few minutes before its arrival. Any train beginning with the letter S, such as Sara, Sam and Sven go to St. Quentin en Yvelines. DON'T GET ON THESE. (Those who do can rectify the error by getting off at any station before Station Viroflay R.G. and waiting for the correct train.) Only board a train whose name starts with a V. Vick, Vony, Vaal and Vurt go to Versailles R.G. Depending on where the RER is boarded, the ride is 20 to 30 minutes to Station Porchefontaine. Station Porchefontaine is the one after Station Viroflay R.G. (One word of caution--on our first trip to the campground, we couldn't get the door open to get off at the correct station, so had to ride to the next station and come back. Observe how others get the door open, consider practicing at an earlier stop, and beware a door nobody uses as it might still be broken.) Trains that begin with P, such as Paul, Polo and Puma only go as far as Blvd. Victor, where you must get off and wait for a train starting with V. If you're boarding the RER prior to Invalides Station, train LARA only goes as far as Invalides Station.

From **Invalides Station**, the last train going to Porchefontaine is 11:23pm. Later trains are listed on the departure schedule, but before counting on them check with the information clerk at the station to verify that the later trains operate for that particular day.

Facilities The campsite is large, heavily wooded and on a slight slope, though a flat tentsite can be carefully selected. The ground is hardpacked dirt and leaves. A wood fence surrounds the camp. The campground is uncrowded, even around Bastille Day, July 14, when we were there. As you enter camp, the office is on the left. Registration and public telephones are here. Across from the office is the main facility. On one side are separate mens and womens restrooms containing sinks with both hot and cold water, free hot showers and one toilet, not of the conventional type but the kind you squat above. (Are you still with me? If not, the other Paris campgrounds have conventional toilets.) Additional identical toilets are located in tiny buildings throughout the camp, and are used by either sex. On the other side of the main building are a dishwashing room, laundry room for handwashing clothing and a large day room with 4-person tables and chairs. We always had the day room to ourselves whenever we used it for eating breakfast. Should you arrive at camp late at night and it's raining, the day room presents the option of a place to sleep. Camp can be set up in the morning. There are no clotheslines, but we tied a cord to hang laundry between two trees next to our tent. In the morning, a small kiosk near the main facility is open and sells limited items such as fresh croissants, bread (baguette size), yoghurt, milk and other basics.

If it's a Wednesday, be sure to visit the **open market** in Porchefontaine on the paved square you passed on the way to camp. Hours are early morning until noon and prices are very low, much less than in Paris. Fruits, vegetables, cheese, sandwich meats, pate and fresh meat are all available. There's no bakery in Porchefontaine anymore, but a small grocery store and a good deli are on the way to the station.

PARC DE CAMPING PARIS-OUEST-BOIS DE BOULOGNE (bow-LONE-yuh) is the official name of the Paris campground. It is also called Camp du T.C.F. for Touring Club of France which owns it. The camp is at the far western edge of the 2,500 acre Bois de Boulogne park. It is located next to the Seine River and near the eastern edge of the bridge, Pont de Suresnes. The camp is on street, Alle du Bord de L'Eau, across from Jeu de Polo. It is not shown on the tourist office map as that shows only the eastern part of the park. It is indicated as "Camp du T.C.F." on the map of Bois de Boulogne in the Michelin green guide for Paris. In metro stations, the map on the wall, Paris et Peripherie, shows it as *Camping du Touring Club de France*.

The camp is open all year and is very crowded in summer but people arriving on foot are never turned away. Fees are adult/13F and tent/13F, but figure in the cost of taking the private camp bus for 12.50F as public buses to camp do not run very late.

Take the metro, direction Pont de Neuilly, to Porte Maillot. From inside Porte Maillot station, take exit Boulevard Andre Maurois. If you did this, you will find the taxi and bus stop visible on your left. You should be on the overpass above the freeway. If you turn around, way across the highway is the modern Palais de Congres. If you emerge from the metro and haven't taken the correct exit, look for an underground passage and take it. One passage brings you to the edge of the Bois de Boulogne where a large silver modern sculpture of pipe and bullet shapes is visible. Continue underground past it and you will reach the bus stop. The white TCF camping bus is full size with CAMPING in big letters written in green. It stops in front of the taxi stand 20 meters from the covered bus shelter for bus 244. The fare for the TCF bus is 12.50F. The fare for bus 244 is 2 tickets if you haven't an Orange Card or other pass. Note the directions for reaching the camp on the wall of the bus shelter. Get off at the stop, Route des Moulins. The stop is still in zone 2, but then the bus goes over the bridge and into zone 3. Bus 244 operates M-F 6:30am-8pm and SaSu 8:20am-7:30pm. Bus 244 departs Porte Maillot weekdays at 6:30am, 6:48, 7:05, 7:20, 7:33, 7:46, 7:58, 8:11, 8:24, 8:38, 8:53, 9:10, 9:30, 9:50, and then 10, 30 and 50 minutes past the hour until 3:50pm, and 4:06pm, 4:20, 4:33, 4:46, 4:58, 5:11, 5:24, 5:37, 5:51, 6:06, 6:19, 6:33, 6:49, 7:07, 7:25, 7:45 and 8pm.

You can also take bus 244N from outside Port Auteil metro station. Bus 244N operates M-F 7am-7:55pm and SaSu 8;20am-7:30pm.

Bus 144A/B runs later than bus 244 and can be taken from metro station, Pont de Neuilly. The exits from Ponte de Neuilly station are clearly marked with bus numbers. Once outside, a 20-meter wide "island" lined with covered bus stops will be visible. Bus 144A/B is the last one. Though these buses are listed as operating M-Sa 5:30am-12:33am and Su 6:05am-12:33am, in actual fact the last departure is 9:05pm and a note to this effect is posted by the schedule. This bus is in zone 3 and you get off near Pont de Suresnes, but on the other side of the river from the campground. To reach camp, walk across the bridge and then along Allee du Bord de l'Eau. The walk is farther with bus 144A or 144B than it is for bus 244.

Facilities. The 9-acre camp is wall to wall tents in summer and the facilities are average. On the grounds are a small grocery-variety store, snack bar serving soft drinks and hot plates (fries and chicken for example), automatic washing machine and dryer, pay telephone and an office which sells stamps, changes travelers checks and has a large map of Paris posted outside. The restrooms have sinks with cold water only.

CAMPING AIROTEL INTERNATIONAL. This 4-star camp has much better facilities than Versailles or Boulogne. It's in the town of Maisons-Laffitte on rue Johnson on an island, I'lle de la Commune, in the Seine River outside Paris. Open all year, adult/19F, tent/11F.

Take a commuter train (banlieue) from Gare St. Lazare in Paris to Maisons-Laffitte Station, a 21-minute ride. Then a 10-minute walk. Eurailpass is valid on banlieue train routes. Those buying an orange card should purchase it for four zones. At Gare St. Lazare, find the clearly marked banlieue section of the train station. Take a train marked Banlieue Maisons Laffitte or Banlieue 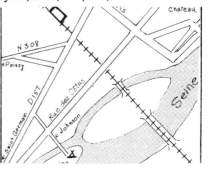 Poissy, which usually leave from tracks 7 and 8. Trains leave from 5:38am to 1:18am. During rush hours service is every 10 minutes. Bus 262 from Puteaux, outside Station La Defense on RER Line A, also goes to Maisons-Laffitte. Get off at the terminus, and then a 10-minute walk.

Facilities include free hot showers, hot water in sinks, hot water in laundry sinks, automatic washing machine, store and restaurant. This is the highest rated camp in the greater Paris area.

CAMPING PARIS SUD The campground is next to the youth hostel at 125, Avenue de Vileneuve St. Georges in the suburb of Choisy-le-

Roi, 14 km. south of Paris. The camp is in zone 3. Open Feb 15-Nov 15, adult/12F and tent/12F. Take RER line C (direction Jourdan or St. Martin D'Etampes) to Choisy-le-Roi. Outside the station, cross the Seine River, turn right and walk 30 minutes. Restrooms have water in the sinks, toilets are modern, plus 3 automatic washers, dryer, cafe and lounge with television. Lunch (12:30-1:30) and dinner (6:30-8:30) are served.

CAMPING DU PARC ETANG is 30 km. from Paris, farther than the other campgrounds. It's being included because it's part of a large recreation area. Apr 1-Sep 30, adult/13.50F, tent/15.50F, registration fee/10F, camping carnet required. The camp is in zone 5.

You can reach station St. Quentin-en-Yvelines either by taking the banlieue (commuter train, free with Eurailpass) from Gare Montparnasse or RER line C. For the latter, see directions under Camping Versailles. This is the same RER line, but you must take any train beginning with the letter S. The ride is 35 minutes and trains leave every 30 minutes, on both the RER and banlieue. From St. Quentin-en-Yvelines station, walk 10 minutes.

Camping du Parc Etang

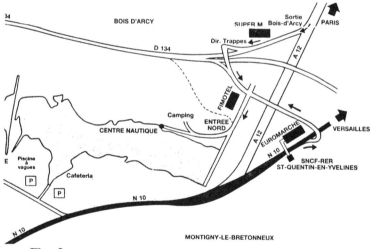

The 3-star camp has hot water in the sinks, free hot showers, automatic washer, store, snack bar, exchange and guided tours of Paris. The camp is on a small lake, part of a recreation area of sailing, fishing, golf, swimming pool with artificial waves, restaurant and children's playground.

CAMPING PARIS EST-LE TREMBLAY (pronounced trahng-bler) is operated by the Touring Club of France and is open all year. Located in the affluent suburb of Joinville-le-Pont (pronounced shown-veel-lah-pahnt), the camp takes longer to reach than the other campgrounds without any reward of better restrooms. The camp is in zone 3. Fees are adult/12F and tent/6.50F.

Take RER line A, direction Boissy St. Leger, to Joinville Le Pont Station. (Nation is a major metro-RER interchange point for RER line A.) Only take a train in the direction of Boissy St. Leger, not Marne-La-Vallee. From Joinville Station, take bus 108N to camp or walk there in about 20 minutes. To walk, from outside the station at the intersection of Avenue

Jean Jaures and N4, note the camping sign marked TCF and follow it. You should be walking straight ahead to the bridge. After crossing the bridge, take the steps down to the river's edge and walk beside the river with the river to your left. Large, beautiful homes, modern apartments and an athletic club line the opposite shore. In about 10 blocks, two discos are passed and the camp is just beyond them.

The site is grassy and partly shaded. The new freeway passes on a ridge behind the campground. The restrooms have individual sink cubicles, but with cold water only. Drying lines and sinks outside the building are provided for laundry. The store stocks lettuce, tomatoes, yoghurt, cheese, butter, ham, weiners, fruit such as oranges and apples, croissants, brioches, dessert tarts and bread. The snack bar sells hot dogs, croque monsieur (grilled cheese sandwich), fries, rotisseried chicken, coffee and orange juice. Next door are miniature golf and boats for rent.

SIGHTSEEING We recommend buying the Michelin green guide to Paris, English edition, for detailed information on the sights of Paris. The Louvre and the Chateau de Versailles are packed in July and August.

To avoid the lines, get to **Versailles** before the castle opens. Take RER line C and ride to the end station, Versailles R.G. (See detailed instructions under Camping Versailles, because the stop is the one after the stop for the campground.) Outside Versailles R.G., turn right and walk to the intersecting main street, Av. de Paris, and then turn left. The Chateau is straight ahead, about a 7-minute walk total. At the Chateau, you have your choice as to which line to enter. The longest line is the one for entrance into the Chateau that doesn't include a guided tour. This line forms on the right hand side of the Chateau as you face it. The smart thing to do is to get in the line on the left side of the courtyard and wait for a guided tour. There may not be a line, because most people see the first line and assume that's the only way in, but cross the courtyard and look for the ticket window. For 20F, you don't have to wait so long and get to see the more spectacular parts of the castle accompanied by a charming and delightful Frenchwoman. The tour was the best one we'd had in Europe.

PRONUNCIATION OF SIGHTS

L'Arc de Triomphe	lark duh tree-awnf
La Palais de Chaillot	luh paleh duh shah-yoh
La Conciergerie	la Kawn-see-ehr-zhree
L'Hotel des Invalides	loh-tel day zen-vah-leed
Ile de la Cite	eel duh la see-TAY
La Louvre	luh loov-ruh
Montparnasse	MAWN pahr nass
Montmarte	mawn-MAR-truh
L'Opera	loh-pay-rah
Le Pantheon	luh pahn-tay-awn
Les Quais	lay kay
Le Palais de Luxembourg	luh pa-leh dew lewk-sahn-boor
La Sainte Chapelle	la sent shah-pehl
La Tour Eiffel	la toor ay-fehl
Les Tuileries	lay twee-luh-ree

FREE LIBRARY Want someplace to sit, relax and read the *Tribune*, *U.S.A. Today* and other European papers for free? Go to the Centre

Pompidou (metro Hotel de Ville, Rambuteau or Chatelet) and turn left after the entrance. A large, comfortable, free library, open M-F noon-10pm and SaSun 10am-10pm (closed Tuesday) awaits you.

CHEAP TRANSPORT TO LONDON   At the Organisation pour le Tourisme Universitaire (OTU), 137, Blvd. Saint-Michel, (metro Port Royal) these are the least expensive rates for air, rail or bus travel from Paris to London in 1989. For flights, make the reservation a few days ahead of the date to assure space, though often seats are available at the last minute. Non-students can also use their services.

All year round you can get a flight from Paris to London (Gatwick Airport) on Friday evening on a comfortable Boeing 737 with 148 seats for 290F. There is no age limit. During summer, there will be additional flights on other days. The flights depart from a small airfield at the town of Beauvais; the bus ride to the airport is included in the price. In Paris, passengers meet outside Gare Routiere Internationale, 5 Av. Porte de la Villette, to board the bus to Beauvais. Take the metro (direction La Courneuve) to Porte de la Villette, and follow the signs from the station to Gare routiere internationale, located outside the metro station. (There is no provision for luggage checking at this bus station.) For our flight, the bus left at 6pm and we checked in at the airport at 9pm. Then we walked outside onto the air strip and climbed the steps into the Boeing 737. The actual flight was about 25 minutes, but we arrived at Gatwick Airport in London at 8:45pm because London time is one hour earlier. (By the time we retrieved our packs, took the train into London, and the bus out to Hackney Camaping, it was 11pm when we registered and set up the tent. I would do the same thing again, because it enabled us to sightsee all day in Paris and then spend the evening sitting down enroute to London. The morning of our flight, we checked our packs at Gare d'Est which is on the metro line to the bus station at Port de la Villette.)

Students under 26 can buy a **BIGE** train ticket to London for 268F one way. Open to anyone, the cheapest way to London is via **EuroLines bus** for 235F. There are three departures daily at 9am (ar. 5pm), 12:30pm (ar. 8pm) and 10pm (ar. 7:30am). A reservation should be made at the OTU travel office or a EuroLine office, such as the one at the bus terminal. All departures are from the bus terminal, Gare Routiere Internationale, 3-5 av. de la Porte de la Villette. Take the metro to Porte de la Villette and the bus station is across from it. (There is no luggage checking at the bus station.) Arrival in London is at Bay 20, Victoria Coach Station. This arrival point saves the fare and the time between airport and town. EuroLines is part of National Express Coaches, based in London. If you plan to ride this line in Britain which is a cheaper way to tour than by rail, consider buying their BritExpress card for 50F. The card gives a 30 percent discount from the published prices on all their lines in Britain for one month. It may also be purchased in Britain.

To Amsterdam, leave Nord Station at 7:48am (ar. 2:02pm), 10:24am (ar. 4:34pm), 2:38pm (ar. 9:01pm), 4:44pm (ar. 10:32pm) and 11:15pm (ar. 8:01am).
To Antibes and the Riviera, trains leave Lyon Station at 7:40am TGV (change at Marseille, ar. 13:37pm), 9:37am (ar. 8:04pm), 10:23am TGV (change at Marseille, ar. 5:48pm), 11:42am TGV (change at Marseille, ar. 6:46pm), 3:40pm TGV (change at Marseille, ar. 10:50pm) and 8:45pm (ar. 8:20am).
To Avignon, a TGV departs Lyon Station every hour. The trip is 4 hours.

154

To Brussels Midi Station, leave Nord Station at 7:10am EuroCity (ar. 9:37am), 7:48am (ar. 10:48am), 10:24am (ar. 1:16pm), 1:30pm EuroCity (ar. 4:20pm), 2:38pm (ar. 5:36pm) and 4:44pm (ar. 7:31pm).

To Carcassonne, leave Austerlitz Station at 9:39am (ar. 6:12pm) and 10:21am (ar. 6:12pm). The latter train is makes fewer stops.

To Chamonix, leave Lyon Station at 7:24am TGV (ar. 1:36pm) and 1:01pm TGV (ar. 7:24pm). Change trains at Annecy. At St. Gervais-le-Fayet you must change to the cogwheel train.

To Cherbourg to connect with Irish Continental Lines ferry to Ireland, leave St. Lazare Station at 3pm Turbotrain (ar. 6:14pm, except on Saturday ar. 6:53pm). On Saturday outside of July 4 to August 29 you must change at Caen.

To Geneva, a TGV leaves at 7:35am (ar. 11:08am), 10:36am (ar. 2:05pm), 2:32pm (ar. 6:16pm), 5:42pm (ar. 9:13pm) and 7:13pm (ar. 10:46pm).

To Le Havre to connect with Irish Continental Lines ferry to Ireland, leave St. Lazare Station at 12:35pm M-Sa (ar. 2:34pm) and 1:45pm SaSu (ar. 4:03pm).

To Les Eyzies, leave Austerlitz Station at 9:39am (change at Limoges, ar. 3:21pm) and at 1:33pm (change at Limoges, ar. 7:42pm).

To London (Victoria Station), trains leave from Nord Station. The three basic crossings are Calais to Dover, Boulogne to Dover and Boulogne to Folkstone. Calais to Dover is the shortest crossing. The crossing can be made on a regular ship or a faster and more expensive hydrofoil. Trains leave at 8:05am (Calais to Dover, ar. 2:23pm), 9:20am (Boulogne to Dover via hydrofoil, ar. 1:53pm), 10:45am (Boulogne to to Folkestone, ar. 5:23pm), 11:25am (Boulogne to Dover via hydrofoil, ar. 3:53pm), 12:22pm (Boulogne to Folkestone, ar. 6:23pm) and 1:15pm (Boulogne to Dover via hydrofoil, ar. 5:53pm).

To the Loire Valley, trains leave Austerlitz Station for Blois at 7:05am (ar. 8:49am), 9:20am (ar. 10:53am) and noon (ar. 1:32pm) plus other departures. From Blois, trains connect with locals that stop at smaller villages.

To Lucerne, leave Est Station at 9:03am (change at Basel, ar. 4:04pm), 1:02pm (change at Basel, ar. 8:04pm), 10:40pm (change at Basel, ar. 7:12am).

To Madrid (Chamartin Station), trains leave from Austerlitz Station. Trains depart at 6:51am M-Sa only (change to Talgo at Irun at 1:49pm, ar. 9:38pm), 2:21pm (change at Irun at 10:45pm, ar. 8:57am), 5:45pm Puerta del Sol-reservation required-Rapide (no change at the border, ar. 9:55am), 8pm Talgo-no seats or couchettes, must pay for sleeper (no change at border, ar. 8:55am) and 10:15pm (change at Irun at 7:26am, ar. 5:33pm).

To Mont St. Michel, the fastest way is to take the train from Montparnasse Station to Rennes and change there for Pontorson, the closest railhead to Mont St. Michel. If you're staying at Versailles, you don't need to go into Paris but can take a train from Versailles Station. Not every train to Rennes stops in Versailles, but it's possible to take a train from Versailles to Le Mans and connect there for Rennes. The distance is less but it takes longer to go via Folligny. On this route, you would leave Montparnasse Station on a train to Granville but change at Folligny to a train to Pontorson (direction Rennes). The best departure is the 11:37am train to Rennes (ar. 3pm). This same train stops in Versailles at 11:54am. Then it leaves Rennes at 4:17pm and arrives in Pontorson at 5:10pm. A later departure leaves Montparnasse Station at 2:37pm (ar. 5:54pm). This train does not stop in Versailles. Then leave Rennes at 6:20pm except Saturday (ar. Pontorson 7:12pm). On some days, these trains carry coaches for St. Malo. In that case, don't get off in Rennes but in Dol and change there for Pontorson.

To Munich, leave Est Station at 7:52am (ar. 4:35pm), 1:24pm (ar. 11:10pm) and 11:15pm (ar. 9:32am).

To Nantes, leave Montparnasse Station at 1:49pm (ar. 5:10pm), 5:27pm EuroCity (ar. 8:27pm) and 7:24pm (ar. 10:48pm).

To Rome, leave Lyon Station at 7:24am TGV (change at Aix-les-Bains, change at Torino, ar. 10:52pm) and 8:56pm (ar. 1:35pm).

To Strasbourg, leave Est Station at 7:52am EuroCity (ar. 11:42am), 8:30am (ar. 1:38pm), 1:24pm (ar. 5:56pm), 4:32pm (ar. 9:04pm) and 6:45pm EuroCity (ar. 10:36pm).

To Venice, leave Lyon Station at 7:14am TGV (change at Lausanne to EuroCity, change at Milan to Rapido, ar. 5:50pm), and 6:50pm (ar. Venice Mestre only 6:55am).

NORMANDY

The ferries included in Eurailpasses leave for Ireland from Le Havre and Cherbourg. The most famous sights are Mont St. Michel and Bayeux.

LE HAVRE (luh AHV-ruh)   Irish Continental Lines ferries to Ireland, included in Eurailpasses, depart from Le Havre. A small port tax is charged at the port, route de Mole Central. A bus marked "Irish Ferries" meets incoming trains that connect with ferry departures and goes directly to the ferry terminal (10F). City bus 4 leaves from the station but after getting off the bus you must still walk 15 minutes to the ferry terminal. Bus 4 also leaves from Hotel de Ville where the tourist office is, 11 blocks west of the station. Turn left from the train station and walk on Blvd. de Strasbourg to place de l'Hotel de Ville. The market is on Rue Voltaire, 3 blocks south of Place de l'Hotel de Ville.

     Irish Continental ferries leave for Rosslare at 6pm Jun 25-Aug 30 on M, W and Sa, and Aug 31-Sep 16 on Th and Su. Arrival in Rosslare is 2pm the next day. To Cork, ferries leave at 6pm from June 25 to August 30 on Thursday. Arrival in Cork is 2:30pm the next day. The ferry leaves for Rosslare only, during the rest of the year on Tuesday and Thursday at 5pm.

     The **municipal campground**, Foret de Montgeon, is an excellent camp within the Montgeon Forest and Park, 4 km. from the main station (Central). Take bus 5 from in front of the station and get off at Cimetiere du Nord. Then it's a 1300-meter walk through the park. Open Apr 12-Sep 30; adult/10F, tent/7F. Store, hot water in sinks, free hot showers and day room.

     The ferry arrives at 3pm (Rosslare) or 3:30pm (Cork). Trains to Paris St. Lazare leave 5:07pm Su all year, M-Th & Su Jun 6-Aug 30 (ar.7:10pm), 5:07pm Sa (ar. 7:27pm) and 5:09pm (ar. 7:10pm).

MONT ST. MICHEL (maun sen mee-SHELL)   To get here, take the train to Rennes from Paris Montparnasse and change at Rennes for Pontorson, the closest rail head. Then take a bus the remaining 9 km.. There are a few through trains from Paris to St. Malo, in which case get off in Dol and change for Pontorson. From the station in Pontorson, STN buses leave about 6 times a day until 6pm for the Mont. The fare is 18F round trip. Upon arrival, simply follow everyone else to the Abbey. English-language tours start at 10:30am, noon, 2:30pm and 4:30pm; entrance fee is 23F, 18-25 years 13F, Sunday half price but the saving does not justify the crowds.

     You can camp at the inexpensive campground in Pontorson, 800 meters from the station, or outside the causeway at Mont St. Michel. In Pontorson, **Camping Pont d'Orson**, on rue de la Victoire, is a 10-minute walk from the station (adult/5F, tent/3F). The municipal camp is a pleasant wooded site on the bank of the Couesnon River. **Camping du Mont Saint Michel** is 1.8 km. south of the Mont on the Pontorson-Avranches fork in the road at the Motel Vert. Apr 15-Oct 30; adult/12F, tent/10F; restroom sinks with hot water, exchange, automatic washing machine, store, restaurant and day room. The illuminated Mont can be seen from camp.

BAYEUX   Home of the famous Bayeux tapestry and an interesting town in its own right, mainline trains between Paris St. Lazare and Cherbourg stop here. The ancient houses and narrow streets of Vieux Bayeux (old Bayeux) are officially protected. The train station is south of the old town and the campground north of it.

156

Pontorson
(use for Mont St. Michel)

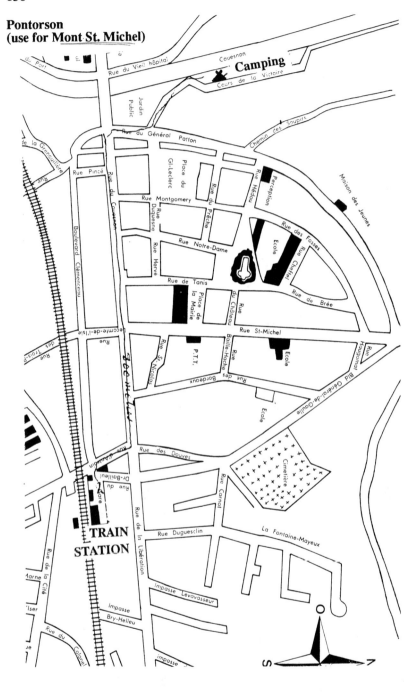

Rue du Port

Rue du Vieil hôpital

Couesnon

Camping

Cours de la Victoire

Jardin Public

de la Grandvillière

Chemin des Soupirs

Rue du Général Patton

Rue Pinçé

Rue du Couesnon

Place du Gl.-Leclerc

Rue Hédou

Perception

Maison des Jeunes

Rue Montgomery

Rue du Prêche

Boulevard Clémenceau

Rue Duquesne

Rue des Fossés

Ecole

Rue Chélhel

Rue Notre-Dame

Rue Hervé

Rue de Tanis

Rue de Brée

Place de la Mairie

du Château

Rue Lecomte-de-l'Isle

Rue Troisp

Rue St-Michel

Rue St-Nicolas

P.T.T.

Baille-Hoche

Rue des Bordeaux

Rue

Ecole

Bld Général-de-Gaulle

Rue Hauguinat

Rue

Ecole

Rue des Douves

Rue du Dr-Bailleul

Rue Carnot

Cimetière

Rue de la Gare

TRAIN STATION

Rue Duguesclin

Rue de la Libération

La Fontaine-Mayeux

Rue de la Cité

Impasse Levavasseur

Marne

Iser

Impasse Bry-Hellieu

Rue du Colonel

impasse

S

O

N

E

Bayeux

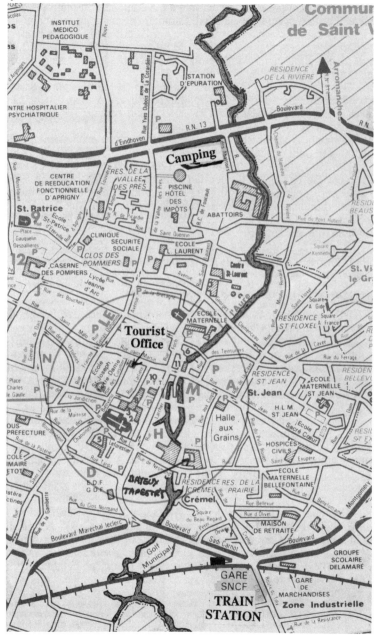

Municipal Camping, Blvd. d'Eindhoven, is 1500 meters from the train station. There are no buses but it's a pleasant walk through the center of town. The scenic route is via Blvd. Carnot, continuing on the main street as it leads to the old town. Stop off at the tourist office (#7 on the map) and then head for the campground. Open Mar-Oct; adult/10.50F, tent/12.90F. This is a very good camp with free hot showers, shade trees and the town swimming pool nearby.

The **Tapestry** is in Centre Guillaume le Conquerant, Rue de Nesmond, open May 13-Sep 17: 9-7; Mar 16-May 12 & Sep 18-Oct 15: 9-12:30 & 2-6:30; Oct 16-Mar 15: 9:30-12:30 & 2-6. Adult/20F, student/10f. The Cathedral is open Jul-Aug 9-7, otherwise 8-12 & 2-7. In July and August, an audio-visual historical presentation is given each evening. The Cathedral is floodlit on summer evenings.

The **1944 Battle of Normandy Memorial Museum**, Blvd. Fabian Ware, traces the 76 days of the conflict following the D Day landing. There are authentic documents, 100 life size models displaying uniforms, equipment, dioramas and a video presentation. Open Jun-Aug 9-7; Mar 16-May 31 & Sep 1-Oct 15: 9:30-12:30 & 2-6:30; Oct 16-Mar 15: 10-12:30 & 2-6. Adult/16 F, student/9F.

To Cherbourg, leave at 7:46am, 9:22pm, 11:13am, 3:17pm and 5:14pm not Saturday. The last departure arrives in Cherbourg at 6:14pm, time enough to transfer to the Irish Continental Lines ferry which leaves at 9pm two days a week.

To Paris St. Lazare, leave at 8:15am, 8:35am, 3:16 (Jun 27-Sep 6), 4:57pm, 5:57pm M-Sa and 7:16pm. The trip is two hours 10 minutes.

CHERBOURG (shehr-BOOR) Irish Continental Lines ferry, free with Eurailpasses, sails from Cherbourg on Tuesday and Sunday at 9pm between June 25 and August 30, and on Tuesday and Saturday from Aug 31 to September 16. Arrival in Rosslare, Ireland, is at 2pm the next day. (Ferries arrive in Cherbourg from Rosslare at 11am.) The Saturday sailing continues for the rest of the year, but leaves 1 hour earlier starting about the third week in September. A small port tax is payable in French Francs at the ferry line office.

There's no bus transportation between the ferry and train station but it's only a 10-minute walk. The ferry leaves from Quai de France near Gare Car-Ferry. From the station, turn right to Av. Millet, cross it and walk on Avenue Carnot, which is shortly renamed Avenue A. Briand, straight ahead to the docks. From the ferry to the train station, walk on Av. A. Briand which becomes Av. Carnot, turn right on Av. Millet and the train station is across the street.

The main **tourist office** 2 Quai Alexandre II at the north end of the canal, Bassin du Commerce, on the downtown side (the west). A branch is open in summer at Gare Maritime by the docks. The market is 4 blocks from the main tourist office. The closest **campground** is La Saline at Equeurdreville-Hainneville, located on a street jutting perpendicularly off D901 to the west of town. Open all year. Take bus 1 from the station or it's a 45-minute walk.

To Bayeux and Paris, take the 1:58pm train which arrives in Paris at 5:10pm.

To Mont St. Michel, take the 1:58pm train (direction Caen or Paris) and get off at 2:55pm at Lison. Leave Lison (direction Rennes) at 2:59pm and get off at Pontorson at 4:34pm, then a bus to the Mont for the final 9 km.. Other departures from Lison for Pontorson are 5:33pm (Friday only) and 7:27pm (ar. 9:12pm).

Cherbourg

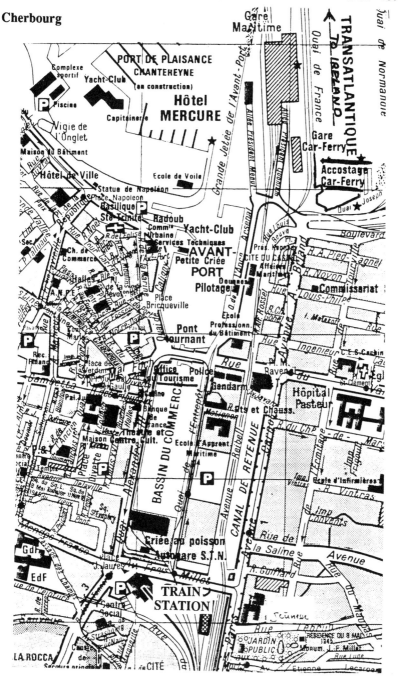

Quai de Normandie

Gare Maritime

TRANSATLANTIQUE To Ireland

Quai de France

Gare Car-Ferry

Accostage Car-Ferry

Quai Joseph

PORT DE PLAISANCE CHANTEREYNE (en construction)

Complexe sportif

Yacht-Club

Hôtel MERCURE

P Piscine

Capitainerie

Vigie de l'Onglet

Maison du Bâtiment

Hôtel de Ville

Ecole de Voile

Statue de Napoléon
Place Napoleon

Basilique
Ste-Trinité

Radoub
Comité Urbaine
Services Techniques

Yacht-Club

AVANT-PORT
Petite Criée

Grande Jetée de l'Avant-Port

Allée Président Menu

Rue Louis Beuve

Pres. Heredia

CITÉ DU CABLE
Affaires Maritimes

Boulevard

R.A. Pieg-agne

H. Novon

Commissariat

I. Metairie

Ch. de Commerce

R.de l'Église

Douanes
Pilotage

Place Bricqueville

Ecole Professionn. du Bâtiment

J. Matatere

Halles Bler

A.N.P.E.

Pont Tournant

Rue Ingénieur C.E.S. Carbin

P. M. Ravenel

Rec. Finland

Place de Verdun

Office du Tourisme

Police

Gendarm.

Hôpital Pasteur

St-Clement

Egl

Rue

Pal. Just.

Banque de France

Théâtre et Centre Cult.

Ecole d'Apprent. Maritime

Pts et Chauss.

R. du Chp

Maison

Rue de la Marianne

Rue de Retenue

BASSIN DU COMMERCE

P

L'Entrepôt

Avenue de Paris

CANAL DE RETENUE

Ecole d'Infirmières

R. Vintras

Imp Convents

Criée au poisson
Autogare S.T.N.

Gdr

EdF

Rue de la Saline

Avenue

R. Guiffard

P

TRAIN STATION

J. Jaures

Rue Millet

Jeunesse

JARDIN PUBLIC

RÉSIDENCE DU 8 MAI 1945

Museum J.F. Millet

Rue Lune

LA ROCCA

de CITÉ

Etienne

Lecaroc

BRITTANY (BRETAGNE)

Bretagne (bruh-TAN-yuh) in French, Brittany is the western peninsula that intrudes into the Atlantic.

QUIMPER   Replete with a fine old quarter with cobblestoned streets, Quimper lies at the end of the rail line from Nantes. In 1989, the tourist office is temporarily on the first floor of the covered market on rue St. Francois. The market *(Les Halles)* is open M-Sa 9-12 & 2-7, Su 9-noon. The open market (W, Sa all day) is by the Cathedral which you pass when walking to the municipal campground. A free tour is given by the porcelain studio, Faienceries Keraluc, outside of town from M-F 9-12 & 2-6. Take bus 4 (direction Bourdonnel) from the stop for Camping de Lanniron. A tour is given (10F) through Les Faienceries de Quimper Henriot, located opposite Notre-Dame. Hours: M-F 9:30-11:30 & 1:30-5:30, on F to 4pm.
   The closest and least expensive campground is the good **Camping Municipal**. Adult/3.50F, tent/2F. Either walk 20-30 minutes from the station or take bus 1 (direction Penhars) to Chaptal stop. Slightly farther from the station is the more expensive **Camping Orangerie de Lanniron**, open May-Sep 15. Take bus 4 (direction Bourdonnel) leaving from Rue du Parc and the bus stop on the side of the Bank B.N.P. about 5 blocks from the station. Get off at Creach Gwen stop.

NANTES (nahnt)   Nantes is the largest town in the area and an important rail junction. The area is easily reached from the Loire Valley (Tours or Saumur) and Paris. The main station is Gare d'Orleans. The market operates Tu-Su 9-1 in place du Bouffay, where you take the bus to the campground.
   Camping du Petit Port is on bus route 25, 51, 53 and 86. From the station go to Boulevard Stalingrad and walk west. In the next block, it is renamed Cours J. Kennedy. Walk beyond the intersection of Rue de Strasbourg to the Bouffay bus stop and take bus 53 (direction Fresche Blanc). Or take tram 1 (direction Bellevue) from the station to Bouffay stop and change to bus 53. Bouffay is the second stop after leaving the station. (The tourist office is the third stop after leaving the station.) Open all year; adult/7.30F, tent/11F. The camp has all facilities and shares a large park with the Petit-Port Sports complex which has a swimming pool, skating rink, bowling alley and restaurant.

   To Cherbourg, take the train to Paris but change at LeMans, or take the train to Rennes and then change to a minor rail line for Cherbourg.
   To La Baule, leave at 7:51am (M-Sa), 9:25am, 10:16am, 11:04am, 12:35pm, 3:17pm, 4:45pm (M-F), 5:20pm, 6:29pm (M-Sa), 7:45pm, 8:30pm, 9:36pm and 10:03pm. The trip is 1 hour and 15 minutes.
   To Paris Montparnasse, leave at 8:26am, 10:24am, 12:18pm, 2pm, 4:18pm, 5:28pm, 6:49pm (Sunday only), 6:58pm, 7:04pm, 7:29pm and 8:08pm. Three hours.

LA BAULE   The area is called La Cote D'Amour. La Baule is a well established resort town whose beautiful sand beach on a small bay maintains its above average price structure. La Baule's frequent rail connections with Nantes make the resort easy to reach. Station Escoublac is the main rail station, but Station Les Pins is closer to Camping Municipal. Both stations have a tourist office within 200 meters. The market operates mornings at Av. Marche and Av. des Petrels.

Quimper

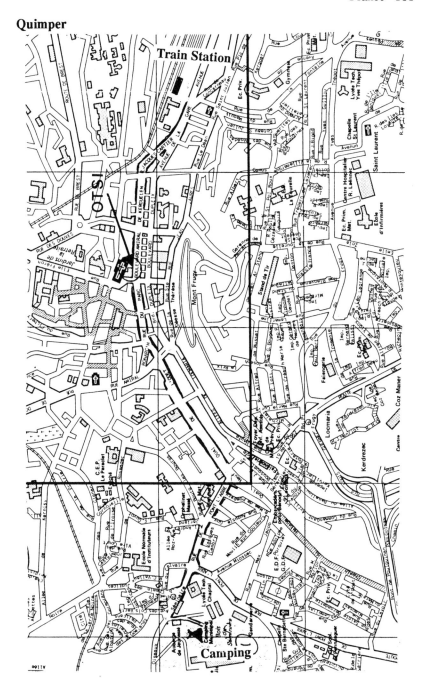

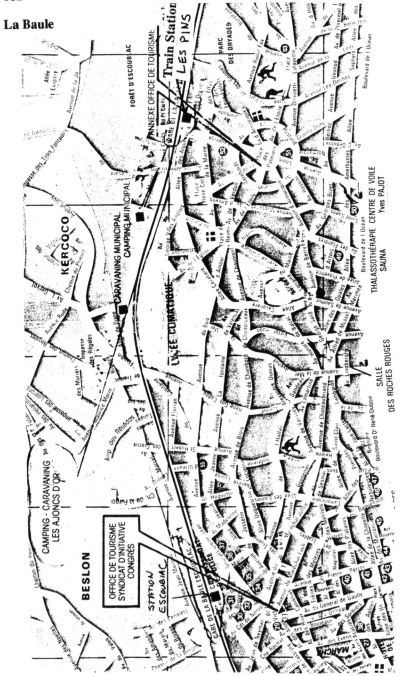

Camping Municipal is part of the forest of Escoublac, 900 meters from the beach and 200 meters from Gare Les Pins and the tourist office. The entrance to the segregated tent area is on Av. Paul Minot. Open Mar 24-Sep 30; tent site including 2 people is 35F, and extra person is 11F (a bargain in this resort). The very good campground is in a rustic, wooded area and the sites are not marked off. The restroom sinks have hot water. Go downtown for food. Another campground, Les Ajoncs D'Or, on ch. du Rocher in Beslon is 3 km. from either train station, and no bus.

The picturesque port of Le Croisic is 13 minutes by train from Les Baules. Trains leave Gare Escoublac at 6:35am, 9:07am, 10:19am, 11:13am, 12:01pm, 1:31pm, 4:12pm, 5:55pm, 6:19pm, 7:44pm, 8:43pm, 9:25pm, 9:29pm, 11:01pm, 10:32pm and 11:49pm. The last train from Le Croisic to La Baule is at 10:48pm. In Le Croisic, the tourist office is near the station.

To Nantes, leave Gare Escoubiac at 7:09am, 9:10am, 10:58am, 12:42pm, 1:34pm (Jun 27-Sep 5 M-Sa), 3:16pm, 3:34pm, 4:15pm (M-F), 5:37pm, 6:55pm, 7:28pm, 9:39pm and 11:04pm.

BASQUE REGION

The French portion of the Basque culture lays next to the border with Spain. Most international express trains stop at Hendaye on the Atlantic Coast on the French side of the Spanish-French border, where passengers must get off and change trains due to the variance in track width between the two countries. This makes it easy to get to Hendaye, a pleasant resort with a fine beach. The resort is less popular than it might be because of its distant location, but if you're passing by anyway and merely want a day of rest, it's a good place to come.

HENDAYE   The fine sand beach of Hendaye-Plage extends 3 km. and is safe with a gentle slope. Restaurants are cheaper in Hendaye than Hendaye-Plage. At Hendaye you must change to the shuttle train that leaves several times daily for Hendaye-Plage Station near the campgrounds and beach. There is also a bus that stops 100 meters from the camps or you can walk.

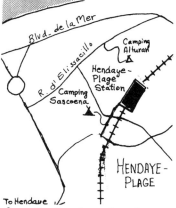

Camping Sascoenea, rue des Lilas, is a 10-minute walk from the beach station. The camp is on a slope overlooking the ocean. Open Easter-Sep 30; adult/12F, tent/5F. The campground is very attractive and has tent sites on terraces. Free hot showers, lounge with television and ping pong, store and restaurant. The beach is a 15-minute walk.

Camping Alturan, though farther from the beach station, is even more attractively situated being only 100 meters from the beach. Open Jun1-Sep 30; adult/9.40F, tent/8F.   Terraced sites, store, restaurant, automatic washer.

ALSACE-LORRAINE

In an area of France long dominated by Germany, the towns show an unmistakable Germanic flavor. Tucked away in Alsace-Lorraine are a string of picturesque wine villages and a remarkably attractive main city, Strasbourg. You can choose between basing yourself in Strasbourg, the main junction for international trains, and visiting the villages on day trips, or staying at a village campground. Though Mulhouse to the south of the villages does not compare with Stasbourg, staying there has the advantage of being within 30 minutes of both Basle, Switzerland, and Alsace-Lorraine.

STRASBOURG The capital of Alsace, Strasbourg (strahz-bour) retains its picturesque atmosphere in the old city, despite being a modern day small metropolis. Gare Centrale SNCF is at the western edge of the old city, across the bridge, Pont Cuss. Exchange in the station is open 9am-8pm. A branch of the tourist office is across from the train station. A bus ticket is 6F, or 5 tickets for 21F at tobacconists, valid one hour.

 Camping Montagne-Verte is in town at 2 rue Robert Forrer. Open Mar 1-Sep 30; adult/8.20F, tent/8.20F. From the station, walk to the bus stop, Ancien Abattoir, at quai Altorffer by walking through the Rue du Maire Kuss on the right, a 5-minute walk. Take bus 3, 13 or 23 (direction Lingolsheim) and get off at bus stop Nid de Cigogne. Then the campground is a 5-minute walk to rue R. Forrer. The last bus leaves at 11:15pm. It's also possible to walk from the station. The 4-star camp has free hot showers, hot water in sinks, automatic washer and store.

 To Colmar and Mulhouse leave at 6:27am, 7:43am M-Sa, 8:04am, 8:30am, 9:58am, 10:59am, 11:40am Friday only, noon, 2:37pm Friday only, 3:37pm no Friday, 5:14pm, 5:48pm, 6:23pm, 7:40pm, 8:12pm, 8:42pm and 10:47pm. Most of these trains also stop at Selestat. In addition, local trains go to the smaller villages.

 To Amsterdam, leave at 9:49am (ar. 6:07pm) and 2:41pm EuroCity (change at Brussels Nord, ar. 10:32pm).

 To Basel and Mulhouse, leave at 8:23am M-Sa, 10:59am M-Sa, 12:11pm, 2:55pm (change at Mulhouse), 5:03pm EuroCity and 9:18pm. To Basel is 80 minutes.

 To Frankfurt, leave 9:10am (ar. 11:48am), 11:50am (change at Offenburg, ar. 2:15pm), 3:15pm (change at Karlsruhe, ar. 6:15pm) and 7:40pm (change at Offenburg, ar. 10:15pm).

 To Munich, leave at noon (ar. 4:35pm) and 6:07pm (ar. 11:20pm).

 To Paris Est, leave at 7:55am (ar. 11:59am), 10:23am (ar. 2:18pm), 12:45pm (ar. 4:58pm), 3:42pm (ar. 8:07pm), 5:10pm TEE not Saturday from May 31-Aug 5 (ar. 8:59pm), and 7:11pm (ar. 11:01pm).

WINE VILLAGES Numerous attractive villages are in the area between Strasboug and Mulhouse.

 Colmar, with its perfectly restored center, is easily reached by train in 30 minutes. Camping de I'lll is at Colmar-Horbourg, 300 meters from town near the beach at the right Ill river bank near the bridge to Neuf-Brisach. Most people walk, but bus 1 (direction Wihr) also goes there. Open Feb-Nov; adult/9F, tent/4F. A 3-star camp with store, restaurant, sinks with hot water. Trains to Strasbourg leave at 7:09am, 8:07am, 9:11am, 10:10am M-F, 10:59am, noon, 1:11pm M-F, 4:17pm, 4:28pm, 5:15pm, 5:25pm, 6:17pm M-F, 6:47pm, 7:52pm, 8:37pm, 9:52pm not Sa and 11:08pm not Sa.

 Molsheim is another good village. It's on a small rail line to Donon. The 2-star municipal campground is on Rue de Sports between the canal and La Bruche, an easy walk from the station. Open May 1-Sep 15; adult/5F, tent/2.50F, one of the cheapest camps in the area. A nice camp but few facilities: cold showers, swimming and a day room.

Obernai, with its completely preserved ramparts and towers from the Middle Ages, is one of the best places. Two-star Camping Municipal is 100 meters west of town at Route d'Ottrott on road N426. Open all year; adult/7F, tent/4F. Few facilities. In Obernai, the Park Hotel serves a well recommended but very expensive Sunday buffet.

Also picturesque are **Ribeauville** and **Riquewihr**, the latter being famous for its beauty and having wineries open to visitors. In Ribeauville, Camping Pierre de Coburbetin is a 4 star camp within the town. Open Apr-Oct; adult/11F, tent/5.50F. One km. from town is a very simple camp having few facilities. **Camping des Trois Chateaux** is open July and August only and charges a mere adult/4.30F and tent/2.20F. In Riquewihr, Camping Intercommunal is at the road to Mittelwihr, 1 km. from town. Open Apr-Oct; adult/11F, tent/5F. The train does not go to Riquewihr.

Rosheim, another picturesque village can also be reached by train but its closest campground is 8 km. from town. **Selestat**, the capital of old Alsace and noted for its flowers, has Camping Les Cigognes just outside town on R.N.83, 900 meter walk, May-Oct 15; adult/6F, tent/2.50F, 2-stars.

International trains stop at Strasbourg, Mulhouse and sometimes Colmar. Slower trains stop also at Selestat. Local trains stop at Molsheim, Obernai, Ribeauville and Rosheim.

MULHOUSE (pronounced either mool-HOW-zen in German or Moo-LOOZ in French) The town itself is modern and of little interest. You come here to visit its famous automobile museum, to use the campground to commute to Basel, Switzerland, or as a base for day trips to wonderful medieval wine villages such as Colmar. There is freqent train service between Mulhouse and Basel, a 30-minute ride, and to Colmar and Strasbourg. The train station has foreign exchange, daily 7:30-12 and 1-6:30.

The **tourist office** is one block from the station. Open M-F 9-7, Sa 9-6, Jul-Sep: M-Sa 9-8, Su 10-1. Leave the station and cross the canal in front. Find Avenue Mar.-Foch which is the street that goes north from the east (right) side of the landscaped area. The tourist office is at the end of the block on the left side of street at 9 avenue Foch. The market is Tu, Th and Sa at 3 locations: Du Canal Couvert, Place Drouot and Place de La Paix. The first location also has a flea market the second Saturday of each month.

Camping L'Ill, rue Pierre de Coubertin on the shore of L'Ill River, is open Easter-Sep 9; adult/11.85F, tent/11.85F. It's a very good camp within about a 20-minute walk from the station. Or take bus 7 from Pont d'Altkirch near the station to bus stop Banlieue and walk from there. Turn left as you exit the station and walk one block to Pont d'Altkirch (bridge). Don't cross the bridge but turn left to the bus stop. The last bus leaves at 8:15pm. The ride is 10 minutes. From the center of town at Porte Jeune Schuman, you can take bus 1 (direction Camus) to the bus stop, Patinoire, and walk from there. The last bus leaves at 8:10pm. Both buses leave 2 to 3 times each hour. To walk, turn left as you exit the station, cross over the canal and follow Quai d'Isly in the same direction (that is, away from the station). The canal will be on your left. After where the railroad tracks cross over, watch for rue Pierre de Coubertin on the right and take it. If you reach the stadium, you've come too far. The camp is between the river and the canal.

Rail Lines - Paris and the Loire Valley

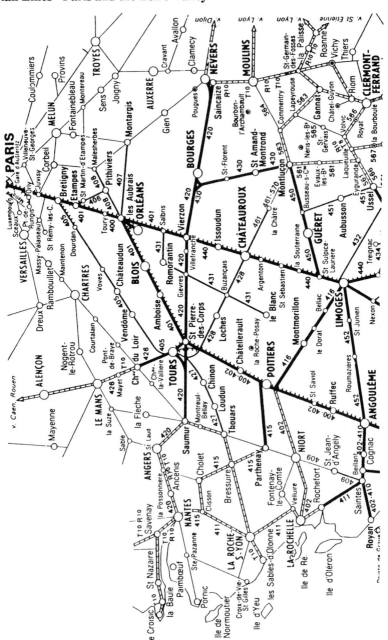

Musee Nationale de L'Automobile, 192 Avenue de Colmar, was opened in 1982 and shows at least 500 cars including a new Formula I Ferrari, the historical Dion Bouton, and the transparent body car Bugatti T16 Garros. The collection is considered one of the best in the world. Open 10-6pm, closed Tu except Jun 1-Sep 30; 37F, student and youth 6-18/14F.

Musee du Chemin de Fer (French Railways Museum) houses the biggest group of historical railway equipment in Europe. You can see the St. Pierre of 1844, the Saloon-Car used by Napoleon the Third's aides-de-camp in 1856. Apr 1-Sep 30, daily 9-6; Oct 1-Mar 31, 9-5. Adult/28F, student and youth 6-18/12F. Joint ticket with automobile museum, adult/48F.

CHATEAUX OF THE THE LOIRE

The Val de Loire (pronounced lwah), about a two hour train ride from Paris, stretches only 70 km. along the River Loire, but contains a density of over 100 castles, cathedrals and curiosities representing seven centuries from the Middle Ages to the 18th century. This area was the seat of power during the 15th and 16th centuries when the kings and queens of France and the lesser ruling nobility built their castles. You can see fortified strongholds, the undulating castle of Chenonceaux spanning the River Cher (often reproduced on posters) and the only existing example of a 16th century formal French garden. At night, castles all along the Loire are illuminated. The area is composed mostly of small towns, each having grown around a castle. This makes for delightful walking tours in the twisting, narrow alleys of the medieval towns. In large cities where remnants of the past are interwoven among the developments of the day, getting any sort of feeling for a past period is more difficult. Here the past comes alive in the lovely French countryside.

The food is great, this being the "garden" of France, and wines are pleasant. The river yields salmon, pike and carp which are sauced and served at reasonable prices. Most villages have a municipal campground that is 10 to 20 minutes on foot from the train station.

The Michelin green guide, *Chateaux of the Loire*, is an excellent resource for historical information and includes small maps of the towns. Chateaux are generally open 9am to 6 or 7pm in summer and cost 20 to 30F with students paying half or slightly more. Some close for lunch between 12 and 2. Often you are not allowed to wander at will but are given an English-language or French tour of the premises. The following places can be reached by train: Angers, Azay-le-Rideau, Beaugency,, Blois, Bourges, Chambord, Cheverny, Chinon, Fontevrault, Gien, Langeais, Loches, Lude, Orleans, Saumur, Usse, Villandry and Amboise. The major train stops are Orleans, Blois, Amboise and Tours. Local trains stop at the other towns. The Loire can also be done as day trips from Paris, but then you miss out on the campgrounds with a view of the illuminated chateaux.

Which chateaux are the best? The Castle of Chenonceaux is seducer for the region, built over the River Cher with the graceful curves of its arches predominating. Chambord is an immense, 440 room elaborate 16th century castle. The Chateau of Villandry houses a fine arts museum, but its elaborately coiffed 16th century formal gardens are of more interest. Loches is of an entirely different character, a fortified stronghold built during the Middle Ages. Azay-le-Rideau is like Disneyland's sleeping beauty castle.

Try to be at your first castle when it opens to beat the tour buses. All of the most important chateaux are floodlit evenings. The Sound and Light shows of Chenonceaux and Amboise have an English version. Guided bus tours, visiting three or four chateaux in a day, leave from Blois and Tours train stations, but the same tour can be done more cheaply on your own. Local buses often connect the villages more frequently than trains. They leave from Gare Routiere in the towns.

ORLEANS   Orlean (or-lay-AHN) is Michelin rated 1 star and is the largest town in the region.   Many trains from Paris do not come all the way into Orleans, but only go as far as Les Aubrais. From Les Aubrais, connecting trains go to Orleans. The tourist office is outside the station and ahead towards the right. The major sight is The Cathedrale de Ste-Croix. The market is off Place du Chatelet, open Tu-Sa 8-6. Restaurant prices are very competitive for the area if not even slightly lower than in small towns. Camping Gaston-Marchard at St. Jean de la Ruelle can be reached by busline D (ligne D) of the bus company, SEMTAO Reseau Urbain d'Orleans, in the direction of La Chapelle, at Place Albert 1er in front of the station. The bus stop is Roche Aux Fees, the 13th or 14th stop. Buses leave every 45 minutes. The camp charges 15F for one person with a tent.
   To Beaugency, Blois, Onzain, Amboise and Tours leave Orleans Station at 11:40am (Sunday only), 2:50pm, 5:12pm and 5:55pm (not Saturday or Sunday). From Orleans-Les Aubrais Station at 8:07am (Sunday only) and 10:27am.

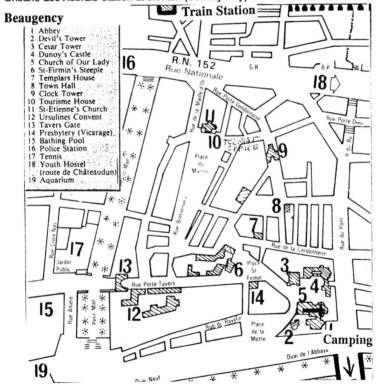

Beaugency

1. Abbey
2. Devil's Tower
3. Cesar Tower
4. Dunoy's Castle
5. Church of Our Lady
6. St-Firmin's Steeple
7. Templars House
8. Town Hall
9. Clock Tower
10. Tourisme House
11. St-Etienne's Church
12. Ursulines Convent
13. Tavers Gate
14. Presbytery (Vicarage)
15. Bathing Pool
16. Police Station
17. Tennis
18. Youth Hostel
    (route de Châteaudun)
19. Aquarium

BEAUGENCY   Beaugency (BO-sjahn-see), a Michelin rated 2 star town, gives a good glimpse of the Middle Ages in its wonderful old town. Beaugency is 30 km. from Orleans or 35 minutes by train. The tourist office, Place du Martroi in the central square, has a free walking tour brochure. From the station, walk forward two short blocks and cross the main road (Rue Nationale). Continue on Rue de la Maille d'Or which leads in one block to Place du Martroi.

A 15-minute walk from the station through the old town brings you to a beautifully situated camp on the banks of the Loire. **Camping Municipal Val de Flux**, is on the Loire River across from the town. Open Apr-Sep; adult/7F, tent/5F. From the campground you can look across the river and see the bridge with its arches. A short path leads to sand dunes and a jetty. During July and August a snack bar is open at the beach. The grassy camp has cottonwood trees, individual sink stalls with cold water, outdoor dishwashing sinks, and turkish toilets except for one conventional. The helpful proprietors speak English.

To Blois, Onzain, Amboise and Tours leave at 7:03am (M-F, change at Blois), 8:26am (Sunday only), 10:46am, 12:09pm (Sunday only), 3:10pm, 5:39pm and 6:15pm (M-F) From Beaugency to Tours is 1 hour.

BLOIS   Blois (blwah), a Michelin 3 star town, has an important chateau which is only a 10 minute walk from the station. Three campgrounds are out of town but inconvenient for backpackers. As this town is one of the larger ones in the area most trains stop here.

To Onzain, Amboise and Tours, leave at 7:47am (M-F), 8:47am (SaSu), 11:07am, 12:36pm (Sunday only), 12:50pm (M-Sa), 3:31pm, 5:35pm (M-F), 6:07pm, 6:35pm (M-F) and 6:43pm (to Amboise and Tours only).

CHAUMONT-SUR-LOIRE   Michelin rated 2 stars, the beautifully sited 16th century chateau is set within a large park. The train goes to Onzain, a town across the Loire River from Chaumont s. Loire. Onzain train station is actually between the Loire and the town of Onzain. From the station to the chateau is an easy 1.7 km.. On your way you pass Camping Grosse-Greve which is on the banks of the river in the area beneath the bridge spanning the Loire. Open Mar-Sep; adult/5F, tent/5F. From the station, take the exit for pedestrians which leads to the main road across the river. After crossing the river, turn right and double back under the bridge at the riverside. To reach the chateau, turn right after crossing the bridge on to the main road and the entrance is at the main intersection. The castle has lots of turrets and is particularly lovely. On the grounds are 2 foot bridges that are connected by stairs within a hollowed out tree trunk. Open 9-12 & 1:30-5; 22F, student 12F.

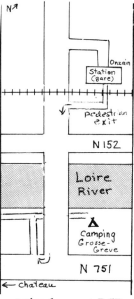

From Onzain Station to **Amboise and Tours**, trains leave at 7:57am (M-Sa), 8:57am (Sunday only), 11:23am, 1:02pm, 3:49pm, 5:47pm (M-Sa), 6:31pm and 6:44pm (M-F).

AMBOISE (ahn-BWAZ)   This Michelin 2 star town has a historically important chateau. The train station is across the river from the old town. The tourist office is at quai General de Gaulle on the same side of the river as the old town. A bus for Chenonceaux stops near the tourist office. The

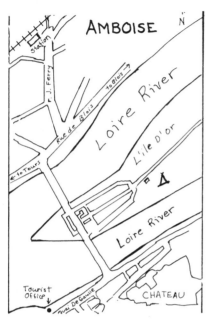

market is across from the tourist office, F & Su 7-5. The chateau is open Jul-Aug 9-7, Sep-Jun 9-5:30; 25F, student 15F.   A bakery (*boulangerie*) is on the right as you turn left off the bridge to the campground.

Camping Ile d'Or occupies part of an island in the middle of the Loire River directly across from the chateau. Evening brings a tentside view of the illuminated castle and its ramparts.   The camp is a 20-minute walk from the station. Walk forward on J. Ferry, then right on Rue de Blois and left across the bridge onto the island where the camp is.   Here you'll pick up signs.   Space is always available in this 25-acre camp. Open Mar 18-Sep 15; adult/10.80F, tent/13F.   Turkish toilets with 1 conventional, hot showers are open 8-12 & 4-8, and there is a day room.   The town swimming pool and tennis courts share the grounds.

To Tours, leave at 8:07am (M-F), 9:09am (Saturday and Sunday only), 11:34am, 1:18pm, 4:01pm, 6:03pm (not Sunday), 6:47pm, 6:55pm (M-F) and 7:01pm. The trip is 20 minutes.

To Paris Austerliz, leave at 9:13am, 10:53am, 1:31pm (M-Sa), 4:10pm, 7:15pm and the last train leaves at 9:37pm (ar. 10:20pm).

TOURS (tour) This is the largest town in an area where time is best spent in the villages. You may need to change trains here but should continue to a small town to camp. The tourist office is outside the train station in the round glass building across the street. The station restaurant is Michelin listed and worth a splurge.

To Azay-le-Rideau and Chinon, trains leave at 6:40am, 9:38am (Sunday only), 12:25pm (not Sunday), 5:20pm (M-F), 6:24pm and 8:15pm (Friday only). The ride to Azay-le-Rideau is 20-30 minutes, to Chinon, 1 hour.

To Chenonceaux-Chisseaux (direction Vierzon), 3 trains daily, 35-minute trip.

To Loches, leave at 6:28am (M-Sa) , 6:32am (not Sunday before July 1 and after September 9), 12:22pm (M-Sa, change at Cormery in 5-minutes), 5:15pm (M-F), 6:28pm (Sa-Th), 6:50pm (Friday only), 8:18pm (Friday only). The trip is about 1 hour.

To Paris, at least 1 train per hour, last leaves at 9:45 (ar. 11:43pm).

To Hendaye on the French-Spanish border, there are through trains.

CHENONCEAUX (shen-on-SEW). The chateaux rates Michelin 3 stars. Don't miss. The train station, *Chenonceaux-Chisseaux*, is between the towns of Chenonceaux and Chisseaux on the rail line between Tours and Vierzon. In the station is a map showing two possible routes to walk to the castle and the location of the municipal campground, Fontaine des Pres. From station to camp is about 1-1/2 km. and the chateau is 500 meters beyond. The castle is open Mar 16-Sep 15: 9-7; Sep 16-30, 9-6:30; (closes at earlier rest of year); 30F, student 20F. At 10pm and 10:45pm, is the 45-minutes Sound and Light show in French only (30F). The tourist office is near the entrance to the Chateau. Restaurant Au Gateau Breton in Chenonceaux is listed in Michelin and has a 55F menu. There are 4 trains a day to Tours and to Vierzon.

Chenonceaux

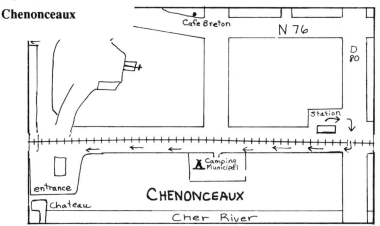

Camping Municipal is an attractive but very small camp. Open Apr 15-Sep 30; adult/3.10F, tent/3.10F. Turkish toilets, 2 free hot showers, restroom, dishwashing and clothes washing sinks, a clothesline, slide and teeter totter comprise the facilities.

Tours, Langeais, Chinon, Azay-le-Rideau, Amboise

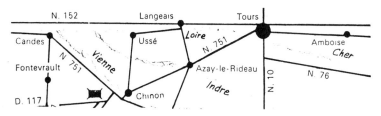

LANGEAIS (lahn-SJAY) Langeais is the station after Cinq-mars on the rail line from Tours (direction Saumur). Rated Michelin 2 star and a 5-minute walk from the station, the 15th century chateau was built within only four to five years and has remained pure as no remodeling has been done. The castle interior is shown in group tours. Meanwhile the gardens are yours to enjoy until summoned by a bell. The tour is in French but a written English translation is provided. Open Mar 15-Nov 2 9-6:30; 20F, student 10F. There are 8 trains a day to Tours.

    Camping Municipal is off N152 on the road to Tours, near a small lake and the town swimming pool. The camp is 1.2 km. to the chateau and less to the train station. The modern white restroom facility has conventional toilets and free hot showers--one with sink and bidet in the womens. Open Jun 15-Sep 15; adult/4.70F, tent/4.70F.

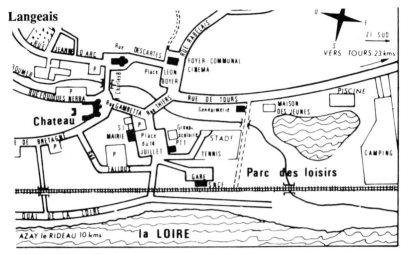

AZAY-LE-RIDEAU (ah-zeh-leh-ree-DOH)   Rated Michelin 2 star, Chateau d'Azay is a beautiful Renaissance chateau, smaller than Chenonceaux. From the train station, which is outside town to the west, to the chateau is 1.6 km. and the camp is then an additional-5 minute walk. The entire way is level ground or slightly downhill. Open Apr 1-Jun 30 & Sep 9:30-12:30 & 2-6; Jul-Aug 9-7, Oct 1-Ma4 31 10-12:30 & 2-5; adult/22F, 18-25 yr/12F, 7-17 yrs/5F. The castle is shown by group tour in French. The Sound and Light show in the evening costs 38F.

   Camping Parc du Sabot, east of the chateau, is off D84 and next to the Indre River by the town swimming pool. Mar 12-Oct 18; adult/6.50F, tent/5F. Good restrooms with conventional toilets, hot water in the sinks.

   To Chinon at 7:20am (M-F, SNCF bus from downtown Azay at Bellevue and Rue Nationale), 10:12am (Sunday only), 1:05pm (M-Sa), 5:54pm (M-F), 7:08pm, 7:55pm (M-Th), 8:49pm (Friday only). Trip is 25 minutes.

   To Tours at 6:55am (M-Sa), 7:31am (M-F), 11:21am (Sunday only), 1:05pm (M-Sa), 5:50pm (M-Sa, SNCF bus from downtown Azay at Bellevue and Rue Nationale) and 8:06pm (Sunday only). 35-minute trip.

CHINON (she-KNOWN)   The town is rated Michelin 2 star. This is the Middle ages and the chateau is a stern medieval fortress overlooking an old town which is extremely evocative of the period. The chateau is 1 km. from the station, reached by walking uphill through the old quarter to its position above the town. Open Jun 1-Sep 30 9-6; 15F, student/10F. The public market is all day Thursday and morning only on Saturday in the town square by the tourist office.

   Camping Municipal de L'ile Auger is across the river from the old town and beside the Vienne River near the bridge. The distance from the train station is 1.5 km.. Open all year; adult/6F, tent/4.50F, hot shower/5F, rental trailer/400F per week in Jul-Aug. Good restrooms, conventional toilets, automatic washer, outdoor clothesline; bakery, cafe, canoe and paddle boat rentals are nearby.

Chinon

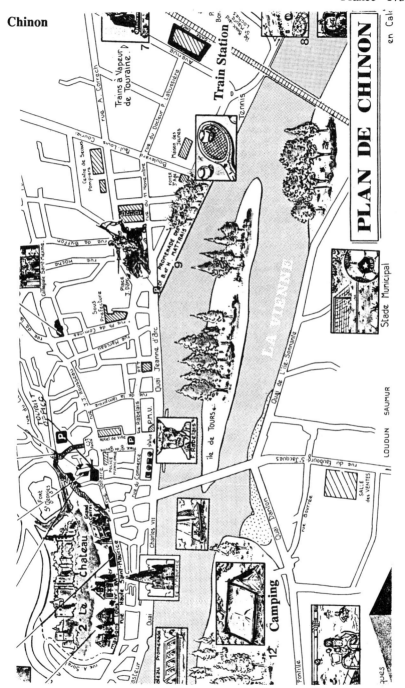

174

Loches

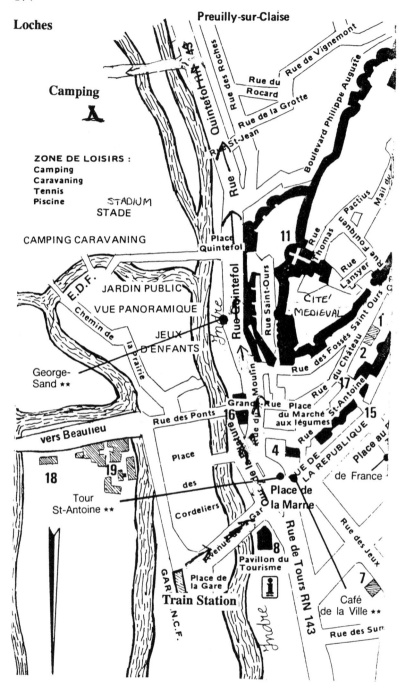

Preuilly-sur-Claise

Quintefol-HA 45

Rue des Roches

Rue du Rocard

Rue de Vignemont

Rue de la Grotte

Boulevard Philippe Auguste

Rue St-Jean

Rue

Mail du

Pactius

Rue Fontuen

Camping

ZONE DE LOISIRS :
Camping
Caravaning
Tennis
Piscine

STADIUM
STADE

CAMPING CARAVANING

Place
Quintefol

Rue
Thomas

Rue
Lansyer

11

E.D.F.

JARDIN PUBLIC

VUE PANORAMIQUE

Chemin de la prairie

Rue Quintefol

Indre

Rue Saint-Ours

CITÉ MEDIEVAL

JEUX D'ENFANTS

George-Sand ★★

Rue des Fossés Saint Ours

1

2

Rue du Château

17

Rue des Ponts

Rue du Moulin

Grande-Rue

16

Rue de la Closure

Place du Marché aux légumes

Rue St-Antoine

15

vers Beaulieu

Place

des

Cordeliers

4

RUE DE LA RÉPUBLIQUE

Place au

18

19

Gare Quintefol

de France

Place de la Marne

Rue des Jeux

Tour St-Antoine ★★

AVenue

8

Rue de Tours RN 143

Pavillon du Tourisme

GAR. N.C.F.

Place de la Gare

Train Station

Indre

7

Café de la Ville ★★

Rue des Sur

Trains to Azay-le-Rideau and Tours leave at 6:29am (M-Sa), 7:07am (M-F), 10:57am (Sunday only), 12:30pm (M-Sa and goes only as far as Azay-le-Rideau), 5:25pm (M-Sa) and 7:31pm (Sunday only).

LOCHES (low-SHAY)   The medieval town and the castle with its fortifications are both rated Michelin 3 star. The tourist office is half a block from the station. The castle, 400 meters from the station, is open Jul-Aug 9-6, May & Sep 9-12 & 2-6; 15F, student 10F.

Camping Municipal is on N143 south of the old town, 800 meters from the train station. It is next to the stadium (stade General Leclerc) and on the shore of the Indre River. The camp is a grassy field next to the town swimming pool. The chateau is visible from the campground. Open Easter-Sep 30; adult/4.90F, tent/4.95F. In the same building as the office are conventional toilets in tile lined stalls and good hot showers, each provided with a small bench and a hook for clothes. Another building has more showers and semi-private sinks.

To Tours leave at 6:38am (M-Sa), 7:33am (M-Sa), 12:29pm (only Jul 1-Sep 7 and not Sunday), 4:51pm (M-Sa, Sep 8-Jun 30, change at Cormery), 5:02pm (M-F) and 7:36pm (SaSu). Buses leave from Gare Routiere for Tours at 7:45am, 8:35am, 1pm, 3pm and 7:10pm.

HAUTE SAVOIE (THE FRENCH ALPS)

The Haute Savoie (oh suh-VWAH) is often overlooked by travelers who go to Switzerland to see those incredibly beautiful peaks, but France is equally good and cheaper because the narrow gauge railway leading to Chamonix is included in railpasses and French campgrounds charge less. The prime destination in this area is Chamonix for viewing Mont-Blanc, the second highest mountain in Europe at 15,771 feet, and its brother and sister Alps.

CHAMONIX-MONT-BLANC

If you have time for only one close-up view of the European Alps, Chamonix (sha-mo-nee) makes a good choice. We were surprised at the paucity of people in this beautiful village during perfectly sunny and clear weather in July. Anywhere in Chamonix is within 20 minutes on foot. Campgrounds and lift prices cost less than those in Switzerland. Hiking trails abound. The little cogwheel railway that takes you to Chamonix from the French side is included in Eurailpass. Routing your arrival or departure through Martigny in Switzerland will incorporate one of the top scenic rides in Europe, though an extra fare must be paid.

HOW TO GET TO CHAMONIX   If Chamonix is approached from Geneva, Aix-les-Bains, or Annecy, the entire trip is covered by Eurailpass. See those cities for train schedules.

Via Martigny   If you go via Martigny in Switzerland, a private railway fare of 11.40SF must be paid for the distance between Martigny and Le Chatelard, the border town. (A weekly pass for unlimited travel on this train costs 30SF. Ask for a "passeport MC") Eurailpass becomes valid once you're on French soil. Martigny is not marked on the map that comes with Eurailpass, but it's between Sion and Chamonix at the acute angle on the map. Trains coming from Italy headed for Lausanne stop at Martigny. On other trains from Italy, change trains at Brig.

176

Train Route from Martigny to Chamonix

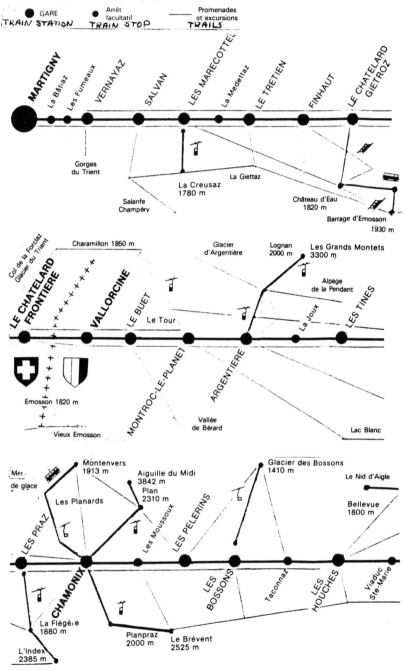

The private railway is worth the fare because it travels high in the Alps, thankfully clinging stubbornly to the steep hillside the entire distance of its rapid ascent through spectacular mountains and waterfalls. Normally only hikers get to see this caliber of scenery.

Trains leave Martigny at 7:31am, 8:50am, 9:50am (June 27-Sept 6), 10:59am, 12:01pm, 1:35pm, 3:26pm, 4:32pm, 5:22pm (May 31-June 26 & Sept 7-26) and 6:27pm (June 27-Sept 6). The last departure is at 7:36pm, but doesn't connect with a train to Martigny at the border. If you take this one, get off at a campground enroute and continue in the morning.

The helpful lone staff member at the station in Martigny speaks English, sells tickets, answers questions and changes money without commission--even on Sunday! Should you need to spend the night here, consult the map on the station wall which marks the location of **Camping Les Neuvilles** at the edge of town, less than 1 km. from the train station. Open all year, adult/4.40SF and tent/2-4SF. Excellent site and facilities with beautiful lawns, hot water for handwashing, dishwashing and clothes washing, automatic washer, sauna, store, cafe and dayroom.

The cogwheel train stops at every "settlement" on the cliffside. If you want to camp enroute, get off at La Medettaz. Camping La Medettaz, visible from the train window, is a 3-minute walk downhill from the station. Fees are adult/2.60SF and tent/2SF, except July and August, adult/3SF and tent/3SF. As the camp is on a cliff overlooking a gorge and a sheer dropoff, you will not find a more spectacular setting. Individual sink cubicles with cold water, dishwashing sinks with hot water, store, cafe and sauna.

Almost to the frontier, the train passes a reservoir and power plant at Chatelard-Gietroz. End-of-the-line is Le Chatelard-Frontiere where passengers change to the waiting French cogwheel train for the remaining distance to Chamonix. The train is still climbing as it leaves the frontier. The summit is at Le Buet and Montroc-Le-Planet, and then the train starts downhill. At Argentiere, a fairly large village, a campground is visible next to a hill about a 15-minute walk from the station. The entire trip from Martigny to Chamonix takes 2 hours.

TRAIN STATION   The small station is at the edge of downtown Chamonix. Travelers checks can be cashed at the station at a higher rate and without commission than anywhere else in town, including banks.

TOURIST OFFICE   The tourist office is at place de l'Eglise. It sells an indispensable trail map for 12.50F. Large readerboards showing which lifts are operating have been erected in the town.

REGIONAL TRANSPORTATION   The cogwheel train which connects the villages sharing the same valley on the following schedule.

The train goes **north towards Vallorcine** at 7:50am, 9:17am, 10:08am, 11:26am, 12:21pm, 1:41pm, 3:07pm, 4:53pm, 6:05pm and 7:23pm. Trains return from Vallorcine at 7:05am, 8:35am, 10:18am, 11:25am, 12:31pm, 1:07pm, 3:04pm, 3:55pm, 5:30pm and 7:26pm.

The train departs **south for St. Gervais-le-Fayet** at 7:06am, 7:42am, 8:42am, 9:13am, 12:03pm, 1:43pm, 3:42pm, 4:31pm, 5:39pm, 6:36pm and 8:05pm. The train returns at 6:57am, 7:52am, 8:35am, 9:26am, 10:44am, 12:59pm, 2:26pm, 4:40pm, 5:30pm, 6:43pm and 8:14pm.

Buses run twice an hour up to 8pm and leave across from the tourist office.

CAMPGROUNDS   The area is saturated with campgrounds, but these are the most convenient, being 10-15 minutes on foot from Chamonix station.

Chamonix

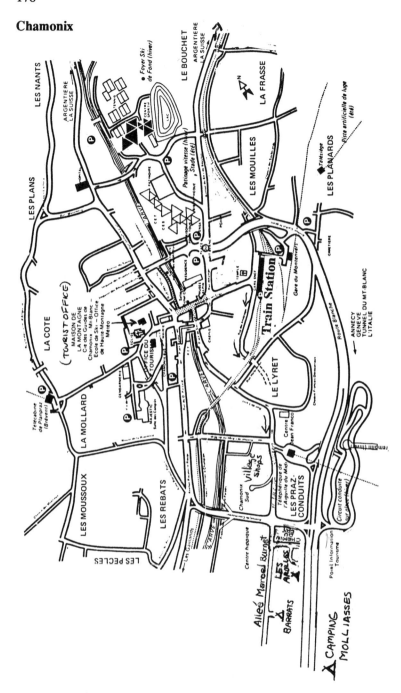

The closest is tiny **Les Arolles** which charges only adult/14F and tent/10F. The camp is open June 25 to September 30. The site comprises beautifully mowed grass on three terraces. The small restroom building has only sinks with cold water, a free hot shower and conventional toilets. When we camped here in July, only three other groups of campers appeared so the few facilities were adequate. There's no place to register; the owner, Mr. Burnet, apparently comes around to collect but we never saw him while we were there. A slot in a door will accept the camp fee. To reach the camp, with your back to the train station, turn left. This road will take you on the underpass beneath the tracks (see map). After passing the lift, telepherique de l'Aiguille du Midi, you will be on Allee Marcel Burnet. After the next block, watch for tiny Chemin du Cry, and turn left. In one block turn right, and the campground is a short block ahead.

Camping L'ille des Barrats, open Jun 15 to Sep 15, is a few minutes farther to walk than Les Arolles. Access is from the street, des Pelerins. The small site is partially wooded and facilities include sinks with cold water, hot showers, laundry tubs with hot water and a day room. Follow the directions for Les Arolles, but keep walking for another block on Allee Marcel Burnet, instead of turning left on Chemin du Cry.

Across the major highway leading to Chamonix, is the morre expensive **Les Moliasses**, three times as large as the other two, and open June 1 to September 9. The wooded site is in terraces. Hot showers, plus both laundry and handwashing sinks have hot water. To reach the campground, walk to Camping Les Arolles and then through the camping area to the back corner where there is a trail to the highway. From the corner, Les Moliasses is visible across the highway.

Close to Chamonix, the train also stops at **Les Bossons**. A campground is within a 5-minute walk from the station. A chairlift has its terminal in Les Bossons. Any town beyond Bossons is probably too far from Chamonix and its attractions.

SIGHTSEEING   Chamonix is high enough itself so the majestic mountains surround your campsite, but most people take a lift to get even higher. If the day isn't perfectly clear and sunny like it was when we were there, inquire of local people when is the best time to go up as they know the cloud patterns for predicting the weather. Chamonix is a major hiking center. The tourist office sells a trail map for 20F, which classifies trails according to difficulty. Most people take a lift up and then begin hiking.

L'Aiguille du Midi telepherique (cablecar) ascends to the Mont Blanc massif in two stages. The first is to Plan de l'Aiguille, 7,500 feet. This stage costs 38F one way or 48F round trip. The hike down takes about two hours. The second stage ascends all the way to the top to Aiguille du Midi, 12,600 feet. The cost is 86F one way or 114F round trip from Chamonix. The telepherique station is a 5-minute walk from the campgrounds.

Telecabine de Planpraz (Brevent) costs 35F one way or 42F round trip to Planpraz. The lift for the rest of the way to Le Bravent was being renovated in 1988. The cablecar operates from 9am-12:20pm and 1:30pm to 5pm. The last ride up leaves at 4:30pm and the last lift down at 5pm. The terminal is a few minutes walk from the tourist office in downtown Chamonix. Restrooms are in the terminal in Chamonix and at Planpraz. If you pass through the cafeteria at Planpraz, there are tables on a terrace

180

overlooking Chamonix below. Colorful hang gliders catch the air currents above and come billowing down in front of the terrace to land in a field below.

The other major excursion is the trip to the glacier, **Mer de Glace**, and le Montenvers. The 6-km. journey takes 20 minutes via private railway. The terminal is beside the SNCF train station in Chamonix. The fare is 30F one way, 43F round trip.

To Martigny, Switzerland, Eurailpass is valid to the Swiss frontier; then a fare of 11.40SF must be paid. Trains leave at 7:50am, 9:17am, 10:08am, 11:26am, 12:21pm, 1:41pm, 3:07pm, 4:53pm and 6:05pm. The connecting train at the frontier for the 4:53pm departure runs from May 31-June 26 and Sept 7-26. The connecting train at the frontier for the 6:05pm departure runs from June 27 to Sept 6.

To Annecy, Aix-les-Bains and Paris, the cogwheel train leaves at 9:13am, 12:03pm, 1:43pm, 3:42pm (except Sa), 4:31pm, 6:36pm and 8:10pm. At St.-Gervais-le-Fayet, change to the connecting regular train. A through train to Paris leaves Chamonix at 3:42pm (except Sa) and arrives at Paris (Gare de Lyon) at 9:53pm. At Annecy the train is a TGV.

To Geneva (Eaux-Vives Station), leave at 9:13am (ar. 12:53pm), 12:03pm (ar. 2:23pm), 1:44pm (ar. 4:04pm) and 4:35pm M-F (ar. 6:57pm). Change from cogwheel to regular at St.-Gervais-le-Fayet.

AIX-LES-BAINS

The spa town is on Lac du Bouget which is lined with campgrounds. Camping Municipal Sierroz (oz is silent) is 2 km. from the station. Open Mar 15-Nov 15; adult/12F and tent/23F. Camaping Alp'Aix is 2.5 km. from the station. Open Apr 15-Oct 15; adult/12.50F, tent/23F. For both camps, buses leave twice an hour from the station or you can walk. With your back to the station, turn left on av. du Grand Port and go in the direction of the lakeside promenade, *Esplanade*. Open market, pl. Clemenceau is W & Sa.

To Chamonix, trains leave at 6:08am, 8:20am, 10:41am turbotrain, 2:10pm, 4:14pm turbotrain, 5:48pm and 8:06pm. Turbotrains are fast trains. Change to cogwheel train at St. Gervais-le-Fayet.

To Paris (Gare de Lyon), trains leave at 7:38am TGV (ar. 10:54am), 10:22am (ar. 1:59pm), 12:29pm (ar. 3:44pm) and 6:47pm TGV (ar. 9:53pm).

To Rome, a through train leaves at 6:34pm (ar. 7:10am).

ANNECY

A wonderful off-the-beaten-track medium size town, Annecy overlooks a clear blue lake in the French Alps. The tourist office is no longer by the lake, but in the building *bonlieue* about 7 blocks from the station. (Upon leaving the station, turn left, walk 5 blocks and then turn right.)

Sightseeing consists of the arcaded old town of Annecy, the beautiful lake, and Les Gorges du Fier (a waterfall, admission fee), 12- minutes by bus or train. For the latter, get off at Lovagny Station on the Aix-les-Bains line.

In Annecy, **Le Belvedere camping** is 1.5 km. south on the road to Semnoz, but don't go there as it's at least a 30-minute uphill walk and no bus. It's far preferable to take a bus from the train station to one of the many camps on the lake. All buses leave from the train station and then go to Hotel de Ville (city hall) by the lake before turning onto the lakeshore road. Upon request, the driver will let you off at a camp, rather than in a village. The lakeside beauty spot is the small town of Taillores. The bus passes **Camping Au Coeur, Roc and L'Horizon** (the closest) before entering the village, about a 20-minute ride.

At Bout-du-Lac at the opposite end of the lake from Annecy are two campgrounds. The bus ride (direction Albertville) is about 30 minutes. First is **Camping International du Lac Bleu**, a 2-minute walk from the bus stop. Open April 1 to October 15. The clean, hedged camp is on the water with mostly Dutch and British clientele with their daysailers and inflatables. Free hot showers, cold water in sinks, no individual sink compartments, all toilets nonconventional except one, store, ping-pong, swimming, dock, rocky beach. A 5-minute walk further on is **Camping Municipal**, open June 15 through August and cheaper than Lac Blue.

To Chamonix, leave at 6:29am, 7:04am, 9:01am, 11:20am turbotrain, 2:53pm, 4:52pm turbotrain and 6:30pm. Turbotrains are fastest. A change of train to a red cogwheel one at St. Gervais-le-Fayet is required for the ascent through the valley to Chamonix. Sit on the righthand side of the train.

To Paris Gare de Lyon, leave at 7:11am TGV (ar. 10:54am), 9:51am TGV (ar. 1:59pm), 12:02pm (ar. 3:44pm), 6:20pm TGV (ar. 9:53pm) and 11:20pm (ar. 7:09am).

GRENOBLE

A large city in a beautiful area with a good campground, but why would anyone want to stay in anything but a village in the Alps? The tourist office is in the center of town but a small branch is maintained outside the train station. The market is held in the morning M-Sa at place Ste-Claire.

The **municipal campground**, Le Bachelard, is on Avenue Beaumarchais, off rue Albert-Reynier and cours de la Liberation, and near the athletic field. Open all year with fees of adult/4.45F and tent/2.40F. The campground is shown towards the lower lefthand corner on the map on the back of the tourist office map. To walk to camp, turn right outside the train station and follow the road, rue Joseph Rey, beside the tracks. In 4 blocks it leads into the important street, Cours Jean Jaures. Turn right onto Jean Jaures. In one long block it is renamed Cours de la Liberation. In five blocks, turn right on rue Albert Reynier. Or take bus 1 or 8 (fare 5F or 10 tickets for 31F) and get off just before reaching the elevated highway. Facilities include sinks with cold water, store and cafe.

PROVENCE

Provence is the center of Roman monuments in France. Avignon is only 4 hours from Paris on the TGV. It's well to use the city as an excursion base as camps aren't available that can be reached by public transport in Arles, Nimes, Orange and Pont-du-Gard.

AVIGNON (ah-veen-yawn) The train station is just outside the town walls at Porte de la Republique. The branch of the tourist office at the train station will change money. The main street, Cours Jean Jaures, extends perpendicularly from in front of the station and leads inside the ramparts. In the third block on the right is the tourist office (Maison du Tourisme et du Vin). The market is on Place Pie, open Tu-Su mornings. The Palace of the Popes (Palais de Papes) has a guided tour in English at 10:45am and 3:30pm; 20F, student 12F.

Camping Bagatelle is on l'ile de Barthelasse, 2 km. north off the road to Nimes and about a 20-minute walk from the station, or bus 10 from Porte de la Republique in front of the station. As you exit the station, turn left. A bus leaves every 10 minutes to 7:40pm, travels outside the walls, crosses the Rhone River and stops 8 minutes later within a 5-minute walk of the campgrounds. Open all year: 1988 prices adult/9.90F, tent/4.50F, tax/1F. The Palace of Popes and the original bridge of Avignon can be seen from camp. This is an excellent camp with free hot showers, individual sink compartments, store, cafeteria, washing machine, dryer and exchange. The camp also has 8 rooms holding 4 to 6 people that rent for 37F per person per night. The island has 3 other camps, this is closest but the others are less.

Avignon

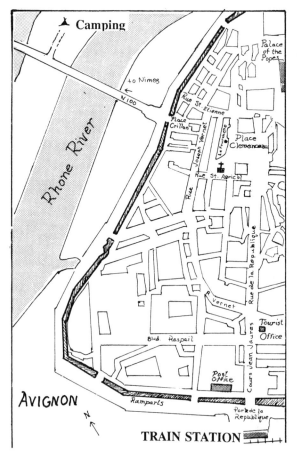

Pont-du-Gard is the Roman aqueduct, 19 centuries old, where no mortar was used in placing its precisely cut blocks. Take the bus to Remoulins from Avignon; no train. **Orange**, a 15-minute train ride in the direction of Valence, has the best preserved of all Roman theaters in France; plays and concerts are given in summer. In the other direction towards Marseille, Arles is a 20 minute ride and Nimes one hour. Departures every 1 to 2 hours. For Aix-en-Provence, take the train to Marseille and change.

ARLES (arl)   Arles is a compact town and easy to walk around. It's known for its Roman ruins and Museum Reattu which shows works by Picasso. No campground for backpackers, but most everything of interest is about a 10-15 minute walk from the station.   A ticket good for all monuments is sold at any monument for 35F (student 22F).   Arles' most famous site, the Roman Arena, is open 8:30-7, 4.80F if bought individually. Bullfights are held in the arena each Sunday at 9:30pm, beginning in June. See also: Theater Antique, Cloitre St. Trophime and les Alyscamps. Musee Reattu shows many of Picasso's paintings and drawings in the last two rooms (8:30-7, 8F). The train ride to Nimes is 45 minutes. Through trains depart at 9:24am, 11am, 1:01pm, 1:31pm, 5:06pm, 6:55pm and 9:08pm.

NIMES   Famous for its monuments from the Roman occupation of Gaul, its Maison Carree, within walking distance of the station, is called the gem of Roman architecture in France. It dates from the Augustan age, a small beautiful temple only 27 by 13 yards in dimension. Also see the arena. No campground.   (If you have limited time, Arles is more attractive than Nimes.)   The indoor market (halles), rue General Perrier, is open M-Sa mornings. The outdoor market is Monday morning on Blvd. Gambetta.
   Camping Domaine de la Bastide, route de Generac, 4.5 km. from the station, is only 6 years old. Take the city bus (T.C.N.) #4 from in front of the train station to the campsite.   Buses depart frequently during the daytime. Open all year; 42.50F for 2 people. The 3-star campsite is fully equipped: hot showers, hot water in sinks, washer, store and restaurant.
   Through trains **to Arles** leave at 8:45am, 10:29am, 12:21pm, 1:41pm, 3:11pm, 5:04pm 6:19pm, 8:39pm and 10:21pm.

LA GRANDE MOTTE   If you want to see the futuristic side of France, come where the French middle and upper middle class vacation.   The surrealistic ultra-modern architecture in this totally preplanned resort on the Green Coast will surprise, amuse and delight you. Accommodations are mostly apartments that are rented ,by the week or condominiums. (Depending on the season a studio apartment rents from 825 to 1745F per week.) An entire section of the resort is set aside for several campgrounds. The tourist office is open 9-8, information on the sailing school, tennis, golf, computer and English lessons, daycare in July and August and scenic walks.
   To get here, the best way is to take the train to Montpellier and then a bus for the 20-minute ride to La Grande Motte. There are 13 trains a day to Montpellier and about hourly buses (18.30F) from Montpellier to La Grande Motte. The last bus is 6:20pm. If you're in Nimes, you can take a bus from Nimes to La Grande Motte for 35.50F. Or you can take a train from Nimes to Le-Grau-du-Roi and then a bus for the 10-minute ride to La Grande Motte. There are 4 trains a day to Le-Grau-du-Roi and then a bus leaves the train station about hourly for La Grande Motte. Last bus leaves at 7:50pm.
   Seven camps are next to each other and a 10 to 20 minute walk to the resort center. Prices are the highest from the last weekend in June through August. The camps charge about 87F for a tent and up to 3 people. The least expensive but farthest camp in the cluster is Les Cigales (adult/10.20F, tent/27.50F). These camps have deluxe facilities equipped with modern restrooms with individual sink compartments, and all conveniences. For a cheaper camp, go to beachfront Camping Boucanet which is in Le Grau-du-Roi but within walking distance of Le Grande Motte. Coming from the Le Grau-du-Roi, before reaching town the bus passes the camp.

184

Provence and Riviera Rail Lines

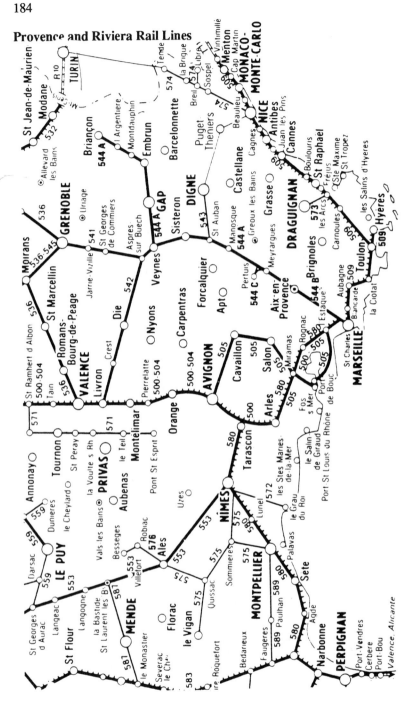

Discovering all the fantastic architecture in this resort will take 1 to 2 hours, and then the beach is wide, safe and sandy. Prices are rather high in this resort community but no where else will you find such an astounding variety of fanciful modern architecture in one place. While you're nearby, an excursion should be made to **Aigues-Mortes** (egg-mort) with its intact ramparts. The town can be reached by bus all the way, or by bus to Le-Grau-du-Roi and then the train. The train ride is 10-minutes.

AIX-EN-PROVENCE (ecks) The tourist office is at place du General deGaulle, open 8-7 and to 10pm Jul-Sep. From the train station, go straight ahead two blocks, turn left on Victor Hugo and go three blocks to Place deGaulle. The market, place Verdun, is Tu, Th and Sa mornings. The best train connections are to Marseille with about hourly for the 20-minute ride.

Don't miss the **Fondation Vasarely** (vahz-sah-HEE-lee), Ave. Marcel Pagnol, Jas de Bouffan, built on the outskirts of Aix as a showcase for the op artist. This is not a museum in the sense of hanging pictures already created by an artist, but an environment designed especially for the works planned by Vasarely for the Foundation. The result is superb and a living experience in op art. His gigantic pieces, some woven like a tapestry and others made of an original assortment of materials, completely engulf the visitor. Open 9:30-12:30 & 2-5:30pm, closed Tu, 20F, student 10F. Take bus 8 from La Rotonde near the tourist office. The Fondation appears silver and black marked with alternating black and silver circles.

Airotel Camping Chantecler, Val St. Andre, is 2 km. from the train station. Take bus 3 from the station, then a 10-minute walk. Open all year; adult/16F, tent/21F. Free hot showers, store, washing machine and free swimming pool.

THE FRENCH RIVIERA

The Riviera has a large colony of artists and writers, and its most important attraction, besides its beaches which can be pebbly, narrow and crowded, is the collections of contemporary art found in the towns. Camping season extends from May into October and any campground that fronts directly on a beach will likely have been filled by prior reservation in August. Campgrounds are more expensive in this area than in the rest of France.

The beaches of the Cote d'Azur (koht-da-zeur) can become polluted during the summer months. Purification plants are being built and in the past local authorities have closed a beach if it became really bad. There are a few free public beaches, otherwise if the campground doesn't have one, admission consists of renting a chair and umbrella for a daily fee.

The best strategy for seeing the Riviera with a railpass is to base yourself in one town and make day excursions from there. The campgrounds across from Biot train station near Antibes make a good base. EuroCity and international trains stop at San Rafael, Cannes, Antibes and Nice, where you can change to a local train for the villages. Try to avoid having to stay in San Rafael (san-rah-feh-EL), but if you can't, Camping Beausejour can be reached via the bus to Cannes from the bus station next to the train station. In 2 km. get off at the bridge. Open May-Sep, 50F for two.

CANNES (can) The tourist office is at the train station. Cannes-la-Boca Station is by the beach in Suburban Cannes. The market (*marche Forville*)

186

is 1 block north of l'Hotel de Ville (City Hall). **Ranch Camping** is 8 km. west of Cannes. Take bus 6 or 10 from the bus station near l'Hotel de Ville, 500 meters from the station. The bus stops at the camp. Open Mar-Oct, by reservation only Jul 15-Sep 15; 70F for two.

LA NAPOULE Don't get off the train at La Napoule for these two camps, but at station Pinede de la Siagne (see-ahg-nay) located between La Napoule and Cannes. The station is not a building, but merely a shelter with a sign. To reach the station from the ground, note the sign on the steps and be sure to go up the Nice side to go to Cannes since once upstairs, crossing the tracks is not allowed. To reach the campgrounds, walk in the same direction the train was going if you came from Cannes. It's a short distance to road D92 and then turn right. There are two campgrounds: de Bosquet, for which you turn right at the intersection, and La Siagne which is reached by continuing straight ahead. They are both about a 10 minute walk from the station. These camps are isolated out in the woods, cost less than other camps, the facilities are not on a par with those in Biot and you must take the train to get to a store. Trains leave for Cannes at approximately 6:45am, 9am, 11:45am, 2:20pm and 7pm (check the schedule at the station).

VALLAURIS Take the train to Golfe Juan (the closest) or Cannes and then a bus from either train station to Vallauris. There are about 20 buses a day. Picasso's noted painting, *War and Peace*,is in the 16th century Castle of the Monks of the Lerins Islands, which is now the Musee National d'Art Moderne. The painting covers three sides of the crypt walls in the chapel. Open 10-12 and 2-5. In the central square is Picasso's bronze sculpture, Man with a Sheep. The town hosts a permanent exhibition off pottery, some of it by Picasso, at A.V.E.C., 15 rue Sicard, open M-F 10-12 and 2:30-6 in summer. The shop Madoura sells authorized copies of Picasso's pottery. In even-numbered years, is the Ceramic Arts Biennial of international scope.

ANTIBES (on-TEEB) EuroCity and international expresses stop here. The tourist office is in Place DeGaulle. From the station, turn right on main street, Robert Soleau, which leads to Place DeGaulle in 5 blocks. Antibe's campgrounds are by the train station of Biot, a 4-minute ride from Antibes. These campgrounds have excellent facilities and are not directly on the beach so their charges are less. They provide the best base for touring the Riviera. (See Biot.)

    Musee Picasso in Chateau Grimaldi contains 175 works done by Picasso during his stay in Antibes in 1946 and which he donated to the town. The museum is behind the ramparts and faces the sea in the old quarter of Antibes, about a 15 minute walk from the station. Open Jul-Sep 10-12 & 3-7 closed Tu; Oct-Jun, 10-12 & 2-6, closed Tu; 15F, student 8F. Antibes also has an archaeological museum and Naval and Napoleonic Museum. The market is at Place Massena, one block inland from Musee Picasso, open mornings.

    To Avignon, trains leave about every 1 to 2 hours. At Marseille it's possible to connect with a TGV. The trip is about 3 hours.

    To Barcelona Sants, leave at 12:16pm (change at Avignon to EuroCity, ar. 9:25pm) and 10:45pm (change at Port Bou to a Rapido, ar. 9:29am).

    To Genoa, leave at 6:48am (ar. 11:33am), 7:29am (ar. 12:03pm), 8:43am (ar. 1:33pm), 9:51am (change at the border, ar. 2:47pm), 10:28am (change at border, ar. 3:33pm), 11:44 (change at border, ar. 4:58pm), 2:14pm (ar. 6:55pm), 3:29pm (ar. 7:33pm), 4:29pm (ar. 9:33pm) and 5:54pm (ar. 11:02pm).

To Paris Lyon, you can change at Marseille and experience the TGV. For instance the 9:12am departure arrives in Paris at 7:23pm without changing at Marseille, but arrives at 4:59pm if you change to the TGV in Marseille. Other departures that connect with the TGV are at 11:42am, 2:27pm and 3pm. Regular through trains leave at 1:02pm (ar. 7:51pm) and 6:20pm (ar. 6:25am).

BIOT (bee-AWT)   Biot makes the best excursion base for the Riviera, being located 11 km. from Nice and 9 km. from Cannes with about hourly train service in both directions.   Those arriving via an international train should check to make sure it stops in Biot. Most don't so you will need to get off in Antibes and take a local train or bus for the 4-minute ride to Biot Station. Four campgrounds are within 500 meters of Biot Station and these camps are more deluxe than those at La Siagne and cheaper than comparable camps that have a beach location. Within 100-200 meters of these camps is Luna-Park (amusement park), Aqualand (water park), Marineland, La Jungle des Papillons (butterflies) discotheques and a casino.

   Camp du Pylone, a 3-star camp on route de Biot, is well recommended. Open all year; adult/25F, tent/15F. Free hot showers, hot water in the sinks, automatic washer, store, bakery, The Inn (restaurant, TV room, records with dancing 8-11pm), snack bar, swimming pool (fee of 10F in Jul-Aug only). The grounds are well organized and taken care of. Tent campers have their own area away from the noise of the cars. The sites are divided by a few small trees on either side and each section is divided by waist-high hedges.

Biot Campgrounds

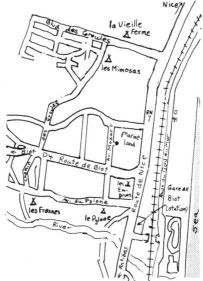

        La Vieille Ferme, also on the Boulevard des Groules, is technically in Villeneuve Loubet Plage. Open all year, 4-star camp, backpackers: 1 person/32F, 2 persons/49F. Free hot showers, store, washer and dryer, hot water in sinks, 2 swimming pools, game room with TV, table tennis. The camp is within a city park with a jogging trail.
        Camping Les Embruns is across from the station at 63 Route de Biot. This is a small 4-star camp situated 100 meters from the beach across

the highway. Open May 1-Sept 30, hot showers, hot water in sinks, snack bar, fresh bread delivery, tennis.

Camping Les Fresnes, on quai de la Braque, is a 4-star camp. Open Jun 6-Sep 30, free hot showers, store, restauant, washer.

From Biot Station, trains going in the **direction of Marseille stop at Antibes, Juan-les-Pins, Golfe-Juan Vallauris, Cannes, Cannes-la-Boca, Pinede-de-la-Siagne, Mandelieu-la-Napoule, Theoule-sur-Mer, Le Trayas, Antheor-Cap-Roux, Agay, Le Ddramont, Boulouris-sur-Mer and St. Raphael Valescure. Trains operate from 6:22am to 11:22pm. Some trains go only as far as Cannes-la-Boca.**

Trains going in the **direction of Ventimiglia** stop at Villeneuve-Loubet-Plague, Cagnes-sur-Mer, Cros-de-Cagnes, St. Laurent-du-Var, Nice St. Augustin, Nice-Ville (downtown), Nice-Riquier, Villefranche-sur-Mer, Beaulieu-sur-Mer, Eze, Capd'Ail, Monaco, Cap-Martin-Roquebrune, Carnoles and Menton (mahn-TOHN). Trains leave at approximately 6:43*, 7:24, 12:43 (request stop), 1:30*, 2:52, 3:34, 4:40, 6, 7, 7:38 (request stop), 8:37 and 10:24pm*. Note: * indicates trains going only as far as Nice-Ville. Request stop means you must let the conductor at the station know that you wish to take that train so he can signal the train to stop. On these same trains, if you want to get off at Eze or Cap d'Ail, the conductor must be notified on the train.

Musee National Fernan Leger is 1.9 km. uphill from Biot train station. Follow the signs on route de Biot. (Just before the museum is Camping L'Eden, another good camp with similar prices to those near the station.) The white contemporary style museum was built especially for Leger's works. Open 10-12 & 2-6, closed Tu, 15F, student 8F, free Su.

SAINT PAUL DE VENCE (san-pohl-deh-VAHNS) Called St. Paul for short, the town is 7 km. from Cagnes-sur-Mer and 4.5 from Vence. Buses leave about once an hour from both Gare Routiere in Nice or from the closer SNCF Station in Cagnes. The town itself is a picturesque medieval fortified village with ramparts that can be walked upon. The Foundation Maeght (mag) is before you reach the town proper so ask the bus driver to let you off there. From the stop, the Foundation is a 10-minute walk, partially uphill. The goal of Marguerite and Aime Maeght in creating the foundation was to achieve a total environment for modern art. This was attained by the skillful blending of terraces, sculpture, pools and gardens into a rich natural setting. On the grounds are an amphitheater, chapel with stained glass windows by Braque and Ubac, library, movie theater, live theater, artists' accommodations and workshop for creating lithography, etchings and ceramics. The gallery shows paintings, sculpture and mosaic of the foremost modern artists of our time. The sales room of reproductions is one of the best. Open Jul-Sep 10-7, Oct-Jun 10-12:30 & 2:30-6, 26F, student, 21F.

VENCE (Vahns) Take the same bus from Cagnes-sur-Mer as you would for St. Paul. The trip is 40 minutes. Matisse thought the Chapel of the Rosary, built under his direction in 1950, was his best work. The graphic interior is done with black outlines on white ceramic tile walls, complemented by stained glass windows of blue, green and yellow in a modern design. Open Tuesday and Thursday, 10-11:30 and 2:30-5:30. The bus to Vence lets you off at place du Grand-Jardin, which is also the location of the tourist office. The chapel is outside town and about a half hour walk.

NICE   (neece)   International expresses stop at Nice. Nice's stations are Nice-St. Augustin, Nice-Ville and Nice-Riquier. Nice-Ville is the centrally located downtown station. The train station is at the edge of a shopping area and seven blocks from Prisunic Department store and its excellent supermarket. The tourist office is outside the station on the left. Local trains to Provence depart from Chemin de fer de Provence at 33 Ave. rue Malaussena, 7 blocks from Nice-Ville Station. There's no campground in Nice, but it's an easy commute from Biot. The market is at Place Massena. The Matisse Museum and Musee National Marc Chagall are in the hills surrounding Nice. Take bus 15 from the downtown station for both. The Matisse Museum is open Tu-Sa 10-12 & 2:30-6:30, Su 2:30-6:30,, free. The Marc Chagall Museum is closed Tuesday and open 10-12:30 & 2-5:30, from Jul-Sep open 10-7, closed Tuesday, 22F (11F on Sunday), student 11F. The Musee des Beaux-Arts Jules Cheret and Musee Massena are both free.

VILLEFRANCHE-SUR-MER   The town is on the main train line just beyond Nice heading towards Monaco. Jean Cocteau's frescoes decorate the walls of Chapelle St.-Pierre (Fishermen's Chapel), Sa-Th 9-12 & 2:30-7, 5F.

EZE-SUR-MER   A famous tiny village of jumbled narrow streets, shops and seaside views, Eze is between Villefranche and Monaco. The train stops at Eze, but at a much lower level than the village. You must take the trail from the train station and hike up. Be sure the train stops at Eze.

PERIGORD

Perigord is a wonderful off-the-beaten-track area with cliff-hanging towns, caves where prehistoric man dwelt and notable cuisine. Rail entry points are Perigueux and Brive, the latter being a major stop on trains from Paris.

BRIVE-LA-GAILLARDE   Brive is a main rail junction. The tourist office is on place 14 Juillet (Jul-Aug M-Sa 9-12:30 & 2:30-7, Su 10-1; Sep-Jun M-Sa 10-12 & 2:30-6). The market is Tu, Th and Sa mornings on place 14 Juillet.   **Camping des Iles**, Boulevard Michelet, is on the shore of the Correze River about a 30-minute walk from the station; no bus. Adult/8F, tent/5F. To **Les Eyzies** take the train to Niversac and change to the Agen line for Les Eyzies. **To Rocamadour**, trains leave at 8am, 11:43am M-Sa, 2:40pm and 6:12pm. 45 minutes.

PERIGUEUX   The town is a relatively large city (50,000) in the Dordogne and the rail gateway to Les Eyzies, the prehistoric capital. Perigueux's Musee de Perigord exhibits prehistoric finds of tools and a skeleton of early man. Similar items are displayed in the museum of Les Eyzies. It's best to continue to tiny Les Eyzies for the night as its camp is only a few minutes walk from the station, but buy some food to take along as grocery shopping is limited to one tiny store though restaurants are available.

The tourist office is at 1 Av. Aquitaine, a 5-block walk from the station, in the direction of the old town. **Camping Barnabe Plage** is on the Isle River, 2 km. east of town. Camping extends to both sides of the river, but the main portion with the most facilities is on the east shore. A boat on a pulley system crosses back and forth. From the train station, first walk to the tourist office for a map and then continue to camp, about a 30-minute walk. The camp is beautifully situated with a beach in front and short falls nearby

Perigord Rail Lines

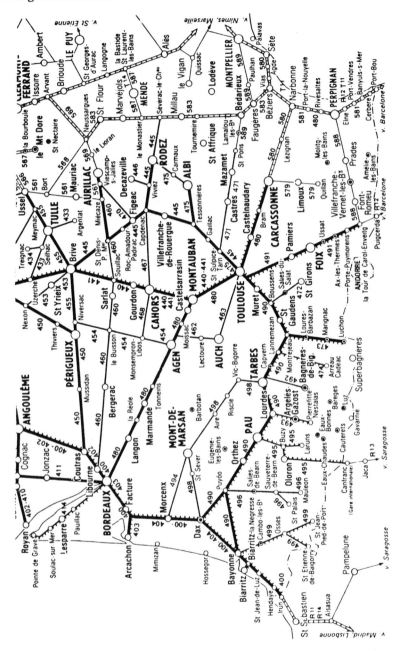

where early morning fishermen cast their lines. The large white round cafe features a spacious courtyard with tables under the spreading trees. Open all year; adult/9F, tent/7.30F.

To **Les Eyzies** (direction Agen) leave at 7:14am, 12:17pm 2:52pm and 7:02pm. The trip is 30 to 40 minutes.

To **Sarlat**, use the same departure times as for Les Eyzies but change at Le Buisson, the stop after Les Eyzies. Trains leave Le Buisson for Sarlat at 8:22am, 6:29pm M-Sa and 8:18pm. The trip is 30 minutes.

LES-EYZIES-DE-TAYAC Les Eyzies is a wonderful one street village in the Perigord and the center of prehistorical finds in France. The town is on the Paris-Agen railway line. The tourist office is on the main road across from the turn off for the museum and will change money. Try to bring some groceries with you to Les Eyzies as there is only one small grocery store.

Camping La Riviere is 200 meters from the station. At the end of the narrow road leading from the station, turn right onto highway D47, walk until you see the camping sign and turn left. The camp is a grassy field surrounding a large house in which meals are available. Open Apr-Oct; adult/12F, tent/10F. Canoe and kayak rental.

Camping La Riviere

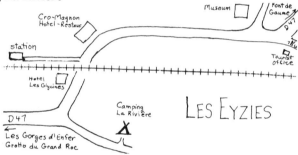

Musee National de Prehistoire is 500 meters from the train station. After emerging from the station road onto the highway, go towards your left passing by the Cro-Magnon Hotel and continuing until the museum sign. Open 9:30-12 & 2-6, closed Tuesday, 10F, 18-25 years 5F, half price on Sunday. Inside are excavation finds from various caves, photographs of cave drawings and an entire piece of rock with an embedded relief sculpture.

Grotte de Font-de-Gaume (fohn-duh-GOH-meh) is 1.5 km. from the train station. Follow directions to Prehistory Museum, but continue on the main road until the sign to Sarlat. Follow the sign to Sarlat and the cave is on the right hand side of the road, one km. from Les Eyzies. Open Apr-Sep 30, 9-11 & 2-5, closed Tuesday; 10F, 18-25 years old 6F. Visitors are guided through the cave in groups. The commentary is in French. The cave is electrically lighted and neither cold nor damp. The interior contains somewhat faded pictures of animals on the walls drawn by prehistoric man and is worthwhile seeing. Only a small part of the extensive cave is shown on the tour. On weekends in summer you need to get there as early as possible to buy a ticket.

Several attractions are on road D47 going towards Perigueux. This is the main road beyond the campground. Musee de la Speleologie is the closest. Open daily 9-12:30 & 2-6; 7F. Next comes Les Gorges d'Enfer

192

with prehistoric caves and rock shelters within an animal preserve. Open 9-6:30, 10F. The caves were inhabited by Neanderthal and Cro-Magnon man. Trails lead to 8 sites classified as historical monuments. Bison, Prejalski horse and a wild donkey of the same species that lived in prehistoric times live in the animal reserve. There is also sort of a semi-enclosed zoo. The third attraction and the farthest from the station at 1.5 km. is Le Grand Roc, a natural cavern of crystal formations. Open Jul-Sep 15, 9-6:30; Apr-Jun & Sep 16-Nov 15, 9-12 & 2-6; 22F. The visit takes 30 minutes.

To Perigueux leave at 8:28am, noon, 4:01pm, 5:35pm, 8:24pm and 10:47pm. The last departure is a through train to Paris Austerlitz, arriving there at 7am.

To Carcassonne, the best way is to leave Les Eyzies at 7:51am for Agen (ar. 9:51am) and change trains there for Carcassonne. Trains leave Agen at 10:15am (change at Toulouse), 12:42pm and 3:54pm.

To Sarlat take the train to Le Buisson and then change.

Rocamadour

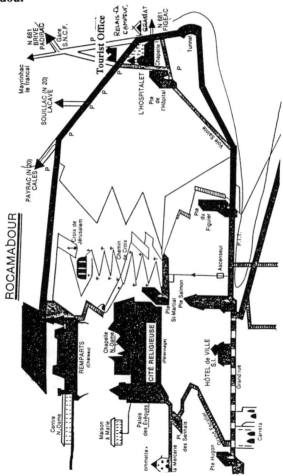

ROCAMADOUR   The cliff-hanging chapel of Notre-Dame has drawn worshippers to Rocamadour since the 12th century.   The train station is 4 km. or 40 minutes from Rocamadour.   On the way you pass Relais du Campeur, 3 km. from town. Open Apr-Sept; adult/12F, tent/12F.
To Brive, leave at 9am M-Sa, 11:51am, 4:06pm and 8:51pm. All except the last departure continue to Paris Austerlitz.
To Toulouse, leave at 3:19pm and 7:03pm. For more departures, take the train to Capdenac and change. Frequent trains to Carcassonne from Toulouse.

SARLAT-LA-CANEDA   Sarlat is a picturesque medieval town but the closet camp is very expensive and a one km. uphill climb from the old town, while the train station is outside town at the opposite end.   **Le Buisson**, between Perigueux and Agen, is the rail gateway to Sarlat.   Trains leave Sarlat for Le Buisson at 6:10am M-F, 7:40am, 3:10pm and 7:27pm.

LANGUEDOC-ROUSSILLON

The area is in the south of France, close to Spain.   Toulouse is the most important town.   The best place, equivalent to Rothenburg in Germany or Bruges in Belgium, is the walled city of Carcassonne.

TOULOUSE   Matabiau is the main station. The top attraction in Toulouse is St. Sernin Cathedral, located 7 blocks from the station.   Walk forward and cross the bridge, walk on Strasbourg, turn right, go one block and turn left (8-12 & 2-7). Bus stops have maps of SEMVAT transit.
Camping Municipal Du Pont de Rupe is on avenue des Etats-Unis, 6 km. from downtown Toulouse.   Open all year; adult/6.70F, tent/3.10F. From the station take bus 2, 40, 72, 75, 76 or F to Jeanne D'Arc and change to SEMVAT P. Ask the driver to let you off at camping. This 3-star camp has free swimming pool, store and day room. **Camping La Bouriette,** 201 Chemin de Tournefeuille, is open May-Oct. Take SEMVAT bus 64. A 2-star camp. **Camping Les Violettes**, 9 km. from Toulouse on N113 towards Narbonnne, has the most facilities including an automatic washer, store and restaurant. From Toulouse Matabian Station, walk to the bus station (gare routiere) which is one block north of the train station on the same side of the street, Boulevard de la Gare. With your back to the station, turn right. Take the bus to Villefranche de Lauracais. The bus stops in front of camp. Open all year; adult/12.30F, tent/12.30F,4-star camp.
To Albi (direction Rodez), leave at 8:11am (Jun 27-Aug 30), 12:36pm and 5:42pm. The trip is 50 minutes.
To Barcelona Sants, leave at 10:13am (ar. 5:22pm) or 2pm (ar. 9:35pm). Change trains at the La Tour-de-Carol, the border.
To Carcassonne, leave at 7:14am, 7:56am, 8:17am, 9:06am, 10:30am, 11:39am, 11:52am, 1:58pm, 5:05pm, 5:15pm, 6:44pm and 9:12pm.
To Les Eyzies, leave for Agen at 8:10am (ar. Agen 9:29am, change for Les Eyzies, lv. 10:22am (ar. noon); leave for Agen at 11:35am (ar. Agen 12:40pm, change trains, lv. 3:58pm (ar. Les Eyzies 5:35pm) or leave for Agen at 4:50pm (ar. 5:52pm, change trains, lv. 6:24pm, ar. Les Eyzies 8:24pm).
To Paris Austerlitz, leave at 7:37am, 9:17am, 10:19am, 10:33am, 1pm and 2:33pm. The last departure arrives at 9:35pm.

ALBI   Albi is a 60-minute train ride from Toulouse in the direction of Capdenac and Rodez.   A fairly large town, Albi has a famous Cathedral and a Toulouse-Lautrec Museum.   The tourist office is across from the Cathedral which is next to Musee Toulouse-Lautrec in the Palais de la Berbie--a 15 minute walk from the train station.

Camping Parc de Caussels is 2 km. east of Albi by N99 and D100 in the direction of St. Juery. From the station, take bus 1 to the hospital and change to bus 5 to Caussels. The hospital is the third stop after leaving the station. Caussels is the last stop on bus 5. Line 1 leaves about every 10 minutes, line 5 once or twice an hour. Bus fare is 3.30F. After the bus lets you off, cross the street and follow the signs. A huge L'Univers shopping mall is across from camp. The camp is a wooded, hilly site with conventional toilets, private sinks, free hot showers and store. The town swimming pool is adjacent. Tent plus 2 persons is 33F.

Musee Toulouse-Lautrec, open daily 9-12 & 2-6 Easter to Oct.1 (otherwise 10-12 & 2-5 closed Tu); 18F, student 9F. The turretted fortress-like castle of the Archbishops who ruled Albi from the 13th century to the time of the revolution now houses this museum. The Comtesse de Toulouse-Lautrec donated her son's paintings following his death in 1901. Other gifts made over the years have resulted in 13 rooms on the first floor containing the artist's paintings, posters and memorabilia, the largest collection of his works in one place. The museum excels in tracing the development of Lautrec since boyhood. His sketches show that he was accomplished by the age of nine. The castle, built between the 13th and 18th centuries overlooks the Tarn River. A beautiful, formal garden and grape arbor in the rear is open to the public. A wonderful view of this can be seen from the circular balcony protruding off the Lautrec section of the museum. The museum store sells large poster reproductions for 30F and postcards for 10F.

To Rocamadour, leave at 12:31pm (change at Tessonieres, ar. 4:06pm) or 5:26pm (ar. 8:51pm). These trains continue to Brive.

To Toulouse, leave at 7:41am, 6:53pm (Jun 26-Aug 29) and 9:54pm (change at Tessonieres).

CASTRES   Built on each side of the Agout River and once the site of a Roman defense station, Castres is a fine town in the Tarn district. (Take the train from Toulouse in the direction of Capdenac or Rodez and change at St. Sulpice.) In the 1619 Bishop's Palace with lovely formal French gardens is the Goya Museum. The tourist office, place Alsace-Lorraine, is about 4 blocks from the station. A good market is on Place Jean Jaures, Tu, Th, F and Sa mornings.

Camping Gourjade, avenue de Roquecourbe on shore of l'Agout River, is just off highway D in the direction of Vabre or Burlats. The camp is a 30-minute walk, or take bus 5 at the bus station. Get off at the stop "Bourriatte" then take the foot bridge over the river to Gourjade Park. The last bus leaves at 7:15pm. Newly opened in 1988, the camp has excellent restrooms, grocery and cafe; 17F for 2 persons plus a tent. In the park is mini golf and a playground.

Musee Goya, well sited in a castle overlooking the river, is open Tu-Sa 9-12 & 2-6, Su 10-12 & 2-6; 5 F. Pass through the first rooms quickly as Goya's works are father along in the last three rooms of Musee Goya wing. His 24 drawings of *The Disasters of War* hang in a nook. Goya's humorous *Les Caprices* series take up a separate room. Others are his *Los Proverbios series: Sottise Feminine, Sottise de Frayeur, Sottise de Niais and Sottise Ridicule*; and a bullfight-toreador group. His mastery of social commentary is well displayed.

Carcassonne

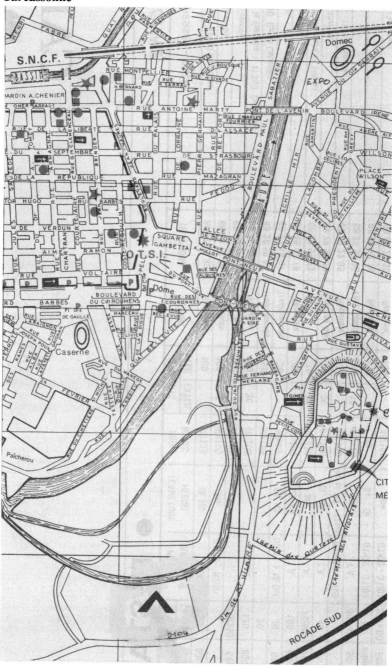

CARCASSONNE Don't miss Carcassonne, a superb medieval walled town in the south of France near the Spanish border. The ramparts are complete with 50 towers dating from the 5th, 12th and 13th centuries. The choicest item within the old town is Basilique St. Nazaire's best ever 14th and 16th century stained glass windows. There is no charge to enter La Cite or the Basilica.

Those traveling between Barcelona and the French Riviera should get off in Narbonne and change for Carcassonne. Trains leave Narbonne at 12:40pm, 6:57pm, 7:24pm and 10:24pm. The trip is 50 minutes.

The **station** is in the lower and newer town and you can walk or take bus 4 (direction St. Georges) from the station up the hill to the old town *(la cite* lah-sit-TAY) on the bluff. Bus 4 leaves at 23 and 53 minutes past the hour between 7:23am and 6:53pm; 14-minute ride. Bus 4 returns from La Cite at 21 and 51 minutes past the hour between 7:21am and 6:51pm. The **tourist office** has a branch at Porte Narbonnaise in La Cite open Apr-Oct. The main office is on Boulevard Camille-Pelletan near Place Gambetta and changes money when banks are closed. Market days are Tu, Th and Sa mornings at Place Carnot. It's possible to walk everywhere in Carcassonne, but city buses operated by C.A.R.T. are available. Either purchase a single ticket or the more economical carnet of 10. From July 30 to August 15, the Medieval Festival turns Carcassonne into a recreation of the Middle Ages.

Opened in 1987, **Camping de la Cite** is located below the Old City. Open all year, about adult/10F, tent/10F. Take bus 4 (direction St. Georges) to Place Gambetta, the seventh stop and the major square in the modern part of Carcassonne. Change to bus 5 (direction Charlemagne) which leaves Place Gambetta at 40 minutes past the hour from 7:40amd to 6:40pm (except not 4:40pm). Get off in 5 minutes at the fourth stop, *Route de Cazilrac*. Then a 5-minute walk. To go from camp to the Old City, take bus 5 (direction Gambetta) to the bridge, *Pont Vieux*, and change to bus 4 (direction St. Georges) to La Cite. Bus 5 leaves Route de Cazilrac bus stop at 8 minutes past each hour from 8:08am to 7:08pm.

To Antibes, leave at 9:51am (change at Marseilles, ar. 3:47pm), 12:39pm (ar. 7:13pm) and 2:49pm (ar. 9:26pm).

To Barcelona, in most cases you must take the train to Narbonne, and change for Barcelona. However, a through train leaves Carcassonne at 8:50am, arrives in Port Bou (the border) at 11:02am where you must change trains and arrives at Barcelona at 3:32pm. If you miss that train, another one leaves Carcassonne at 9am, arrving in Port Bou at 11:50am, in time to make the same connection as the 8:50am train. The difference is the 9am train is slightly slower and only carries second class coaches.

To go in style, leave Carcassonne at 6:21am M-Sa, and arrive Narbonne at 6:53am, just in time to board the Rapido that leaves at 7:04am. The Rapido arrives at the border (Port Bou) at 8:59am. Then change to the TALGO which leaves Port Bou at 10am and arrives at Barcelona Sants at 11:56am. The Rapido is a summer train, operating between May 31 and September 26. Eurail Youthpass holders must pay a supplement to ride the Talgo. The Talgo makes the run between the border and Barcelona in two hours, whereas a regular train with only second class leaves at 10:38am and arrives at Barcelona Termino at 12:57pm, taking an extra 25 minutes.

Other trains **leave Narbonne for Barcelona** at 9:32am (ar. Port Bou 11:02am, change trains, lv. 12:05pm all second class (ar. Barcelona Termino 2:41pm) and at 5:41pm (EuroCity in France and Talgo in Spain, no change at border, ar. 9:25pm). To connect with the 5:41pm departure, leave Carcassonne 2:49pm, ar. Narbonne 3:27pm).

To Paris Austerlitz, a through train leaves at 1:29pm (ar. 9:35pm). This same train stops at Brive (change for Les Eyzes and Rocamadour) and Vierzon (change for Chenonceaux).

To Toulouse, leave at 9:07am, 10:36am, 12:43pm, 3:49pm, 4:58pm, 5:42pm, 7:19pm, 7:33pm, 7:55pm and 10:21pm. One hour trip.

GERMANY

Castles on the Rhine, medieval Rothenburg, rococo castles of "mad" King Ludwig, and Munich, the capital of Bavaria, draw most visitors for their first trip to Germany. The modern German city is oriented towards the pedestrian, and rapid transit is thoroughly developed. Most Germans under 35 seem to speak English, or at least the ones you're likely to encounter.

CURRENCY The German mark (Deutsch Mark) is abbreviated DM. One U.S. dollar equals 1.8DM. Each mark is divided into 100 pfennig.
It's hard to avoid the high fee, often DM4-5, extracted by banks when cashing travelers checks. The fee amount varies from bank to bank. Sometimes the fee is calculated according to the amount exchanged. In some banks, no fee is charged to change currency, only travelers checks. Deutsche Verkehrs Kredit Bank seems to have a monopoly on station exchange services and charges high fees of DM2-5 per transaction.

WEATHER Camping weather extends from June through September, but the warmest and driest period is usually August. German weather follows the rain pattern of northern Europe. Remain flexible and if the weather is beautiful, do the things that require good weather and save museums for cloudy days. Remember to look out the train window before getting off. On the other side of the Alps is a completely different weather picture; Italy is only a day ride away.

CAMPING Available from the German tourist office before you go, the brochure, *Camping 1989-90*, contains a map of the country with campgrounds marked and a listing describing general rating, basic facilities, noise level and dates of operation. Germany has excellent to satisfactory campgrounds in every area you're likely to want to tour. Nightly fees are generally adult/DM4-6 and tent/DM3-5. The practice of charging an extra DM1.50 for a hot shower is widespread. Any camp listed as having a washing machine will also have a dryer.

TRAINS German trains are excellent. The railways connect all major cities and most small towns with frequent, comfortable and uncrowded trains. The German Federal Railroad (abbreviated DB for Deutsches

Bundesbahn) carries 1.5 billion passengers annually. Reservations are never needed for travel within Germany as trains run every hour between major cities. Germanrail also operates buses (bahnbus), passenger ferries and commuter trains (the S-Bahn). Almost all are included in Eurailpass.

Trains are classified as follows. EC are **EuroCity** deluxe trains that connect major European cities speedily and in style. IC are **InterCity** trains that are fast, deluxe and travel within Germany. Many are former TEE trains. IC trains provide hourly service between major cities, usually at the same number of minutes past each hour. (Should you not have a Eurailpass, the required supplement for EuroCity and InterCity trains includes a reservation and can be purchased from the vending machine at the station or a ticket counter. If the supplement isn't paid before boarding, the conductor will collect DM6 on board the train.) Only slightly slower than IC trains, D trains are **schnellzug** and provide express service. Service within Germany is not as frequent for D trains as for IC trains. Often international express trains are classified as D. The FD train is **Fern-Express**, a D train that is equipped with a Quick-Pick restaurant car. E trains are **eilzug**, slower than D category trains and usually stopping at every village along the way. Some trains have no letter designation and these **nahverkehrszug** are the slowest. The **S-Bahn** are operated by the German railroads and connect central areas of cities with their suburbs; free with Eurailpass.

A **seat reservation** costs DM3.50 but the only time one might be needed would be traveling south to sunny Italy on a Friday during July and August. Reservations for buses of Germanrail are made at the train reservation window of the train station, and often the bus leaves from outside the train station. **Free train schedules** are available from racks in the train information office of all major cities. Both individual timetables and a booklet containing out and back schedules to German and European destinations from that city are available. Free baggage carts *(koffer-kulis)* are provided at the larger stations. Coin-operated lockers cost 1 DM for small and 1.50DM for the large size per 24 hours. Luggage checking rooms are also available at the stations. Special rail plans available at train stations in Germany include a Senior Citizen Ticket *(Senioren Pass)* for women of 60 and men of 65 to buy train tickets at half price and receive discounts on long-distance buses. Children 5 through 11 travel at half fare on trains, 4 thru 13 pay half on buses. A child under 4 rides free.

zug	train (tsoog)	auskunft	train information
wagen	coach	platz	seat
gleis	track	platzcarte	seat reservation
abfahrt	departures	reisedatum	date of departure
ankunft	arrivals	abfahrtszeit	time of departure
ab	departure time	So	Sunday
an	arrival time	Mo	Monday
taglich	daily service	Di	Tuesday
nur	except	Mi	Wednesday
bis	until	Do	Thursday
an		Fr	Friday
sonntagen	Sunday only	Sa	Saturday

EURAIL BONUSES (1) Railpasses are valid on the following **bus lines** of the integrated bus transport Post/Railroad bus union: **Kiel** - AutoKraft

GmbH, **Luneberg**, Kraftverkerhr GambH-KVG Stade and KVG Luneberg, HANOVER - Regionalverkeh Hanover GmbH, **Cologne** - Koln GmbH, **Munich** area - Oberbayern GmbH and **Schwaben** area - Schwaben-Allgau GmbH. (2) The bonus listed as the ferry crossing between **Puttgarden, Germany and Rodby, Denmark** is simply the crossing used by international trains between Germany and Denmark. The trains roll onto the ferry and then passengers are free to get off and go upstairs to the lounges and duty free shop. In a few cases, where an extra train has been added to carry the overload, passengers may have to get off the German train, walk onto the ferry, and on the other side walk onto a waiting Danish train. (3) The **S-bahn** has been constructed by the German Federal Railroads in several cities to link the suburbs with the downtown center and these DB trains are included in the railpasses.

(4) **Romantic Road Eurapabus** Line 190. The *Romantishe Strasse* Eurapabus between Wiesbaden/Frankfurt and Munich is included in railpasses. The English-speaking guide provides commentary as the bus passes by some of the more picturesque towns in Germany, the most scenic part being between Wurzburg and Augsburg. A free reservation may be necessary for the direction Frankfurt to Munich. The other direction is less popular and a reservation is not needed. In Frankfurt, make the reservation in the Eurapabus office outside the train station. You may stop off overnight or join the bus from another town enroute, but this should be indicated when the reservation is made or upon boarding if without a reservation. The bus operates daily in each direction from March 14 to November 2. The journey breaks for two hours in Rothenburg and and about one hour in medieval Dinkelsbuhl. Bring lunch to eat enroute so precious layover time may be used for sightseeing. More details are under "Munich."

I think the best way though is to make it a jpday trip from Frankfurt (or neighboring villages) to Rothenburg. You arrive in Rothenburg at noon and then change to the other bus for your return at 5pm. This gives more time to see Rothenburg, the most interesting village, and avoids the long boring bus ride from Munich.

A second bus operates solely between Augsburg and Wurzburg. About hourly train service is provided between Frankfurt and Wurzburg, and Munich and Augsburg. Information on the trip from Munich to Frankfurt is given under Munich.

Highlight of the tour is the two hour stop in **Rothenburg** (pronounced ROW-ten-burg), a fascinating old walled village of the Middle Ages, now designated as a museum town. This town on the Tauber River was a free city of the Holy Roman Empire from 1274 to 1803. Its architecture is mostly Gothic and Renaissance, and though packed with tourists, Rothenburg remains a highpoint of a trip to Germany. The town is also served by train, though service is so infrequent it's of little use. (Camping Tauber Idyll is 3km north of Rothenburg on Romantische Strasses, open Apr-Oct, should you wish to spend the night.) Another stop is made in **Dinkelsbuhl** which is not so determinedly picturesque as Rothenburg and its architecture is more relaxed. A good and convenient campground within walking distance is just outside the walls across the moat beyond Wornitz Castle.

Romantic Road Europabus
Linie EB190   ROMANTISCHE STRASSE

Wiesbaden / Frankfurt/M. – Würzburg – Augsburg – München / Füssen

A tägl. daily	tägl. daily	14. März – 2. November	A tägl.*) daily	tägl. daily
–	7.00 ab	Wiesbaden, Theater/Kurhaus .... an	20.45	–
–	7.05	Wiesbaden, Hbf./Ost, Omnibusbf. Bstg. 1 .. ▲	20.40	–
–	8.15 ▼	Frankfurt/M., Hbf./Süd, Touring-Büro ...	19.55	–
– / 9.00¹)	– an / 10.15** ab	Würzburg, Hbf., Omnibusbf. ...... ▲ {ab 18.10 / an –}		– / 19.20
{	10.35	Ochsenfurt, Mainbrücke	17.45	{
}	10.55	Uffenheim, Rothenburger Str........	17.20	}
9.40	}	Tauberbischofsheim, Bf.	}	18.40
10.05	{	Bad Mergentheim, Bf...........	{	18.15
10.25 / 10.45	an) / ab)	Weikersheim, Marktplatz .... {ab 17.55 / an –}		17.55 / –
10.55	{	Röttingen, Marktplatz .... ▲	}	17.40
11.10	{	Creglingen, Omnibusbf. .... ▲	}	17.30
11.15 / 11.30	an) / ab)	Creglingen, Herrgottskapelle ..... ● {ab / an}		– / –
12.00 11.35 an / 13.30 13.45 ab		Rothenburg o.d.T., Schrannenplatz²) ● {ab 17.00 17.00 / an 15.15 15.35}⁴⁾		
13.35 –		Rothenburg, Bf.		– 15.30
13.55 –		Schillingsfürst, Gasthof „Post"		– 15.15
14.15 14.30 ▼		Feuchtwangen, Omnibusbf.		14.30 14.55
14.30 14.45 an / 15.00 15.30 ab		Dinkelsbühl, Schweinemarkt³) ... ▲ {ab 14.15 14.40 / an 12.35 13.10}		
15.20 16.00 ab		Wallerstein, Sparkasse .... ab		12.00 12.35
15.25 16.05		Nördlingen, Rathaus .... ▲ {ab 11.55 12.30 / an 11.40 –}		
15.55 –		Harburg, Marktplatz .... ▲		– 12.15
16.10 16.35 ▼		Donauwörth, Stadtpfarrkirche .... (Richtung Rothenburg Kaufhaus Nassel)		11.05 12.00
16.55 – an / 17.05 17.40 ab		Augsburg, Hbf., Bstg. F .... ▲ {ab 10.20 11.10 / an – 11.00}		
	17.55 ✦	Friedberg, Marienplatz .... ✦	9.55	
	18.55 an	München, Hbf., Starnberger Bf. .... ab	9.00	
		Arnulfstr. Bstg. 21		

Augsburg – Füssen

A tägl. daily		14. März – 2. November	A tägl.*) daily	tägl. daily
17.55 – an / 18.15 – ab		Landsberg, Hauptplatz .... {ab / an}		– 10.15 / – –
18.30 –		Hohenfurch, B17		– 9.55
18.35 –		Schongau, Bf.		– 9.50
18.40 –		Peiting, Meierstraße		– 9.45
18.45 –		Rottenbuch, Post		– 9.35
18.50 –		Echelsbacher Brücke		– 9.30
18.55 –		Wildsteig		– 9.25
18.57 –		Abzw. Ilchberg		– 9.22
19.00 – ▼		Kohlhofen, Abzw. Wies		– 9.20
– – an / – – ab		Wieskirche .... {ab / an}		– 9.15 / – ▲8.50
19.05 –		Steingaden, Postamt		– 8.40
19.15 –		Trauchgau		– 8.35
19.20 –		Buching		– 8.30
19.25 –		Schwangau, Verkehrsbüro		– 8.25
19.30 – ▼		Hohenschwangau		– 8.20
19.35 – an		Füssen, Bf. .... ab		8.15

A = vom 31.5.–5.10.   letzte Fahrt Füssen – Würzburg 6.10
) Letzte Fahrt München – Wiesbaden am 3.1
**) Zusteigen nur möglich bei noch freien Plätzen in der Zeit vom 31.5.–5.10.1987 zwischen Würzburg und Rothenburg.
✦ Keine Verkehrsbedienung Friedberg – Augsburg – Friedberg.

Linie EB 189

Castle Road Europabus „Die Burgenstraße"
Mannheim – Heidelberg – Langenburg – Rothenburg o. d.Tauber – Nürnberg – (Augsburg – München – Füssen)

Schienenfahrausweise, EURAIL- und EURAIL YOUTHPÄSSE werden anerkannt.

täglich/daily			31. Mai – 26. September		täglich/daily	
7.15	–	ab	Mannheim, Hbf.	an	–	20.45
7.30	–	an�	Heidelberg, Hbf.	⎰ab	–	–
7.45	–	ab		⎱an	–	20.25
7.57	–		Neckargemünd, Bf.		–	20.19
8.05	–		Neckarsteinach, Bf.		–	20.11
8.10	–		Neckarhausen, Bf.		–	20.06
8.15	–		Hirschhorn, Schiffsanlegestelle		–	20.02
8.26	–		Eberbach, Neckaranlagen		–	19.52
8.31	–		Lindach, Schiff		–	19.46
8.34	–		Zwingenberg (Baden), Anker		–	19.43
8.48	–		Neckarelz, Schulzentrum		–	19.29
8.53	–		Neckarzimmern, Rathaus		–	19.23
9.12	–	ab	Bad Friedrichshall-Jagstfeld, Bf.	ab	–	19.09
9.39	–		Öhringen, Stadthalle		–	18.37
9.49	–		Neuenstein, Schloß		–	18.27
9.57	–		Hohebuch-Waldenburg		–	18.19
10.02	–		Kupferzell, Rathaus		–	18.14
10.16	–		Braunsbach, Marktplatz		–	18.00
10.35	–	an	Langenburg, Rathaus	⎰ab	–	17.40
11.20	–	ab		⎱an	–	–
11.35	–		Blaufelden, Bf.		–	17.25
11.43	–		Schrozberg, Friedhof		–	17.17
11.56	–		Rothenburg o.d.Tauber, Bf.		–	16.54
12.00	–	an	**Rothenburg o.d.T.**¹), Schrannenplatz²)	ab	–	16.50

Anschluß Nürnberg (DB-Bus)

16.30	–	ab	Rothenburg o.d.T.¹), Schrannenplatz²)	an	–	10.45
18.30	–	an	**Nürnberg,** Hbf./ZOB	ab	–	8.45

Anschluß „Romantische Straße" (A / EB 190)

A					A	
13.30	13.45	ab	**Rothenburg o.d.T.**¹), Schrannenplatz²)	an	15.15	15.35
13.35	–		Rothenburg, Bf.		–	15.30
13.55	–		Schillingsfürst, Gasthof „Post"		–	15.15
14.15	14.30		Feuchtwangen, Omnibusbahnhof		14.30	14.55
14.30	14.45	an	Dinkelsbühl, Schweinemarkt	ab	14.15	14.40
15.00	15.30	ab		an	12.35	13.10
15.20	16.00	ab	Wallerstein, Sparkasse	ab	12.00	12.35
15.25	16.05		Nördlingen, Rathaus	ab	11.55	12.30
				an	11.40	–
15.55	–		Harburg, Marktplatz		–	12.15
16.10	16.35		Donauwörth, Stadtpfarrkirche		11.05	12.00
			(Richtung Rothenburg Kaufhaus Nassel)			
16.55	–	an	**Augsburg,** Hbf., Bstg. F	⎰ab	10.20	11.10
17.05	17.40	ab		⎱an	–	11.00
	17.55	♦	Friedberg, Marienplatz	♦	9.55	
	18.55	an	**München,** Hbf., Starnberger Bahnhof	ab	9.00	–
			Arnulfstraße, Bstg. 21			
17.55	–	an	Landsberg, Hauptplatz	⎰ab	–	10.15
18.15	–	ab		⎱an	–	
18.30	–		Hohenfurch, B17		–	9.55
18.35	–		Schongau, Bf.		–	9.50
18.40	–		Peiting, Meierstraße		–	9.45
18.45	–		Rottenbuch, Post		–	9.35
18.50	–		Echelsbacher Brücke		–	9.30
18.55	–		Wildsteig		–	9.25
18.57	–		Abzw. Ilchberg		–	9.22
19.00	–		Kohlhofen, Abzw. Wies		–	9.20
–	–	an	Wieskirche	⎰ab	–	9.15
–	–	ab		⎱an	–	▲ 8.50
19.05	–		Steingaden, Postamt		–	8.40
19.15	–		Trauchgau		–	8.35
19.20	–		Buching		–	8.30
19.25	–		Schwangau, Verkehrsbüro		–	8.25
19.30	–		Hohenschwangau		–	8.20
19.35	–	an	**Füssen,** Bf.	ab	–	8.15

Left/right margin section labels: DB-Bus · EB 190 · EB 190 A

¹) Für Fahrgäste nach oder von München, Füssen und Nürnberg: Umstieg in Rothenburg.
²) Bei offizieller Sperre des Schrannenplatzes ist der Bahnhof Ausweichhaltestelle.

(5)   **Castle Road Europabus** line 189.   The bus goes between Mannheim, Heidelberg, Heilbronn, Rothenburg ob der Tauber, Ansbach and Nuremberg.

(6) **Rhine River Cruise**   Railpasses are valid on ferry passenger liners operated by Koln-Dusseldorfer-Deutsche Rheinschiffahrt (KD line) on regularly scheduled runs on the Rhine River between Dusseldorf and Frankfurt. The hydrofoil Rheinpfeil is not included. The most scenic portion is between Koblenz and Binger, which takes 2-3/4 hours downstream (Bingen to Koblenz) or 4-3/4 hours upstream.   Once a day express service, *schnell-fahrt* leaves Bingen at 10:45am and arrives in Koblenz at Rheinwerft near Deutsches Eck at 1:45pm.   Several small towns along the Rhine have a campground within a 5 to 10-minute walk from the ferry dock.   Campground directions are included for Bacharach (the most picturesque stopover), St. Goar, St. Goarshausen and Boppard.   Schnellfahrt (express) service is the same in other months, but ordinary service is curtailed.

(7) **Mosel River Cruise.** Eurailpasses are valid between Koblenz and Cochem on regular daily runs of the steamers operated by the KD German Rhine Line.   (8) 50 percent reduction on normal fares for the ferry crossing Lubeck-Travemunde to Trelleborg, Sweden, on the TT Line.   (9) 50 percent reduction on regular steamer services on Lake Constance (Bodensee).   (10) Reduced fares on the following **mountain railroads**: **Garmisch**-Partenkirchen   Grainau   Zugspitze   (Schneefernerhaus)   and **Freiburg** (Breisgau) Schauinsland: 50 percent on ordinary tickets.   (11) 25 percent reduction on the roundtrip bus fare **Braunschweig-Berlin** or vice versa operated by Bayern Express and P. Kuhn Berlin GmbH for students producing a valid student ID card.   (12) 20 percent reduction on some half-day or full-day excursions out of Munich operated by the Oberbayern GmbH.   (13) 10 percent off on Munich city tours of by Oberbayern GmbH.

CASTLES ON THE RHINE CRUISE - BINGEN TO KOBLENZ

On either side of the middle Rhine River gorge between Bingen and Koblenz lies a succession of terraced vineyards, small wine villages and beautiful castles. The area can be leisurely enjoyed by riding a ferry down its length, or quickly viewed in 45 minutes from the train as it speeds by. Throughout the summer, the castles along the Rhine are floodlit and can be glimpsed through the train windows even at night because the tracks parallel the river.

Eurailpass is valid on ferry passenger boats operated by Koln-Dusseldorfer-Deutsche Rheinschiffahrt (**KD line**) on regularly scheduled runs on the Rhine River between Dusseldorf and Frankfurt. The hydrofoil, Rheinpfeil, requires a supplement. Bring lunch as food is expensive. The most **scenic portion** of the Rhine is between Koblenz and Bingen which takes 2-3/4 hours downstream (Bingen to Koblenz) or 4-3/4 hours upstream. Once a day express service (schnell-fahrt) leaves Bingen at 10:45am and arrives in Koblenz at Rheinwerft near Deutsches Eck at 1:45pm. Express service does not stop at all the smallest villages, but only the most important ones: Assmannshausen, Bacharach, St. Goar, St. Goarhausen, Boppard and Braubach. Regular service leaves Bingen at 10:10am, stops at every village and arrives in Koblenz at 1:50pm. The loading dock is marked "KD".

Rhine River Upstream, Summer Schedule (mid-June to mid-September)

Upstream

41	43	61	19	15	35	13	1	/1	23	9	27	Daily
					Tue,Sun from 19.7. to 30.8. only	Mon, from 18.7. to 29.8. Thu,Sat also	Schnell-fahrt Koblenz-Mainz with sur-charge	Hydro-foil excl. Mon				Limited service on July 4 and August 8
							7.00	9.00	9.15		11.00	dep Köln
									10.00		11.50	Porz
									10.40		12.33	Wesseling
					8.15	8.15	9.15	9.40	11.50		14.00	Bonn
									12.00			Bn-Bundeshaus
					8.50	8.50	9.45		12.27		14.35	Bn-Bad Godesbg.
					9.05	9.05	10.00	9.55	12.50		14.50	Königswinter
					9.25	9.25	10.17		13.10		15.10	Bad Honnef
					9.45	9.45	10.35		13.31		15.31	Unkel
					10.00	10.00	10.50	10.10	13.46		15.46	Remagen
					10.20	10.20	11.05	10.15	14.07		16.07	Linz
				8.45	10.50	10.50	11.30	10.25	14.38		16.38	Bad Breisig
				8.50	10.55	10.55	11.35		14.43		16.43	Bad Hönningen
				9.35	11.45	11.45	12.15	10.38	15.30		17.30	Andernach
				9.55	12.05	12.05	12.35				17.50	Neuwied
			9.00		11.30	13.35	13.35	14.00	11.05	14.30	19.03	Koblenz
	9.24				11.55				14.55			Niederlahnstein
	9.33				12.05				15.05			Oberlahnstein
	9.45				12.15				15.15			Rhens
	9.58				12.25	14.25	14.45		15.25		19.50	Braubach
9.00	10.40		12.15		13.15	15.15	15.25	11.30		16.15	20.30	Boppard
9.10	10.50		12.25		13.25					16.25		Kamp-Bornhofen
9.20	11.00		12.35		13.35					16.35		Bad Salzig
10.10	11.50		13.30		14.30		16.25			17.25		St. Goarshausen
10.15	11.55		13.40		14.40		16.30	11.50		17.35		St. Goar
10.45	12.20		14.10		15.10		16.50*			18.05		Oberwesel
11.00	12.37		14.25		15.25					18.20		Kaub
11.20	12.55	13.55	14.45		15.45		17.25	12.08		18.40		Bacharach
11.35	13.07	14.07	15.00		16.00					18.55		Lorch
11.45	13.12	14.12	15.10		16.10					19.05		Niederheimbach
12.25	13.50	14.50	15.40		16.40		18.10			19.35		Assmannshausen
12.55	14.20	15.20	16.05		17.05		18.35	12.28		20.00		Bingen
13.10	14.30	15.30	16.20		17.20		18.50	12.33		20.10		Rüdesheim
		16.35			18.25		19.55					Eltville
		17.20			19.10		20.40	13.00				Wiesbaden-Biebrich
		17.45			19.30		21.00	13.10				Mainz
		18.30										Rüsselsheim
		19.55										Frankfurt-Höchst
		20.45										arr Frankfurt (M)

Column 13: Rhine-Moselle excursion — arr. Winningen 14.45

Column 1: stops only in July and August

Column 9: Koblenz-Boppard excl. Sat (arr. Koblenz 20.00)

RHINE ↓→	Königswinter	Remagen	Linz	Bad Breisig Bad Hönningen	Andernach	Neuwied	Koblenz	Boppard	St. Goarsh. St. Goar	Bacharach	Assmanns-hausen	Bingen	Rüdesheim	Wiesbaden Biebrich	Mainz
Köln (Cologne)	26,20	34,80	37,80	41,80	49,80	52,60	59,60	71,60	80,80	90,60	97,60	99,80	101,—	114,20	117,—
Bonn	9,—	17,60	20,40	24,60	32,60	35,40	42,40	54,40	63,60	73,40	80,20	82,60	83,80	97,—	99,80
Königswinter	-	10,80	13,60	17,60	25,60	28,60	35,40	47,60	56,80	66,40	73,40	75,60	76,80	90,—	93,—
Koblenz	35,40	26,80	24,—	20,—	11,80	9,—	-	14,20	23,40	33,20	40,—	42,40	43,40	56,80	59,60
Boppard	47,60	38,80	36,—	32,—	24,—	21,—	14,20	-	11,20	21,—	28,—	32,20	31,40	44,60	47,60
Bingen	75,60	67,—	64,20	60,20	52,20	49,20	42,40	30,20	21,—	11,20	4,40	-	3,20	16,40	19,40
Rüdesheim	76,80	68,20	65,40	61,40	53,20	50,40	43,40	31,40	22,20	12,40	5,60	3,20	-	15,40	18,20
Wiesbaden-Biebr.	90,—	81,40	78,60	74,60	66,40	63,60	56,80	44,60	35,40	25,60	18,80	16,40	15,40	-	5,—
Mainz	93,—	84,40	81,40	77,40	69,40	66,40	59,60	47,60	38,40	28,60	21,60	19,40	18,20	5,—	-

Rhine River Downstream, Summer Schedule (mid-June to mid-September)

Downstream

Daily — Limited service on July 4 and August 8	20	10	2	24	22	34	14	40	70	42
	from 6.7		Schnellfahrt Mainz-Bonn with surcharge			Tue,Sun from 19.7. to 30.8. only	Mon. from 18.7. to 29.8. Thu,Sat also		Hydrofoil excl. Mon	
Köln Frankenwerft arr			18.20	19.30	20.40				18.05	
Porz				19.05						
Wesseling				18.38						
Bonn opp. Rheingasse			17.00	18.00	19.15	20.15	20.15		17.30	
Bn-Bundeshaus				17.50						
Bn-Bad Godesbg. (N.-u. O.dollendorf)			16.40	17.40	18.55	19.55	19.55			
Königswinter (Drachenfels)			16.30	17.30	18.45	19.45	19.45		17.20	
Bad Honnef Grafenwerth			16.15	17.10	18.30	19.30	19.30			
Unkel (Rheinbreitbach)				16.55	18.15	19.15	19.15			
Remagen (Bd. Neuenahr, Ahrtal)			15.55	16.45	18.05	19.05	19.05		17.03	
Linz (Westerwald, Bd. Kripp)			15.40	16.30	17.50	18.50	18.50		16.58	
Bad Breisig (Rheineck)			15.25	16.15	17.35	18.35	18.35	19.30	16.50	
Bad Hönningen (Arenfels)				16.05	17.30	18.30	18.30	19.25		
Andernach (Laacher See, Eifel)			15.00	15.40	17.05	18.05	18.05	19.00	16.38	
Neuwied (Rengsdorf)			14.45		16.50	17.50	17.50	18.45		
Koblenz K.-Adenauer-Ufer		13.50	14.05*			16.05	17.05	17.05	16.20	20.00
Niederlahnstein (Bad Ems, Lahn)		13.30					15.37	16.37	17.37	19.42
Oberlahnstein (eck, Stolzenfels)		13.25					15.30	16.30	17.30	19.35
Rhens (Königstuhl)		13.15					15.23	16.23	17.23	19.30
Braubach (Marksburg)		13.05	13.15				15.15	16.15	17.15	19.20
Boppard (Hunsrück)	11.45	12.35	12.50			15.45	14.45	16.45	15.55	18.50
Kamp-Bornhofen (Feindliche Brüder)	11.35	12.30					14.35	16.35		18.40
Bad Salzig	11.25	12.15					14.25	16.25		18.30
St. Goarshausen (Burg Katz, Loreley)	11.00	11.45	12.10				14.00	16.00	15.40	18.10
St. Goar (Rheinfels, Loreley)	10.50	11.35	12.00				13.50	15.50		18.00
Oberwesel (Schönburg)	10.30	11.20				62 daily	13.30	15.30		17.45
Kaub (Pfalz, Gutenfels)	10.17	11.08					13.17	15.17		17.33
Bacharach (Stahleck, Steeg)	10.05	10.55	11.30				13.05	15.05		17.20
Lorch (Wispertal)	9.55	10.45					12.55	14.55		17.11
Niederheimbach (Sonneck)	9.50	10.40					12.50	14.50		17.05
Assmannshausen (Rheinstein)	9.30	10.25	11.00				12.30	14.30		16.48
Bingen (Bad Kreuznach)	9.15	10.10	10.45			13.00	12.15	14.15	15.05	16.35
Rüdesheim (Niederwald)	9.00	9.50	10.25			12.45	12.00	14.00	15.00	16.20
Eltville (Schwalbach)				9.25	10.55	11.55				
Wiesbaden-Biebrich				9.05	10.35	11.35			14.33	
Mainz Am Rathaus				8.45	10.15	11.15			14.25	
Rüsselsheim			* arr. 13.45			10.20				
Frankfurt-Höchst						9.10				
Frankfurt (M) Eiserner Steg dep						8.15				

Rhine-Moselle excursion dep. Winningen 16.00

Day excursions Koblenz – Cochem

daily from 10.5. to 18.10.	Mon from 15.6. to 5.10.; Thu, Sat from 18.7. to 29.8.			Mon from 15.6. to 5.10.; Thu, Sat from 18.7. to 29.8.	daily from 10.5. to 18.10.
10.00	13.35	dep. **Koblenz** arr.		17.00	20.10
10.40	14.15	Moselweiß		16.25	19.20
11.05	14.45	Winningen		16.00	19.00
11.30		Kobern-Gondorf			18.40
12.15		Alken			17.55
12.25		Brodenbach			17.45
13.00		Moselkern			17.15
13.45		Treis-Karden			16.35
14.30		arr. **Cochem** dep.			16.00

Rhine-Moselle excursion (dep. Bonn 8.15) · Rhine-Moselle excursion (arr. Bonn 20.15)

If coming from Munich, a good strategy is to arrive the night before and stay in Rudesheim, take a morning or afternoon cruise to Boppard or Koblenz and then change to the train to reach your overnight destination. Koblenz is a medium size city that has frequent InterCity train departures, but a bus fare must be paid to reach the station from the ferry dock. The hassle of a busy town and the bus ride can be avoided by getting off the ferry in **Boppard**, the only small village between Bingen and Koblenz in which at least D category trains stop. If you have the time and inclination, an overnight stop in the lovely town of Bacharach is enjoyable.

To reach Rudesheim by train from Munich, take any train to Wiesbaden and then change. Trains leave Wiesbaden for Rudesheim at 7:42am (ar. 8:06am), 10:15am (ar. 10:37am), 11:20am (ar. 11:49am), 2:19pm (ar. 2:49pm), 4:49pm (ar. 5:14pm), 6:19pm (ar. 6:50pm), 7:19pm (ar. 7:49pm), 8:12pm except Saturday (ar. 8:41pm) and 9:15pm (ar. 9:44pm).

Ferries cross the Rhine, connecting the towns on either side, between Boppard and Kamp-Bornhofen, St. Goar and St. Goarhausen, Bacharach and Kaub, and Bingen and Rudesheim. Towns usually have more than one dock, called a landing stage (landebrucke), used by the various ferry lines. It is possible, of course, to take a local train on either side of the Rhine which connects all villages on the respective side.

Numerous campgrounds border the Rhine and getting off the boat wherever you like will probably place you within 3 km. of a campground. However, two towns in particular are worthwhile. Both have campgrounds a short walk from both dock and train station. **Bacharach** is the nicest for daytime visiting with its attractive authentic architecture, but for evening entertainment nothing beats the wine taverns on the Drosselgasse in **Rudesheim**. Besides exploring the villages, time can be spent visiting the castles overlooking the river. Trails lace the terraced vineyards on both sides of the Rhine, and trail maps are available at local tourist offices.

Stopping at any small town on the Rhine or Mosel Rivers between July and mid-October, posters announcing the dates of a nearby **wine festival** will be posted on train station walls. Though called a wine festival, the date usually has no relation to the actual harvest which occurs between mid-September and November depending on the weather. Instead these are local summer celebrations, often ending with Saturday night fireworks on the Rhine, called *Rhein in Flammen* (Rhine in Flames). Consider yourself lucky if you happen to find one in progress.

KOBLENZ (COBLENCE) The tourist office is in the round building across from the train station. Use the pedestrian underpass to get there. Open M-Sa 8:30-8, Su 1:30-7. The post office is outside the station to the right. Bus 1 leaves from in front of the three small shops in the plaza in front of the station and terminates at the monument, Deutsches Eck. The ferry dock, Rheinwerft, is only a short distance from there. Koblenz hosts fireworks, *Rhein in Flammen*, on the second Saturday night in August.

Camping Rhein-Mosel is opposite Deutsches Eck at the confluence of the Rhine and Mosel rivers on the left bank of the Mosel. Apr 1-Oct 15; adult/DM3.75, tent/DM3.75, hot shower/DM1. If you've arrived by ferry, walk to the Deutsches Eck monument (you can't miss it) and then go past it and walk to the edge of the Mosel and find a tiny wood dock where you must wait for the motorboat to come from across the river. A DM.60 charge is made for the ride and the last boat leaves at 7pm. Coming from the train station, take bus 4 to Schwarzerweg and then walk, or bus 1 to Deutsches

206

Eck and then the boat. Hot water in the sinks, automatic washing machine, cafe and lounge. The closest store 500 meters.

BOPPARD   Camping Sonneneck is north of town, 5 km. from Boppard, located between the highway and the river. Local buses from Boppard station go to the campsite; last bus is 11:41pm. Apr-Oct; adult/DM7, tent/DM4; hot water in the restroom sinks, automatic washing machine, store, restaurant (half chicken DM10), lounge, table tennis, fishing and large solar-heated swimming pool plus childrens pool. The 24-acre site bordering the Rhine River has extensive mowed lawns, trees and shrubbery. The Boppard tourist office is at Karmeliter Strasse 2.
    To Koblenz and Cologne (Koln), leave at 9:19am (ar. Koln 10:44am), 10:44am (ar. Koln 12:27pm), 1:17pm (ar. Koln 2:38pm), 4:32pm (ar. Koln 5:56pm) and 8:19pm (ar. Koln 9:48pm). Koblenz is reached about 12 minutes after leaving Boppard. Trains leaving Boppard and ending in Koblenz leave at 2:33pm, 5:36pm, 6:41pm and 10:21pm. At Koblenz, train connections can easily be made for the faster EuroCity and InterCity trains traveling north to The Netherlands or south to Munich or Switzerland.

ST. GOAR   Camping Loreleyblick, on the southern edge of town along the main riverside highway, Bundestraseee, is 1 km. from the train station and ferry dock. From the station, walk to the river and turn right onto Bundestrasse, the highway. The camp is directly on the beach and open all year, but is not as good a camp as the one in Bacharach. Burg Rheinfels, the castle, is a 20-minute walk from the campground (daily 9-6, adult/DM3, student/DM1.50). The tourist office, Heerstrasse 120, is open M-F 8-12:30 & 2-5. A ferry shuttles between St. Goar and St. Goarshausen.

ST. GOARSHAUSEN Across from St. Goar, the rock of Loreley serves as the landmark for this small town on the Rhine that grew where the river narrows the most. **Camping Clause**, Wellmicher Strasse, is north of town about 1 km. from either the ferry dock or train station. With your back towards the dock, turn left and walk north along the river. From the station, facing towards the river, walk to your right (north). The tourist office, at Bahnhofstrasse 8 in the town hall 1 block from the train station, distributes a map of the town and surrounding countryside on which 6 hiking trails are marked, each taking 2-4 hours. St. Goarhausen's *Rhine in Flames* is the third Saturday in September, and its wine festival starts the weekend before and extends through the Sunday following Rhine in Flames.
    To Rudesheim, Wiesbaden and Frankfurt, leave at 6:19am, 8:37am M-F only, 10:53am, 12:45pm and 6:48pm. The ride is about 30 minutes to Rudesheim, an hour to Wiesbaden and 1-1/2 hours to Frankfurt. Other trains going only as far as Rudesheim and Wiesbaden leave at 3:42pm, 4:42pm and 9:50pm.
    To Koblenz, leave at 6:08am M-F only, 8:29am, 11am, 12:14pm, 3:14pm, 7:17pm, 8:13pm, 9:05pm except Sa and 10:08pm. The trip is about 30 minutes.

KAUB The village is the closest one across the river from Bacharach and a ferry shuttles back and forth. One of the least expensive but accessible campgrounds on the middle Rhine is here, but it is only open during July and August. Small **Camping Am Eisieinbad** is by the swimming pool at the road to Weisel, 2 km. from Kaub. Adult/DM2.80, tent/DM2.80. The attractive camp has sinks with cold water only, 2 hot showers, 6 toilets, and sinks for hand washing clothes. For food you must go to Kaub. Remember that only regular KD ferry service stops here, not express service.

BACHARACH This especially attractive wine village has **Camping Anmeldung**, only 200 meters from the station or 500 meters from the ferry dock (*landebrucke*). The somewhat windy camp is next to the Rhine River. The site provides shade trees, good restroom facilities, store and medium priced restaurant with a terrace overlooking the Rhine River. Adult/DM4.50, tent/DM4, hot shower/DM1.50. The tourist office is at Oberstrasse 1. Bacharach is probably the best overnight stop on the middle Rhine, from both a campground and village standpoint.

BINGEN Fast trains from Mainz and Cologne stop at Bingen bahnhof. Across the street on the right is the tourist office, open M-Sa 9-7, Su 9-12. The ferry dock for the Rhine excursion boats is three blocks away. It's nicer to take the ferry across the Rhine and stay in Rudesheim, but if you want to stay on this side of the Rhine, a campground can be found on the Rhine River east of town in the suburb of Kempten. The bus to Kempten leaves every 20 minutes across the street from the station. The ride is 10 minutes plus there is a five-minute walk to camp. Bingen's second train station is Bingen-Bingerbruck, from which trains depart to Basel, Switzerland, and some to Munich.
    From Bingen station to Mainz, where InterCity trains stop, leave at 6:10am M-F only, 6:55am M-F only, 7:36am M-F only, 8:11am, 9:55am, 11:54am and 4:51pm.
    To Munich, a through train leaves Bingen at 9:55am (ar. 3:20pm).

RUDESHEIM AM RHEIN Frequent ferries shuttle back and forth across the Rhine between moderate size Bingen and small Rudesheim. Rudesheim, with its narrow alleys, overhanging houses with flower boxes and atmospheric wine taverns along the Drosselgasse, is by far the better place to stay. The town architecture is not authentic as it was reconstructed after World War II, but it was nicely done and the town itself attracts an exceptionally lively crowd. The Asbach-Uralt plant near the dock offers a free guided tour through its brandy-making facility. Rudesheim's annual wine festival always begins on the third weekend in August and lasts for four days. The tourist office is near the dock at Rhinestrasse 16. Campingplatz am Rhein is the closest campground, only 600 meters from the ferry dock, located between the main thoroughfare, Promenadenweg, and the Rhine. May-Sep; adult/DM5.15, small tent/DM4.70, 5-minute hot shower/DM2 (buy token in office); hot water in sinks, washer, store.
    To leave Rudesheim by rail, take the train to nearby Wiesbaden, a major train interchange, and then transfer to a faster InterCity or EuroCity train. Trains leave Rudesheim for Wiesbaden at 6:47am (ar. 7:23am), 9am (ar. 9:27am), 10:10am (ar. 10:16am), 11:13am (ar. 11:40am), 1:06pm (ar. 1:31pm), 4:06pm (ar. 4:39pm), 5:08pm (ar. 5:40pm), 7:15pm (ar. 7:52pm), 9:12pm (ar. 9:40pm) and 10:15pm (ar. 10:47pm).
    To travel north, trains leave for Koblenz at 6:42am, 8:06am, 10:37am, 11:49am, 2:49pm, 5:25pm, 6:50pm, 7:49pm, 8:41pm not Sa, and 9:44pm. One hour.
    To St. Goarshausen, leave at 8:06am, 10:37am, 11:49am, 2:49pm, 5:14pm, 6:50pm, 7:49pm, 8:41pm except Saturday, and 9:44pm. The trip is about 23 minutes.

MOSEL RIVER CRUISE - KOBLENZ TO COCHEM

Terraced vineyards, picturesque towns with half-timbered houses and a few castles in the green Mosel Valley can be seen from the KD cruise ship as it steams from Koblenz to Cochem. Eurailpass is valid on ferries operated by the "KD German Rhine Line" making regular runs on the Mosel River between Koblenz and Cochem. From about May 5 through October 18, there is one sailing daily at 10am from Koblenz and 4pm from Cochem. See schedule in introductory section to Germany.

In **Cochem** are 2 campgrounds within 1 km. of the station. **Camping am Stadion** is the closest at the sports field on the right Mosel bank near the Youth Hostel. Apr 11-Oct 15; adult/DM4, tent/DM3.50; sinks with hot water, store. **Camping Schausten** is 1 km. from the river. May 11-Nov 15; adult/DM3.50, small tent/DM3.50; sinks with hot water, store. The dock and train station are 4 blocks apart in Cochem.

COLOGNE (KOLN)

Cologne's magnificent world famous Gothic Cathedral, the focal point for the city, rises directly beside the train station. The dual spires of the cathedral are visible from the train window as it approaches Cologne from the north. Even if you don't want to take the trouble of going out to a campground, it's worthwhile to stop off in Cologne, check your pack, and at least tour the Cathedral. If there's extra time, visit the excellent modern museum complex that begins across from the Cathedral. In no other German city are found so many major sightseeing attractions clustered immediately outside the train station.

TRAIN STATION   Cologne is a busy railway junction with over 200 international connections a day. The enormous terminal is always busy and has myriad eateries, shops and services. Train information is open daily 6am-10pm. The Deutsche Verkehrs Kredit Bank is open M-Sa 7am-9pm, Su 8am-9pm, and charged a fee of DM2 to cash $40 in travelers checks.

TOURIST OFFICE   *Verkehrsamt* is not located in the train station, but outside at 19 Unter Fettenhennen opposite the main entrance of the Cathedral (M-Sa 8am-10:30pm, Su 9am-10:30pm). Ask for *Between Rhine and Ring*, a booklet describing walking tours.

CITY TRANSPORTATON   Buses, tram and U-Bahn are integrated into one system operated by the Cologne City Transport (KVB). The campgrounds are within the A-Karte zone, comprising zones 1 and 2. The price for a single ticket (*einzelfahrscheine*) valid for zones 1 and 2 is DM2,40. A 4-ride card for zones 1 and 2, called an A-Karte, is sold for DM8. Purchase tickets at the KVB office in the train station or from vending machines. Trams and buses have no conductor but the driver sells individual tickets. On board the bus or tram or at the entrance to the U-Bahn, validate the ticket in the machine, which stamps the date, hour and direction on the ticket. Transfers are allowed in the same direction within one hour and tickets can be used interchangeably on bus, tram or U-Bahn. A 24-hour tourist ticket (*24-Stunden-Karte*), valid on the entire network except bus 170, is sold by any ticket office for DM7. Remember that Eurailpass is valid on buses of the Koln GmbH bus company, operated by the railroads, and the few S-Bahn stops in Cologne.

CAMPGROUNDS   Koln-Poll Camping, Weidenweg 46, is the municipal campground (Stadtischer Familienzeltplatz) for families. May 1-Sep 30; adult/DM4.50, small tent/DM3. Outside the station, board bus 132 and ride to Bayenthal. Get off and transfer to bus 130 (direction Rodenkirchen) and ride as far as the bridge over the Rhine used by the autobahn. Walk across the bridge (Rodenkirchener Brucke) and look for stairs to the land below. Cold water in the sinks, automatic washer, store, cafe and lounge.

Koln-Poll Camping, Alfred Schutte Allee, is the municipal campground for young people and is open only during school vacations, Jul-Sep 15; a bargain at adult/DM1, tent DM,80 (1989). It is located near Koln-Poll Camping on Weidenweg, but you can get closer to it by taking the U-Bahn to Neumarkt, changing to tram 7 and then changing to bus 139. Ask the tram driver when to change to bus 139 as the stop is easy to miss.

Camping Berger, in the district of Rodenkirchen at Uferstrasse 53A, is open all year; adult/DM5, tent/DM5. Outside the station, board bus 132, then ask the driver to let you know when to transfer to bus 130, and ride as far as Bayenthal, the street on which you change.   Transfer to bus 130 (direction Rodenkirchen) and ride to its terminus.   Then there is a several block walk to camp. Hot water in the sinks, automatic washing machine, store and restaurant.

SIGHTSEEING   This 2,000 year old city founded by the Romans displays art treasures and monuments from every period in its generously budgeted museums.   A 3-day museum pass is sold at all museums, valid for all municipal museums. Students receive a reduced rate.

Cologne - The Station, Cathedral and Museums

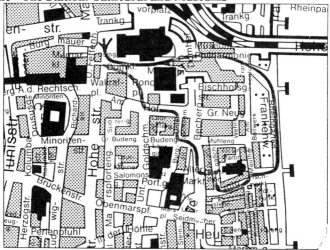

First priority should be given the **Cathedral** (Dom), begun in 1248 and completed in 1880.   Among its treasures is the 12th century Golden Shrine of the Magi (5:45am to 7:30pm). The Cathedral Treasury in the north transcept is open M-Sa 9-4 and Su 12-4. Guided tours in German starting from the altar are presented M-F at 10, 11, 2:30, 3:30 and 4. The 95-meter high gallery in the south spire can be ascended by climbing 509 steps. On the way up, the bell chamber is passed which houses the largest swinging church bell in the world. On a clear day, the view from the top extends over the city to the countryside and foothills.   In summer, organ concerts are presented on Tuesday evenings at 8pm.

Next priority goes to the **Wallraf-Richartz Museum/Museum Ludwig** building built in 1986 (F-Su 10-6 & Tu-Th 10am-8pm, adult/DM3, student/DM1). It forms part of a new complex that occupies the area in front of the Cathedral and extends down to the Rhine. Included are the Philharmonic Concert Hall, small theaters and a Rhine Garden recreation area. From a historical perspective, first visit the Wallraf-Richartz Museum which shows medieval painting, 17th and 18th century Dutch masterpieces and paintings by German and French artists to 1900. Then visit the Ludwig Museum which houses a large collection of modern art, including impressionists, an impressive pop art collection, and contemporary art.

The **Romano-Germanic Museum** on the southside of the Cathedral cost 25 million marks to build in 1974 (F-Su & Tu 10-5, W-Th 10am-8pm; adult/DM3, student/DM1). The building, display methods and contents are all worth seeing. Two of its most prized possessions are the Dionysos mosaic from the second century A.D. and the 40 foot high funeral monument of Poblicious from the first century A.D. Both of these items can be viewed from outside the museum through a window provided for that purpose. Inside, innovative display techniques include the use of T-bars of steel painted in pompeian red, instead of the usual stone or marble bases, for head sculptures and fragments. Life sized copies of the exterior of a Roman guard tower and Roman coach are shown.

Elsewhere, Cologne's **Museum of Ethnology**, Rautenstrauch Joest Museum at 45 Ubierring, is one of the largest in Europe with 60,000 exhibits. The Kathe Kollwitz Museum, Neumarkt 18-24, contains over 200 sketches, printed graphics and sculptures of the artist. Hours are M-W 9-4:30, Th 9-6, F 9-3:30.

DAY TRIP TO DUISBURG North of Cologne, Duisburg is an industrial city of little interest except for its excellent museums. There is no campground. Its tourist office, Konigstrasse 53, is 4 blocks from the train station. For modern art enthusiasts, Duisburg's museum of modern sculpture opened in 1964 is only 500 meters from the train station. **Wilhelm-Lehmbruck Museum**, Friedrich-Wilhelm Strasse 42, is open W, Th, Sa, Su 10-5, Tu & F 2-10pm; DM3. The striking steel and concrete museum is within a city park whose benches are convenient for picnics. Even when the museum is closed, most of the sculpture can still be seen by walking around outside. Inside, some walls are textured cement that look like rough hewed lumber and provide a background for lots of Lembruck's nude sculptures, male and female.

Train Schedules InterCity trains leave at least hourly for all major German cities.

To Amsterdam, leave at 7:55am (ar. 11:14am), 8:55am (ar. 12:14pm), 9:49am (ar. 1:14pm), 11:10am EuroCity (change at Duisburg, ar. 2:14pm), 12:55pm (ar. 4:14pm), 4:04pm EuroCity (ar. 6:58pm), 4:57pm EuroCity (ar. 7:59pm), 6:04pm EuroCity (ar. 8:58pm) and 6:55pm (ar. 10:14pm).

To Copenhagen, leave at 7:10am (change at Hamburg, ar. 4:29pm), 11:10am EuroCity (ar. 8:45pm) and 8:10pm (change at Hamburg, ar. 6:38am).

To Paris (Nord Station), leave at 7:30am (ar. 1:11pm), 8:18am EuroCity (ar. 1:40pm), 1:20pm EuroCity (ar. 6:56pm) and 5:08pm EuroCity (ar. 10:09pm).

To Rome, leave at 7am EuroCity (change at Milan, ar. 11:05pm), 2:03pm EuroCity (change at Basel, ar. 8am) and 11:58pm reservation required (ar. 5:50pm).

STUTTGART

Stuttgart (pronounced STUT-gahrt) is a prime example of German urban planning where 60 percent of the land has been reserved as open space for parks, gardens and woods.

TRAIN STATION The station is a large complex with a tram terminal, bus station, tourist office, restaurants, shops and travel services. The exchange office is open M-Sa 8am-8:30pm, Su 9-8. In front of the station, Koenigstrasse has been converted to a pedestrian street and contains the historical Schlossplatz, palace square. Next to the station, the large park, Schlossgarten, extends 4 km. and features fountains, lakes and playgrounds.

CITY TRANSPORATION A dense network of S-Bahn trains, trams and buses is available. Tickets are sold singly, in multiples at savings or as a 24-hour ticket. The S-bahn is free with Eurailpass.

CAMPGROUND Camping Cannstatter Wasen is located across the Neckar River in Stuttgart-Bad Cannstatt, next to the site of the autumn festival, Cannstatter Volksfest. Apr-Oct, adult/DM5,50 and tent/DM5. From the main station, take the S-Bahn line S1 to Bad Cannstatt, a 5-minute trip. Get off at Bad Cannstatt train station. Then walk 15 minutes in the direction of the river. Or, take a tram from near Stuttgart Train Station and get off at Mercedes Strasse after the tram crosses the Neckar River. Facilities: sinks with cold water only, automatic washer and dryer, store.

SIGHTSEEING Stuttgart has a number of interesting museums including the Stuttgart Municipal Art Gallery (Galerie der Stadt Stuttgart) at Schlossplatz, 4 blocks from the station. Within are 19th and 20th century sculpture and paintings. Staatsgalerie Stuttgart, Konrad Adenauer Strasse 32, 2 blocks from the station, shows notable Old Masters, an excellent early 20th century French collection and modern art. Manet, Renoir, Bonnard, Cezanne, Gauguin, Modigliani, Braque, Gris, Picasso, Leger, Kirchner, Nolde, Barlach, Beckmann, Klee, Feininger are all represented. Wurttembergisches Landesmuseum, Altes Schloss, 6 blocks from the station, exhibits art and culture of Swabia beginning with the Stone Age, the Wuerttemberg crown jewels, and a clock collection. The Linden Museum for Ethnology, Hegelplatz 1, 6 blocks from the station, covers the Amazon, ancient Peru, New Guinea and Southern Africa. Unique to Stuttgart is the Daimler-Benz Museum, Unterturkheim.

A "must" excursion is to **Ludwigsburg Palace**, the largest Baroque palace in Germany. Mar 15-Oct 15 daily 9-12 and 1-5. Take S-Bahn line S5 from the train station to Ludwigsburg, and walk 4 blocks. The **Wilhelmina Zoological and Botanic Gardens** is the only one in Germany of its kind and visited each year by 1.5 million people, making it the most popular attraction in the entire Baden-Wuertemberg area. Take the S-Bahn.

Train Schedules There are one to two trains per hour between Stuttgart and Munich. Last departure is 11:01pm which arrives at 1:50am at only Pasing Station in Munich. Travel time is about two hours. There are frequent departures to all major German cities, and south to Switzerland.

Though the distance is short, it is more difficult to travel east to **Strasbourg**, France. Take the train to Karlsruhe and then change for a train to Strasbourg. Trains leave Stuttgart for Karlsruhe at 7:41am (ar. 8:50am), 8:38am (ar. 9:50am), 9:36am (ar. 10:46am), 10:01am (ar. 11:05am), 11:39am (ar. 12:48pm), 12:18pm (ar. 1:30pm), 1:37pm (ar. 2:50pm), 2:40pm (ar. 3:50pm), 3:49pm (ar. 5:05pm), 4:35pm (ar. 5:39pm),

4:56pm (ar. 6:09pm), 5:39pm (ar. 6:49pm) and 6:41pm (ar. 7:50pm). Trains leave Karlsruhe for Strasbourg at 9:01am (ar. 10:06am), 9:36am (ar. 11:13am), 11:10am (ar. 12:21pm), 1:04pm (ar. 2:17pm), 1:58pm EuroCity(ar. 3:13pm), 2:59pm (ar. 4:31pm), 4:58pm EuroCity (ar. 6:13pm), 5:42pm (ar. 6:44pm), 6:47pm (ar. 7:51pm) and 7:58pm InterCity (ar. 9:55pm).

MUNICH (MUNCHEN)

Most people who come to Germany for the first time visit Munich. Munich was one of the earliest cities to transfrom its historic center into a pedestrian sector, a practice widespread in Europe today. The city's Deutsches Museum easily qualifies as the best of its kind in Europe, even outranking Paris' new science museum. The memorial museum of the former Dachau concentration camp is educational and tremendously moving. After these sights, Munich makes a good base for day trips to King Ludwig's famous castle, Neuschwanstein; to the mountain resort of Garmisch; and even to Salzburg if you only have a day to spend there.

TRAIN STATION (HAUPTBAHNHOF) The station is large, busy and connected to surrounding businesses by escalator. Train information across from track 22 has a rack of free schedules. The tourist office is across from track 11 at the end of the hall. Within the enormous station are a bakery, international newsstand, pharmacy, luggage storage, bank, grocery store and numerous restaurants. The large size lockers are big enough for a pack and take two DM1 coins per 24 hour period. Avoid the station's Deutsche Verkehrs-Kredit-Bank which charges DM5 to cash travelers checks. It's useful to know that usually the same banks that charge DM4-6 to cash travelers checks will change currency into marks without additional charge. Changing a few dollars will get you to Camping Thalkirchen where travelers checks can be changed without commission. The station bakery and grocery shops may be convenient but are more expensive than elsewhere.

    Starnberger Station (bahnhof) is adjacent to the Hauptbahnhof's track 26. Its tracks seem like a continuation of the main station's, except the track numbers are higher. Local trains to nearby towns and villages generally leave from Starnberger Station. The Europabus office (Deutsch Touring GambH) is in Starnberger Station. A reservation for the Romantic Road Europabus is theoretically made here, but when we attempted to do so we were told that no reservations were needed in the direction Munich to Frankfurt and to just show up at the bus stop marked "romantische strasse" across Arnulfstrasse outside Starnberger Station. We arrived at the last minute and still found seats, although the bus was full when we left. If possible, try to arrive at least 15 minutes early. A charge of DM2 is made for your pack, but many people take the excursion as a day trip.

    Munich's suburban stations are **Ostbahnhof** (east station) and **Pasing**. Many long distance trains arriving from the south and southwest, stop at small Pasing Station before arriving at the main station, Hauptbahnhof. Get off at small Pasing Station if you plan to stay at Camping Obermenzing and avoid the size, long distances and complexity of the Hauptbahnhof. Pasing Station serves both long distance trains and the S-Bahn. Trains leaving from track 4 go to downtown Munich. A bakery, grocery-deli, train information office, reservations office and baggage check are inside Pasing Station. Outside the station is a small shopping area.

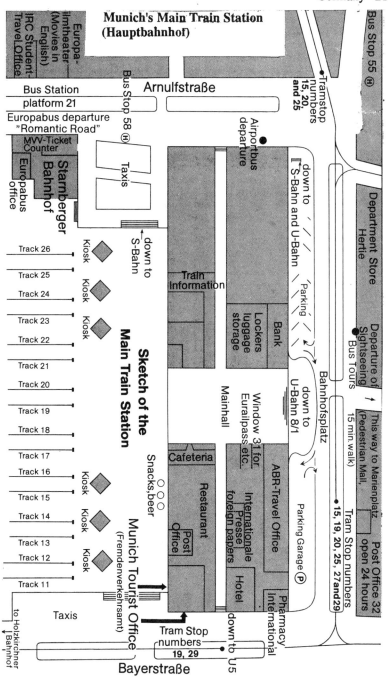

Munich's Main Train Station (Hauptbahnhof)

Bus Stop 55 (H)

Tramstop numbers **15, 20, and 25**

Bus Station
platform 21

Arnulfstraße

Bus Stop 58 (H)

Europabus departure "Romantic Road"

MVV-Ticket Counter

Europabus office

Starnberger Bahnhof

Taxis

Airportbus departure

down to S-Bahn and U-Bahn

Department Store Hertie

Track 26

Kiosk

down to S-Bahn

Track 25

Track 24

Kiosk

Track 23

Train Information

Parking

Departure of Sightseeing Bus Tours

Track 22

Kiosk

Lockers luggage storage

Bank

This way to Marienplatz (Pedestrian Mall, 15 min walk)

Track 21

Track 20

down to U-Bahn 8/1

Bahnhofsplatz

Track 19

Sketch of the Main Train Station

Track 18

Track 17

Mainhall

Window 31 for Eurailpass etc.

Post Office 32 open 24 hours

Track 16

Kiosk

Cafeteria

Snacks, beer

Track 15

Track 14

Kiosk

ABR-Travel Office

Tram Stop numbers

15, 19, 20, 25, 27 and 29

Track 13

Restaurant

Internationale Presse foreign papers

Parking Garage (P)

Track 12

Kiosk

Post Office

Hotel

Track 11

Munich Tourist Office (Fremdenverkehrsamt)

Pharmacy International

Taxis

down to U5

to Holzkirchner Bahnhof

Tram Stop numbers

19, 29

Bayerstraße

Europa-Filmtheater (Movies in English)

IRC Student Travel Office

214

Munich - S-Bahn and U-Bahn (subway)

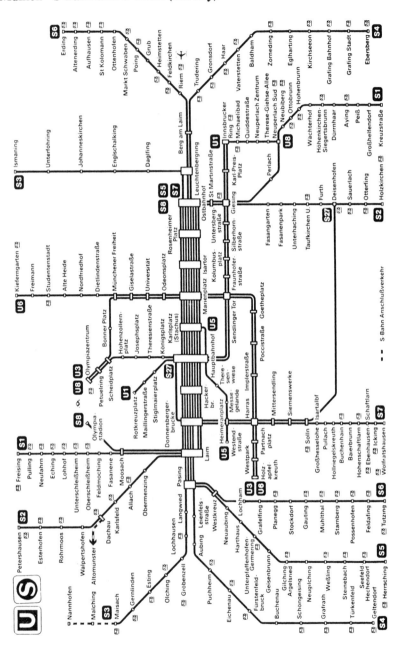

MUNICH ORIENTATION   The core of downtown is a pedestrian mall (the Fussgangerbereich) that stretches for a half-mile beginning at the Stachus (Karlsplatz), along Neuhauser Strasse and Kaufinger Strasse to Marienplatz, center of the old town (altstadt).   Within the area are department stores, shops and historical buildings.   Pedestrian underpasses (stairs and escalators) and underground shopping malls connect the "people only" area with surrounding streets.   Both Marienplatz square and Stachus shopping mall have a subway terminal where U-Bahn and S-Bahn lines criss-cross.

TOURIST INFORMATION   *Fremdenverkehrsamt* is in the main train station across from track 11 at the Bayerstrasse exit.   Hours are 8am to 11pm; expect at least a short line.   The city map costs DM.30, and the most helpful city brochure in Europe, *Young People's Guide to Munich* is DM.50 and useful for all ages.   Also request the free brochures, *Combined Transport in Munich--Travel Fare and Tickets*, *Verkehslinienplan--Staat and Region*, and *Rendevous with Munich*, all dealing with public transportation, *Castles in Bavaria* and leaflets on both campgrounds.

CITY TRANSPORTATION   Munich's trams, buses and two subways, S-Bahn and U-Bahn, are coordinated.   The same ticket is valid for all and connecting buses wait at subway exits.   The S-Bahn is free with a Eurailpass, but not the U-Bahn.   At each bus stop, the name and schedule are posted.   Buses are blue and cream colored.

For determining the fare, the greater Munich area is divided into zones.   The inner blue zone comprises two zones and includes all transporation to Camping Thalkirchen and Camping Obermenzing, the Olympic Stadium and the BMW factory.   The only place you're likely to be going outside this area is the Dachau Museum.   For very short trips, defined as any trip between two open circles on the transporation map, a special red K ticket is sold.   This ticket isn't very useful because even after getting off the S-Bahn, the ride to either camp is longer than the distance between two open circles.

Tickets are sold from vending machines indicated by a white K on a light green background.   Look for the *Mehrfahrtenkarten* machines in the U-Bahn and S-Bahn stations.   Purchase your ticket for the U-Bahn while you're at the S-Bahn station in the Hauptbahnhof to avoid having to detour back to the entrance when changing from S-Bahn to U-Bahn.   Children 4 through 15 qualify for reduced fares and should purchase the red K ticket, which when used for childen is valid for 4 zones by cancelling a single strip.

Einzelfahrkarte is a single ticket valid in two zones and costs DM2.30.   The cost per two-zone trip is reduced from DM2.40 to DM1.90 by purchasing a 10-strip ticket (*kleine Streifenkarte*) for DM9.50.   A 16-strip ticket (*groBe Streifenkarte*) is sold for DM15, but the additional savings is so miniscule that you're better off with the 10-strip ticket.   The strip tickets can be used by more than one person as long as a minimum of two strips are cancelled per trip per person.   To cancel, fold the ticket on the line between strips 2 and 3 and insert in the cancelling machine in the direction of the arrow printed on the ticket.   A single ticket must also be cancelled in the machine.   The validity period on all the above tickets is two hours in the same direction, including any changes.

The red **K** *Streifenkarte* (the 10-strip red ticket) is DM6.50, but is not very useful as the ride can only be between two of the empty circles on the map and most backpackers would simply walk that distance. On the K red ticket, the validity period is one hour. Each ride requires that two strips be cancelled per person.

The **24-hour ticket** (*24-Stunden-ticket innenraum*) for the inner blue zone costs DM7.00. Both campgrounds, the Olympic Stadium, and the BMW Museum are all within the blue zone. The most important exception is the Dachau Museum. Don't cancel the ticket until your first ride. A weekly ticket is sold at Starnberger Station at the Hauptbahnhof and is a good buy if you plan to base yourself in Munich for at least 5 days. Purchasing and cancelling tickets is on the honor system. Inspectors wear short sleeved light blue shirts and dark pants in summer. We were checked once on the U-Bahn after leaving Marienplatz. Those caught without a valid ticket are escorted off the U-Bahn to purchase one and perhaps pay a fine.

CAMPGROUNDS Two are accessible by public transportation, the close-in and crowded Camping Thalkirchen or the farther out and more spacious Camping Obermenzing.

Camping Thalkirchen (pronounced thal-kir-ken), the municipal campground in Munich, ranks right up there with the municipal campground in Florence as being the most crowded in Europe. But don't let that deter you--we overheard some fascinating conversations while trying to sleep in our tent. As always, don't worry about being turned away as management always lets backpackers squeeze in wherever they can find a space. We had an interesting time here but next trip I plan to walk the 15 minutes back and forth from the bus stop for Camping Obermenzing, which is more wooded, less crowded and has larger campsites. But I'll miss the friendly and large contingent of 16 to 21 year olds camping in the tent area at Thalkirchen. The other campgrounds in the Munich area are difficult to reach by public transportation.

Camping Thalkirchen is across the river from Hellabrunn Zoo (*Tierpark*) about 4 km. south of downtown Munich. Apr 1-Oct 31, adult/DM4.90, small tent/DM3.00, large tent/DM4.50 . Two people walking in with a small tent pay a tent fee of DM3.00; 3 pay DM4.50.

From the Hauptbahnhof, take the S-Bahn from the station for two stops to Marienplatz and change to U-bahn lines 3 (direction Westpark) or 6 (direction Holtzapfelkreuth) to Implerstrasse. (The S-Bahn is free with Eurailpass, but not the U-Bahn. The 24-hour ticket for DM7.00 is probably your best buy, but don't start it until the U-Bahn ride.) From inside Implerstrasse station, exit in the direction of the bus symbol and then choose *Tierpark 57* to get topside on the correct side of the street for the bus stop for camp. After getting off the escalator, the bus 57 stop is about 50 meters ahead at the bus shelter with seats. (Just beyond the bus stop is a grocery store.) I don't think we ever rode bus 57 without there being other campers on board. Ride the bus past the Thalkirchen stop and the Maria Einsiedelbad to the end of the line, the eighth stop, campingplatz. The bus ride is 12 minutes. After getting off, walk back to the intersection and cross both Benediktbeuerer Strasse and Zentralland Strasse. The rear of the campground is visible through the wire fence. Walk forward on the path beside the fence to the entrance, a 5-minute level walk.

Munich - Camping Thalkirchen

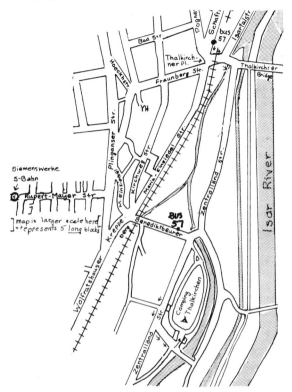

Bus 57 leaves Implerstrasse stop for Thalkirchen from 8:10am to 1:28am. The earlier buses listed on the post as leaving at 5:25am don't go all the way to camp. Returning to Munich from the campingplatz stop, the first bus on Monday through Saturday is 8:23am and on Sunday, 8:38am. If you need an earlier bus, walk back for about 5 minutes to an earlier bus stop where buses leave Monday through Saturday from 5:06am to 1:53am, but on Sunday only from 8:38am to 1:53am. Departures are every 10 minutes on weekdays and Saturday, less frequently on Sunday.

If you have a Eurailpass and are willing to walk about 2 km., bus and U-Bahn fare can be avoided by taking the S-Bahn. The closest S-Bahn stop to Camping Thalkichen is Siemenswerke, the sixth stop on lines S7 (direction Wolfratshausen) and S27 (direction Deisenhofen), which leave from the S-Bahn Station outside the door by the tourist office across from track 11. After getting off, walk east on Rupert-Mayer Strasse for 1.8 km.

The office will cash travelers checks at almost as good a rate as at a bank, and you actually come out ahead as no commission is charged. Camper rigs and trailers are separated from tents. The quite small tent campsites are delineated by short peeled logs. The terrain is dirt, grass and gravel broken by a few clumps of trees. Some parts of camp are noisy, especially the areas with small tents, and the voices don't quiet down until midnight. Camping tour groups are accepted and they occupy their own reserved area. Two or three buses were always there during our stay.

The camp has a well stocked store, restaurant (not a good deal) and a large area of roof-covered outdoor tables and benches useful for cooking and eating your own or store bought food. Prices in the store are reasonable, such as a half liter carton of milk for DM.85, chocolate milk for DM1.20.

Each section of the camp has its own restrooms. The showers take a DM1 token purchased at the office, have a shower stall and outer dressing area and provide 8 minutes of hot water. The toilets are exactly what we're used to and the oversized toilet paper rolls never run out. There are both rows of sinks, and sinks in private compartments. All handwashing sinks have cold water only. Separate sinks for either handwashing laundry or dishwashing are provided.

In the building across from the office are 5 washing machines and 3 dryers. The washing machine costs DM5 for a token purchased at the office. The store sells individual bags of detergent. In the evening, a line usually forms to use the washing machine. The washing cycle takes one hour. The dryer takes 50 pfennig coins. To dry a normal load of clothes on hot (the black solid symbol), we found three coins to be required. If you've got Levis, it will take 4 coins. Each coin is worth 6 minutes of drying time. You can't put in all the coins at the beginning, but must insert each coin individually at the end of each 6 minutes. This may sound tedious, but there's always interesting fellow campers to chat with. If you have trouble with the machines, ask for help at the office.

Camping Obermenzing is on Lochhausener Strasse 59 in the Obermenzing district, northwest of the main station. It's near the beginning of the Stuttgart autobahn and set within a park. (March 15-Oct 31, adult/DM6.90, tent/DM4) During Octoberfest, the last week in September, arrive as early as possible as the camp becomes full. Otherwise, backpackers will have no trouble being admitted.

From the Hauptbahnhof, the main train station in Munich, take the S-Bahn to either Station Obermenzing or Pasing. Buses run later and more frequently from Pasing, but the bus ride from Obermenzing is slightly shorter.

Via Station Obermenzing, take S-Bahn line S2, direction Petershausen, to Station Obermenzing. Buy a ticket at the station for the bus if necessary. Outside walk one block in the direction of uphill to the bus stop for #75. There are food stores between the S-Bahn and the bus stop. You will be on the same side of the street as the H. Bank and Boutique. Bus 75 leaves from the Obermenzing Post stop M-F, 5:15am-7:18pm. On Saturday and Sunday, the buses don't run until after 8am. The bus ride is five minutes. Get off at the fifth stop, Lochhauserstrasse. Take the left fork of the road, Lochhauserstrasse, and walk for 14 minutes. The way is level and Camping Obermenzing is on the left side.

Via Pasing train Station. Most long distance trains arriving from the south stop at Pasing Station before continuing to the Hauptbahnhof in central Munich. If your train stops at Pasing, be sure to get off here as the station is small and less confusing than the Hauptbahnhof. If you are at the Hauptbahnhof, S-Bahn lines S3 (direction Maisach), S4 (direction Geltendorf) and S5 (direction Herrsching) all stop at Pasing Station. At Pasing Station, be sure to leave by the the front entrance, rather than the rear where the parking lot is. The bus stop for #76 is to the right as you exit the station from the main entrance. Don't cross the street to the other bus stop or you'll be going in the wrong direction. Buses run Monday through Friday from 5:40am to 1:05am, every 20 minutes during the daytime. On weekends, bus 76 operates from 6:25am to 1:05am. Get off at the seventh stop, Lochhausener Strasse. (This is the same stop where bus 75 from Obermenzing Station brings you.) Then walk on the left fork of the road, Lochhausener Strasse, for 14 minutes to the camp which is also on the left side of the road.

    The campground is large and grassy with a good number of trees. No tour groups are accepted at Camping Obermenzing and the large sites prevent that crowded feeling. The restrooms have hot water in the sinks which are separated by privacy curtains. Purchase a token for DM1.50 at the office for a hot shower. The camp store and cafe has a small outdoor eating area, but it is smaller and not covered like the one at Thalkirchen. (If you plan to cook much, stay at Thalkirchen.) The three automatic washing machines hold 7 kilos and cost DM5 per load. The dryer takes 50 pfennig coins. Handwashing laundry sinks are also provided.

FOOD Food is rather expensive in the small shops of the Viktualienmarkt, three blocks from Marienplatz. Prices are better in the basement of the Kaufhof department store in Stachus (Karlsplatz). The only reasonable place to eat prepared meals is at the University dining halls, the mensas. The mensas are closed in August and September. At other times they are open M-Th until 4:45pm and on Friday for lunch only. No one checks for student ID even if you're not of student age and visiting one is an experience in itself. Each mensa offers meals at three prices, DM2.30, DM3.15 and DM4.20. Buy your ticket from the cashier booth whose sign has the price of the meal you want. Then find the appropriate cafeteria line for that priced meal. The meals are two or three courses and you have a selection for each course. Generally the choice is among salad or vegetables for one course, a main dish for the second, and dessert such as yoghurt or applesauce for the third. An easy mensa to visit for lunch while your're at the fine arts museums is the Technical University's at Arcisstrasse 17, across the street and park of the Alte Pinakothek. Merely walk into the entrance of the University and follow the students to the cashier booths. Another convenient one is in Schwabing at Leopoldstrasse 13. Take U-Bahn line 6 (direction Kieferngarten) or line 3 (direction Olympiazentrum) to Universitat or Giselastrasse. The mensa is midway between the two stations and is marked on the map from the tourist office.

SIGHTSEEING The **Deutsches Museum** is far and away the best thing in Munich. It's the largest science and technical museum in the world and no where else will you find such diversity in one convenient place. The museum is on Isarinsel, an island in the Isar River. To get there take the S-Bahn to Isartor and follow the signs outside the station for the 5-minute walk to the museum. Admission is adult/DM4 and student/DM2.

    The museum has 300 rooms on the subjects of (1) mining and metallurgical techniques (walk through salt and coal mines, tours at 9:45 and 1:45, ground floor; casting of metals such as aluminum at 10:30 and 2:30, ground floor; film, "The Path from Iron Ore to Steel," 11:30 and 2:30, ground floor; (2) engines; (3) electricity (high voltage plant demonstrations at 11, 2 and 4, ground floor); (4) cars; (5) trains (model railroad, 10am and each hour following, ground floor); (6) planes (from WW1 and later); (7) chemistry (plastics made at 11:30 and 3:30, second floor; (8) astronomy (Zeiss Planetarium at 10, 12, 2 and 4, sixth floor, and observatory at 12 and 3, sixth floor); (9) meteorology; (10) watchmaking; (11) musical instruments; (12) marine navigation (full size ship); (13) physics (pull handles and work levers that demonstrate basic lawas); and (14) aeronautics (history of development of rocket, space vehicles).

Don't miss the actual reconstructions in the basement of **four mines:** iron ore, salt, potash and coal. The mines are closed during the excellent free guided tours from 9:45 to 10:30 and 1:45 to 2:30. The entrance to the mining section (bergbau) is from the Open Pit Mining room. To reach it, after entering the museum, turn left and pass through the Mineral Resources room into the Open Pit Mining room. The exhibits have English subtitles and the mines take at least 30 minutes to walk through on your own.

Another must are the **full scale ships.** After entering the museum, walk straight ahead to the fully rigged sailing ship. If you look up at the ceiling, you will be amazed to see at least 30 full scale planes suspended from the ceiling. A very interesting reproduction of the **Altamira Cave** in Spain and its prehistoric drawings is located next to the room of Glass on the second floor. If you aren't going to be visiting any prehistoric caves, this is a rare opportunity to see a reproduction.

Memorial Site Concentration Camp Dachau   The site and museum are open daily 9-5 except Monday, free. The English-language film is shown at 11:30am and 3:30pm in the auditorium. To reach the auditorium, pass through the first exhibits.

To reach the museum, take S-Bahn line S2, direction Petershausen, to Dachau Station. As you leave Dachau Station, turn left out the main entrance to board the waiting connecting bus 722 to the Camp. Don't follow the sign to Dachau in the Station unless you plan to walk the 20 minutes to the museum. The sign points to the rear exit and the parking lot. Bus 722 leaves from the front entrance shortly after the arrival of the S-Bahn and is easily missed if you don't go directly to it. The entrance to the Dachau Museum is a four-minute walk after getting off bus 722.

Returning to Dachau S-Bahn Station, bus 722 leaves from bus stop Dachau Robert-Boschstrasse near the museum at 10:29am, 11:08, 11:49, 12:28pm, 1:08, 1:48, 2:28, 3:08, 3:48, 4:28, 4:48, 5:08, 5:28, 5:48, and 6:28pm. On Saturday, the last buses leave at 3:08pm, 3:48, 5:08 and 6:31. On Sunday, the last buses leave at 3:50pm, 5:08 and 6:30.

Free BMW Factory Tour   The BMW factory offers complete free guided tours in English of their Munich plant. We found this a very complete and interesting industrial tour. We first saw sheets of unstamped metal and at the end the completed cars rolling off the assembly line in the same manner as a car rolls off the conveyor belt in a car wash. The plant is largely automated and shows the latest techniques of assembly, but they keep the hood ornaments out of the way! It's best to reserve a place by calling 3895-3639 from the campground as soon as you arrive in Munich. The tours are weekdays at 9:30am and 1pm and you must be 14 or older. They usually fill 2 days in advance, except if you arrive about 30 minutes early and put your name on standby you may replace a "no show."

To reach the plant, take U-Bahn line U3 or U8 (direction Olympiazentrum) to the end station, Olympiazentrum. The BMW plant is across the street from the station and from there signs point the way to the BMW Museum, where the tour assembles. If you're on the list for the 9:30am tour, take the 8:23am bus from Camping Thalkirchen, change to U3 at Implerstrasse and you will arrive at 9:10am at the BMW plant, including about a block walk to the Museum.

There are lockers for checking belongings at the Museum and on the tour. The required DM1 coin returns to you after removing your things. The Museum itself, which features the latest in audio-visual techniques, is not included in the tour. (Daily 9-5 but must arrive by 4; adult/DM4.50, student/DM3, includes booklet and free use of earphones.)

While you're in the area, check out the site of the former Munich Olympic Games, across the street from Olympiazentrum Station. Restaurants in the area are expensive, but the Olympic Park provides good potential picnic sites.

DAY TRIP TO SCHLOSS NEUSCHWANSTEIN   The famous travel poster, cliff-perching castle of King Ludwig II was built in 1868 to 1886 in a scenic mountain area above Poellatgorge. Architecturally interesting and sumptuously furnished, the castle is visually delightful inside, outside and inside looking outside. To get there take a train to Fussen and from there a bus to Hohenschwangau. The best departure is train D2162 that departs Munich Hauptbahnhof track 17 at 8am and carries a through coach (all second class) to Fussen, arriving at 10:30am. All other departures require a change of train at Buchloe or Kaufbeuren. The next train, E3172, leaves from track 28 at 10:04am and arrives in Kaufberen at 12:07 where you must change trains. Train E3924, leaves Kaufberen at 12:48pm and arrives Fussen at 1:04pm.

The frequent bus from Fussen train station to Hohenschwangau is free with Eurailpass, a saving of DM2. At Hohenschwangau, a 30-minute fairly steep uphill trail punctuated by benches and connected to the road about midway, will bring you to the spectacular castle. Alternatively, horse-drawn taxi-carts are available. The castle is open daily 9-5:30 and expect a 30-minute wait in line. Entrance fee is adult/DM6 and student/DM3, including an English-language tour.

Returning to Munich, the only train with through cars (second class only) leaves Fussen at 7pm and arrives at 9:15pm. An afternoon train leaves at 3pm and arrives in Kaufbeuren at 5:04pm, where you must change trains. The next train to Munich leaves Kaufbeuren at 6:03pm (ar. 6:12pm).

FREE ROMANTIC ROAD BUS DAY TRIP TO ROTHENBURG   See schedule in introductory section to Germany. The bus leaves across the street from Starnberger Station on Arnulfstrasse, near stop 21, daily at 9am. A reservation (free) is needed only in the direction Frankfurt to Munich. For Munich to Frankfurt, places are always available according to Europabus personnel.

The bus carries a driver, plus a tour guide who commentates in both German and English and presents historical background on the sights along the route. The modern, comfortable buses have large, clean windows equipped with pull down shades and each seat has a reading light and air control. The air conditioning was somewhat weak on our bus in July. No restroom is on the bus, but sufficient stops are made.

Each passenger receives a bus schedule on board. After leaving Munich, the bus stops in Freiburg at 9:55am for a 10-minute rest stop. On Ludwigstasse, the street behind where the bus stops, a supermarket is one block down on the righthand side. After passing Augsburg and Donauworth, at 11:40am a 15-minute stop is made in Nordlingen by a church. On the street by the church is the open market with fruit and vegetable stands. A wurst stand presents an opportunity to sample the delicious white wurst, characteristic of the area. Two long, thin grilled ones with roll cost DM2.10. This makes a tastier and less expensive lunch than you're likly to find in Dinkelsbuhl, the official lunch stop. Along the same street are a pastry shop and supermarket. Prices are lower here than in Munich. A lunch break from 12:35 to 2:30pm is made in the walled town of Dinkelsbuhl. The entire old town can be explored within the allotted time if you don't have to spend time at a restaurant.

Rothenburg

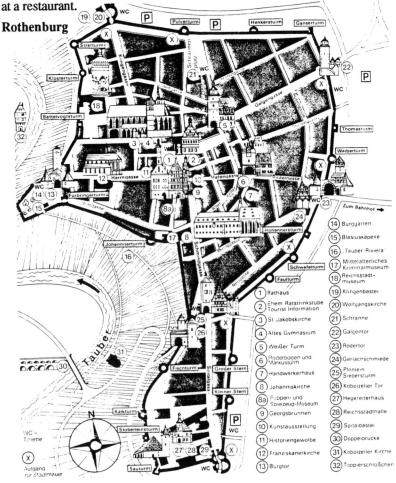

Before the bus arrives in Rothenburg at 3:15pm, the driver distributes a handy, free leaflet/map of the town, *Objects and Facts of Interest.* Unfortunately the time scheduled for Rothenburg is too short to see everything. The fascinating Medieval Criminal Museum can easily absorb the entire time. The Romantic Road bus departs from Rothenburg at 5pm and arrives in Wurzburg at 6:10 at the train station. This is where you should get off if you need to return to Munich. An InterCity leaves Wurzburg at 6:37pm, arriving Munich at 9:18pm. A later InterCity leaves daily except Saturday at 7:56pm, arriving 10:19pm. After Wurzburg, the bus continues to Frankfurt, arriving at the train station at 7:55pm, and to Wiesbaden, arriving at its train station at 8:40pm. If you plan to take the Rhine cruise in the morning, the bus guide announces directions to take the subway to Mainz from Frankfurt to be in the same town as the start of the Rhine cruise.

If you're heading for Heidelberg and want to change to the Castle Road Europabus in Rothenburg, your luggage can stay on board while you tour Rothenburg but will be available 10 minutes before the Castle Road bus leaves at 4:50pm.

It's not possible to leave the Europabus and take a later train from Rothenburg to Munich as none leave after 3:10pm. It is possible to stay at the campground 3 km. outside of Rothenburg and take a morning train. Please note that the buses listed on the schedule are operated by Deutsch Bundesbahn and are free with Eurailpass. The Rothenburg train station is outside the walls of the old city.

BEER, BANDS AND BELCHES Any first timer to Munich will want to include an evening visit to one of the great beer halls sponsored by Hofbrau, Lowenbrau, Spatenbrau, Hackerbrau, Augustinerbrau or Pschorrbrau beer companies. Liter glass steins of beer, wurst, soft pretzels, lederhosen garbed bands, costumed waitresses, group singing and clapping all contribute to what the French Michelin guide calls the "extraordinary atmosphere" and "astonishing spectacle." The noisiest, most boisterous room is the ground floor of the Hofbrauhaus at Platzl 9 downtown, where a half liter of beer is *eine halb*, and a whole liter, *eine mass* costs DM6.20. Light beer is *hell* and dark is *dunkel.* A glass of apple juice costs DM2. Be sure to visit after 9pm when things begin to get lively. Hofbrauhaus T-shirts and sweatshirts are for sale at the entrance.

OKTOBERFEST is the last two weeks in September, or specifically the third Saturday in September to the first Sunday in October. Parades are held during the first weekend. At 11am on the first Saturday, the opening parade features marchers, bands and horses pulling gaily decorated gigantic beer kegs. The parade route starts on Josephspitalstrasse and leads to the festival grounds at Theresien Meadow. Grandstand seats are sold but the parade can be watched free from the the sidewalk just as easily. That night there is usually a folklore entertainment with dancing, singing and music by groups who have come to town to appear in the parade. Tickets should be bought in advance. The next day, Sunday, the best parade called "Oktoberfest Costume and Marksmen's Procession" starts at 10am at Max II Memorial, later passing through the old town on its way to the festival grounds. Ask at the tourist office for a current schedule of events for Oktoberfest.

At the Theresien Meadow fairgrounds, mammoth portable tents are erected, each functioning as a beer hall. Inside in the middle is a lederhosen-garbed brass band on a revolving stage and long narrow tables for fairgoers. Beer is served in one liter steins and huge signs translated into six languages warn not to take the steins home as souvenirs. Waitresses carry six to eight steins in one hand and can also manage to carry an order of rotisseried chicken if necessary. Throughout the evening, the band plays and everyone joins in, standing and linking arms. As the evening draws late, an elderly man faints in the aisle and the medical man comes. It's an exercize in mass convivality and worth seeing, but go on a weekend evening when things are liveliest.

To Amsterdam, EuroCity trains leave at 9:38am (ar. 6:58pm) and 11:56am (ar. 8:58pm). For overnight trips, an international express leaves at 11:10pm (ar. Koln 6:52am, change trains, leave Koln 7:13am, ar. Amsterdam 10:44am). An InterCity train leaves at 10:56am (ar. Duisberg 5:42pm, change to EuroCity train and leave 5:46pm, ar. 7:59pm).

To Brindisi to connect with ferry departures, take the Brenner express at 11:20pm and arrive in Bologna at 7:50am. A rapido leaves Bologna at 8:42am, arriving Brindisi at 5:02pm.

To Salzburg, trains leave at 7:45am (ar. 9:30am), 8:22am (ar. 9:59am), 9:07am (ar. 11:01am), 9:26am (ar. 11:10am), 9:44am (ar. 11:25am), 10:22am (ar. 12:29pm), 11:35am (ar. 1:40pm, 12:21pm InterCity (ar. 2:06pm), 1:37pm EuroCity (ar. 3:11pm), 2:50pm (ar. 4:41pm), 2:55pm (ar. 4:56pm), 3:27pm (ar. 5:30pm), 4:47pm (ar. 6:21pm), 7pm EuroCity (ar. 8:35pm) and 8:54pm (ar. 10:58pm). Remember to take your passport, something easily overlooked for a day trip.

To Venice, the 8:06am Alpen express arrives in Verona at 2:20pm, where you must change trains. Trains leave Verona for Venice at 2:30pm Rapido (ar. 3:50pm), 3:33pm (ar. 5pm), 4:30pm Rapido (ar. 5:50pm), 6:30pm Rapido (ar. 7:57 at Venice-Mestre only), 7:33pm (ar. 9pm), 8:30pm (ar. 9:50pm) and 10:30pm (ar. 11:56pm). The next train operates between July 26 and September 26 and leaves Munich at 10:04am (change at Bolzano and change again at Verona, ar. Venice S.L. 7pm). Overnight expresses travel over the scenic Brenner pass in the dark. The first express operates between May 30 and September 25 only and leaves at 10:35pm (ar. 8:45am). The Brenner express leaves at 11:20pm (ar. 8:45am).

To Vienna, leave 7:45am (change in Salzburg, ar. 1pm), 8:22am (change in Salzburg, ar. 2pm), 9:44am (change in Salzburg, ar. 3pm), 9:44am direct train (ar. 3:17pm), 10:22am (change in Salzburg, ar. 4pm), 12:21pm InterCity (change in Salzburg, ar. 6pm), 1:37pm EuroCity (change in Salzburg, ar. 7pm), 1:56pm (change in Salzburg, ar. 8pm) and 3:27pm (change in Salzburg to EuroCity, ar. 9pm).

GARMISCH-PARTENKIRCHEN

In the German alps, Garmisch-Partenkirchen is a ski resort in winter and a hiking center in summer that grew beneath towering Zugspitze mountain. The name is pronounced GAR-mish PAR-ten-kir-ken. The tourist office, Kurverwaltung at Bahnhofstrasse 34, is in front of the station to the left as you exit (M-Sa 8-6 & Su 10-noon). Behind the main station, hauptbahnhof, is the small station for the expensive private cog railway up Zugspitz. Eurailpass holders receive a discount on the mountain railway.

Camping Zugspitze is on the road from Garmisch to Grainau, 4 km. from Garmisch. The highly rated camp is open all year; adult/DM6,70, tent/DM4,50. From in front of the station, take the blue bus of the Eibsee line marked "Schmolz"(DM2,20); last bus 8:03pm. From camp to the train station, the last bus leaves at 8:31pm. The campingplatz is located between the road where the bus stops and the river Loisach. Hot water in the sinks, automatic washer, store, swimming, fishing, canoeing and bavarian evenings with live music.

To Munich, trains leave at 7:34am (ar. 8:57am), 8:34am (ar. 9:57am), 9:34am (ar. 10:57am), 10:25am Rapido (ar. 11:39am), 11:25am EuroCity (ar. 12:39pm), 12:31pm (ar. 1:57pm), 1:37pm (ar. 2:57pm), 2:34pm (ar. 3:57pm), 3:27pm (ar. 4:58pm), 4:30pm (ar.5:59pm), 5:30pm (ar. 6:57pm), 6:31pm (ar. 8:01pm) and 8:08pm (ar. 9:33pm).

To Innsbruck and South to Italy, there are frequent departures to Innsbruck and from Innsbruck trains travel to Verona in Italy via the Brenner Pass. At Verona, change trains for Venice. Trains leave for Innsbruck at 7:34am (ar. 9:23am), 9:27am (ar. 10:51am), 10:26am (ar. 11:46am), 1:29pm (ar. 3pm), 3:23pm (ar. 4:45pm), 4:39pm EuroCity (ar. 6:05pm), 5:27pm (ar. 7:13pm) and 7:31pm (ar. 8:57pm).

HAMBURG

A major trade center, well developed industry, international seaport and second largest consular city in the world after New York, Hamburg makes a worthwhile stop on the way to Copenhagen.

It is also a gateway to Berlin. (For a reduction, students should buy their ticket from the border to Berlin at the Transalpino office at Rothenbaumchaussee 61, open M-F 9-6 & Sa 9-noon. To reach this office, get off at Bahnhof Dammtor. Hamburg University is north of the station. Rothenbaumchaussee is the main street leading north from the older part of the University. The walk is about 4 long blocks past the older University.)

TRAIN STATIONS   Hamburg has three important ones. Hauptbahnhof (abbreviated Hamburg-Hbf) is the main station and the largest. It is so large that its two ends are designated Hauptbahnhof Sud (south) and Hauptbahnhof Nord (north). Also important is Hamburg-Altona, west of the Hauptbahnhof and closer to the campgrounds. The third station is Hamburg-Dammtor, located about midway between the other two stations.   All stations are in central Hamburg and all are connected by S-Bahn. Many international and domestic trains stop at all three.   If coming from Copenhagen, trains arrive at Altona, Dammtor and then Hauptbahnhof. The order is reversed for trains from the south.

The **Hauptbahnhof** has all tourist services. Luggage check is open 6am to 11:30pm; Deutsche Verkehrs-Kredit-Bank on the main concourse (daily 7:30am-10pm), and on the south concourse (M-Sa 7:30am-3pm & 3:45pm-8pm, Su 10-1 & 1:45-6pm); tourist office (Hotelnachweis der FVZ) at Kirchenallee exit, daily 7am-11pm; and post office, all hours. The other side of the station leads into Glockengiesserwall, a pedestrian tunnel to Spitalerstrasse, and the shopping street, Moenckebergstrasse.

Bahnhof Hamburg-Altona, Hamburg's second largest station, received a new building in 1979. Deutsche Verkehrs Kredit Bank is open M-Sa 7:30am-3pm & 3:45pm-8pm, Su 10-1 & 1:45-6pm. At one end of the station is a department store. The station is connected with a large shopping mall, Neue Grosse Bergstrasse. In front of the station is Altonaer Bahnof Platz, marked by a sculpture and fountain. Continuing south, across from the platz is a park, Platz der Republik, featuring the Stuhlmann fountain. Across the street from the park is the Altona government building and the Kaiser Wilhelm monument. Continuing south to the port, another park, Altona Balkon, serves as a good viewpoint of the port and Elbe River.

Bahnhof Hamburg-Dammtor is within three blocks of the Alster (lake), next to the park, Planten un Blomen and the Botanical Garden and close to Hamburg University. If it's a nice day and you have a layover between trains, for relaxation, get off at this station which is practically surrounded by park areas.

TOURIST OFFICE   Besides the hotel booking/tourist office in the Hauptbahnhof, there are two other tourist offices in Hamburg. The main office is in the Bieberhaus on Hackmannplatz, near the Hauptbahnhof (M-F 7:30-6, Sa 8-3). Another is at the Port, St. Pauli Landungsbrucken (S-Bahn S1, S2 or S3 Landungsbrucken), and is open daily 9-6.

The Hamburg tourist office has prepared some of the most informative free booklets in Europe. Be sure to ask for: *The Museums, The Port, Elbe Banks* (contains map of area around Altona Station), *Old-Hamburg, Bergedorf, The Alster* (has a map showing Dammtor Station and the University area for cheap eats), *Hamburg Guide and HVV Information*.

CITY TRANSPORTATION   The S-Bahn, free with Eurailpass, is of more use in Hamburg than in other German cities. Most of the lines are S-Bahn rather than U-Bahn. The S-Bahn goes within about a 15 to 25-minute walk of the campgrounds and to most sightseeing attractions. AKV lines are private subway lines that tack onto the end of S-Bahn and U-Bahn lines. HVV (Hamburg Transport Association) is a group of 8 companies using the same tickets. Hence a ticket can be used interchangeably on subway, bus or regular boat services on the Alster and around the harbor. Individual tickets vary from DM1-DM3, with the average fare being DM1.80. Children up to 12 years old pay DM1 on all routes.

A variety of tickets is available for the city transportation system of S-Bahn, U-Bahn, AKV-Bahn and buses. Tickets can be bought from the ticket machine or from bus drivers. The 9 O'clock City Ticket (T on the ticket machine) is valid from 9am weekdays, or all day Saturday or Sunday, in zones 1 and 2 which covers all of Hamburg and includes the campgrounds and most sightseeing attractions. The ticket costs DM7. Children under 12 are free when with a parent. The 24-Hour Ticket is valid for 24 hours starting from the time it is purchased on the entire HVV network (not just zones 1 and 2). Children under 12 are free when with a parent. The cost is DM12.50; push button N on the ticket machine. The two kinds of Family Tickets are valid weekdays from 9am, or all day Saturday or Sunday, for up to 4 adults and 3 children. The City Family Ticket costs DM10 and is valid in zones 1 and 2; push button F on the ticket machine. The Network Family Ticket is valid within the entire HVV network and costs DM14; push button FN. There are also more expensive Tourist Tickets which can be bought in advance and the validity will start later. These cost an extra mark for the advance purchase privilege and can only be bought from tourist offices.

The Elbe passenger ferries are considered part of the city transportation network and are included in the special tickets described above. They provide a view of the port without the expense of a tour. Stops are marked on the tourist office map.

In the Hamburg Guide, an article entitled, *See the sights for free*, makes this suggestion about who qualifies as a "family." *Make up a family of your own (no one will ask to see your marriage certificate) and a network of buses, trains and ferries is at your beck and call...for only DM10.*

CAMPGROUNDS   The most convenient campgrounds are on Kieler Straase in the general vicinity of the zoo (tierpark). (Look for the circled number 3 on the rapid transit map.) All of the campgrounds are in the

Hamburg-Eidelstedt area and open all year. The closest S-Bahn is line S2 or S3 (direction Pinneberg) to Stellingen or Eidelstedt. Camping Park is the highest rated. For Camping Park, get off the S-Bahn at Stellingen, the station before Eidelstedt, and then a 25-minute walk. From Eidelstedt, it's about a 15 to 20-minute walk to Camping Anders. You can reach the campgrounds more quickly by getting off the train at Hamburg-Altona Station, rather than Hamburg-Hbf (Hauptbahnhof). For your arrival in Hamburg, we suggest paying the fare and taking bus 183 (direction Schnelsen) from outside Altona Station on Max-Brauer Allee. Bus 183 travels northeast on Max-Brauer Allee until it intersects with Holstenstrasse. Then it turns north (left) on Holstenstrasse which in a few blocks is renamed Kieler Strasse. The bus continues along Kieler Strasse, passing all four campgrounds on its way to Schnelsen.

From the Hauptbahnhof, take the S-Bahn to Altona and then bus 183, S-Bahn to Holstenstrasse and then bus 183, or U-Bahn line U2 (direction Niendorf-Markt) to Schlump and then bus 182 in front of Schlump station to the campgrounds. (For Camping Anders, get off at bus stop marked Reichsbahn Strasse and then a five-minute walk.) Going all the way by bus from the Hauptbahnhof and spending about 40 minutes on buses, take bus 188 from Steintorplatz outside the south end of the Hauptbahnhof to the last stop. Change to bus 183 which runs along Kieler Strasse, where the campgrounds are.

Camping Anders, 650 Kieler Strasse; adult/DM4, tent/DM5, hot shower/DM1; sinks with cold water, washer, store, cafe and lounge. **Municipal Camping**, 620 Kieler Strasse; adult/DM4.50, tent/DM6. **Camping Park**, 539 Kieler Strasse and 86 Ecke Kronsaalsweg; adult/DM4.50, tent DM6; sinks with cold water and store. **Camping Buchholz**, 374 Kieler Strasse and 74 Lokstedter Steindamm; adult/DM4, tent/DM7.50; sinks with cold water , 2 hot showers, store, cafe and lounge.

FOOD The produce market is near the main station at the market halls and is open M-F 12-6 & Sa 10-4. The 6 to 9:30am Sunday fish market sells fish, fruit, flowers and plants and has become a minor flea market. Look for it between Hexenberg and Grosse Elbstrasse near the Elbe River. Take S-Bahn lines 1 or 3 to Landungsbrucken, Reeperbahn or Konigstrasse, and then a 4 to 8-block walk. The Reeperbahn Station is closest.

For prepared meals, the University mensa is cheapest. One convenient to Dammtor Station is at Schluterstrasse 7, open weekdays for lunch. From Dammtor Station, walk north about three blocks past the old University to the new University Park. Schluterstrasse leads north and is the next street west of Rothenbaumchaussee. (The Alster tourist office brochure has a map of this area.) Purchase your ticket, about DM2-4 for a full meal, and then get in the line corresponding to the meal price.

SIGHTSEEING There's plenty to see and do in Hamburg. Most museums are closed on Monday. North of the Hauptbahnhof are grouped two contemporary art museums. The Hamburg Art Gallery (Hamburger Kunsthalle), Glockengiesserwall, is open Tu-Su 10-5 and charges adult/DM3, student/DM.70. Within its vast collection are works by French Impressionists, Klee and Friedrich and Runge. Next door, the Kunstverein, shows changing exhibitions of contemporary art and is open Tu-Su 10-6 and W until 8pm. To the south of the Hauptbahnhof is the Museum of Arts and

Crafts (Museum fur Kunst und Gewerbe) at Steintorplatz 1, open Tu-Su 10-5, admission adult/DM4, student/DM2. Items date from the Middle Ages to the present, including a famous and impressive Art Nouveau section.

With the *Old-Hamburg* brochure in hand, you can easily and knowledgeably explore the old town. Take S-Bahn S2 or S3 to Stadthausbrucke. A choice item within Old Hamburg is **St. Michaelis Church** (St. Michaelis Kirche), the most important Baroque church in northern Germany. The steeple can be reached by elevator for DM3 or via 400 stairs for DM1.80 from M-F 9-4, Su 11:30-4. **The Museum for Hamburg's History** (Museum fur Hamburgische Geschichte) at Holstenwall 24, is Tu-Su 10-5. Inside are a navigation section with models of ships from the Vikings to modern day ocean liners, model of **Hammaburg Castle**, a large model railway and more. Conducted tours of the Rathaus (City Hall) are given in English every hour M-F 10:15-3:15, SaSu 10:15-1:15, DM1. At the edge of Old-Hamburg, St. Pauli-Landungsbruecken is lined with restaurants, shops and offices which are supported by six floating ferro-concrete pontoons, 2,625 feet long. The pontoons rise and fall about nine feet with the tidal movement. Between this street and the shipyards on Steinwerder is the old Elbtunnel that was burrowed 70 feet beneath the Elbe River and is used for cars and pedestrians.

Neuengamme Concentration Camp Memorial In 1981, the Museum for the History of Hamburg opened its House of Documents which chronicles the World War II concentration camp of Neuengamme, set up in 1938. The site is open Tu-Su 10-5. Take S-Bahn S2 (direction Bergedorf) or S21 (direction Friedrichsruh) to Bergedorf, then bus 327 to the House of Documents on Neuengammer Heerweg. Both S-Bahn and bus are barely within fare zone 2. On the site are an original barracks and its furnishings, a reconstruction of the camp fence, and the remains of some trucks, a clay pit, the watch tower at the entrance, the brick factory, crematorium and bunker. Inside the House of Documents, a shattering chronological pictorial account of the concentration camp is displayed.

To Amsterdam, the only through train is the Holland-Scandinavian Express, which leaves Hbf 3:30pm (ar. 9:32pm). For the following Inter City trains, you must change at Osnabruck. Trains depart Altona 7:37am, Hbf 7:50am except Sunday (change at 9:37am, ar. 1:32pm), Altona 9:39am, Hbf 9:52am (change at 11:37am, ar. 3:32pm), Altona 11:39am, Hbf 11:52am (change at 1:37pm, ar. 5:32pm) and Altona 1:39pm, Hbf 1:52pm (change at 3:37pm, ar. 7:32pm).

To Berlin, trains leave Altona 7:32am, Hbf 8:02am (ar. 11:51am), Hbf 1:42pm (ar. 5:36pm), Altona 5:09pm, Hbf 5:32pm (ar. 10:17pm) and Altona 7:57pm, Hbf 8:14pm (ar. 12:06am). The portion through East Berlin is not covered by Eurailpass and can be paid on the train if you didn't buy the ticket beforehand. Price is about DM45, one way, second class. A free transit visa will be issued on the train.

To Copenhagen, trains leave Altona 6:33am, Hbf 6:58am (ar. 12:09pm), Altona 8:18am, Hbf 8:36am EuroCity (ar. 1:54pm), Hbf 11:12am (ar. 4:29pm), Hpf 1:52pm (ar. 7:09pm), Hbf 3:33pm EuroCity (ar. 8:45pm), Altona 5:19pm, Hbf 5:39pm EuroCity (ar. 10:50pm) and Altona 11:54pm, Hbf 12:22am (ar. 6:38am).

To the Rhine Area, the best train is EuroCity Mont Blanc which leaves Hamburg Altona at 9:49am, Hbf 10:02 and arrives in Frankfurt at 3:25pm (change for Rudesheim) and in Freiburg at 5pm. If the weather isn't good when you get here, stay on the train to Geneva, where you can change for a train that runs overnight to Barcelona, arriving in the sunny south at 9:24am. Or you can get off somewhere along the Rhine and change for a train to Italy. A train leaves for Frankfurt at least once a hour from all three stations in Hamburg.

To Munich, a train leaves Hbf at 7:07am, 7:55am, 8:55am except Sunday, 9:57am EuroCity, 10:57am, 11:57am, 12:57pm except Saturday, 1:57pm, 2:57pm except Saturday and 3:57pm. All departures pick up at Altona Station about 13 minutes earlier.

HANNOVER

Hannover is a major rail hub and the most convenient gateway to Berlin, unless you're coming from Scandinavia. Eurailpass is valid to the border town of Helmstedt and then a fare of about DM45 (one way, second class) must be paid either before boarding or on the train. Reduced fare tickets may be purchased at student travel agencies throughout West Germany. Also Eurailpass entitles you to a 25 percent reduction on the roundtrip bus fare between Braunschweig and Berlin operated by Bayern Express and P. Kuhn Berlin GmbH for students. Braunschweig is a border town on the rail line from Hannover.

Hannover's main sight is the free Great Herrenhausen Garden (Grosser Garten Herrenhausen); U-bahn 1 or 2 (direction Stocken) to station Herrenbauser Garten. Those here the first week in July can enjoy the city's summer beer fest with parades and fireworks on weekends. The train station has a tourist office and foreign exchange. Buses, trams, S-Bahn and U-Bahn comprise the transportation network. There are single tickets, ticket booklets and tourist tickets. Coaches of the Regionalverkehr Hannover Gmbh are free with Eurailpass. The one campground, Camping Birkensee, requires a 4-km. walk, but you can camp at the Youth Hostel, Ferdinand-Wilhelm Fricke Weg 1, for DM5. Take bus 24 (Stadionbrucke) from the bus station in front of the opera. Camping Birkensee, at Hannover-Laatzen at the bank of Birkensee (lake), is open all year, adult/DM4, tent/DM5. Facilities include free hot showers, sinks with hot water, automatic washing machine, dryer, store, restaurant, lounge and water activities.

Day Trip to Goslar   Every area has its particularly picturesque village where time seems to have stood still, and Hannover's is Goslar. From the train station in Goslar, walk about 10 minutes to the tourist office located in the ancient village square to pick up a free map and historical guide. (On Tuesday and Friday mornings the open market is held in this square.) The train ride takes about 1-1/2 hours and trains leave about once an hour.

To Amsterdam, trains leave at 6:53am (ar. 11:32am), 8:38am (ar. 1:32pm), 10:47am (ar. 3:32pm), 12:57pm (ar. 5:32pm), 2:36pm (ar. 7:32pm) and 4:57pm (change at Amersfoort, Netherlands, ar. 10:02pm).
To Berlin, trains depart Hanover at 3:04am (ar. 7:19am), 7:38am (ar. 11:34), 10:17am (ar. 2:12pm), 1:04pm (ar. 5:22pm), 2:58pm (ar. 7pm), 4:58pm (ar. 8:55pm) and 6:58pm (ar. 10:50pm).
To Hamburg and Scandinavia, trains leave for Hamburg about every hour. Trains to Copenhagen from Hannover leave at 9:17am (ar. 4:29pm), 9:41am (ar. 4:29pm), 1:41pm (ar. 8:45pm), 1:47pm (ar. 8:45pm), 3:41pm (ar. 10:50pm) and 3:47pm (ar. 10:50pm). Overnight trains leave at 9:03pm (ar. 6:38am) and 9:41pm EuroCity (ar. 6:38am). The train rolls onto the ferry at Puttgarden so you can sleep through.
To Munich, leave at 7:12am (ar. 1:04pm), 8:12am weekdays only (ar. 2:28pm), 8:39am (ar. 2:43pm), 9:12am EuroCity (ar. 3:04pm), 10:12am weekdays only (ar. 4:24pm), 12:12pm (ar. 6:04pm), 2:12pm not Saturday (ar. 8:04pm) and 3:12pm (ar. 9:28pm).

BERLIN

Eurailpass is valid only to the border of East Germany and then a fare must be paid the rest of the way. A free transit visa is issued on the train. The place to cross for the cheapest train fare to Berlin is Helmstedt, near Hannover, or Buchen near Hamburg. It's also possible to enter at Hof or Ludwigstadt, convenient if coming from Munich, but the train fare is more. A ticket can be purchased on board the train for the portion through East Germany, at the station, or more cheaply at a student travel agency.

The trip to Berlin from Hannover takes 4 hours (7 trips daily). Trains depart Hanover at 3:04am (ar. 7:19am), 7:38am (ar. 11:34), 10:17am (ar. 2:12pm), 1:04pm (ar. 5:22pm), 2:58pm (ar. 7pm), 4:58pm (ar. 8:55pm) and 6:58pm (ar. 10:50pm). The fare from the border to Berlin is about DM45, less if bought at Transalpino in Hannover. **From Hamburg**, there are 3 departures for the 4-hour trip. Trains depart at 8:02am (ar. 11:51am), 1:42pm (ar. 5:36pm) and 5:32pm (ar. 9:39pm).

Train Station Trains arrive at Berlin-Zoo station, downtown. The station has a tourist office, foreign exchange and post office. A branch tourist office is in the station, open 8am-11pm. The main office is east of the station in the Europa Center at the entrance to Budapesterstrasse 2. To get there walk past the ruined Gedachtniskirche (church). A city information office is across from the station and has free booklets about Berlin.

The S-Bahn is not free with Eurailpass, but the U-Bahn is necessary anyway to reach the campgrounds. A single tickets costs DM2.70, a *sammelcarte* for 5 tickets is DM11.50, a 24-hour tourist pass is DM9. One ticket allows 2 hours of travel any direction.

The best camp is **Camping Cladow**, next to the Wall on Krampnitzer Weg 111-117. Open all year; adult/DM6, tent/DM5. (One camper wrote to say while camping off season here, a young man came across the wall and ran smack into his tent in the middle of the night so he invited him in to hide.) From Berlin-Zoo take the U-Bahn to Ruhleben, the terminus. Change to bus 35 and ride about 30 minutes to Krampnitzer Weg. Then walk about 1.5 km. on this road to the Wall and the camp is on the left at the end of the road. Bus 35E goes closer to the campground, leaves from where you get off bus 35, but only runs during rush hours. Check the schedule for bus 35E posted at the stop for bus 35. Returning to town, bus 35E is scheduled to arrive opposite the stop for bus 35 a few minutes before a bus departs for Ruhleben. Very good facilities: sinks with hot water, washer and store.

Another good campground is **Camping Kohlhasenbruck**, to the south on the lake, Wannsee. Apr-Sep; adult/6DM, tent/5DM. Take the U-Bahn to Oskar-Helene-Heim and change to bus 18. Sinks with cold water only, store, swimming and boating.

East Berlin The minimum cost for the day will be DM5 for a one day transit visa and DM25 which must be exchanged for 25 East German marks in order to obtain a visa. East German marks cannot be reexchanged into West German marks, but must be spent in East Berlin--bring your shopping bag for groceries and save all receipts. Take your passport and ride the U-Bahn to Kochstrasse, or the U-Bahn or S-Bahn to Friedrichstrasse, two crossing points to East Berlin. Checkpoint Charlie and Friedrichstrasse are open day and night, but there is a 5-minute break at midnight. The crossing Heinrich HeineStrasse which has to be used by Germans coming from the FRG, opens at 6am.

To Hannover, leave at 6:07am (ar. 10am), 8:02am (ar. 12:04pm), 10:05am (ar. 2:01pm), 12:32pm (ar. 4:37pm), 3:22pm (ar. 7:19pm) and 4:22pm (ar. 8:01pm).
To Hamburg, leave at 7:43am (ar. 11:43am), 1pm (5:03pm) and 5:05pm (ar. 9:02pm).

GREECE

Anyone with a Eurailpass should seriously consider going to Greece. Its islands, sand beaches, bright blue water, craggy landscapes with scrub pine, luscious cheap fruit and wonderful archeological sites will leave Greece clearly etched in your mind. Go to Athens, Delphi and the Peloponnese for classical history, to northern Greece for Byzantine and Hellinistic artifacts and to the 1,425 islands in the Aegean for brilliant light and color.

The Greek Tourist Office publishes a wonderful folder which includes guidebook quality details about archeological sites for each region and group of islands. They also stock good maps of the country, Athens, Thessaloniki, Rhodes, Corinth, and Iraklion. Take the pertinent ones with you to read on the ferry to Greece. Otherwise pick them up at the tourist office in Patras, your arrival point in Greece.

If you already know the Greek alphabet you have a head start in reading signs. Usually the destination sign on the front of the bus has the city in Greek letters, and you must do some guessing and deciphering to make sure you have the correct bus.

Even when words are printed in our alphabet, the names of places can be spelled several different ways. The most interchangeable letters are K for C, I for Y, E for AE, H for CH and F for PH. For example, Aegina (Egina), Alphios (Alfios), Chalki (Halkida), Chanea (Hania), Cyclades (Kiklades), Herakleion (Iraklio), Mykonos (Mikonos), Mycenae (Mikines), Salonika (Thessalonika), Pireaus (Pireas), Rhodes (Rodos), Sparta (Sparti).

CURRENCY   One U.S. dollar is worth 150 drachma. The National Bank of Greece gives a good rate and only charges 60dr commission.

WEATHER   During what the press calls a "Balkan heat wave," temperatures soar into the 90's. Usually the hottest temperatures come in July and August. *The International Tribune* and *U.S.A. Today*, available throughout Europe, will alert you to the prevailing weather pattern. We arrived during a Balkan heat wave in late June 1987 and found it bearable. The most uncomfortable part was the stifling heat in the Archeological Museum in Athens. Wonderfully, the campground outside Athens had a cooling breeze and the humidity everywhere was dry and comfortable.

Rail Lines in Greece

ΒΟΥΛ
BULGA

ΓΙΟΥΓΚΟΣΛΑΒΙΑ
YOUGOSLAVIE

ΣΟΦΙΑ
SOFIA

ΒΕΛΙΓΡΑΔΙ
BEOGRAD

Κούλατα
Koulata

Προμαχώνας
Promachonas
Στρυμώνας
Strimonas
Δράμα
Drama

Ροδοπόλη
Rodopoli

Γευγελή
Gevgelija

Ειδομένη
Idomeni

Σέρρες
Serres

ΣΚΟΠΙΑ
SKOPJE

Κρεμένιτσα
Kremenica

Κιλκίς
Kilkis

ΑΛΒΑΝΙΑ
ALBANIE

Νέος
Neos
Καύκασος
Kafkasos

Μεσονήσια
Mesonissia

Έδεσσα
Edessa

ΘΕΣΣΑΛΟΝΙΚΗ
THESSALONIKI

Φλώρινα
Florina

Αμύνταιο
Aminteo

Πλατύ
Plati

Πτολεμαϊδα
Ptolemaida

Βέροια
Veria

Κατερίνη πόλη
Katerini ville

Κατερίνη
Katerini

Καζάνη
Kozani

Καλαμπάκα
Kalambaka

Κραννών
Krannon

ΛΑΡΙΣΑ
LARISSA

Τρίκαλα
Trikala

Καρδίτσα πόλη
Karditsa ville

Ορφανά
Orfana

Βελεστίνο
Velestino

ΒΟΛΟΣ
VOLOS

Καρδίτσα
Karditsa

Παλαιοφάρσαλος
Paleofarssalos

Αλόννησος
Alonnisos

Δομοκός
Domokos

Σκιάθος
Skiathos

Σκόπελος
Skopelos

Λαμία πόλη
Lamia ville

Στυλίδα
Stilida

Λευκάδα
Lefkada

Λειανοκλάδι
Lianokladi

Λαμία
Lamia

Μπράλος
Bralos

Αμφίκλεια
Amfiklia

Ιθάκη
ithaki

Αμφίκλεια πόλη
Amfiklia ville

Τιθορέα
Tithorea

Ορχομενός
Orchomenos

Χαλκίδα
Chalkida

Εύβοια
Evia

Λεβάδεια
Levadia

ΠΑΤΡΑ
PATRA

Αίγιο
Egio

Λεβάδεια πόλη
Levadia ville

Θήβα
Thiva

Οινόη
Inoi

Κεφαλονιά
Kefalonia

Διακοπτό
Diakopto

Μέγα Σπήλαιο
Mega Spileo

Ξυλόκαστρο
Xilokastro

Κιλλήνη
Killini

Καβάσιλα
Kavassila

Καλάβρυτα
Kalavrita

Κιάτο
Kiato

Λουτράκι
Loutraki

ΑΘΗΝΑ
ATHINA

Βαρθολομιό
Vartholomio

Πύργος
Pirgos

Κόρινθος
Korinthos

Σαλαμίνα
Salamina

ΠΕΙΡΑΙΑΣ
PIREAS

Ζάκυνθος
Zakinthos

Κατάκολο
Katakolo

Ολυμπία
Olimpia

Αργος
Argos

Αίγινα
Egina

Μακρόνη
Makroni

Ζαχάρω
Zacharo

Μεγαλόπολη
Megalopoli

Τρίπολη
Tripoli

Πόρος
Poros

Καλόνερο
Kalonero

Λεύκτρο
Lefktro

Ύδρα
Idra

Κυπαρισσία
Kiparissia

Ζευγολάτιο
Zevgolatio

Μεσσήνη
Messini

Ασπρόχωμα
Asprohoma

Σπάρτη
Sparti

Σπέτσες
Spetses

Καλαμάτα
Kalamata

Γύθειο
Githio

Γραμμή κανονικού πλάτους.
Ligne à voie normale.

Γραμμή στενή.
Ligne à voie étroite.

Διπλή γραμμή.
Ligne à double voie.

---- bus

Οι αριθμοί στό χάρτη παραπέμπουν στούς
πίνακες πού περιέχουν τό δρομολόγιο.

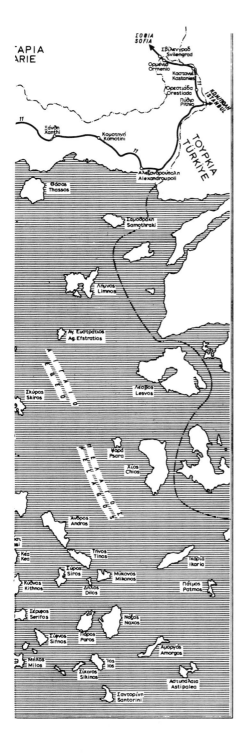

Greek Alphabet

A	α	alpha
B	β	beta
Γ	γ	gamma
Δ	δ	delta
E	ε	epsilon
Z	ζ	zeta
H	η	eta
Θ	ϑ	theta
I	ι	iota
K	κ	kappa
Λ	λ	lambda
M	μ	mu
N	ν	nu
Ξ	ξ	xi
O	o	omicron
Π	π	pi
P	ϱ	rho
Σ	σ¹	sigma
T	τ	tau
Y	υ	upsilon
Φ	φ	phi
X	χ	chi
Ψ	ψ	psi
Ω	ω	omega

TOURIST INFORMATION   Besides offices of the National Tourist Organization of Greece (NTOG) (pronounced toor-is-MOHSS), many towns have Tourist Police (pronounced touristiki as-tee-no-mia) which function as tourist offices. The letters EOT also signify a tourist office.

CAMPING   NTOG campgrounds are licensed by the National Tourist Organization and are generally large and comfortable with numerous services. High season is June 15 to September 15, low season is the remainder. The busiest period is July 15 through the first few days in September. The 1989 high season charges are adult/530dr or 460dr, small tent/380dr or 420dr, sleeping bag only/210dr or 190dr depending on classification of camp. Low season costs are adult/390dr or 330dr, small tent/300dr or 250dr, sleeping bag only/140dr or 130dr. Another group of excellent campgrounds is operated by the Hellenic Touring Club. Many more good campgrounds exist in Greece than are listed in the official tourist office publication or *Europa Camping and Caravanning*. Typical prices are 300-400dr per adult and per tent. Camping is officially forbidden outside of organized campgrounds, but occurs anyway on remote and isolated beaches. You see a few young adults at each campground who are using sleeping bags without a tent. This is comfortable in summer because you are cooler and there's no morning dew.

In general the price differential between camping and staying at a rock bottom hotel is narrower here than in any other European country. In small towns you might want to consider the convenience of merely taking a room rather than going out to the campground. We did this twice but found that between the church bells and the traffic noise we didn't get much sleep. And the price always turned out to be greater than we expected, what with extras and price rises. At a campground, the charges are set, you have only friendly relations with campground personnel, and you're away from the noises and stuffy heat of hotel rooms.

TRAINS   Trains in Greece are operated by the state Hellenic Railways Organization (O.S.E.), whose head office is at #1-3 Karolou Street in Athens. The main line runs northward from Athens to Thessaloniki and into Yugoslavia, Bulgaria or Turkey (reservation fee 150dr). Smaller lines branch off the main line to Volos, Kalambaka and Stylis.

The other line is the Pelopponese line which provides transportation on the Pelopponese peninsula. The Pelopponese trains have narrow gauge tracks, smaller coaches and are fairly slow because of the terrain. A train will often have only 3 or 4 cars and the majority of seats will be second class. The few first class seats will occupy one end of a coach. A reservation can be made on this line in Athens, but as reserved seats are not marked in the coaches you may have to uproot an existing passenger.

A **bus network** makes up for the lack of railway density and archeological sites can often be reached by combining train and bus. During the tourist season, buses run frequently to the sites. During the rest of the year bus schedules are curtailed. Those on a tight schedule and wishing to visit archeological sites more efficiently should rent a car for a day from a local agency in the town. A U.S. driver's license is valid in Greece.

train	treno
station	strathmos
information	pliroforia

luggage check	apodhiksiston poskevon
exchange	sarafiko
timetable	dhomoloyion
non-smoking compartment	dhya mi kapnistas
waiting room	ethusa anamonis
ticket window	thiris
entrance	eisodros
exit	exodhos
ticket	biletto

EURAIL BONUSES   (1) **Ferry crossings** on the Adriatica and Hellenic Mediterranean Lines between **Patras, Greece and Brindisi, Italy.** This is deck class--a reclining seat costs an extra $10, but is less desirable than a mattress and sleeping bag on deck in the fresh air. All year a port charge of 400dr must be paid upon embarkation. If a reservation is made, the fee is the equivalent of $2.00. Between June 10 and Sept 30, a surcharge of 1200dr is made for any Eurailpass. If a stopover in Corfu is planned, tell the agent when obtaining your boarding pass. Anyone with an advance reservation, before boarding check in at the shipping line office at the pier. Hellenic Mediterranean Lines office in Athens is at Leoforos Amalias 28, near Syntagma Square. See additional information under Patras. (2) Railpasses are also valid for a 30 percent reduction on Libra Maritime Line between Piraeus and Haifa or Ancona.

FOOD   Food is much less expensive in Greece than in the rest of Europe, whether you're shopping for groceries or eating out. As always, the open market provides the cheapest and freshest food. Common vegetables are zucchini, eggplant, green pepper, artichokes, cucumbers, lettuce and tomatoes. Melons, apricots, oranges and peaches represent some inexpensive fruits, with oranges being the cheapest at 110dr per kilo in 1988. Out in the countryside, apricots freshly fallen from trees that often line the roads are yours for the bending over. Bread commonly costs 70dr per 500 grams. Besides bread, Greek bakeries sell very good apple, cheese and meat turnovers. In the grocery store, small bags of roasted garbanzo beans, eaten like peanuts as a nutritious snack, are sold for 80dr per 250 grams. Soft drinks and mineral water cost 55dr to 75dr. Better quality unresinated wines are bottled according to European Economic Community standards and are labeled VQPRD on the label.

For prepared meals, head for the typical Greek taverna. Lunch is eaten between 1 and 3 and dinner between 8 and 10. Throughout Greece, the custom in small restaurants and tavernas is for the customer to go into the kitchen and select from what is on the stove, usually slowly simmered stewed lamb, beef or chicken served with rice, noodles or semolina--always a tasty dish. Anything to be grilled or deep fried will be on the menu and is prepared individually.

What is **the least expensive entree**, that is always reliably cooked and delicious? Fresh, **deep fried baby squid--***Kalamari*! With a flavor similar to clams, that tasty dish will cost only between 234dr to 350dr in simple tavernas. Combine it with a salad of sliced tomatoes and cucumbers, or the more elaborate and expensive typical Greek country salad: sliced tomatoes, cucumbers, olives and feta cheese, dressed with olive oil and

236

lemon juice. The Greek country salad is listed as a Greek salad on the menu in most tavenas.

Two standbys that are found everywhere, but vary in quality according to class of establishment are *dolmadhes*, vine leaves stuffed with rice and ground lamb, and *moussaka*. Greek chefs make moussaka by slicing a layer of potatoes in the bottom of individual earthenware casseroles, adding a half-inch of ground and seasoned meat (usually lamb), arranging eggplant over the meat, putting in another layer of potatoes, topping the casserole with grated cheese and baking it in the oven. As it is freshly made for each meal, expect to be able to enjoy a salad before it will be ready to be served. Because Greek working men prefer a slightly sour taste to dolmadhes that westerners are not used to, this dish served in the cheapest taverna may be unpalatable.

Lamb is the most frequently found meat, and the basis of the Greek skewered and grilled meat, *souvlaki*. These shish-ke-babs also go by the names *suvlakia* or *doner kebab*. The meat of souvlaki varies in tenderness and quality from place to place, but is always served with bread. In the snack bar coach on the train from Athens to Patras, snack-sized freshly grilled tender souvlaki with one piece of bread is served for 60dr. As the snack bar had only two tables, the waiter went up and down the aisle selling it to passengers at their seats.

Fish is widely available as nowhere in Greece are you far from the sea, but easily can be **the most expensive entree** on the menu. The main drawback to ordering fish is not knowing in advance what it is going to cost because the price on the menu is by weight. The fish is weighed before being cooked. If you're going to go for the big splurge (fish), always order the cheapest fish on the menu, which won't be cheap but only less expensive than the rest! We found the cheaper fish to have the most delicate texture, whereas the most expensive fish is usually similar to red snapper, much prized by Greeks. After ordering fish, the waiter will ask whether you want it fried or grilled. Never order fish unless you can get it grilled because the wood fire makes all the difference in taste. The memory of simply grilled fish served on the veranda under large desiduous trees of a taverna in Corinth evokes thoughts of one of our best meals in Greece.

Usually we never took dessert with our taverna meals, but purchased something from a pastry shop, called *patisserie* even in Greece, if we happened to come upon one. From the delicious sticky baklava to French-style buttercream-filled layer cakes, you'll find desserts hard to resist. For cool refreshment try an ice cream bar from a vending cart for 40dr to 100dr.

SIGHTSEEING Admission to archeological sites and museums is 150dr to 300dr. Students of any age with an identity card pay half price.

POLLUTION As long as you don't swim around the port city of Piraeus (or any closer than perhaps Glyfada), Corfu and other major ports, the Greek coastline and islands are free of pollution.

CORFU ISLAND (KERKIRA, KERKYRA)

This is one Greek island that Eurailpass holders can get to free as a stopover on the ferry between Patras, Greece and Brindisi, Italy. That is almost free. There is a 300dr port tax due when leaving Corfu for Patras, 800dr for Italy.

If you plan to visit Corfu, you must tell the ferry official of your intention when receiving your boarding pass in Brindisi or Patras. Laying over in Corfu provides respite from city touring and breaks the long ferry ride. Most people come for the beach scene of rocky inlets and sand beaches rather than the attractions of its largest town, Corfu. The same clear blue water and secluded coves found on other Greek islands are duplicated here, but Corfu enjoys more vegetation because of its latitude and greater moisture.

Corfu Island

Corfu
KEPKYPA
(Kérkira)

The **10pm ferry departure from Brindisi, Italy**, stops enroute at the island of Corfu, arriving at 7am. Remember that Corfu time is one hour earlier than Brindisi time. From the other direction, **the 10pm ferry from Patras arrives in Corfu at 9am.** Departure from Corfu varies, but usually doesn't happen until a half hour after arrival time. In any case, you will need to stop in the port building and pay the port tax. The receipt must be shown before boarding. New in 1989 is Hellenic Mediterranean Lines/Adriatica daily service on the Apollonia between Brindisi, Igoumenitsa and Corfu as follows.

238

Corfu Town

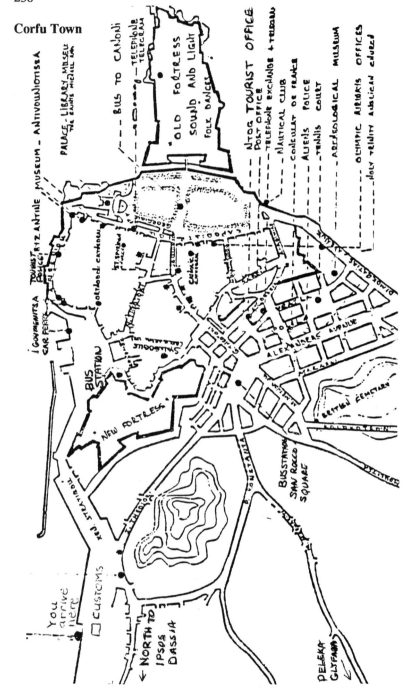

		7/27/89 8/08/89	8/14/89 9/05/89
Corfu	lv.	9:30pm	8:15pm
Igoumenitsa	lv.	11:50pm	11:00pm
Brindisi	ar.	8:30am	8:30am
Brindisi	lv.	1:00pm	noon
Corfu	lv.	9:00pm	7:30pm
Igoumenitsa	ar.	11:00pm	10:00pm

Foreign exchange is in the customs building at the new port where the ferry docks. The clerk at the information counter has maps of Corfu. Outside the port building, those high walls you see are the sanitarium, Lofos Avrami.

TOURIST OFFICE   The NTOG tourist office, Pl. Eleftherias 1, is near San Rocco Square in an uninteresting part of town.   You're better off walking to the Tourist Police office at 35 Arseniou Street.   If you turn left outside the port building and follow the coastal road with the sea to your left, in about 15 minutes you will arrive at the Tourist Police Office (7:30am-11pm).   On your way you pass by the New Fort, *Neo Frourio*, and just beyond it the New Fortress Square bus terminal.

BUS STATIONS   City buses and those to Kontokali and Dassia leave from San Rocco Square, in downtown Corfu.   To get there turn left when leaving the port building and then in two blocks turn right at the main intersection. Walk on Avrami Theotoki which leads into San Rocco Square.

The **bus terminal** for the outlying beaches is closer to the port and the route is level. Buses to the more remote beaches such as **Paleokastritsa, Glyfada, Ag. Gordis and Pelekas** leave from Neo Frourio Square (New Fortress Square).   To reach New Fortress Square, turn left as you leave the port facility and walk along the coastal road. The sea should be on your left. It's about a seven minute walk to the bus station.   An inexpensive bakery selling bread and turnovers is on the right hand side of the road on the way. It's well to buy a loaf to take with you as bread is cheaper and fresher here than in the stores by the campgrounds. When you see several buses parked together you know you've arrived at the square. You'll have to read Greek to decipher the destinations, or else ask the drivers or waiting passengers. Buses carry both a ticket seller and a driver, so get on board and the fare will be collected once underway. Alert the ticket seller to where you're going so he will have the bus stop at the campground. Fares are very reasonable to anywhere on the island. The tourist office in downtown Corfu distributes a printed bus schedule.

CAMPGROUNDS   Corfu's abundance of campgrounds are located near Corfu town as well as all around the shoreline of the island.   Select a campground according to whether public transportation is available early enough to return you to the port in time to board the ferry. Public buses go from Corfu to all the major beaches on the island. The problem is the first bus leaves Corfu usually around 8 or 8:30am and the first bus returning from the beaches usually starts at 8:30 or 9am. Obviously, this presents a problem if your ferry is leaving at 7:15am to 7:30am, as it does for Patras. You're in better luck for Brindisi as the ship doesn't leave Corfu until 9:15am or later.

If you are enroute to Patras, two strategies should be considered. The first possibility is to stay at a campground whose representative has met the ferry with a van and promises return transportation in time to get the ferry when you leave. Other island beaches can be visited by renting a moped. The second approach is to base yourself at a campground near Corfu that is served by Corfu city buses as they operate early enough to meet the ferry. Then you can take a day trip by public bus to a different beach each day.

Upon debarking at Corfu, you will be stopped by representatives of hotels and campgrounds with offers of accommodation. They will quote a camping price to you, or give you a brochure with prices. Prices per adult and per tent generally range from 400-600dr. In evaluating these offers, keep in mind that areas on the west side of the island near the beaches of Paleokastritsa, Glifada, Agios Gordis and Pelekas are some of the most scenic. Also consider whether you want the campground to be immediately on the beach or are willing to walk to it.

Corfu is one of those places where prices drop dramatically once the main tourist season is over. If you're here during that season, it's hardly worthwhile to camp because the gap between camping and hotels is small. Less expensive hotels are mainly located in the old part of Corfu. An area that's easy to find is two blocks beyond the New Fortress bus station near the ferry dock for Igoumenitsa. The Hotel Constantinopolis at 11 Zavitsianou is one. Convenient, but more expensive C class hotels Ionion and Atlantis are across from the port building where ferries arrive from Patras and Brindisi. For cheaper rooms in private homes, go to the Tourist Police office and ask them for the tourist office list and assistance in calling.

Camping Vatos Pelecas is on the west coast of Corfu. Its green van is parked outside the port building and its representative meets incoming ferries and offers free transportation to and from the camp. The camp is near beautiful beaches, being 800 meters from Ermones Beach, 1.5 km. from the nudist beach, Mirtiotissa, 3 km. from Glifada beach and 3 km. from Pelekas. The camp has hot showers, a washing machine and mopeds for rent.

Those planning to base themselves in Corfu should consider **Camping Dionysus** at Gouvia Bay, 8 km. from town. Take bus 7 from San Rocco Square. A bus departs every half hour and stops outside the campground. Facilities include hot showers, store, restaurant, automatic washing machine and a disco with Greek dancing. Offered occasionally at extra charge are a boat tour of the island and a special Greek dinner with spit roasted lamb and Greek dancing. The camp is near the youth hostel and caters to college age travelers, but accommodates campers of all ages. The beaches in this area close to Corfu town do not equal the beauty and clearness of those on the west coast, however.

Another close-in camp is **Kormarie Camping International**, opposite the Chandris Hotel, near Dassia. Take bus 7 from San Rocco Square, or a local bus marked *Ypsos, Pirgi* or *Kassiopi* from New Fortress Square. Fees are adult/240dr and tent/180dr. Facilities include free hot showers, store and cafe.

Camping Paleokastritsa on the west side of the island is up the hill from the beach cove of Paleokastritsa. Fees are adult/350dr and tent/350dr. (This would be my first choice for where to stay because of the beauty of

Paleokastritsa except that the bus doesn't leave early enough in the morning to catch the ferry.) The peaceful and attractive terraced camp has hot showers and the manager speaks English. A store is across the road. It's an easy 20-minute walk downhill to the beach from camp, and you can take an hourly bus back to camp for 55dr to avoid the uphill trek. The bus to Paleokastritsa leaves from New Fortress Station in Corfu town. Tell the ticket seller that you are going to Camping Paleokastritsa, which is directly on the road, so he will stop there before descending to the cove. See Day Trip to Paleokastritsa for bus schedules and more information. Outside summer if you aren't traveling alone, you can probably pick up a "room to let" deal down at the beach for not much more than this campground costs. In that case, ride the bus all the way to the beach. If you can't find anything, you can always take the next bus back up the hill to the campground.

Two campgrounds are at Ipsos, 14 km. north of Corfu town. **Camping Ipsos Ideal** is the second one on the Ipsos Road. Fees are adult/250dr and tent/250dr. Facilities include a sand beach, restaurant, disco, store, moped rentals and hot showers. **Wooden Pier Camping** is also at Ipsos. Buses leave from New Fortress Square.

Further north is **Karoussades Camping**, outside Karoussades in the direction of Roda. Take the bus to Roda from New Fortress Square and ask to get off nearest to the campground, then a 10-minute walk.

FOOD   The market is open 7-12 at the north end of S. Dessylla Street. A supermarket is on Solomou Street near the New Fortress Square bus station.

SIGHTSEEING IN CORFU   The most interesting area is the old town, centered on the narrow, twisting streets behind Spianada, the grassy esplanade by the old fort, Paleo Frourio. From May 15 to September 30, the Sound and Light (*Son et Lumiere*) show in English takes place at 9:30pm in the Old Venetian Fortress. At the same spot, folk dances are performed at 9pm before the show. A combo ticket costs 400dr (students half price).

DAY TRIP TO PALEOKASTRITSA   Paleokastritsa, a beauty spot on the west coast 26 km. from Corfu, is known for its sandy beach and clear deep blue waters. Four tavernas and several outdoor "stores" inhabit the cove. At one stand located beyond the bus stop, a woman sells reasonably priced and nicely designed silver jewelry handcrafted by her husband. An attractive silver ring was 600dr. Typical price for a postcard is 15dr and the striking pictorial calendars you see sold throughout Greece are priced at 350dr for the small size. Peddle boats can be rented for 200dr per hour to explore the cave just outside the cove. If you're splurging for a lounge chair and umbrella on the beach, the rate is 200dr each. Be forewarned that if a second person even momentarily sits on the end of the lounge, the lady who operates the chair and umbrella concession will immediately come over and let you know that only one person is allowed to use the chair. **The 13th century fort**, Angelokastro, overlooking the cove can be visited by hiking up the winding road to it. The ascent takes about 20 minutes. In many ways, Paleokastritsa is one of the most interesting spots on the island.

Buses leave New Fortress Square in Corfu town (130dr one way, 30-minute ride). A bus leaves Corfu for Paleokastritsa M-Sa 8:30am and every half hour until noon, and 2:30pm, 3:30, 4:00, 5:00, 5:30 and 7:00pm. On Sunday and holidays, a bus leaves at 9:00am, 10:00, 10:30, noon, 2:30pm, 3:30, 4:00, 5:30 and 7:00pm.

A bus leaves Paleokastritsa for Corfu on Monday through Saturday at 9:15am, 9:45, 10:45, 11:15, 11:45, 12:15pm, 12:45, 3:15, 4:15, 4:45, 5:45, 6:15 and 7:45pm. On Sundays and holidays a bus leaves at 9:45am, 10:45, 11:15, 12:45pm, 3:15, 4:15, 4:45, 6:15 and 7:45pm.

THE PELOPPONESE (PELOPONISSOS)

The city of Patras, port of the Pelopponese, is where Adriatica Line ferries (included in Eurailpass) arrive from Brindisi, Italy. The isle of Pelops, now connected by bridge at Corinth to mainland Greece, compactly presents 4,000 years of history through imposing ruins, archaeological sites (some being currently excavated as at Corinth) and museums. The most important sites from the second millennium B.C. are the Lion gate and beehive tombs at Mycenae, the Cyclopean walls at Tiryns, and Nestor's palace at Pylos. Also important are the Greek and Roman ruins in Olympia and Corinth, the theater in Epidaurus, the temple of Bassae and the walls of Messini. Illustrative of later times are the medieval castles of AcroCorinth, Tornese and Karitena and the Byzantine Mistra and Monemvassia. Still later in history are the Venetian fortresses of Nauplion and Methoni. Nauplion, Methoni and Monemvassia are particularly charming small villages as well as archeological sites.

Of the towns mentioned, Olympia, Mycenae and Corinth are on a rail line. The best base for visiting Mycenae, Tiryns, Epidarus and Nauplion is the selection of campgrounds in the tiny beach resort hamlet of Tolo, a 15-minute bus ride from Nauplion. Nauplion with its great Greek ambience is what a Greek village ought to be. An entire day could be happily spent here, strolling, exploring and shopping.

Trains are operated by the Pelopponese branch of the Hellenic Railways. The speed and comfort of the narrow diesel trains (automotrices) on this branch are of a lower standard than in the rest of Greece and Western Europe. Departures are generally infrequent making efficient touring difficult. This lack in the railways is more than compensated by the long distance bus network, KTEL. Green and cream colored KTEL buses connect nearby towns often on a half-hourly basis and fares are low. Bus service is reduced from October through May.

Through trains follow these routes: (1) Pirghos (Pyrgos), Kavassila, Patra (Patras), Diakopto, Xylocastron, Corinthia (Corinthia, Korinthos), Athinai (Athens) and Piraeus, and (2) Kalamata, Tripolis, Arghos (Argos), Mykine (Mikenes or Mycenae), Korinthos (Corinth), Athinai (Athens) and Piraeus. Note that both routes duplicate the portion between Piraeus, Athens and Corinth. At Corinth, trains either turn south to Kalamata or continue west to Patras. Once you get off these 2 main paths, departures lessen considerably. Trains operate 3 times a day on the line between Kalamata, Zevgolatio and Pyrgos, the remaining leg on the circular train route on the peninsula.

Additionally, there are rail spurs off the main route at Kavassila for Killini and Loutra, at Pyrgos for Olympia, and at Kalonero for Kyparissia. At Zevgolatio, some trains go onward to Argos and others go to Messina and Kalamata. Also a small rail spur goes to Megalopolis. Near Patras at Dhiakofto, the scenic, short Kalavrita Railway runs to Zakhlorou where there is a walk to a monastery. The train leaves 3 times daily for the 45-minute trip.

The best strategy is to rail to a main town and change to KTEL buses to the sites. The best train service is on the direct Patras-Corinth route as it originates in Athens and carries the most traffic. It's hardly worth waiting very long for the next train departure for short distances when a bus is sure to be leaving within the hour and the few drachmas paid easily compensate for the time saved. If an archeological site is not accessible by train, in almost every case a bus will be available. The bus station is usually one to two blocks from the train station. Railway personnel will point the way. If you haven't a Eurailpass, take buses as they are modern, and more frequent and quicker than the train.

In the rare event of not finding a bus, a taxi will be easy to find. Taxis are charged per taxi, not per person, and the fare initially quoted by the driver is subject to negotiation. If you look like you might walk or hitch instead, the price will invariably drop. Also be sure to agree that everything is included to avoid being surprised with extras. Have the driver write down the price before you get in, and pay the driver after he has returned you to your originating point. Round trip fare normally includes some waiting time, usually one hour, at the site.

OVERNIGHT TOUR TO OLYMPIA FROM PATRAS BEFORE GOING TO ATHENS   Take the train to Olympia, overnight at a campground, explore the site and museum the next morning, then take train #313 leaving Olympia at 1:27pm. This train arrives in Athens at 9:15pm, allowing sufficient time to ride the bus to the campground. Between about June 24 and September 8, expect the train to become packed with ferry arrivals when it stops in Patras. (But you'll have a seat because you got on first.)

FIVE NIGHT TOUR, PATRAS TO ATHENS   This itinerary follows a semi-circular route beginning in Patras and ending in Athens. Five nights are spent in campgrounds, one in Olympia and two nights each in Methoni and Tolo. Methoni and Tolo are used as bases for day trips to surrounding archeological sites. KTEL buses provide connections between local towns. **Day 1 (Olympia):** Rail from Patras to Olympia and spend the night at one of the 2 campgrounds in this basically one-street village. **Day 2 & 3 (Methoni):** The next morning, make an early visit to the site and museum which open at 7:30am. Take the train from Olympia to Pyrgos at 10:38am. If you need more time in Olympia, a KTEL bus may be taken so long as you can connect with the 1:11pm train to Kyparissia. From Pyrgos, take the 1:11pm train (direction Kalamata) to Kyparissia which arrives at 2:28pm. Take the bus to Methoni from Kyparissia. Spend two nights at the campground in Methoni, and then take a morning bus to Kalamata. In Kalamata, board the train 3:16pm and get off in Arghos at 7:02pm. Walk to the bus station and board the bus to Nauplion, and in Nauplion the bus to Tolo. (Both bus rides are 15 to 20 minutes each.) Select from among the campgrounds in Tolo. **Day 4 & 5 (Tolo):** The next day visit delightful Nauplion and Mycenae, Epidaurus or Tiryns. Spend the evening exploring Nauplion or at a Greek play in Epidaurus, returning to Tolo for the night. In the morning, take the bus to Nauplion and then to Arghos and board the train which leaves at 11:02am and arrives in Athens at 1pm. There are also later trains. It is also possible to stop in Corinth to see the archeological site before continuing to Athens.

PATRAS (PATRA)

The only good reason to visit Patras is because the Adriatica-Hellenic Lines ferry to and from Italy which is "free" with Eurailpass uses this port. Many rail options are open to those who arrive at 1pm on the direct ferry from Brindisi, Italy. Most travelers will squeeze aboard the 2pm train for Athens which arrives at 6:48pm in plenty of time to reach a campground and set up. A better strategy is to go in the opposite direction and take the 2:50pm train to Olympia, arriving at 6:48pm. For those who arrive in Patras at the less desirable time of 6pm, either stay overnight at the campground and take a morning train or board the 6:54pm departure for Athens, get off in Corinth at 9:09pm, and stay at a hotel or take a taxi (150dr) to the campground. The train arrives in Athens too late to connect with the bus to Voula Camping. If you must arrive in Athens the same day, purchase a ticket for 1200dr while on board the ferry for the connecting bus to Athens, which arrives at 10pm while city buses to Voula Camping are still running.

FERRY ARRIVALS FROM ITALY The Adriatica-Hellenic Lines ferry from Brindisi, Italy, arrives at either 1pm or 6pm. You will arrive at the dock in front of the Port facility. Restrooms, a water cooler with a drinking fountain and spout useful for filling water bottles, and a branch of the tourist office are located at the far right of the outdoor area of the complex, as you face it. The bus to Athens provided by the ferry line will be waiting in the general area of the port building.

The train station is located about 500 meters to the right of where the ferry docks. After disembarking, turn right and walk straight ahead along the main street until you see the small train station on the right hand side of the road. The walk takes about 5 minutes and you will have lots of company. Station personnel will not accept reservations for the ride to Athens and it becomes an "everyone-for-themself" proposition. The train to Athens that connects with the ferry arrival is always overcrowded in June through August. Do your best to get a seat once the train arrives. The unlucky sit on their packs in the aisle. (People were in the aisle even in late June when we were there and that was before the main tourist season.) Also, you might enquire at the train station whether a second train will be added for the overload.

FERRY DEPARTURES TO ITALY Assuming you have arrived by train, this is what you must do to take the Adriatica-Hellenic Lines ferry to the island of Corfu, or Brindisi, Italy. This is the line which provides "free" passage to Eurailpass holders. The 10pm departure operates year around and stops enroute at Corfu. The 6pm departure is available from June 21 to September 10 and sails direct to Brindisi. The busy season from Patras to Italy is August 14 through September 5. Though ferry officials advise a reservation during this period, travelers report it's unnecessary. Passengers with advance reservations must obtain their boarding pass at least 2 hours prior to the ship's departure time. Failure to comply may result in cancellation of the reservation and the space reallocated to standby passengers.

Ferry Schedule - Patras to Brindisi, Hellenic/Adriatica Line

1 9 8 9 — SAILINGS FROM GREECE

(MONTH)	DEPART TIME
JAN	22.00
FEB	22.00
MAR	22.00
APR	22.00
MAY	22.00 / 17.00
JUN	22.00 / 17.00
JUL	17.00 / 22.00
AUG	17.00 / 22.00
SEP	17.00 / 22.00
OCT	22.00
NOV	22.00
DEC	22.00

From 03/01 to 31/12/89

ATHENS (by coach)	DEP	13:30
PATRAS	DEP	22:00
IGOUMENITSA		07:00
CORFU		09:00
BRINDISI	ARR	17:00

From 21/06 to 10/09/89

ATHENS (by coach)	DEP	09:30
PATRAS	DEP	17:00
CEPHALONIA *		20:30
BRINDISI	ARR.	09:30

* 14.07 to 09.09.89

1989 Sailings from Greece to Italy*

		01/03/89 12/12/89	6/21/89 9/10/89
Athens (bus)	lv.	1:30pm	9:30am
Patras	lv.	10:00pm	5:00pm
Igoumenitsa	ar.	7:00am	
Corfu	ar.	9:00am	
Brindisi	ar.	5:00pm	9:30am

*The 5pm departure from Patras is daily. It also stops at 8:30pm at Cephalonia between July 14 and September 9, 1989. The 10pm sailing is daily from March 16 to October 15, 1989. Please refer to chart for sailing dates in other months.

First, depending on the time interval before ship embarkation, consider checking your pack at the train station. Then, turn left from the station exit facing the street and walk about 300 meters to the main Adriatica Lines Office at #8 on the right hand side of the road. The signs are gold and orange, or yellow and red and read, *Adriatica Embarkation*. Inside, pay the 1200dr Eurailpass supplement if it's high season and the 400dr port tax. If you are stopping over on Corfu, be sure to mention this so that the ticket will be properly endorsed. A ticket be issued and a separate receipt attached for the port tax and supplement. This same procedure can be accomplished at the Adriatica and HML window in the Port Building, but the main office at #8 opens sooner than the Port Office window. If the main office is closed, it will open anywhere from 2 to 5 hours prior to sailing time. The office at the Port is open 2 hours before sailing time. Once you have your ticket, continue walking for another 300 meters to the Port. At the Port, go into the large waiting room and look for the sign, passport control. Step up to the window and obtain a white card, complete it, and return it along with your passport to the officer in the window. He will stamp your passport and hand you a white boarding pass.

About 1-1/2 to 2 hours before departure, passengers are allowed on board. People start amassing early in the area to be first aboard to "reserve" their favorite floor space. Once boarding begins, the official takes your ticket, you go inside, and the immigration officer takes your boarding pass.

TRAIN STATION The Station's luggage check stays open 24 hours and charges 60dr per piece. Across the street is the Tourist Police office, whose man on duty speaks English and has free brochures available.

BUS STATION Halfway between the Port building and the train station is the KTEL bus station, on the left as you walk towards the train station. The bus company operated by the railways is OSE and its station is next to the train station. Both companies operate buses to Athens, Pyrgos and other destinations. Their fare to Athens is about 200dr less than the coach fare sold by Adriatica, but the Adriatica bus is easier and worth the difference.

TOURIST OFFICE A branch is at the Port facility, a good chance to pick up English language brochures on all areas of Greece that you plan to visit.

CURRENCY EXCHANGE A bank and post office are in the Port facility. The National Bank of Greece is next to the Tourist Police office across from the train station. Open M-F 8am-1:30pm, and 5:30-7:30pm on days when ferries arrive during that time.

Patras (Patra)

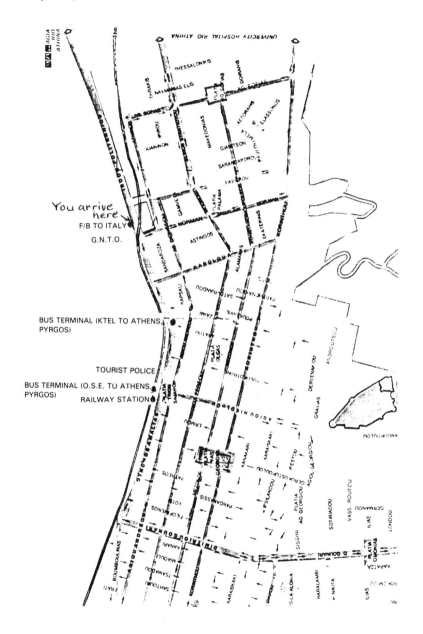

CAMPGROUNDS   Agia (Aya) Patron Camping, a N.T.O.G. camp, is on the beach 3 km. southwest of Patras. Open all year, high season adult/460dr, small tent/380dr, sleeping bag/190dr. To reach Camping Agia, walk across the street from the train station, enter the tourist police office and go out the back door. This puts you on the next street, Agiou Andreou. Across the street and a little to the right is a bus stop. Take Bus 1 with *Plage* (beach) on the front to reach the campground. Bus 1 departs every 20 minutes and the last departure is at 10:30pm. The very attractive camp has hot showers, sinks with hot water, store, cafe, lounge, skin diving and boating.

Another option, the close-in **Youth Hostel,** allows camping on its grounds. Fee is adult/130dr. To reach it, as you disembark from the ferry, turn left and walk along the coastal road, Iroon Politechniou, for about 10 minutes to #68. (The sea should be on your left as you walk towards the Youth Hostel.)

Camping Rion is on the beach, 8 km. northeast of Patras, 300 meters south of the Rion ferry dock and 500 meters from the train station of Rion (Rio). Open Apr 1-Oct 31, adult/560dr, tent/560dr, 30 minutes by bus from Patras. Facilities include hot showers, hot water in the sinks, automatic washing machine, store, and cafe equipped with a barbeque for preparing souvlaki.

FOOD   The **Taverna Bienza** has tasty stewed meat with noodles or semolina for 345dr. To reach it from the train station, turn left and walk one block to Kolokotroni, turn right and it's in the third block, across from the park. Walk up to the serving counter, look over the day's dishes and simply point to what you want.

To Corinthia (Korinthos) and Athens

lv.	am	am	am	pm	pm	pm
Patras	6:48	8:09	11:01	2:00	4:47	6:54
Diakofto	7:15	9:17	12:01	3:15	5:50	7:51
Xylocastr		10:14	12:47	4:11	6:39	8:34
Korinthos	8:26	10:57	1:21	4:50	7:17	9:11
Athens	10:00	1:00	3:00	6:48	9:15	10:54
Piraeus	10:30	1:38	3:35	7:22	9:49	11:20

To Kalamata, trains leave at 2:02am (ar. 7:16am), 6am, 10:58am (ar. 4:25pm) and 2:50pm (ar. 8:20pm).

To Olympia, trains leave at 7am, 10:58am (ar. 2:30pm), 12:22pm and 2:50pm (ar. 6:48pm). The trip takes about 1-1/2 hours.

To Pyrgos, trains leave at 7am, 10:58am (ar. 1:11pm), 12:22pm (ar 2pm), 2:50pm (ar. 5:01pm), 5:11pm (ar. 6:56pm) and 8:30pm (ar. 10:45pm).

Pyrgos to Olympia, trains leave Pyrgos at 6:30am (ar. 7:06am), 9:46am (ar. 10:22am), 12:45pm (ar. 1:27pm), 2:17pm (ar. 2:59pm) and 7:06pm (ar. 7:42pm). The distance is 21 km.. There are also hourly KTEL buses between Pyrgos and Olympia.

Kavasila to Killiny, trains leave Kavasila at 6:40am, 8:06am, 9:56am, 12:25pm, 2:06pm, 4:15pm and 6:25pm. NTOG Camping Kyllini at nearby Vartholomio, open Apr-Oct, is 500 meters from a bus stop. Take the bus from Killini to Vartholomio. Excellent site directly on the beach; sinks with hot water, cafe, boating and fishing, adult/530dr and tent/420dr.

Pyrgos to Katakolo, trains leave Pyrgos at 8:44am, 11:16am, 2:18pm, 3:44pm and 5:15pm. Katakolo is a small port west of Pyrgos.

Bus to Delphi No train, but 2 bus routes are available. First, you can take the Thessaloniki bus from the OSE Bus Station near the train station to Itea and then change for a bus to Delphi. Three buses go daily from Patras and many buses the short distance from Itea to Delphi.

Olympia Archeological Zone

A Entrance
1. Gymnasium
2. East Portico of the Gymnasium
3. Palaestra (Wrestling School)
4. Theokoleon (Priests' House)
5. Heroon (Heroes' Memorial Building)
6-7. Phidias' Workshop - (Early Christian Basilica)

8. Leonidaion
9. South Portico
10. Bouleuterion (Council House)
11. Echo Portico
12. Stadium
13. Treasuries
14. Nymphaeum
15. Metroon

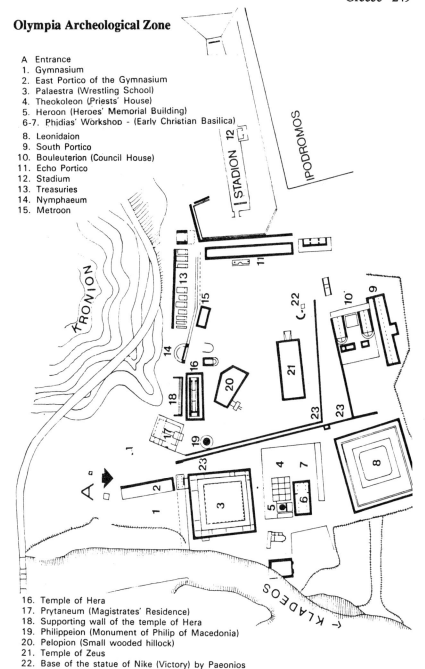

16. Temple of Hera
17. Prytaneum (Magistrates' Residence)
18. Supporting wall of the temple of Hera
19. Philippeion (Monument of Philip of Macedonia)
20. Pelopion (Small wooded hillock)
21. Temple of Zeus
22. Base of the statue of Nike (Victory) by Paeonios
23. Enclosure of Sacred Altis

OLYMPIA (OLIMBIA) *ΟΛΥΜΠΙΑ*

Birthplace of the Olympic Games, the sanctuary is now within a 5,000 acre national park. See map page 249. The new beautiful Archeological Museum is open M-Sa 7:30am-7pm (except Tu noon-6pm) & Su 8am-6pm; 300dr. The top rated sculpture is the Hermes by Praxiteles. From the train station it's an easy 15-minute walk to the site, and **Camping Olympia** (Arkhala Olimbia) is closer. Open all year, adult/280dr and tent/230dr. **Camping Diana**, behind the museum, is newer and higher rated. Open all year, adult/300dr, tent/250dr, hot water in the sinks, store, cafe, lounge and television, nicely shady site. The heavily touristed, though still pleasant, basically one street town, has a bank, post office, bakery, grocery stores and interesting boutiques.

To Kalamata, trains leave at 7:13am, 2:30pm (ar 4:17pm) and 6:48pm (ar. 8:24pm).

To Patras, trains leave at 7:30am (ar. 10:56am), 10:38am (ar 1:50pm) and 1:40pm (ar. 4:44pm).

To Pyrgos, trains leave at 7:30am (ar. 8:08am), 10:38am (ar 11:14am), 1:40pm (ar. 2:16pm),4:09am (ar. 4:50pm), 7:52pm (ar. 8:18pm). 45 minutes by either train or bus. Buses depart at least hourly from 6:30am to 9:30pm and the fare is 100dr.

From Pyrgos to Patras, Corinth and Athens

lv Pyrgos	5:50am	9:10am	11:37am	2:37pm	5:03pm
ar Patras	8:06am	10:56am	1:50pm	4:44pm	6:51pm
ar Corinth	10:52am	1:19pm	4:47pm	7:15pm	9:09pm
ar Athens	1:00pm	3:00pm	6:48pm	9:15pm	10:54pm

PYLOS (PILOS) AND METHONI

If you follow the coast south from Patras, you will find Pylos and Methoni nestled near the tip of the peninsula. The closest major rail town is uninteresting Kalamata. In summer 9 buses link Kalamata with Pylos for a fare of about 250dr. The rail towns of Kiparissi (Kyparissia), on the coast south of Patras, and Messini, west of Kalamata, are actually closer to Pylos and also are connected by bus. If coming from Patras or Olympia, rail to Kiparissi and then take a bus. Pylos is extremely attractive itself, but the walled medieval town of Methoni is even better. The latter village is very picturesque and boasts a notable and interesting Venetian fortress. Buses leave frequently from Pylos at the main square on the waterfront and go to Methoni for 75dr, to Nestor's Palace (130dr) and Chora (museum).

Camping Methoni (May-Sept) at the beach by the village has store, cafe, boating and waterskiing.

If you've come from Patras or Olympia with the intent of following a semi-circle to Corinth and then continuing to Athens, take the bus to Kalamata and board a train there. Those having time for further explorations should take the bus to Kalamata and then a bus to Sparta, gateway to Mystra and Monemvassia. People traveling in the other direction should take a bus to Kyparissia and then a train to Pyrgos or Patras. For Olympia, change trains at Pyrgos.

Kyparissia to Pyrgos and Patras

lv Kyparissia	8:00am	1:34pm
ar Pyrgos	9:10am	2:57pm
ar Patras	10:56am	5:02pm

KALAMATA *ΚΑΛΑΜΑΤΑ*

Kalamata is an important seaport and the end station on the main rail line from Athens. The only reason for coming here is to connect with the train or buses for towns not served by the railroad. The train station is downtown and travelers checks may be cashed across the street at a bank.

The bus station is several blocks from the train station and is located on Artemithos Street. To get there, first find your way to the central square, Platia Georgion, two blocks north of the train station. From the square, take the main street, Aristomenous Street, and walk four blocks to Platia 23 Martiou. Cross the bridge and then turn left. There are 10 buses a day for Pylos, about 250dr; 8 buses daily for Argos, Corinth and Athens, 9 buses daily for Koroni (fewer on Sunday), and 2 buses daily for Sparta (about 175dr) and Patras. Even though the distance is shorter, the bus ride to Sparta from Kalamata takes two hours, twice the time the bus takes to get there from Tripolis. The reason is that the famous, scenic Kalamata-Sparta road twists along as it proceeds to Sparta. And why go to Sparta? Sparta is 5 km. from Byzantine Mistra and its convenient campground and is the gateway for buses further south to Monemvassia.

Several **campgrounds** are along the beach to the east of town. Take either bus 1 or bus 1 marked Motel Philoxenia. Service is every half hour until 11:30pm. Camping Sea and Sun is well rated, open all year and 6 km. east of Kalamata on the coastal road. Store, cafe, lounge, boating, fishing and skin diving.

Kalamata to Tripolis, Argos, Mycenae (Mikines), Corinth and Athens

lv Kalamata	6:40am	8:30am	10:25am	3:16pm
lv Tripoli	9:34am	11:13am	1:09pm	5:44pm
lv Argos	11:02am	12:35pm	2:38pm	7:02pm
lv Mikines	11:16am	12:47pm	2:52pm	----
ar Corinth	12:09pm	1:41pm	3:42pm	7:59pm
ar Athens	2:04pm	3:40pm	5:35pm	9:40pm
ar Pireaus	2:11pm	3:48pm	5:42pm	9:50pm

Kalamata to Kyparissia, Olympia, Pyrgos and Patras

lv Kalamata	8:15am	11:24am	8:45pm
lv Kyparissia	---	1:34pm	10:48pm
lv Olympia	10:35am	1:27pm	----
lv Pyrgos	11:37am	2:37pm	11:55pm
ar Patras	1:50pm	4:44pm	1:58am

SPARTA, MYSTRA AND MONEMVASSIA

Sparta is the jumping off point for Mistra and its deserted Byzantine village, 5 km. away. The closest rail town is Kalamata, but if you're coming from Athens, Corinth, Argos, or Mycenae, you'll do better getting off the train at Tripolis and taking a bus from there. The fare is about 310dr and the ride one hour. Coming from Methoni, Olympia or Patras, get off the train at Kalamata and take the shorter scenic route to Sparta, a two-hour twisting bus ride costing about 190dr.

The **bus to Mistra** leaves from Agisilaou and Leof. Lykourgou. Please note that this is not the main bus station of Sparta. Fare is about 75dr and buses leave every hour and a half until 8:40pm for the 15 minute trip. The bus passes a campground (behind the gas station) enroute to Mistra. Ask the driver to let you off and then flag the next bus down when you're ready to continue. To go to the site, don't get off the bus in the tiny town of

Mystra itself, but stay on the bus until the last stop. You must then walk uphill to the archeological site (open M-Sa 9-7, Su 10-4, 250dr).

Another outstanding excursion from Sparta is to **Monemvassia**, a fortified 13th century byzantine village connected to the mainland by causeway. Two buses daily depart Sparta for Monemvassia, a distance of 98 km., at a fare of about 310dr. Two buses return to Sparta each day. Instead of returning to Sparta, you can go direct to Pireaus, the port of Athens, via car ferry three times weekly for about 1200dr or take a faster hydrofoil for 2750dr. If you opt for the water ride, be sure to stop off at the island of Hydra (Idra) enroute, and you may want to stop at Aegina island to camp overnight before continuing by frequent ferry to Pireaus.

When it's time to leave, those who are heading towards Corinth or Athens, should take the bus to Tripolis and the train from there. Those going to Methoni, Olympia or Patras should take the bus to Kalamata to connect with the train.

MEGALOPOLIS, ANDRITSENA AND BASSE

West of Tripolis, a small rail spur from the main rail line between Tripolis and Kalamata leads to the modern town of Megalopolis. This rail town is the closest you can come to **Basse** (ba-SEH). Basse is 12 km. from the town of Andritsena, and the famous Temple of Basse is 11 km. from Andritsena. A once daily KTEL bus leaves Megalopolis in the early afternoon for Andritsena. The bus stops at the picturesque village of Karitena on its way to Andritsena. A taxi for the 14 km. from Andritsena to Vassae runs about 1200dr roundtrip per car, after you've bargained. Be sure to pay after the trip is complete and you're back in Andritsena. The distance can be covered on foot, either by going up the road, or by taking the trail that begins near the KTEL (bus) office. The uphill hike to the isolated temple takes 3 hours. Allow 2-1/2 hours for the downhill trek. Because of the paucity of departures for Andritsena and the difficulty in reaching the site by public transportation, you might save this one for when you have a car.

ARGOS, MYCENAE, NAUPLION, EPIDAURUS, TOLO
ΑΡΓΟΣ   ΜΥΚΗΝΑΙ   ΝΑΥΠΛΙΟΝ   ΕΠΙΔΑΥΡΟΣ

The towns are all close to each other. The best thing to do is base yourself at a campground in the beach community of Tolo and explore the other sites by day. To reach Tolo, take the train to Argos, then a bus to Nauplion and a bus from Nauplion to Tolo. This is less complicated than it sounds because you're boarding the buses in small towns and the rides are only 15 to 20 minutes each.

ARGOS   Argos is a main town on the rail line, hosts the regional fruit and produce market, is only 13 km. from Mycenae and has an archeological area itself that contains an amphitheater.

Argos is where you take the bus to Nauplion. From the train station, cross the street and walk straight ahead for one block. Turn left and across the street is the bus stop for the KTEL bus to Nauplion. The brown and cream building with KTEA lettered on it is the bus station. You must stand in front of the station for the bus to Nauplion. Returning from Nauplion, the bus stops across the street, and to reach the train station, turn right at the corner and walk one short block. Fare to Nauplion is 70dr one way. The driver will stow your pack in the luggage compartment beneath the bus. Buses leave every 30 minutes on the hour and half hour, 7am-9:30pm.

If you aren't taking the train directly to Mycenae, buses for Mycenae leave from the bus station 6 times daily.

To Korinthos, trains leave at 11:01am (ar. 12:08pm), 12:34pm (ar. 1:39pm), 2:32pm (ar. 3:34pm) and 6:54pm (ar. 7:52pm).

NAUPLION   One of the most pleasant small towns of the Peloponnese with fine squares and a relaxed ambiance, Nauplion rests on the shores of the Gulf of Argolis. Not on a rail line, the town is reached conveniently by bus from Arghos. No campgrounds are close in and it's best to take a bus to the beach resort town of Tolo and camp there.

Orientation   The bus from Arghos lets you off at the KTEL bus station. Straight ahead on the hill is the fortress and the steps leading to it, there being no buses only taxis. (Fort Palamedes closes at 6:30pm, not 7pm as guidebooks tell you, and it takes 15 minutes climbing to reach the entrance.)   Facing the fortress, on your right are the picturesque streets of Nauplion, C and D class hotels and the port area. Walking towards your right will eventually place you at the main square of the port where a tourist office assists travelers. (Ask for their free booklet, *This Summer in Nauplion*, which contains a map and historical information on Mycenae, Nauplion, Tolo, Tiryns, Argos and Epidaurus.) On your left and two blocks down the main street paralleling the fortress is the excellent Saturday morning fruit and produce market. On this same street, but just across it and on your left from the KTEL bus station are two roofed bus stops. Buses for Tolo and Epidaurus leave from the second. Departure times and fares are listed at the stop.

Campgrounds   Nauplion Camping is 2 km. from Nauplion along the road to Argos. On the bus from Argos, the camping sign is visible on the left hand side. Though the camp is listed as being open, the entrance looked abandoned as we rode by. If you do plan to get off here, alert the ticket taker early so the bus driver will stop.

Bus Schedules   Buses to **Tolo** leave from the second roofed bus stop on the hour from 7am to 5pm and then at 6:30pm, 7:30pm and 8:30pm. One way fare is 75dr.

Buses to **Epidaurus** leave from the second roofed bus stop at 9am, 10:15am, noon, 2:30pm, 5pm and 7:30pm. One way fare is 170dr. Buses return from Epidaurus at noon, 1pm, 4pm and 6pm.

From the KTEL bus station, buses leave for **Arghos**, 8 km. from Nauplion, every 30 minutes from 7am to 9:30pm. Fare is 70dr and the ride is 20 minutes. (The same schedule is in effect from Arghos to Nauplion.)

To **Mikines** (Mycenae), buses leave from in front of the KTEL station at 10am, noon and 1:30pm and return from Mikines at 11am, 1pm and 3pm.

Car Rentals   Staikos Tours and Rent-A-Car at Bouboulinas 18, the street facing the sea, rents cars on a daily basis for 2200dr for 24 hours, including 100 free km.. Additional km. cost 23dr each plus a 16 percent tax is levied. Minimum age is 23 and a deposit of 6000dr must be left. Optional insurance costs an additional 800dr per day and covers collision and damage

Nauplion
(Náfplion)

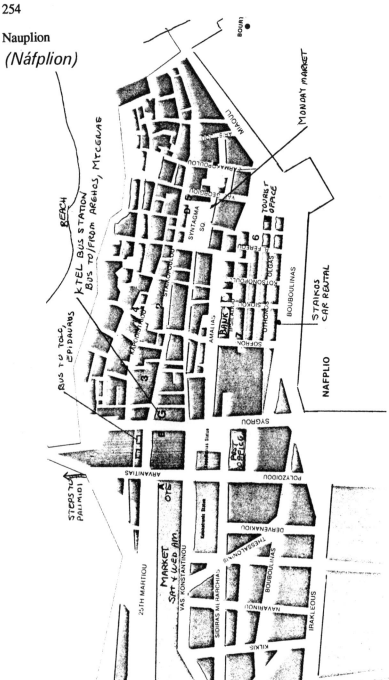

waiver. An Opel Corsa costs 2400dr per day plus 25dr per km.. Weekly rentals with unlimited mileage are 38,100dr for the smallest car, or 40,600kr for an Opel. Rates are about 200dr less during months other than Jun through Sep. They have an office on the main street in Tolo, in Athens at Sygrou 40-42, phone 92 38 941, and in Porto Heli in Argolida.

TOLO (TOLON)   A major seaside resort 7 km. from Nauplion, Tolo provides 4 campgrounds within 2 blocks along the town's main drag which parallels the sea. The shore begins 20 meters from the main street which runs the length of the town. Tolo is reached by bus from Nauplion. Just before the bus from Nauplion approaches the area of hotels and shops, on the left will be visible one of the better sand beach areas. The beach in front of the hotels and shops is narrow and rocky.

Tolo makes a good base for exploring the area. As it's fairly inefficient piecing together train and bus schedules to visit the archeological sites, you might consider renting a car for a day. You can see in one day with a car what it would take two to cover by bus.

Campgrounds   In town amidst hotels, shops, restaurants and cafes, are four campgrounds. The first one, visible from the bus on the right side, is **Swiss Camping**. Fees are adult/180dr and small tent/200dr. A reed-covered roofing above packed earth and parched grass provides shade, but much of the terrain is gravel. The clean bathrooms have conventional toilets with seats, hot showers and a clothes washing area. Registration is handled by Hotel Flivos, across the street.

In the next block, again on the right side, is **Camping Lido 1**. Fees are adult/350dr and small tent/250dr in July and August. Fees are lower the remainder of the year. Being larger than Camping Swiss and having greater areas with reed roof coverings, tents can be placed farther from the main road. The hard packed dirt and sparse grass cover flat terrain; conventional toilets of the type without seats.

The next camp, this time on the left and directly facing the beach, is small **Camping Tolo**. Fees are adult/350dr and tent/250dr, less outside July and August. The campsite is reed covered and affords a beautiful view of the blue water and small island offshore. The beach itself is rocky, but it's only a few minutes walk from any of these campgrounds to the sandy beach.

Further along, **Camping Stars** is 200 meters off the main street. Its two camping areas are situated in front and behind the hotel of the same name and have either canvas or reed covering. The area behind the hotel is terraced and especially quiet. This camp is the most attractive and highest rated. Hot water in sinks, store and restaurant.

If you prefer to be outside the center of town in quiet and solitude rather than staying at one of the four camps already mentioned, ask the driver to let you off at **Camping Xeni**, located on the road to Tolo at Palia Assini, before the bus passes the sand beach immediately before Tolo. Camping Xeni is 100 meters from a much more private beach than found in Tolo. Open all year, adult/300dr and tent/200dr, sinks with hot water, automatic washer, store, restaurant and indoor lounge.

Foreign Exchange, Shops and Food   About halfway down the street and beyond the campgrounds, a sign points around the corner on the right to a combination post-exchange office. Travelers checks are cashed for a 140dr commission at a good rate and stamps are sold. The office is open Saturday and Sunday as well as weekdays. At the Grill-House Argiris on the left side of the main street in the block before the post office sign, a half rotisseried chicken to go is priced at 400dr. Cafes, restaurants, C and D class hotels, rooms and apartments for rent, grocery stores, a laundromat, supermarket and all kinds of small shops abound along the main street. A branch of the Staikis car rental agency is here. See prices under Nauplion. Off season, prices fall dramatically on apartments and hotels. If you're traveling outside of summer and want a respite from camping, hole up in an apartment here for a week. Prices start at 700dr for a room to 1200dr for an apartment, all prices subject to bargaining. These values are only available off season of course when a plentiful supply of vacant rooms occurs.

Bus to Nauplion   Buses return to Nauplion from the 4 unmarked bus stops along the main street on the half hour from 6:30am to 5:30pm and at 7pm, 8pm and 9pm, the last bus. Fare is 75dr one way. The closest bus stop to the sandy beach as you enter town is outside the Solon Hotel. If you're the only one waiting for the bus, it is well to signal to the driver to stop by facing the oncoming bus and stretching your right arm straight out parallel to the ground with palm down.

TIRYNS (TIRINTHA)   The excellent archeological site, with more remaining than at Mycenae, is celebrated for its fine Cyclopeon Walls. The site is open M-Sa 9-7, Su 10-5, adult/150 dr. Tiryns is 4 km. from Nauplion in the direction of Argos. Take any of the buses going to Argos, but purchase your ticket only to Tiryns.

MYCENAE (Mikines, pronounced mi-KEY-nez)   The ancient city where Agamemnon once ruled is about a km. uphill from the one street village of Mikines. Bring your flashlight for illuminating the dark beehive tombs at the archeological zone. The site is open M-Sa 7:30 to sunset, Su 10-1 & 3-6. Save your ticket for admission to Agamemnon's tomb.

If you're staying in **Tolo**, it's best to take the bus direct from Nauplion. If you're coming from Corinth or Argos, you might as well take the train. Mikines is between Corinth and Argos, but only 19 km. from the latter. The slower trains stop at Mikines Station, which is not at the village but on the outskirts. The small station has no luggage check, but the helpful official will lock your pack in the office until 5pm when it closes. (However, you may not wish to wait around for a return train. In that case take your pack with you as the bus to Arghos and Nauplion is boarded at the archeological site.)   Around the corner from the train station is the bus stop for Mikines. Facing the tracks and with your back to the station building, turn left, walk down to the main road, turn right and the stop is a few meters up the road by an apricot tree on the side you're on.

The green and cream colored KTEL bus comes at 10:50am, 12:50pm and 2:50pm and costs 55dr to the archeological site. The bus goes up the hill and passes the entrance to Camping Atreus just before entering the one street town of Mikines and stopping across from the Belle Helene Hotel. The more convenient Camping Mycenae is 50 meters farther on from this bus stop. (Camping Mycenae is very small, has reed roof covering and charges adult/250dr and tent/200dr. Camping Atreus is more attractive with more amenities and similar charges, but less convenient to the bus stop.

As buses come infrequently and it's a hot walk uphill to the archeological zone, you may want to remain on the bus. At the site, the ticket seller may be willing to watch your pack. Unusual beehive tombs in which Kings were buried erect and the Lion Gate are the most famous sights in this extensive archeological area. Two refreshment trailers cater to thirsty visitors at the site. The bus departs from the archeological site at 11am, 1pm, 3pm and 6:30pm and stops in Mycenae at the Belle Helene Hotel before continuing to Nauplion. You can also walk down to Mikines in about 15 minutes as we did. Be sure to mention to the ticket seller on the bus that you want to get off at the train station, if that's where you're going, as the stop it extremely difficult to spot until after you've passed it by. (Yell *stassis* to make the bus stop if you've gone by.)

Mycenae (Mikines) to Kalamata

lv Mikines	9:33am	12:20am	2:48pm	4:27pm
lv Argos	9:43am	12:32am	2:59pm	4:44pm
lv Tripolis	11:04am	2:03pm	4:30pm	6:11pm
lv Zevoglotia	12:47pm	4:02pm	6:33pm	8:07pm
lv Aspracham	1:18pm	4:37pm	7:12pm	8:40pm
ar Kalamata	1:25pm	4:44pm	7:19pm	8:47pm

EPIDAURUS The archeological site of Epidaurus (E-pee-DAV-ros) is open M-Sa 9-7, Su 10-6, closed Tu; 150dr. Purchase tickets for the evening's 9pm performance (in Greek) at the box office after 5pm. Classical plays are presented Saturday and Sunday between July and September 15 with cheapest seats being 250dr. To reach Epidaurus, take the thrice daily bus from Nauplion. An extra bus operates to and from the performances from these towns and costs 200dr.

CORINTH (KORINTHOS) The main attraction is the archeological site of Acrocorinth, or Old Corinth. This site is more complete than the one in Mycenae. (M-Sa 8am-7pm, Su 10-5; 200dr).

Acrocorinth is reached by bus. Alternatively, to walk to the bus station from the train station, walk one block on Agiou Nikolaou Street, then turn left onto Anistasis Anaxartesias Street. Go four blocks and turn right on Koliatsou which leads into the park. Facing the park with your back in the direction of the Port, you will notice that the park has two halves. On the street on the port side of the park at the far corner, is where buses leave for Mycenae. On the street on the side of the park farthest away from the port is where the KTEL bus station is located, near the middle of the park at Ermou and Kolianou Streets. The bus station is beige with green painted woodwork. The bus leaves from in front of the blue sign with white lettering, reading *KTEA KOPINOIAE*. Underneath it at the far right are the words "Ancient Corinth" in English. Buses depart on the hour 7am-8pm, and cost 60dr for the 20-minute ride. Buses return on the half hour.

Next to Acrocorinth are restaurants, a grocery store, shops and cafes. Across from the exit of Acrocorinth and to the right is Themi's Place. The gracious proprietor here speaks English and suggested we buy picnic fixings at the store across the way and bring them back to his place to eat. We did just that and bought cheese, lunch meat and fresh rolls for the three of us for 180dr and brought them back to Themi's Place. We were directed to tables on a cool, shady terrace in the back that overlooks the valley. It's not apparent from out front that this wonderful back patio even exists as everyone else is out on the sidewalk tables in front. We ordered a sprite, lemon soda and bottle of cold mineral water and the bill came to 180dr. We lingered as long as we could enjoying the view and the solitude until the bus arrived for the return trip to Corinth.

Two km. from Ancient Corinth on top of the mountain is the medieval castle of Acrocorinth, about a 30-minute hike.

Two km. out of Corinth, the bus to Acrocorith passes by **Corinth Beach Camping** on the left side of the road. It's more convenient to take the bus from the stop 50 meters from the train station. Look for a blue city bus. Departures are every 20 minutes (50dr). The last bus leaves about 8:05pm. After that you must take a taxi which should cost about 150dr. Alert the ticket seller on the bus to let you off at camping. This is the best and most convenient camp in the area. Adult/350dr, tent/300dr, reduction for students, free hot showers, free gas burners, automatic washing machine/160dr, store, restaurant (breakfast, lunch, dinner), volleyball, ping pong and stamps for sale. The flat and grassy terrain is planted with shade trees and flowers. The bus to Acrocorinth leaves once an hour from the camp bus stop.

To Athens, leave at 8:26am (ar. 10am), 10:57am (ar. 1pm), 12:11pm (ar. 2:04pm), 1:21pm (ar. 3pm), 1:44pm (ar. 3:40pm), 3:44pm (ar. 5:35pm), 4:50pm (ar. 6:48pm), 7:17pm (ar. 9:15pm), 8:02pm (ar. 9:40pm) and 9:11pm (ar. 10:54pm).

To Patras, leave at 8:25am (ar. 10:55am), 10:09am (ar. 12:18pm), 12:10pm (ar. 2:46pm), 2:52pm (ar. 5:08pm), 5:43pm (ar. 8:24pm), 8:03pm (ar. 10pm) and 11:32pm (ar.1:59am). All the above trains except the 8:03pm departure continue to Pyrgos after reaching Patras.

To Mikines, Argos, Tripolis and Kalamata (Change at Zevgolatio after Tripolis to reach Kyparissia, Pyrgos and Olympia.)

lv Corinth	8:52am	11:30am	2:07pm	3:43pm
lv Mikines	9:40am	12:23pm	2:52pm	4:35pm
lv Argos	9:47am	12:36pm	3:07pm	4:46pm
lv Tripolis	11:11am	2:10pm	4:40pm	6:21pm
ar Kalamata	1:41pm	4:51pm	7:33pm	9:00pm

ATHENS (ATHINAI, ATHENAE) ΑΘΗΝΑΙ

The archeological zone of the **Acropolis** and Agora, and the National Archeological Museum are the glories of Athens. Allow two days to tour the highlights of this metropolis. Additional time might be spent on a day trip to the Temple of Poseidon at Cape Sounion or a nearby island. Two excellent campgrounds occupy prime waterfront property and provide a welcome relief to the high temperatures of downtown Athens.

TRAIN STATIONS   Larissa Station serves trains heading north to Thessaloniki and beyond. Tourist Police office, luggage check (6am to 11:30pm), bank and post office. Trolleybus 1 (direction Kallithea) leaves every few minutes from in front and goes through downtown Athens passing Omonia Square and Syntagma Square. Fare is 30dr.

Behind Larissa Station is Pelopponese Station (S.P.A.P.) which handles trains to and from the Pelopponese. The luggage check is open irregular hours--it closes whenever the attendant is at lunch or on a break. Allow plenty of time to retrieve your luggage prior to boarding. To reach Pelopponese Station, go through Larissa Station to the back and take the footbridge and metal stairs down to the street below. Across the street and one block ahead on the left is Pelopponese Station.

During the last two weeks in August and first few days in September, it's wise to make a reservation at the downtown railways office for the train to Athens which connects with the ferry departure. The downtown office of the railways is located midway between Syntagma and Omonia Square at 6

Athens - Bus Stop for Camping Voula

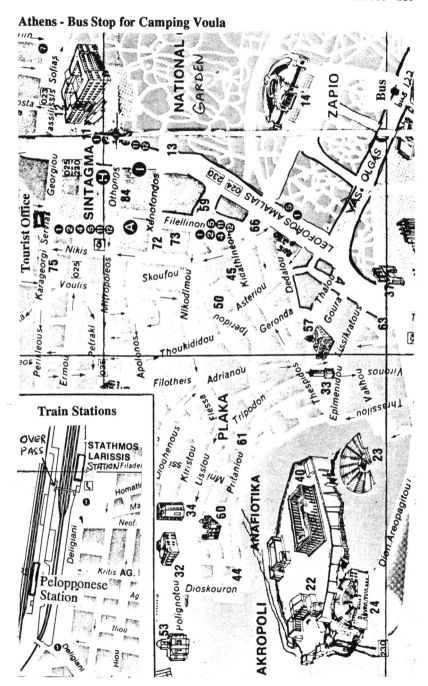

Sina. From the bus terminal on Vas. Olgas, turn right on main street Amalias and take trolleybus 1 past the Tomb of the Unknown Soldier and then get off at the fifth block (or you can walk). Turn right on Sina and the office is midway up the block. Hours are M-Sa 8:30am-6pm. For international departures, a more convenient office is at 17 Filellinon Street. Filellinon Street parallels Amalias, and trolleybus 1 travels on this street when coming from the train station and going to the bus station on Vas. Olgas. When coming from Camping Voula, from the bus terminal on Vas Olgas, turn left, cross Amalias and turn right. At the fourth short "block" turn left and then immediately right onto Filellinon.

TOURIST INFORMATION   The most convenient branch is at 2 Karageorghi Servias Street inside the National Bank of Greece on Syntagma (Sintagma, Constitution) Square. Hours are M-Sa 8-8. Ask for a leaflet on each town or island you will be visiting as well as a map of Athens and a ferry schedule. American Express, 2 Ermou Street, is nearby. Hours are M-F 8:30am-5:30pm and Sa 8:30am-1pm.

FOREIGN EXCHANGE   The National Bank of Greece, 2 Karageorghi Servias Street, is a convenient place to change money because it's also the location of the Tourist Office. Bank hours are M-F 8am-9pm and SaSu 8-8. A good exchange rate is given and the commission is 60dr.

HELLENIC MEDITERRANEAN LINES   The Athens office is at Leoforos Amalias 28, near Syntagma Square. The main office is in Pireaus in the electric railway station building. The busiest period is the last two weeks in August and the first few days in September. Though shipping line officials recommend that a reservation be made during this period, travelers have told us they had no trouble getting on without a reservation. Please see Patras for timetable of 1989 sailings from Greece to Brindisi.

PUBLIC TRANSPORTATION   Yellow trolleycars, blue city buses, the subway, and orange and white long distance coaches comprise the public transportation system of Athens. Fares for the first three are 30dr. The more expensive long distance buses charge according to distance.

Trolley stops are yellow and city bus stops are blue. Trolley or bus number and final destination are listed at the stops. Trolley 1 connects Larissa Train Station with Omonia and Syntagma Squares. Trolley 5 goes to the National Archeological Museum. Both of these can be boarded on Amalias. From the bus terminal on Vas. Olgas, turn right on Amalias until you come to the stop. For the Acropolis, take bus 230 from Amalias, but from across the street on the same side as Syntagma Square.

The subway (metro or electric train) travels every few minutes from 5:30am to 12:10am between Piraeus (port, ferries to islands) - Neo Faliron - Kallitha - Thission - Monastiraki (near Plaka) - Omonia (downtown Athens) - Victoria Square (near train station) - Patisia - Nea Ionia - Neo Iraklion - Maroussi - Kifissia (Camping Nea Kifisia). Tickets are sold by machine.

CAMPGROUNDS   Several campgrounds in the Athens area are accessible by bus. The best one, Camping Voula, is operated by the National Tourist Organization of Greece on prime seafront real estate in the suburb of Voula. The attractive camp has excellent facilities, its own beach, and a welcome cool breeze flowing onto shore. As in Rome, it's wonderful to leave a sweltering city and spend the night on the outskirts where temperatures are several degrees cooler.

Camping Alipedeon Voula is 20 km. from Athens on the beach at Voula on the road to Sounion. Buses to Voula and other south coast beaches leave from the terminal at Vas. Olgas. The camp charges adult/530dr, small tent/300dr Jun 16-Sep 15, 1989; and adult/390dr, small tent/300dr other months, plus 11 percent tax. City bus fare is 30dr.

Directions to the campground: If you arrived from the Pelopponese, you are at the Pelopponese Station. You must go to the Larissa Station. Walk out the front of Pelopponese Station and turn left. Walk along and before the end of the block cross the street when you can. You are now outside the rear of Larissa Station. Look ahead until you spot the outdoor metal stairway that leads upward over the building. Take those steps and you'll be in Larissis Station. Go out the front of the station and the stop for trolley 1 is in front. The trolley departs every few minutes. On board and watching out the window, you'll soon notice where the streets circle around a large fountain of water and lots of people get on the bus. That's Omonia Square, the heart of Athens and where the department stores are. A little while further, you will see a sunken park on the left. That's Syntagma Square. American Express and the main tourist office are near here. On the other side of Syntagma and across busy Amalias Street is the Tomb of the Unknown Soldier, with a throng of tourists photographing the Greek soldiers in their short uniforms. Extending forward from the Tomb is the National (Royal) Garden and its building, the Zappeon. Get off at the second stop past Syntagma Square. You should be on the busy thoroughfare, Leoforos Amalias. Amalias is easy to recognize because it's a main street with the lanes separated by a divider of trees and flags. Walk one block farther to where Vas. Olgas intersects Amalias, and cross Amalias, but not Olgas. On Olgas, you'll find a series of bus shelters. Walk down Olgas, past the entrance to the Royal Garden, until you come to the shelter for bus 122 which goes to Voula. The fare is 30dr and buses leave every 20 minutes from 5:30am to 11:30pm. The last bus has arrived at the shelter by 11:20pm and leaves at 11:30pm.

The ride to the campground takes you through a downtown office building section of Athens, and to the coastal road that heads south past the airport at Glyfada and up the coast. The trip lasts about 30 minutes. When you see the airport on the left, you have reached Glyfada. Its yacht basin and luxury hotels are about 15 blocks beyond the airport. The next luxury enclave is Voula. After passing Hotel Triton and immediately after the sign, *Hotel Bungalow*, the flag poles outside Camping Voula may be seen on the right hand side of the road. The bus stops at a shelter directly outside the campground, a few meters before the entrance.

Directions from Camp Voula to Athens: To return to Athens, board bus 122 across the road from the campground and ride to its terminus on Olgas. After getting off the bus, turn left and walk to the main street, Leoforos Amalias. Turn right and walk until you reach the trolley stop for #1. Actually, it's shorter to cut through the park surrounding the Zappeon. Trolley 1 will take you back to the train station or to other parts of Athens. To the Acropolis, cross Amalias and take bus 230.

Facilities. Registration is in the office, the building on the right as you enter. The campground extends forward from the office until it reaches the beach. The best area for small tents is way at the back by the beach. Midway in the campground is a well-stocked store. There are several restroom facilities and we were often the only ones even using the one closest to our tent. Plenty of free hot showers and hot water in the sinks. There's no automatic washing machine and dryer, but large laundry rooms have plenty of hot water. An enclosed drying area with lines is adjacent. The drying area is rather windy so if you don't have clothespins, clothes must be tied, snapped and buttoned to the line. If you've done a fairly decent job wringing out, clothes will dry overnight on the line. You can feel perfectly secure leaving clothes on the line all day while you're gone as we found nothing was ever disturbed. The honor system that seems to be prevalent throughout the campgrounds in Europe has never failed us.

The entire campground is surrounded by cyclone fencing. This same fence separates the camping area from the beach, except for one opening for an entrance. The beach itself is immaculate, wide, sandy and uncrowded. Beach chairs are provided free on the beach and can be brought out to the immediate camping area behind the fence for the use of backpackers. In the evening we could sit on the beach and admire the lovely colors of the Greek sunset. One of the best areas for small tents is the grassy area immediately outside the fence separating the beach from the campground. In the middle of the area are paved rectangles, some covered with a roof. It's worth taking some thought as to where to pitch your tent. If it is placed towards the left side of the grassy area next to the cement area as you face the beach, the roof over the adjacent paved area will shelter the tent from the hot morning sun. Even though Athens was in the 90's while we were there, evenings at the campground were very comfortable and we enjoyed a breeze coming in the windows of the tent during the night.

Athens Camping, Anolofos-Peristeri, at 198 Leoforos Athinon Street near Shell City Information, is the closest camp to Athens. It's located 7 km. from downtown Athens (Omonia Square), on the Athens-Corinth-Patras highway. Open all year; adult/350dr and tent/225dr. It's connected with Athens and Pireaus by bus from 5am to midnight daily. The last bus leaves at midnight from both Athens and Pireaus. From in front of Larissa train station in Athens, take trolley bus 1 to Trochea stop, leaving every 10 to 15 minutes. Trochea is one stop before Omonia Square. Trochea is close by the bus terminal on Deligiorgi Street where the bus to camp leaves. Take bus 822, 823 or 873 to the bus stop, Camping Athens. From the port of Pireaus, take bus 802 or 845 from Karaiskaki Square to the Camping Athens bus stop. To return to Athens or Pireaus, take the same numbered bus, but at the stop across the road from the camp. This highly rated camp has cold water in sinks, store, cafe, lounge and travel information office.

Camping Dafni is only 10 km. from Athens, but is not as attractive or nicely situated as the beachfront camp, Camping Voula. Its advantage is its closeness to Athens and the nearness of the sightseeing attraction of the Dafni Monastery, celebrated for its Byzantine mosaics (open daily 9-3, 200dr). The camp is open all year. Take bus 853, 864, or 873 from Eleftherias Square. Buses leave every half hour to about 11:45pm. Fare is 30dr and trip 30 minutes. On the shady site are free hot showers, cold water in the sinks, store, cafe and a pavillion for folk dances during the evening. The camp is crowded during the wine festival held 7pm to 12:30am from mid-July to mid-September, next to the campground. At the festival, one entrance fee of 300dr entitles you to sample wines from all over Greece.

Camping Nea Kifisia at Nea Kifisia Eleon 12, which is about 12 km. northeast of Athens in the attractive and classy suburb of Kifissia, can be reached by frequent buses from the Kanigos bus terminal on Kaningos Square (see map), four blocks northeast of Omonia Square. The trip is 50 minutes. Alternatively, take the subway to its terminal station, Kifissia, and then take a bus for the short ride to Nea Kifisia. Ask the driver to let you off at the campground. Market day in Kifissia is Wednesday. The camp is open all year. Facilities include hot showers, store, cafe and lounge.

Varkisa Beach Camping is on the beach at Varkisa (Varkiza), farther along the coast than Camping Voula. Buses leaves from Vassilissis Olgas Avenue, the same place as for Camping Voula, but find the shelter with Varkisa as the destination. Also, bus #149 stops at Varkisa. Fare is 30dr. After the bus passes Vouliagmeni, alert the driver to let you off at Varkisa Camping. The camp is before the town of Varkisa. The beach at this camp is part rock; open all year; adult/450dr, small tent/310dr including tax (cheaper than Voula); automatic washing machine, free hot showers, hot water in the sinks, store and cafe. If you're looking for a small, private cove for sunbathing, take a bus that goes beyond Varkiza and watch out the window. Soon after leaving Varkiza you will discover several such secluded sites visible among the boulders and scrub vegetation.

Camping at Rafina, 27 km. from Athens, is a good idea if you plan to take a ferry to the Cyclades in the morning. Ferries are cheaper than from Pireaus, and Rafina is an attractive, small port, much preferable to Pireaus. Buses to Rafina leave every half hour from 7:45am to 9:15pm from the Green Park Terminal at Patission Street and Alexandras Avenue. The ride is 45 minutes. (Buses to Sounion also leave from here.) Only 1 km. from the ferry pier, Kokkino Limenaki Camping occupies several small terraces overlooking the beach. Hot showers, sinks with hot water, store, pebble beach, bus stop one block away, adult/300 dr, tent/200dr.

FERRIES TO THE ISLANDS Pireaus (pronounced pi-refs) is the main port for boats to the Greek Islands, but if you're going to the Cyclades (Mykonos, Tinos, Siros, Paros, Naxos), the port of Rafina (45-minute bus ride) is less expensive, charming and easier to navigate. In either case boat schedules change frequently. In general most departures occur between 7:30 and 9:30am. Consult the Tourist Office's weekly listing. Plan to arrive at the pier and buy your ticket at least 30 minutes before departure. Besides the large ferries, quicker and more expensive hydrofoils are available to the more popular islands.

To get to the following places by ferry from Pireaus takes the indicated number of hours. Crete (12), Ios (11), Samos (10), Kos (14), Kythnos (4), Milos (8), Mykonos (5.5), Naxos (8), Paros (7), Patmos (8), Rhodes (18), Santorini (12), Syros (4.25), Tinos (4.75).

From Rafina, the Chryssi Ammos Line boats leave at 7:45am daily for Andros, Siros, Tinos and Mykonos and also for Siros, Paros, and Naxos. There is a second departure during summer only to the first 4 destinations, and off-season the schedule is reduced to 5 times a week to the last 3 islands. There is weekly service to Amorgos. For Karystos, Evia and Andros, take a boat of the Anne L. Ferry line which provides daily service.

264

DAY TRIP TO CAPE SOUNION   Who can resist visiting the striking white marble Temple of Poseideon at Cape Sounion? Bring your swimsuit if you want to cool off at the beautiful beach below. The ride is one hour and 17 minutes from Camp Voula. The cheapest way to get to Sounion from Camp Voula is to take a blue city bus for 30dr as far up the coast as you can and then transfer to the more expensive orange and white KTEL bus, the only public bus that goes all the way. KTEL buses charge by distance. For instance Athens to Sounion by the coastal road is 370dr, but farther up the coast, Varkiza to Sounion is only 220dr. For the latter you take a 30dr city bus, such as #149, to Varkiza or father up the coast and change to a KTEL bus. KTEL buses for Cape Sounion leave Varkiza somewhere between 15 and 30 minutes after the hour. The trip takes one hour. On a KTEL bus, press the button in the ceiling above the center aisle to signal when you want to get off. Some KTEL bus stops have shelters, but out in the countryside, the stop is marked by a blue round sign with "KTEA" lettering, attached to a waist high pipe in the ground. Board the bus at the rear and purchase a ticket from the ticket seller on board. KTEL buses will stop between official stops on country roads if you face the bus and signal by holding your right arm out parallel to the ground with palm facing downwards.

The bus goes all the way to the site, its terminus. KTEL buses leave Sounion for Athens via the inland route on the half hour from 7:30am to 8:30pm. This is the departure to take if you want to go into Athens as it's faster than the coastal route. KTEL buses depart on the hour from 6am to 8pm for Athens via the coastal route. Select this route if you're returning to Camping Voula. Buy your ticket only as far as Varkiza and at Varkiza board a blue city bus for a cheap 30dr to Athens or Camping Voula.

While you're at Cape Sounion, you'll notice Hotel Aeghion below at sea level. Look around and find the path leading to the Hotel and the beach. Beyond the hotel is an inexpensive cafe which serves souvlaki for 430dr, deep fried baby squid for 250dr and a salad for 100dr. Once you're down at the beach it's easier to walk up the road at the entrance to the beach and wait there for the bus, rather than trekking back uphill to the site. Be careful that you're waiting at the correct bus stop. After the road from the beach meets the highway, turn right and walk to the intersection and find the metal bus stop post on the left across the street for the coastal route bus. The bus following the coastal route will travel along the highway that the road from the beach leads from. The bus following the inland route will not come on that road, but after leaving the site will turn to its right at the intersection. The bus stop is near the intersection on the bus' right hand side of the road.

To Patras (and Corinth) leave from the Pelopponese Station. Corinth is reached about 2 hours after leaving Athens. Leave at 6:25am (ar. 10:55am), 8:21am (ar. 12:18pm), 10:13am (ar. 2:46pm), 1:03pm (ar.5:08pm), 3:47pm (ar. 8:24pm), 6:27pm (ar. 10pm) and 9:41pm (ar. 1:59am). (Hellenic Lines ferries from Patras to Brindisi depart all year at 10pm and also between Jun 21-Sep 10, 1989 at 5pm.)

To Argos (and Corinth and Mycenae), leave from Pelopponese Station. Arrival in Corinth is 2 hours after leaving Athens. The stop for Mycenae is about 9 minutes before Argos. The trains continue to Kalamata. Trains leave at 7:07am (ar. 9:47am), 9:38am (ar. 12:36pm), 12:12pm (ar. 3:07pm) and 1:48pm (ar. 4:46pm).

To Delphi, take the train to Levidia (direction Thessaloniki or Larissa) and then a connecting bus (270dr) to Delphi for the remaining kilometers. Trains leave from Larissa Station at 7am (ar. 8:59am), 11am (ar. 12:43pm), 2:25pm (ar. 4:25pm), 3:30pm (ar. 5:47pm) and 5:20pm (ar. 7:29pm).

Delphi Archeological Zone

To Thessaloniki from Larissa Station, leave at 7am (ar. 2:48pm), 8am Akropolis Express reservation mandatory (ar. 3:22pm), 11am (ar. 6:05pm) and 2:25pm (ar. 10:15pm).

To Meteora, take any northbound train to Larissa or Thessaloniki and get off at Paleopharsalos. Change to the Trikkala train and get off in Kalambaka. The best departures from Athens are 7am (ar. 11:15am), 8am reservation required (ar. 12:37pm) and 11am (ar. 3:09pm). Trains leave Paleofarsalos for Kalambaka at approximately 12:55pm (ar. 2:35pm) and 4:10pm (ar. 5:51pm).

DELPHI (DELFI) *ΔΕΛΦΟΙ*

The Delphi archeological site is often considered to be the number one such site in Greece. The closest rail station is Levadia. Frequent bus service is provided between Levadia and Delphi. The bus from Levadia stops on the town's main street, Frederiki, next to the youth hostel.

Delphi Camping is 3 km. from Delphi in the direction of Amfissa. When coming from Patras, ask the driver to let you off at the camp, which is on the highway, rather than going all the way into Delphi. From Delphi, take the bus to Amfissa from Frederiki Street, next to the youth hostel. The camp is open all year, store, restaurant and swimming pool.

Caparelis Camping is on the beach at the road to Delphi two km. from Itea. Itea is 15 km. from Delphi. Open all year, adult/35dr, tent/150-200dr. From Delphi, take the bus to Itea that leaves from Frederiki Street, next to the youth hostel. The highly rated site provides sinks with hot water, store, cafe, lounge, beach and water sports.

The **Archeological Site and Museum** entrance is about a 10 minute walk from Delphi. M-Sa 8:30am-7pm, Su 10-2:30, closed Tu; 200dr.

Day Trip to Arachova Frequent buses leave Frederiki Street next to the youth hostel for the charming mountainside village of Arachova, 10 km. north of Delphi. Fare is 60dr.

To Athens, take a bus from Frederiki Street to Levadia and then the train to Athens. Trains leave Levadia for Athens at 8:19am (ar. 10:36am), 11:07am (ar. 1:20pm), 12:11pm (ar. 2:26pm), 2:04pm (ar. 4pm), 4:23pm (ar. 6:02pm) 6:29pm (ar. 8:47pm), 8:04pm (ar. 10:03pm) and 9:10pm (ar. 11:06pm).

To Patras, take the bus to Itea and from there a direct bus to Patras.

To Meteora, take the bus to Levadia and then the train to Paleofarsalos in the direction of Thessaloniki. Change at Paleofarsalos for Kalambaka.

METEORA *ΜΕΤΕΩΡΑ*

In the rivalrous 14th century, the towering rocks of Meteora were used as a safe refuge for monks who built their hermitages high among the inaccessible pinnacles. Originally ropes were lowered and raised to gain entrance to these refuges, but in modern times steps have been built.

The Meteora area is reached by the **Trikkala train from Paleofarsalos** on the Athens-Thessaloniki line. Kalambaka is the final stop on the Trikkala line. The largest monastery is closed Tuesday, and another important one, Varlaam, is closed Friday. Tourist Police in Kalambaka is at 33 Rammidi Street. If you have extra time in Kalambaka, visit the Byzantine Mitropolis Church, rebuilt in 1309.

CAMPGROUNDS Camping Vrachos Kastraki is on the road to Kastraki 800 meters from the station in Kalambaka. Adult/400dr; swimming pool, store, restaurant and attractive shaded campsites with the famous rocks of Meteora as a backdrop.

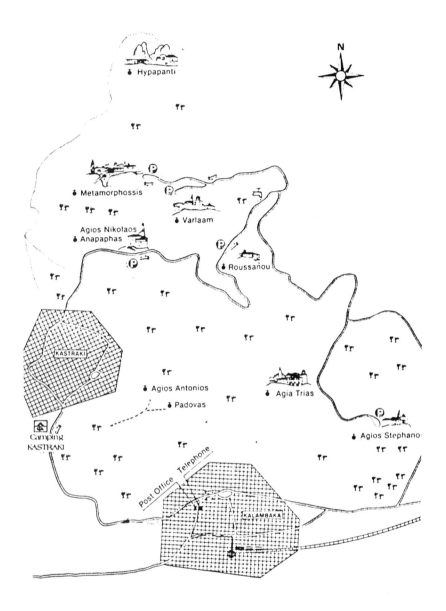

DAY TRIP TO THE MONASTERIES   Dress with your legs and arms covered to conform with the dress code for entrance into the monasteries, and bring lunch. Stand on the road to Meteora and signal the bus to stop by extending the right arm parallel to the ground with palm down. Local buses to Meteora leave Kalambaka from Vass. Pavlou Street, near the turnoff for the Ioannina and Kastoria highway, at 9am, 11:30am and 1:30pm (75dr).

These buses pass Ag. Nikolaos Monastery (open daily 8-1 & 3-6:30pm) and then the largest one, Metamorphosis, Grand Meteoron Monastery, (open W-M 9-1 & 3-6:30pm).   This is as far as public transportation will take you. It's not difficult to walk to nearby Varlaam Monastery (open Sa-Th 9-1:30 & 3-6:30pm). The last 2 monasteries, Ag. Trias (open daily 8-1 & 3-6:30pm) and Ag. Stephanos (open Tu-Su 8-1 & 3-6:30pm), are 5 km. farther along the road. It's possible to have the campground manager arrange a taxi that will visit all 5 monasteries with time to tour each for about 2500dr per taxi.

From Kalambaka to Paleofarsalos, trains leave at 6am, 10:40am, 3:09pm and 6:35pm. Trip is about 1 hour and 40 minutes.
From Paleofarsalos to Thessaloniki, trains leave at 11:43am, 12:37pm (reservation required), 3:09pm and 7:09pm, about a 3-hour trip.
From Paleofarsalos to Athens, trains leave at 7:53am, 9:04am, 11:11am, 1:54pm, 3:11pm, 5:14pm and 6:25pm, about a 5-hour trip.

THESSALONIKI

Greece's second largest city makes a good stopover for those enroute to Yugoslavia or Turkey, but its attractions don't warrant a special trip.

TRAIN STATION   The new train station on Monastiriou Street is about 18 blocks from the tourist office and downtown Thessaloniki.   Within the station are a Tourist Police office, foreign exchange and luggage storage which is open all hours. Bus 1 from outside the station goes to Plata Aristotelous, the central square and home of the tourist office (open M-F 8-8, Sa 8-2). (The produce market is on V. Irakliou Street, 2 blocks from the tourist office.)

CAMPGROUNDS   The closest campgrounds can be reached by bus 10 from the train station to Platia Dikastirion (Dikastirion Square), and then bus 73 for Camping Aghia Triada, which stops directly at the camp, or bus 69 to the Epanomi NTOG campsite. Camp Aghia Triada is very pretty with terraced sites facing the beach, and good facilities including store, snack bar, laundry, and hotplates. The bus ride to camp is 25 km. or 60 minutes.
Camping Epanomis is on the beach 34 km. south of Thessaloniki. Adult/460dr, small tent/380dr, sleeping bag only/190dr for Jun 15-Sept 15, less other months. Facilities are very good with hot showers, hot water in sinks, store, cafe, lounge, fishing, skin diving, boating, waterskiing and tennis.

SIGHTSEEING   The one indispensable sight is the excellent Archeological Museum (open 9-5, except Su 10-5, closed Tu). There are fine churches to see such as the Byzantine Aghia Sophia.

TRAIN SCHEDULES   From Thessaloniki, trains follow three routes across international borders, entering Yugoslavia, Bulgaria and Turkey.

To Athens, trains leave at 8:00am (ar. 4pm), 11am (ar. 6:02pm), 1:50pm (ar. 10:03pm), 3:10pm (ar. 11:06pm), 9:30pm (ar. 6:45am) and 12:15am (ar. 8:33am).

THE ISLANDS

If you haven't come to Greece for the archeological sites of its golden age, then you've heard about its islands. For the most part you can gauge the popularity of an island by the frequency of ferry departures. To find an untouristed island, choose one that has sailings to it no more than twice a week. If you find yourself on an island with more people than you like, there's usually another more remote island that can only be reached by boat from the harbor of the more popular one. Tourism is at its peak during the last two weeks in July and the month of August. Outside of summer, even the most popular islands see a drastic drop in visitors.

If the duration of the ferry ride is at least 8 hours, usually there will be both a daytime and overnight sailing. If you want to save time or money, opt for the overnight trip and sleep on deck in plenty of company. Most people purchase the least expensive fare, usually called third class or deck class. Tickets should be purchased at the port before getting on board ship. Tickets purchased on board may cost an extra 20 percent.

Informal beach camping is more or less condoned on isolated beaches where no organized campgrounds exist. Even though no listing is found in the standard guidebook, *Europa Camping and Caravanning*, don't assume the island has no campground. It probably does as there are more unlisted than listed campgrounds on the Greek islands. The best guidebook to the Greek Islands is the one you compile yourself on the spot by being friendly and talking with other campers, campground personnel and whomever you happen to meet.

THE SARONIC GULF ISLANDS

These are the closest to Athens and serve as weekend getaways for the city's residents. Obviously, the best time to visit is on a weekday. The frequency of departures make the islands good daytrips, or you can camp on a tiny island just offshore Aegina. Ferries and the faster and more expensive hydrofoil make frequent voyages even in the evening from Pireaus to Aegina and Hydra. The islands also can be used as stepping stones for island hopping across the sea from Pireaus to Monemvassia, the Byzantine village on the Pelopponese peninsula.

AEGINA AND HYDRA (IDRA) Aegina and Hydra are the most popular islands in this group. Hydra being designated an architectural preservation site and having outlawed motorized vehicles in its port makes it the best of the Saronic Gulf islands to visit. There is no camping on Hydra. For camping, stay at **Moni Camping** on the isle of Moni, 20 minutes by boat from Aegina. The campground is operated by the Hellenic Touring Club. To get there take the bus from Aegina town to the beach enclave of Perdika. At Perdika, a boat shuttles campers back and forth to tiny Moni island.

THE CYCLADES

Ferries from both Piraeus and Rafina travel to the celebrated Cyclades. These are the islands whose whitewashed houses contrast with the bright blue Aegean Sea on posters and calendars. During August, the strong *meltimi* blows from the south onto the southern Aegean islands. During that time be prepared with tent stakes and tolerance for blowing sand. The boats out of Rafina cost less money and take less time. Rafina is a 45-minute bus ride from Athens. Arrive the night before and stay at the nearby campground ready to board the boat first thing in the morning. (See Athens.

MYKONOS   We'll start with the most well known and popular of all the Cyclades, Mykonos. The island has been established as an official architectural landmark preserving for all time its famous appearance of sparkling whitewashed houses freshly washed with lime, twisting byways, windmills, numerous small "churches," and, hopefully, its greeting committee of pelicans.

Ferries arrive at the port of **Chora** where you'll find banks and a post office, but no tourist office. Behind the port, narrow alleys and pathways lead to the many unexpected delights of the village. Thankfully, motorized vehicles are prohibited in town, but the rest of the island is served by buses, taxis, rental mopeds and feet. The nearby island of Delos, one of the best archeological sites in Greece, is reached by small boat from Mykonos.

Paradise Camping occupies one of the best beaches on Mykonos, Paradise Beach.   (Jul 1-Sep 30: adult/400dr, tent/200dr; Oct 1-Jun 30: adult/300dr, tent/150dr.)   To get there, take the bus of Paradise Camping from the Port which meets each incoming ferry. Otherwise, you can take a bus to Plati Yialos and then transfer to a small motorboat, called a caique.

DELOS   Delos, a sacred sanctuary during the Golden Age, is now a large, highly interesting archeological site.   Boats leave from Chora harbor in Mykonos daily at 9am for a roundtrip fare of 500dr for the 40-minute ride by small boat.   The site is open 8:30am to 2:30pm.   Admission is 150dr. Unfortunately (or fortunately if you're staying here) boats return at 12:30pm, which allows insufficient time to thoroughly explore the island.   After the boat leaves, Delos becomes deserted as there is only a four room hotel and a small 2,000 square meter camping area on the island.   Those who prefer peace and solitude in beautiful surroundings and campfire comaraderie over the wild but highly interesting nightlife in Mykonos will enjoy staying the night.

Camping Delos is open year around and is near the house of the archeologists and the closed museum.   Facilities are minimal with only toilets and cold water sinks, A small store and cafe are available, but it's less expensive if you bring your own food. Open campfires are permitted at the campground. The island coves invite private swimming and sunbathing.

PAROS AND ANTIPAROS   Paros will remind you of Mykonos, but enjoys more relaxed living and less concentrated charm. Ferries land at the main village, Paproikia.   There you'll find a tourist office, bank, post office, bus station with luggage check, laundry, supermarket and bakery.

Camping Koulas is a 15-minute, 800 meter walk from the dock. From the pier and the windmill which you will spot immediately, turn left onto the beachfront road and walk north past the bus station, marina, and several hotels to Livadhi Beach and the campground.

ANTIPAROS is the small island opposite Paros, reached by small boat from Paros. Camping Antiparos is on a beach north of the port, about a 15-minute walk. The island is devoid of group tourists and informal camping occurs on isolated beaches on the unpopulated north end.

IOS A campground is near the beach outside Gialos where the ferries dock. **Camping Stars and Soulis Camping** are at Milopatas Beach. They can be walked in about 25 minutes, or a bus connects Gialos to Milopatas. Two buses leave each hour between 8am and 10:30pm.

SANTORINI A beautiful island, ferries dock at Fira (Thira), Ia or Athinios. Athinios is connected to Fira by bus. Fira is the most important village and has a bank, post office, shops and tour agents. From Fira, buses run every half hour until 11pm in summer for the 15-minute trip to Perissa, where you'll find **Perissa Camping** next to a volcanic black sand beach, typical of the island. The beach is used by both topless and nude sunbathers. Inland, **Pyrgos Camping** is at the Elias Monastery near Pyrgos and Thira. Minimal facilities: toilets, running water, small store and lounge.

TINOS Fewer foreigners visit Tinos, than Mykonos, Paros, Ios or Santorini. **Tinos Camping** is open Apr-Oct; adult/400dr (Jul-Aug), 350dr (Apr-Jun & Sep-Oct), tent/200 dr.(Jul-Aug), 150dr other months. Located 150 meters from the harbor and 80 meters from the beach. Sinks with hot water, laundry room, store, nice restaurant, bungalows (2500dr for 2).

THE WESTERN CYCLADES You've probably never heard of **Serifos, Milos, Sifnos and Kimolos** and that's good reason for coming. Ferries from Pireaus depart about four times a week for this group of islands. It's 5 hours to Serifos, 6 to Sifnos and 8 to Milos and Kimolos. Milos has remnants of Minoan civilization.

THE SPORADES

The Sporades are more difficult to reach, less celebrated but still beautiful, and with fewer tourists. To get here, take the ferry from Pireaus, Ag. Constantino or Volos. Departures from Volos, north of Athens, charge the lowest ferry fare to **Skiathos**, around 750dr. Ferry service between Skiathos and **Skopelos** departs three times daily and costs about 350dr. To reach Volos from Athens, take the train to Paleofarsalos and change trains for Volos. From Thesssloniki, change trains at Larissa. Trains leave Larissa for Volos at 7:30am, 9, 10:40, 12:05pm, 13:26, 14:51, 4:36, 6, 8, 9 and 9:50pm.

SKIATHOS The campgrounds are reached by bus from the port town of Skiathos. Buses leave from the harbor every half hour from 7:30am to 10:30pm and travel along the southern coast terminating at Koukounaries. Ask to get off the bus at the road to inexpensive **Aselinos Camping** at Megalos Aselinos beach. After the bus lets you off, it's a 25-minute walk to the beach.

Beaches on the north coast are reached by caique, small boats, from the harbor in Skiathos town. Trips to the remains of Kastro village and to some caves in this area are offered by caique.

SKOPELOS   Skopelos is less touristed than Skiathos. The island's major settlements are Skopelos town and Loutraki. In Skopelos town, a tourist office is on the main street. Buses leave from the harbor.

Traveler Sara Dolph reports her favorite campground in Greece was on Skopelos Island. *In Skopelos Island take the bus from Skopelos town to Agnontas Bay (last bus leaves at 6pm), then take the boat around to Illuminasis Bay (last boat leaves around 4:30pm). The boat is free to the bay and about 150dr for the return. However there is a footpath, about a 25-minute walk, for the return trip to Agnontas. The campground is on very uneven ground, but very inexpensive. The beach is absolutely beautiful, especially the clear water. The tourists all leave by 4:30pm, only a few campers are left. There is a cafe that serves dinner--moussaka, fish, or lamb, and a Greek salad, plus retsina was very reasonable. The dinners were served after 9pm and the atmosphere was very friendly--the cook usually would sit down and have a glass of retsina with you.*

ALONISSOS AND SKYROS   Less popular than either Skiathos or Skopeles, Alonissos and Skyros remain underdeveloped.   On Alonissos boats dock at Patitiri harbor where you'll find a tourist office and the bus station. Ikoros Camping is on Steni Vala beach. Skyros has an official campsite on the beach by Skyros village.

CRETE (KRITI)

Crete, birthplace of the brilliant Minoan civilization which reached its zenith about 1600 BC, is about an 11-hour boat trip from Pireaus. In summer, the large overnight car ferries leave at 6pm, 6:30pm, 7pm or 7:30pm for Herakleion (Iraklion), largest town on the island, or Chania. The trip is shorter if the ferry is boarded at Gythion on the Pelopponese. From Santorini, one boat departs each day during high season.

On Crete you can get everywhere by bus. Pick up a schedule from a tourist office. The two indispensable sights are the Archeological Museum in Herakleion and the archeological site at nearby Knossos. After that you can enjoy the beaches without feeling guilty. The most famous natural attraction is the Samaria Gorge and the 17-km. trail that leads through it-- downhill all the way! If you take the bus from Herakleion to Chania, you can camp in Chania and make the gorge trip from there. The the return to Pireaus can be made from Chania.

HERAKLEION   Pick up the island bus schedule from the tourist office, located across the street from the Archeological Museum near Eleftherias Square.   The Archelogical Museum (closed Monday) contains Minoan objects from the excavations and is considered the second best museum in Greece. Bus 2 leaves for the excavations at Knossos (M-F 8-5, SaSu 8:30-3) from the bus terminal and from Eleftherias (Lions) Square every 10 minutes from 7am to 10:30pm for the 20-minute ride. The open market is on 1866 Street, off Venizelou Square.

Camping Iraklion is 5 km. west of the city and reached by bus 6 from Eleftherias Square. Fees are adult/350dr and tent/160dr.

MALIA   The ruins of the Minoan Palace of Malia are 3 km. from Malia. The site is open M-Sa 8:45-3pm, Su 9:30am-2:30pm, entry free.

Camping Asimenia Akti is 35 km., a one hour ride from Heraklion, on a beautiful, white sugar sand beach near Malia. Take the half hourly bus from the bus station which is between the harbor and the walls of the old city, 400 meters from the port of Heraklion. **Malia Camping** is 1.5 km. from Malia and has hot water in the sinks, automatic washing machine, store, cafe, lounge, television and water sports.

MATALA AND AG. GALINI   These towns are on the opposite side of the island from Heraklion. Matala Camping is behind the beach on the road to Phaestos. Go past the Bamboo Sands Hotel and turn right. Camping Agia Galini is 3 km. south of Ag. Galini. The beach camp is open all year and charges about adult/210dr and tent/140dr. Facilities include sinks with hot water, store, cafe, lounge and water sports.

RETHYMNON (RETHIMNO)   At Rethymnon, 78 km. from Heraklion, three beachfront campgrounds are east of town along the Rethymnon-Heraklion national road.   About 4 km. out are Camping Arkadia and Camping Elizabeth, and at 15 km. is Camping George. Take the local bus from Moatsou Street to the campgrounds on Rithymna Beach and Skaleta. Camping Arkadia is open all year, charges adult/250dr and tent/200dr, and has sinks with hot water, store, cafe, lounge and water sports. The higher rated Camping Elisabeth is open April 15 to October 15, charges adult/300dr and tent/280dr and has cold water only in its sinks, a store, cafe and lounge. The Rethymnon market is Thursday, between Moatsou and Kountouriotou Streets, on the square next to the city park.

CHANIA (HANIA)   You can arrive or depart from attractive Chania or Pireaus. The tourist office is at the harbor at 6 Akti Tombazi. Ferries leave from Souda, and buses for Souda leave from Venizelou Square.   Two campgrounds at the town of Chania (Khania) are Camping Shell which has a cafe but is not on the beach and Camping Gatt Alfredos.   The covered market in Chania is on Venizelou Square.

SAMARIA GORGE   The popular 17-km. hike from Xyloskalo by inland Omalos to Aghia Roumeli at the beach takes about 6 hours. The trail is administered by the government parks agency and is open April through October. Excursion operators unload buses of tourists at the start of the path in mid-morning so try to be off as early as possible. Pack your daypack with food, water, swimsuit and towel. No camping is allowed in the area which is a national park. However, once at Aghia Roumeli, freelance camping occurs in secluded areas away from the village.

Buses leave Chania at 6:15am, 8:30, 9:30 and 4:30pm for Omalos and Xyloskalo, the start of the trail. The bus ride takes about 90 minutes for a fare of 245dr. At the end of the trail in Aghia Roumeli, boats motor east five times daily between 1 and 5pm for Loutro and Chora Sfakia for a fare of about 550dr. The boat ride lasts slightly over an hour. It's possible to get off at Loutro and hike for about two hours past secluded coves to Chora Sfakia. To return to Chania, take the bus from Chora Sfakia.

HUNGARY

An Eastern European tourist heads for Budapest as the Paris of the Eastern bloc. To western eyes the resemblance may seem meager, yet the spirit is there and Hungary has much to offer at less cost than even Greece or Portugal. Budapest occupies the geographical center of Europe, being equidistant from Moscow and London, Kiev and Paris, and Stockholm and Istanbul. A visa is required to enter Hungary. If you didn't get one before leaving home, you can get one in Vienna from IBUSZ, the official Hungarian tourist agency. Eurailpass was extended to the railroads of Hungary in 1989, the first Eastern European country to be included.

Traveling in Hungary is more difficult than western Europe because it's not as well organized to receive foreign visitors. Figuring out how to ride the buses and getting to sights on your own is not as simple so you may want to consider taking an inexpensive guided tour in Budapest. What isn't a problem is paying for an elegant restaurant meal, which can be had for $5.

CURRENCY   Hungarian forint. One dollar equals about 47 forints. You are allowed to bring 100 forints in coins (no bills) into Hungary. Pick them up at a bank in Vienna as the rate outside of Hungary is much higher. When in Hungary, exchange only the amount of dollars into forints that you will need as changing it back is difficult and time consuming. Save receipts from currency transactions in case you're asked for them.

BUDAPEST

Budapest is divided into two parts. Buxom Buda is separated from plain Pest by the Danube River. Both campgrounds are on the hilly Buda side. Downtown is in Pest.

TOURIST OFFICE   IBUSZ, the official government tourist agency, has branches in the train stations. Express Youth and Student Travel Bureau caters to young people. Its central office is at Semmelweis utca 4, Budapest V. (metro Astoria) and a branch is in Keleti Pu Train Station (open daily 24 hrs. metro Keleti Pu). These offices exchange money, book sightseeing tours, provide rooms in private homes, and give brochures and maps.

TRAIN STATIONS   Coming from Vienna, you will arrive at the East Station, Keleti Pu. Both Ibusz and Express have branch offices here. The next most important station is West Station, Nyugati Pu, which handles tranffic to Yugoslavia, Czechoslovakia and Romania. South Station, Deli pu, serves Lake Balaton and some points in Austria. The quickest way between these stations is by metro. Minoe stations are Kelenfold, Zuglo, Ferencvaros and Kobanya-Kispet (to Beograd).

CITY TRANSPORTATION   Blue buses, red trolleys, yellow trams, the metro and the green coaches of the suburban trains (HEV) comprise the crowded public transportation system. A bus ticket costs 3ft, and tram, trolley and metro cost 2ft. regardless of distance. All tickets must be bought in advance of boarding from bus or tram terminals, metro office, railway station or tobacconist (Trafik) shop. You punch your ticket in the machine after boarding. Bus tickets can be used on the cog-wheel railway which goes to Szechenyi Hill, from which trails begin. Rush hours are 7-9 and 4-5:30 and to be avoided. If you can't, be prepared to step lightly as drivers do not consider necessary that the passenger have more than one foot on board before departing.

CAMPGROUNDS   Harshegy Camping, Budakeszi Ut and Denes Utca, has the most facilities. Sixteen acres of park-like, grassy ground with a view of the city attracts largely Eastern European tourists. Though 1500 campers can be accommodated, the camp never receives that many at one time. Adult/35ft, tent/50ft;modern restrooms (220 volt, 50 cycle current as in Western Europe), hot showers, grocery store, office with English-speaking clerk and safe deposit box, souvenir store, snack bar/restaurant, indoor lounge, cooking facilties and cabins for rent (360ft.). Take bus #22 from Moszkva Ter to Harshegy.

   Romai-Part Camping is at Roman Beach (Romai-part or Romai Furdo) next to the Danube River, Romai-part III. The flat and grassy site has similar facilities as Harshegy but with a barber and hairdresser (very cheap); adult/20ft, tent/30ft. Take the metro to Batthyany ter. Change to HEV (suburban train) to Station Romai-part, across from the campground.

SIGHTSEEING Heroe's Square (Hosok Tere) and City Park (Varosliget) are next to each other at the end of avenue Nepkoztarsasag Utja in Pest. The area includes a superb fine arts museum and the Vajdahunyad complex of buildings. Heroe's Square, built in 1896-1929 as a Millenary Memorial, in the middle of a broad expanse of pavement, hosts a semi-circular statuary of national heroes. The circular column in front depicts 7 Hungarian Chieftains on horseback, and a colonaded semi-circle behind holds statues of 14 historical figures. The Fine Arts Museum, 41 Dozsa Gyorgy Ut (the main street in front of the memorial) displays works by Goya, Rembrandt, Titian, Raphael and other important artists including some French Impressionists. The Mucsarnok (exhibition museum) is next door in the building resembling a Greek temple in granite. Also see City Park, Castle Hill (Varhegy).

   TRAIN SCHEDULES   To Vienna Westbahnhof, trains leave Keleti Station at 7am (ar. 10:40am), 9:45am The Orient Express (ar. 1:34pm), 4:25pm (ar. 8:15pm). To Vienna Sudbahnhof, a train leave Deli Station at 6:30pm (ar. 9:18pm), reservation required.

   To Prague, trains leave Keleti Station at 1:45pm reservation required (ar. 5:58pm), 9:20pm (ar. 7:08am).

   To Zagreb, Yugoslavia, trains leave Deli Station at 12:10am reservation required (ar. 6:50am), 6am from Keleti Station (ar. 12:20pm), 12:35pm (ar. 7:40pm).

IRELAND

Ireland is divided into Northern Ireland (Ulster), comprising the six counties which are under British rule, and the South, an independent country called the Republic of Ireland or Eire. All information refers to the Republic.

If you have a Eurailpass, it seems logical in planning your trip to take the free ferry from France to Ireland and then the ferry from Ireland to Britain. This is fine except that there's no inexpensive ferry that goes between Ireland and Britain, no matter what crossing is selected. However, students do alright as they receive 50 percent off certain crossings with a TravelSave stamp. Anyone of any age with a youth hostel card receives a reduction on the Sealink service between Dun Laoire and Holyhead, and Rosslare and Fishguard; and on B+I Line between Liverpool and Dublin, Holyhead and Dublin, and Pembroke and Cork. For others, it's cheaper to cross via the English Channel.

CURRENCY   One Irish pound equals 100 pence (100p). The British pound is called the pound sterling. One Irish pound is worth $1.58 U.S.

WEATHER   Always be prepared for the possibility of rain, but don't be discouraged at the thought. At the least, if you have a Eurailpass, take the free overnight ferry from France and spend a few days here. The friendliness of the Irish is worth a little liquid sunshine.

CAMPING   The Irish Tourist Board publishes a free pamphlet, *Caravan and Camping Parks 1989*, which lists and decribes campgrounds. Most campgrounds charge by tent and by person, or by person alone.

TRAINS   CIE (Coras Iompair Eireann) operates the trains. Eurailpass and Eurail Youthpass are valid in Ireland. If you don't have a pass, CIE offers one-day roundtrip train tickets, called Day Excursion, for the price of one way. Weekend travel tickets offer a discount for trips leaving on Friday, Saturday and Sunday and returning by the next Tuesday. A variation on Weekend Travel is an Eight Day Return Ticket that discounts a trip of 8-day duration. ISIC Student Card holders can purchase a TravelSave stamp for L5.50 which is valid for 50 percent off on trains and buses in Ireland, including the ferry between Ireland and Britain. Rambler Tickets give unlimited travel by rail alone or by rail and coach for 8 or 15 days. Children under 15 pay half fare in Ireland. Trains are classified InterCity, first and standard. Reservations are not necessary.

EURAIL BONUSES   (1) Ferry crossings on the **Irish Continental Line** from Rosslare, Ireland to Le Havre, France (21 hours), Rosslare, Ireland to Cherbourg, France (17 hours), and Cork, Ireland to Le Havre, France (21-1/2 hours).   Port taxes are extra and payable in Irish pounds.   Advance reservation is only compulsory if cabin accommodation is requested.

Two ferries are used on the crossings. St. Patrick weighs 7,984 tons and holds 1630 passengers and 300 cars. The cheapest cabin is 4-berth on the lower deck. St. Killian, weighs 10,256 tons and carries 2,000 passengers and 380 cars. If a cabin is wanted, the cheapest is a berth in a 6-berth cabin. Most backpackers manage to sleep well on board ship without a cabin. Both ferries carry restaurants and snack bars, duty free shops, discotheque, lounges and movies on closed circuit television. It's a good idea to bring some food in lieu of paying shipboard prices.

On fridays only, a ferry leaves Cork for Le Havre at 5pm Jun 25-Aug 30 (ar. 3:30pm the next day). From Rosslare to Cherbourg on monday and saturday (Jun 25-Aug 30) and monday and friday (Aug 31-Sep 16), a ferry leaves at 5pm (ar. 11am the next day). From Rosslare to Le Havre on Tu, W, Th and Su (Jun 25-Aug 30) and Tu, W, Th, and Su (Aug 31-Sep 16), a ferry leaves at 5pm (ar. 3pm the next day). The schedule is reduced the remainder of the year. Check period and sailing days before you go.

(2) **Expressway buses** owned and operated by the Irish Railroads (CIE) except the services to and from Northern Ireland operated jointly with a foreign carrier.

GAELIC   Public toilets are sometimes classified in Gaelic--*Fir* is men's, *Mna* is women's.

SHOPPING   A Value-added tax (VAT) is 25 percent and applies to items like furs, cameras, glassware and china.   On some items the rate is 10 percent, and no tax is assessed on clothing, food and shoes. VAT is always included in the displayed price.   Merchandise sent out of the country or delivered to your plane can be sold free of VAT, but you must ask.

ROSSLARE

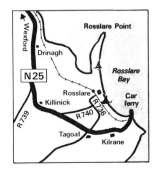

Irish Continental Lines ferries, free with Eurailpasses, arrive at Rosslare at 2pm. Starting from the dock, the three train stations of Rosslare are called Rosslare Harbor (pier), Rosslare Harbor (mainland) and Rosslare Strand (town). It's about 5 miles from the dock to the town. (See train schedule to Dublin for trains to Rosslare Strand.) Irish Continental Line ferries included in Eurailpasses leave at 5pm for France. (See details under Eurail Bonuses.)

CAMPGROUNDS   Rosslare Caravan and Camping Holiday Park is within walking distance of Rosslare Strand train station. May 31-Sep 19; L4 per tent for backpackers; automatic washer. Two miles north of Rosslare Strand, **Burrow Caravan and Camping Park** is open Mar 14-Nov 9; the normal charge is L6 per unit, but a reduction is given for backpackers. The **Holiday Inn Caravan and Camping Park**, 2 miles from Rosslare Harbor near Kilrane, open May 15-Sep 15; adult/L1.50, tent/L4 with on site special Irish nights, roller skating, dancing, bingo, camper's kitchen and store. Cheapest is **Carne Beach Caravan and Camping**, 6 miles south of Rosslare Harbor, charges hikers L2.50 per unit. Ten miles from Rosslare, the town of Wexford is on the main rail line. **Ferrybank Caravan Park** is located half a mile from town on Dublin Road. Easter to Sep 15; tentsite/L6.

   To Dublin Connolly Station, trains leave Rosslare Harbour Pier at 7:55am (M-Sa), 9:15am (Su), 2:55pm (M-Sa) and 6pm (daily); 3-hour trip. These trains stop at Rosslare Strand (town), 11 minutes after leaving the Pier Station. Stops enroute to Dublin are Wexford, Arklow, Wicklow and Bray.

   To Killarney, take the train to Limerick, but get off at Limerick Junction and change for Mallow. At Mallow, change for Killarney. To reach Killarney in one day, take the 7:20am departure from Rosslare Strand.

   To Kilkenny, go to Waterford and change there. Trains leave Waterford for Kilkenny M-Sa at 7:40am, 10:50am, 3:25pm and 6:15pm; and Su at 9:50am and 6:05pm. The trip is 40 minutes.

   To Waterford and Limerick, trains leave Rosslare Harbour at 7:15am (M-Sa) and 7:40pm (M-Sa). The 40 miles to Waterford takes one hour and 15 minutes, and to Limerick about 4 hours. Free guided tours M-F of the Waterford Crystal Factory are given in Waterford. Trains return to Rosslare from Waterford at 5pm (M-Sa) and 6:22pm (M-Sa).

CORK (CORCAIGH)

On Fridays at 2:30pm, an Irish Continental Line ferry arrives in Cork, Ireland's major city at its southern tip. The ferry returns to Le Havre at 5pm the same day. (See Eurail Bonuses for details.)

   Cork is the closest arrival point via Irish Continental Lines to the most scenic area of Ireland, the Southwest. Rather than staying in Cork for the night, push on to Killarney, a typically Irish city in a beautiful area.

CAMPGROUNDS   **Cork City Caravan and Camping Park**, on Togher Road 2 miles southwest of the city center, is open June 1-Sept 30. Take bus 14 which leaves every 20 minutes from downtown Cork. The bus stop is in front of the campground. Adult/75p, tent/L2.90; store and lounge with television.   **Cork Caravan Company Caravan and Camping Park** is loacted 3-1/2 miles southewest of Cork on L42 road to Kinsale and Cork Airport. Open all year; TV lounge, washer, 200 yards from a grocery store.

TRAIN SCHEDULES From Cork Kent Station on Lower Glanmire Road, the main rail line goes to Dublin. A less important route follows the main rail line as far as Mallow, turns west to Killarney and continues to Tralee at the coast.

   To Dublin Heuston Station, trains leave 11:20am (M-F), 11:30am (Sa), 2:30pm (Su), 2:45pm (M-Sa), 5:30pm (M-Sa), 6:20pm (Su), 6:50pm (M-Sa) and 6:55pm (Su). The trip is 3 hours.

   To Killarney and Tralee, trains leave 10:40am M-F (change at Mallow), 10:55am Sa (change at Mallow), 11:05am Su (change at Mallow), 12:30pm (M-F & Su), 12:45pm (Sa), 3:15pm (M-Sa) and 8pm M-Sa (change at Mallow). The trip is 2 hours to Killarney, 2-1/2 hours to Tralee.

National Express Coach to London

DUBLIN FROM LONDON & BIRMINGHAM BY *Rapide* INCLUDING HOSTESS SERVICE — 553

OUTWARD JOURNEY				OPERATED BY:			RETURN JOURNEY			
553	CIE	553	CIE	*Supabus* NATIONAL EXPRESS/BUS EIREANN			CIE	553	553	CIE
15 Apr to 30 Sep	1 Apr to 30 Sep	18 June to 30 Aug†	18 June to 30 Aug				18 June to 30 Aug	18 June to 30 Aug	15 Apr to 30 Sep†	1 Apr to 30 Sep
DAILY	DAILY	DAILY	DAILY				DAILY	DAILY	DAILY	DAILY Excl. SUN
0900	–	2130	–	Dep.	LONDON, Victoria Coach Station	Arr.	–	1045	2240	–
1130	–	2359	–	Dep.	BIRMINGHAM, National Express Coach Station, Digbeth	Arr.	–	0830	2025	–
1400	–	–	–	Dep.	CHESTER, Delamere Street Bus Station	Arr.	–	–	1755	–
1525	–	0335	–	Dep.	BANGOR, Garth Road, Bus Terminus, Stand No. 8	Arr.	–	0455	1620	–
1600	–	0410	–	Arr.	HOLYHEAD, Sealink Terminal Coach Park	Dep.	–	0420	1545	–
1715	–	0530	–	Sail	HOLYHEAD, Sealink/B + I Ferry	Arr.	–	0345	1515	–
2045	–	0930	–	Arr.	DUBLIN, Ferryport B + I Terminal	Sail	–	2300	1145	–
2120	–	1000	–	Arr.	DUBLIN, Busaras	Dep.	2200	1030		
2300		1105A		Dep.	DUBLIN, Busaras	Arr.	2000B	–	–	1020
–	2359	–	1215A	Arr.	DROGHEDA, Bus Office	Dep.	1845B	–	–	0930
–	0045	–	1315A	Arr.	DUNDALK, Market Square	Dep.	1745	–	–	0645

† – TIDAL RESTRICTIONS AFFECTING B + I SAILINGS: On the following dates the 553 service will operate at earlier departure times as follows: Ex London – 11 July, 9 & 10 August will depart one hour earlier than advertised. Ex London – 8 August will depart two hours earlier than advertised.

A – On Sundays departs DUBLIN 1210, DROGHEDA arrives 1315, DUNDALK arrives 1405.   B – On Sundays departs DROGHEDA 1835, arrives DUBLIN 1945.

SUPABUS RAPIDE

DUBLIN FROM LONDON & BIRMINGHAM — 851 / 853

OUTWARD JOURNEY		OPERATED BY:			RETURN JOURNEY	
853	851	*Supabus* NATIONAL EXPRESS/BUS EIREANN			851	853
1 Apr to 17 June and 31 Aug to 30 Sep	25 June to 14 Sep				26 June to 15 Sep	1 Apr to 17 June and 31 Aug to 30 Sep
DAILY	DAILY				DAILY	DAILY
1800	1900	Dep.	LONDON, Victoria Coach Station	Arr.	0800	0815
–	1920	Dep.	KILBURN, Outside Thatchers Travel, 221 Kilburn High Road	Arr.	0740	–
2030		Dep.	BIRMINGHAM, National Express Coach Station, Digbeth	Arr.		0540
2300		Dep.	CHESTER, Delamere Street Bus Station	Arr.		0310
0035		Dep.	BANGOR, Garth Road, Bus Terminus, Stand No. 8	Arr.		0135
0110	0115	Arr.	HOLYHEAD, Sealink Terminal Coach Park	Dep.	0145	0100
0315	0315	Sail	HOLYHEAD, Sealink Ferry	Arr.	0015	0015
0645	0645	Arr.	DUN LAOGHAIRE, Sealink Terminal	Sail	2045	2045
0740	0740	Arr.	DUBLIN, Busaras	Dep.	1940	1940

Service 851 is a shipside service. The coach does not travel on the ferry, passengers board or leave the coach at the ferry terminal.

SUPABUS SERVICE

DUBLIN

Discovering James Joyce's well-loved city takes some doing. Pick up the Joyce map from the tourist office. The Guinness Brewery, largest of its kind in Europe, offers a free film on the brewery and a glass of brew.

TRAIN STATIONS Connolly Station handles trains going north. Heuston Station is used by trains going south and west. In both stations, luggage checking is open M-Sa 7:30am-9pm, Su 8am-9pm.

DUBLIN'S SUBURBAN TRAINS (DART) go north and south from Dublin Connolly Station. Trains going north stop at Killester, Harmonstown, Raheny, Kilbarrack, Howth Junction, Portmarnock, Malahide, Donabate, Rush & Lusk, Skerries and Balbriggan. From Howth Junction, a rail spur goes to Bayside, Sutton and Howth. South from Dublin Connolly Station, the train stops at Tara Street (Dublin), Dublin Pearse Station, Landsdowne Road, Sidney Parade, Booterstown, Blackrock, Monkstown & Seapoint, Dun Laoghaire, Sandycove, Glenageary, Dalkey, Killiney, Shankill, Bray and Greystones.

BUS STATION CIE Expressway buses (free with Eurailpasses) leave from Store Street, near Connolly Station.

TOURIST OFFICE Located at 14 Upper O'Connell Street, 7 blocks from Connolly Station. Open M-Sa 9-5, currency exchange. The office near the ferry terminal of Dun Laoghaire is more convenient (8am-8pm daily).

CAMPGROUNDS **Donabate Caravan Park** is beside the sea in the village of Donabate. Take the suburban rail line from Connolly Station north to Donabate. Open May 1-Oct 1; about L5 per tentsite.

Cromlech Caravan and Camping Park, Killiney Hill Road, is in Ballybrack, south of Dun Laoghaire. The camp is 10 miles south of Dublin and half a mile south of Ballybrack village. This is the closest camp to Dun Laoghaire; take bus 46a from Dun Laoghaire ferry terminal for three miles to the campground. From Dublin, take bus 46 or the suburban train south to Ballybrack. Open Apr 17-Sep 19; backpacker tent/L3.50, adult/50p.

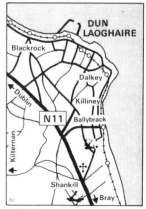

Shankill Caravan Park has 55 tent sites and is located just past the village of Shankill on the right hand side of Bray/Wexford Road, 12 miles south of Dublin. Take bus 45 or 84 from Dublin, bus 45a from Dun Laoghaire ferry terminal, or the suburban train south to Shankill plus a walk. (Walk south on N11 past Shanganagh Inn Pub; camp is on right hand side of road). The buses stop directly at the camp entrance. The seaside town of Bray is 2 miles from the campground. Open Easter to Sep 30; backpacker tent/L3, adult/50p.

To Cork, trains leave Dublin Heuston Station at 7:30am (M-F), 8:20am (Sa), 8:50am (Su), 9:05am (M-Sa), 10:10am (Su), 10:35am (M-Sa), 1pm (M-Sa), 2:05pm (Su), 2:40pm (M-Sa), 4:45pm (F), 5:30pm (M-Sa), 6:25pm (M-Sa), 6:40pm (Su), 6:50pm (M-Sa), 8:40pm (M-Sa) and 9:20pm (Su). The trip is 2-1/2 hours.

To Galway, trains leave Heuston Station M-Sa at 8am, 11am, 2pm, and 6:35pm; Su at 9:20am, 6:50pm and 8:10pm. The trip is 5 hours.

To Killarney, take the train to Cork, but change at Mallow. Trains that are through or have good connections leave from Dublin Heuston Station at 8:50am (Su), 9:05am (M-Sa), 10:10am (Su, change at Mallow), 10:35am (M-Sa, change at Mallow), 1pm (M-Sa), 5:45pm (F), 6:25pm (M-Sa) and 7:10pm (Su).

To Rosslare Harbour Pier, trains leave Connolly Station at 9:35am (M-Sa), 10:25am (Su), 1:35pm (M-Sa), 6:05pm (Su) and 6:30pm (M-Sa). The 1:35pm departure train arrives at Rosslare Pier at 4:35pm, in time to board the ferry. On Sunday, take the 10:35am departure which arrives at 1:15pm.

To Holyhead, Wales and London, leave Dublin Connolly Station by CIE bus at 8am daily. The bus arrives at Dun Laoghaire harbor to connect with the ship that leaves at 8:45am. Holyhead in Wales is reached at 12:15pm. On M-Sa a train leaves Holyhead at 12:45pm and arrives in London Euston Station at 4:57pm. On Sunday, the train leaves Holyhead at 1:05pm and arrives in London Euston Station at 6:06pm. The trains to London do not stop at Llandudno Junction in Wales. Instead take a local train from Holyhead to Llandudno Junction.

For **night service**, the bus leaves Dublin Heuston Station at 7:30pm daily, picks up at Connolly Station at 7:50pm and arrives in Dun Laoghaire in time to board the ferry which leaves at 8:45pm. Holyhead is reached at 12:15am. The train leaves at 1am M-Sa (ar. London 5:20am) or 12:45am Su (ar. 6:21am).

You can also sail from the port of **Dublin to Liverpool** and then take a train to London. The overnight sailing is best because there's enough time to get a full night's sleep. The ferry leaves M-F at 11pm, arrives in Liverpool at 7am. The train leaves Liverpool Lime Station at 8:20am and arrives London Euston at 11:08am.

BY COACH TO BRITAIN Coach fares are cheaper than train fares. Fare is according to season. Two large operators are the B & I Line and National Express.

National Express Coach (Bus Eireann). Standard fare season is about Apr 21-Jul 2; peak season about Jul 3-Sep 30 costs about 25 percent more. A reservation at Bus Eireann, Busaras Bus Station in Dublin, should be made for these trips. The fares below are given in British pounds. A Period Return fare is a roundtrip ticket valid for 3 months. Students with a National Express Coach Card receive a student discount. **Services 851, 551 or 853 are the least expensive.** Service 858 from Dublin port via Liverpool to London is about L10 additional. During peak season, **service 851** has the least expensive fare of about L32 single (one way) or L44 period return. During standard season the fare is about L29 single and L38 period return. Bus Eireann leaves Dublin Busareas at 7:40pm. Passengers get off the bus and board the ferry at Dun Laoghaire, Sealink Terminal, sailing at 8:45pm. Holyhead, Wales is reached at 1:45am, where passengers board a National Express coach for the trip to London, arriving at Victoria Coach Station at 8am. Service 851 operates from June 6 to September 15. **Service 553** has both a daytime and overnight trip. For the overnight run, the bus leaves Dublin, Busaras, at 8pm; the ferry sails from Dublin port at 10pm. The ferry arrives at the Sealink terminal in Holyhead, Wales at 3:45am and the coach arrives in London at 10:45am. This service operates daily from about June 18 to August 30. For a daytime sailing, from April 15 to September 30, a bus leaves Dublin, Busaras, at 10:30am, sails from Dublin port at 11:45am, arrives Holyhead at 3:15pm and London at 10:40pm.

B & I Line has a walk-on special between Holyhead and Dublin or Pembroke Dock and Rosslare for (1989) L20 one way and L32 rountrip Jul 14-Aug 20, 1989, and L15 one way, L27 roundtrip rest of the year. (British pounds.) B & I sails daily. From Dublin leave at 11:45am (ar. 3:15pm) and 11pm (ar. 3:45am). Pedestrians must obtain a "control ticket" in advance for the following dates on the 11:45am departure: Jun 2,3,10,17,24,25, Jul

1,7,9,13,15,21-23,27-31, Aug 3-21, 26,28,29, Sep 2. From Rosslare to Pembroke leave at 9am (ar. 1:15pm) and 8:30pm (ar. 12:45am). No control tickets are needed. For all routes you must check in at least 20 minutes prior to sailing. Some ships leave an hour earlier due to tides; check exact departures in Ireland. Through fares to London via coach are available for about L32 one way and L43 roundtrip high season.

GALWAY

Gateway to the rocky west coast, this Norman port provides some good wanderings through its narrows streets (Shop Street, Middle Street, Abbeygate Street and St. Augustine Street). For solitude, take the boat from Galway Pier which reaches the Aran islands in 3 hours.

The **train station** is on Eyre Square, the center of the city. The tourist office, one block east, is open M-Sa 9am-6:45pm.

Salthill Caravan Park is half a mile from the village of Salthill. This is the closest camp to Galway. The bus to Salthill from Galway train station leaves twice an hour and stops at the site. Open Apr 1-Oct 1; backpackers/L2 each. This is the most convenient and least expensive camp for backpackers. **Barna House Caravan and Camping Park**, Barna Road on R336 at Barnabeach, charges L5.50 per tent. Nearby, **Hunter's Silver Strand Caravan and Camping Park**, on the main coast road to Barna and Spiddal, is 2 miles from Salthill. Its entrance is just past Barna House Camping. Charges are tent/L4.40, adult/20p. The same bus goes to all 3 camps; take any bus going to Spiddal, Carraroe or Lettermullen. Departures at 9:15am, 11:30am, 1pm, 2:30pm, 4:20pm and 5pm.

Trains for Dublin Heuston leave M-Sa at 8am, 11:35am, 3:10pm and 6:25pm; Su at 10:05am, 3:10pm and 6:15pm.

SOUTHWEST IRELAND

Beautiful Southwest Ireland provides the backdrop for many a holiday. The train goes as far as Tralee. Killarney is the main town in the area. On Dingle peninsula, what you hear is Gaelic being spoken.

KILLARNEY Worth noting in this town are St. Mary's Cathedral on New Street and the Folk Museum in the National Park.

Three campgrounds are within 3-1/2 miles of Killarney. The closest is **Whitebridge Caravan and Camping Park**, located one mile east of Killarney off the road to Cork. The camp is between the railway and the the the River Flesk; the entrance is 300 yards from the road. Take the bus from Killarney train station in the direction of Cork. Open Mar 15-Sep 30; backpackers L4 per tent. This camp received an award of excellence, one of eight campgrounds so distinguished. The camp has excellent facilities including automatic washing machines and dryers, store, lounge with television and fishing in the river. **Beech Grove Caravan and Camping Park** is 3 miles west of Killarney in the direction of Killorglin on the main Ring of Kerry road, and next to the golf course and Hotel Europe. Open Mar 14-Sep 30; backpacker tent/L4.50, adult/25p. Take the bus to Killorglin and get off at campground.

Fossa Caravan and Camping Park, 3-1/2 miles west of Killarney, just beyond Beech Grove Camping. Open Easter-Sep 30; backpacking tent/L4. Very good facilities including automatic washer and dryer and store.

For trains **to Cork and Dublin**, see the schedule under Tralee. Trains depart from Killarney 30 minutes after departing from Tralee. **To Tralee**, trains leave at 12:37pm (Su), 12:43pm (M-Sa), 2:16pm (Su), 2:19pm (M-Sa), 4:51pm (M-Sa), 9:19pm (F), 9:32pm (M-Th & Sa), 9:39pm (F) and 10:27pm (Su). The trip is 30 minutes.

TRALEE The last week in August, Tralee hosts the Rose of Tralee International Festival featuring an array of free entertainment.

Bayview Caravan and Camping Park is one mile from town on the road to Ballybunion. The 3-acre camp is open Apr 1-Oct 31; tent and 1 person/L2.50, tent and 2 people/L4, tent and 3 people/L5, maximum stay 2 nights. No camping during festival week.

Trains to **Killarney, Cork and Dublin** leave at 7:30am M-Sa (change at Mallow for Cork), 8:05am Su, 10:05am M-Sa (change at Mallow for Dublin), 1:50pm Su (change at Mallow for Cork), 2:45pm M-Sa (change at Mallow for Cork), 5:25pm Su (for Dublin only), 5:35pm M-Sa, and 5:50pm Su (for Cork only). The trip to Cork takes 2 hours, to Dublin, 4-1/2 hours.

KENMARE Kenmare is 18 miles from Killarney off the Ring of Kerry Road. A bus goes on the Ring of Kerry road and connects the towns in the area. **Ring of Kerry Caravan and Camping Park** is 2.5 miles west of Kenmare on the Ring of Kerry Road, N70. Open Mar 1-Sep 30; backpackers/L2.50 each. The 10-acre camp has excellent facilities including automatic washer and dryer, camper's kitchen, eating room and dayroom with fireplace in which management allows campers to sleep in bad weather!

GLENBEIGH A village off the Ring of Kerry road, located 7 miles from Killorglin, the beach of Glenbeigh is on Dingle Bay. Bicycles may be rented in Glenbeigh. Glenross Caravan and Camping Park is in Glenbeigh village beside the Glenbeigh Hotel. Open May 16-Aug 31; backpackers/L3.50. The site has a sun lounge and barbeque patio.

ITALY

Italy has it all. Some of the world's greatest art, the world's greatest walking city--Venice, St. Peter's, wonderful cuisine, and a spontaneity and vigor are a few of its magnets. Most visitors tour at minimum the triumphirate of Venice, Rome and Florence. Be forewarned that the major sights in these cities acquire long lines during July and August.

If you aren't going to Greece, Italy represents a great opportunity for viewing early Greek civilization. Two magnificent sites are the temples at Paestum, just south of Naples, and those at Agrigento on the island of Sicily. An air-conditioned train swiftly journeying down the scenic boot of Italy will bring you to Sicilian life in comfort.

Those destined for Greece during the last week in July or first week in August should make ferry and connecting train reservations immediately after their arrival in Italy. Reservations may also be needed on either side of this period.

CURRENCY Italy uses the lira (lire is plural) as their monetary unit. One U.S. dollar equals 1200L.

Be certain to inquire in advance about the fee charged to change travelers checks as it varies widely and can be even L5000 per transaction as at the Banco di Roma, which is best avoided. However, there is a L500 government tax imposed per transaction no matter where you go. American Express office policy varies by city, but often only the tax is charged.

WEATHER During July and August camping is best in the Alps and Dolomites and on the beaches and coasts. The main cities can be rather warm in these months although it's always cooler out in the open air in the campgrounds. Rarely will rain be encountered during summer outside of mountain areas, and should a slight drizzle occur, the warm air rapidly absorbs the moisture. Of course if you can manage it, late spring and early fall are wonderful times to visit the south of Italy. Fall color is spectacular while early spring vegetables and June raspberries are delicious. Sicily, so jampacked with attractions it's called the archeological museum of Europe, is the place to head for a winter camping vacation. The sun shines an average of six hours a day.

CAMPING   Camping is well entrenched in Italy and campgrounds are filled with both vacationing Italians and northern Europeans. A map and campground list are available free from the national tourist office before you go.   The government classifies campgrounds just as it does hotels. Campgrounds are restricted to charging within the range that is allowed for its category. Campgrounds have up to three charging periods: high season, shoulder season and low season. High season is generally mid-July to mid-August. Usually the tent or site fee is reduced for a two-person tent, which is sometimes called a Canadian tent for two. Clearly mentioning that you have only a small tent when you register will often result in a reduced tent or site fee. The UPIM department store chain sells reasonably priced camping equipment if you're in need of a stove or other equipment.

campeggio	camping
entrata	entrance
uscita	exit
venvenuti	welcome
andate lentamente	drive slowly
informazioni	information
orario spaccio	hours open
direzione	office
tende	tent
luce	child
moto	motorcycle
acqua potabile	drinking water
acqua non potabile	water not for drinking
W.C. uomini	mens restroom
W.C. donne	womens restroom
non gettate gli assorbenti igienici nei W.C.	do not throw sanitary napkins in the toilet
ma negli appositi recipienti	use the wastebasket
docce	showers
lavabo	sinks for washing hands
lavatoio stoviglie	sinks for washing dishes
vietato lavare	no washing allowed
lavatoio biancheria	clothes washing room
rifiuti	garbage disposal
spiaggia	beach
noleggi sedie a sdraio, ombrelloni	deck chairs, umbrellas for rent

TRAINS   FS is the symbol for Ferrovie dello Stato, the Italian railroads. FS operates some buses, but never in competition with train routes. Eurailpass is valid on these buses. Be aware that trains are more crowded here, especially in second class, than you may have become used to in northern Europe. Whereas you may never have bothered with a reservation in northern Europe, you may need to in Italy, especially during late July and early August. Be sure to note which station your particular train uses. The station name is listed following the city name in the schedules. Several cities have more than one station and some trains will only stop at one.

   Strikes Italian railroads are also subject to occasional strikes. You may find out about an impending strike by noting headlines carrying the word *sciopero* in the Italian press, or from youth on the street practicing their English by letting you know one is coming.   If a strike occurs, enough nonstriking and management personnel are available to maintain international train schedules.   Domestic trains are the most likely to be affected.   If a strike occurs, don't necessarily believe people who tell you no trains are operating.   Just show up at the station and you'll likely find trains running and with available seats because everyone else is standing in the reservation line.

Timetables   All train information offices distribute the free, 3" x 5" pamphlet, *Principali Treni*, which lists schedules for all the mainline trains in Italy.   The footnotes contain information about which arrival or departure station the train uses and restrictions on the days it operates, if any.   Pink highlighted areas denote InterCity, Rapido and EuroCity trains.   The blue highlighted area indicates trains carrying couchettes.

Reservations   For some trains, a reservation is mandatory as indicated by the "R" in the schedule, and costs L2200 at the counter marked "prenotazione posti."   Also train reservations can be made for the same fee at travel agencies with the FS insignia in the windows.   Of course you can board any train requiring mandatory reservations without one, but on board the conductor will collect an extra L1000 on top of the regular L2200 unless you can convince him the computers were down at the station so you couldn't make one, which occasionally is actually the case.

Seat Reservation Receipt

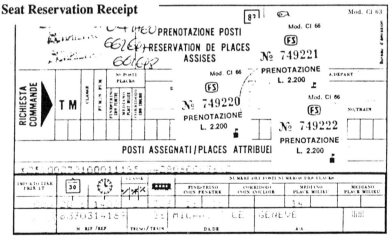

During early July we found reservations weren't necessary in first class, and though more crowded still weren't being made for second class. Ultimately, this is a situation that you have to play by ear once you get there. If you don't make one, at worst you may have to sit in the aisle or nurse an overpriced drink in the refreshment car, if any.   But there is one situation where you should prebook and that is the train to and from Brindisi.   So many Eurail and InterRail pass holders funnel into and out of that city that a reservation may make the difference between a seat or the aisle floor.   Also, if you ever are going to treat yourself to a couchette in Europe, the time to do it is on any overnight journey from Brindisi in July or August.   If you've arrived on the late ferry, many of those passengers will be continuing on the overnight trains to Rome. Even if you snag a seat, you won't get any sleep as there will be no vacant compartments on that trip. Get off the ferry, head for the station and reserve a couchette before they're all taken! Then check your bags and you're free to wander the pleasant back streets of Brindisi and have dinner before the train leaves.

Train Categories The best trains are: **EuroCity** (EC), **InterCity** (IC) and **Rapido** trains. The next best are long distance **Expresses**, though they don't have the air-conditioning the deluxe trains are supposed to have. The next slower train is **Diretto** (called Fast in this book and in Cook's timetable). The slowest trains are **Locales** which stop at every station, usually only have second class, and are not listed in either Cook's timetable or *Principali Treni*. Check the local station for these schedules.

Train Splitting Beware of the train that splits enroute, especially on trains leaving Rome where cars to both Milan and Venice are strung together at the outset but midway the coaches for Venice are detached and connected to another engine for the journey east to Venice. Always check the destination nameplate inside and outside the door of each coach for its ultimate destination.

FS	Italian State Railways
ferrovia	railway
binario	track
treno	train
carozza	car
posta	seat
da	from
a	to
data del viaggio	date of departure
treni en partenza	trains that are departing
treni en arrivo	trains that are arriving
prenotazione	seat reservation
baglio a mano	luggage storage

Theft on Trains No one can travel by train in Italy without hearing stories about thefts of luggage from compartments while people are sleeping. We never encountered anyone to whom this actually happened, but an easy precaution to take is to secure your pack to the luggage rack by attaching the straps through the metal rods.

EURAIL BONUSES (1) **Free ferry to Greece** Eurailpass, Eurail Saverpass and Eurail Youthpass travelers may use the steamers, Appia, Egnatia, Espresso Grecia, Castalia and Lydia, operated by the Adriatica di Navigazione and Hellenic Mediterranean Lines between Brindisi, Italy, and Patras, Greece, and vice versa at no charge. However, from June 10 to September 30 inclusive, a US $8.00 high season surcharge must be paid. A reservation may be made for a fee of US $2.00. Special accommodations such as airline type reclining seats and cabins, as well as port taxes, are extra. Before boarding, all passengers must check in at the shipping line pier office. Passengers who wish to stop over in Corfu must say so upon delivery of the steamer ticket. Holders of a ticket to Corfu as the final port of destination can in no way continue their voyage to Patras. (2) **To Alexandria** Reduction of 30 percent on the published full fares of the Adriatica Line between Venice-Piraeus-Candia-Alexandria and vice versa on the M.S. Espresso Egitto, except between Piraeus and Candia. Contact local Adriatica offices.

TOURIST OFFICES   E.P.T. are offices of the provincial tourist boards. A.A.S.T. are tourist offices operated by the city or town. Pro loco is a tourist office in a village. Ask for a map (*carta*).

CITY TRANSPORTATION   Buses and trams are the usual conveyances, but in Rome, Milan and Naples, subways are available too. Buy your ticket before boarding from tobacconists or at newstands. On buses and trams, the usual procedure is to enter at the rear door, insert your ticket into the stamping machine, and exit at the front. For subways, tickets are stamped as you pass through the turnstyle. Phone directories contain a handy map of the public transportation system. For safety's sake, always cross the street at the black and white striped crosswalks (*passaggi zebrati*) and watch the traffic signals (*semafori*).

FOOD   The food is a joy, no matter what class establishment you patronize. The only places to avoid are those that have someone on the sidewalk trying to hustle you inside as you walk by. Breakfast of fresh rolls, yoghurt and fruit (bought at the market previously) will cost L1800. A lunch consisting of a ready-made sandwich bought at a bar or slice of hot pizza to-go purchased at a pizzeria and fruit purchased by the kilo at the market or grocery store will cost about L2500 to L3500. A full-course meal bought at a self-service bar will cost L5000 to L10000. The least expensive restaurant will cost from L8000 to L15000. An ice cream cone is L1200 and up.

The best-value restaurants lauded in *Europe on $30 a Day* and *Let's Go* in dominant tourist cities such as Venice and Florence are generally very crowded, often even with lines, and can be disappointing. We were more satisfied by asking for a recommendation of a local person in the neighborhood we happened to be in when it came time to eat. Usually the places turn out to be small, family-operated restaurants, with 100 percent Italian clientele, excellent food, and very good value, although they may not always be the absolute cheapest.

The average Italian spends about 40 percent of his income on food and beverages and most of this is spent in the farmer's market and small food shops. The freshest food and lowest prices are usually found at the open market, but the option remains of small shops and supermarket chains such as Standa, G.S., SMA and IN'S. Buy cheese, butter and delicatessen items by the "etto" which is 100 grams or about three ounces.

The cheapest ready-to-eat foods are the sandwiches (*tramezzini*) which you'll notice in the windows of food bars, and the to-go offerings of the tiny *pizzerie rustiche* shops that sell hot pizza by the slice and sometimes rotisseried chicken. In these shops are various varieties of pizza baked in long rectangular pans and cut into slices. You indicate the piece you want and it will be weighed to determine the price and then wrapped in paper ready for immediate consumption. Often payment is made first at a separate cashier island. Expect to pay about L1500-L3000.

To eat cheaply in Italy is to eat pasta (spaghetti, macaroni, etc.), salad, bread and fruit. Meat is relatively expensive, though veal and chicken remain staples in this category. American-style beef is extremely expensive in Italy as grazing land is in short supply. The important agricultural crops are wheat, much of which is the hard type used in pasta, olives and wine. Corn and citrus fruits are also cultivated and cheese is an important industry.

Pasta is the basic food and comes in numerous sizes and shapes and a variety of colors. Green is made from spinach flour. Macaroni is a result of hard red wheat and boiling water. Other varieties such as ravioli and canneloni have egg added to the macaroni dough. Pasta is not served as the main course but as a separate first course (*plato primo*) following *antipasto* (appetizers).

Restaurants come in several types. The **ristorante** ranges from deluxe to reasonable. A **trattoria** has a regular group of neighborhood customers, more informal service, straight-forward decor and generally cheaper prices. Even less expensive and easier for ordering, but still very good, are self-service places such as *pizzeria, rotisserie or tavola calda* which serve quick simple meals with various seating or standing accommodations ranging from resting your plate on a shelf to counter stools or small tables and regular chairs. Aim for a noon to 2pm lunch (*colazione*) and a 7-9pm dinner (*pranzo*) for the best freshly prepared food.

The usual restaurant meal has four courses, beginning with *anitpasto*, appetizers which can be hot (*caldo*) or cold (*freddo*). Usually a platter of small amounts of lightly dressed raw vegetables and perhaps a slice of ham or pork sausage are served. Pasta or soup follow (*plato primo*) and you always are given a choice often between a thick, vegetable soup (*minestrone*) or two or three kinds of pasta. A small dish of freshly grated parmesan cheese often is served as garnishment. If the option of lasagne, cannelloni, ravioli or tortellini is given for the pasta dish, these are usually more interesting than spaghetti or macaroni because they always incorporate a nicely seasoned meat and cheese mixture. A basic lettuce salad with oil and vinegar dressing is sometimes served with the pasta or soup. The entree (*plato secondo*) is often a meat, fowl or fish dish served with vegetable or rice. Dessert is frequently fruit, your choice between a peach or grapes perhaps, or a baked dessert may be available. Wine normally is taken with the meal. When requesting water, you will be served and charged for bottled water unless you make it clearly known that it's tap water you want, which is, of course, safe throughout Italy.

Restaurants offer two kinds of set menus. A *prezzo fisso* is the restaurant's daily special for which the restaurant sets policy. The *menu turistico* is government controlled and required to have an appetizer, entree with vegetable, dessert and beverage (1/4 liter wine, glass of beer or orange pop, etc. or 1/2 bottle mineral water). The quoted price includes bread, cover, service and taxes. In all but very simple restaurants, you'll encounter a cover charge (*pane e coperti*) and usually a service charge (*servicio*) figured as a percentage of the bill. A cover charge of L1000 is typical of an inexpensive restaurant. Classier restaurants assess higher cover charges. Restaurants are required by law to issue a receipt.

SIGHTSEEING   The least expensive sightseeing is merely wandering around or visiting churches as there is no entry fee. The drawback is that many of the art works that were originally commissioned for cathedrals have been removed to safer museums. Museums are closed usually on Monday, and on Sunday and holiday afternoons. Some museums are free one day a week, but in some cities the policy is suspended during the summer. Italy has a plethora of public holidays including Easter Sunday and the following

Monday, April 25 (liberation day), May 1 (labor day), Ascension Day, Corpus Christi, June 2 (national day), June 29 (St. Peter and Paul) and August 15 (*Ferragosto*).

Italy has so many museums, art galleries, cathedrals and monumental architecture that the traveler must be very selective to avoid sensory overload. Try to include something from the following periods. (1) **Etruscan**. Archeological finds at Tarquinia, Volterra, Cerveteri and Veio are prominent. But much of the uncovered art has been removed to the Archaeological Museum in Florence, Etruscan Museum in Rome (first choice), and Municipal Museum in Bologna. (2) **Greek Civilization**. You needn't visit Greece to see ancient Greek architecture. Some of the most impressive examples are on Sicily and south of Naples at Paestum. (3) **Roman Civilization**. You will stumble upon many a remnant of the Roman Empire during your visit in Italy so you can henceforth ignore the less complete Roman museums in northern Europe. Triumphal arches, colosseums and roads are prolific. Rome, Pompeii, Herculaneum and Ostia (suburb of Rome) host the most important excavations. Naples National Museum is the elite because they have all the good pieces from nearby Pompeii, but good examples are everywhere. (4) **The Middle Ages**. Sculpture and paintings are found in many museums and galleries. The Uffizi and Gallery of Ancient and Modern Art in Florence are two. (5) **Renaissance**. Florence is the most notable for this period, but every large city has a collection. If you are staying in Italy for any length of time, it's worthwhile to buy the green English language Michelin sightseeing guide to Italy. If southern Spain or Portugal isn't on your itinerary, Moorish architecture can be seen in Palermo on the island of Sicily.

POSTOFFICES It's best to avoid mailing a package from Italy because it's a hassle complying with regulations on packaging (including little lead balls having to be clamped on any loose ends of twine) and it can take two months to arrive by surface mail. The post office at the Vatican is a separate system and the best place for mailing letters and packages in Italy. Otherwise, visit a tobacconist who will help you comply with rules. (Tobacco is a state monopoly and is sold in shops with the sign *Sale e Tabacchi*. They also sell bus tickets, stamps, postcards, candy, etc. and are open Sunday morning.)

POLLUTION Pollution is a problem on beaches near cities and towns and mouths of rivers, the coastline between Venice and Ravenna and the Ligurian coast except the Cinqueterre. We also avoid eating shellfish that come from the Venetian lagoons or the Bay of Naples.

THEFT While in Italy it is important to be especially careful about your railpass, money and travelers checks. Rome, Brindisi and Naples are the spots to watch, but this is written so the visitor will not be careless, rather than to discourage him from touring this beautiful country. We personally have not experienced any theft or received any letters from people who have.

MILAN (MILANO)

The heart of the downtown area and tourist Milan is the pedestrian sector centered in Piazza del Duomo. Flanking the piazza are Italy's largest and celebrated Gothic Cathedral, the Museo del Duomo, the entrance to the arcade of shops, Galleria Vittorio Emanuele II, and the tourist office. Milan functions as the major rail gateway between northern Europe and Italy so you're likely to find yourself here if only to make connections. If you have two hours between trains, you can check your pack and head for the Piazza del Duomo to see the Cathedral.

TRAIN STATIONS Stazione Centrale is the main station and all normal services including luggage check, currency exhange, post office and tourist office are found in this huge structure. Heeding the pictorial signs will save time locating them. Note the separate office for making reservations. Other stations are Stazione Milano Garibaldi and Stazione Lambrate. Metropolitana line M2 (green) connects all three stations.

CITY TRANSPORTATION Buses, trams and the metropolitana or MM (subway) are operated by Azienda Trasporti Municipali (ATM). Tickets must be bought in advance for L800 at news kiosks with the sign *Vendita Biglietti* or from yellow vending machines at many stops. Tourist offices and ATM offices sell a one-day pass for L3200 valid on all buses, subways and trams. Enter the rear of the tram or bus and cancel the ticket in the machine. Metro Line 1 (red) goes to P. del Duomo and intersects with line 2 (green) at Cadorno and Loreto. Two trams, 29 and 30, follow the route of the ring road circling the city. Tram 1 and bus 65 leave from Stazione Centrale and go to P. del Duomo.

CAMPGROUNDS Three campgrounds are accessible from Milan. In suburban San Donato Milanese on Via Emilia at km. 320 near the autostrada (freeway) is **Camping Agip**. Fees are adult/L4000 and tent/L3500. Eric Wolterstorff writes, *This camp is tricky to find the first time around. Take the clockwise ring-road tram 30, or from the station, tram 9, around to Porta Romana, where the Corso di Porta Romana runs out of the center of town like the spoke of a wheel and on through the Roman Gate. Walk one block down this street, away from town--it becomes Via Lobdi. The stop for the suburban buses is at the next intersection. They'll be gray and blue, not orange like the city buses, and will be facing into town toward the Roman Gate. Ask the driver or conductor for a bus going to San Donato. The buses run about every 15-20 minutes all day, slightly less often in the evening and Sunday. The fare is 800L one way, and the ride took 10-12 minutes. Look for the sign on the right side of the road which says San Donato, or ask the conductor to show you the stop, which is at the bus shelter immediately past the sign. Walk about 50 meters father down the road, and cross the bridge over the concrete-lines gulley to the campground.* The grassy camp has hot showers, lounge, store and a restaurant serving good, reasonably priced food.

Campeggio Autodromo di Monza is in Parco Villa Reale next to the famous racing track in suburban Monza. The camp is open April through September. From Stazione Centrale, trains to Monza leave about once an hour and the trip is 11 to 21 minutes. Local trains to Monza leave from Stazione Garibaldi at 6:30am, 8:30am, 12:30pm, 1:30pm, 2:14pm, 4:30pm, 6pm, 7:30pm, 8:30pm and 9:30pm for the 16 to 18-minute trip. From the train station in Monza, a city bus goes to the campsite. ATM buses to Monza leave from Piazzale Duca d'Aosta in front of Stazione Centrale and stop about 150 meters from camp. The attractive camp has hot showers, store and a swimming pool.

Campeggio II Bareggino, in Bareggio on via Corbettina, is open all year. Fees are adult/L4000 and tent/L4000. The camp can be reached by bus. The site is grassy and amenities include hot showers, store, lounge and swimming pool.

To Venice leave Stazione Centrale at 6am (ar. 9am), 7:05am-InterCity (ar. 9:50am), 8am (ar. 11am), 9:05am-InterCity (ar. 11:50am), 11:50am (ar. 3pm), 1:05pm-InterCity (ar. 3:50pm), 2pm (ar. 5pm), 2:20pm (ar. 6:44pm), 3:05pm-InterCity (ar. 5:50pm), 4pm (7pm), 5:05pm-InterCity (ar. 7:57pm Venice-Mestre only), 6pm (ar. 9pm), 7:05pm InterCity (ar. 9:50pm) and 8pm (ar. 11pm).

To Florence leave Stazione Centrale at 7:55am-InterCity (ar. 10:46am), 8:55am InterCity (ar. 11:46am), 11:20am (ar. 3:20pm), 12:55pm InterCity (ar. 3:46pm), 1:55pm InterCity (ar. 4:46pm), 3:55pm InterCity (ar. 6:46pm), 4:55pm InterCity (ar. 7:46pm) and 5:55pm InterCity (ar. 8:46pm). All these departures stop at Bologna about 1-3/4 hours out of Milan and continue onto Rome after reaching Florence. Milan to Rome on an InterCity train takes 5 hours. Only one train listed above is not an InterCity, but other departures using slower stock are listed at the station.

To Genoa leave Stazione Centrale about once an hour. Through trains from Stazione Centrale in Milan to Sestri Levante leave at 6:55am (ar. 10:17am), 8:25am SaSu only (ar. 11:36am), 2:15pm (ar. 5:16pm), 5:15pm Su only InterCity (ar. 7:37pm), 6:15pm EuroCity Carlo Magno (ar. 8:48pm) and 7:15pm InterCity (ar. 9:48pm). You needn't wait for the departures above; merely go to Genoa and board a local.

To Brindisi to connect with the ferry to Greece, your best bet is the InterCity Adriatico departing Stazione Centrale at 6:55am and arriving Brindisi at 5:02pm. Reservations advised during the last two weeks in July and first week in August, and possibly before and after this period.

To Cremona, leave from Stazione Centrale in Milan at 6:30am (ar. 7:44am), noon (ar. 1:04pm), 5:20pm (ar. 6:20pm) and 6:45pm (ar. 8:01pm). One hour trip.

To Switzerland and Germany, trains take two main routes. One goes via Domodossola and through the Simplon tunnel to Brig. At Brig some trains follow the route Visp, Sierre, Sion, Martigny, Montreux and Lausanne. For Zermatt, change trains at Visp. For Chamonix, change trains at Martigny. The other trains continue via the Lotschberg tunnel to Spiez, from where trains to Interlaken depart, before continuing to Bern and points north. The other main route from Milan is via Como, Chiasso, Lugano and through the St. Gotthard tunnel. At Arth-Goldau, trains heading to Lucerne and Basel take the route to the left while those destined for Zurich continue straight ahead. Both of these route are especially scenic in the Italian and Swiss Alps.

To Martigny and Chamonix, take a through train to Martigny (direction Lausanne or Geneva), change to a private cogwheel train to Vallorcine, and then board a waiting connecting French railways train to Chamonix. The portion Martigny-Vallorcine is not included in any Eurailpass and a small fare must be paid for this extremely beautiful mountainside-hugging steep stretch. Departures from Milan Stazione Centrale are 7:23am (ar. 10:40am), 9:10am EuroCity Lutetia (ar. Sion 11:45am where it's an easy change for Martigny), 10:15am (ar. 1:39pm), 12:20pm (ar. 3:39pm) and 2pm EuroCity Cisalpin (ar. Sion 4:45pm where it's an easy change for Martigny). The latter is the latest train that can be taken to arrive in Chamonix that night. Be sure to sit in the coach that is destined for Montreux, Lausanne or Geneva, NOT Bern or Basel. Arrival times are for Martigny.

Trains leave Martigny for Chamonix via Vallorcine at 7:31am, 8:50am, 9:50am (Jun 27-Sep 6 only), 10:59am, 12:01pm, 1:35pm, 3:26pm, 4:32pm (May 31-Jun 26 and Sep 7-26 only), 5:22pm and 6:27pm (Jun 27-Sep 6 only). A change of trains is required at Vallorcine. There are two later departures, 6:50pm and 7:36pm, from Martigny that end at the Swiss border, Le Chatelard. If you get off at Les Marecottes, the fourth stop out of Martigny, you can camp for the night 300 meters away and be on your way in the morning.

To Zermatt, take the same trains as for Chamonix above, but get off at Visp, the station after Brig. At Visp, a private train not honoring Eurailpasses leaves at 5:10am, 6:10am, 7:23am and then once each hour at 23 minutes after the hour until 8:23pm, except on Fridays a 9:23pm train runs.

To Spiez and Interlaken, take a train in the direction of Bern or Basel and change trains at Spiez for Interlaken. Be sure to sit in a coach that has Bern or Basel on its nameplate or you may find yourself headed to Lausanne after passing Brig. Arrival times are for Spiez. Departures from Milan Stazione Centrale are 7:23am (ar. 11:09am), 9:10am EuroCity Lutetia (ar. 1:09pm), 10:15am (ar. 2:09pm), 12:20pm (ar.

4:09pm) and 2pm EuroCity Cisalpin (ar. 5:33pm), 3:25pm (ar. 6:33pm) and 5:25pm (ar. 9:09pm). Trains depart from Spiez for Interlaken West and Interlaken Ost at 8:01am and one minute past each hour until midnight. There are also 2:29pm and 6:34pm departures which connect with arriving trains. To Interlaken Ost is 20 minutes.

      To Lucerne, trains leave Milan Stazione Centrale at 7:30am (ar. 11:39am), 9:30am (ar. 1:39pm), 11:30am EuroCity Carlo Magno (ar. 3:39pm), 1:30pm (ar. 5:39pm), 3:30pm (ar. 7:39pm) and 6pm (ar 10:25pm). Be sure to sit in a coach with Lucerne or Basel on the nameplate as these same trains may carry cars for Zurich.

      To Zurich, trains leave Milan Stazione Centrale at 6:30am (ar. 10:53am), 8:30am (ar. 12:53pm), 10:30am (ar. 2:53pm), 1:30pm (ar. 5:53pm), 3:30pm (ar. 8:07pm), 4:30pm (ar. 8:53pm) and 5:30pm (ar. 9:53pm). Be sure to sit in a coach destined for Zurich as these same trains may carry cars for Lucerne and Basel.

RIVIERA DI LEVANTE

The eastern part of the Italian Riviera, known as the Riviera di Levante, stretches 112 km. from Genoa to La Spezia. The area contains delightful cliff-hugging villages overlooking the blue Mediterranean, and two very scenic trails. The two magnets for the area are the beautiful Portofino peninsula and the picturesque five villages forming the Cinqueterre. The once brightly painted houses which allowed fishermen to recognize their homes from offshore, now present a spectacular picture in contrast to the green trees and blue sea. The resort town of Sestri Levante makes a good base from which to tour the area as it's relatively small yet still a stop on the major train lines. A campground is 10 minutes on foot from the station.

      Trains to Riviera di Levante   Both international expresses and Italian Intercity trains stop at both Sestri Levante and La Spezia, which are between Genoa and Pisa. From northern Europe, Sestri Levante is the end station on the excellent EuroCity train Carlo Magno that originates in Dortmund, Germany at 5:43am and makes major stops in Cologne, Koblenz (dep 7:56am), Mainz, Basel (dep 12:08pm), Lucerne (dep 1:19pm), Milan (dep 6:15pm) and Genoa (dep 7:53pm), before arriving in Sestri Levante at 8:48pm, not too late to set up camp, get a good night's sleep and be ready to explore in the morning. On the Genoa - Pisa - Rome train line, the fast trains stop at La Spezia, slower ones stop also at Sestri Levante, while the really slow ones will stop at Monterroso, part of the Cinqueterre, as well.

      If you find yourself in Genoa, be aware that local trains leave more frequently from Stazione Brignole, than from Stazione Principe (P.P.). Most EuroCity trains and Intercity trains stop at both stations, but some medium fast trains do not. Coming from Milan, if a train stops at both, Stazione Principe is first, followed by Stazione Brignole.

LOCAL TRAINS   Frequent local train service up and down the coast simplifies daytripping. La Spezia is to the south of the Cinqueterre, an 8-minute local train ride north to the first hamlet, Riomaggiore, or a 20-minute ride to the furthest village, Monterroso. The local train departs once or twice an hour depending on time of day. Positioned somewhat in the middle, Sestri Levante is north of the Cinqueterre yet south of Portofino. It's 22 minutes from Monterroso and, in the opposite direction, 24 minutes to S. Margherita where the bus is taken to Portofino.

CAMPGROUNDS   There are no campgrounds in the Cinqueterre, the closest being at Levanto, a town on the train line north of Monterroso. Acqua Dolce Camping, Via G. Semenza 5 at the beach, has hot showers, store, cafe and is open May-Sept. There are 3 other campgrounds available so you are bound to find something here. The train also stops at nearby Deiva Marina where you can camp at La Mammmola, Via Provinciale in Arenella, open all year; Camping Fornaci al Mare, foce de l Torrente Devia; or Camping Valdevia, via Ronco 1 on the beach.

The Cinqueterre - Trails

MONTEROSSO AL MARE
Pianta dei Principali Sentieri
TRAILS

Trail	Time
MONTEROSSO/LEVANTO (Via Punta Mesco)	2h. 30m.
MONTEROSSO /LEVANTO (Via Colla di Gritta)	1h. 50m.
MONTEROSSO/PUNTA MESCO (Semaforo)	30m.
MONTEROSSO/SANTUARIO DI SOVIORE	1h. 20m.
MONTEROSSO/VERNAZZA (via Santuario di Soviore)	1h. 40m.
MONTEROSSO/VERNAZZA (litoranea)	1h. 30m.
MONTEROSSO/RIOMAGGIORE (via Vernazza, Corniglia, Manarola)	4h. 30m.
MONTEROSSO/PORTOVENERE (via Crinale principale)	10h. 30m.
RIOMAGGIORE/TELEGRAFO (strada dei Santuari)	1h. 40m.
VERNAZZA/CORNIGLIA	1h. 30m.
CORNIGLIA/MANAROLA	1h.
MANAROLA/RIOMAGGIORE	30m.

294

The Cinqueterre - Monterroso

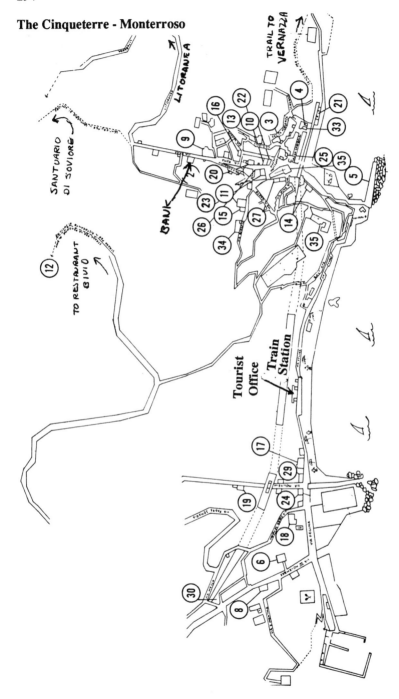

La Spezia   Accessible from La Spezia, which itself is devoid of campgrounds, are several campgrounds in nearby Lerici. From in front of the train station of La Spezia, Stazione Centrale, take the frequent bus L to Lerici. Camping Maralunga, between Via Maralunga and the sea, is open Jun-Sep; adult/L7300, small tent/L5700. The camp is 1500 meters from the Lerici bus station. The very nice small grassy site is studded with shade trees, and has a store, cafe, and dayroom. Alternatively, try Camping Gianna, on Via Fiascherino, which is 400 meters from the bus stop Lerici-Tellaro. Adult/L7300, small tent/L6700.

Carrara   To the south, the coastline between Carrara and Marina di Massa is chock ful of campgrounds. Get off the train at Carrara. Lots of campgrounds off the main street, Viale delle Pinete, host many caravans and vacationing Italian families, in this somewhat crowded beach area.

Sestri Levante   The big attraction here is the campground within walking distance of the train station, and Sestri Levante's proximity to both the Cinqueterre and the artists' colony/fishing port of Portofino. The tourist office, on via XX Septembre, is 5 blocks from the train station and open June-Sept M-Sa 9-noon and 5-6pm .

The closest campground, **Camping Cava Santa Ana**, charges adult/L4600 and tent/L3800. To reach the campground, walk forward from the station to Viale Mazzini and turn right. Then follow the map and signs. The walk is about 10 minutes.

Farther away but higher rated and with more amenities is **Camping S. Vittoria**, Via Villa Rocca 12, which is open all year. The owner, Santanna Enzo, writes that he will offer a 40 percent reduction of camp fees from L12000 to L7200 for 1 adult and 1 small tent upon showing this guidebook. To reach Camping S. Vittoria, take the bus for "S. Vittoria" from the bus terminal in front of the train station and ask the driver to let you off at the camping stop (fermata del carpeggio S. Vittoria). Buses leave about every 10 to 15 minutes and the ride is 5 minutes for the 2-km. distance. If you wish to walk, the route is shorter if you walk on Via Antica Rumana behind the station. The grassy site has store, cafe, lounge with television, shows movies, and allows campfires.

DAY TRIP TO THE CINQUETERRE   Five small picturesque villages perched against the steep, rugged hillside opposite the Ligurian Sea along the Italian Riviera are known collectively as The Cinqueterre. These winegrowing and fishing villages are connected by rail and trail. Exploring them for a day makes a delightful diversion from city touring. This area west of La Spezia is Michelin-rated two star, and the most interesting village of the five is Vernazza, which is given one star. The five villages are, in order, Monterroso al Mer, Vernazza, Corniglia, Manarola, and Riomaggiore. Monterroso is the largest and the only one with a developed beach. Of the other four tiny villages, Vernazza and Riomaggiore are the most rewarding.

One approach is to take the train to Riomaggiore, the southern most village and from there follow the road and trail to Vernazza. The touristed and famous Via dell'Amore (Road of Love), hewn from rock, connects Riomaggiore with Manorola and takes about 20 minutes to walk. From Manarola the trail to Corniglia takes about one hour, and Corniglia to Vernazza, 90 minutes. The path extends further to Monterroso, but the train might be boarded here because the last stretch is less easy, takes another two hours and you've already seen the best part. Corniglia and Manarola each have a small medieval church and Monterrosso has a developed beach at the southern end of the inlet. Vernazza rates a Michelin star with its bell-towers, narrow streeets, ancient houses, and tiny plazas. In Monterroso below the train station is the Pro Loco, tourist office, open June-Sept M-F 9:30am-12:30pm and 5:30-7:30pm, Sa 9:30am-noon.

DAY TRIP TO PORTOVENERE   Portovenere, 12 km. south of La Spezia, can be reached by twice hourly ATC bus P (L800) from in front of La Spezia train station. The winding corniche road itself merits a Michelin star and the bus passes through olive groves along the ridge of the gulf, a 30-minute scenic trip. To go by water, take one of the summertime six daily departures of an In-Tur boat (L3000) from the waterfront of La Spezia.

Portovenere is characterized by its 12th-16th century fortress, ancient houses and labyrinthe of narrow streets. A tourist office, Pro Loco, near the bus terminal, is open Jun-Sep daily 10am-12:30pm and 3-7pm. You can walk up to the promontory at the edge of the village to see the Church of St. Pietro and enjoy the vista. Ferry service links Portovenere with La Spezia, Vernazza and Monterosso.

DAY TRIP TO THE PORTOFINO PENINSULA   Michelin rates the Portofino peninsula as two stars and has long given the beautiful village of Portofino three stars and the hamlet of San Frutuosso, two stars. To reach Portofino, take the train to S. Margherita, north of Sestri Levante in the direction of Genoa, and then walk to the waterfront and look for the Tigullio bus terminal on piazza Martiri della Liberta. Bus fare to Portofino is L800. To journey by sea, boats leave from the harbor for L3500 one way to Portofino, L3000 one way (L5000 round-trip) to San Fruttuoso. The tourist office in S. Margherita, via XXV Aprile 2B, can be reached by turning right as you exit the station and staying on this street when it is renamed via Roma until you come to largo Giusti. Its hours are M-Sa 8:15-11:45am and 3:15-5:45pm, plus July-Sept Su 9:15-11:45am. An early morning fish market is held weekdays on L. Marconi on the waterfront.

PORTOFINO   A tourist office is at via Roma 35, open June-Sept M-Sa 9am-8pm, Su 9:30am-12:30pm and 3:30pm-7:30pm. After enjoying the aspect of the port and its colored houses set amidst verdant nature, there are two worthwhile trails to take. Passeggiata al Faro, the path to the Lighthouse, takes one hour roundtrip, and rewards you with a panoramic view of the Gulf of Rapallo all the way to La Spezia. The view is at its spectacular best during sunset. Follow the signs, *al faro*, to the lighthouse by climbing the steps from the port to the Church of St. George (San Giorgio). With the church to your right, keep walking on to the lighthouse, enjoying the view of Portofino below, the bay, clear streams, olive trees, yews, and pine. A longer trail leads from Portofino Vetta through a nature reserve to tiny San Frutuosso. This trail takes 4-1/2 hours roundtrip and the section near San Frutuosso is harder, but not really difficult. In summer only, a boat leaving several times a day connects the villages and hamlets along the coast. For example, Portofino to San Fruttuoso costs L2500, but if you plan a round trip by boat, buy the ticket at the outset as the fare is then L4500 roundtrip.

SAN FRUTTUOSO, Michelin rated two stars, is a lovely, small fishing port at the head of an inlet under Monte Portofino, connected by boat to the towns of Portofino, Camogli, S. Margherita and Rapallo, and by trail to Portofino. No bus, as there is no road to speak of. Across from the tiny harbor, the buildings of the Benedictine Abbey show the development from Romanesque to Gothic architecture. You can visit its thirteenth century main building, an exquisite eleventh-century church, and the Romanesque cloisters holding the tombs of the Dorias. The bronze statue, Christ of the Depths, in the bay commemorates those lost at sea.

To Switzerland and Germany, your best bet is the EuroCity train #4, Carlo Magno, which originates in Sestri Levante at 8:20am and follows the route Genoa (ar. 9:12am), Milan (ar.10:45am), Lugano, Lucerne (ar. 3:39pm), Basel, Freiburg, Mainz (ar. 8:11pm), Koblenz, Cologne and Dortmund (ar. 11:17pm). To Lucerne, leave Genoa at 10:53am (ar. 5:46pm), and 1:15pm-change at Milan-dep. 3:30pm (ar. 7:46pm).

To Amsterdam and Belgium overnight, go to Genoa and then take the 3:15pm train to Milan and change for the Holland-Italy Express which departs Milan (Stazione Centrale) at 6pm and arrives in Brussels at 7:27am and Amsterdam at 9:38am. Be sure to board a coach which is bound for your destination as the train reassembles in the upper Rhine and the coaches bound for Belgium continue with another engine. It's still daylight when this train passes through the scenic Alps. Then you can sleep (hopefully) through the industrial area along the lower Rhine. If you awaken early at 4:30am to view the castles along the Rhine River between Bingen and Koblenz, at 5:10am you can return to slumbering until early morning northbound businessmen start boarding and fill the empty seats.

To the French Riviera and Antibes, go to Genoa and then change trains. Trains depart for Genoa from Sestri Levante at 7:03am, 7:37, 9:01, 10:27, 11:21, 1:58pm, 3:52pm, 4:40pm, 7:11pm, 8:38pm, 10:31pm and 11:34pm. In all cases you will arrive at Stazione P. Principe in Genoa within one hour. From Genoa, trains leave for Antibes at 8:02am (ar. 12:48pm), 8:23am-Ligure/Rapido-(ar 11:40am), 9:13am (ar. 2:42pm), 10:02am (ar. 3:16pm), 1pm (ar. 5:50pm), 2:02pm-Rapido (ar. 6:56pm), 4:02pm-Rapido (ar. 8:03pm), 4:02pm-not Rapido (ar. 8:21pm) and 5:12pm (ar. 10:45pm). The Italian-French border is at Ventimiglia. Some coaches go right on through, but for some trains you have to get off the coach, go quickly through customs and board another connecting train to continue. In the latter case, make haste as the connecting train has a schedule to meet and doesn't wait for laggards.

To Barcelona, overnight, leave Genoa at 6:15pm (ar. Barcelona 9:29am.

To Paris, overnight on the Napoli Express, leave Sestri Levante at 8:28pm, arrive Rapallo 8:58pm and change trains, depart Rapallo at 9:17pm, arrive Paris (Gare de Lyon) 8:52am.

To Florence, take any train to Pisa and then change trains for Florence. Trains leave Sestri Levante for Pisa at 7:50am, 9:42am, 12:52am, 1:51pm, 3:09pm, 3:14pm, 4:50pm, 6:27pm, 7:56pm and 8:34pm. The trip is one hour, 40 minutes. These same trains pick up in La Spezia about 30 minutes later. Trains leave Pisa for Florence about twice an hour up to 7:10pm and then once an hour until 11:37pm. The trip is 1-1/2 hours.

To Venice, you can go either via Florence or Milan and each requires a change of train in those cities for Venice. Sestri Levante to Florence takes about 3-1/2 hours and Florence to Venice, 3 hours. Sestri Levante to Milan is 2-1/2 to 3 hours and Milan to Venice is 3 hours. Trains leave about once an hour from Milan.

To Rome, a fast train can be picked up from either Rapallo, 15 minutes north of Sestri Levante, or La Spezia. Direct trains from Sestri Levante to Rome leave at 7:50am M-Sa only (ar. Roma Ostiense 1:05pm, Roma Termini 1:15pm), 9:42am (ar.Roma Termini 4:05pm), 1:51pm (ar. Roma Termini 7:25pm), and 3:14pm (ar. Roma Ostiense 8:22pm, Roma Termini 8:35pm). Faster trains leave from RAPALLO, at 8:29am (ar. Roma Termini 1:25pm), 8:47am (ar. Roma Termini 1:35pm), 10:46am Rapido reservation required (ar. Roma Termini 3:30pm) and 6:26pm Rapido (ar. Roma Termini 11:10pm). All trains pick up from La Spezia about 30 minutes later.

VERONA

To say Verona is a main rail junction, which it is, belies its red, ochre and pink colored beauty and its wonderful historical center. Though it is only second in importance to Venice as an art center in this region, it receives only a fraction of the tourists which throng to the latter in July and August. Though Verona is well worth more than a day, if you find yourself changing trains here, consider checking your pack at the train station and exploring the historical center for the day, taking a late train to your final destination.

Verona

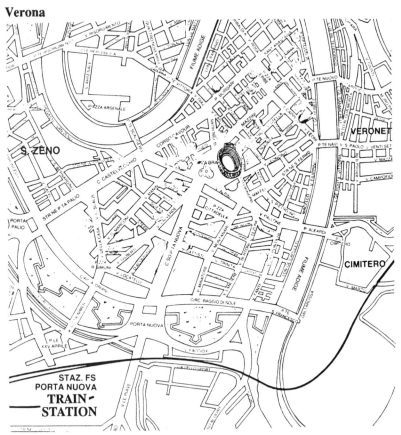

TRAIN STATION   The main train station is Verona Porta Nuova. The plaza in front of the station is P. le XXV Aprile and terminus for both local and long distance buses. Luggage check within the station is L800. The town center is far enough away from the station that you should take bus 1 (direction S. Michele) or bus 2 (direction Ospedale C.) from across the street in front of the station to the arena (colosseum), center of the historical area. Bus fare is L800 and the ticket is good for one hour. Purchase your ticket from the kiosk in the square, board by rear door and stamp the ticket in the machine. To walk to the historical center from the station takes about 20 minutes. Turn right after leaving the station and then turn left, passing through Porta Nuova and continuing on this main street until reaching Piazza Bra, the town center and site of the Roman arena. The tourist office is across the street from the arena. The main outdoor market is in piazza delle Erbe, the former Roman Forum.

CAMPGROUND   Camping Romeo e Giulietta, Strada Bresciana, 54 in the S. Massimo part of town 5 km. from Verona, is open all year. The camp is located in square A3 at the edge of the tourist office map.   Fees are adult/L4700, camping site/L12,400. If you're still interested, take the blue bus (direction Brescia) from across the plaza in front of the train station. The bus leaves once an hour and ask the driver to let you off at camping. Free hot showers, store, cafe, swimming pool. If you have a youth hostel card, you can camp at the close in Ostello Verona, Salita Fontana del Ferro, 15, for L3000. Open all year.

VENICE (VENEZIA)

Venice is made of passageways, narrow waterways, curved footbridges, stone buildings and pigeons. St. Mark's Square, its focal point, is a paved plaza of football field dimensions extending forward from the great domed Basilica San Marco. Pedestrians reign supreme here in Europe's premier walking town.   Once an island, Venice is connected to the mainland at Mestre by a three mile road and railway bridge built in 1933. Multi-story covered parking and the bus station are at Piazzale Roma, the end of the road. Venezia S.L. train station is at the end of the tracks.

TRAIN STATION   All trains to Venice S.L. stop first at Venice-Mestre Station in the modern city of Mestre before proceeding down the causeway to Stazione S. Lucia (Venezia S.L.) in Venice itself. Some trains go only as far as Venice-Mestre and don't go into Venice, itself. Those not camping in Mestre should be sure to check the schedule or question the conductor that their train does go to Venice S.L. If yours doesn't another train going to Venice will come along momentarily.   In Stazione S. Lucia, cafeteria, waiting rooms, reservation counter open until 10pm, tourist information, foreign exchange but with a hefty commission, luggage storage, and post office are available.

FOREIGN EXCHANGE   Beware the high commission charge at most banks.   American Express, at Salizzado S. Moise 1471 near San Marco, imposes no commission but only the L500 government tax that is assessed everywhere. Hours are Monday to Saturday 8am to 8pm.

TOURIST OFFICE   Three convenient offices are at Piazzale Roma where the bus lets you off, in Stazione S. Lucia, and in St. Mark's Plaza.

CITY TRANSPORTATION   Public transportation is needed to get from the campground to Venice. Once there you can depend on your legs or take boat rides as desired. A 24-hour ticket *(biglietto turistico 24 ore)* is sold for L9000 and a 3-day ticket *(biglietto 3 giorni)* for L17,000 at any ticket kiosk, including the one outside Venice-Mestre Station.   It includes rides on both buses and boats in Venice, Mestre, Jesolo Peninsula and the greater Venice area, as well as the conveyance of one piece of luggage. (Normally an extra fare is charged for luggage on a vaporetto, the boats plying the canals of Venice.)   The 3-day ticket should be seriously considered by anyone staying at Camping Miramare, and for everybody for their first 3 days when heavy usage of public transportation is made. If you figure the cost of reaching camp (L500 for bus to Mestre, L1700 for vaporetto plus L2500 for ferry to Miramare), then going to Venice (L600 bus from Mestre or L2500 ferry from Miramare), taking a cruise down the Grand Canal that bisects the island (L1700 for Mestre only as this was done on the way to Miramare), a boat ride around Venice's outer edge (L1700), return to the campground (L600 for bus to Mestre or L2500 for ferry to Miramare), plus any short vaporetto rides or trips to Murano or the Lido and the return to Venice the next day, you're bound to come out ahead during the 3-day period.

The regular fare for a ride on a vaporetto, even for only three or four stops, is L1700. Buy individual tickets only if you need a long ride--for short hops it's a lot cheaper to walk. In the evening, ticket sellers for the vaporettos have gone home and if you haven't already bought a ticket, one must be purchased on board for an extra L500. The fare between Piazzale Roma or Stazione Venezia S.L. and San Marco, Schiavoni in Venice and the Lido (the beach), and for the ride around the outside of Venice is L1700 in each instance. The ferry ride from Schiavoni in Venice to Punta Sabbioni on the Jesolo Peninsula is L2500.

Another money saving option is to purchase a Venice Card (*Cartavenezia*) for L10,000, valid 3 years for discounted boat and bus fares. With the card for example, ferries normally costing L1700 to L2500 (including the ferry to Punta Sabbioni) are reduced to only L600 or L800. A passport type photo is needed to purchase the card which is sold at the ACTV office in Corte dell' Albero, west of San Marco and in the general vicinity of the Sant Angelo vaporetto stop on the Grand Canal. The ACTV office is open Mondays to Saturday from 8:30am to 12:30pm. It's sold also at the ACTV office in Mestre at Via Ca Savorgnan and at the Piazzale Roma ACTV office.

Ferries are classified into three kinds. (1) **Linee interne vaporetti** start at Piazzale le Roma and follow the internal canals to San Marco with some boats continuing to the Lido. **Line 1** boats (accelerato) motor down the Grand Canal and stop at all docks, whereas the faster line 3, 4 (*diretto*) vaporetti follow the same route making only a few stops. *Line 2* vaporetti take a shortcut through a side canal and provide the fastest transpotation to San Marco. (2) **Linee circolari** boats circle Venice from the outer perimeter, stopping at the bus and train stations and making a few other stops in Venice and detouring out to the islands in the Venetian Lagoon. (3) **Linee esterne ferries** stay out of the Venetian Canals altogether and connect Venice to Punta Sabionni, the Lido and other islands in the Lagoon.

Vaporetto **Linee Interne line 1** follows the Grand Canal to San Marco and then on to the Lido. It stops at (1) Piazzale Roma (bus station), (2) Ferrovia (train station), (3) Riva di Biasio, (4) San Marcuola, (5) San Stae, (6) Ca d'Oro, (7) Rialto (the fancy bridge and on the other side, the market), (8) San Silvestro, (9) Sant' Angelo, (10) San Toma, (11) Ca Rezzonico, (12) Accademia, (13) S.ta M. del Giglio, (14) Salute, (15) San Marco (St. Mark's), (16) San Zaccaria, (17) Arsenale, (18) Giardini-Esposizione, (19) Sant'Elena, (20) Lido. From the other direction, the vaporetto starts from the Lido and goes to Piazzale Roma.

Linee Interne line 2 boats stop at Ferrovia (train station), Piazzale Roma (bus station), S. Samuele, Accademia, San Marco, S. Zaccaria, S. Elena and the Lido.

St. Mark's Plaza (San Marco) - Tourist Office and American Express

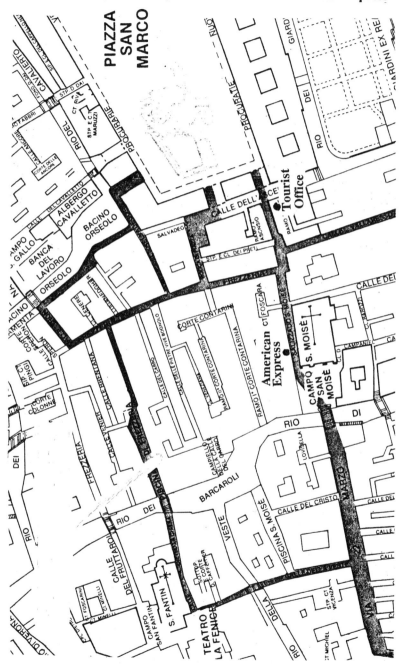

Traghetti, the gondolas that ferry passengers across the Grand Canal from one side to the other, leave every few minutes and cost L300 in exact change. They cross between Santa Maria del Giglio and San Gregorio, San Barnaba and San Samuele, Sant' Angelo and San Toma, Riva del Carbon and Riva del Vin, Santa Sofia and Pescheria (the outdoor fish market), San Marcuola and Fontego dei Turchi, and Ferrovia (at the train station) and San Simeon Piccolo.

CAMPGROUNDS   There are no campgrounds in Venice itself, but several are found at the rail junction of Mestre just outside Venice and about 27 populate the Jesolo peninsula which juts out from the Italian seacoast east of Venice. Get off at Mestre Station if you plan to camp in Mestre. Otherwise continue onto Venice Santa Lucia Station (Stazione Venezia S.L.) for the campgrounds on the Jesolo Peninsula. When it comes time to leave Venice, especially if you're taking an early morning train, it's easier if you're already staying in the rail junction town of Mestre. However, Camping Miramare on the Jesolo peninsula is a quiet and neatly tended camp. It's more romantically situated requiring commuting by boat rather than bus so it's a hard decision to make.

We've included details on only three camps, Camping Rialto in Mestre, Camping Fusina in Fusina and Camping Miramare on the Jesolo peninsula. The former is the most convenient campground in the area but is not as nice as Miramare or Fusina. If you wish a better camp in Mestre, merely get off the bus at Camping Venezia which is about two blocks before the bus reaches Rialto. As both Rialto and Venezia close September 30, you may wish to consider two that stay open all year. Camping Fusina is the one listed in *Let's Go* and has lots of college age people as it has 200 beds available and gets the overflow from the youth hostel. Also open all year is Camping Alba d'Oro in Tessera. All except Miramare can be reached by bus from Mestre. Camping Miramare is a very good camp and the most convenient on the peninsula, that also happens to be one of the least expensive in this high priced area. Many of the other camps on the peninsula are mammoth affairs catering to Northern Europeans on holiday who devote inordinate amounts of time to the beach.

A final note, there is so much water surrounding Venice the campgrounds have a few mosquitos which can be bothersome in the evening, warranting bringing along insect repellant if mosquitos are fond of you. The only other place in Europe you're likely to encounter any would be in northern Scandinavia towards the Arctic circle.

Camping Rialto in Mestre, at Via Orlanda, 16, is open May through September. Fees are adult/L4000, small tent/L2500 during high season. (You must tell the proprietor that you have a small tent or you will be charged for a large one.) Directions: From in front of Mestre Train Station, look across the street and to the right to the end of the block in front of Telefono Publico, to find the bus stop for bus 9. Last bus leaves at 9:36pm. The ride is 10 to 15 minutes and the fare is L500. Sit on the righthand side of the bus. After leaving the downtown and industrial area, you will first see the sign for Camping Venezia, which requires a few minutes walk away from the highway to camp. The camp has nicer grounds than Rialto, charges adult/L4000 and camping site/L5000, has hot showers and a store and is open April through September. After passing Camping Venezia, to get off at

Camping Rialto push the stop button in the bus when you see the green API gas station sign on the righthand side. Camping Rialto has a sign on the road and the camp is directly on the highway. To return to the Mestre Train Station, take bus 85 (L600) across the street from Camping Rialto to its end stop, Stazione FS.

The grounds have been pretty much left in their natural state making Camping Rialto more rustic appearing than the other more neatly landscaped and manicured camps. Basically the camp is a grassy field with areas divided by bushes and a few trees here and there and a road down the middle. The noise from the highway penetrates the area near the store so you may want to consider pitching your tent deeper into the campground. The small grocery store has a meat/deli section and the owner will slice lunch meats and cheese to order. There is also fruit, a good wine selection, dairy products, bread, freezer meats and vegetables. Sample prices are cheese for L1000 per etto (about 4 ounces), an individual serving of yoghurt for L800 and 250 grams of thin crispy breadsticks for L1550. Outside, the tiled patio with fiberglas roofing is home to one black and one grey cat, and tables and chairs for dining form a nice shaded area cooled by a pleasant summer breeze. The free, very hot showers are open 7:30-11am and 6pm to midnight. Women have two tiled restrooms and there are outside clothes and dishwashing sinks. Checkout is 2pm.

Camping Rialto to Venice. Fare is L600 for the 15-minute ride to Piazzale Roma in Venice. Bus 19 leaves from across the street from camp at 10 minutes before the hour. Bus 5 leaves at 20 minutes past the hour from around the corner from camp. To reach the bus stop for bus 5, turn right upon leaving camp, turn right again at the first intersection and the stop is across the street, about a three-minute walk. Fare for either is L600 and tickets are sold in the camp store. Buses 5 and 19 from Mestre deposit you conveniently at Piazzale Roma in Venice. A tourist office branch is next to the bus ticket office at Piazzale Roma. After getting off the bus you can either go straight down to the water, buy a ticket and board a vaporetto or start walking and explore Venice on foot. You can glide down the Grand Canal to St. Mark's (San Marco Piazza) by boarding vaporetto #1 for a slow ride which makes all the stops, or #4 for a faster limited stop cruise. Another choice which you're likely to make after your initial Grand Canal cruise, is to board line 2 (Linea Diretto) for the fastest way to San Marco via a side canal and S Samule and Accademia. Depending on exactly where your bus has stopped in Piazzale Roma, when you go down to the canal you may first find the boat landing stage for line 2, the direct line to San Marco. To the left of line 2 are two other landing stages, the last one being line 1, the slow route down the Grand Canal to San Marco. Single fare between Piazzale Roma and San Marco is L1500.

Venice to Camping Rialto. From Piazzale Roma, bus 5 leaves from 6:35am to 11:35pm at 35 minutes past the hour and bus 19 leaves from 7:05am to 11:05pm at 5 minutes past the hour.

Camping Fusina is across the lagoon from Venice. Open all year, backpacker special/L6500, tent/free. To get here from Mestre, buy a L600 bus ticket from the ACTV ticket booth outside Mestre train station. Then cross the street in front of the station and look for the underground passage to Marghera. The passage is visible from the station and looks like any metro access, except it's a walkway passage. You emerge from the passage on the other side. Now cross the road, leading left. You should be on a busy 4-lane road. Walk straight to the next bus stop and wait for bus 13. The bus leaves at 10 minutes past each hour. Ride to the last bus stop, which is at the campground. From Venice, in summer only vaporetto 16 leaves from Zattere every half hour for Fusina, and then a few minutes walk to camp. The last boat leaves at 11:45pm.

The camp is on the lagoon, but not the beach so there's no swimming. Free hot showers, 5 washing machines & 3 dryers, store and a lively pub. The camp is larger and has more and nicer facilities than Camping Rialto. They also have rooms with 8 bunks each at L9000 per person. In winter, the bunk cost is L10,000 to pay for the heat. Their trailers rent for L25,000 plus L6500 per person. Total bed count is 200. The campground management is especially accommodating to backpackers and young people.

Camping Miramare, romantically situated on the Jesolo Peninsula, is open April 1 to September 30. The management writes it has reduced prices for " walkers with a tent." Normal fees are adult/L3600, tent/L5250 (May & Sep 13-30); adult/L4200, tent/L6850 (Jun 1-21 & Aug 31-Sep 13) and adult/L4750, tent/L7350 (Jun 21-Aug 31).

Get off the train at Venice Santa Lucia Station and walk to the canal and buy your ticket for the vaporetto. Seriously consider buying a 3-day pass as the vaporetto fare to San Marco is L1500 and then the ticket to the Jesolo Peninsula is another L2500 and you'll want to return to Venice after setting up camp unless it's quite late. Besides, the all pass includes luggage, whereas another fare is payable for it on the vaporetto. The delightful cruise down the Grand Canal to San Marco can be taken in the limited stop vaporetto #4 or the slower all stop vaporetto #1. Get off at San Zaccaria, the stop following San Marco. Turn right and line #14 is just beyond the footbridges. If you got off at San Marco, turn right and walk along the seaside promenade, past the opening to St. Mark's Square and over the footbridges. Look for #14 with Punta Sabbioni lettered on the front of the pier sign. Passenger ferry line 14 leaves for Punta Sabbioni on the Jesolo Peninsula from this pier, Riva Schiavoni. Single fare is L2500 and the ride is 30 minutes with a brief stop at the Lido (the famous beach) enroute. (If you get off at the Lido you have to pay another L2000 fare to continue on to Punta Sabbioni. The fare between the Lido and Venice is L1500.) On a hot summer day, this very breezy trip makes for a refreshing interlude.

Ferry schedule - Venice to Punta Sabbioni. From June 16 to September 13, ferry line 14 leaves Venice (Riva Schiavoni) for Punta Sabbioni at 5:05am, 5:55, 6:20 (M-F only), 6:40, 7:45, 8:15, 8:45, 9:15, 9:45, 10:15, 11:15, 12:15pm, 1:15, 1:45, 2:15, 2:45, 3:15, 3:45, 4:15, 4:45, 5:15, 5:45, 6:15, 6:45, 7:15, 7:45, 8:15, 9:15, 10:15, 11:00pm, 12:28am and 3:08am. From September 14 to June 15, the ferry leaves at 5:05am, 6:00 (M-F only), 6:45, 8:05 and then at 5 minutes past each hour until 8:05pm, and then 9:35, 10:44pm, 12:28am and 3:08am.

Ferry schedule - Punta Sabbioni to Venice. From June 16 to September 13, ferry line 14 leaves Punta Sabbioni for Venice (Riva Schiavoni) at 5:55am, 6:45, 7:10, 8:30, 9:00, 9:30, 10:00, 10:30, 11:00, 12:00 noon, 1:00pm, 2:00pm, 2:30, 3:00, 3:30, 4:00, 4:30, 5:00, 5:30, 6:00, 6:30, 7:00, 7:30, 8:00, 8:30, 9:00, 10:00, 11:00, and 11:45pm. Sep 14-Jun 15, the ferry leaves at 5:50am, 6:45am, 7:10am, 8:58am and then at 58 minutes past each hour until 7:58pm, and 9:08pm, 10:25pm and 11:30pm.

Enroute to Punta Sabbioni as the ferry approaches the peninsula, the yellow painted pole archway announcing Camping Miramare is visible off the right side of the boat. Concession stands dominate the area of debarkation, and the connecting orange buses that head up the peninsula and pass within three or four blocks of the other campgrounds wait across the

Venice Area Train Stations

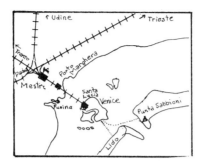

Venice - Campgrounds on the Jesolo Peninsula

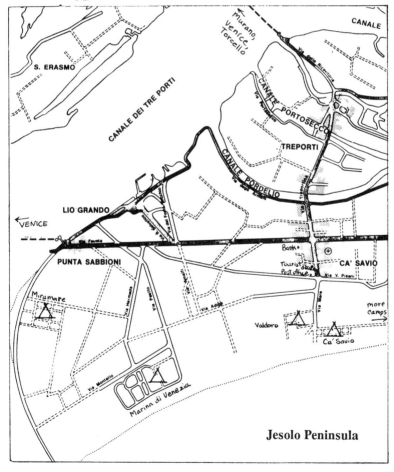

306

street. Nearby, an attendant in the kiosk with the blue sign, "ATVO Biglietteria Bus," sells tickets, and a 4 km. ride to Treporti, for example, costs L1000. But there really isn't any point paying another bus fare when you can merely get off the boat, turn right and walk 500 meters or about 10 minutes along the gravel rode beside the beach to Camping Miramare.

This is a very neat, well landscaped camp with 20 or so small cabins and a paved road within the campground. Trees carefully planted in straight lines delineate each individual camp site. Two sections are for tents, each site marked by trees and some equipped with a small cement bench. Behind the restrooms, an extra covered area large enough for three small tents is tucked away. A six foot high cement brick wall surrounds the entire camp. Children play on the small sand beach across the street. There are 2 restrooms, each having free hot showers, hot water in the sinks and separate basins for washing clothing and dishes. Use of the automatic washing machine is L3500; there is a store. The office is open 8-1 and 3-10. Checkout is noon. The 4-person cabins without a toilet rent for L37,000, L32,000 or L27,000 total according to season and the 5-person cabins including toilet facilities command L53000, L41000 or L36000. These should be reserved in advance by March by writing to Camping Miramare, Punta Sabbioni, 30010 Treporti (VE), Italy. Phone is 041-966-150.

FOOD   The market (*erberia*) is on the left bank of the Grand Canal in S. Polo near the end of the Rialto Bridge and is open Monday to Saturday, early morning until early afternoon. A good self-service place is Rosticceria S. Bartolomeo, 5423 Calle della Bissa, near Campo San Bartolomeo in the vicinity of the Rialto Bridge. You are likely to come upon it while wondering from San Marco to Rialto. Purchase your meal and take it to the narrow counter against the wall where stools are provided. A typical main course costs L3000, a first course, L2400 and snack foods, L800. Closed on Monday. If you happen to be near the train station, a full course lunch is available at the Mensa DLF (Dopolavoro Ferroviario), railway worker's subsidized cafeteria, for L9000 to L11000. The exact address is 19 Fondamente S. Lucia, located to the right at the bottom of all those broad steps leading away from the station. Look for a plain, modern structure not resembling a commercial restaurant and only go between noon and 2:30pm.

The ferry to Murano (glass factories), Torcello (church) and Burano (lace factories) leaves Venice from Fondamente Nuove at 5:00am (M-F only), 7:17, 8:05, 9:05, 9:55, 10:55, 11:35, 12:35pm, 1:35, 2:35, 3:35, 4:35, 5:35, 6:35, 7:35, 8:35, 9:35 and 10:35pm. From Treporti on the Jesolo Peninsula, the ferry to Burano, Torcello, Murano and Venice leaves at 5:30am, 6:30, 8;40, 9:25, 10:15, 11:05, 1:50pm, 2:50, 3:55, 4:45, 5:45, 6:45, 7:50 and 8:55pm. To reach Treporti from Punta Sabbioni, board an ATCV bus at Punta Sabbioni and get off at the dock.

To Brindisi for the Ferry to Greece, first take a train to Bologna and then change trains for Brindisi. The trip is very scenic after Rimini as the train hugs the coastline. There's only one really good connection and that is a fast category train which leaves Venice S.L. at 6:25am and Venice-Mestre at 6:36am and arrives in Bologna at 8:22am. In Bologna, change to the air conditioned InterCity Adriatico that leaves at 8:42am and arrives in Brindisi at 5:02pm. The InterCity requires a mandatory reservation for first class. Because a reservation is required regardless and this train can be completely prebooked in at least the last half of July through the first week in August, it is prudent to make a reservation as soon as you reach Venice-Mestre or Venice S.L. We rode this train in late June, having chosen Camping Rialto in Mestre specifically for its convenience to Venice-Mestre station. We did not know of the mandatory reservation for the InterCity as Cook's Timetable did not indicate it. We found out about it from others who were waiting on the platform for the InterCity to arrive and who said they couldn't make a reservation because the computer was down. Many people boarded at Bologna with the result that the train was three-fourths full in second class and half full in first class. Because of the computer breakdown, on board the conductor collected only the normal reservation fee, L2200.

To Brindisi by overnight train, an express leaves Venice S.L. at 9:04pm, Venice-Mestre at 9:16pm and arrives Brindisi at 9:01am. This through train carries coaches with seating in compartments for both first and second class and couchettes. If you take this train, a good strategy upon arrival is to check your pack at the train station, walk to the port office, go upstairs and pay the fees, secure your boarding pass and the customs control card, return to the station and be off daytripping. A good destination is non-touristy Lecce, the premier example of southern Italian Baroque architecture and only 30 minutes south by train.

To Florence, trains leave frequently with some requiring a change of trains at Bologna. All trains pick up at Venice-Mestre about 10 minutes after Venice S.L. An InterCity leaves Venice S.L. at 7:25am (ar. 10:08am), noon but requiring mandatory reservation in first class (ar. 3:08pm) and 6:25pm (ar. 9:08pm). Other trains depart Venice S.L. at 9:52am express(ar. 1:22pm), 9:52am (ar. 1:22pm), 11:25am change at Bologna (ar. 3:20pm), 1:25pm (ar. 4:40pm), 2:25pm change at Bologna (ar. 5:46pm), 3:25pm change at Bologna (ar. 6:46pm) and 5:25pm change at Bologna (ar. 8:46pm).

To Milan, an InterCity departs Venice-Mestre at 8:21am (ar. Centrale 10:55am) and 12:10pm (ar. Centrale 2:55pm). The earliest express leaves Venice S.L. at 10:45am (ar. Centrale 1:45pm). Later expresses leave Venice S.L. at 12:45pm, 2:45pm, 4:45pm, 5:29pm and 6:45pm. To make connections in Milan, the rail hub from Italy to northern Europe, try to take the early 8:21am departure. See Milan for departures from Milan.

To Ravenna, take any train to Ferrara which is a stop on trains between Venice and Florence; then change to a train to Ravenna for the remaining 74 km. Through trains Venice to Ravenna (direction Rimini), and lower category than "fast" depart Venice S.L. at 10:25am second class only (ar. 1:27pm), 11:25am (ar. 3:08pm), 2:25pm (ar. 5:22pm), and 5:25pm second class only (ar. 9:31pm).

To Rome, all the trains to Florence also go to Rome with the exception of the 1:25pm departure which ends in Florence. For InterCity trains, arrival time in Rome is two hours and 19 minutes later. The others arrive in a little under three hours.

To Chamonix, France, an InterCity leaves Venice-Mestre only at 8:21am and arrives in Milan Centrale at 10:55am. Change trains to an express for Geneva which leaves Milan Centrale at 12:20pm and arrives Martigny at 3:39pm. Change to private railway to Chamonix. See Chamonix for schedule.

To Innsbruck and Munich, in general take a train to Verona and then change to an express over the scenic Brenner Pass, through Austria and into Germany. A good through express train leaves Venice S.L. at 10:55am (ar. Innsbruck 6pm, ar. Munich 8:12pm.). A through train overnight to Munich leaves Venice S.L. at 9:30pm (ar. Munich 6:16am).

To Paris, an overnight international express leaves Venice S.L. at 2:45pm (ar. Paris Lyon 6:40am).

To Switzerland, the best train is EuroCity Monteverdi, departing Venice S.L. at 2:10pm (ar. Brig 7:48pm, Sion 8:17pm, Geneva Cornavin 9:47pm).

To Salzburg, take any train for Vienna but then change at Villach unless the train has through cars. The Gondoliere Express leaving Venice S.L. at 7am has through cars to Salzburg, arriving 3:49pm.

To Vienna (Wien), the best train is the EuroCity Romulus that leaves Venice-Mestre only at 12:16pm and arrives Vienna Sudbahnhof at 8:38pm. For an overnight run, the international express Remus leaves Venice-Mestre only at 12:44am and arrives Vienna Sudbahnhof at 9:05am. Other options are the Austria-Italy express which departs Venice S.L. at 8:35pm and arrives Vienna Sudbahnhof at 6:53am, and the Gondoliere Express leaving Venice S.L. at 7am and arriving Wien Sudbahnhof at 6pm. Any train leaving Venice S.L. will pick up at Venice-Mestre 10 minutes later.

RAVENNA

Ravenna dazzles the visitor with the finest mosaics of early Christian art in Europe. It became capital of the Roman Empire when Honorius left Rome for Ravenna in 402 A.D. Outside Ravenna, at Marina di Ravenna and Porto Corsini fishermen enjoy breakwaters extending two km. into the sea. Ten km. from Ravenna at Lido Adriano is the International Center of Studies for Mosaics which offers two week classes throughout the summer for an instruction and materials fee of L200,000. Housing is available in campgrounds, apartments, pensiones and the youth hostel. For information write directly to Assessorato All'Istruzione del Comune di Ravenna, Piazza del Popolo, 48100 Ravenna, Italy.

Stazione F.S. is east of the central square, Piazza del Popolo, a seven block walk. Buses leave from the square in front of the station. The tourist office, Via S. Vitale 2, is four blocks from Piazza del Popolo. It's easier to go directly to a campground and pick up a free map there. No campgrounds are in Ravenna itself, but the beach towns of Ravenna (starting from the north and going south) of Casal Borsetti, Marina Romea, Porto Corsini, Marina di Ravenna, Punta Marina, Lido Adriano, Lido di Dante, Lido di Classe and Lido di Savio, offer numerous large resort campgrounds, most accommodating between 600 and 2000 people. All campgrounds remain open only May through September. The highest rates are charged during high season from the second week in July through the third week in August. High season fees are generally adult/L3500-L6000 and camping site/L6000-L8000. Often a lower price is charged for a site for a small tent if it is specifically requested. All campgrounds are linked to Ravenna by ATM buses which leave from the square in front of the train station. Bus fare is L800 and the campgrounds take 20 to 40 minutes to reach.

Lido di Dante

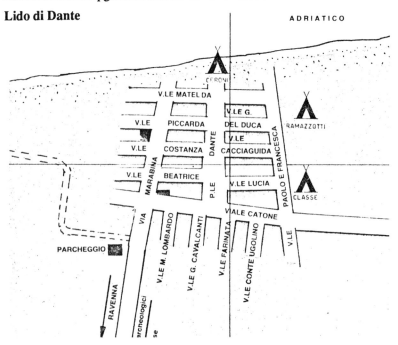

The only small campground in the area is simple **Camping Ceroni**, Via le Matelda 245, in **Lido Di Dante**, 10 km. from Ravenna. The camp is next to the beach and takes 140 people, charging adult/L3100, site/L5400.

Only 8 km. from Ravenna is Lido Adriano, the resort before Lido di Dante. **Camping Adriano**, Via dei Campeggi 7, charges adult/L4900 and small tent/L5200. All facilities including free hot showers, store, restaurant, pizzeria, 2 swimming pools, German language TV room, windsurfing and sailing school, stage with shows, and excursions.

Marina di Ravenna is the closest resort requiring only a 15 to 20-minute bus ride. In Marina di Ravenna on viale delle Nazioni on the other side of the road from the beach, the first camp, **Piomboni**, charges adult/L4600 and camping site/L7500 and has automatic washing machines. The next camp, **Rivaverde**, charges adult/L4450 and camping site/L8000. Several ATM bus lines stop at Marina di Ravenna. The earliest bus leaves at 5:30am and the latest at 10:30pm. The market is held Wednesday and on Saturday afternoon in town, where you will also find foreign exchange, post office, stores and restaurants.

Oasi Camping is composed of 5 campgrounds situated 17 km. from Ravenna along the coast between Casal Borsetti and the mouth of the river Lamone. The least expensive are Camping Villaggio Pineta, Via Spallazzi 5, adult/L3900, site/L7300, and Camping Reno, Via Spallazzi 11, adult/L4180 and site/L6970. (All fees are plus taxes.) The ATM bus line is Linea Ravenna - Marina Romea - Casal Borsetti. Earliest departure from the square opposite the Ravenna train station is 7:20am and latest is 7pm. Return buses leave Casal Borsetti between 6:50am and 7:40pm. The market is held Wednesday, Saturday and Sunday in this small fishing port. Also in town are post office, foreign exchange, restaurants and stores. A moped can be rented on Via Spallazzi.

FOOD   A covered market is in the center of Ravenna at Piazza A. Costa, near Via Cavour. The open market is at Piazza della Resistenza.

Train Schedules   Ravenna is on a minor rail line and doesn't enjoy very frequent service. The closest town on the main rail line is Faenza, which is enroute to Florence. See "To Florence" for departure times. Though the distance is longer, better service is available on the rail line to Ferrara. See "To Venice" for departure times.

To Brindisi, take the train to Rimini and then change for Brindisi. Trains leave Ravenna for Rimini at 7:29am (ar. 8:20am), 8:36am (ar. 9:30am), 9:45am (ar. 10:39am), 10:38am (ar. 11:42am) 1:32pm (ar. 2:30pm), 3:23am (ar. 4:27pm), 7:07pm (ar. 8:10pm) 7:54pm (ar. 8:49pm) and 9:36pm (ar. 10:38pm). Outside of May 31 to September 26, departures are reduced.   For Brindisi, trains leave Rimini at 9am express--approx. Jun 26-Sep 6 only--(ar. 5:41pm) and 9:53am InterCity (ar. 5:02pm). There are later departures, but they don't arrive in time to make ferry connections.

To Florence, the selection is poor. An all second class train leaves at 4pm (ar. 7:01pm) and 6:30pm (ar. 10:03pm).

To Venice, trains leave at 7:53am (ar. 10:44am), 10:30am (ar. 1:44pm), 1:06pm (ar. 4:44pm), 4:32pm (ar. 8:44pm) and 6:35pm (ar. 9:44pm).

FLORENCE (FIRENZE)

Almost everything of interest in this lovely city of the Italian Renaissance can be reached on foot without very long distances. The only bus that needs to be taken is the one to the campground. This is indeed a town where the early bird gets the worm when applied to the Uffizi and Academia Galleries where you must arrive by the opening time of 9am to beat the long lines in July and August. By 9:15am, tour buses will have arrived and lines formed a block long. In the past when lines have become too long, the Uffizi has extended its closing time.

310

Florence - Train Station and Campground

1) - CHIESA DI S.CROCE
2) - CHIESA DI S.LORENZO E CAPPELLE MEDICEE
3) - CHIESA E MUSEO DI S.MARCO
4) - ACCADEMIA BELLE ARTI (DAVID)
5) - CHIESA DI S.M.NOVELLA
6) - GALLERIA DEGLI UFFIZI
7) - BARGELLO (MUSEO NAZIONALE)
8) - PALAZZO PITTI E GIARDINO DI BOBOLI
9) - CHIESA DI S.SPIRITO
10) - PALAZZO VECCHIO
11) - DUOMO, BATTISTERO E CAMPANILE DI GIOTTO
12) - STAZIONE CENTRALE
13) - CAMPING

TRAIN STATION   The Station, known variously as Santa Maria Novella, Firenze S.M.N. and Stazione Centrale, is downtown.   A handy small booklet, Principali Treni, free from the train information window, contains schedules for major train lines within Italy.

Station Orientation   With your back to the tracks, you will find an exit to your left, to your right and straight ahead.   On the right, train information and the second class waiting room are across the aisle. Restrooms are near track 5.   On the left across the aisle are a newstand (which sells bus tickets), the first class waiting room, a self-service cafeteria and a tourist office.   On the left by track 16 is luggage checking which is open 24 hours and charges L800, and a pharmacy.   If you go out the exit on the left, you will find one group of bus stops and an ATAF ticket booth. From the tracks walking straight ahead, you will pass train ticket windows on the right, see an exchange office on the left and by turning right come to the reservation (prenotazione) windows.   If you go out the door you will see a parking area and across the plaza on the right is the SITA terminal for long distance buses.   Straight ahead is the busy intersection, the station plaza. **The bus stop for bus 13 (black) for the municipal camp is across the street, and reached via underground passage beneath the plaza.**

ORIENTATION   Florence is divided by the River Arno.   The train station, main market and most of the important museums, churches and galleries are on one side, while the Pitti Palace, American Express and municipal campground are across the river.   The most famous bridge across the Arno is the Ponte Vecchio with its shops and ornamental facade.   The landmark of Florence is the Duomo (Cathedral) and its accompanying Baptistery, which you will pass on the bus if you stay at the municipal campground.

TOURIST OFFICE   An office with lines is in the train station, and a small glass booth without a line is outside on the station plaza.   To reach either, after leaving the tracks, turn left and the tourist office is just on the other side of the large self-service cafeteria.   For the booth, keep going and leave the station.   Then turn right and you will see the kiosk ahead.   Specifically request their booklets *Florence for the Young* and the pink *One, three, five days in Florence* which contains a much better map than the one dispensed to most people.   They also offer a folder listing opening hours of museums and galleries and current fees.   A third branch is by the Duomo (Cathedral) and generally doesn't have a line.   Also, the municipal campground distributes a free map.

CITY TRANSPORTATION   A bus ride in Florence costs L600.   Tickets can't be obtained on the bus, but must be bought before boarding at the ATAF kiosk outside Stazione Centrale or at the Piazza del Duomo 57r, newspaper/tobacco stands, some bars or the municipal campground.   Once inside the bus, stamp your ticket in the machine provided.

CAMPGROUNDS   Both campgrounds in this tremendously popular city are crowded in July and August.   Italiani e Stranieri is sponsored by the city and has a capacity of 960 persons.   Villa Camerata is on the grounds of the youth hostel and can hold 220 persons.

The municipal campground is the largest. Camping Italiani e Stranieri/Parco Communale di Campeggio at 80 Viale Michelangelo, spreads across a hillside overlooking the city. During July and August, often tents will be separated by only five to ten meters. This isn't all bad as it assures that you're going to meet your neighbors, and they are ever changing as some depart and others take their place. No backpackers are ever turned away. Apr-Oct; adult/L4500, tent/L4000. Maximum stay is 15 days.

Directions After leaving the tracks in the train station, turn left and go past the self-service cafeteria and the tourist office and leave the station. Then turn right and pass the glass tourist office booth up ahead. With your back to the end of the train station, you will see a main street (actually the station plaza, piazza Stazione) ahead of you. Bus 13 leaves every 20 minutes for the campground, but there are two bus number 13's, one red and one black, each making a circular route from opposite directions. The bus stop for bus 13 on the station side of the plaza is 13 red. Don't wait here but go down the steps under the street and catch bus 13 black from across the street. The shortest distance to camp is a 15-minute ride via bus 13 black which follows the route Piazza Stazione, Duomo, P.le Michelangiolo, Viale dei Colli and Pte. S. Niccolo. Try to sit on the right hand side to be able to follow the route and get off at the right place. Soon after the bus leaves the stop near the train station, it halts on the middle bus island of Via dei Pecori, the street diagonally across from the Baptistery of the Duomo, and the closest stop to Florence's landmark cathedral. About four minutes later, the bus stops at Piazza san Firenze where the Museo Nazionale (Bargello) is located. Then heading towards the Arno River, the bus stops outside the Museum of Science immediately before the river. Next the bus turns left and follows the River Arno, stopping before the bridge, Ponte Alle Grazie, which it then crosses. Once across, there is another bus stop and then the bus ride parallels the river and shortly turns inland to start climbing the hill. As it travels upward, on the right the bus passes tennis courts and an athletic field with bleachers. Then a stone wall comes into view and the camp stop is immediately beyond that. There is a clock, the tents below are visible, and the entrance is marked by a flagpole carrying two flags. If you miss the correct stop, the next one is the scenic turnoff at the crest of the hill and you can easily walk back down.

From camp to downtown A convenient bus back to town leaves at 7:45am, but many people prefer to hike directly down as it's a nice route away from the roads and takes only 15 minutes. To walk to town, turn right as you leave the campground and walk about two minutes slightly uphill to the scenic turnoff, a popular spot for tour buses. Near the large statue are two sets of broad stairs descending to the road below. Take the lefthand stairs as you face downtown and from there the path is obvious.

Facilities The camp terrain is hardpacked dirt with some grass and limited shrubbery of pines affording some shade. As the camp is on a hillside, it takes a practiced eye to select a nice flat campsite. Facilities include free hot showers, cold water in sinks for personal washing and sinks for handwashing clothes (no washing machine), hot water in dishwashing sinks, and store. Sample prices at the store are croissant/L700, roll/L300, milk/L700, and yoghurt/L950. A large covered patio outside the store has a jukebox and tables and chairs where you can cook, eat and enjoy a magnificent view of Florence. Checkout is 4pm. Registration is open 6am to midnight. Information office hours are 8am to 8pm. Travelers checks can be cashed between 8 and 10am without a fee.

The Youth Hostel Campground, Villa di Camerata shares the grounds of the youth hostel (ostello della gioventu) on Viale Augusto Righi, 2/4. Open all year; adult/L3900, 2-person tent/L4600, large tent/L6550. Take bus 17B from the train station, about a 25-minute ride. To find the stop, after leaving the tracks turn right and use that exit. After getting off the bus, there is a 10-minute walk up the private road leading to the Villa. Hot showers, store, restaurant.

Campground at Fiesole (pronounced fee-A-so-lay) If you absolutely can't stand a crowded campground and love to hike uphill in the hot sun with a pack, then Camping Panoramico above the villa-studded village of Fiesole is for you. Fees are adult/L6250 and tent/L4000.

Directions: Bus 7 goes to Fiesole at 6:30am, 6:50 and every 20 minutes until 9:25pm, and then 9:55pm, 10:25, 11:25 and 12:30am. From the Florence train station, leave the tracks, turn left and go outside. Cross to the cement island in the center and the stop for bus 7 is on the left. Buy a ticket (L600) at the ticket booth on the second island, or if it's closed, return to the station and buy one at the tabacchi counter. (Bus 7 also stops near the Duomo close to the Baptistery and at Piazza San Marco.) Ride the bus out of Florence and through the countryside as it climbs upward to the town of Fiesole, the last stop and where you get off. The trip takes 35 minutes. If you're lucky, at Fiesole you can transfer to bus 70 which runs every hour and stops only 300 meters from the camp. Otherwise, keep walking uphill beside the highway for about 25 minutes until the sign to the camp directs you to leave the highway and turn right, where you now have another 10-minute walk to the campground. (But what a view when you get there!)

Camping Panoramico is lovely, shady, cool and uncrowded, with a marvelous view of Florence and the surrounding countryside. Facilities include free hot showers, hot water in the sinks which are divided for semi-privacy, washing machine, store/cafe with tables and chairs provided, playground and a bird aviary with parakeets, guinea pigs and turtles.

In tiny downtown Fiesole itself are a tourist office, Roman theater and archeological museum (closed Monday), a notable cathedral and the Bandini Museum, all uncrowded and without the lines found in Florence.

FOOD The public market is indoors in the marble building on Piazza del Mercato Centrale about five blocks from the train station. The food counters are open only from 8am to 1pm, closed Sunday. Another food market is at Piazza S. Spirito, three blocks from the Pitti Palace and open mornings only, closed Sunday.

SHOPPING The outdoor shopping area is along Via dell' Ariento and Piazza S. Lorenzo. We were able to bargain successfully on a leather jacket, but had no luck with T-shirts. The flea Market (mercator delle pulci) is on Piazza de' Ciompi, four blocks from Casa Buonarroti at the intersection of Borgo Allegri and via Pietrapiana, open daily 9am to 7pm.

AMERICAN EXPRESS The office Universalturismo on via degli Speziali, 7r, near piazza della Repubblica, does not handle American Express client mail. For that you must go to American Express across the Arno River on Via Guicciardini, the street that you're are on after crossing Ponte Vecchio, the bridge with shops and reserved for pedestrians. However, Universalturismo will change any brand travelers check for only the L500 bank tax, whereas the other office of American Express charges an additional L500 for EACH non American Express check besides long lines.

DAY TRIP TO SAN GIMIGNANO Only 55 km. southwest of Florence, this is a delightful 14th century town whose medieval appearance has been preserved. Ramparts surround the town and 14 towers have survived. You can get most of the way to small San Gimignano by train, and then transfer to a connecting bus. The town has an excellent, accessible and uncrowded campground, useful for escaping the crowded one in Florence. Camping Boschetto is at the road to Poggibonsi, 2-1/2 km. downhill from Porta San Giovanni, where the buses arrive. Buses (L500) go to camp or you may wish to walk. Open April through September. Fees are adult/L3000 and tent/L1500. The shady, pretty site offers free hot showers, hot water in sinks, store, restaurant, indoor lounge with television and tennis courts. The market is Thursday and Saturday morning at Piazza del Duomo.

    Directions To get to San Gimignano, take any train to Siena and get off before Siena at Poggibonsi, 80 minutes out of Florence. See "Day trip to Siena" for departure times. In front of the Poggibonsi train station, frequent buses depart for the small remaining distance to San Gimignano, a 20-minute ride. Buses arrive at Porta San Giovanni and there is a tourist office nearby and also one at Piazza del Duomo, in the center of town. The tourist office sells bus tickets and has the bus schedule. Trains leave from Poggibonsi to Florence at 8:27am, 9:10am, 12:02pm, 1:57pm, 5:02pm (change at Empoli), 7:07pm, 8:01pm, 9:41pm and 11:08pm.

    If you don't have a train pass, you may wish to take the faster bus. It leaves from the SITA bus terminal at Via S. Caterina da Siena, 15r. With your back to the train station and facing the station plaza, SITA is across the plaza on the righthand corner. The fare is L5000 one way, requires a change of buses at Poggibonsi and takes one hour and 40 minutes to get all the way to San Gimignano. The woman at the information counter in the SITA terminal will give you a schedule of buses from Florence to Poggibonsi and the times of the connecting bus to San Gimignano. To Poggibonsi there are nonstop buses taking 50 minutes and buses that stop at each town and take 90 minutes. The nonstop buses pick up at the main SITA terminal, Porta Romano and Galluzzo and then go direct on the Superstrada (highway). The two nonstop buses that allow enough time in the village leave Florence at 7:10am and 10:10am. Inquire at SITA information for the bus bay number of the departure you want. The last two nonstop buses returning from Poggibonsi to Florence, leave Poggibonsi at 6:06pm and 8:56pm. The 8:56pm bus is the last departure from Poggibonsi and arrives in Florence at 9:45pm. (If the bus is missed, the train has later departures.) Do not confuse this public bus route with the day excursion to Siena and San Gimignano offered by SITA for L38,000.

    If you are staying at the municipal campground in Florence, there's no point in going all the way to the main SITA terminal by the train station as the SITA bus picks up at Porta Romana ten minutes after the main terminal. Instead take bus 13 (black) from in front of the campground. It will continue uphill to the turnoff and then start downhill and go to Porta Romana before continuing to the river and the train station. The nonstop buses for Poggibonsi leave Porta Romana at 7:15am and 10:15am. Likewise on the return trip, get off at Porta Romana, the stop before the main terminal and after the stop at Galluzzo.

DAY TRIP TO FIESOLE Though Fiesole doesn't compare with San Gimignano, it makes a pleasant and relaxing day trip through the Florentine countryside to an attractive tiny town with only a handful of tourists, and offers a chance to see a Roman arena as well. To get there, see directions under "Campground in Fiesole" in the campground section of Florence. This trip can also be made in a half day if necessary. Avoid Mondays when the Roman Arena and Archeological Museum are closed.

DAY TRIP TO PISA The Leaning Tower draws people to the famous square of Pisa. Most of the trains carry only second class coaches and are either "fast" category or no category. Departure times are 7:10am (ar. 8:05am), 7:30am (ar. 8:25am), 7:55am (ar. 8:59am), 9am (ar. 9:54am), 9:20am (ar. 10:30am), 11:20am (ar. 12:38pm), noon (ar. 12:54pm), 12:25pm (ar. 1:45pm), 1:10pm (ar. 2:40pm), 2:20pm (ar. 3:42pm), 3pm (ar. 3:54pm), 4pm (ar. 4:54pm), 4:30pm (ar. 5:42pm) and 5pm (ar. 5:54pm). See "Pisa" for more information.

DAY TRIP TO SIENA Siena is reknowned for its harmony between the red clay hills and its medieval architecture. Trains carry second class coaches only. Trip is about 90 minutes. Departure times are 8:10am, 11:42am, 12:25pm (change at Empoli), 2:15pm, 3:30pm, 5:10pm, 6:10pm, 7:10pm and 8:10pm. As a full day is needed in Siena, the 8:10am departure is best. See "Siena" for more information.

To Brindisi, you must either go to Bologna or Rome and there change trains for Brindisi. There's only one train you can take by day and still arrive in Brindisi for the 10pm ferry departure to Greece. The train leaves from Rome. To reach Rome, either leave Florence on an express at 9:24am (ar. Rome Termini 11:53am) or on an InterCity at 10:17am (ar. Rome Termini 12:27pm.). Then depart from Rome Termini for Brindisi on an express at 1:05pm (ar. Brindisi 8:54pm). This leaves sufficient time to walk to the port, pay the fees and board the ferry. For an overnight trip to Brindisi, the best way is to go to Bologna and there change trains for Brindisi. Either leave Florence on an InterCity at 8:29pm (ar. 9:32pm) or an express at 9:08pm (ar. 10:15pm). Depart Bologna either on an express leaving at 9:55pm (ar. 8:13am) or an express at 11:24pm (ar. 9:01am).

To Milan (Centrale), InterCity trains leave at 7am (ar. 9:50am), 10:19am (ar. 1:10pm), 11:19am (ar. 2:10pm), 3:19pm (ar. 6:10pm), 4:19pm (ar. 7:10pm), 5:19pm (ar. 8:10pm) and 6:19pm (ar. 9:10pm). Express trains leave at 7:23am (ar. 10:25am), 8:49am (ar. 12:10pm), 9:12am (ar. 12:20pm), 9:38am (ar. 12:55pm), 2:44pm (ar. 5:45pm) and 7:42pm (ar. Lambrate Station 10:55pm).

To Riviera di Levante, take a train to PISA and there change to a train to La Spezia or Sestri Levante (direction Genoa). See "Day Trip to Pisa" for train departure times from Florence to PISA. Trains from Pisa to Sestri Levante leave at 12:08pm (ar. 1:58pm), 1:23pm (ar. 4:33pm), 2:08pm (ar. 3:52pm), 4:20pm (ar. 7:02pm) and 5:27pm (ar. 7:11pm). These trains also stop enroute at La Spezia.

To Rome (Termini), Intercity trains leave at 10:27am (ar. 12:27am), 10:55am (ar. 1:05pm), 1:55pm (ar. 4:05pm), 3:17pm first class only and reservation required (ar. 5:27pm), 3:55pm (ar. 6:05pm), 4:55pm (ar. 7:05pm), 6:55pm (ar. 9:05pm) 7:55pm (ar. 10:05pm) and 8:55pm (ar. 11:05pm). Express trains leave at 7:26am (ar. 9:55am), 9:24am (ar. 11:53am), 1:31pm (ar. 4:25pm), 3:29pm (ar. 5:50pm) and 5:24pm (ar. 7:53pm).

To Venice (S.L.), a EuroCity train leaves at 9:29am (ar. Venice-Mestre only 11:59am). InterCity trains leave at 2:24pm (ar. 5:05pm) and 4:29pm first class only and reservation required (ar. 7:32pm) and 8:29pm (ar. 11:10pm). Express and fast trains leave at 7:23am (ar. 10:44am), 10:19am change at Bologna (ar. 1:44pm), 11:25am (ar. 2:44pm), 3:19pm change trains at Bologna (ar. 6:44pm), 5pm (ar. 8:44pm) and 6:25pm (ar. 9:44pm).

PISA

It's 294 steps to the top of the famous Leaning Tower (Torre Pendente). The Tower is part of Piazza del Duomo, the Michelin-rated three-star Cathedral Square. **Stazione Centrale** is outside the walls of the original settlement. A branch of the tourist office is at the station. To reach the Leaning Tower, take bus 1 from in front of the station.

    Camping Pisa (Torre Pendente), Viale Delle Cascine 86, is several blocks outside the walls of the old town, but within walking distance of the Leaning Tower. Open April through October. Fees are adult/L6000 and tent/L3000. From outside the train station, take bus 4 which leaves every 15 minutes. The ride is 15 minutes. Camp has hot showers, store, snack bar.

    Pisa is about an hour ride from both Florence and the Riviera di Levante. Because there is about hourly train service on these routes, Pisa is conveniently seen on daytrips from either of these cities.

SIENA

The central core of lovely Siena is restricted to foot traffic and the entire medieval city blends with the red clay hills. The town rates Michelin three stars. Siena is on a minor train line that carries second class coaches only. To reach the heart of Siena, Piazza del Campo, take a bus (L500) from in front of the train station, get off at Piazza Gramsci and follow the signs to P. del Campo.

    Camping Siena Colleverde, strada Scacciapensieri 47, is 2 km. from the center and located behind the station at the road to Hotel Scacciapensieri. Open Apr-Oct; adult/L6650, tent free. Take any bus from the station to P. Gramsci at the edge of the pedestrian zone. Then change to bus 8 for the campground. Last departure is 10pm. The camp is good and attractive with shade trees, grass, sinks with hot water, hot showers, store, restaurant, and lounge.

    To Florence, trains leave at 6:37am (ar. 8am), 8am (ar. 9:25am), 8:48am (ar. 10:10am), 11:36am (ar. Empoli 12:41pm and change trains, ar. Florence 1:25pm), 1:30pm (ar. 3:12pm), 4:34pm (ar. Empoli 3:55pm, change trains, ar. Florence 6:20pm), 6:34pm (ar. 7:59pm), 7:36pm (ar. 9:12pm), 9:18pm (ar. 10:36pm) and 10:40pm (ar. 12:17am).

    To Rome, through trains to Rome leave at 8:05am (ar. 12:38pm), 2:58pm (ar. 6:35pm) and 7:11pm (ar. 10:35pm).

    To Riviera di Levante, take the trains listed for Florence but change trains at Empoli for Pisa. At Pisa, change trains again for the towns of the Riviera di Levante.

ROME (ROMA)

The eternal city is monumental, huge and requires at least five days to see. Though there is a good subway and frequent buses, walking is still the best way to rub shoulders with this ancient town and its intimate byways. The pedestrian only zones provide fine strolling where you can leisurely stop, look, understand and submerge yourself in the Roman culture. A good area for this starts in front of the piazza del Pantheon. As an added bonus, wandering forward from the Pantheon you're bound to come upon the nearby modern Giolitti ice cream parlor at degli Uffici del Vicario, 40, which is acclaimed as having the best ice cream in Italy (from L3500 and up,

closed Monday).   The frequently encountered letters--SPQR stand for
Senatus Populusque Romanus or "The Roman Senate and People."

TRAIN STATIONS   Most trains arrive at Stazione Termini (Terminal
Station), an enormous building with almost every conceivable service
including a tourist office, foreign exchange, post office, various eating
establishments, and downstairs the *albergo diurno*, at which you can grab a
quick shower for a fee, or pay a substantial charge to use their restroom.
The albergo diurno is the most expensive place to store luggage for a day,
charging a high L1100. The procedure here is to first pay the cashier and
then take the receipt to the counter which stays open 8am to 2am.

A cheaper baggage check charging only L800 is upstairs on the
ground floor across from track 1 on the right side as you leave the tracks. In
this same area are restrooms and waiting rooms. After passing through the
gates separating the track area from the rest of the station, you will see a
tourist information window across from track 1.   Usually this window
doesn't have a line because it is kept closed unless there is a client, but the
person inside is there to answer questions and has a free map of Rome to
distribute. Regardless of your age, be sure to specifically ask for their free
publication, *Young Rome*, which serves as a mini guidebook and describes
good walking tours.   Other useful free publications include *Here Rome*
which lists eating establishments and describes monuments, churches and
museums and *Tourist Itineraries in the Province of Rome.*   Most
campgrounds provide a free map, and many shops and travel agencies stock
the free *Taxi News* map of Rome which is supported by advertising.

On the ground floor but looking across the concourse, you will see
two red and white signs with the letter M, indicating stairs down to the
metropolitana (subway) level. The downstairs level is Stazione Termini of
the Metropolitana. There are two lines of the Metropolitana, the newer line
A and the older line B, and signs directing you to them.

Returning to the ground floor of Stazione Termini, beyond the metro
signs you will come to another large lobby where the ticket and reservation
windows are located as well as a post office and bank. Outside the front of
the station in the large square are the stops for the buses.

A few trains stop only at the smaller Tiburtina Station and don't
come into Termini Station at all. A train's arrival and departure station is
noted in the timetables. Actually, arrival in Rome is easier at Tiburtina
Station because of its size and simplicity, although the services of Termini
are not available. Bus 9 outside Tiburtina goes to Stazione Termini.

PUBLIC TRANSPORTATION   Buses, a tram and the subway,
metropolitana, will serve your needs while in Rome. Any ticket valid for a
bus is also valid on the tram. A one calendar day ticket valid on buses and
metro costs L2800, a half day ticket valid only on buses between either
6:00am and 2pm or 2pm to midnight is L1000, and an 8-day ticket for buses
only for L10000 can be purchased at ATAC bus kiosks such as the one
outside Stazione Termini in piazza dei Cinquecento or at Stazione Tiburtina.
A single bus or metro ticket costs L700 and a combination single bus and
metro ticket is L1000. Tickets must be bought before boarding the bus or
metro and are sold at tobacco shops, bars or newsstands which display the
ATAC sign. After boarding the bus, stamp your own single ticket in the red
machine. Bus riding is on the honor system enforced by inspectors who

reputedly don't like riding the crowded buses which is why no visitor has ever seen one. After the last bus leaves sometime between 11pm and midnight, special night buses operate infrequently, and their schedule is posted on the green post at each bus stop.

The relatively new metropolitana has two lines, A and B which operate until 11:30pm. Metro stations are marked with the letter M and tickets are sold at tobacconists and newstands by the metro or from vending machines inside. Entrances to the metro are inside Stazione Termini while city buses depart from in front of Stazione Termini. The phone book contains a subway and bus map in its *Tutto Citta* section.

There is also a train, called both Cristofo Colombo and Roma-Lido which connects Rome to the Lido, its beach town, and on which neither a Eurailpass nor day ticket is valid.

Tram 30, a streetcar, can provide a "free" sightseeing tour of the city if you already happen to have a day or half day pass. You can catch it at Piazza Risorgimento, near St. Peter's and four blocks from Otaviano subway stop on line A. It crosses the Tiber and passes through some interesting sections of Rome, past University City, the Basilica of St. Lawrence, St. John Lateran and to the Colosseum, where it's a good idea to end your tour. On the other hand, you'll no doubt be venturing into these areas anyway as you visit the city's many attractions so those short of time might forego this ride.

Metro Line A

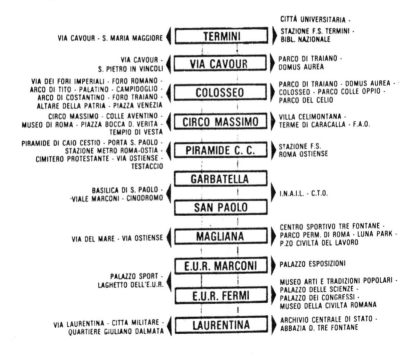

Metro Line B

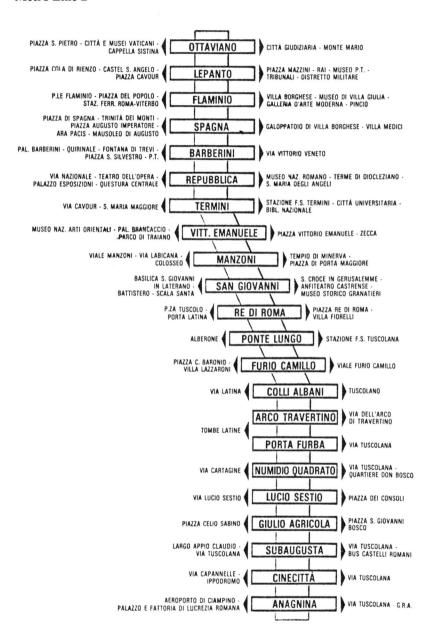

PIAZZA S. PIETRO - CITTÀ E MUSEI VATICANI - CAPPELLA SISTINA ◄ **OTTAVIANO** ► CITTÀ GIUDIZIARIA - MONTE MARIO

PIAZZA COLA DI RIENZO - CASTEL S. ANGELO - PIAZZA CAVOUR ◄ **LEPANTO** ► PIAZZA MAZZINI - RAI - MUSEO P.T. - TRIBUNALI - DISTRETTO MILITARE

P.LE FLAMINIO - PIAZZA DEL POPOLO - STAZ. FERR. ROMA-VITERBO ◄ **FLAMINIO** ► VILLA BORGHESE - MUSEO DI VILLA GIULIA - GALLERIA D'ARTE MODERNA - PINCIO

PIAZZA DI SPAGNA - TRINITÀ DEI MONTI - PIAZZA AUGUSTO IMPERATORE - ARA PACIS - MAUSOLEO DI AUGUSTO ◄ **SPAGNA** ► GALOPPATOIO DI VILLA BORGHESE - VILLA MEDICI

PAL. BARBERINI - QUIRINALE - FONTANA DI TREVI - PIAZZA S. SILVESTRO - P.T. ◄ **BARBERINI** ► VIA VITTORIO VENETO

VIA NAZIONALE - TEATRO DELL'OPERA - PALAZZO ESPOSIZIONI - QUESTURA CENTRALE ◄ **REPUBBLICA** ► MUSEO NAZ. ROMANO - TERME DI DIOCLEZIANO - S. MARIA DEGLI ANGELI

VIA CAVOUR - S. MARIA MAGGIORE ◄ **TERMINI** ► STAZIONE F.S. TERMINI - CITTÀ UNIVERSITARIA - BIBL. NAZIONALE

MUSEO NAZ. ARTI ORIENTALI - PAL. BRANCACCIO - PARCO DI TRAIANO ◄ **VITT. EMANUELE** ► PIAZZA VITTORIO EMANUELE - ZECCA

VIALE MANZONI - VIA LABICANA - COLOSSEO ◄ **MANZONI** ► TEMPIO DI MINERVA - PIAZZA DI PORTA MAGGIORE

BASILICA S. GIOVANNI IN LATERANO - BATTISTERO - SCALA SANTA ◄ **SAN GIOVANNI** ► S. CROCE IN GERUSALEMME - ANFITEATRO CASTRENSE - MUSEO STORICO GRANATIERI

P.ZA TUSCOLO - PORTA LATINA ◄ **RE DI ROMA** ► PIAZZA RE DI ROMA - VILLA FIORELLI

ALBERONE ◄ **PONTE LUNGO** ► STAZIONE F.S. TUSCOLANA

PIAZZA C. BARONIO - VILLA LAZZARONI ◄ **FURIO CAMILLO** ► VIALE FURIO CAMILLO

VIA LATINA ◄ **COLLI ALBANI** ► TUSCOLANO

ARCO TRAVERTINO ► VIA DELL'ARCO DI TRAVERTINO

TOMBE LATINE ◄ **PORTA FURBA** ► VIA TUSCOLANA

VIA CARTAGINE ◄ **NUMIDIO QUADRATO** ► VIA TUSCOLANA - QUARTIERE DON BOSCO

VIA LUCIO SESTIO ◄ **LUCIO SESTIO** ► PIAZZA DEI CONSOLI

PIAZZA CELIO SABINO ◄ **GIULIO AGRICOLA** ► PIAZZA S. GIOVANNI BOSCO

LARGO APPIO CLAUDIO - VIA TUSCOLANA ◄ **SUBAUGUSTA** ► VIA TUSCOLANA - BUS CASTELLI ROMANI

VIA CAPANNELLE - IPPODROMO ◄ **CINECITTÀ** ► VIA TUSCOLANA

AEROPORTO DI CIAMPINO - PALAZZO E FATTORIA DI LUCREZIA ROMANA ◄ **ANAGNINA** ► VIA TUSCOLANA - G.R.A.

Piazzale Flaminio - enroute to some campgrounds

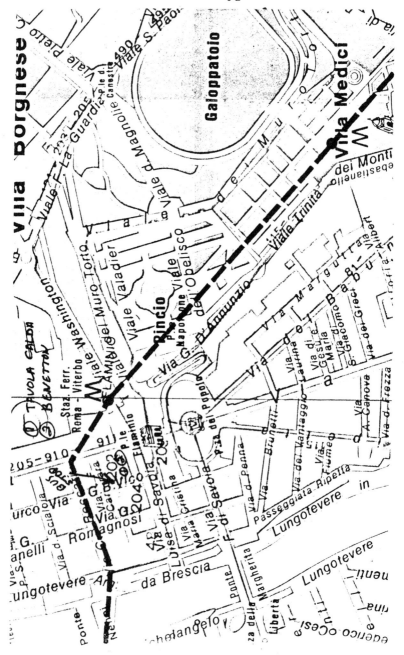

CAMPGROUNDS   About 11 campgrounds serve travelers visiting Rome, but we are including only those that are convenient for the rail traveler. **Camping Flaminio** is easy to reach with public transportation, quiet and large enough to accommodate all comers and still result in 20 to 30 meters between tents even during the busy part of July.   **Camping Salaria** is new, has frequent public transportion to downtown Rome, is inexpensive because it is offering a special rate to users of this guidebook, has 32 hot showers (more than Flaminio even though it takes fewer campers) and makes an excellent choice for those not addicted to an automatic washing machine. The other campgrounds are not likely to be crowded either because there are so many good choices in the Rome area. We have omitted Camping Pineta Fabulous and Capitol Camping Club because the commute is 1-1/2 hours.

Camping Flaminio, via Flaminia Nuova, at Km 8.2, is one of the best camps for tent campers in Rome and is open all year.   Fees are adult/L6100 and tent/L2800. The somewhat grassy and tree shaded grounds extend into several separated areas including three used solely by backpackers.   Facilities include free hot showers, washing machine and clotheslines, and a large terrace outside the store and restaurant providing picnic tables and benches for cooking and eating meals. Flaminio is easily reached by public bus, and the stop is immediately across from the camp, plus a few minutes walk between the entrance and the actual camping area which is set well back from the traffic and noise of the highway.

Directions From either Stazione Termini or Stazione Tibertina, you must first reach Piazzale Flaminio and then transfer to a bus to the campground. From Stazione Termini the fastest way to get to P.le Flaminio is by subway, the Metropolitana. After leaving the track area, look for the red and white signs with the letter M which indicate the stairs to the lower metro level.   Once downstairs, follow the signs to line A, and select the platform marked **Ottaviano** which is the end station in the direction you want to go.   Assuming you have a goodly amount of change, you can purchase your ticket from the vending machines on this lower level. Otherwise it can be bought from a news kiosk in the station. After the metro leaves Termini, it will stop at Republica, Barberini and Spagna and then you get off at the fourth stop, **Flaminio**. You are now beneath P.le Flaminio. To exit closest to where you'll be catching the bus, follow the *uscita* (exit) signs marked P.le Flaminio and then choose Via Flaminio. This brings you up to street level of the square. While you're at P.le Flaminio, note the archways at one side of the square. These mark the entrance to the Piazza del Popolo. If you were to pass through the archways, on your left would be the large park, the Villa Borghese and straight ahead numerous shopping streets. The tobacconist in the plaza sells bus tickets in multiples only and requires exact change. Refer to the map for the location of the bus stop for buses 202, 204 or 205, on the street Vico.   The last bus from P.le Flaminio for the campground leaves around midnight. Then there are a few later nighttime buses. Get off the bus when you see the Phillips sign in large blue block lettering upon a white background on top of a rectangular office building on the right side of the highway.   The entrance to the camp is immediately across the road.

Lucky is the person who arrives in Rome at the small Stazione Tibertina. Pass through the station, purchase your bus ticket outside at the kiosk near the buses and take any bus that lists P.le Flaminio on its route, such as bus 490 or 495. Get off at P.le Flaminio, which is easily recognized by the large stone arches on your left and the signs for the metro with the letter M. Then transfer to bus 202, 204 or 205 and follow directions from P.le Flaminio above under Stazione Termini. However, should you be so fortunate as to ride bus 204 from Stazione Tibertina which only runs on Sunday, no transfer is necessary as the bus goes directly to camp.

Returning to downtown When leaving camp, only take buses 202, 204 or 205, NOT 203, as the latter does not take you to P.le Flaminio. The camp office sells only the day ticket for L2800 and the single bus ticket for L700. It doesn't sell the half day ticket for L1000 for buses only or the combination single bus/metro ticket for L1000. Once at the convenient P.le Flaminio, you can take the metro, bus or walk to many sightseeing attractions.

Facilities The office at the entrance will change traveler's checks and foreign currency. Hot showers are free; sinks have cold water only. To use the small washing machine adjacent to the restrooms, purchase a token at the store for L3000 including soap. The well stocked store is open 7:30am to 1pm and 3:30pm to 9pm daily and sells fresh rolls for L200, 125g plastic container of fruit-laced yoghurt for L900, 500 ml. of chocolate milk for L1000, can of lentils for L1000 and most other essentials. The camp restaurant serves a L12000 menu and is open from 7:30am to 11pm. Every night at 9:30pm, the owner shows older American movies on a small screen in the informal lounge next to the bar. This is especially fun for watching uninhibited European reactions to shows featuring such stock characters as cowboys (they cheer) or Nazis (they boo). There is no charge and you don't need to buy anything to drink either. The chalk blackboard outside the store posts the nightly movie which changes each day. Up the road from the store is the swimming pool. Address for camper's mail is Camping Flaminio; Via Flaminia Nuova, km. 821, 00191 Rome, ITALY, telephone 3279006.

Camping Salaria, Via Salaria 2141, is a new campground, 9 km. north of downtown. The camp operates from April through October. For 1989 the Director, Pasquale Carroccia, will give a discount upon request for readers of this book. Its regular prices are adult/L5500 and tent/L2900. From the square in front of Stazione Termini, take bus 319 to the last stop, Piazza Vescovio. Then change to bus 135 in Piazza Vescovio and get off at the last stop. Bus 135 travels along Via Magliana Sab, Viale Somali and then onto Via Salaria where the camp is situated in the suburb of Settebagni. The camp is 50 meters from where the bus lets you off. Both buses leave every 15 minutes.

The site is grass covered with shade trees. Registration office is open 7am to midnight and offers a free map of Rome and guided tours for a fee. Travelers checks can be cashed at the cashier, open 7am-noon and 4-8pm. Hot showers are included; sinks have cold water only. On the grounds you'll find a store (open 7am-10pm), restaurant (7am-midnight), swimming pool, playground and video-bar.

Roma Camping, Via Aurelia, km. 8,2 is 4 km. from the Vatican and 8 km.from downtown Rome. Open all year; adult/L6300, tent/L2750. From outside Stazione Termini take bus 64 to Ponte Vittorio, change to bus 46 and get off at Piazza Irnerio, and transfer to bus 246. The last bus 246 leaves at midnight. The camp is visible on the left side of the road before reaching the stop where you get off, and there is a half block walk to camp. The entire ride takes about one hour.

Checkout time is 1:30pm. The camp is in terraces and several small restrooms are scattered throughout the area. Amenities include hot showers, cold water in sinks, store and restaurant. To leave camp, bus 246 departs every 15 minutes and terminates at Largo Boccea where you can change to bus 46 to go to Saint Peters (San Pietro) and Piazza Venezia, bus 49 for the Vatican Museums, or bus 490 for Via Veneto and Piazza Croce Rossa (800 meters from Stazione Termini).

Camping Nomentano, Via delia Cesarina at the corner of Via Nomentano km. 11.5, is about 10 km. north of Rome. Open Apr-Oct; L5600/adult and L2900/tent. From the plaza outside in front of Stazione Termini, board bus 36 and transfer at Piazza Sempione to bus 337. Bus 60 also goes to the campground. The camp has free hot showers, hot water in sinks, store, restaurant and lounge with television.

Camping Tiber-Roma, Via Tiberina km. 1,400, is 1.5 km. from Prima Porta and 8 km. north of Rome. Open Mar 1 - Nov 10; adult/L6100, tent/L3200. A 10 percent reduction is given upon request when showing this guidebook.

From Stazione Termini, take metropolitana line A to Piazzale Flaminio (see directions under Camping Flaminio). Change to the small electric train, Roma Nord, to Prima Porta which leaves every 15 minutes (L700) with the last departure at 9:26pm. Or you can take bus 205 until midnight from Piazzale Flaminio to Prima Porta. From Prima Porta the camp minibus (L350) leaves for the campground every ten minutes between 8:10am and 1:10pm and then later in the afternoon between 3:00pm and 10pm. The camp minibus leaves camp for Prima Porta every 5 minutes from 8am to 1pm and 3pm to 10pm.

The English-speaking office personnel will change travelers checks, and there is a box for outgoing mail, free use of an iron upon request and a free brochure with an updated train schedule and suggested sightseeing itineraries. The site has free hot showers, cold water in sinks, automatic washing machine (at office buy token for L3500 without soap), store (open 7am to 11pm), lounge, restaurant and separate disco. In the store a map is posted showing all bus and metro routes. Camper mail can be addressed to Camping Tiber, Via Tiberina km. 1,400, 00188 Prima Porta, Rome, ITALY.

Happy Camping, north of Rome at Via Prato della Corte 1915, is open March 15 to October 31; adult/L6500, tent/L3400. The management grants a 10 percent reduction in fees upon request when this guidebook is shown. From Stazione Termini, take metro line A to P.le Flaminio, change to the small train, Roma Nord, and get off at Prima Porta Station. The Happy Camping bus waits outside the station from 8am to 10pm. (For more detailed directions on reaching P.le Flaminio see Camping Flaminio, and for the Roma Nord train see Camping Tiber.)

The attractive site is grassy with shade trees. Facilities include store, restaurant, foreign exchange, swimming pool, free hot showers, hot water in wash basins and lounge with television.

Camping Seven Hills, Via Cassia 1216, is 4 km. north of Rome. Open Apr-Oct;adult/L6000, tent/L2900. From Stazione Termini, take the metropolitana line A to Piazzale Flaminio (see directions under Camping Flaminio) and change to bus 911 on Via Flaminia. The bus travels along Via

Flaminia and crosses the Tiber River on Ponte (bridge) Duca d'Aosta, turns right and parallels the river until Ponte (bridge) Milvio. Get off at Ponte Milvio and change to bus 201. Be sure to catch bus 201 going in the correct direction--the bus should be heading away from the river, rather than continuing on parallel to it in the same direction you were coming on bus 911. Ask the bus driver to let you off at Camping Seven Hills on Via Cassia from where the camp runs a minibus to the campground every half hour from 8am to 7pm.

The camp is divided into terraced sites and has office (7am-11pm), foreign exchange, store, restaurant, free hot showers, sinks with hot water, swimming pool and disco.

SIGHTSEEING   For budgeting purposes, figure that admission charges range from L3000 to L7500 with reductions for students. Many monuments can be viewed for free from outside and no admission is charged for churches, fountains and parks.

WALKING TOUR STARTING FROM P.LE FLAMINIO   In the piazzale you will notice a large archway, La Porta del Popolo or People's Gate. Pass through that archway into Piazza del Popolo (People's Square). Across the square on the left is the outdoor used book market (but English titles aren't carried). Of the three main streets across from the archway, choose the one on the left, Via dei Babouino and walk (or ride bus 81) for the nine blocks to Piazza di Spagna (the Spanish Steps). Now is a good time to check for mail at American Express in the Piazza if you left that address. If you go up the Spanish Steps you will come to the large park, Villa Borghese. Turn left and walk 200 meters to the viewpoint, Pincio, from which there is a view of Rome, St. Peter's, churches and palaces. Also within the large park are the excellent Etruscan museum in Villa Giulia and the Borghese Gallery. Returning to Piazza di Spagna, walk on the well known shopping street, Via Condotti, for 4 blocks until it intersects with Via del Corso. Turn left and walk 7 blocks to the sidestreet, Via de Sabini. Turn left onto this street which leads in two blocks to the famous Trevi Fountain. Find your way back to Via del Corso, the main street of Rome, and turn left and go four blocks to Piazza Venezia and the imposing Victor Emmanuel Monument. Walk down the right side of the monument as you face it, and take the steps leading to the Santa Maria d'Aracoeli Church of 1250. Leaving the church, you are in Piazza di Campideglio and the area of the Roman Forum. To return to P. le Flaminio, board bus 90 at Piazza Venezia.

COLOSSEUM/ROMAN FORUM   You can get here various ways. From P.le Flaminio, near the magazine stand, bus 90 will take you to Piazza Venezia, marked by the striking Victor Emmanuel monument. From there you can walk to the Roman Forum and then to the Colosseum or transfer to bus 85, 87 or 88 to go directly to the Colosseum. Or, you can take metro line A to Termini and transfer to metro line B to the Colosseum (metro station Colosseo) and the next door Roman Forum (Foro Romano). A third approach is to walk through the archway (La Porta del Popolo--people's gate) across from P.le Flaminio and take bus 81 from Piazza del Popolo (People's Square). The bus travels along Via de Savoia, arrives at the square and then follows Via del Babuino, passes Piazza di Spagna (Spanish Steps and American Express) and goes to the Colosseum and Forum.

Colosseum and Roman Forum

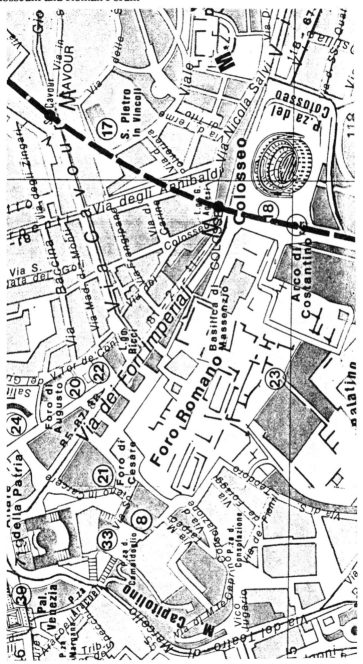

326

COLOSSEUM TO THE CATACOMBS Then from the Colosseum, bus 118 leaves for the catacombs about every half hour. We caught the 1:55pm bus from the stop behind the Colosseum. To find the bus stop, from outside the entrances to the Colosseum, walk around to the back where the restrooms stand against the hillside, climb the stairs and turn right. The bus passes the Baths of Caracalla (Terme di Caracalla) on the right and later barely squeezes through a narrow Roman archway, an original gate to the city. In about 15 minutes from the Colosseum, get off immediately when you see a sign on the right hand side for the first catacomb. The next catacomb, San Sebastian, is only a few meters away. We toured San Sebastian and caught the 3:10pm bus back to Rome from across the street.

THE VATICAN MUSEUMS To reach the Vatican Museums, from P.le Flaminio take metro line A to Ottaviano and then walk five blocks to the entrance. An alternative way and one which eliminates crossing the Tiber River for those staying at Camping Flaminio, Tiber or Seven Hills is to take bus 32 from Via dei Robilant near Stadio d. Farnesina (check the top lefthand corner of the free tourist office map). Incidentally, we found the cheapest T-shirts in Italy to be sold at the street stands on Via Leone around the corner from the Vatican Museum where they were priced at L5000, compared to the L8000 to L10000 you have to pay in Florence. The entrance to St. Peter's is about a 10-minute walk from the Museums.

OSIA ANTICA To reach Ostia Antica, take metro line A to Termini and change to metro line B to Piramide Station and then change to the Roma-Lido line, also called Cristofo Colombo. Neither our day pass nor Eurailpass was accepted on this line and we had to pay L700. (A single combo train/metro ticket is L1000.) The stations of this line are shown on the map in the train. Get off at Ostia Antica for the ruins, a five-minute well signed walk from the station. On the way, you pass the stop for bus 4 to the beach town, the Lido. Returning to Rome, get off at Station Magliana to change to metro line B.

TIVOLI Buses for Tivoli leave frequently from Via Gaeta near the plaza in front of Stazione Termini, but those with a Eurailpass may prefer the train. Some trains on the line Roma-Avezzano-Sullmona-Pescara stop at Tivoli, 44 minutes out of Rome. Not all trains on this line stop in Tivoli, so caution is advised. Those that do stop leave Termini for Tivoli at 6:55am, 8:05am, 2:10pm, 5:23pm, and 6:35pm. A train leaves Tiburtina Station for Tivoli at 11:00am only. Trains return from Tivoli to Termini at 6:27am, 8:24am, 10:07am, 1:25pm, 5:14pm, 9:30pm, and 11:23pm. Trains return from Tivoli to Tiburtina Station at 4:04pm, 8:31pm and 10:34pm.

FOOD The main MARKET is at Piazza Vittorio Emanuele, about eight blocks from Stazione Termini. Metro line A Station Vittorio is underneath the piazza of the market. To walk from Stazione Termini, with your back to the end of the tracks, you want to go outside and double back along the left hand side of the station on Via Giovanni and then turn right onto V. Cap Pellini which leads into Vittorio in three blocks. The market is open daily except Sunday.

In P. Le Flaminio, just around the corner from the bus stop for Camping Flaminio and on the same street as the Benetton shop, is a convenient take-out snack shop that has rotisseried chicken and sells several varieties of delicious freshly baked pizza by weight. A piece of pizza usually will come to about L1300, and you can purchase fruit from the small vendor in the square to complete the meal.

DAY TRIP TO GUBBIO   This makes a good trip to take after you've spent two or three days in Rome and have worn out your feet. Gubbio is a choice medieval town in the Umbrian region, visited by Italians and Europeans but not much by others. After relaxing for 3 hours on the train from Rome to Fossato di Via, the closest railhead, board a connecting bus for the 30-minute ride to Gubbio and the wonderful explorations it provides. This is a long day trip but worth it, especially if you're experiencing Rome fatigue.

The City of Silence, as it is known, seems to have stood still since medieval times. The town rates Michelin two stars for its well preserved Middle Ages architecture and atmosphere. Gubbio is also known for its ceramics and retains the methods used in the Middle Ages. If you would rather spend the previous night in the region thereby gaining extra time in the village, try stopping at the campground in Spoleto, 90 minutes out of Rome, and visiting Gubbio the following day. (See Spoleto for more information.)   The scenic region of Umbria is serviced by the Rome - Ancona train line. To have sufficient time in Gubbio on a day trip, take no later train from Rome than the 9:10am departure. The train goes as far as the village of Fossato di Vio (where you get off) and then connecting buses travel the remaining 19 km. to Gubbio. Bus fare is L1850 for the hour ride and buses leave about once an hour.

Trains leave Rome Termini in the direction of Ancona at 6:50am InterCity Perugino (ar. Spoleto 8:11am, ar. Fossato Di V. 10:07am), 9:10am (ar. Spoleto 11:06am, ar. Fossato Di V. 12:07pm), 1:25pm (ar. Spoleto 3:04pm, ar. Fossato Di V. 4:07pm), 2:50pm InterCity first class only reservation mandatory, doesn't run on Sunday, stops at Spoleto only between approximately June 22 and July 14 (ar. Spoleto 4:07pm), 3:25pm (ar. Spoleto 5:04pm, ar. Fossato Di V. 6:07pm), 5:25pm (ar. Spoleto 7:04pm, ar. Fossato Di V. 8:07pm), 6:50pm InterCity Federico (ar. Spoleto 8:09pm, ar. Fossato Di. V. 8:57pm) and 7:25pm (ar. Spoleto 9:04pm, ar. Fossato Di V. 10:07pm). All of the above trains not noted as InterCity are "fast" category.

Trains from Fossato di via to Rome (Termini) leave at 8:28am InterCity Federico (ar. 11am), 12:53pm (ar. 3:35pm), 4:54pm (ar. 7:35pm), 6:53pm (ar. 9:38pm) and 8:35pm InterCity Dorico (ar. 10:58pm). If visiting Gubbio on a day trip, don't figure on starting the return journey before the 6:53pm departure.

TRAIN SCHEDULES   To Brindisi for the 8pm ferry (ferry operates approx. June 24 to September 6), the best train is the InterCity Mercadante that leaves Stazione Termini at 7:15am and arrives in Brindisi at 2:05pm. Alternatively, an express train leaves Stazione Termini at 9:05am and arrives in Bari, the end of the line, at 2:50pm. At Bari, you can either take an express at 4:30pm, arriving in Brindisi at 5:41pm, or the InterCity Adriatico at 3:42pm, arriving in Brindisi at 5:02pm. During the last week in July and first week in August, train reservations are needed. How far on either side of these dates reservations may be necessary will have to be determined when you get there by asking at the train reservation window how many vacant seats are available for the departure you want.

To Brindisi for the 10:00pm ferry, an express train departs Stazione Termini at 1:05pm and arrives Brindisi at 8:54pm. During the last week in July and first week in August, this departure is extremely risky. It arrives too late to secure a boarding pass should any happen to be available and too late to meet the required check-in time for those with advance reservations.

To Florence, Trains leave Termini about every hour. InterCity trains not requiring a mandatory reservation leave Termini at 9am (ar. 11:10am), 12:05pm (ar. 2:15pm), 1pm (ar. 3:10pm), 2pm (ar. 4:10pm), 3:02pm from Tiburtina (ar. 5:10pm), 4pm (ar. 6:10pm), 5pm (ar. 7:10pm) and 7pm (ar. 9:10pm). Express trains leave Termini ar 8:25am (ar. 10:55am), 12:15pm (ar. 2:35pm), 1:40pm (ar. 4:51pm), 5:10pm (ar. 7:33pm) and 6:30pm (ar. 8:59pm).

To Naples (Napoli), trains leave about once an hour. For instance, expresses leave Termini at 8:50am (ar. Centrale 10:55am) and 9:40am (ar. Centrale at noon); fast trains at 4:20pm (ar. Centrale 6:50pm), 5:20pm (ar. Centrale 7:50pm) and 6:20pm (ar. Centrale 8:50pm); InterCity Aspromonte leaves Termini at 4:10pm (ar. Mergelina 5:55pm, P. Garibaldi 6:08pm), and an all first class Rapido leaves Termini at 7pm (ar. Campi Flegrei 8:41pm, Mergellina 8:47pm, P. Garibaldi 9pm). The last one is good to take as you can get off at Campi Flegrei and avoid the confusion of the downtown Naples station. None of these trains requires mandatory reservations. An early afternoon InterCity and Rapido, not listed here, do.

To Pompeii, take the 5:20pm fast train from Termini and arrive at 8:35pm. An all first class Rapido leaves Termini at 7pm and arrives Pompei at 9:23pm.

To Riviera di Levante. For the town of Sestri Levante, expresses leave Stazione Termini at 10:20am (ar. 15:52pm), 1:25pm (ar. 7:11pm), and 5pm (ar. 10:31pm). For La Spezia, express trains leave Stazione Termini at 12:03pm (ar. 4:34pm), 12:30pm (ar. 4:56pm), 3:40pm (ar. 7:48pm) and 4:15pm (ar. 8:32pm). A Rapido train that requires a mandatory reservation leaves Termini at 2pm (ar. La Spezia 6:05pm). Frequent local trains connect La Spezia to Sestri Levante.

To Sicily, an express leaves Termini at 8:50am and arrives Siracusa (Syracuse) at 8:50pm. For an overnight trip, depart Stazione Tiburtina at 10:46pm and arrive Siracusa at 10:18am. There are several trains that travel overnight and only carry sleeping cars and couchettes, thus taking some of the passenger load off this express with seating compartments. For the most comfortable trip, take the air conditioned InterCity Peloritano that departs Termini at 7am and arrives Siracusa at 5:40pm and Palermo at 6pm. This train requires a mandatory reservation in first class as for all InterCity trains.

To Venice, a EuroCity train leaves Termini at 7:10am (ar. Venice-Mestre only 11:59am). InterCity trains leave Termini at 8am (ar. 1:44pm), 12:05pm (ar. 5:05pm), 1pm (ar. 6:44pm) and 2:10pm (ar. 7:32pm). Express trains leave Termini at 1:40pm (ar. 8:44pm) and 10:55pm (ar. 6:10am). The above trains have through cars to Venice.

SPOLETO

Spoleto makes a good base for exploring the jewel hill towns, Gubbi and Todi, of the region of Umbria. Perugia is the dominant city of touristic interest in the area, meriting two Michelin stars, but the campgrounds of Spoleto are more accessible. Spoleto resides on a major rail link between Rome and Ancona. An important cultural festival is held between mid-June and mid-July, and fills the town with visitors. The city itself rates Michelin one star for its medieval aspect but this is not evident as you leave the train station and are confronted with an Alexander Calder sculpture in the piazza.

Either walk forward from the station to the old part of town or take a bus (L400) from the station to Piazza della Liberta. Pick up a map from the tourist office in the Piazza (open June 15-Aug daily 8-8, Sept-June 15, 8-2 and 4-7). It is important for finding the campground to have a map so try to schedule your arrival prior to closing hours.

Camping Monteluco is behind the church of San Pietro and can be reached on foot from the tourist office in about 15 minutes. When you reach the church, you need to go beyond it to the trail that veers towards the right and leads to the campground. Open all year; adult/L4500, tent/L4500.

For a more developed site, try **Camping Villaggio Turistico Il Girasole**, 9 km. from Spoleto, at Petrognano. Take bus Circolare "C" Spoleto-La Bruna from outside the train station. The bus leaves at 7:10am and 10 minutes past the hour until 8:40pm. Get off at the stop "Petrogreno" which is 2 minutes after the stop "S. Brizio." Open all year; adult/L4500, tent/L4000. The large, attractive site offers grass cover and shade trees; hot water in sinks, automatic washer, store, restaurant, lounge with television, swimming pool, tennis and horseback riding. Mountaineers often stay here.

A **regional market** is held mornings, Monday through Saturday, in Piazza del Mercato. Between Camping Monteluco and p. della Liberta is likly the least expensive restaurant in town, the subsidized **Ristorante Economico** on via San Carlo 7 (L8000).

Day Trip to Gubbio   Gubbio is a choice well preserved medieval town in the Umbrian region, visited by Italians and Europeans but not much by others. The City of Silence, as it is known, seems to have stood still since medieval times. The town rates Michelin two stars for its well preserved Middle Ages architecture and atmosphere. Gubbio is also known for its ceramics and retains the methods used in the Middle Ages. The Gubbio tourist office has free descriptive literature on the town. Take the train to the village of Fossato di Vio, about one hour from Spoleto in the direction of Ancona on the Rome - Ancona line. At Fossato di Vio, board a connecting bus to Gubbio (L1850) for the 35 minute ride over 19 km..   (Otherwise, buses leave about once an hour, less often on weekends.)

Trains leave Spoleto for Fossato di Vio at 8:11am InterCity (ar. 9:03am), 9:02am (ar. 10:07am), 11:06am (ar. 12:07pm), 3:04pm (ar. 4:07pm) plus later departures. Afternoon buses leaving Gubbio for the connecting train are at 1:40pm, 4:15pm, 5:20pm and 7:05pm. Trains leave Fossato di Vio for Spoleto at 12:53pm (ar. 1:55pm), 4:54pm (ar. 5:55pm), 6:53pm (ar. 7:55pm) and 8:35pm InterCity (ar. 9:36pm) plus earlier departures. The last departure arrives in Spoleto at 9:49pm.

Day Trip to Todi   A day trip to the charming, ancient town of Todi, rating Michelin two stars, can be made from Spoleto. The town is equally delightful as Gubbio, but public transportation is not as frequent. Take the private Umbrian train (Ferrovia Centrale Umbra) or an ASP bus from Spoleto or closer Terni. Eurailpass is not valid on the Umbrian train. To save money you may want to board it or take a bus at Terni. Italian State Railways trains leave Spoleto for Terni at 6:11am (ar. 6:48am), 7:06am (ar. 7:32am), 9:19am InterCity (ar. 9:40am), 1:55pm (ar. 2:21pm), 5:55pm (ar. 6:22pm) and 7:55pm (ar. 6:22pm). Outside the station of Todi, board the connecting bus to the old city, a distance of 3 km..   There are no campgrounds in Todi, but the Todi tourist office has free pamphlets on the town. Trains return from Terni to Spoleto at 4:38pm (ar. 5:04pm), 6:38pm (ar. 7:04pm), 7:47pm InterCity (ar. 8:09pm) and 8:38pm (ar. 9:04pm).

Trains to Rome (Stazione Termini) from Spoleto leave at 6:11am express (ar. 8:10am), 7:06am fast (ar. 8:40am), 8:10am M-Sa InterCity Perugino, first class only, reservation mandatory, only stops at Spoleto about June 22 to July 14 (ar. 9:12am), 9:19am InterCity Federico (ar. 11am), 1:55pm fast (ar. 3:35pm), 3:56pm M-Sa fast (ar. 5:35pm), 5:55pm fast (ar. 7:35pm), 7:55pm fast (ar. 9:27pm) and 9:36pm InterCity Dorico (ar. 10:58pm).

NAPLES (NAPOLI)

Italian life gets louder and more animated the farther south you go. If you are coming here mainly to visit nearby Pompeii, you may wish to forego the cultural experience of Neapolitan life and stay at the campground across from the excavations in Pompeii.

TRAIN STATIONS   Stazione Centrale (Napoli C.) is the main station and contains a tourist office (Ente Turismo), seat reservations office (open 7am-10pm), foreign exchange and luggage storage. Many buses and trams leave from Piazza Garibaldi in front of Stazione Centrale. One level beneath

Stazione Centrale and Piazza Garibaldi is Stazione Garibaldi (Napoli P.G.) which is reached through Stazione Centrale. For the metropolitana (subway), go to platform 4 in Stazione Garibaldi.

Most trains arrive at Stazione Centrale but a few stop only at outlying stations, Mergellina or Campi Flegrei. Knowing the arrival station of your train is necessary to get off at the right time. The conductor can give you this information, or check the train schedule posted in the station. If you are coming from the north, such as Rome, and your train stops at Campi Flegrei station, get off here as it is the closest station to Camping Solfatara and Camping Citta di Napoli. In any case, if your train stops at either Campi Flegrei or Mergellina Stations, get off the train at one of those stations rather than Centrale or P. Garibaldi to avoid the hotel hawkers who meet the trains at Centrale. Both Campi Flegrei and Mergellina are also stops on the subway, the Metropolitana, which is part of the state railway system and free with Eurailpass. Mergellina Station has a reservation office, tourist office and foreign exchange.

Both Circumvesuviana Railway and Cumana Railway are private railways and do not take Eurailpasses. The former serves Ercolano, Pompeii, Vesuvius and Sorrento. It originates at Stazione Circumvesuviana on Corso Garibaldi, about six blocks from Stazione Centrale, and one-minute later picks up at Stazione F.S., reached through Stazione Centrale by travolator. The Cumana Railway serves Marina di Licola and Torregaveta on the coast and departs from its own Stazione Mergellina.

TOURIST INFORMATION Ente Turismo (ENIT) offices are at both Central and Mergellina Stations. Ask for its monthly publication, Qui Napoli, which lists sightseeing, restaurants, campgrounds, and train, bus and boat schedules.

PUBLIC TRANSPORTATION The metropolitana (subway) is part of the state railway system (ferrovie dello stato) and hence is included in Eurailpasses. The subway route is Napoli Gianturco - PIAZZA GARIBALDI (Central Station) - Piazza Cavour - Montesanto - Piazza Amedeo - Stazione MERGELLINA (Mergellina Station) - Piazza Leopardi - Stazione CAMPI FLEGREI (Campi Flegrei Station) - Cavalleggieri Aosta (Citta Napoli Camping) - Bagnoli - Pozzuoli Solfatara (Camping Solfatara). Bus, tram and subway fare are L800.

CAMPGROUNDS **Citta di Napoli**, Viale Giochi del Mediterraneo 75, is in Mostra d'Oltremare, a modern cultural center featuring a swimming pool stadium, sports arena, zoo and amusement park, Edenlandia. Open all year. Fees are adult/L6600 or 2 adults/L10900. Store, automatic washer.

If your train arrived at Stazione Campi Flegrei then you can merely walk to camp. If you are at Stazione Mergellina, take the metropolitana to Stazione Cavalleggieri Aosta and from there walk to camp. From Stazione Centrale, go down to Stazione Garibaldi underground and take the metropolitana from platform 4 to Stazione Cavalleggieri Aosta. Alternatively, bus 152 from Corso Novara in front of Stazione Centrale can be taken. It follows the route Corso Novara, Corso Garibaldi, the waterfront (Via Marina, Via Cristoforo Colombo), Viale Augusto, and Mostra d'Oltramare where you get off (it continues to Solfatara and Pozzouli).

Camping Internazionale Vulcano Solfatara borders the grounds of the Solfatara Volcanic Crater in the suburb of Pozzuoli. This camp has a country-rural feeling as opposed to Citta di Napoli which is part of a large city cultural complex. Open Apr 21-Oct 15. High season (Jun 6-Sep 9) fees are adult/L7000 and small tent/L4000. The shady camp has store, cafe, hot showers for an extra charge, swimming pool and exchange.

You can follow directions for bus 152 for Camping Citta Napoli but remain on the bus until the Solfatara stop and then walk 100 meters to camp. A faster arrival is achieved by taking the metro to Pozzuoli Solfatara Station. Then the campground is about a 15-minute partially uphill walk, or take the bus from via Solfatara to the campground. The area is well signed and if you follow the signs to the Crater from the station, the camp will be passed on the way.

FOOD   Pizza was invented here and is still made in the traditional brick ovens. Your basic Neapolitan pizza is Pizza Margherita made of tomatoes, mozzarella cheese, olive oil and a fresh sprig of basel on top.   More expensive pizzas have more expensive ingredients such as Pizza Calzone with salami and cream cheese.

DAY TRIP TO POMPEII   Pompeii is the famous excavated Roman town buried by volcanic eruption in 79 A.D. Open daily 9am to one hour before sunset. A few Italian State Railway trains stop at Pompeii, but none are feasible for a daytrip.   Instead, ride the private narrow gauge Circumvesuviana Railway which doesn't honor Eurailpass and costs L1300, but stops at Pompeii near the Villa d. Misteri on its route to Sorrento.

Departure times from Circumvesuviana Station (direction Sorrento) are: 7:34am, 9:14am, 9:04am, 9:34am, 10:14am, 10:54am, 11:34am, 11:54am 12:14pm, 12:54pm, 1:14pm, 1:54pm, 2:14pm, 2:45pm, 3:14pm, 3:54pm, 4:34pm, 5:14pm, 5:54pm, 6:14pm, 6:34pm, 7:14pm, 7:45pm, 8:14pm, 8:34pm, 9:05pm, 9:14pm, 9:31pm, 10:14pm, 10:48pm. These same trains stop one minuute later at Stazione F.S., connected to Centrale by travolator. The trip to Pompeii takes 26 to 36 minutes. The reverse schedule is just as frequent; check departure times at the station in Pompeii.

The Circumvesuviana also has a Pompeii line that leaves equally frequently and stops at Pompeii Station (don't get off at Pompeii Scavi), a few minutes walk from the site. See train schedules for Italian State Railways' departures. However upon returning to Naples from Pompeii, you may want to take the State Railways' 8:29pm departure which arrives at Stazione Centrale at 8:55pm.

DAY TRIP TO THE GREEK TEMPLES AT PAESTUM   If you aren't going to Greece or Sicily, it would be a shame to miss the three beautiful Greek temples at Paestum, 41 km. southeast of Salerno.   Paestum was founded in the 6th century as a Greek colony and the ancient city stands all alone in a grassy field inhabited only by crickets and lizards. The site is open daily from 9am until two hours before sunset. The museum is open Tu-Sa 9am-1:30pm and Su 9am-30pm. Admission to the site (including museum) is L3000. Outside the site is a restaurant.

Directions   Take a train south to Battipaglia, 20 km. beyond Salerno, and change to a local train to Paestum. Connections can also be made from Salerno. Should you miss the local train connection, board a local bus to Paestum (L1500 to L3000) rather than wait the likely two hours for another train. The best InterCity train departs from Stazione Mergellina at 8:45am and P. Garibaldi at 8:58am (direction Reggio C./Sicily) and arrives in Salerno at 9:37am where you must change to a local train or bus to Paestum. Morning departures for Battipaglia (direction Taranto) leave Stazione Centrale at 7:56am express (ar. 8:52am) 8:10am fast (ar. 9:14am) and 12:10pm (ar. 1:20pm). **Returning to Naples**, a fast train leaves Battipaglia at 7:53pm (ar. Stazione Centrale at 8:55pm). An InterCity leaves Salerno at 7:20pm (ar. Stazione Garibaldi 7:54pm, Stazione Mergellina 8:08pm). An express leaves Salerno at 9:48pm (ar. Stazione Campi Flegrei 10:47pm). The last train, an express, leaves Battipaglia at 11:38pm, Salerno at 11:53pm (ar. Stazione Centrale 12:30am).

In Salerno, you can pick up a map at the tourist office outside the train station. Should you have a layover, the town itself is worth exploring. Walk to the waterfront and follow Lungomare Trieste, a seashore promenade affording views of the Gulf of Salerno. The old quarter is also interesting, especially along Via Mercanti, which rates Michelin one star. The major architectural sight is the Cathedral (Duomo) in Sicilian-Norman style.

To Pompeii (direction Salerno) trains of the Italian State Railways leave Central Station at 1:10pm--all first class Rapido and reservation mandatory but maybe the conductor won't check for such a short time--(ar. 1:35pm), 2:10pm (ar. 2:35pm), 8:10pm (ar. 8:35pm), 8:41pm from Campi Flegrei, 8:47pm from Mergellina and 9pm from P. Garibaldi (ar. 9:23pm) and 9:10pm (ar. 9:35pm). The private Circumvesuviana Railway (which doesn't honor Eurailpass) has trains leaving for Pompeii about twice an hour from both Circumvesuviana Station and Station F.S. The cost is L1300. See schedule under daytrips.

To Rome, the best train is the all first class Rapido (reservation mandatory) that leaves Stazione Mergellina at 8am and arrives Stazione Termini at 10am. InterCity trains stopping at both Stazione Garibaldi and Stazione Mergellina and arriving at Stazione Termini depart at 12:07pm (ar. Termini 2:05pm), 4:45pm (ar. 6:52pm) and 7:54pm (ar. 9:50pm). An InterCity leaves Stazione Centrale at 1pm and arrives Stazione Tiburtina at 2:48pm. A Rapido leaves Stazione Campi Flegrei at 11:46am (ar. Termini 1:40pm). Express or fast trains leave Stazione Centrale for Stazione Termini at 7:05am (ar. 9:20am), 7:15am (ar. 9:45am), 8:15am (ar. 10:55am), 9:15am (ar. 11:52am), 12:15pm (ar. 2:45pm), 1:15pm (ar. 3:45pm), 1:50pm (ar. 3:55pm), 1:57pm (ar. 4:30pm), 2:15pm (ar. 4:45pm), 4:15pm (ar. 6:45pm), 5:15pm (ar. 7:45pm), 6:15pm (ar. 8:45pm), 6:47pm (ar. 8:50pm), 7:15pm (ar. 9:45pm), 8:15pm (ar. 10:45pm), 8:45pm (ar. 10:55pm), 9:15pm (ar. 11:45pm) plus later departures.

To Sicily by day, the best trains are the InterCity that leaves Stazione Mergellina at 8:45am, Stazione P. Garibaldi at 8:58am (ar. Syracuse 5:40pm, Palermo 6pm), an express which leaves Stazione Centrale at 7:56am (ar. Syracuse 6:05pm) and an express departing Stazione Centrale at 11:07am (ar. Syracuse 8:50pm, Palermo 9:24pm). An overnight train leaves Stazione Centrale at 12:52am (ar. Syracuse 10:18am).

POMPEII

Thirty minutes south of Naples in the direction of Salerno, Pompeii is the famous excavated Roman town buried by volcanic eruption in 79 A.D. Open daily 9am to one hour before sunset. Admission L5000.

TRAIN STATIONS Pompeii is served by both the Italian State Railways and the private Circumsuviana Railway (Eurailpass not valid). If you have taken the Sorrento line of the Circumsuviana Railway, get off at the Villa D. Misteri station at the west entrance to the site. The actual Villa D. Misteri is physically outside the gate, but a part of the site. If you took the Pompeii line, don't get off at Pompeii Scavi but at Pompeii Station, a short walk to the East entrance of the ruins. The Italian State Railways' station is farther away, about a 10-minute walk to the site.

CAMPGROUNDS Immediately across from the ruins is Camping Spartacus on Via Plinio and Via della Guiliana. Open all year with high season fees of adult/L4800 and tent/L2000. The attractive camp has store, cafe, and two automatic washing machines. Nearby is Camping Pompeii.

To the Greek Temples at Paestum, a train leaves (direction Paola) at 1:35pm (ar. Battipaglia 2:15pm). At Battipaglia, either wait for a local to Paestum or take a local bus (L1500). Returning, leave Battipaglia at 7:53pm (ar. 8:29pm).

To Naples, trains of the Circumvesuviana Railway leave about twice an hour and cost L1300. Trains of the Italian State Railways going to Naples, and also Rome in most cases, leave at 7:29am (ar. Naples Centrale 7:55am, ar. Rome Termini 10:55am), 7:59am (ar. Naples Centrale 8:25am, Rome Termini 11:52am), 11:29am (ar. Naples Centrale 11:55am), and 8:29pm (ar. Naples Centrale 8:55pm, ar. Rome Termini 11:45pm).

To Sicily, it's preferable to backtrack to Naples to connect with a train going south, but there is the following departure from Pompeii that requires a change of trains at Salerno. It leaves for Salerno at 1:35pm, arriving at 1:57pm. Then an InterCity which requires reservations leaves Salerno at 3:45pm and arrives Messina at 10:30pm.

BRINDISI

You come to Brindisi solely to catch the ferry to Greece that's included in Eurailpass. The hustle (and lots of it) and bustle are largely confined to the one main street linking the port with the train station. Two blocks away in either direction reveals peace and serenity. There is no campground in Brindisi; try nearby villages.

TRAINS TO BRINDISI If you make only one reservation in Europe, let it be for the train to Brindisi, especially during high season of July 24 to August 16 and, for those who want to play it safe, during the rest of July.

A comfortable train is the InterCity that leaves Milan at 6:55am, Bologna at 8:42am and arrives in Brindisi at 5:02pm. This arrival allows ample time for embarkation formalities and dinner before departure time at 8pm or 10pm. The train is air-conditioned in first class and has both aisle and compartment seating. We took the 6:36am departure from Venice-Mestre which arrives in Bologna at 8:22am and then changed to this InterCity train. Another good InterCity train leaves Rome, Termini Station, at 7:05am, and arrives in Bari at 12:15pm. Then from Bari, another train leaves at 12:24pm and arrives in Brindisi at 2:05pm, putting you first in line if you haven't a reservation, and a lot of time on your hands. A direct train from Rome leaves Termini Station at 1:05pm and arrives in Brindisi at 8:54pm in time for the 10pm departure only. This arrival time is safe only outside of high season when space is generally available.

TRAIN STATION Central Station F.S. is about one km. and a 20-minute walk from the ferry dock. Luggage checking is available and remains open late at night until the last train to Rome leaves. A tourist office is in Piazza Crispi, on the other side of the square in front of the station and towards the right.

FERRY TO GREECE The period when you either have an advance reservation or you don't go is the last week in July through the first week in August. Other than that period, you are likely to get on without an advance reservation according to Adriatica line officials. However, people say they didn't have any trouble getting on then. Those with advance reservations still need to report to the Adriatica Embarkation office a minimum of two hours prior to the ship's departure time. Failure to comply may result in the cancellation of the reservation and space reallocated to "standby" passengers. In 1987 the direct boat to Athens started its run a week earlier than scheduled so it's well to inquire if you're interested.

334

Brindisi

1 S. Maria del Casale
2 Monumento al Marinaio d'Italia
3 Colonne Terminali della Via Appia
4 Loggia Balsamo
5 Castello Svevo
6 Fontana Tancredi
7 Chiostro di S. Benedetto
8 Tempio di S. Giovanni al Sepolcro
9 Porta Mesagne
10 Piazza Cairoli
11 Porta Lecce
12 Chiesa del Cristo
13 Cripta di S. Lucia
14 Sede A.A.S.T.
15 Ufficio Informazioni AAST
16 Ufficio Informazioni EPT
17 Sede E.P.T.
18 Municipio
19 A.C.I.

20 Camera di Commercio
21 Museo Provinciale
22 Approdo navi traghetto
23 Aeroporto Civile "Papola"
24 Stazione marittima
25 Prefettura - Questura - Provincia
26 Ostello per la Gioventù
27 Camping "Materdomini"
28 Stazione Ferroviaria
29 Duomo
30 Chiesa di S. Paolo

Ferry Schedule - Hellenic/Adriatica Lines - Brindisi to Corfu/Patras

1 9 8 9 – S A I L I N G S   F R O M   B R I N D I S I

(MONTH) DEPAR. TIME:	1	2	3	4	5	6	7	8	9	10	11	12	13	14	15 16	17	18	19	20	21	22	23	24	25	26	27	28	29	30	31
JAN 22.00				L	L	L	L	L	L	L	L	L	L	L	L	L	L	L	L	L	L	L	L	L	L	L	L	L	L	L
FEB 22.00	L	L	L	L	L	L	L	L	L	L	L	L	L	L	L	L	L	L	L	L	L	L	L	L	L	L	L	–	–	–
MAR 22.00	L	L	P	P	P	P	P	P	P	P	P	P	P	P	P	P	P	P	P	P	P	P	P	P	P	P	P	P	P	L
APR 22.00	L	L	P	P	P	P	P	P	P	P	P	P	P	P	P	P	P	P	P	L	L	L	L	L	L	L	L	L	L	–
MAY 22.00	L	L	P	P	P	P	P	P	P	P	P	P	P	P	P	P	P	P	P	L	P	P	L	L	L	L	L	P	P	P
JUN 21.00	P	P	L	P	L	L	L	L	L	C	C	P	C	P	C	C	C	C	C	P	P	P	C	P	P	C	L	C	C	C
JUL 20.00	C	C	C	C	C	C	C	C	C	C	E	P	P	P	P	P	P	P	P	C	C	C	C	P	P	C	C	P	P	P
AUG 20.00	P	P	C	C	C	C	C	C	C	C	C	C	L	C	L	L	L	L	C	C	C	C	C	C	E	C	C	L	C	P
SEP 20.00	E	E	E	E	E	E	E	E	E	E	E	E	E	E*	E	E	E	P	E	E	E	E	E	E	P	E	E	P	E	
OCT 22.00	L	L	L	L	L	L	L	L	L	L	L	L	L	P	L	L	L	L	L	L	L	L	L	L	L	L	L	L	L	L
NOV 22.00	L	L	L	L	L	L	L	L	L	L	L	L	L	L	L	L	L	L	L	L	L	L	L	L	L	L	L	L	L	
DEC 22.00	L	L	L	L	L	L	L	L	L	L	L	L	L	L	L	L	L	L	L	L	L	L	L	L	L	L	L	L	L	L

From 04/01 to 31/12/89		
BRINDISI	DEP	22:00
CORFU		07:00
IGOUMENITSA		09:00
PATRAS	ARR	17:00
ATHENS (by coach)	ARR	22:30

From 22/06 to 11/09/89		
BRINDISI	DEP	20:00
CEPHALONIA *		09:30
PATRAS	ARR	13:00
ATHENS (by coach)	ARR	18:00
* 01/07 to 25/08/89		

	From 28.07.89 to 13.08.89		From 14.08.89 to 05.09.89	
BRINDISI	DEP	13:00	DEP	12:00
CORFU		21:00		19:30
IGOUMENITSA	ARR	23:00	ARR	22:00

Daily services by m/n "APOLLONIA"

1988 Ferry Prices Without Eurailpass (Add 8% for 1989)

All rates are subject to increase without notice. **1988**

PASSENGERS RATES PER ADULT MEALS EXCLUDED **USA $**	from BRINDISI to	
	CORFU or IGOUMENITSA or vice versa	PATRAS ● or vice versa
PASSAGE - without accommodation	72	83
SEATS	83	97
PULLMAN BERTHS (4 berth compartments)	86	105
3 AND 4 BERTH CABINS	95	115
2-BERTH CABINS *	125	150
2-BED CABINS WITH PRIVATE BATH ●	165	195
STUDENTS AND YOUTH (Students up to 30 years of age, holder of Student Card; young people up to 26 years of age):		
PASSAGE - without accommodation	64	70
SEATS	70	80
PULLMAN BERTHS (4-berth compartments)	80	90
● For single occupancy: 50% supplement ESPRESSO GRECIA: 2-bed cabins with shower/wc ● Supplement for coach connection Patras/Athens or vice versa: $9. per adult.		
PASSENGER - DRIVEN VEHICLES RATES PER VEHICLE		
CARS: 1) up to 4.25 m. length	51	57
2) over 4.25 m. length and Minibuses to 2 m. height	58	69
BICYCLES	FREE	FREE
MOTORCYCLES and SCOOTERS	22	29
BAGGAGE TRAILERS up to 3m overall length	36	43
CAMPERS, CARAVANS, COMBICARS, MINIBUSES over 2 m. height, TRAILERS, BOAT TRAILERS:		
1) up to 5 m. overall length	98	109
2) over 5 m. overall length	116	138

To reach the Adriatica Lines Embarkation Office, leave the train station, and walk straight ahead through Piazza Crispi and along the main street, Corso Umberto, lined with travel agencies, foreign exchange offices, shops and restaurants. A little over half way to the waterfront, the main street angles slightly to the left and becomes Corso Garibaldi, which leads directly to the harbor. Total distance is one km. which can be covered in 15 minutes by a fast walker. Before reaching the waterfront you will see a two story beige building, the port offices. Turn to your right on the waterfront side of the building and in about the middle of the building are stairs to the second floor. Upstairs, go to the Adriatica Embarkation Office and stand in line to make a reservation and obtain a boarding pass. The clerk will collect L14000 from Jun 10-Sep 30 for the Eurailpass supplement and L6000 all year around for port taxes. If you plan to stop over on the island of Corfu, you must tell the clerk at the time the supplement is paid unless you made an advance reservation and did it then. Be aware that another port tax will be due upon leaving Corfu and that Adriatica will allow re-embarkation only if space allows. The only probable period this might happen is the last week in July and first week in August. (Remember to set your watch ahead one hour upon arrival in Corfu.)   The Adriatica office is open 9am to 1pm, and 4pm to sailing time.

With your sailing papers in hand, go next door to passport control where you will be issued a customs card to be turned in to the official as you get on board. The foreign exchange office located next to passport control charges no commission and offers a decent rate for Lire, but a wretched rate for Drachma. (First they change it to Lire and then from Lire to Drachma and much is lost during the conversions.) It's open daily 8:30am to 8pm. Also on the second floor are benches in the hallways and a large waiting room in the tourist office. A baggage check is on the street floor on the non-waterfront side of the building and charges L800 for 24 hours, but is not very helpful as it closes at 6:45pm. Food bought on board is expensive, so shop for provisions before boarding.

The Cyprus Star is berthed in front of the port offices, whereas the Appia and Grecia leave from about 200 meters to the right as you face the water.   For 10pm departures, boarding theoretically starts at 8pm and passengers start assembling a couple of hours earlier. For our trip, boarding didn't actually start until 8:35pm and then was very slow and disorganized without lines, but with everyone in a crowd funneling up to the official guarding the gangway and collecting boarding passes. On board at the door to the inside cabin, the white customs card from passport control must be turned in (or completed if you don't have one) and your passport stamped. Then you're free to go where you please. Passengers planning to sleep outside on deck, and most people on board fall into this category, try to board early in order to secure an advantageous spot.

In 1988, three ships were used on the Brindisi-Patras route, the Appia, Grecia and Cypress Star. The timetable shows ship assignments by day and sailing time. The newest and prettiest boat is the Appia. Its wood decks make it the best for sleeping out. The outdoor sleeping areas around the swimming pool on the top deck fill fast and travelers are quick to "reserve" the few tables and chairs there. On the floor below, the scattered deck chairs on either side of the ship become quickly occupied, followed by floor space. The advantages of this deck are the protection afforded by the three foot overhang of the top deck and suspended lifeboats, and fewer people. Available to deck class passengers are an indoor lounge with comfortable lounge chairs, television, a bar area with tables and chairs, restaurant serving L7000, L15000 and L18000 snacks or meals, and a duty free store. The room containing rows of airplane type recliner seats which can be reserved for a fee is virtually unoccupied as most deck class passengers prefer a good night's sleep stretched out in the open air. The women's restroom has both hot and cold water in its sinks, conventional toilets, and two free hot showers. The air conditioned Appia is 12310 meters long, 1880 meters wide, weighs 6100 tons, travels at 15 knots and carries 1130 passengers and 150 vehicles.

The Grecia is 12550 meters long, 1850 meters wide, weighs 5200 tons, travels at 19 knots and can carry 835 passengers and 210 vehicles. The cement decks of the Grecia make this ship less comfortable for sleeping than the Appia, otherwise its facilities are similar.

During the passage, the sale of tickets costing 1100 drachma for a connecting bus to Athens is announced. Upon arrival in Patras, the buses wait outside the port offices for the ship's arrival. Paying for the bus avoids the wait at the train station and the ensuing mad scramble for seats on the train departing for Athens.

FOOD   The main market is held daily except Sunday from 6am to 1pm in Piazza della Vittoria next to the Post Office, near the intersection of corso Umberto and corso Garibaldi. Avoid any restaurant on the main streets, corso Umberto and Garibaldi, whose employee hustles you as you walk by for much better food is found off the main drag.

We ate at the small Ristorante Pizzeria da Carlo on Via Terribile, 20 meters off the left of the main street and four blocks before the port as you walk from the train station to the port. A sign is posted on the main street and the Ristorante is beneath the sign for The British School and next to a pharmacy. For L8500, we had our choice of a first course of very good cannelloni, spaghetti, pizza or vegetable soup; a second course of meatballs, breaded veal cutlet or excellent veal with melted mozzarella cheese; and salad, bread and either mineral water or 1/4 liter of wine, including service and taxes.

Train Schedules   Adriatica Lines ferries from Patras arrive at 10am and 5pm. The most comfortable train out of Brindisi is the InterCity Adriatico that carries both first and second class and leaves at 1:20pm. It arrives at Bari at 2:35pm, Foggia at 4:07pm, Bologna at 9:42pm and Milan at 11:30pm. If you want to go to **Rome**, you can change to an express train at Bari which departs at 3:11pm for Rome, or stay on the InterCity longer and change at Foggia and ride the same train which then departs at 4:32pm. The express reaches Caserta at 6:50pm and arrives Rome (Stazione Termini) at 9:05pm. For **Naples**, get off at Caserta at 6:50pm, change to a category "fast" train and depart Caserta at 7:12pm and arrive Naples (Stazione Centrale) at 7:40pm. (Trying to reach Venice or Florence on the InterCity is possible but puts you into these cities too late to comfortably reach camp and set up.)

For 5pm ship arrivals, your earliest train out of Brindisi is a tight 5:27pm departure on a slow train to Bari where you can transfer to an express that departs Bari at 7:45pm and travels overnight to Milan, arriving there at 6:05am. For an overnight trip to Torino, depart Brindisi at 6:15pm on an express, arrive Tortona 6:31am, and arrive Torino 8am where there are connections to Paris and the French Alps. To go to Genoa and the Riviera di Levante, get off at Tortona at 6:31am, change to an express train to Genoa which leaves at 6:58am, and arrive in Genoa at 7:42am. From Genoa, local trains depart frequently for the towns along the Riviera di Levante.

For 5pm ship arrivals heading to Florence, your best bet is the 7:47pm express to Bologna which arrives at 5:30am. Then you can change to an InterCity that departs at 5:42am (ar. Florence 6:46am) or an express that departs at 6:07am (ar. Florence 7:17am). A later express leaves Brindisi at 10:02pm, arrives Bologna at 7:36am, change to an express, depart Bologna at 8:05am (ar. Florence 9:15am). If you consult a rail map, it looks like you should get off at Faenza and change trains there. Indeed that is possible, but the trains from Faenza run infrequently and with inferior slow trains carrying only second class that you're better off speeding rapidly along to Bologna and then backtracking to Florence.

For 5pm ship arrivals going to Venice, you can depart Brindisi (direction Bologna) on an express at 7:47pm, arrive Bologna 5:30am, change to another express, depart Bologna at 6am, arrive Venice-Mestre 7:58am and Venice S.L. 8:10am. A later express leaves Brindisi at 10:02pm, arrives Bologna at 7:36am, change to fast train, depart Bologna at 7:44am, arrive Venice-Mestre at 9:33am and Venice S. L. at 9:44am.

For 5pm ship arrivals who want to go to Rome, there are two overnight express trains from which to choose. The first leaves at 8:57pm and arrives at Rome (Stazione Tiburtina) at 7am. The second leaves at 10:27pm and arrives at Rome (Stazione Termini) at 8:25am. In early July 1987, we took the 8:57pm departure, were just barely able to find seats without a reservation and sat upright the entire way to Rome. This ride ranks as the most uncomfortable on our entire trip! My advice is to go to the station as soon as the ferry arrives, reserve a couchette, check your pack, have dinner, explore the areas of Brindisi away from the main street, and return in time to board the train. If you don't want to spring for a couchette, then consider waiting for the later 10:27pm departure which is less crowded as most people from the ferry opt for the first one. Another plan is to take the 5:43pm departure south to nearby Lecce, eat a picnic dinner on the train, arrive 6:35pm, check your pack, look around at what is called the Baroque Florence, and then board the same train you would have in Brindisi but earlier and ahead of the rest of the people waiting to board in Brindisi. The two trains for Rome leave Lecce at 8:21pm and 9:45pm. In Lecce, see the Piazza del Duomo, rated Michelin 1 star, and the Basilica of the Holy Cross (Santa Croce), a two star attraction.

SICILY (SICILIA)

Fewer travelers go south of Naples but those who do are well rewarded. If you aren't going to Greece or visiting the Greek temples at Paestum, then Sicily is your last chance in Italy to see magnificent Greek architecture.

Because of its vulnerable geographical position, Sicily has seen a succession of rulers. The southern and eastern coasts were colonized by the Greeks who built fantastic cities with the aid of the native Sicels for five centuries until they were destroyed by the Carthaginians who wanted to keep the western Mediterranean for themselves. Then came the Romans who first ruled from Rome until it fell, then continued their domination from Constantinople. Subsequent ruling Arabs, Moors, Spaniards and Saracens were succeeded in time by the well-liked Normans.

During the Middle Ages, numerous aristocratic landowners took control. Peasants reacted to years of foreign rule by banding together into secret societies of mutual aid. Centers of Mafia activity are reportedly Monreale and Corleone but the visitor has no awareness of this presence. The most important places to visit are Syracuse, Agrigento and Palermo.

WEATHER Camping is good the year around and half the campgrounds stay open all year. The main tourist season is April through October; February and March are the next most frequented months; November through January see the fewest visitors. July and August can be hot inland though the coast is always cooled by a breeze. Occasional rain and strong wind appear outside high season, but the sun shines through it all and sea bathing is possible even though skiers may be on the slopes of Mt. Etna.

RAILWAYS Trains arrive at the boot of Italy at Villa S. Giovanni to make the sea crossing to Messina on the island of Sicily. The crossing takes 35 minutes. Skip modern and uninteresting Messina and travel onward. Messina is the junction where the train splits with coaches continuing west to Palermo or south to Syracuse. Syracuse and Palermo are end stations for fast international trains. Travel is slower to areas not on these lines. Remember too that Eurailpasses are valid on the numerous buses operated by the Italian State Railways (FS).

FOOD Sicilian specialties are wines, almonds, almond paste, early seasonal vegetables, lemons, oranges, tangerines, artichokes, apricots and a variety of celery, finocchio.

AGRIGENTO Just outside town is the Valley of Temples (Vallata dei Tempi) site of five magnificent Greek temples of the Doric order, other ruins and an archeological museum. The most romantic views are obtained at sunrise or sunset, and the temples are floodlit at night. In town, you will find an interesting medieval section of narrow alleys lying behind Piazza Roma. A tourist office shares the Banco di Sicilia towards the left of the train station as you exit.

    Camping San Leone, at San Leone at the beach, is open April though September. Its tightest period is August 10 to 25. Fees are adult/L4200 and small tent/L4000. Bus 8 from in front of the station goes both to the temples and to the campground. You can also take the bus marked San Leone. The shady camp has hot showers, cold water in the sinks, store, restaurant, lounge and water sports.

    To Palermo, trains leave at 7:10am (ar. 9:12am), 8:20am (ar. 10:35am), 12:47pm (ar. 3:20pm), 1:40pm (ar. 3:55pm), 5:02pm (ar. 7:05pm) and 8:06pm (ar. 10:15pm).

    To Catania, trains leave at 3:20pm (ar. 8:15pm) and 7:10pm (ar. 8:58pm).

CATANIA Catania is a seaport and the second largest town in Sicily after Palermo. A tourist office is in the train station. Bus tickets can be bought at the station newstand. **Camping Jonio**, Via Acque Casse 38, below the cliffs of Ognina in a residential area, offers shady trees on a level site next to the sea. Open all year. Fees are adult/L4400, tent/L8300. From the square in front of the train station, take a local bus to Piazza Duomo or Via Etna and transfer to bus 34 (direction Scogliera). Get off at the stop at the crossroads of Via Acicastello and Via Villini Al Mare. The camp has cafe, store, token-operated hot showers, and sells bus tickets. Catania's market operates Monday through Saturday mornings in the vicinity of via Garibaldi near Piazza Duomo. For train schedules, refer to those for Syracuse. Trains depart Catania about an hour after leaving Syracuse.

PALERMO This is Italy at its most expressive--a city of honking horns, transistor radios, animated conversations and fast breaking life. The capital of Sicily shows a variety of architecture reflecting past domination by Romans, Byzantines, Saracens and Normans, but the Saracen (Arab) influence predominates.

    A branch of the tourist office is in the train station. The city bus terminal is outside. Buy bus tickets for L600 in advance from the newstand. The market is at Via del Bosco, off Via Maqueda, and piazza Bellaro.

    Camping Internazionale Trinacria, Via Barcarello, is 10 km. from Palermo between Monte Gallo and the bay of Sferracavallo. Open all year.

A flat fee of adult/L6000 is charged, inclusive of tent, car, etc. From the train station, take bus 16 which leaves every 30 minutes between 5am and 11pm. Fare is L600. This is a resort camp on the beach and features shady grounds, hot showers (L600), hot water in sinks, store, restaurant, lounge with television, and water sports such as waterskiing and boating.

For sightseeing, first see the center of town (quattro canti) at Via Maqueda and Corso Vittorio Emanule--you can't miss the walls. Next visit the exquisitely decorated Palentine Chapel in Palazzo dei Normanni, about 15 blocks from the city center. Be sure to visit the chapel upstairs on the "first" floor. Two blocks south of the Palace is the Church of San Giovanni which has mosque-like domes. The Catacombs in Donvento di Cappuccini are some of the more startling ones to be seen. (Not for young children.) Bodies have been mummified and are propped against the walls in lifelike vertical position--babies, young children and adults. Heads are not wrapped and have become basically skeletal. Other mummies rest in interminable rows of horizontal bunk bed arrangement.

A huge Norman Cathedral is 14 km. away in Monreale.   A Benedictine Abbey and Cathedral form a large Norman church with overtones of Arabic decoration. The Abbey functioned as sort of a Camp David for royalty.   Highlight is the 12th century mosaics pictorially representing the story of the old and new testaments. Also interesting are the gardens and cloisters.

To Agrigento, trains leave at 7:18am (ar. 9:26am), 9:36am (ar. 12:16pm), 1:25pm (ar. 3:58pm), 2:22pm (ar. 4:50pm) and 6:08pm (ar. 8:18pm).

To Naples and Rome, InterCity Peloritano leaves at 7:40am (ar. Naples 4:45pm, ar. Rome 6:25pm), express Archimede leaves at 8:40am (ar. Naples 6:35pm, ar. Rome 8:50pm), and an overnight express leaves at 8:40pm (ar. Naples 6:53am, ar. Rome 9:;20am).

To Riviera di Levante, the express Treno del Sole leaves at 1pm and arrives in La Spezia at 6:07am and Genoa at 7:52am.

SYRACUSE (SIRACUSA)   The extensive ruins of the ancient city of Syracuse, once a rival to Athens, draw visitors. The noted archeological area is on a hillside outside of town. Most notable is the 5th century B.C. Greek Theater (Teatro Greco) in such good condition that classical plays are presented there in spring and summer. The original seats, hollowed out of rock and curved to fit the body, are still used. Nearby is a park-like area of five quarries (latomie) from which most of the town was built. Orecchio di Dionisio (Ear of Denys) quarry's acoustical properties enable a whisper from inside to be heard a great distance outside the quarry.   There are some catacombs but the ones in Palermo are more fantastic. **Central Station** is at the edge of downtown and has a tourist office. Other tourist offices are located at the entrance to the archeological zone and in the historical center at Via Maestranza 33. Ask for the excellent red city map, Archeological Map of Syracuse and its Province, and the booklet, Syracuse City of Art.

The least expensive camp in the area is **Camping Agritourist Rinaura**, 4 km. south of Syracuse in an olive grove in the countryside about two km. from the sea. Open all year; adult/L3500 and small tent/L3700. From the train station, turn left and follow Via Francesco Crispi for 300 meters to Piazza Marconi and take bus 34/S, 34/D, 35/S, or 35/D from across the Piazza at the corner of the park and Corso Umberto. Bus 34/D leaves M-Sa at .6:45am, 9:45, 12:45pm, 3:45 and 6:45pm. Bus 34/S leaves daily at 8:15 am, 11:15, 2:15pm, 5:15 and 8:15pm. Bus 35/D leaves M-Sa at 7am,

342

10, 1pm, 4:00 and 7:00pm.   Bus 35/D leaves Sundays and holidays at 6:45am, 9:45, 12:45pm, 3:45 and 6:45pm. Bus 35/S leaves M-Sa at 8:30am, 11:30, 2:30pm, 5:30 and 8:30pm. The bus arrives on Corso Umberto, turns to run alongside the park, continues onto Corso Gelone, turns left onto Viale Paolo Orsi, and passes the archeological park on your right.   After getting off the bus 4 km. from Syracuse, walk 1 km. to the campground. Camp has a store supplied with fresh produce from its fields. When returning from camp to Syracuse, keep in mind that the two main sightseeing areas are the archeological park which the bus passes and the island of Ortigia which can be reached by remaining on the bus to its terminus, Riva della Posta.

Syracuse - Camping Agritourist Rinaura

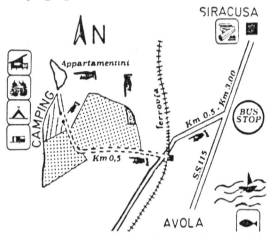

Camping Fontane Bianche, at Fontane Bianche 14 km. south of Syracuse, is open April through October. Fees are adult/L4500 and small tent/L4500. Same directions as for Camping Agritourist, except only take bus 34/S or 34/D and remain on the bus for 10 more km.   The camp is in an almond grove across the street from beautiful blue water and a beach.

Day Trip to Noto A relaxing day trip can be made to the small town of Noto to see the Baroque palaces and church lining its main street, Corso. This wonderful example of 18th century town planning, a result of the earthquake of 1693, is 32 km. from Syracuse and can be reached via the train to Modica which leaves about once an hour. Alternatively, SAIS buses leave about once an hour. The most convenient bus stop is at Ospedal Provinciale on Corso Gelone, the same street the bus takes from Camping Agritourist and Fontane Bianche.

To Agrigento, you must backtrack to Catania and then take a local line to Agrigento. Departures for Catania early enough to make the connection, are 8am InterCity (ar. 9:05am) and 8:50am express (ar. 10:08am).   Trains leave Catania for Agrigento at 9:16am (ar. 1:56pm) and 10:18am (ar. 3:15pm).

Naples and Rome, the best train is the InterCity Peloritano which departs at 8am (ar. Naples 4:45pm, ar. Rome 6:52pm). The next best is an express which leaves at 8:50am (ar. Naples 6:35pm, ar. Rome 8:50pm). For an overnight train, there are two expresses, as well as several trains carrying sleeping accommodations only.   The overnight express trains with seating compartments depart at 6:20pm (ar. Naples 4:01am, Rome 6:11am), 7:05pm (ar. Naples 4:41am, Rome 6:50am) and 8:55pm (ar. Naples 6:53am, Rome 9:20am).

THE NETHERLANDS

Holland is a wonderful, compact country with good grassy campgrounds near everything of interest and fast frequent trains to get you there. Low camping fees, the National Travel Ticket for city transportation, the Museum Pass, delicious Indonesian rice dishes, and excellent low priced Dutch cheese combine to make this delightful country one of the least expensive to visit in Europe. For those with Eurailpasses, either Utrecht or Amsterdam makes a convenient base for daytripping to other towns.

CURRENCY   Guilders (also called florins, abbreviated f or fl) and Dutch cents. Figure 2 guilders to one U.S. dollar. If you change travelers checks just anywhere, you are likely to pay the almost ubiquitous 5 guilder fee for this service. If you can't avoid it then be sure to change sufficient money so you won't have to pay it again. However, there are places that charge less than this standard fee or none at all and the rates are usually just as good or only slightly less. Invariably, these places aren't at the train station. Many campgrounds charge a lower fee, but also give a slightly lower rate. The best place we found to change money is American Express in Amsterdam, where surprisingly we encountered no lines yet there was no fee for any brand travelers check and the rate was equivalent to other exchange offices.

WEATHER   Similar to the Pacific Northwest, there is always the possibility of cool evenings or rainfall. The warmest and driest weather is during high season, mid-July through August.

CAMPING   The Tourist Office in the U.S. distributes free their combination map and campground directory, *Holland Camping '89*. Campground personnel generally stock some sort of free map of the town, always speak English and are willing to help with sightseeing plans. Because of the marine climate, almost every campground has a lush lawn for pitching your tent. Restroom facilities are uniformly modern and clean. The bus or tram driver that takes you to the campground invariably speaks English and will alert you to your stop upon request. The campgrounds in Utrecht and Amsterdam are inexpensive and convenient.

TRAINS   The very modern Dutch National Railways (abbreviated NS) has built a dense network of tracks with service at least half-hourly or hourly on most lines. Its intercity network provides express service between major Dutch cities two or more times an hour. Utrecht is the rail center of the country and has the most convenient connections.

Train information offices will give you their free mini-timetable of main train connections for the Netherlands and European destinations. The official timetable, *Het Spoorboekje*, contains all the timetables for Holland, plus European destinations and is for sale, but isn't necessary to have. Train information offices also distribute free a booklet of one day unescorted excursions to various sightseeing destinations. A ticket can be bought for both the rail and sightseeing admissions, or for only the latter which is then called an "attraction ticket." They aren't worthwhile if you have a Eurailpass or Museum Card already.

Arrival is *ankomst*, departure is *vertrek*, and track is *spoor*.

TOURIST INFORMATION   Look for its symbol, VVV, pronounced vay-vay-vay.

CITY TRANSPORTATION   All buses, trams and subways in the country have coordinated rates based on zones. One zone is about 4-1/2 km.. A National Strip Ticket can be bought for f8.75 for 15 strips only at NZH transport company offices and postoffices. Two or more strips are cancelled per person per ride depending upon its length. Transfers are included and the ticket can be used by more than one person. This strip ticket is the cheapest way transportation tickets can be purchased and represents a 65% savings over buying tickets individually. Single tickets are often sold from vending machines at the stops and smaller strip tickets are sold by bus and tram drivers, but the cost per strip is higher than the 15 strip ticket. *Ingang* means entrance and *uitgang* is exit.

FOOD   The open markets offer a mouth-watering array of produce, cheese and other delectables, making picnics or camp cooking highly recommended. The tastiest and least expensive meals are the rice and noodle dishes called nasi goreng or bami goreng served at the many Indonesian-Chinese restaurants. These are fried rice or noodle dishes with bits of meat and vegetables and make an inexpensive lunch or dinner. The one mandatory splurge is *rijsttafel* (pronounced rye-staf-fel), the Indonesian rice table multi-course lunch or dinner consisting of many small deliciously sauced dishes served with steamed white rice. The procedure is to first cover the plate with a thin layer of rice and then take one or two spoonfuls from each dish and place them around the edge of the plate, filling the center last. Typical of a rijstaffel are *kroepoek* - a large freshly cooked prawn cracker, *sate babi* - pork in a peanut sauce, *loempia* - like Chinese egg or spring rolls, *bebottok* - steamed meat in coconut sauce, *fricadel* - meatball, *sambal telor* - egg in red sauce, and *gado gado* - cold vegetables in peanut sauce.

THE MUSEUM PASS   Except for the briefest stay, consider buying a Museum Pass or Cultural Youth Passport (CJP). The Museum Pass (*Museum Kaart*) gives free admission to over 300 museums, virtually all of them except a few privately owned ones in The Netherlands, and is good for a calendar year. It costs f25 (26-65 years), f7.50 (under 26), f12.50 (over 65). Purchase it at a VVV Tourist Office or any participating museum. The CJP is sold only to those under 26 for f9.50, is valid May through August and gives free admission to the same museums as on the Museum Pass and but also includes discounts on cultural events. The CJP requires a photo and is sold by VVV Tourist Offices.

AMSTERDAM

A city of canals, narrow gabled houses, Rembrandt and Van Gogh, Amsterdam offers outstanding hospitality to campers. Camping Vliegenbos, a mere 10 minute bus ride from Central Station, charges only f3.75 for ages 15 through 30; others still pay only f5.00. Because the country is so compact and train service so frequent, consider making Amsterdam your base for day trips into the surrounding countryside. The Wednesday cheese market of Alkmaar, the market village of Purmurend, the charming towns of Haarlem, Gouda or Delft and the Dutch government seat of The Hague are only a few of the varied day trips awaiting you.

SCHIPHOL AIRPORT A wonderful airport for your European arrival, merely follow the pictorial signs to the trains, have your Eurailpass validated at the train information office and be off to Amsterdam or any other destination with minimum fuss. Be sure to pick up a free "Minitimetable" of Holland trains while you're there. If you don't want to start the validity on your Eurailpass, purchase a ticket in the ticket office next to the train information office for only f4.40 for the 19-minute ride to Central Station in Amsterdam. Trains leave every 15 minutes for Amsterdam, Leiden and The Hague. In addition, there are hourly services to Antwerp and Brussels in Belgium and to some cities in Germany. For venturing further afield, frequent connections to major European cities are easily made from Amsterdam. However, if you wish to make a reservation, do so while at the Airport Station to avoid the long wait for your turn at Central Station.

All services that travelers expect of an airport can be found at Schiphol. In the baggage claim area of the arrivals section are free baggage carts, two bank offices for buying guilders, and clearly marked pictorial signs leading to the Railway Station. Schiphol's duty free shops are renowned for their low prices for name brand goods of electronics, liquor, perfume, chocolates, toys, clothing and jewelry. A 400-gram triangular Swiss Toblerone chocolate bar costs f8.75, and three bundled 100 gram bars sell for f6.95. A boarding pass for your outgoing flight obtained during baggage check-in must be shown to buy at a duty free store.

TRAIN STATION All trains stop at Central Station, the main station located on one edge of Amsterdam's major section of touristic interest. Minor stations are Zuid, RAI and Amstel. Trains coming from the direction of Arnhem and the German cities of the Rhine often will stop at Amstel Station before arriving at Central Station. Those who plan to make Camping Gasper their home should get off here if they have a choice because Amstel Station is closer on the metro line to Gasperpark Station. Everyone else should arrive at Central Station.

Facilities Fortunately there's little reason to stand in the horrendous line for luggage checking (open M-F 5am-1am, SaSu 6am-1am, f1.25) as campgrounds are so close to downtown. Lockers are provided near the luggage check, but empty ones do not abound. A locker large enough for a pack takes four f.25 coins.

In the **Information/Reservation** office, take a number and be prepared for a long wait. The reservation counter is open M-F 8am-8pm, SaSu 9am-5pm. Trains for Schiphol Airport leave from track 4a; purchase your ticket at the usually line-free ticket counters.

346

Amsterdam - Bus Routes

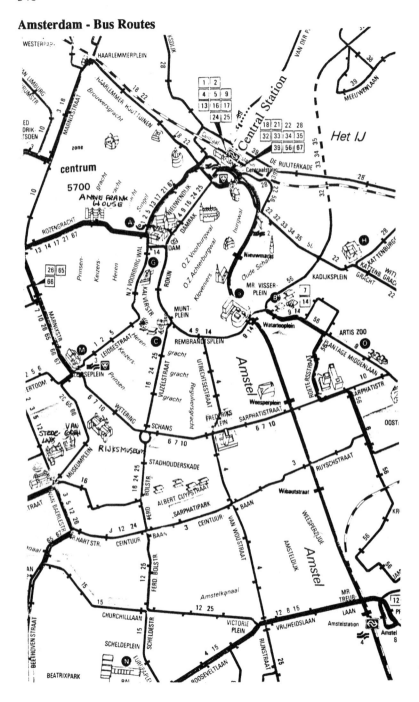

Currency exchange is open until 10:45pm but a hefty f5 commission is charged per transaction. Instead, head up Damrak, the street leading perpendicularly away from the station, for about five minutes to American Express at #66 on the right hand side where no commission is extracted regardless of brand of travelers check, give good rates and lines are actually minimal. Open M-F 9-5, Sa 9-12, Su 10-2. Alternatively and second choice, campgrounds will change money at a slightly lower rate for a fee of f2. Beware of the f4-5 charged at most banks and Thomas Cook offices to cash traveler's checks and for the fee to change currency.

The **tourist office, VVV,** is outside the entrance to the station (look beyond the trams) at Stationsplein 10. Open Easter-June and Sept M-Sa 9am-11pm, Su 9-5; July-August daily 9am-11pm. It's not worthwhile standing in line as the same free transportation map is available at campground offices and campground personnel speak English and can answer most questions.

Infinitely more worthwhile is a stop at the **bus/tram/metro office** also located outside the station. Here you can buy strip tickets the most cheaply or purchase a pass (see city transportation), and usually lines are not more than three deep.

ORIENTATION Central Station anchors one end of the main street, Damrak, which leads to bustling Dam Square. Successive semi-circular rings of canals surround the station until they are stopped on either edge by the River Ij which flows parallel to the rear of the station. The major sights of Amsterdam, clustered as they are in various parts of this area fanning out from Central Station, makes the city seem like an easily toured small town and requiring only minimal use of public transportation. Amsterdam and its suburbs actually comprise a rather extensive area, and residential districts can be seen during the ride to the campground.

Terminal stops for the metro, trams, city buses and long distance buses are each grouped together in front of Central Station. As you exit from the main entrance, you will notice the tram stops immediately in front and slightly to your left. Next to the trams is a metro entrance and adjacent to the entrance is the GVB transportation office which sells day passes and the best value 15-strip national ticket. On your left are the bus stops for buses within Amsterdam and where you catch the bus to the Vliegenbos and Zeeburg campgrounds. Across the canal towards your left you will see a church. In front of the church is a sign with the letter H, which marks the terminal for the network NZH long distance buses connecting the towns of Holland. Buses for Alkmaar, Volendam, Purmerend, Edam and Marken usually leave half-hourly or hourly from here. Schedules are marked on the signs by the bus stops. For example, line 114 bus departs for Alkmaar about every half hour from 7:30am to 11:03pm.

CITY TRANSPORTATION Trams, GVB (city) buses and metro (subway) all use the same ticket and zone system. On a pay-as-you-ride basis, the best buy is the 15-strip ticket (Nationale Strippen Kaart) sold for f8.85 which represents a 65 percent discount over tickets bought individually. It is sold only at GVB offices and some postoffices. (The cost is the same, but for only 10 strips, if purchased from bus or tram drivers.) The GVB public transportation office is in front of Central Station beyond the trams and adjacent to a metro entrance. Even in July, the lines were not more than 1 to 3 people long and the office stays open M-F 7am-10:30pm, SaSu 8am-10:30pm. The GVB Amstel Station office is open M-F 7am-8:30pm, SaSu 10:15am-5pm. Tickets from the strip ticket can be used by more than one person and anywhere in The Netherlands for city transporation and for buses connecting towns and cities.

Day tickets (*Dagkaart*), offering unlimited rides on city buses, trams and metro are sold for f8.85 for one calendar day, f11.80 for 2 days, and f14.50 for 3 days plus f2.75 for each additional day. This makes a 4-day ticket cost f17.25 and a 5-day ticket f19.75. Bus and tram drivers sell the one day ticket, but the better value multi-day tickets are sold only at GVB offices and postoffices. As the actual touring area of Amsterdam is quite compact, it would be impossible to break even on a one day ticket. However, the 2 to 4-day tickets should be considered and you definitely come out ahead even with only 2 trips a day on a 5-day ticket.

One trip leaving Camping Vliegenbos and one trip returning requires 6 strips total. For many campers, this is all the public transportation needed because distances between sightseeing attractions are all walkable in 15 to 25 minutes. For example, the three major museums: Rijksmuseum, Stedejlik and Van Gogh, are within two blocks of each other. The cancellation of three strips makes the ticket good for an hour which gives a generous allowance for transfers for that initial ride into the city and again when returning. The city itself can be covered in two or three days depending on the amount of time spent in the wonderful museums, and then day trips to other towns can easily consume another rewarding two to four days.

If you are under 18 and plan to stay five or more days within the same calendar week, a Week Ticket may be your best bet. A week ticket costs f28.50, as opposed to a 7-day ticket which would cost f24.75, but those under 18 receive a 40 percent discount on a week ticket, bringing the cost down to f17.10. Remember that the Week Ticket is valid for a calendar week, whereas a 7-day pass can start any day of the week. The Week Ticket requires a passport type photo and may be purchased at any GVB ticket office such as the one outside Central Station.

Day tickets must be stamped with the date in the yellow stamping machines before being used for the first time. Strip tickets work in the following manner. For example, two people going to Camping Vliegenbos need three strips cancelled for each. Assuming you are both using the same completely unused strip ticket, fold your card between the fifth and sixth strip, then the bus driver will stamp the sixth strip for you. The yellow stamping machine is located at the rear of trams and near the escalator to the trains for the metro and for these you must do your own stamping. Always start counting from the last stamped strip, and then stamp only the last strip of the strips needed for the ride. A 2 or 3 strip cancelled ticket is valid for one hour for transfer to bus, tram or metro in any direction. A 4-strip cancelled ticket is good for 1-1/2 hours. Trips within the Centrum Zone which encompasses virtually all sightseeing attractions in Amsterdam need only two strips cancelled.

Riding the trams and metro is on the honor system reinforced by inspectors who collect a f26 fine for those without a ticket. We saw inspectors one time during our stay when our tickets were checked on the metro returning from Camping Gasper.

On buses, enter at the front and show the driver the ticket. For trams and the metro, pushing the *deur open* button will open the door automatically. Doors close automatically and never try to get on or off the metro after the bell has sounded. On a tram the lowest step controls the closing of the door; as long as you keep your foot on the lower step the door will not shut.

The relatively new metro is the cleanest and least used of any in Europe. Both elevators and escalators are available in all metro stations except Waterlooplein. The metro stations in downtown Amsterdam are Centraalstation, Nieuwmarkt (red light district and Indonesian restaurants), Waterlooplein (flea market), Weesperplein, Wibautstraat and Amstel (connection with train station). The free folder, *Tram/bus/metro Amsterdam*, available at campgrounds, GVB and Tourist Offices, tells how to reach all sightseeing attractions. Also, note that the route for that particular bus or tram is listed on a sign at the stop. If you lack the folder, bus or tram stops with shelters have a map posted of the entire system.

How to reach sightseeing attractions from Central Station:
Rijksmuseum, Van Gogh Museum, Stedelijk Museum, Heineken's Brwery: bus 67, tram 2, 5, 16. Ann Frank House: bus 21, 67, tram 13, 17. Rembrandt's House: tram 9.

CAMPGROUNDS   Camping Vliegenbos   Fees are f4.2 for ages 15-30, f5.50 for over 30, no charge for tent, and f1.25 for a hot shower. Transportation cost is f1.75 for 3 strips, based on a 15-strip ticket price of f8.75. A well tended, clean campground designed to accommodate those without cars, this camp is the closest to downtown Amsterdam and very popular with both young adults and families, even though it's noted as particularly suited for youth. Still the camp was not that crowded even in mid-July. Tents were 10 to 30 meters apart and the policy of management if the camp is near capacity is to turn away campers with a car, but never to refuse a guest arriving on foot. The camp is divided into two green grassy level areas onto which only tents are allowed to trespass. Cars are relegated to the parking lot, and a gravelled area is provided for vans.

To get there, from in front of Central Station, look towards your left until you spot the buses and the large blue and white signs, one with a letter C and one with the letter B. Bus stop for the most convenient bus, #32, is between these signs. Bus 32 leaves Central Station M-F from 6:21am-12:15am, Sa 6:50am-12:15am and Su 7:30am-12:15am at about 15 minute intervals. Cost is three strips, which are then good for one hour, time enough to get to camp, set up and return to town. Ask the bus driver, who all seem to speak English, to let you off at the stop for the campground. The ride is 10 minutes. The bus travels through the tunnel underneath the Ij River, turns right, then turns left. Get off immediately at the first bus stop (Meeuwenlaan) after the bus makes that lefthand turn. The camp is in Vliegenbos Park on the same side of the road as the bus stop. Once off the bus, to reach the camping area, look for the camping sign and walk up the herringbone-paved road that passes in front of the Technical School entrance which is within meters of the bus stop and perpendicular to it; then take the first road to the left. This junction is not marked with a camping sign, but 50 meters along the road you'll see a sign pointing to the right and the camp is nearby. The walk from the bus stop is less than 5 minutes.

Other buses that go to the camp are bus 39 from Central Station via Buiksloterweg ferry, Hagedoornweg, Meeuwenlaan and Vliegenbos; and bus 31 which offers rush hour service M-F 7-9am and 4-5:30pm and follows the route Central Station, Buiksloterweg ferry, IJ tunnel, Vliegenbos.

English-speaking personnel work in the office, give away the free public transportation map of Amsterdam and sell day passes and strip tickets for the bus/tram/metro, but not the better value 15-strip or 2 or more day passes. Also sold are shower tokens for f1.25 and tokens for f7 for the automatic washing machine and dryer which are inside a room to the rear of the reception building. Check out is 12 noon; maximum stay 3 weeks.

The grocery store is open 9am-9pm and will cash travelers checks for a f2.0 fee. Across from the store is a small covered area furnished with wood benches arranged in squares, log-cabin fashion, and also functioning as tables for eating what you brought or bought at the grocery store. Two recently built brick buildings with curved skylighted ceilings reveal clean white tiled bathrooms with brightly painted orange doors, conventional toilets without seats (bring your own toilet paper), sinks, footbaths, and hot showers (token required). There are three stainless steel sinks for diswashing. All water is cold only, except for the pay showers.

By the tent area at the far end of camp are two picnic tables. Further exploration will reveal a square cement block paved patio with an outdoor fireplace, five log seats and a sleepy yellow cat! Parallel to the tent area are seven small snug cabins, each equipped with four bunk beds without mattresses, a table and four chairs, counter for a campstove, and electric lighting. An interesting option for late or early season campers, each rents for f40 total, but should be reserved far in advance: Meeuwenlaan 138, 1022 AM Amsterdam, Netherlands. Phone is 020-36 88 55.

Camping Gasper Fees are f4.50 per adult, f3.25 per small tent and f1.25 for a hot shower. Transportation cost is 4 strips. Spacious and larger than Vliegenbos with its lawns only one third full even in the middle of July when we visited, this carefully tended campground in Gasper Park offers the same warm welcome as Vliegenbos. Thanks to the new metro line, Camping Gasper is only a 20-minute ride from Central Station to Gasperplas, the terminal metro station, plus a 7 minute walk.

To get there, from in front of Central Station you will see two entrances to the Metro, one on your left almost next to the station building and one in front and slightly to the left on the far side of the trams. Head for this latter entrance if you need to buy a multi-day pass or strip ticket from the GVB office adjacent to the entrance. In the metro station, remember to stamp your ticket in the yellow stamping machine and only board the train if Gasperplas is listed as the destination on the overhead signboard. If Gasperplas isn't listed at the moment, then Gien will be. Do not take any train with Gien listed as the terminus as the train leaves the main line for Gien a few stations down the tracks after leaving Central Station. Gasperplas is the name of the terminal station and is where you get off.

The metro leaves Central Station M-F 6am-12:15am, Sa 6:37am-12:15am, Su 7:37am-12:15am. From the other end, Gasperplas, trains leave M-F 5:38am-12:03am, Sa 6:15am-12:03am, Su 7:15am-12:03am. Trains leave at about 7 minute intervals, and Central Station terminal to Gasperplas terminal is a 19 minute ride. We never saw the sparkling clean metro more than 20 percent full. After passing Amstel Station, the metro speeds along above ground for a lifeseeing trip into the suburbs of modern suburban highrise mass housing, a startling contrast to quaint Amsterdam! Gasperplas Station is the last station on the metro line, and clearly identified by a modern sculpture of a three-piece set of luggage made of theft-free brick, should you miss the large signs on the walls.

After getting off, turn left, take the escalator or elevator downstairs, note the camping sign with the arrow on the wall across from the escalator, and turn left out of the station and cross the red brick plaza. Follow the arrows to "camping" painted in white on the ground, a 7 minute walk to the campground. The 4-strip ticket is good for 1-1/2 hours, enough time to reach camp, set up and return to town. Should your train happen to stop at Amstel Train Station, as trains from the direction of Arnhem and the German cities on the Rhine often do, you can take the metro from Amstel Station to the campground. Also for day trips and leaving Amsterdam, inquire if your train stops at Amstel Station which if it does will save the extra 10 minutes to Central Station.

The English-speaking registration clerk will answer any questions you may have about Amsterdam and upon request give the same free transportation map distributed by the Tourist Office. Money can be exchanged in the office for a low f2.0 commission with rates only f0.06 lower than in town. The fenced camp is completely closed at night. The night attendant on duty from 11pm to 7am will let you in if you ring the buzzer outside the gate. Beyond the office is a small grocery store and across the street, a large cafe which closes at midnight. Use of the automatic washer and dryer cost f8.50; purchase token at office. Both the cafe and office accept Visa and Mastercharge, an uncommon occurrence among campgrounds! Checkout is 12 noon. One area of the camp is set aside for permanent mobile homes, while the large expanse of thick, green lawn is for guest campers.

The recently built facilities include on both ends of the buildings restrooms which open directly to the outdoors and contain both a seatless conventional toilet and sink in each compartment. (Furnish your own toilet paper.) Inside the building are showers with an outer dressing room and stool in each compartment (buy token at office), private rooms containing a sink and located across from the showers, a row of sinks, and a large round stainless steel basin for handwashing clothing. A separate room inside the building contains sinks for dishwashing. Sinks have cold water only, but the f1.0 token can be used for hot water in the dishwashing, clotheswashing and outdoor sinks.

Camping Zeeburg, Zuider Ijdijk 44, is in the eastern part of Amsterdam and, though only about 10 minutes by car to downtown Amsterdam, requires a change of bus when using public transportation. For this reason we place it third on our list of recommended campgrounds. Charges are f4.50 per person, f1.0 per tent and f1.25 for a hot shower. The camp rents tents for f8.0 which includes the per person fee, trailers bedding three for f25 inclusive (early or late season travelers might keep these in mind), and bikes for f7.50 per day. The camp is open April through September. Registration is open 9am to midnight during July and August and closes from 1pm-5pm during the other months.

From Central Station, take bus 22 at the blue and white sign with the large letter B towards your left as you leave the Station. Bus fare is three

352

strips and validity is one hour. Tell the bus driver where you're going and ask him to alert you when it's time to transfer to bus 37. As you leave the bus, ask the driver to point in the right direction for catching bus 37. The bus stops very near the camp. Bus 22 leaves Central Station M-F 6:17am-12:15am, Sa 6:45am-12:15am, Su 7:30am-12:15am. Should your train happen to stop at Muiderpoort Station, a minor rail station of Amsterdam, bus 37 stops outside the Station. At 11:15am and 8:15pm, the camp runs a free taxi-bus from Central Station direct to the campground, a 15-minute trip. It leaves from in front of Central Station to the left of the main entrance as you exit the station (see map). The free taxi-bus leaves Camping Zeeburg for Central Station at 11am and 8pm, arriving 15 minutes later.

Camping Zeeburg

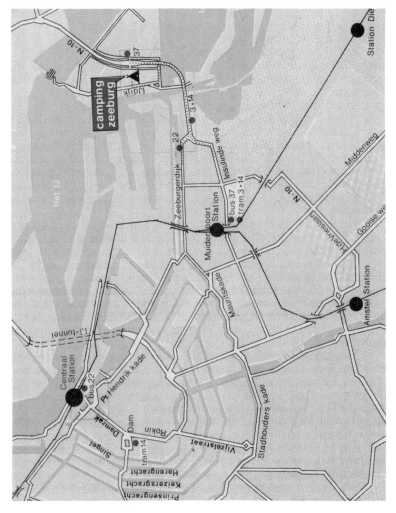

FOOD   Amsterdam's largest outdoor market operates Monday through Saturday, 9-5 at Albert Cuypstraat to the east of the grouping of the three important museums.   Take tram 4, 16, 24, or 25 from Central Station to within one block of the street.

SIGHTS   Most visitors will save money and see more by purchasing a Museum Pass (Museum Kaart) which gives free admission to over 300 museums in The Netherlands and costs f30 (26-65 years), f15 (under 26), f20 (over 65) from a tourist office or participating museum.

Within Amsterdam, the Museum Pass is good for admission to Rijksmuseum (admission f6.50), Van Gogh (f6.50), Stedjlijk (f5), Rembrandt's House (f3.50), Maritime Museum, Our Lord in the Attic Museum (Amstelkring), Maritime Museum, Jewish Historical Museum, Biblical Museum, Museum Willet-Holthuysen, Museum Van Loon and virutally all others.   Average size museums, such as most of those listed above, generally charge f3, larger and more important ones f5-f6.50.   Those under 18 or over 65 receive reduced prices, generally about half, on the regular admission.   Neither the Museum Pass nor the CJP includes the Anne Frank Museum, which is owned by a private foundation.

The innovative Tourist Office introduced in 1987 a **Museum Boat** which leaves 5 times a day from Central Station and stops at the following museums: Anne Frank House, Amsterdam Historical Museum, Rijksmuseum, Van Gogh Museum, Stedelijk Museum, Rembrandt House, Jewish Historical Museum and Maritime Museum.   A one-day ticket costs f7.50 and the first departure is at 9:30 daily, except Sunday and Monday. The last boat returns to Central Station at 3:45pm.   The entire boat trip takes 75 minutes, but you are free to exit and reenter at any point throughout the entire day.   A member of the Dutch Guides Association accompanies each boat.   This ticket is more worthwhile for the canal tour it provides than for transportation to the museums themselves.   During July and August, there are lines at the Anne Frank, Van Gogh and Stedelijk Museums, making it difficult to see more than 2 or 3 in a day.   Besides, they can be reached on foot, or more quickly by bus or tram than by boat.

DAY TRIPS   These trips must be made on the specified day of the week.
Wednesday Trip to Folk Market in Hoorn and Zuiderzee Open Air Museum in Enkhuizen.   Wednesday in Hoorn from about Jul 1-Aug 26, occurs a folk market with dance groups in traditional Dutch costumes, oldtime craft demonstrations, cheese, art, antiques and food.   The town itself developed as a fishing port and powerful medieval trade center and comprises picturesque buildings and colorful canals, making it a pleasant destination to explore.   Taking the 8:19 or 8:49 morning trains from Amsterdam allows ample time for enjoying Hoorn and its market.   Then if you will continue by train to the even better preserved and interesting town of Enkhuizen, you can visit its fascinating outdoor museum comprising the choicest buildings dating from the nineteenth century standing in the way of a land reclamation project--the building of the Afsluitdijk enclosure dam in 1932.   The **Zuiderzee Museum** shows how the Dutch lived in this area between 1880 and 1932 and includes 135 houses and tradeshops grouped into a village.   From the train station in Enkhuizen, simply follow the signs to the ferry which will transport you to the ticket office and then the museum entrance. Admission fee is f7.50.   Want to go further than Enkhuizen?

Remember that Eurailpass holders receive free passage across the inlet between Enkhuizen and Stavoren on the ships of BV Rederij Naco which operate between May 14 to early September.

Trains leave Central Station in Amsterdam daily at 7:16, 7:49, 8:19 and then every 30 minutes until 11:19, 11:52 and 12:29. After leaving the station, the train stops 8 minutes later at Sloterdijk, arrives in Zaandam in 8 more minutes, then Purmerend in 10 minutes and 18 minutes later in Hoorn. Trip from Amsterdam to Hoorn takes 42 minutes (42 km.). The train then continues to the end of the line at Enkhuizen, another 20 minutes from Hoorn or about an hour from Amsterdam. For the return trip trains leave Enkhuizen at 7:35am, 8:08, 8:38 and every 30 minutes until 10:38pm, with the last train leaving at 11:08pm. Trains leave Hoorn at 8:07am, 8:37, 9:07 and every 30 minutes until 11:07pm with the last train leaving at 11:38pm.

Thursday trip to Cheese Market in Purmerend, 600-year-old town of Hoorn and Zuiderzee Museum in Enkhuizen. Follow the directions above for the Wednesday excursion, but instead get off in Purmerend for the morning cheese market held at the foot of the Town Hall each Thursday from about June 18 to August 13. The exact dates vary each year. Then on Tuesday mornings, Purmerend hosts a pig, cattle and horse market. Trains leave Purmerend for Hoorn and Enkhuizen at 7:41am, 8:12, 8:40 and every 30 minutes until 11:40pm, and then 12:13am and 12:50am. The distance is 19 km. to Hoorn, an 18-minute ride.

Friday trip to the Cheese Market at Alkmaar with Extension to either Haarlem or Zuiderzee Museum at Enkhuizen. A traditional cheese market is held every Friday from 10-12, mid-April through mid-September in Alkm.aar's town square. Trains leave Central Station (direction Den Helder) at 7:16am, 7:49, 8:19 and every 30 minutes until 11:19pm, and then 11:52pm, and 12:29am and arrives 37 minutes later. Between the third week in June and third week in August, a special Cheese Express (kaasexpres) train leaves Central Station each Friday at 9:02am. Although hostesses ride this train dressed in traditional costumes and give away free cheese samples, an earlier train will allow you to beat the crowds and find a closer vantage point to watch the colorful ritual of carrying, weighing and auctioning the large round cheese wheels. Trains return to Amsterdam at 8:08, 8:38 and every 30 minutes to 11:08pm, with the last train at 11:38pm. From Alkmaar, the towns of Haarlem, Leiden and The Hague (Den Haag) share the same train line and are conveniently reached. The trip is 34 minutes (35 km.) to Haarlem (see Haarlem), one hour (64 km.) to Leiden and 73 minutes (79 km.) to Den Haag. Trains leave at 8:35am and every 30 minutes until 8:35pm and then 9:35, 10:35 and 11:35pm.

On this same train line, but going in the opposite direction, you will reach Hoorn in 23 minutes and then can transfer to another train for Enkhuizen. Trains leave Alkmaar for Hoorn at 8:02am, 9:02 and every 30 minutes until 8:02pm, and 9:02, 10:02, 11:02pm and 12:02am. Trains leave Hoorn for Enkhuizen on the half-hour and hour.

Thursday trip to the Farmers Market at Schagen. Thursday mornings in Schagen from about June 25 to August 27, gather a West Frisian folk market with sheep shearing, goat competition, farmers in traditional clothing, and West Frisian folkdancing. Trains leave Central Station for Den Helder, stopping at Schagen on the way, at 7:22, 7:52 and every 30 minutes to 10:52pm and then 11:22pm. Trains return at 7:46, 8:26 and every 30 minutes until 10:46pm, and then 11:16pm. If you wish to prolong the daytrip, when the return train reaches Alkmaar, get off and change trains for Haarlem, Leiden, Den Haag, or Hoorn. (See directions under Alkmaar.)

Day Trip to Leiden to see the Windmill. Korenmolen De Valk is a 5-minute walk from the station. From in front of the station, walk up Stationsweg, the street that is perpendicular to it. In 2 blocks, turn left at the sign to the windmill. (Tu-Sa 10-5, Su 1-5, f3.50F.)

LEAVING AMSTERDAM   To London, for cheap bus fare see Budget Bus at Rokin 10, (tel. 020-275151), for round trip fare on EuroLines of f135. Office hours are M-F 9:30-17:30, Sa10:00-16:00.

TRAIN SCHEDULES   Train service is at least hourly to domestic destinations and main Belgium towns.
   To Bern, leave at 8:55am EuroCity, change at Basel (ar. 6:09pm) and 7:51pm, change at Basel (ar. 8:09am).
   To Brussels, leave at 26 minutes past the hour from 8:26am to 8:26pm.
   To Cologne, leave at 6:45am, 7:56am EuroCity, 8:55am EuroCity, 9:49am, 10:56am EuroCity, 12:49pm, 2:49pm, 3:49pm, 5:15pm, 6:49pm and 7:51pm. 3 hours.
   To Copenhagen, leave at 8:02am (ar. 7:09pm), 10:02am (change at Osnabruck, ar. 8:45pm) and 8:02pm (ar. 8:09am).
   To London, the best bet is the overnight train via the Hook of Harwich which leaves at 8:31pm and arrives at Liverpool Station at 9am. This allows for a good 7 hours of sleep on board. Other departures via Dover are 8:56am (ar. 4:23pm), 11:56am (ar. 7:05pm) and 2:56pm (ar. 10:05pm).
   To Paris Nord Station, leave at 7:03am (ar. 1pm), 8:53am EuroCity M-Sa (ar. 2:15pm), 10:53am (ar. 4:55pm), 3:53pm (ar. 10:06pm and 10:15pm (ar. 6:50am).
   To Strasbourg, leave at 8:28am (change at Brussels Nord, ar. 5pm) and 12:28pm (change at Brussels Nord, ar. 8:35pm).

UTRECHT

Utrecht serves as the rail hub of The Netherlands. Most international trains pass through here and it also serves as a good base from which to see the rest of Holland. For example, six trains an hour make the 25 minute trip to Amsterdam and 4 trains each hour leave for The Hague. Connected by covered passageway to Central Station is Hoog Catharijne, the largest shopping mall in the country. Beyond the mall is Utrecht's medieval city center with the landmark Cathedral.

   Central Station is downtown and directly connected to the shopping mall. Foreign exchange office in the station is open M-Sa to 9pm and Sunday to 6pm. Tourist information is open M-Sa 9:30am-5:30pm. They sell a good map for f1.25 which has the bus routes marked and shows the campground in the upper right section, but the last page of the free booklet, *Utrecht*, has an adequate smaller map that also shows the campground. The camp is marked "C1" in the upper right hand corner.

   Camping De Berekuil, 5-7 Arienslaan--2 km. from the downtown area, is set within a larger recreational complex, 'de Voorveldse Polder, comprising bowling, riding, tennis and fishing. Open Apr-Oct. From the Central Bus Station beside the Central Train Station, take Centraal Nederland Company bus 57. The bus leaves every half hour and passes the shopping center, medieval area and then eventually skirts the recreational complex before it arrives at the last stop in Utrecht, Veemarkt, where you get off. Then it's a 5 minute walk to the campground. The last bus leaves daily at 12:27am for the campground. The camp charges adult/f3.95, tent/f2.75, hot shower/f1. Facilities include store, snack bar, playground with wading pool, basketball and football fields and the camp itself is surrounded by canals where people fish. The 10-acre grassy camp has about 200 places, the most popular ones being next to the water.

ARNHEM AND HOGE VELUWE NATIONAL PARK

Two outstanding attractions are in this convieniently situated city on the main rail line between Amsterdam and the German cities on the Rhine. The Kroller-Muller Museum within the huge Hoge Veluwe National Park (pronounced ho-kah vay-lu-vah), shows 270 works by Van Gogh, and a large collection of modern sculpture is erected in the surrounding woods. Inside Arnhem, the National Folklore Museum presents the past in a reconstructed village of peasant houses and tradesmen's shops.

The main **Station N.S.** is downtown and has foreign exchange. The tourist office, VVV, Stationsplein 45, is on the left of the plaza in front of the train station. Its summer hours are June, M-F 9-8, Sa 10-4; July-Aug, M-F 9-8, Sa 10-5; Sept M-F 9-6, Sa 10-4.

Campgrounds   Camping Warnsborn, closest to town at 5 km. on Bakenbergseweg 257, is set within a wealthy residential area on a large estate with trails through its surrounding woods. This is the best camp for backpackers. Open April 1 to September 15. From the train station, take bus #11 (direction Schaarsbergen), a blue bus, opposite the train station. Buses leave every 30 minutes. A camping sign is visible from the bus stop which is one block from the campground. Fees are adult/f4, tent/f3, and hot shower/f1.25 for 6 minutes.   The site is grassy and there is a store, playground, bike rentals, washing machine and dryer.

Camping Arnhem (Kampeercentrum), 7 km. from town at Kamperbergerweg 771, in a wooded area, is open Mar-Oct. From the train station, take bus #11 (direction Schaarsbergen), a blue bus, opposite the train station.   The bus stop closest to camp is on Kemperbergerweg and from there the camp is one km. down a narrow road through the forest. Fees are adult/f4, tent/free. Store, snack bar, washing machine, dryer, and bikes (including tandems) for rent.

Rijks-Museum Kroller-Muller shows modern art, a few old masters and an exciting collection of sculpture within a beautiful natural setting in De Hoge Veluwe National Park. Tu-Sa 10-5, Su 11-5, closed Monday. The Sculpture park opens early at 11am on Sunday and closes early every day at 4:30pm. Museum is free, but entry to the National park costs adult/f6.25. Allow a minimum of two hours and three or four hours could easily be spent here. The benches in the sculpture garden provide a good picnic site.

Unfortunately, reaching the museum is a little involved.   The museum is 8.8 km. from the Arnhem entrance to the National Park.   A bicycle can be rented at the campgrounds and pedaled over completely flat terrain to the museum. Between the end of June and mid-August, a special blue city bus marked Hoge Veluwe, leaves from opposite the train station 3 to 6 times a day for the museum entrance. Otherwise, a regular VAD bus #107 (direction Lelystad) leaves from opposite the station at 15 minutes past every hour M-Sa and every other hour on Sunday. The ride takes 45 minutes to the Otterlo entrance where you can rent a bike or walk 3.5 km.

NORWAY

A land of spectacular fjords and snow-patched green mountains where a fourth of Norwegian families maintain vacation homes, Norway beckons the traveler far from the maddening crowds. Norway is a good country in which to break away from the capital city circuit, camp beside lake and mountain and go hiking. English is widely spoken due in part to the system of education in which compulsory education ends at 16, but to proceed to the gymnasium (higher) level requires passing exams in English, Norwegian, German and mathematics. Being the only industrial country in Europe that's a major exporter of oil has brought inflationary pressures to bear on the country. The government has slowed price rises by limiting oil production and allowing only part of the oil revenue to feed back into the economy. Even so, Norway is the most expensive of the Scandinavian countries.

CURRENCY   Norwegian krone. One krone equals 100 ore. There are about 6.5 kroner to the U.S. dollar.

WEATHER   July and August are the warmest and most rainfree months. In summer it never gets really dark so arriving late is no problem.

TOURIST INFORMATION   All tourist offices publish a free English-language city guide that includes descriptions, opening times, fees and public transportation to museums and sights; campgrounds, restaurants and cafeterias and miscellaneous information about the city.

CAMPING   Norway has excellent campgrounds and the Norwegians themselves are avid campers. Most are open June 15 to August 25, except those in cities and major tourist areas have longer seasons.

TRAINS   The Norwegian Railways (*Norges Statsbaner* or NSB) have very good trains. Most routes pass through spectacular scenery, especially those between Oslo and the coast. The three main rail lines are the southern railway from Stavanger to Kristiansand and then to Oslo; the Bergen line from Oslo; and the northern link from Oslo to Trondheim and on to Bodo. The train from Stockholm goes from Kiruna, Sweden to Narvik, Norway, in the land of the midnight sun. This rail line is the farthest north in Norway.

Norwegian trains are classified **Ekspresstog** (express), **Hurtigtog** (fast) and **Persontog** (slow). All seats on express trains are reserved. The conductor will collect the normal reservation fee of 13kr from those with Eurailpasses without a reservation. Norway has no supplements. Free schedules (NSB Lommeruter) are available in train information offices. A

358

reservation is made at the ticket window (*billetter*) and may be advisable in summer on main rail routes. The trip to Copenhagen is particularly in demand. Children 4 through 15 pay half price. The Nordic Tourist Pass valid for 21 days throughout Scandinavia is available, but would only be useful for those arriving and departing in Scandinavia.

spor	track
avgaende tog	departures
ankommende tog	arrivals
vindusplass	window seat
hverdager	monday through saturday
hverdager unntatt lordag	monday through friday
son og helgedag	sunday and holidays
plassreservering	seat reservation
lommeruter	schedule

EURAIL BONUS   Thirty percent reduction between Kristiansand and Hirtshals on the normal fares of the steamship comapny KDS.

FOOD   Fresh fish is always good in Norway, but lutefisk has a strong taste Americans are not used to.   The country's catch of herring is one of the largest in the world. Herring is canned, its oil is used in production of margarine, the fish scales yield a chemical necessary for making artificial pearls and scraps and skin are made into cattle feed. In restaurants, herring is served plain, smoked, pickled, in sour cream and in wine.

Restaurants begin serving the last meal at 4pm but most people eat at 5 or 5:30. Some restaurants will start to close as early as 6pm. As food is expensive, cafeterias and markets are your best bet. Fish is usually the cheapest main dish. The entree is normally garnished with one or two vegetables, often boiled potatoes. To save money, buy all beverages in a store and drink water when eating out. Whole milk (*helmelk*) and skim milk (*skummet melk*) are both available and delicious.

Few Norwegian families eat a hot breakfast. The usual children's lunch is a glass of milk and open faced sandwiches of egg, canned fish, perhaps goat cheese or meat. People start work at 8:30am and finish at 4:30pm. They take a scant half hour for lunch which is a snack brought from home or open faced sandwiches (*smorbord*) in a restaurant.

MIDSUMMER'S EVE   This June 23rd holiday ranks second in popularity only to Christmas with the Norwegians. This shortest night of the year finds people celebrating by the woods or lakes where they build bonfires, sing, dance and watch fireworks.

HIKING   This is the best way to get to know Norway. Tourist huts are found along the trails. Those willing to pay a nightly fee, need carry only a towel, soap, clothing and personal items. No one is turned away even if a hut is full. At the least you will be provided with mattress and blanket on the floor. Included in the nightly fee are dinner, breakfast, a sack lunch and a thermos full of coffee or tea. Some huts are self-service for which a sleeping bag or liner must be carried and food is for sale. Blankets are available. Also, you can carry your own tent and buy meals at the huts.

Trails and huts are coordinated by the Norwegian Mountain Touring Association (Den Norske Turistforening or DNT). DNT offices sell maps to a scale of 1:100,000 and 1:50,000. Free rough maps of the area with suggested routes and average hiking times are available to help decide what scale maps will be needed. Some unstaffed huts are locked and require a standard key from DNT. Conducted hikes of varying difficulty sponsored by DNT provide a good introduction to hiking in Norway for the experienced hiker who can keep up. In Norway, backpacking is a national sport. The Oslo branch of DNT is at Stortingsgaten 28, or ask at the tourist office of the location you're in.

Hardangervidda, Hardanger Plateau, easily reached from the route of the Bergen-Oslo railway, is a popular hiking area dotted with small lakes with good fishing. Wild reindeer can often be seen. Tourist huts have been placed within a day's hike of each other. Gateway towns are Hardanger, Numedal and Telemark. Itinerary and topographical maps are available from the Oslo DNT office. Trails are marked with red paint on trees and signed at junctions, forks and bridges.

OSLO

Fjords were formed in the Ice Age when glaciers scooped out the granite mountains in their pathway leaving behind very deep ocean beds. Oslo grew beside just such a fjord.

TRAIN STATIONS After May 1989 all trains arrive and leave Central Station (Oslo S or Oslo Sentralstasjon). The station has foreign exchange (7:30am-10:30pm), hotel reservations office *(inkvartering)* and luggage lockers. Obtain tourist information at the hotel reservations office (7am-11pm) or train information office (8am-11pm).

TOURIST OFFICE The main office is in the City Hall. Their *Oslo Guide* contains all information on museums, transportation and camping sites. The campgrounds stock some of the same brochures found at the tourist office.

CITY TRANSPORTATION The basic fare for bus, tram and subway is 13kr. A *trikkekort* valid for 4 rides is 40kr, 12 rides 120kr. A 24-hour tourist card is 40kr. Most buses stop downtown at Wessels Plass. The subway *(tunnelbane, T-bane)* has two lines that are independent of each other. One line runs west from the National Theater and the other east from Central Station Square *(Jernbanetorget)* andthe Parliament. Stations are designated by a T.

The Oslo Card *(Oslo Kortet)* costs 80kr for 1 day, 120kr for 2 days and 150kr for 3 days. It is valid for all transportation, admission to museums and sights and reductions in some restaurants. Buy it at the Hotel Reservations office, campgrounds or tourist office.

CAMGPROUNDS The best and most convenient camp is **Ekeberg Camping**, Ekebergsletta, 4 km. from downtown in a wooded residential area on a hillside overlooking central Oslo. Jun 20-Aug 20; tent/50kr. From Central Station, take bus 24 or 72 in front of the station on Jomfrubraten. The camp will appear on the right as the bus travels uphill. The stop is a half block from the entrance. From the National Theater downtown, take bus 72. The camp is all good lawn. Excellent facilities: cafeteria, grocery and souvenir store, cooking facilities, laundry room, post office and exchange. The camp is adjacent to a city park with a wading pool.

Bogstad Camping, 8 km. from the city center, is less convenient and so large that you have to walk vast distances within the campground if your tent site is not at the busy front of the camp. The facilities are on a par with Ekeberg however. Open all year; tent/50kr. From Central Station, take bus 41 (direction Sorkedalen) that has hourly service from 7am to 9pm. The last bus leaves around 11pm. The route is Gronlands Torg, Central Station, Wessels Plass, National Theater, Solli Plass, Frogner Kirke and so on until the bus arrives 32 minutes later at Woxen bus stop across the street from the campground. Post office, exchange, automatic washers and dryers, freezer, cooking room with coin-operated burners, cafeteria with outdoor terrace (chicken and fries, hamburger and fries, etc.), grocery and souvenir store, playground, teen pavillion with jukebox and 20 vacation cabins.

A private campground, **Stubljan Camping**, is located south of the city on the highway to Oslo. The camp is more expensive, less convenient and not as good as the others. Jun 1-Aug 31; tent/55kr. Bus 75 (direction Ingierstrand) from Central Station.

FOOD   Three outdoor food markets operate M-Sa 7am-2pm. The most centrally located is Stortorvet, the open plaza marked by the Cathedral that opens off Karl Johans Gate. Others are at Youngstorget and Gronlands Torv. The new Aaker Brygge Market is on Stranden 1-3.

SIGHTSEEING   The viking ships are Norway's most prized historical possessions. These 9th century vessels were grave-ships in which Viking chiefs and queens were buried with their possessions. The bodies were covered with a blue mud which helped to preserve them. When the ships were recovered, workmen found chest-of-drawers, wood plates and cups, hoes and iron scissors along with the bones. Three viking ships are in Viking Ship Hall on Bygdoy Peninsula, open May-Aug 10-6, Sep 11-5; 10kr, student/5kr. Take bus 30 (Bygdoy) from Wessels Plass or the half hourly ferry in summer from dock C at City Hall.

Nearby on **Bygdoy**, the Norwegian **Folk Museum** (*Norsk Folkemuseum*), is a collection of farm buildings which recreate Norwegian life in earlier times. The 12th century staved church, made entirely of wood with pieces being cut and fitted without nails, is the outstanding feature. The ends of the gabled roof are decorated with ship's figureheads attesting to the workmens' experience as shipbuilders, having only converted to Christianity a century before. Folklore programs are given in summer. Same hours as Viking Ships, 25kr, student 20kr. Also on Bygdoy is the Polar Expedition ship **Fram** used in 1893-96 and 1910-12. Open May 16-Aug 31 10-5:45, Sep 11-4:45; 10kr, student 5kr. The **Maritime Museum** and **Kon-Tiki Museum** are here also, the latter containing the raft used by Thor Heyerdahl as he and his companions drifted to determine if the South American Incas could have discovered the South Pacific.

The **Munch Museum**, Toyengate 53, contains much of the lifetime output of the expressionist Edvard Munch, Norway's greatest contemporary painter. Open Tu-Sa 10-8, Su noon-8; 20kr, student 10kr. Free guided tours in English on Thursday at 6pm. Take bus 29 from Central Station or T-bane from Parliament Station to Toyen. The museum is east of downtown, beyond the Akerselva River and across the street from the Botanical Gardens. Across the street are the University's Natural History Museums, Sarsgate 1, Toyen. Tu-Su noon to 3; all free. The Paleontological Museum has collections of prehistoric plants and animals. The recently modernized Zoological Museum has a good exhibit showing animals from beneath sea level up to a mountain plateau. Also a Mineralogical Geological Museum.

The **National Gallery** (Nasjonalgalleriet), 13 Universitetsgata, has works of Norwegian painters from the 19th and 20th century. The 45 paintings by Munch give a good sampling of his gloomy outlook and forlorn sense of man's isolation, and of his expressive technique. Open M-Sa 10-4, Su 12-3, plus 6-8pm on W & Th, free.

Henie-Onstad Art Center, Hovikodden, Baerum, is 12 km. from downtown Oslo. The contemporary building sets on a small promonatory within a park. Only a small portion of the foundation's permanent collection is on view at any one time. Open M-F 9-9:30, SaSu 11-9:30; 20kr, student/10kr. Take bus 151, 153, 161, 162, 252, 261 from University Square to Hovikodden. Two buses an hour, 25-minute ride. From Bogstad Camping, transfer from bus 41 at Lysaker. The Center is out of the way considering the limited works on view.

To **Bodo** leave 3:15pm (change at Trondheim, ar. 9:42am) and 10:55pm (change at Trondheim, ar. 7:20am). Reservation required.

To **Copenhagen**, leave at 7:35am reservation required (ar. 5:24pm), 11am reservation required (ar. 8:51pm), 1pm May 31-Aug 30 (ar. 10:51pm) and 10:35pm reservation required (ar. 8:54am). **Use same departures for Gothenberg**.

To **Stockholm** leave at 8:55am (ar. 3:27pm), 3:54pm May 31-Oct 30 (ar. 10:30pm) and 10:50pm (ar. 6:55am). Reservation required.

To **Trondheim** leave 7:55am (ar. 2:35pm), 9:25am (ar. 6:10pm), 3:15am (ar. 10:05pm, 10:25pm not Sa (ar. 7:45am), 10:55pm (ar. 7:20am). Reservation required.

OSLO - BERGEN RAILWAY

Three-fourths of Norway's land is covered by mountains. The Oslo-Bergen train ride gives a good idea of them. Trains leave Oslo's Central Station at 7:35am (ar. 2pm), 10:20am (ar. 6:05pm), 3:45pm (ar. 10:20pm), 10:50pm (ar. 7:20am), 11:30pm Sunday only (ar. 7:52am). The 3:45pm departure does not stop at Myrdal. To get to Flam for the night, depart Oslo no later than 10:20am.

There are two very scenic rail spurs, one at Myrdal and the other at Voss, that can be taken by breaking the journey at those points. The train on the **Myrdal-Flam line** is equipped with five independent sets of brakes, enabling the tracks to decline 2,845 feet in only 12 miles. The train passes through sub-alpine mountains to sea level vegetation at Flam. Flam nestles beside the fjord on the floor of a narrow canyon. **The campground in Flam** is 100 meters from the train station, tent/50kr. The train leaves Myrdal for Flam at 5am, 7:40am M-Sa only, 11:45am May 31-Aug 30 only, 12:15pm, 4:20pm May 31-Aug 30 only, 5:10pm and 7:15pm. The 20-km. journey takes 50 minutes. Trains return from Flam at 7am M-Sa, 10:10am May 31-Aug 30, 11am, 2:55pm, 3:25pm May 31-Aug 30, 5:20pm and 6:20pm M-F only. Trains leave Myrdal for Oslo at 12:13pm, 4:31pm, 5:07pm reservation required and 5:47pm Friday only. Trains leave Myrdal for Bergen at 7:45am not Sunday, 12:10pm reservation required, 3:56pm, 4:29pm, 6:12pm and 7:20pm. (If you don't mind paying extra money for more spectacular scenery, from Flam take the ferry to Gudvangen and the bus from Gudvangen to Voss which returns you to the main rail line.)

The Voss-Granvin sidetrip is next best and can be done on a day excursion in either direction. Leave Central Station at 7:35am, change at

Voss and arrive in Granvin at 2:10pm. From Granvin, you can take a train to Bergen or Oslo. Voss Camping is by Vangsvatnet Lake near the center of town within walking distance of the train station. Open all year; tent/40kr. Excellent facilities including automatic washer and store.

BERGEN

Bergen welcomes you with lush green parks, cobbled streets and a lively waterfront. The train station is downtown, 2 blocks from the bus station and 8 from the tourist office.

TOURIST OFFICE To reach the tourist office at Torgalmenning, from the train station walk 7 blocks straight ahead on the main street, Kaigaten, to Torgalmenning (M-S 8:30am-9pm, Su 10-3). Their *Bergen Guide* has all information, including hikes. The Bergen Touring Club, 3C. Sundtsgate, arranges hikes and has information on hiking huts and trails. Open 10-3 in summer.

CITY TRANSPORTATION The basic in-town fare is 11kr. A tourist ticket for Bergen and surroundings for 48 hours costs 48kr. Buy it at the Tourist Office all year or on the buses from May 1-Sep 15. Each city bus is signed with route number and terminus. The central bus station, 8 Stromgaten, is the departure point for all buses serving the environs of Bergen and the Hardanger area. Campground buses leave from here. The ferry across Bergen harbor between Slottsgatan and C. Sundtsgt costs 6kr and has frequent service M-F to 4:15pm.

CAMPGROUNDS Bergenshallens Camping, 24 Vilh. Bjerknesvei, 10 minutes from downtown, is open Jun 20-Aug 15. Take bus 3. Check to make sure this camp is operating.
    Midttun Camping is 13 km. from Bergen. From the train station, turn left as you come out and in about 100 meters, there is a sign to your left, Bergen Busstasjon. Take the bus to Arna at Perrong 22 to your right as you enter (20kr). Buses leave from 6:05am to 12:15am, twice hourly during the day. Pick up a free bus schedule *(Lokalruter)* bus station information office. Immediately after passing a small town and where the bus turns off the main road, pull the stop cord when you see the camping sign on the left, a 20-minute ride. The camp is 100 meters and visible from the stop. Two other Bergen camps, **Grimen near Helldal and Lone near Haukeland** are farther on the same bus route. Bus fare is 25kr to Lone Camping.

FOOD The fish, fruit and vegetable market operates M-Sa 8:30-3 at Torget on the waterfront. The morning fish market is exceptional.

SIGHTSEEING **Bryggen**, the wharf lined with step roofed wooden warehouses built when Bergen met success as a Hanseatic port is now home for the workshops of many artists and craftsmen. The Hanseatic Museum, within a 16th century wood building, displays merchant life in the Hansa days. Jun-Aug 10-4, Sep-May 11-2; 10kr. The Bryggen Museum shows archaeological and historical items, May 1-Aug 31 M, W, F 10-4, Tu & Th 10am-8pm, SaSu 11-3; 10kr. **The Maritime Museum**, Sydneshaugen, is a modern museum showing the development of shipping. Su-F 11-2, 5kr. The **Aquarium** on Nordnes Peninsula, a 10-minute walk from downtown or bus

4 from Markeveien, is one of the best in Europe. May-Sep 9-8, Oct-Apr 10-16; 24kr. **Mount Floien** (pronounced floy-en) is a viewpoint and start of several trails. Take the funicular from downtown Bergen, 8am-11pm, 22kr roundtrip. **Gamle Bergen** (Old Bergen), at Elsesro in Sandviken, contains 30 buildings from the 18th and 19th centuries grouped to form a town. May 11-Jun 13 noon-6pm, Jun 14-Aug 23 11-7, Aug 24-Sep 13 noon-6pm, 15kr. Take bus 1 from the bus station, departures every 8 minutes, fare 9kr.

To Oslo (reservation required) leave 7:30am (ar. 2pm), 10:05am (ar. 5:31pm), 3:15pm (ar. 10pm), 10:20pm Sunday only (ar. 6:31am), 10:45pm (ar. 7am).

STAVANGER

Though the center of Norwegian North Sea oil exploration, Stavanger retains its picturesque old quarter. The train station is downtown facing the lake. Luggage check is open 7:30am-10pm. Bus station is next door.

TOURIST OFFICE   Reiselivslaget for Stavanger is in the modern glass building next to the station. Turn left upon leaving the station. Open Jun 1-Sept 11 8:30am-7pm, Sep 1-Jun 1 M-F 8:30-4, Sa 9-1.

CAMPGROUNDS   Mosvangen Camping, Tjensvoll on Lake Mosvatnet, is next to Mosvangen Youth Hostel. From the train station, turn left and the bus stop for yellow bus 10 is on Musegate street behind the train station. Two buses per hour, fare 9kr. You can walk from camp to downtown in 30 minutes by taking the gravel path around Mosvatnet lake and then following highway 510 into town. Open Jun 1-Aug 31; tent/50kr. **Vaulen Camping** is on route 44, 5 km. south of Stavanger. Open July only. From the train station, take bus 22, 23 or 24 (12kr). No showers at camp, but swimming.

CITY TRANSPORTATION   City buses are yellow and cost 12kr. Suburban buses are blue and leave from the bus station beside and to the right of the train station. The circular route of city bus 10 (same bus as to Mosvangen Camping) is suggested as an excellent unguided tour of Stavanger, passing the most interesting sights.

FOOD   The public market including tanks with live fish is near the Cathedral at Haakon VII's Gate and Skagenkaien. Open M-Sa to 3pm. Eating out is expensive in this oil town. You might try the Mosvangen Youth Hostel next door to Mosvangen camp as it serves all three meals.

SIGHTSEEING   **Old Stavanger** (Gamle Stavanger) between Ovre Strandgate and Nedre Stradgata has cobbled streets, gaslights and wood buildings. An **Iron Age Farm**, Ullandhaug, is a reconstructed farm dating from about 350-550 A.D. on bus line 10, but farther than Mosvangen Campground. The **Ullandhaug Tower**, a telegraph company tower with a public viewing platform is also on bus 10's route at the Gosen bus stop. The **Pulpit Rock** is a sheer cliff face 2,000 feet high above Lyse Fjord. Sightseeing boats charge a hefty price to see it, but it can be done on your own by taking the local ferry to Lysebotn, which passes under the rock.

To Oslo leave at 8:45am (ar. 6:28pm), 1:40pm reservation required (ar. 10:03pm) and 10pm reservation required (ar. 7:15am).

NORTHERN NORWAY

TRONDHEIM The train station is on the edge of the downtown area. It has luggage checking. To reach the tourist office, walk straight ahead on Sondregate for 6 blocks and turn right to the main square, Torvet. Ask for *Trondheim Guide* for complete information on sightseeing attractions.

Flak Camping is 10 km. west of town. Take bus 75 or 76 from the bus station in the center of town (12kr). The bus leaves once an hour in the morning and afternoon, less frequently at night; last bus 11pm. **Sandmoen Camping** is 10 km. south of town. Take bus 44 from the bus station (12kr) which leaves twice an hour during the day, last bus 11:40pm. Open all year; tent/40kr; store, exchange, minigolf and automatic washer. **Storsand Gard Motel and Camping** is 17 km. north of Trondheim. Take the bus from the bus station (22kr). One bus an hour; last bus 11:15pm. Open all year; tent/50kr; store, swimming. Vikhammer Ard and Camping is 15 km. north . Same bus as for Storsand. Open all year; tent/80kr.

To Bodo (reservation required) leave at 8:10am (ar. 7:15pm) and 10:50pm (ar. 9:42am). **To Oslo** (reservation required) leave at 8:40am (ar. 3:25pm), 1pm (ar. 9:40pm), 3:42pm (ar. 10:17pm), 9:45pm not Saturday (ar. 6:47am) and 10:30pm (ar. 7:08am). **To Stockholm or Boden**, leave at 4:45pm (ar. Stockholm 6:25am). For Boden, change at Ange and arrive Boden 7:30am.

BODO The town is across the Arctic Circle and the midnight sun is visible from June 2 to July 10. A favored viewpoint is from the restaurant on Mount Ronvik. The train station is downtown at the edge of the water. This is the end of the line for the rail line from Oslo. Narvik, further north, is reached by train from Sweden. The tourist office is 2 blocks from the train station at Sjoegata 21.

Bodosjoen Camping is 3 km. from the train station near the radio station (Saitfjord), about a 40-minute walk. From the station, turn left onto Sjogata and continue walking until you see camping signs. Or, take the bus (10kr) from a stop about 150 meters from the station; departures every half hour; last bus midnight. May 15-Sep 1; adult/20kr, tent/20kr; store (8:30am-10pm), automatic washers and dryer.

To Oslo (reservation required) leave at 9:45am (ar. 7:08am) and 8:50pm (ar. 3:25pm). Change at Trondheim.

NARVIK This far northern land of the midnight sun town is on the rail line from Stockholm, Sweden. Narvik's fjord-side campground is a little less than 2 km. south of town, a 15-minute walk from the train station. A separate area is reserved for tents/35kr. Store, cooking facilities, boat rental.

To Boden leave 5:15am May 31-Aug 30 (ar. 12:58pm), 8:35am (ar. 3:58pm), 1:20pm reservation required (ar. 8:16pm). **To Stockholm**, leave 8:35am (change at Vannas, ar. 7:20am next day), 1:20pm reservation required (ar. 11:15am the next day).

Narvik

PORTUGAL

Portugal's main attractions are its beaches, especially around the Algarve, and the old quarters of its towns. Interesting architecture is found in Lisbon with its indigenous Manueline Style and in Coimbra and Oporto with their romanesque churches and remnants of past Arab occupation. Prices in Portugal are lower than in the rest of Europe.

CURRENCY The monetary unit is the escudo (pronounced es-HOO-dough), written 1$00. One escudo equals 100 centavos. Centavos are written to the right of the dollar sign. One U.S. dollar is worth 150$00.

WEATHER Summer offers a mild coastline but finds the interior uncomfortably warm. Camping is pleasant in spring or fall, but with occasional rainfall. April is a noted tourist month because of the many folklore festivals. The southern most province, The Algarve, is warm enough for winter camping except watch out for wind. The season for swimming in the Atlantic or Mediterranean is March through October.

TRAINS Companhia dos Caminhos de Ferro Portugueses (CP) is the Portuguese Railways. The best trains ply the international routes, such as the SUD Express, Lusitania Express and the best one, the TER Lisbon Express. Portugal does not have the fast intercity trains of northern Europe. Good service is provided along the coast north of Lisbon and for international connections. The rail line connecting Lisbon, Belem, Estoril and Cascais is now part of the Portuguese Railways.

A reservation made at least a day in advance is free on international and express trains and should be made in summer espcially for the trip to Madrid or Paris. Children under 4 ride free and those 4 to 12 pay half. Persons 65 and over pay half price for tickets for distances over 50 km. Various special tickets are offered, but the country is too small for them to be of interest.

estacao	station
caminho de ferro	railway
chegadas	arrivals
partidas	departures
retrete	restroom
deposito de volumes	luggage check

guard de volumes de mao	luggage check
platforma	track
informacoes	information
sala de espera	waiting room
todos os dias	daily
domingos e feriados	Sundays and holidays

CAMPGROUNDS   Campgrounds are called Parque de Campismo. Camping informally (not in a campground) is legal except in urban areas or less than 1 km. from a campground or public beach. Campers must be careful to not foul the water of srpings and wells, build a fire or leave garbage behind. The tourist office pamphlet, Portugal Camping, lists campgrounds according to area and distance from the bus stop and train station. Campgrounds are graded tourist, first and second class. Small tents are usually given a price break over large ones. From October to May camping fees are reduced 30 to 50 percent.

pessoa	person
tenda	tent
cozinha	kitchen
duche quente	hot shower
lava-loicas	washbasins
lava-roupas	laundry sinks
abastecimento	grocery store
parque infantil	playground
informacoes	information
auto caravana	van
crianca	child
por noite	per night

FOOD   Portugal produces wheat, corn, rice, olives, tomatoes, grapes, almonds, figs and sugar cane. Sardines and wine rank two and three after cork on Portugal's list of exports. Fish is eaten 10 times as often as meat by the Portuguese and dried cod is very popular. Fish is a best buy in Portugal. The carob plant, a short, bushy everygreen, grows in the Algarve.

A delicatessen (*mercearias*) sells pasteurized milk. Tap water is safe in Lisbon, major towns and resorts, though the high mineral content may bother some. Aqua de Lusa is a non-carbonated mineral water. House wine is *vinho de casa*. *Prego* is roast beef or a thin filet steak on a bun, often served in cafes. Eggs are incorporated into many dishes and custard *(flan)* is on every menu. Food is cooked in olive or groundnut oil. For children, you can order a half portion *(meia dose)*. Meal times are 1pm and 8pm. Grocery stores are open 9-1, 3-7 and until 1 on Saturday.

PRONUNCIATION OF TOWNS   Aseitao (az-aye-TAN), Cascais (kash-keish), Estoril (ish-to-REEL), Evora (A-VOO-ra) Faro (FA-roo), Fatima (FA-tee-ma), Portimao (port-i-MAN), Praia da Rocha (PREE-a-da ROH-cha), Sagres (SA-gresh), Setubal (se-TOO-bal), Sintra (SEEN-tra).

LISBON (LISBOA)

Lisbon has its own grand style with broad, modern boulevards contrasting with the Alfama, the old quarter of steep cobbled streets and narrow alleys.

Apolonia and Rossio Train Stations

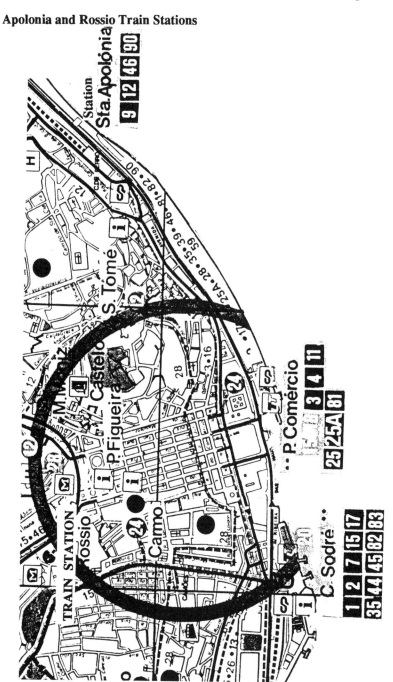

Lisbon Central Area
Rossio Train Station

AIRPORT   Outside the entrance on the right is the bus stop, Rotunda do Aeroporto. Bus 50 goes to the campground. Bus 44 and 45 (both direction Cais do Sodre) travel downtown to Rossio Train Station and the heart of Lisbon. Fare is 60$.

TRAIN STATIONS   The two important ones are Rossio, the central station and focal point of the city, and Santa Apolonia, the main station which handles international traffic. Gare Estoril-Cascais at Cais do Sodre and Gare do Sul e Sueste (T. Paco) at Praca do Comercio are minor. **Santa Apolonia** has an exchange office (8:30am-8:30pm), a combined train information, seat reservations and tourist office (7am-midnight), luggage check (7am-1am), exchange (9am-8pm) and restaurants.   Trains from northern and eastern Portugal arrive here. Trains going to Spain require a reservation.

Bus 9 and 9A go to **Rossio Station**. Rossio serves Sintra, Vila Franca de Xira and western lines, but reservations for any train may be made here. "Servico International" window takes reservations for international trains. The train information office is open 9am-8pm; luggage checking. Outside Rossio Station is Rossio Square (Dom Pedro IV Square) recognized by the monument to Pedro IV of Portugal and the National Theater. The tourist office is nearby at Restauradores Square. The metro station is Rossio.

Gare Cais do Sodre serves the famous resort of Estoril (ish-to-REEL) and Cascais (kash-keish). The latter has an interesting early morning fish auction. The station is next to the Tagus River on bus route 43 from the campground or bus 1, 44 or 45 from Rossio Station. The ride to Cascais is 30 minutes. Estoril and on some trains, Belem, are intermediate stops. There are about four trains an hour.

Sul e Sueste Station (T. Paco), next to Praca do Comercio near the waterfront, handles traffic going south and southeast, such as Baizo Alentejo and the Algarve. Ferry service (Eurailpass valid) is provided between T. Paco Station and Barrerio across the Tagus where the trains begin.

TOURIST INFORMATION   Offices are at Apolonia Station, on Restauradores Square (metro Restauradores) near Rossio Station and at the campground. Ask for *Portugal Welcomes You* which has a map of Lisbon, and *Lisbon, Unforgetables* for its walking tour of Alfama.

CITY TRANSPORTATION   Trams, buses and subway (metro) are good and inexpensive. Tram and bus fares are according to distance. The metro is a flat rate. Carris kiosks sell a 1-week ticket valid on buses, trams and metro for 1000$ and 10-ticket metro books for 300$. A single bus ticket is 85$, a single metro ticket, 35$. Trams start at 35$ for a short trip.

CAMPGROUND   The municipal camp, Parque de Campismo, is in the northwestern corner of huge Parque Florestal de Monsanto which covers one-sixth of Lisbon. The camp is outstanding. Open all year. The camp is served by 3 bus routes; 14 (Outurela) from Praca da Figueira, 43 (Buraca) from Praca da Figueira and 50 (Alges) from Poco do Bispo.

From Rossio Station, walk across the square in front and turn left onto Rua do Amparo to another square, Praca da Figueira. Take bus (carreira) 14 in the direction of Buraca which leaves every 20 minutes. The ride is 30 minutes. The trip gives a good orientation to the city on its way to the campground. After leaving Praca da Figueira, the bus follows R. da Prata straight through downtown to the waterfront, Praca do Comercio. Then it turns right on Av. 24 du Julho, passes Gare M. da Rocha and continues along the shoreline on Av. da India to Belem. At Belem, the bus turns inland on Calcada da Ayuda, passes through Parque Monsanto on Estr. de Queluz and finally reaches the campground. Then the bus continues to Casa de Paulos and terminates at Outurela.

From Apolonia Station (Estacao de Santa Apolonia), take bus 28 to Cais do Sodre and then bus 14 to the campground.

From the airport, take bus 50 (direction Alges) from outside the station on the right. The bus leaves every 15 minutes for the half hour trip. After leaving the airport, the bus travels on Avenida M. Carmona to Estadio da Luz (stadium), then enters the Benfica district, and goes by Alto Boa Vista to the campground. After the camp, the bus continues along E. Circunvalcao, the road bordering Parque Monsanto, to Alges.

The well equipped camp has store, restaurant, tourist office, post office, hair dresser, automatic washing machines, swimming pool, tennis courts, playground, croquet and minigolf.   Open all year; Jun-Sep adult/180$, small tent/150$, hot shower/76$.

FOOD   The main market. Av. 24 de Julho near Cais do Sodre Station, is open M-F 6am-2pm, Sa 6am-5pm. The fruit wholesale market is at Cais da Ribera near the river and opens 6-11am. Neighborhood outdoor markets are on R. da Madalena below Castle of St. George, and between T. Maria da

Fonte and R. Damasceno Monteiro, northeast of downtown. A supermarket is on Rua de Dezembro next to Rossio Station.

SIGHTSEEING Calouste Gulbenkian Museum (Fundacao Gulbenkian), Av. de Berna, is the gift of the Anglo-Armenian oil tycoon and considered one of the best museums in Europe. The collection includes representative items from Egyptian, Greek, Roman, Mesopotamian, Islamic and Oriental cultures in the form of paintings, sculpture, fabrics, pottery, furniture and jewelry. Open T-F & Su 10-5, Sa 10-7, 40$, students 20$. Take bus 31, 41 or 46 (direction Moscavide) from Restauradores near Rossio Station. Buses leave every 10 minutes and the ride is 12 minutes to the modern building on the left side of the street. Coming from Praca da Figueira, terminus of bus 14 and 43 from camp, take the metro to Palhava Station.

The following monuments and museums are open Tu-Su at 10am. Several attractions are concentrated in the Belem area. Belem is on the route of bus 43 from the campground. Jeronoimos Monastery, Praca do Imperio, a masterpiece of Manueline architecture, was built in the 16th century to celebrate the discovery of the trade route to India in 1498. Next door is the Naval Museum with model boats tracing the historical development of water craft, along with a tiny seaplane in which the first crossing of the South Atlantic was made in 1922. The Tower of Belem marks the spot from which Portuguese navigators began their voyages. The Folk Art Museum, Av. Brasilia, exhibits handicrafts from the country. The National Museum of Archaeology and Ethnology, Largo do Carno, shows Roman mosaics, Egyptian mummies, etc. The pier for boats crossing the river is in this area.

The 2,000 year old **Castle of St. George** crowns Lisbon's highest hill. What you see now is the castle after its 16th century remodeling. Entrances are on Largo do Chao da Feira and in the Alfama district, Largo do Menino de Deus. Open 9am-sunset. **Alfama**, the picturesque old quarter, is where the Museum of Decorative Art, Lg. das Portas do Sol, shows 17th and 18th century paintings set within a lovely palace. Adjacent is a craft school. Downtown in Lisbon, the **Cathedral**, Lg da Se, was an Arab Mosque before the 12th century. The bullfight season is Easter to October on Thursday evenings in the Campo Pequeno ring. The bull is not killed in Portuguese fights. The flea market (Feira da Ladra) is on Campo de Santa Clara, Tu and Sa 9-6.

TO THE ALGARVE (direction Tunes), go to T. Paco Station and take the ferry across the river to Barreiro Station. Eurailpasses are valid on the ferry. The departure times given are ferry sailing times from T. Paco Station. The connecting train leaves about 10 minutes after the arrival of the ferry. The best trains are Rapidos and require a reservation. They go as far as Faro and stop only at Tunes and Albufeira. If you want to continue to the Portuguese-Spanish border, a connecting train leaves 7 to 10 minutes after the Rapido arrives. Arrival times are given for the border, Vila Real de Santo Antonio. From T. Paco, the ferry for connecting with Rapido trains leaves at 7:25am (ar. 1:13pm), 2:10pm (ar. 8pm) and 6:05pm (ar. 12:28am). Express departures from T. Paco are at 8:25am (ar. 3:05pm), 6:30pm (ar. 1:18am) and 10:30pm (ar. 7:47am). No reservation needed. For local trains to smaller towns, see schedules under the Algarve.

To Evora, leave T. Paco Station for the ferry trip to Barreiro Station at 7:40am (ar. 10:28am), 12:50am (ar. 3:43pm) and 6:05pm (ar. 8:57pm). The ferry is included in Eurailpasses. The train leaves 10 minutes after the arrival of the ferry.

To Porto (and Coimbra), the best trains are the Intercity Rapidos which carry Corail-type air conditioned coaches with airline style seating. A reservation is required. They leave S. Apolonia Station at 7:15am, 8:25am, 11am, 2:30pm, 5pm and 8:15pm. The trip to Porto is 3 to 3-1/2 hours. All but the 7:15am departure also stop at Coimbra. Arrival in Porto is at Campanha Station. Regular trains leave S. Apolonia Station at 7:20am, 8:50am, 11:35am, 3:25pm and 7pm.

To Madrid, the best train is the TER Lisbon Express, reservation required, which leaves S. Apolonia at 8:10am (ar. 7:23pm). The other through train is the Lusitania Express, leaving S. Apolonia at 9pm (ar. 8:15am). This train is a Rapido in Portugal and an Express in Spain.

EVORA

Evora (A-voo-ra) is Portugal's wonderfully preserved medieval town. Located 150 km. east of Lisbon, it is most easily visited on a daytrip from Lisbon or enroute to the Algarve. If you're here between June 23 and July 2 for their summer festival, consider yourself fortunate.

The **train station** is outside the town walls and you must walk 1 km. to the medieval city. The tourist office is in the central square, Praca do Giraldo 73. Their folder outlines 3 walking tours of the medieval town and describes the buildings.

Camping Orbitur-Evora is 1 km. from town, right of the road to Alcacovas. From the train station, it's a 30-minute walk. Open Jan 16-Nov 15; adult/230$, tent/155$. The shady site has a store.

Trains leave for Lisbon at 8am (ar. 10:50am), 2:14pm (ar.5:05pm), 7:32pm (ar.10:20pm) and 9:20pm (ar. 12:25am). For the Algarve, either backtrack and take the train to Lisbon and change at Barreiro Station or take a slow train south to Funcheira and connect with a train to Tunes.

COIMBRA

Coimbra (kweem-bra) is a fine historical university town. Of its 2 train stations, Coimbra A and Coimbra B/International, the former is closest to downtown. Trains from Lisbon generally only stop at Coimbra B. Connecting trains run to and from Coimbra A and B; 4 minutes apart. If the connecting train from Coimbra B goes beyond Coimbra A to stop at Estacao S. Jose, the latter station is only a 5-minute walk to the campground.

The **municipal campground** is a 20-minute walk from the train station (Coimbra A). See map. In front of the station begins Av. Emidio Navarro. Walk forward on this road keeping the river (Rio Mondego) on your right. This is the road to Guarda. When the road bisects the Botanical Garden it is renamed Rua do Brasil. This street eventually turns left. Follow the road signs to Guarda or to the stadium (*estadio*). The campground is behind the large municipal stadium. You can also take bus 5 (S. Jose) which leaves on R. Ferreira Borges, about 4 blocks from the train station and goes in the direction away from the river. The bus circles around the old city and the botanical garden and does not follow the walking route at all. A small train station (Estacao S. Jose) where only local trains stop is a 5-minute walk from the campground. Open all year; adult/120$, tent/85$. Excellent facilities: 8 automatic washers, swimming pool, store and restaurant.

Trains to Lisbon leave Coimbra B at 7:09am, 9:08am, 9:43am reservation required, 11:16am, 1:45pm, 4:02pm reservation required, 5:18pm, 6:18pm reservation required, 7:12pm, 8:34pm and 9:44pm reservation required.

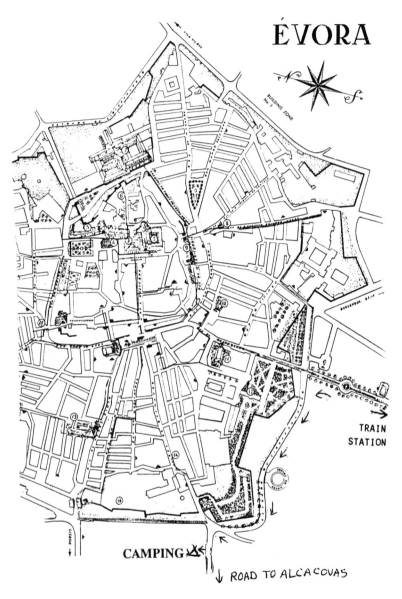

ÉVORA

TRAIN
STATION

CAMPING

↓ ROAD TO ALCACOVAS

1 **TOURIST OFFICE**

Coimbra

374

Porto

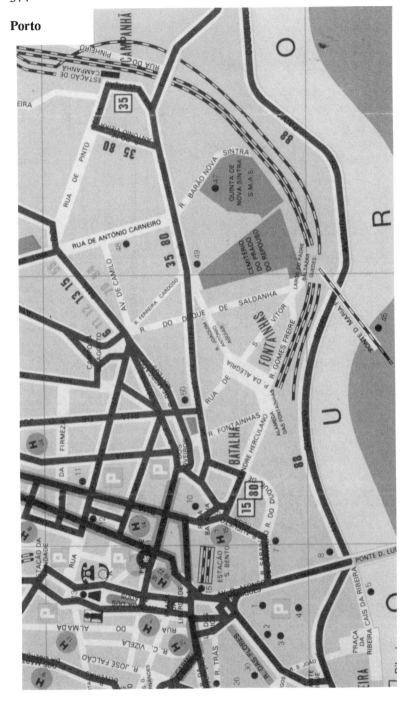

PORTO (OPORTO)

Capital of the north and center of the port wine trade, Porto (oh-POR-toe) is 5 km. inland from the mouth of the Douro River on what once was Portucale in pre-Roman times.

TRAIN STATIONS   The two main stations are Sao Bento, downtown, and Campanha, outside of downtown. From Campanha, take either bus 35 to the last stop at Praca de Almeida Garrett near Sao Bento Station or a local train to Sao Bento Station and the downtown area. Trindade Station serves the coastal area around Porto. To go to northern Spain or France, either backtrack to Pampilhosa and take an international express from there, or take the slower route through north Portugal and Galicia in Spain. For Madrid, go to Encontramento and take the TER Lisbon Express.

TOURIST OFFICE   An office is at Rua dos Fenianos 25, near the town hall and a 4 block walk from Sao Bento Station. The main office is at Praca Dom Joao I near Sao Bento Station.

CAMPGROUND   Camping Prelada, Rua Monte dos Burgos, north of downtown in a public park, is operated by Santa Casa da Misericordia. Open all year; adult/170$, tent/90$. Take bus 35 or 80 from Campanha Station to Praca Almeida Garrett near S. Benito Station. Change to bus 6 at Praca de Liberdade for the campground. Between 9pm and midnight take bus 50. Store and restaurant.

SIGHTSEEING   The tourist office has a brochure on museums and churches. See the Moorish hall inside the Stock Exchange (Palacio de Bolsa), Praca Infante D. Henrique, for its tri-colored red, blue and gold ceiling and Arabesque interior of columns and arcades reminiscent of the Alhambra. Open M-F 10-12 & 2-5. Most port wine firms open their cellars to visitors, but Casa Ferreira even offers a boat cruise on the Douro River which passes wine lodges where maturation takes place before the wine is shipped. The shippers are in Vila Nova de Gaia, across the river from Porto. Tour hours: M-F 9-12 & 2-5:30, also Sa in June. Get information from Instituto do Vinho do Porto, Rua Ferreira Borges.

   To go north to Spain, take the train to Vigo (and then continue to Santiago de Compostela which is more interesting). Trains leave Porto S. Bento for Vigo at 7:27am (ar. 12:41pm) and 2pm (ar. 7:14pm). These trains leave Porto Campanha 8 minutes later. From Porto Campanha only, a train leaves at 6:09pm (ar. 11:01pm).
   To Lisbon S. Apolonia, Intercity Rapido trains (reservation required) leave Campanha at 7:15am (ar. 10:15am) 8:25am (ar. 11:55am, 11am (ar. 2pm), 2:40pm (ar. 6:10pm), 5pm (ar. 8:30pm) and 8:15pm (ar. 11:45pm). Slower Express trains leave Campanha at 7:35am M-F only (ar. 11:35am), 9:30am (ar. 1:50pm), noon (ar. 4:25pm), 3:30pm (ar. 7:55pm) and 6:45pm (ar. 11:10pm). All of these trains stop at Coimbra about 90 minutes later except for the 7:15am and 11am Rapidos.

THE ALGARVE

The extreme southern province provides a cooling summer breeze. It makes a good, sunny year round destination offering sandy beaches, fishing villages and remnants of long past Arab occupation. Campgrounds abound up and down the coast, and by walking some kilometers away from the developments and villages, spots can be found on the beach for freelance camping which is legal in Portugal. Trains from Lisbon go to Tunes, where you must change trains for Lagos if that's your destination. If not, continue on from Tunes to Faro, Monte Gordo (a request stop on local trains only) and Vila Real de Santo Antonio on the Portuguese-Spanish border. Vila Real has two stations of which the second is Guadiana. Ferries (60$) cross the river to Ayamonte in Spain every half hour from 9am to 6pm for the 15-minute trip. From Ayamonte, there are connections to Seville.

Those entering Portugal from Spain will arrive at Vila Real. Three fast Rapido trains leave each day between Faro and Lisbon. Each requires a reservation. From Vila Real, a regular train leaves in time to arrive in Faro about 30 minutes before the Rapido leaves for Lisbon. The fast trains stop only at Albufeira and Tunes before reaching Barreiro Station on the other side of the river from Lisbon. (Then cross on the ferry--Eurailpasses valid--and take a train into Lisbon.) The connecting train leaves Vila Real at 6:40am, 8:10am and 5:40pm. The trip is about 6 hours. Slower express trains leave Vila Real at 8:10am, 1:22pm, 4:10pm and 9pm. These through trains do not require a change at Faro and take 7 hours to reach Lisbon.

Local trains provide service between Lagos, Portimao (port-i-MAN), Alcantarilha, Tunes, Albufeira, Faro, Tavira and Vila Real de San Antonio. Some trains stop only at these towns, while other slower ones will stop at every village on the rail line. From Lagos to Vila Real on a local train takes about four hours. Local trains leave Lagos at 6:30am, 8:33am, 11:30am, 1:20pm, 3:05pm, 4:40pm (goes only as far as Tunes), 6:05pm (goes only as far as Tunes), 7:01pm and 8:25pm. From Vila Real, local trains leave at 5:20am, 7:17am (goes only as far as Tunes), 10:40am, 1:25pm, 4:30pm, 6:15pm, 7:17pm and 9pm (goes only as far a Tunes).

LAGOS   A fishing port with fine beaches, Lagos provides Parque de Turismo de Lagos campground on the beach outside of town, between Porto de Mos and Ponta de Piedade. Open all year; automatic washer, store, bus from Lagos, no camping carnet needed.

FARO (FA-roo)   The largest town on the Algarve, Faro has Camara Municipal de Faro campground in Praia de Faro (PREE-a-da-fa-roo), the beach reached by river ferry. Open all year, adult/75$, tent 120$; store, no camping carnet needed. Take bus 16 (80$) from the station; last bus is 7pm. The Saturday market in nearby Loule is good.

VILA REAL   Two km. west of Vila Real, Camara Muncipal campground in Monte Gordo is 1500 meters from Monte Gordo train station or 200 meters from the bus stop. Open all year, store.

At Vila Real, Torralta Parque Campismo Praia Verde is at the beach. Open all year; Jul-Aug: adult/230$, small tent/140$; Jun & Sep: adult/200$, small tent/120$; Oct-May: adult/120$, small tent/90$. A large, very good camp, sinks with hot water, store, restaurant, swimming and water sports.

From Vila Real, the ferry crosses to Ayamonte in Spain. Remember to set your watch ahead one hour. Portugal uses the same time as Britain, Ireland and Morocco, which is one hour earlier than the rest of Europe. From ferry dock to Ayamonte train station is 2 km.

Trains leave Ayamonte for Seville, a distance of 179 km., at 7am (ar. Huelva 8:20am, change trains, lv. Huelva 9:40am, ar. Seville Plaza de Armas 11:22am), 11am (ar. Huelva 12:25pm, lv. 1:35pm Talgo, ar. 2:52pm Seville San Bernardo), 3:40pm (ar. Huelva 5pm, change trains, lv. 5:10pm, ar. Seville Plaza de Armas 6:43pm). For Madrid, the 1:35pm Talgo from Huelva is a through train arriving in Madrid at 9:02pm.

SPAIN

Spain ranks with Italy, France and Greece in the glory of her past civilization. Distances are great in this large and mountainous country, but the journey is worth it.

CURRENCY There are about 110 pesetas to the U.S. dollar.

WEATHER Spain is a mecca for the off-season camper who could make this country the anchor of his itinerary. The best time for visiting all of Spain is spring or autumn, except the northern coast might be somewhat cold and rainy. May probably provides the best camping weather for an all-around itinerary, with September and early October being next. In summer, the cities of Moorish background, Seville and Cordoba, are very warm. Madrid gets periodically hot in summer with an 84 degree average in July. Average temperatures shouldn't be taken too literally because weather varies from week to week and a heat wave sending temperatures soaring into the 90's can occur even in June. The trick to fitting Madrid into a summer itnerary comfortably is to keep plans flexible, watchdog the weather in the international papers and be ready to move when the temperature is right. For a winter tour, camping is good along the Costa del Sol in southern Spain and on the islands of Majorca and Ibiza.

CAMPING In contrast with the camps of Germany, Switzerland, France and Scandinavia which were first developed for their own countrymen, those of Spain sprouted to meet the needs of tourists from northern Europe, notably the traditional sun-seekers of Scandinavia, Britain and Germany. Because of this, the majority of campgrounds are on the southern coast rather than in Madrid or near the best sightseeing destinations. Some campgrounds on the Costa Brava and Costa del Sol in southern Spain are resort camps with teams of cleaning ladies scouring the restrooms three times daily, resident doctor, store, restaurant, shops and anything else a week-long vacationer needs to enjoy himself.

      The tourist office publishes, *Mapa de Campings*, which pinpoints each camp on a map of Spain and lists opening times and government classification. Camps are categorized deluxe (*lujo*), first, second and third class according to number of facilites and seaside location. From our experiences, we found camp classifications unrelated to restroom quality and, if anything, the smaller family-run camps seemed tidier and more tightly managed. Before each season, the owners of each campground are required by law to obtain a certificate of proof of water quality to show that the water is drinkable. Non-drinking water may only be used for irrigation and in the toilets. Each camp in Spain is required by law to have a surrounding fence, first aid box, watchman, running water, sinks, showers, toilets, lighting and fire extinguisher. The words tent (*tienda*), car (*coche*) and child (*nino*) are used at campgrounds.

TRAINS   The best of the Spanish State Railways (RENFE) trains are comparable to EuroCity trains. Often a reservation is necessary. Reservations are computerized and efficient throughout Spain, but you still must stand in line. Starting with 1989, Eurail Youthpass includes all supplements. In July and August trains on popular tourist routes are fairly crowded in second class, so Youthpass holders might want to figure their itinerary and make all the reservations at once. **Whatever class, be particulary careful to secure a reservation for Granada in advance because only one good train arrives and departs each day and it is often completely reserved a day or two ahead.** All most people need is one day in Granada--its sights are wonderful but few.

Distances are so great in Spain that often trains will arrive late at night. Usually this doesn't present a problem as buses run late too and Spaniards keep late hours. The tracks of Spanish and Portuguese trains are of a broader width than those in France and the rest of Europe (except Finland), so you must change trains at French-Spanish borders except in a few cases where trains are used whose wheels are adjustable in width, such as Spain's premier train, the Talgo. Many Spanish trains have no running water for hand washing in the restrooms. Often only one or two signs identifying the station are visible as the train arrives. You must be alert to catch the name so you know which station it is. Some of the regional trains have no first class.

The best trains are the **Talgo, T.E.R.** (Tren Espanol Rapido) and **E.L.T** (Electrotren), all of which have both first and second class and are air-conditioned. Everybody must either reserve a seat or obtain a free boarding pass before getting on any train in the express category, i.e. any long distance or international train. A reservation made 2 to 3 days in advance is advised for Talgo, TER and ELT trains in summer--if you don't get one you aren't likely to get on--but is not officially required. But if you don't make a reservation, it is still mandatory that a free boarding pass be obtained for the specific train departure at the reservations counter of the train station before you are allowed on the train. The boarding pass is a computerized card like the reservation, is issued the same day as the train departs and doesn't assign a specific seat. Any train categorized as Rapido or Express also requires a boarding pass. A boarding pass is not required for non-express trains: local and commuter trains and slower long distance ones. These are called semi-directo, tranvia and correo and generally leave from the area or station marked as cercanias (local trains which stop at small towns). Long distance trains are categorized as largos corridas and leave from main stations.

Large Spanish cities tend to have more than one train station, so be sure to go to the correct one. The station is listed in parenthesis following the city name on the schedules. Sometimes track assignments are changed at the last minute. If you hear an announcement made over the loudspeaker and everyone on the platform begins to head elsewhere, follow them to the new track. Reservations and boarding passes are obtained at the reservations window. If it's not obvious which is a reservation window, ask at train information. Often the same window both sells tickets and issues reservations and is marked *Taquilla Largo Recorrido*. Stations generally have a tourist office and foreign exchange. Lockers are less abundant than in the rest of Europe, but luggage checking is always available. Sometimes there is a separate cashier who collects the fee and issues a receipt before you proceed to the baggage line. Sometimes one line is for checking and another for receiving.

estacion	station
acceso andenes	to the tracks
asiento	a seat on the train
reserva	seat reservation
cambio	foreign exchange
la consigna	baggage check
llegada	arrival
sala de espera	waiting room
oficina de informacion	train information office
horario de trene	train schedule
trenes de salida	trains ready to depart
venta para hoy	for trains leaving today
venta anticipada	for trains leaving after today
cercanias	local trains
largo recorrido	long distance trains
cerrado	closed
abierto	open
entrada	entrance
salida	exit
senores, hombres	mens restroom
senoras, mujeres, damas	womens restroom
Quiere darme un horario de trene?	May I have a timetable.
Esta ocupado este asiento?	Is this seat taken?

EURAIL BONUS On the normal fares of the Trasmediterranea Company between Barcelona or Valencia and Palma de Mallorca and between Algiciras and Tangiers (Morocco), there is a 20 percent reduction.

FOOD You can eat reasonably in Spain on seasonal fruits and vegetables, chicken, fish and cheese. Chicken breast *(pechuga)* is usually a reliable and tasty dish most anywhere. Veal is good and cheaper than beef. Baby lamb, rabbit and pork are commonly found. Milk and cream are pasteurized. There's also a sterilized milk that is safe. Good apple juice and cider come from the north of Spain. Tap water is safe but the popular and inexpensive Solares mineral water is only slightly effervescent and Font Vella is flat. Sherry is the usual aperitif and dessert wine. Valdepenas, produced in Central Spain, is the most popular and reasonable red wine. A restaurant's house wine will often be Valdepenas. The best and smoothest wines come from the Rioja region in northern Spain. Better quality ones have the name of the vintner *(bodega)* on the label.

The outdoor market sells most everything and has considerably lower prices than the shops or supermarkets. A half kilo is slightly over a pound and a good quantity of fruit to buy. Request *un medio kilo* (MAY-dee-oh KEY-loh). A *panaderia* sells bread and a *lecheria* stocks milk and cheese. Go to a *bodega* for wine, liquor and soft drinks. Try an *ultramarinos* for canned food, vegetables, sausage, cooking oil and wine. Toilet paper, tissue and shampoo are sold at a *perfumeria*. A *churreria* sells churros, rings of deep fried batter which Spaniards eat for breakfast in cold weather. These tiny shops open and close in early morning to reopen later in the afternoon to cook and sell potato chips. Ice cream sold in restaurants, cafes and grocery stores are safe, but those sold by vending carts, most of which have questionable means of refrigeration, are best avoided.

Restaurants are government classified into five categories from deluxe with a five fork symbol to a simple restaurant denoted by one fork. Each restaurant is required to offer a tourist menu (menu turistico) which includes three courses, bread, quarter liter wine and service at a set price. The three courses are normally appetizer or soup, entree and dessert. A minimum of three choices are offered within each course. Some choices may carry a supplemental charge. Many restaurants offer a fixed price meal which changes daily according to the offerings of the local market. This menu is posted outside along with the tourist menu. It is often the better buy, but doesn't necessarily include service or beverage.

The best time to eat in a restaurant is for the "noon meal" which is eaten about 2pm. The evening meal is typically taken at 10:30pm by a Spaniard, though restaurants open earlier for visitors. Sometimes choosing a higher grade restaurant and ordering a la carte costs no more and gives better value than ordering the tourist menu in an inferior place. The reliability of cooking is often greater in a higher class restaurant unless a specific recommendation is being followed. If you wish to avoid fried foods, order a dish marked grilled (*a la parilla*) or roasted (*asado*).

BARCELONA

Barcelona is near the French border and a good choice for those who have time for only one Spanish city. Don't worry if your train arrives late as commuter trains still depart for the suburbs where the campgrounds are.

TRAIN STATIONS   Termino, Sants and Paseo de Gracia are the three main stations. Termino Station is being remodeled so trains may be using Sants instead. Since some trains stop at all three, it's possible to get from one station to another by train. The metro stops at all stations.

Termino   The station is called both Barcelona Termino and Estacion de Francia. It is used by most Talgo, TER, ELT and long distance fast trains, and by trains coming from southern France. Facilities include a tourist office, reservations office (7am-7pm), foreign exchange (8am-10pm), lockers (100ptas), luggage check (5am-11pm) and restaurants. The metro (subway) stop for Termino Station is Barceloneta. Consult the reader board inside the entry to the tracks (*acceso andenes*) for the next departures from the station. A green light flashes next to the departures currently loading. Here is an example of the reader board.

Barcelona - Termino and Barceloneta Station Area

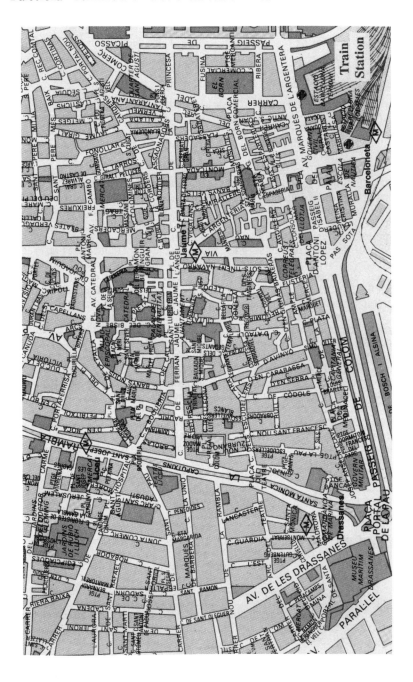

PROXIMAS SALIDAS (next departures)

Tren	Destino	Hora	Via
(train)	(destination)	(departure)	(track #)
Rapido Talgo	Madrid	10:00	7
Catalan Talgo	Ginebra	10:18	8
Electro Tren	Bilbao	12:35	not listed yet
Rapido Talgo	Madrid	13:50	2

Flanking the tourist office (*Oficina Municipal de Turismo e Informacion*) window in Termino Station are two large reader boards which list trains leaving from both central (*Termino*) and Barceloneta (cercanias) Stations. Estacion Barceloneta is beside Termino Station and handles local trains. These two boards show Lina Villanueva and Lina de Mataro. The route is shown in red on the diagram. Note the time of the next train going in the direction you want. Every train leaving from Barceloneta Station stops at all towns on the map. Only *tranvia* and *semi-directo* trains leave from Barceloneta Station. For the most part, trains leaving Termino only stop at the largest towns, but there are a few exceptions. Trains to the campgrounds leave from Barceloneta Station.

Linea de Villanueva goes south of Barcelona and stops at Prat de Llobregat, Gava, Castelldefels, Playa de Castelldefels, Garraf, Vallcarca, Sitges, Villanueva, Geltru and at towns farther up the coast. To go to Castelldefels, take a train in the direction of Taragona or Reus or one of the aforementioned stops. Trains leave about once an hour on this route.

Linea de Mataro extends north of Barcelona along the coast towards France. Its trains stop at Pueblo N., S. Adrian de B., Badalona, Mongat, Montsolis, Masnou, Ocata, Premia, Vilasar, Mataro, Llavaneras, Caldetas, Arenys and other towns until it reaches Blanes. At Blanes, the train turns inland to Port-Bou and the Spanish border. Service is very frequent on this line, about every 15 minutes, with the last train departing at 11pm. Be careful not to take any train in the direction of Gerona Via Granollers as that's the inland route and doesn't go along the coast.

To reach Barceloneta Station, use the side door off the track area of Termino Station. That is, from the tracks, pass the restrooms and the Cantina, turn left and follow the signs to Barceloneta Station (see map). The reader boards in Termino Station are easier to read for Barceloneta Station departures than those in Barceloneta Station, but if you're already here, look for trains leaving under Direccion Villanueva for southern coastal towns and Direccion Mataro for departures for northern coastal towns towards France. These trains are included in Eurailpasses. The normal fare round trip (de ida y vuelta) for nearby towns is very cheap, equivalent to local bus transportation. In front of each track a signpost gives details on the train.

Via 01	(track #1)	
Tren	(type of train)	Tranvia
Destino	(final destination)	Mataro
Salida	(departure time)	17:30 (5:30pm)

Sants Station (Estacio Sants-Central)   Trains for northwest Spain leave from Sants. Similar facilities to Termino including a reservations office (open 7am-8pm), tourist office and luggage storage (5am-11pm).

CITY TRANSPORTATION   Fares are inexpensive on both the metro and buses. A single metro ticket costs 50ptas or a 10-ride ticket for 295ptas.

Barcelona - Metro

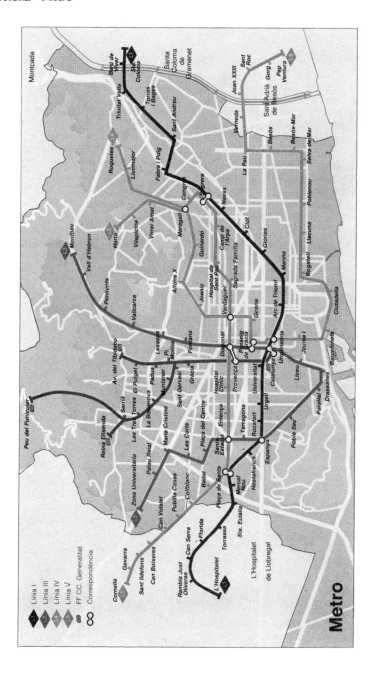

Metro

The bus is 55ptas except on Sunday, 60ptas. A 10-ride ticket is 345ptas good on either bus or metro. A combination metro and bus ticket valid for 10 rides on each costs 490ptas. Purchase tickets at the metro stations. Bus stops are marked *parada*.

CAMPGROUNDS Many camps are located south of Barcelona between the coast and the highway to Castelldefels. These are large, resort type deluxe camps with restaurants, supermarkets, laundries, souvenir stores and wide, sandy beaches. The camps are generally rated deluxe because of the numerous facilities and charge the highest rates for Spanish campgrounds. Smaller and cheaper campgrounds are situated on the coast north of Barcelona towards France. These are easily reached by commuter train and are recommended over those towards the south. Another option is to camp at the lovely resort town of Sitges and commute to Barcelona. All things considered, I prefer staying at Camping Masnou.

Camping Badalona-Playa, Apartado de Correos 77, is in Badalona, 7 km. northeast of Barcelona. Jun 15-Sep 15; adult/250ptas, tent/250pts. From Barceloneta Station, take the train to Badalona Station. (The station is on P. Del Caudillo. Walk one kilometer farther north on the seafront street to the campground. It can also be reached by bus. The campground is quite small with two straight lines of marked campsites with reed roof cover to filter the sun. Clean restrooms, free hot showers, beach in front, automatic washer, store, snack bar, bargain rental apartments.

Camping Don Quijote, is northeast of Barcelona at Montsolis. Jun 1-Sep 30; adult/275ptas, tent/275ptas. From Barceloneta Station, take the train to Montsolis. Then walk northeast farther along the coast on the beach road for one kilometer. Camp is on the left side of the road. Store, automatic washer, snack bar and 200 meters across the road to the beach.

Camping Masnou is more deluxe than the other two camps. The beach across the road is quite nice and better than at the other closer camps, yet the train ride is only another 5 minutes. Open all year; adult/380ptas, tent/380ptas. Camping Masnou is in the town of Masnou, 11 km. from Barcelona. Take the local train (cercanias) from Barceloneta Station to Masnou, the stop after Montsolis. Trains leave approximately every 20 minutes from 6am to 10pm; the ride is 15 to 20 minutes. Masnou Station is 200 meters from the campground. (Also near the station is a beautiful yacht club and marina.) Another way is to take the subway to Badalona and change to bus B29 which stops directly in front of the campground. There is also another bus line which covers the Alella-Barcelona portion by freeway and is therefore faster, but this bus does not run as frequently as the B29 or the train. It stops 100 meters from camp. The camping site has some shade and you get a good breeze close to the water. There's a nice bar with a terrace overlooking the water, store with rotisseried chickens, restaurant, large swimming pool with slide, high and low dive (extra charge), ping pong and foreign exchange. The restrooms have hot showers (charge), no toilet paper, and laundry sinks.

Camping La Ballena Alegre is 12.5 km. south of Barcelona on the highway to Castelldefels. Whereas the other camps are small, this is a huge campground with all manner of services. It's more time consuming and trouble to reach than the others and more expensive because of its deluxe rating due to its number of facilities. Its restrooms are not particularly better. Open Apr 1-Sep 30; adult/375ptas, tent/375ptas. From Termino

Station, take bus 14 from outside the station on the right, near the post office, to Calle de Aribau. Then walk two blocks to Diputacion-Enrique Granados on Calle (street) de Enrique Granados and take the bus to Castelldefels. After about 40 minutes and beyond Barcelona, the bus takes the coastal highway and passes the first camp, El Toro Bravo, on the left. Don't get off here because this camp is a long walk from the highway to the coast whereas others are closer. The next camp, La Ballena Alegre, is immediately across the highway from the bus stop. The bus continues passing several other camps before reaching Castelldefels. Alternatively, a train from Barceloneta Station to Castelldefels can be taken, and then a bus to the campgrounds. Ballena Alegre is very large with shade trees and a wide, sandy beach. All facilities are on site including automatic washers, free hot showers, disco, restaurant, souvenir store, supermarket, snack bar, chicken rotisserie and foreign exchange.

Campgrounds in Sitges A good, cheap Mediterranean resort town with good beaches, Sitges lies 41 km. south of Barcelona. The town is on the main rail line and enjoys frequent train service to all three train stations in Barcelona. The most frequent departures to Sitges originate from Sants Station. Trains not requiring a boarding pass leave Termino (and also stop at Paseo and Sants) at 6:48am, 9am, 10:43am 12:05pm, 12:59pm, 1:58pm, 2:58apm 5:30pm 7:06pm 10:02pm and 10:51pm. Other local trains leave from Paseo de Gracia and Sants. The trip is 45 minutes from Termino, 30 minutes from Sants. The tourist office is at Isla de Cuba 7, a street jutting perpendicularly from the train station. Two campgrounds are within 200 meters of the station: **Camping El Roca**, Carretera S. Pedro Ribas, and Los Almendros, Avenida Capellans. From the Station, cross the tracks on the walkover and walk 5 minutes up the street. **Camping Sitges** is open all year; adult/275ptas, tent/250ptas; store, snack bar, exchange. Los Almendros is open Apr 1-Sep 30; adult/300ptas, tent/280ptas; store, snack bar and exchange.

SIGHTSEEING   Montjuich Park is a stellar attraction with the Pueblo Espanol (Spanish Village), Museum of Art of Catalonia and the new Fundacion Joan Miro. The Spanish Village contains houses and workshops reflecting various regional styles of architecture and decoration, grouped to form a small village. Open 9-8, 250ptas. The excellent Catalonia Museum is open Tu-Su 9-2, 190ptas, free on Sunday. Finally, the Fundacion is open Tu-Sa 11am-8pm, Su 11-230, 300ptas. If you like the Fundacion, you may wish to stop at Figueras on the Costa Brava northeast of Barcelona near the French border to see the Salvador Dali Museum. (The trip is 2 hours from Termino Station.) Designed by Dali, the museum has a cupola painted inside by Dali who has foreshortened the characters so they appear to be emerging towards you with very large feet.

Picasso Museum (*Museo Pablo Picasso*), Calle de Montcada 15, is open m 4-8:30, Tu-Sa 9:30am-1:30pm & 4-8:30pm, Su 9:30-1:30, 190ptas, student free. Mansions and palaces mostly built in the 13th century line Calle de Montcada where the beautiful medieval Aguilar Palace and Baron de Castellat Palace are now home to the Museo Palo Picasso. Don't miss. The largest grouping in the world of Picasso's paintings, sculpture, etchings, lithographs and book illustrations is shown here. Picasso's friend and former secretary, Jaime Sabartes, donated his collection to the museum, and in 1968 and 1970, Picasso gave over 900 items as a memorial to Sabartes.

Alicante

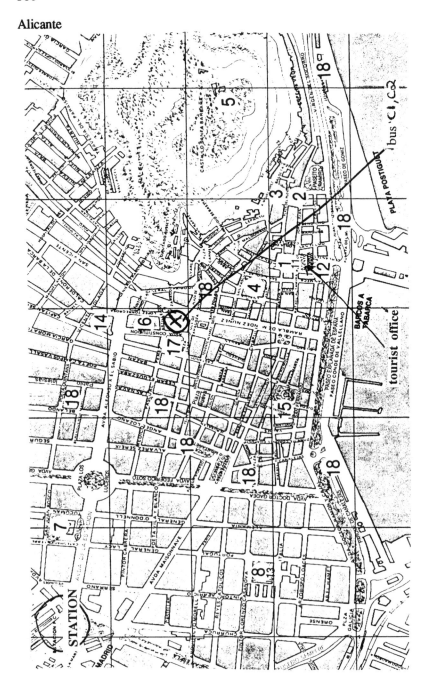

Las Meninas, a satire on Valazquez' famous painting in the Prado in Madrid, is here, consisting of 58 paintings done within five months. The restroom is near the entrance. Good reproductions are sold at the sales desk. The Ramblas, Barrio Gotico and the Cathedral of the Sacred Family (Templo de la Sagrada Familia) by Gaudi are other sights. The latter, at Calle Mallorca and Calle de Ceerdena, is in no recognizable architectural style and somewhat strange, though monumental.

To Granada, an express leaves Sants at 5:50pm (ar. 10:40am).
To Geneva, take the EuroCity (reservation required) that leaves Sants at 9:50am (ar. 7:44pm), or the overnight train leaving Sants at 7:49pm (change at Cerbere, ar. 7:25am).
To France (Montpellier, Cannes, Antibes and Nice) leave Sants at 9:50am EuroCity reservation necessary (change at Avignon, ar. Nice 7:58pm), 10:25am (change at Cerbere, ar. 10:13pm) and 7:49pm (change at Cerbere, ar. 8:05am).
To Madrid Chamartin, the best train is the Talgo that leaves Paseo de Gracia at 10:40am, picks up at Sants (ar. 6:10pm) or the Talgo that leaves Termino at 2:20pm, picks up at Paseo de Gracia and Sants (ar. 9:25pm). A Rapido leaves Sants at 8:25am (ar. 5:28pm). The overnight express Costa Brava leaves Paseo de Gracia at 9:53pm, picks up at Sants (ar. 7:31am). A better overnight train is the air-conditioned Rapido that leaves Sants at 11:05pm (ar. 8:30am).
To Paris Austerlitz, leave Sants at 7:12am Rapido, stop at Paseo de Gracia (ar. 9:35pm); 4:28pm (change at Cerbere, ar. 7:48am); and 8:55pm Barcelona Talgo, reservation required (ar. 8:36am).
To Seville, leave Sants at 7am Rapido Torre del Oro (ar. 8:01pm), or 7:20pm Rapido (ar. 9:33am). Cordoba is a stop on the way to Seville.

ANDALUCIA

Beautiful geometrically patterned Moorish palaces, cathedrals showing Moorish influence and fascinating old quarters are the main attractions. The important cities are Granada, Seville and Cordoba. From Seville, it's possible to enter Portugal from the south and visit The Algarve enroute to Lisbon.

STOPOVER IN ALICANTE ENROUTE TO ANDALUCIA From the station, walk to the bus stop marked on the map and board bus C1 or C2 for the campgrounds. Camping Bahia near a fine sand beach is on Playa Albufereta (Mar 15-Oct15; adult/265ptas, small tent/245ptas, shady site). Camping Lucentrum on Albufereta is inland but in the same vicinity. Open all year; adult/205ptas, small tent/205ptas.

CORDOBA Cordoba (accent on the first syllable) has both a wonderful old quarter and an attractive modern area. The tourist office (Oficina de Informacion de Turismo) on on Torrijos Streetin the the Palace of Congress across from the Mezquita, 15 blocks from the station.

Campamento Municipal de Turismo is on the Cordoba-Villaviciosa highway 2 km. from Cordoba. This is a first class site open all year; adult/250ptas, tent/200ptas. From the train station, turn left and walk to the intersection of Avenida de Gran Capitan. Turn right onto this stree and walk 3 blocks; turn left on Ronda de los Tejares. Take bus 10 or 11. It is possible to walk by turning left on Avenida de American upon leaving the station. Continue beside the station for 2.5 blocks until the street that crosses beyond the railway tracks. Turn left and follow signs to camp. The walk is less than 2 km.. Store, snack bar, swimming pool.

388

The **market** (*mercado publico*) is in Plaza de la Corredera, the public square enclosed by walls, near the street, Rodriguez Marin. The dominant sight is the Mosque (Mezquita-Catedral), open daily 10:30am-1:30pm & 4-7pm, 250ptas. The tourist office pamphlet has other sightseeing ideas and a walk through the old quarter is a must.

To Barcelona Sants, leave 10:22am (ar. 9:25pm), 8:44pm (ar. 8:55am) or 10:39pm (ar. 12:25pm). The first 2 are Rapido; the last slower express.
To Madrid, the best train is the Talgo that leaves at 8:49am (ar. Atocha 1:06pm), 4:30pm (ar. Atocha 8:17pm), and 5:06pm (ar. Atocha 9:39pm, Chamartin 9:49pm). A rapido (leaves at 1:54pm (ar. 7:15pm). A non-express overnight train leaves at 9pm (ar. Atocha 6:50am).
To Seville, the best trains leave at 7:50am, 1:30pm, 6:48pm and 7:35pm. Non-express trains leave at 8:10am 1:55pm, 3:10pm 6:15pm and 8:35pm. 2 hours.

SEVILLE (SEVILLA) Capital of Andalucia, Seville (pronounced say-V-ya) can be the hottest spot in all Spain, the average high temperature reaching 93 degrees in summer. Seville's two train stations are San Bernardo (Estacion de Cadiz) and Plaza de Armas (Estacion de Cordoba). Reservations can be made at the RENFE office, 29 Calle de Zaragoza. The tourist office is one block from the cathedral, or about 14 blocks from San Bernardo Station.

Campgrounds The campgrounds outside Seville can be reached by bus from the bus station in Prado de San Sebastian. From San Bernardo Station, walk across the plaza in front and head towards your left for three blocks. **Camping Sevilla** is 5 km. from Seville on the highway to Cordoba and Madrid. Take the bus to Carmona and ask the driver to let you off at the campground, then a 3 minute walk. Open all year; adult/250ptas, tent/225ptas. Swimming pool, store, snack bar and day room. **Club de Campo** is 12 km. from Seville on the highway to Dos Hermanas, the main Madrid-Cadiz road. Take the bus to Dos Hermanas and get off at the camp. Open Jun-Oct; adult/250ptas, tent/225ptas.

Sightseeing Top priority is the Cathedral, largest in Spain, and its accompanying tower, Giralda. Open May-Sep M-Sa 10:30am-1:30pm & 4:30-6:30pm, Su 10:30am-1pm; 125ptas. The Alcazar, a beautifully decorated moorish (or more accurately mudejar) palace is open 9am-12:45pm & 3-5:45pm, 125ptas. Santa Cruz is the picturesque old quarter.

To Barcelona Sants, leave Plaza de Armas at 8:45am (ar. 9:45pm) and 7pm (ar. 8:55am).
To Caceres, leave Plaza de Armas at 5:30pm (ar. 10:30pm). This is a minor rail route and an all second class, slow train.
To Granada, leave San Bernardo at 7:45am (ar. 12:10pm), 12:10pm (ar. Bobadilla 2:48pm, change trains, lv. Bobadilla 3:20pm (ar. 5:35pm) and 5:05pm (ar. 9:30pm).
To Lisbon, leave San Bernardo at 7:20am Rapido, ar. Huelva Termino 8:50am, change to all second class train, leave Huelva Termino 9:15am, ar. Ayamonte 10:35am, cross on ferry to Vila Real de Santo Antonio in Portugal, lv. Vila Real 12:05pm, ar. Faro 1:45pm, change to Rapido Sotavento, reservation required, lv. Faro 2:15pm (ar. Lisbon 6:30pm). At Ayamonte, the train station is 2 km. from the ferry dock. The ferry to Portugal runs every half hour from 9am-6pm. The ride is 15 minutes.
To the Algarve in Portugal, see above or leave Plaza de Armas at 6:55am, 11am and 2:46pm. Change at Huelva Termino. Leave Huelva Termino at 9:15am (ar. 10:35am), 2pm (ar. 3:25pm) or 5:30pm (ar. 6:50pm). At Ayamonte, walk to the ferry dock, 2 km. from the station, and take a 15-minute ferry for Vila Real in Spain which leaves every half hour from 9am-6pm. At Vila Real, local trains traveling along the coast to Lagos leave at 5:20am, 10:40am, 1:35pm, 4:30pm, 6:15pm (change at Tunes) and 7:17pm (change at Tunes). Trains to Lisbon leave Vila Real at 8:10am (ar. 3pm),

12:05pm (ar. Faro 1:45pm, change to rapido, reservation required, lv. 2:15pm, ar. 6:30pm), 1:22pm Sunday only (ar. 8:40pm), 4:10pm (ar. 11pm) and 5:40pm (ar. Faro 6:55pm, change to Rapido reservation required, lv. 7:05pm, ar. 11:20pm).

To Madrid Atocha, a Talgo leaves Plaza de Armas Station at 7:30am (ar. 1:06pm) and a Talgo leaves San Bernardo Station at 3:09pm (ar. 9:02pm). A Rapido leaves San Bernardo Station at 11:53am (ar. 7:15pm). An express, air-conditioned train leaves Plaza de Armas Station at 11pm (ar. 8am) and another express leaves San Bernardo Station at 12:27am (ar. 8:08am). A non express train leaves Plaza de Armas Station at 8:02am (ar. Cordoba 9:57am, change trains, lv. Cordoba 2:10pm (ar. 6:59pm). All trains stop at Cordoba enroute to Madrid.

GRANADA   The Alhambra draws visitors to this immortalized Moorish town. The plaque at the entrance gate of the Alcazaba translates: Give him alms, woman, For there is nothing in life, nothing, So sad as to be blind in Granada. The Alhambra is open Mar-Sep 9:30am-7:45pm, Oct-Apr closes at 5:15pm, 350ptas, Sunday free after 4pm. You can walk everywhere in town and this is the best way, or buses (4, 5, 9 & 11) run from the train station to the center. RENFE is at Calle de los Reyes Catolicos (M-F 8am-2:30pm). Because of the few trains arriving and leaving Granada, it's important to make your return reservation as soon as you arrive. The tourist office is downtown at C. Libreros.

Campgrounds   Camping Ultimo is just south of the city. From the station, take bus 9 to Al Camping, the end of the line, and change to bus 90 or walk 15 minutes to the campground. The bus stops at the camp entrance every 15 minutes. The attractive camp has lots of shade trees, swimming pool, store and restaurant; adult/275ptas, tent/250ptas. **Camping Motel Sierra Nevada** is on the highway to Madrid (Avenida de Madrid, 79), 1.5 km from the train station. Take bus 3 or 5 in the direction "Almanjayar." Open Mar 1-Oct 30; adult/350ptas, tent/350ptas. This is a good camp (classified 1a) with shady and grassy sites, 2 swimming pools (1 for children), hot water in restroom sinks, free hot showers, store, restaurant, 2 tennis courts and children's playground. **Camping Maria Eugenia** is on the highway to Malaga. Open all year; adult/275ptas, tent/275ptas. All facilities including automatic washer, store, restaurant and swimming pool. Very nice camp. **Camping Reina Isabel** is 4 km. from Granada on the road to La Zubia. Open all year; adult/2750ptas, tent/275ptas. Excellent facilities hot water in restroom sinks, automatic washer, store and restaurant.

Camping Sierra Nevada

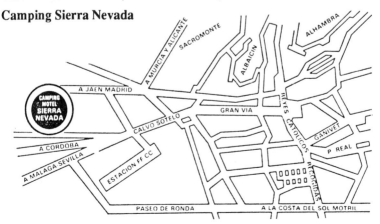

To Barcelona, the only through train is an overnight express, leaving at 3:50pm (ar. 8:43am).

To Madrid, there's only one through train, the Talgo that leaves at 2:25pm and arrives at 8:55pm. This train can be fully reserved two days before departure in summer, so make a reservation as early as possible. The alternative is to take the train to Linares-Baeza, the closest town on the main rail line to Madrid from Malaga. Trains to Linares-Baeza leave at 7:40am (ar. 10:29am) and 3:50pm (ar. 7:09pm). Slower trains leave Linares-Baeza for Madrid at 2:49pm (all second class, ar. 6:59pm), and 11:54pm (all second class, ar. 6:50am).

To Seville, leave 8:20am (ar. 12:28pm) and 5:40pm (ar. 9:55pm). The rail line to Seville is very minor, Rapido trains, second class only.

MADRID

Madrid occupies the economic, political and geographic heart of Spain. It is the only major city in Europe that is somewhat bereft of campgrounds, having only two. Its major sight is the world famous Prado Museum. Madrid also serves as an excursion base for nearby Toledo and El Escorial.

TRAIN STATIONS Madrid has four. They are connected by both trains and the metro. Make reservations at the train stations, or the RENFE downtown office at Alcala 44 (open M-F 8-2:30 & 4-7, Sa 8-1:30).

Chamartin, the newest station, handles most international traffic. Its tourist office has English language brochures for all Spanish cities and towns. Also available are luggage check (7am-midnight, 100ptas), lockers, seat reservations (open 8am-9pm), exchange (open 7am-10pm) and post office. The metro stop is called Chamartin. Chamartin Station is connected with Atocha Station by shuttle train (apeadero) which is part of RENFE and included in Eurailpasses. Trains leave at 15 minute intervals and make two stops enroute, first at Recoletos (Paseo Calvo Sotelo) and then at Nuevos Ministerios (Avenida del Generalisimo).

Atocha, the older station, used to handle international trains before Chamartin was built. It's in an area of hotels, restaurants and pensions, but away from the main shopping area. Trains leaving Atocha serve Granada, Valencia, Seville, Cordoba, the Levant, Extramadura, Toledo, Alcala de Henares, Guadalajara and Portugal. Inside are a reservations office (open 9am-9pm), foreign exchange (8:30am-9:30pm), post office and luggage storage (7am-midnight, 100ptas). Beside Atocha Station is small **Atocha-Apeadero** (Apd.) Station which is directly connected with the subway.

Estacion Norte (Principe Pio) handles traffic to Barcelona, Santiago de Compostela and Salamanca.

TOURIST OFFICE Offices are at Chamartin Station, Torre de Madrid, Plaza de Espana and Alcala 44.

CITY TRANSPORTATION The tourist office map includes a subway map. The bus route map (Plano de Lineas Itinerarios) is separate. Besides regular buses, there are faster yellow mini-buses which are privately owned, cost slightly more and don't allow standing. The subway (metropolitano) operates 6:30am-1:30am. A single ride is 50ptas or a 10-ride ticket for 410ptas. Puerta del Sol (Sol) and Opera are the main interchange stations. City buses are red and cost 55ptas per ride or a 10-ride ticket for 500ptas. The yellow minibuses cost 65ptas a ride or 20 rides for 1300ptas.

CAMPGROUNDS   Camping Madrid, Cerro del Aguila just off the Burgos-Madrid highway, is the closest camp being 11 km. from the center and 3-1/2 km. from Chamartin Station.   Open all year, adult/275ptas, tent/275ptas.   From Chamartin Station, either walk 7 minutes or take the metro to Plaza de Castilla.   Then take bus 129 (Moraleja) that leaves every 20 minutes to the stop at Dominicos Church, 900 meters from the campground. The camp has a swimming pool, store and snack bar.

Camping Madrid

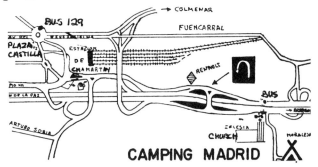

CAMPING MADRID

Camping Osuna, 15 km. from downtown, is on the highway Ajalvir-Vicalvaro in the general vicinity of Barajas Airport.   Open all year; adult/275pts, tent/275ptas.   Take the metro to Canillejas Station.   Outside board bus 105 and then a short walk to the camp. Facilities include store, restaurant, swimming pool and automatic washer.

FOOD   The market (mercado), Cava Baja, is near interesting Plaza Mayor.

SIGHTSEEING   Museo del Prado is alone worth the trip to Madrid for its vast collection of the works of incomparable Goya which show the real and fallible kings and queens of his time, and comment on humanity in his cartoon etchings which include, The Disasters of War 1810-14. Also on display are the best works of El Greco, Velazquez, Zurbara, Ribera, Murillo, Fra Angelico, Rafael, Bosco, Rubens, Titian, Breughel,Bosch, and Van Dyke. Open May-Oct Tu-Sa 9-7, Su 9-2; Nov-Apr Tu-Sa 10-5, Su 10-2; 400ptas, students free.

Plaza Mayor, a nicely proportioned square inaugurated in 1620, marks the heart of a good walking area in picturesque old Madrid. Nearby are inexpensive food shops and the public market at Cava Baja. The City Information office is at Plaza Mayor 3.

Archeological Museum, Serrano 13 (metro Serrano), open Tu-Su 9:15-1:45 (200ptas, students free), shows exact reproductions of prehistoric wall paintings from the Cave of Altamira near Santillana del Mar. The cave reopens later from 4-8pm, entrance to left of main gate.

DAY TRIP TO TOLEDO   Subject of El Greco's famous painting and 92 km. from Madrid, Toledo can be seen on a day excursion from Madrid. From the station take the bus (Santa Barbara) for 45ptas up the hill to the old town, or else a 20 minute walk. Once in town, all sights are within walking distance of each other. The Alcazar (open Mar-Aug 9:30am-7pm, Sept-Oct 9:30-6:30; 100ptas), Cathedral (open Jul-Aug 10:30-1 & 3:30-7, Sep-Ju

10:30-1 & 3:30-6, free), El Greco's House and Museum (Tu-Sa 10-1:45 & 3:30-5:45, Su 10-1:45, 200 ptas.), Transito Synagogue (200ptas) and the Church of Santo Tome (150ptas) in which hangs El Greco's, Burial of the Count of Orgaz, are priority sights. The latter two are open Tu-Sa 10-1:45 & 3:30-6:45, Su 10-1:45.

If you wish to spend the night, **Camping Circo Romano** is the nearest one to Toledo and the train station. Open Mar 1-Sep 30; adult/275ptas, small tent/225ptas. Take the bus from the train station which goes to the main entrance (Puerta de Bisagra) of Toledo where the tourist office is located. From the tourist office, it is a short walk of about 300 meters to the campground. Signs indicate the route. Very good camp with swimming pool, tennis courts, store and snack bar.

Trains to Toledo leave from Atocha Station, carry all second class and depart at 6:55am, 8:30am, 9:20am, 10am, 11:45am, 2:10pm, 4:30pm, 5:30pm 6:25pm, 7:55pm and 9:05pm. Trains leave Toledo for Madrid at 7:35am, 8:43am, 10:20am, 11:45am, 1:20pm, 2:20pm, 4:22pm, 6:30pm, 7:24pm, 8:36pm and 10:10pm. The trip is 1-1/2 hours. The train stops at Aranjuez and Algodor enroute.

DAY TRIP TO EL ESCORIAL The monastery built in the 16th century by Philip II lies 52 km. from Madrid. Open 10-1 & 3-6, 350ptas. El Escorial is on the rail line to Avila. Trains leave Atocha Apeadero at 8:28am, 1:40pm and 6:42pm. From Chamartin departures are 8:42am, 1:54pm and 6:54pm. The trip is one hour. These trains continue to Avila after stopping at El Escorial. Local trains (cercanias) leave Atocha Apeadero at 8:34am, 9:33am, 10:31am, 11:34am, 12:34pm, 1:34pm, 1:34pm, 2:19pm, 2:49pm, 3:34pm, 4:30pm, 5:34pm, 6:34pm, 6:45pm, 7:27pm, 7:34pm, 8:32pm, 9:32pm and 10:49pm. All of these cercanias trains pick up at Recoletos, Nuevos Ministerios and Chamartin after leaving Apeadero. The stop at Chamartin is 13 minutes after leaving Apeadero. Trains return from El Escorial at 6:59am, 4:40pm, 8:32pm and 10:23pm. Local trains (cercanias) leave for Madrid at 7:16am, 7:41am, 9:01am and one minute past the hour until 10:01pm. All trains continue to Chamartin Station.

Valle de los Caidos (Valley of the Fallen), 13 km. from El Escorial, commemorates those who died in the Spanish Civil War. The spectacular monument done in stark modern style consists of a large cross on the mountain top and a cavernous Cathedral carved from the side of the mountain below. A bus from El Escorial leaves about 3pm (240ptas) and starts back about 5:30pm.

Camping El Escorial is a good campground 7 km. from El Escorial enroute to the Valley of the Fallen. Open all year; adult/375ptas, tent/350ptas. Take the bus from El Escorial train station to the village San Lorenzo de El Escorial. Change to the bus to Madrid, which passes by the campground. Then walk 800 meters. The shady site has restroom sinks with hot water, automatic washer, store, restaurant, dayroom, pool.

From El Escorial, trains leave for the walled city of Avila at 9:28am, 2:38pm, and 7:40pm. The trip is one hour. Returning from Avila to Madrid, trains leave at 8:52am Talgo, 2:30pm ELT, 3:38pm, 7:30pm and 9:21pm. The last 3 departures also stop at El Escorial.

To **Barcelona**, leave Chamartin at 9:55am Rapido (ar. Termino 5:01pm), 11:45am Talgo (ar. Sants 7:01pm), 3pm Talgo (ar. 9:56pm), 9:40pm Express (ar. Sants 7:12am) and 10:35pm air-conditioned rapido (ar. Termino 8:30am).

To **Cordoba and Seville**, leave Atocha at 9:05 Talgo (ar. Cordoba 1:30pm, Seville 2:31pm), 10am TER (ar. Cordoba 3:26pm), 11am Rapido (ar. Cordoba 4:08pm, Seville 6:03pm), 2:15pm from Chamartin Talgo (ar. Cordoba 6:55pm), 3pm Talgo (ar. Cordoba 7:30pm, Seville 8:52pm) and 10:20pm express Jun 25-Sep 6 (ar. Cordoba 5:12am, Seville 7:07am).

To **Granada**, leave Atocha at 7:35am all second class (ar. Alcazar 9:25am, change trains, leave Alcazar 9:45am express (ar. 3:22pm).

To **Lisbon**, leave Atocha at 10:10am TER reservation required (ar. 7:05pm) and 11:30pm Lusitania Express (ar. 9:10am).

To **Paris** Austerlitz, leave Chamartin 8:05am ELT reservation required (change at Hendaye, ar. 11:24pm), 12:40pm express (change at Hendaye, ar. 8:15am), 3:15pm Talgo reservation required (change at Hendaye, ar. 7:15am), 6:10pm Puerta Del Sol (ar. 10:27am) and 7:40pm EuroCity reservation required (ar. 8:48am).

NORTH OF MADRID

SALAMANCA   The two closest campgrounds are Regio and Don Quijote. **Camping Regio** is 4 km. from Salamanca at Santa Maria de Tormes. Open all year; adult/330ptas, small tent/280ptas. A very good camp with all facilities: automatic washer, store, restaurant, day room. For Regio, you can take a bus from Calle de Espana each hour. **Camping Don Quijote** is 4 km. from Salamanca on the local road to Aldealengua. The camp is hard to reach as there are only 2 buses a day. Open Jan 20-Dec 10, audlt/250ptas., small tent/200ptas. For **Camping El Cruce**, 52 km. from Salamanca, take a local train (direction Ciudad Rodrigo) to the village of La Fuente de San Esteban and the campground is 300 meters from the station. There are also buses from Salamanca. Open Jun 15-Sep 15; adult/250ptas, small tent/200ptas. A good cheap camp with the necessities but few extras.

BURGOS   Camping Fuentes Blancas is 3 km. from the city. Open Apr 1-Sep 30; adult/225ptas, tent/175ptas. Buses run July and August only. They leave from Plaza del General Primo de Rivera each hour from 10am to 9pm. Automatic washer, store and restaurant.

SAN SEBASTIAN   Camping Igueldo is 7 km. from town. May 1-Sep 30; adult/265ptas, small tent/170ptas. The nearest bus stop to the train station (Del Norte) is at Plaza de Guipuzcoa. Take bus 2 Igueldo (40ptas.) which leaves at 6:50am, 7:45am, 10:05am, 11:05am, 12:05pm, 1:05pm, 2:05pm, 3:30pm, 6:05pm, 7pm, 8:05pm and 10pm. Store, day room.

SANTIAGO DE COMPOSTELA   Located in Galicia the northwestern corner of Spain, the town is famous for its pilgrimages and Cathedral. It lies on the main rail line going north from Portugal. You can leave Portugal by taking trains across the top of Spain and through Galicia.

The closest campground is Camping Las Cancelas, Rua do 25 de Xulio 35, 2.5 km. from the Cathedral. See map. Adult/300ptas, tent/330ptas. You can walk or take bus 6 or 9 leaving every 15 minutes to 300 meters from the campground. The walking route is marked by arrows on the map. From the station, walk forward on the main street, General Franco for 3 blocks past the intersection Santiago de Guayaquil to the bus stop on the right side of the road. Store, restaurant, exchange, swimming.

Santiago de Compostela

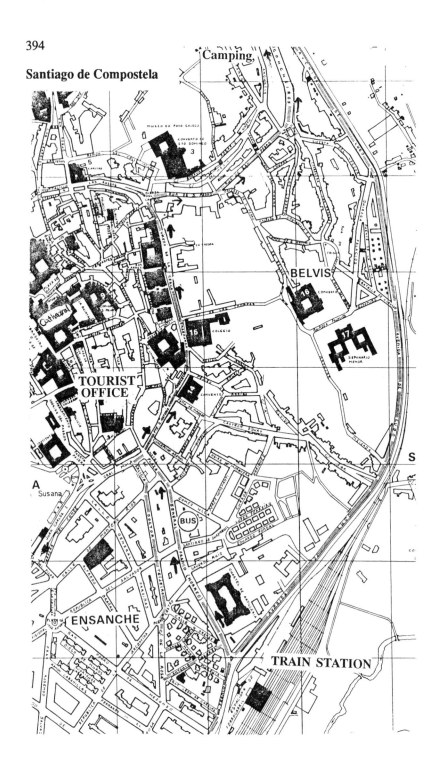

Camping,

MUSEO DO POVO GALEGO

CONVENTO DE STO DOMINGO
3

5

CARITAS

LA XOURA

BELVIS

16
CONVENTO

15
COLEGIO

17
SEMINARIO MENOR

TOURIST
OFFICE

14
CONVENTO

Cathedral

S

A
Susana

BUS

ENSANCHE

TRAIN STATION

SWEDEN

Sweden's Nobel Peace Prizes, smorgasbord and trolls, and its contribution to drama and films are well known. It practices a combination of social welfare programs and private capital with heavy emphasis on redistribution of wealth through taxation. Sweden's birth rate is so low the native population is no longer having enough babies to replenish itself. Swedish citizens enjoy the highest standard of living in Europe and each receives a paid month vacation by law.

CURRENCY   Swedish krona. Each krona is divided into 100 ore. There are 6 kronor to the U.S. dollar. *(5)*

WEATHER   June through the first half of September is the warmest period. Rain sometimes comes even in summer, similar to the Pacific Northwest. Summer days are long where daylight occurs beetween 4am and 10pm and then will be only semi-dark through the night. July is the most popular vacation month.

CAMPING   Many campgrounds require a camping carnet or Swedish Camping Card which can be bought at any campground for 22kr. Most camps are open June through August, except those in tourist areas stay open longer. Camping is permitted anywhere in the country, even on private land, as long as it's not too close to buildings or fenced land.

TRAINS   Swedish State Railways are abbreviated SJ. The trains are very good, and even provide a bottle of drinking water hung on the wall in each compartment. As in all of Scandinavia, second class is not much different than first class. You can travel from Stockholm to Kiruna in Swedish Lapland, and onward to Narvik in Norway by train. Free timetables *(snabbtag)* are available in train information offices.

If you haven't a Eurailpass, traveling by bus is much cheaper. On train fares, the longer the journey the cheaper each kilometer becomes. Persons 65 or older receive a 50 percent discount on all rail tickets except during Easter, Christmas and on weekends in summer.

A seat reservation costs 15kr and is only necessary when it's mandatory, which is all too often on trips between the capitals in Scandinavia. The way to get around it is to travel overnight when a reservation is not required. If a train departure time is marked with an R, the train is an expresstag and the conductor will collect double the reservation fee on board if the required reservation hasn't been obtained before boarding. No supplements are charged for the fast trains in Sweden. The busiest period is Friday afternoon through Saturday morning and on Sunday.

ankomst	arrival
avgang	departure
biljettluckan	ticket office
jarnvagsstationen	train station
ingang	entrance
platsbiljetter	reservation
spar	track
till sparen	to the tracks
utgang	exit
vaxelkontoret	foreign exchange

EURAIL BONUSES   (1)   Steamer service of the Silja LIne between Stockholm and Helsinki and between Stockholm, Aland Islands and Turku. This is an incredible bonus and should be used. See Stockholm for more information. (2) Ferry crossings operated by the Swedish and Danish State Railways between Helsingborg and Helsingor, Denmark. (3) Steamers operated by Stena Line, a private steamship company, between Goteborg and Frederikshavn, Denmark. (4) 50 percent reduction on the Danish Navigation Company, Oresund, for travel on the hydrofoil between Malmo and Copenhagen. (5) 50 percent reduction on normal fares for the ferry crossing Trelleborg to Lubeck-Travemunde, West Germany, on the TT Line.

FOOD   Grocery shopping requires some care. The excellent whole milk (mjolk) and skim milk (skummjolk) are reasonably priced at 4.69kr per liter. Soft drinks cost more than milk. Fruit juice will have "saft" as the suffix, but any canned or bottled juice is expensive. Rye bread is a better value than white bread. Meat, leafy green vegetables and fruit are expensive. Fish, carrots, beets, potatoes and other underground vegetables are reasonable. Breakfast (frukost) is often an all-you-can-eat buffet, a good value often found in train stations, some hotels and on ferries that cross a national border. Dinner (middag) is the last meal. In cafeterias, usually the daily special (dagens ratt) is a good buy.

The best value in smorgasbord is found on the Silja Line ships. An incredible feast is about 80kr.

STOCKHOLM

An air of well being pervades Sweden's capital. The city is built on thirteen islands within an archipelago of 24,000 making it hardly surprising that all four of Stockholm's campgrounds are near water.

TRAIN STATION   The immense and confusing Central Station (*Central Stationen*) on Vasagaten downtown, forms part of an underground plaza of stores and services. All conceivable services are found here: tourist office, foreign exchange (daily 8am-9pm), restaurants, luggage lockers, grocery store, shops and T-Centralen subway station. The tourist office and luggage checking are on the same floor but on opposite sides and ends. A locker large enough for a pack costs 5kr, but empty lockers are not always available. Next to the lockers, luggage checking is open 7am-11pm and charges 8kr per pack. The tourist office (*Hotellcentralen*) is open daily 8-9. Train reservations are made in the ticket office (*fardbiljetter platsviljetter*). Many commuter trains, free with railpasses, leave from Central Station and information is given on airport-type closed-circuit television screens in the station. The Hyllans Restaurang offers a smorgasbord breakfast for 32kr, M-Sa 6:30-9:30am, Su 8-10:30am. Beverages, cereal, cheeses, breads, pastries, sausage and fruit juice.

Stockholm T-Bana (subway)

SILJA LINES CRUISESHIP TO TURKU OR HELSINKI, FINLAND
Eurailpass and Eurail Youthpass are entitled to free deck class passage on Silja Line ships to Turku and Helsinki. Reservations aren't necessary; just show up and you'll be issued a boarding pass. Silja Line Terminal is at Vartahamnen, northeast of Central Station. Take *tunnelbana* (subway) lines 13 or 14 to Ropsten, the last station. Outside, board bus 76, 76E or any bus to Vartahamnen. The bus between Ropsten and the ferry terminal is free. Get off at the last stop, Silja Line Terminal. Allow about 45 minutes to reach the Silja Terminal from the train station.
There are two overnight departures and one daytime sailing. The overnight sailings go directly to Helsinki or Turku. The daytime sailing goes to Turku via Mariehamn in the Aland Islands. Even on the overnight sailings you see quite a bit of the archipelago before it gets dark, but you will see more islands on the daytime sailing. To Helsinki, the ship leaves at 6pm and arrives at 9am. The direct boat to Turku leaves at 9:15pm and arrives at 8am. The day sailing leaves at 8:15am, arrives in Mariehamn (Aland Islands) at 2:35pm, leaves at 2:45pm and arrives in Turku at 8:15pm.

398

Silja Line Schedule (free with Eurailpass)

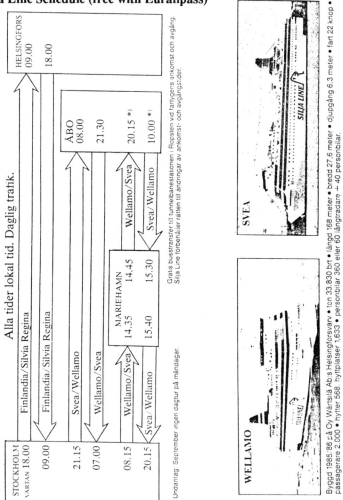

The 6pm sailing to Helsinki has the advantages of leaving early enough so the luxury facilities on board can be enjoyed, giving a free night's sleep, saving an entire day of traveling time, and affording a good panorama of Helsinki as the boat sails into the harbor. But if you've got plenty of time, you can certainly enjoy the amenities of the ship for a day on the day sailing. All Silja Line boats are excellent.

The overnight boat to Helsinki leaves at 6pm, but boarding is allowed starting at 4:30pm. During the last two weeks in July and the first three weeks in August, get there at 4:15pm to be sure to get a free bed. During the rest of the year, you can probably get there an hour ahead and still find one. The situation is similar on the 9:15pm sailing for Turku. It only takes a few minutes to show your Eurailpass and be issued a boarding pass, unless there are lines. No port taxes are due.

Silja Line ships are no less than luxury floating hotels. On overnight sailings from the backpacker's standpoint, their most important feature are the free dorm beds available. Upon boarding the ship, you will be on deck 4. Immediately take the elevator or the stairs to the sleep-in on deck 7. Follow the signs to the Sleep-in or Sitseria. The Sitseria is a room of reclining chairs and the Sleep-in is next to it. The sleep-in has bunks arranged into small 5-bunk groupings. This sleep-in becomes full fast, but there's another on deck 9 that no one seems to know about which has 14 three-layer bunk beds. It's not well signed because it's a converted conference room and you have to poke about to find it, but it's there. The door says "Conference 8" on it. This one has few people and is very quiet. Outside the sleep-in on deck 7 are lockers large enough for a small pack, but not an overnight one. A locker requires two coins worth 1 Finnmark. Leave your pack zipped and with everything inside on the bunk bed to hold your place. Don't leave anything loose on the bunk that would be easily picked up. Then you can leave and no one else will claim it. However, if you don't use it by about 11pm and there aren't enough beds for everyone, someone may preempt it. People commandeer floor space after the beds are all taken.

After the free beds, a camper is most likely interested in the free showers in the luxurious bathrooms. A line forms for the showers in the bathroom by the sleep-in shortly after sailing, so the smart thing to do is to go there immediately after claiming a bunk.

Next, go to the the 8th floor and make a reservation for the smorgasbord. There are two sittings for the evening one, 6pm and 8:30pm, and you will be assigned a table. Families prefer the first sitting. The second sitting is the quickest to become fully booked. The dining room is beautiful; a live combo plays and at the end of the second sitting people start getting out on the dance floor. The smorgasbord is an exceptional value at 58 Finnmark or 77.50 Swedish kroner (excluding beverage but you can drink water), and you should make every effort to treat yourself to it. (Think of what you're saving by not paying for a campground.)

There are four buffet tables at the smorgasbord: a cold table, a hot table, a dessert table and a children's table. On the cold table are several kinds of bread and butter, 6 or 7 kinds of herring, raw salmon, other raw fish, shrimp salad, 6 or 7 other kinds of salads, crayfish, smoked fish, caviar, white turkey meat, roast beef (well done and rare), ham, several varieties of pate, jellied meat loaf, sliced tomatoes, carrot sticks, cauliflowets and sliced cucumbers. On the hot table are baked salmon, baked chicken, roast beef, veal and mushroom stew, green beans, peas, two potato casseroles, small boiled potatoes with dill, meat balls and a mixed vegetable casserole. On the dessert table, are whole oranges and granny smith apples, a variety of crackers and cheese, apple pie, 3 kinds of tortes (layer cakes), 3 or 4 sugarless desserts, mixed fruit salad, melon, cherries, whipped cream and dessert sauces. (There is nothing chocolate however.) The children's table has such items as hot dogs and fries as well as duplications of some of the items on the other tables.

In the Maxim Terrass restaurant, each morning a breakfast smorgasbord is available from 7-9am for 26.50 Finnmark or 35.40 Swedish kroner. Beverages are included and you can get more than your fill of fruit juices, milk, coffee, tea, croissants, pastry, breads, crackers, cereals, jams, butter, cheeses, eggs, meats, fish and fruit. This is an incredible bargain. No reservation necessary; pay as you go in, but be sure to come by 8am at the latest as the ship arrives in Helsinki at 9am.

The ship has several other places to eat ranging from a cafeteria that offers dinner plates and a salad bar to a very expensive first class restaurant. Throughout the ship, either Swedish or Finnish money is accepted, as well as Visa and Mastercharge. Comfortable lounges are available inside and outside the ship.

On deck 4 are foreign exchange (a commission is extracted but so will one be in Finland), tourist information on Finland (you can plan enroute), beauty salon, supervised playroom with toys and a ball-filled play section and facilities for baby changing and heating baby food. The two duty-free shops are on decks 4 and 7 and sell chocolates, cigarettes, liquor clothing, toys, gifts and perfumes. On deck 2 is the swimming pool, pool bar, children's pool and sauna (fee). An elevator connects the sunbathing area on deck directly with the pool. On deck 7 in the evening are a blackjack/roulette table, slot machines and dancing in the Tiffany Disco with a disc jockey playing the top 40 (no cover or entrance fee). Also in the evening live music, dancing and floorshows are enjoyed in the Bar Maxim Terrass on deck 8 for the cost of a drink (no cover or entrance fee). For a smaller room and more intimate atmosphere, go to the pianobar, Silja Club, also on deck 8.

TOURIST INFORMATION Stockholms Turisttrafikforbund, in Sweden House (Sverigehuset) at Hamngatan 27, is 9 blocks from the station. Open June 16-Aug 9 8:30-6, shorter hours rest of year. A branch office is in the train station. Ask for *Stockholm This Week* which contains museum hours, fees and bus #; events, subway map, map of downtown, and describes a do-it-yourself walking tour.

CITY TRANSPORTATION Buses, subway (*tunnelbana*) and local trains make up the public transport network. Tunnelbana entrances are marked with a blue T on a white background. The same tickets are good on all forms of transportation. The entire greater Stockholm area is divided into zones. The downtown area is the inner zone. Tickets are cancelled in machines on the bus or at the subway station. A single ticket within one zone consists of two coupons costing 3.5kr each if purchased singly. To cut costs, buy an 18-coupon ticket book in advance for 45kr which cuts the cost per coupon to 2.5kr. A ticket is good for unlimited transfers within one hour of the latest time stamp. Other limits apply for more than one zone. Children 7-16 and senior citizens pay half. Coupon books are sold at newstands marked Pressbyran, commonly found in main subway stations including T-Centralen. The coupons may be shared among you. Various passes are also offered.

A trip within one zone takes two coupons. Each additional zone costs one coupon for each zone. For trips late at night, two extra coupons are required. It doesn't matter if you change from bus to subway within the same zone, but if another zone is crossed another coupon is charged. However, changes must be made within one hour of the latest time stamp. The maximum fare is 8 coupons which, if paid from the start, is valid for three hours of unrestricted travel throughout the entire transport area. The trip from Central Station to Bredang Camping is five zones, requiring 6 coupons. The cost is 15kr if an 18-coupon ticket book has been purchased. Various kinds of passes (*turistkort*) are sold. Children under 18 and senior citizens pay half price. Because of the distance to the campgrounds, campers come out ahead on these passes. A card valid for 24 hours throughout the entire greater Stockholm area which includes all campgrounds costs 40kr. For just the central area, the cost is 22kr. A 72-hour pass for the greater Stockholm area costs 76kr and includes admission to Skansen, Kaknastornet television tower, and Grona Lund amusement park. The ferry to Djurgarden is included in both passes.

For a longer stay, consider buying a monthly season ticket for 190kr. It consists of a "base card" which requires a photo--bring along an extra passport picture--and a monthly token.

Campers who move fast, don't have a student card, and want to visit a lot of museums, should consider purchasing a Key to Stockholm Card (*Stockholmskortet*) for 70kr for 1 day, 140 kr for 2 days, 210kr for 3 days and 280kr for 4 days. These cards include transportation on the entire bus and subway network including the Tourist Line and free admission to virtually all museums and sightseeing attractions, including Drottningholm Palace, Skansen and the Wasa. Sightseeing admissions are about 10-20kr.

The Tourist Line (*Turistlinjen*) bus passes by the train station, through central Stockholm and Djurgarden Park, stopping near 14 major sightseeing attractions. The bus leaves every 15 minutes. Commentary is in Swedish, but an English language folder is provided. A 24-hour ticket costs 30kr. It would be difficult to break even with this card, but the convenience might be worth something. This tram is included in the Stockholm Card.

Passes and coupon books are sold at Pressbyran kiosks and other SL (Storstockholms Lokaltrafik) sales points such as the tourist office, some agencies of Swedish State Railways, and the Silja Line terminal.

CAMPGROUNDS   The tourist office has a folder on Stockholm's five campgrounds. Bredang, Satra and Malarhojdens are your best bets. The other two have chemical toilets and poorer restroom facilities.

Bredang Camping is the largest and most popular camp in Stockholm, located 10 km. southwest of downtown Stockholm. Open all year, 6am-11pm for new arrivals. Charge is 30kr per tent. From Central Station, follow signs to T-Centralen tunnelbana station designated by a large T. Board train 13 (direction Norsberg) or 15 (direction Satra). Frequent departures. Get off at Bredang Station, the 11th stop and a 20-minute ride. The station is in the shopping area of preplanned Bredang suburban community. Walking out of the station you will see a Bredang (formerly called Satra) camping sign to the left. Turn left, follow the pedestrian underpass, and once across, another camping sign directs you on the other side. Follow street Stora Sallskapets Vag straight to camp. This street parallels the subway tracks for most of the way, a 10-minute or 700-meter walk. Bus 163 also goes to Bredang. The camp has a sauna, hair dryer, snack bar, washing machine (15kr, open 9-5), and dryer. Malarhojden Beach is 350 meters from camp.

Unless you need a washing machine, a better place to stay with fewer people but also fewer facilities is **Angby Camping** located on Lake Malar, 12 km. west of downtown Stockholm. June 1-Aug 31; 30kr per tent. From the train station, follow signs to T-Centralen (subway) station. Board train

17 (direction Vallingby) or 18 (direction Hasselby Strand) and get off at Angbyplan Station, the 13th stop and a 23-minute ride. Then the camp is about a 15-minute or 700-meter walk. It adjoins a sand swimming beach.

Malarhojdens Idrottsplats Camping, open only during peak season approximately Jun 1-Aug 31, is located 10 km. southwest of downtown Stockholm. Tent fee is 20kr. This is an annex to The Bredang Camping site. Take T-tunnelbana line 14 (direction Fruangen) to Fruangen Station, a 16-minute ride and then walk 600 meters to the camp. The camp is by Hotel Gyllene Ratten. Hot water and regular toilets are provided.

Flatens Camping is 17 km. southeast of downtown Stockholm on Lake Flaten. Open May 2-Sep 30; tent/20kr. From Central Station follow signs to T-Centralen (subway). Board train 27 (direction Hagsatra), 28 (Hokarangen) or 29 (Hogdalen). Get off at the fourth stop, Skanstull Station. Outside the station, take bus 804, 811, 814-817 or 828 from Ringvagen. From Slussen Station, take bus 401. The camp is a wooded pastureland with chemical toilets, showers, water slide and boat rentals.

With unattractive and not well kept chemical toilets and no showers, Farstanaset Camping is on Lake Magelungen, 27 km. south of downtown Stockholm. Open May 2-Sep 15; 20kr per tent. From Central Station, follow signs to T-Centralen (subway) station. Board train 18 (direction Farsta Strand) and get off at Farsta Station, the stop before Farsta Strand Station. From outside the station, take bus #744 to Farstanasvagen and then a 10-minute walk. Alternatively, take trains 19 or 29 to Hogdalen, and then bus 744 to Farstanasvagen and then a 10-minute walk. The campsite is a meadow surrounded by pine trees, 300 meters from a public beach.

FOOD   The public market (Hotorget Market or Haymarket) occurs at Hotorget Square in front of the Concert Hall, M-Sa 8-6. Take the subway to Hotorget or walk 8 blocks from Central Station. Another market is on Ostermalmstorg Square near the Royal Dramatic Theater, and a third is at Kornhamnstora. Grocery stores in underground arcades at T-Centralen, Hotorget, Fridhemsplan and Ostermalmstorg subway stations close at 10pm.

SIGHTSEEING   The sights are concentrated in three main areas in central Stockholm. Gamla Stan is the old quarter and site of the Royal Palace. On Djdurgarden the main sights are Skansen and the Wasa Museum. On Skeppsholmen are the two most important art museums. The major sight outside of the downtown area is Drottningholm Castle. The Stockholm Card gives free admission to everything listed here.

On Djurgarden are concentrated several attractions. (With your back to the main entrance to Central Station, cross the street and walk up the sidestreet on the left. Take bus 47 from there, the ferry from Nybroplan, or bus 44 from Karlaplan. Once you get to Djurgarden, an entire day can be spent walking from one attraction to another. **Skansen** is Stockholm's outdoor museum of transplanted farms and dwellings from earlier times. The buildings are open 11-5. Free guided tours in English start on the hour from 11-4, 20 kr. **Wasavarvet** (Wasa Museum) shows the famous warship which sank soon after being launched in 1628. Jun 6-Aug 16 9:30-7, Aug 17-Jun 5 10-5; 15kr. **Prins Eugens Waaldemarsudde** shows paintings including contemporary works, Tu-Su 11-5, W & F evenings 7-9; 15kr. **Biologiska Museet** (Museum of Biology), 10-4, 5kr. **Liljevalchs Konsthall** (Liljevalch Art Gallery) houses special exhibitions, Tu & Th 11-9, W-F-Sa-Su 11-5;

15kr. **Grona Lunds Tivoli** (amusement park), open M-F 7pm-midnight, Sa 2pm-midnight, Su noon-10pm, except June 9-Aug 20 when it opens 2pm weekdays, closed weekdays during first 2 weeks in Sep, closed for season Sep 15; 20kr.

On **Skeppsholmen Island**, the **Moderna Museet** (Modern Art Museum), formerly part of a naval station, was remodeled to become an uncluttered and spacious modern art gallery showing 20th century painting and sculpture. Open daily Tu-F 11-9, SaSu 11-5, adult/15kr, thursday free. Bus 46, 55 or 62 from Ostermalmstorg (subway station on lines 13 and 15) o T-bana Kungstradgarden.   The **National Museum** on peninsula S. Blasieholmshamnen by Grand Hotel, is a 5-minute walk from Moderna Museet or bus 46, 55 or 62 from Ostermalmstorg.   Shown are paintings by Rembrandt, Rubens, Frans Hals, Sculpture, graphic art, French Impressionists, craft items and an exhibit of modern Swedish design in home furnishings. Daily Tu-Su 10-4 & closes at 9 on Tuesday; 20kr, free Tu.

Drottningholm Palace, Sweden's Versailles, and the Court Theater are open M-Sa 11-4:30, Su noon-4:30, palace/15kr, theater 17kr. Take the T-bana to Brommaplan and then the bus. Of lesser interest, but also on the grounds is the Chinese Theater, 10kr.

SHOPPING   The lower level of **Ahlens** Department Store by Central Station contains a large supermarket.   Find the entrance direct from the station. Its third floor has restrooms, baby changing rooms, supervised playroom (*barnparkering*) camping equipment and toys.   Shipping is on street floor and the value added tax is deducted from purchases sent out of the country.   The street floor and all lower levels are open Sundays and evenings until 8pm.

To Copenhagen, leave at 7:05am (ar. 3:35pm), 9:05am (ar. 5:05pm), 11:05am (ar. 7:51pm), 1:05pm (ar. 10:05pm), 9:12pm (ar. 6:21am) and 10:55pm (ar. 7:21am). All departures but the overnight ones require a reservation. We took the 9:12pm departure on a Sunday night in July and found the train two-thirds empty. The train has both compartments and aisle seating.
To Narvik, Norway, a train leaves at 5:30pm (change at Kiruna, ar. 2:15pm and 8:42pm (change at Vannas, ar. 7:15am). Reservation required on both departures.
To Oslo, leave at 8:12am (ar. 2:40pm), 3:30pm (ar. 9:44pm) and 11:10pm (ar. 7:55am). Reservation required for the daytime departures.
To Uppsala, there are about 30 trains a day for the 45-minute trip.

UPPSALA

This old and famous university town in historical Sweden makes a good day trip from Stockholm or you can stay in a campground within walking distance of the train station.

The **train station** is downtown on Kungsgatan. The **tourist office** is 5 blocks away at Gamla Torget (St. Perse. 4) May-Aug M-F 10-6, Sa 10-2. A single bus ticket is 9kr, valid for a free transfer and the return journey if taken within 90 minutes of the start of the bus ride. The market (*Saluhall*) is indoors at St. Erikstorg on M-F 9:30-6, Sa 9:30-3.

Fyris Camping is by the river next to Fyrisbadet swimming pool, 15 blocks from the train station, or bus 5, 7, 20 or 50 from Dragarbrunnsgatan. From the station walk forward and cross the main street Kungsgatan and walk to the next street Dragarbrunnsgatan. Turn right and walk 3 blocks.

404

After crossing Vaksalagatan, the bus stop is in the next block on the right hand side of the street. Open all year; tent/30kr.

Uppsala

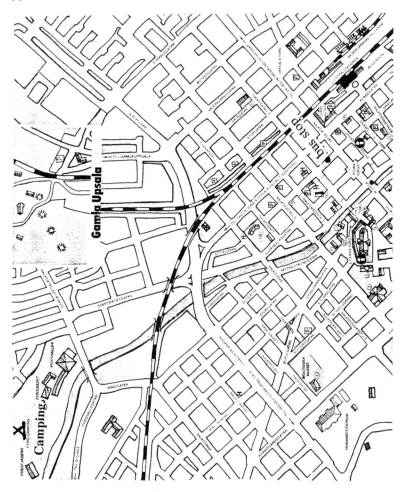

    Graneberg Camping is by Lake Malaren about 7 km. south of the train station. The camp is off Dag Hammarskjolds vag, 20 minutes from town by bus 20, leaving from Nybron by the river on the hour and half-hour (9kr). From the station walk forward crossing the main street, Kungsgatan. Keep walking straight ahead and cross the next 2 main streets. At the next street, Ostra Agatan, turn right. May 22-Aug 31; tent/35kr, 2-bed cabins/50kr.

    To Gamla Uppsala, the old town, take bus 14 or 24 from Kungsgatan in front of the station. Sights are the Viking burial mounds and Disagarden, a museum of old original Swedish farmhouses. Other sights in

Uppsala are the largest Cathedral in Sweden, Uppsala castle, anatomical theater in Gustavianum and Upplands Museum, St. Erikstorg 10, which shows local history. Ulva Mill Craft Center, 9 km. north of town, is an old 18th century mill where craftsmen work and sell their creations: glass, pottery, wood crafts and textiles.

MALMO

In the southern tip of Sweden, across the water from Copenhagen, Malmo can be visited as a day trip. To stay here, try Sibbarp Camping, 7 km. south of town. Take bus 41 from Central Station direct to the campground. Open all year; tent/30kr.   Store, snack bar, washing machine and dryer/15kr together.

LUND

An old and beautiful town with a cathedral and outdoor museum of note, Lund is conveniently located 17 km. from Malmo and makes a good day excursion from Copenhagen. Lund Touristtrafikforening (tourist office) is at S. Petri Kyrkogata 4, three blocks from the station.   The market is at Martens-torget, open M-F 7-1:30, Sa 7-1.   No campgrounds in Lund, but three are 10 km. away in Lomma on the coast. Take the bus to Lomma from Lund bus station. The trip is one hour and buses leave once an hour.

GOTEBORG (GOTHENBURG)

Goteborg is pronounced YER-ta-boy.   Sweden's second largest city is located on the west coast of Sweden on the main rail route to Norway. Its Goteborg Card allows the visitor to do viturally everything in Goteborg, including guided bus and boat tours, for one inclusive price.

TRAIN STATION Centrally located downtown with a branch about 200 meters away at the Nordstan Mall (open M-Sa). Luggage storage is open M-F 6:30am-10pm, Sa 6:30am-8pm, Stena Line ships, free with Eurailpasses, leave Goteborg bound for Frederikshavn, Denmark. To change from train to boat, leave the train station using the exit by the information office. Cross the street and you will see the tram station. Take tram 3 to Stena line stop. **The tram is included in Eurailpasses.**

CITY TRANSPORTATION A single ticket costs 9kr, a 24-hour pass is 20kr and a book of 21 coupons costs 60kr. Two coupons are needed for one ride but the same coupons can be used on the return trip if taken between 9am and 3pm. Eurailpasses are valid on tram 3 when changing from ship to train or vice-versa.

   The **Goteborg Card** costs 70kr for one day, 120kr for 2 days, 165kr for 3 days and 200kr for 4 days. It is valid on all buses and trams, for entrance into museums (regularly 10kr), Lisberg amusement park and 5 night clubs. It includes a guided tour by bus around Goteborg (reserve at tourist office, tour leaves from Kungsportsplatsen on tramlines 1, 4 or 5 and bus lines 40 and 64); a round trip tour on the sightseeing boat, Padden, for departures from 2-6pm (regularly 35kr, leave from Kungsportsplatsen daily); a boat trip to Elfsborg's fortress (regularly 35kr, departure every 75 minutes daily 9:45-5:30pm from Stenpiren, take tram 2, 3, 4, 6, 7 or bus 85, 86 to

406

Lilla Torget.), and a free day trip via Stena Line to Denmark (regularly 70kr, but this is included in Eurailpasses anyway). Other benefits include free entrance to sports center and bathing beaches, free fishing license, free tickets to City Theatre if any are unsold, and free boat travel to the southern archipelago (take tram 4 to Saltholmen for the boat).

CAMPGROUNDS Karralund Camping, open all year, is 4 km. from downtown and has 310 marked sites. Tent/70kr. Because of the amusement park in town, this campground becomes full up with families on weekends. Try to arrive early. From the train station, cross the plaza and take tram 3 (direction Kalltorp) going towards your left when you have your back to the station. The driver sells a ticket for 9kr for the 20-minute ride. After getting off the tram, walk about 300 meters in the direction the tram was going. Then turn left off the main street at the small grocery store, continuing up this road, beyond the miniature golf to the camp--about a 5-minute walk. From downtown Goteborg, take tram 5 (direction Torp) which lets you off across from the grocery store and side road to camp. The attractive camp has hot water for dishwashing, free maps and sightseeing information and marked trails in the nearby woods. Other camps are further out; inquire at the tourist office.

FOOD Within the Nordstan shopping mall two blocks from the station, Ahlens Department store has a supermarket with a good delicatessen section in its basement. Restrooms are on the top floor just outside the elevators. The market is downtown at Kungstorget, open M-F 8-6, Sa 8-1.

SIGHTSEEING   The best museum is the **Maritime Museum** (*Sjofartsmuseet*).   Three floors are packed with all kinds of ship models dating back to the Vikings. Excellent instructive dioramas exhibit fishing boats set within a mock ocean to depict various kinds of gear and techniques used in deep sea fishing. Located at Stigbergstorget, tram 3 from the station. Open May-Aug daily 12-4; Sept-May Tu-Sa 12-4, Su 11-5; adult/10kr.

   Gotaplatsen is the cultural center of Goteborg marked by Carl Milles' statue of Poseidon. The Art Gallery (Konstmuseet) has a good selection of modern Swedish artists, the most comprehensive group of French contemporary art in Sweden, and a few old masters. Daily May-Aug 12-4, Sep-Apr Tu-Sa 12-4, Su 11-5, 10kr.   The art Exhibition Hall (Konsthallen), Concert Hall and City Theater complete the square.

   Liseberg Amusement Park, Orgrytevagen, is very popular with Swedish out-of-towners. Go in the evening when the park is beautifully lighted. Admission is 20kr, a single ride 8kr, but there are ride books.

To Oslo, leave 7:57am, 9:50am, noon, 2:35pm and 5:10pm for the approximately 5-hour trip. To Stockholm, leave at 15 minutes past the hour from 7:15am to 8:15pm; 15kr reservation required for all departures. The trip is 4-1/2 hours. Not requiring a reservation is the overnight journey that leaves at 10:30pm (ar. 6:55am). To Copenhagen, leave at 6am, 7:45am, 9:45am, 12:48pm, 4pm and 6:10pm.

KALMAR

Kalmar is the County seat in southeastern Sweden on the eastern coast, and about a six hour train ride from Stockholm. On the main route from Stockholm to Copenhagen, change at Alvesta. In the early Middle Ages, it was Scandinavia's capital city. The beautiful castle of Kalmar is the most well known Renaissance castle in Sweden.

The tourist office (*turistbyra*) is in the rear of the train station. Stenso Camping, south of Kalmar 3 km. from downtown, can be reached by bus from the station. Open all year; tent/30kr. Full facilities: hot water in restroom sinks, washer, store, restaurant, day room, boating and fishing.

Olands Bridge (6,070 meters), the longest bridge in Europe, stretches from Kalmar to the very different **island of Oland** with its limestone bedrock, wildflowers and birds, prehistoric ruins including stone passage graves, a medieval church and 400 windmills. This is Sweden's sunbelt where Solliden, the Royal Summer Home, was built outside the town of Borgholm. Many campgrounds are in the area, reached by bus from Kalmar.

Kalmar is the gateway city to the **glass factories of Orrefors, Kosta and Boda** which offer free guided tours of their plants and the opportunity to buy "seconds." The Kalmar tourist office offers a guided tour of the factories, or you can go by train from Kalmar for the hour ride to the town of Orrefors which grew around the factory. Prices on goods are about half of what they are in the stores, and the value added tax of about 23 percent is deducted from anything mailed out of the country, which covers postage to the U.S. at least. If anything breaks, a replacement will be sent. This replacement guarantee against breakage is offered throughout Scandinavia, and we found it to be reliable as a broken glass ice cream dish, 1 of a set of 6, was replaced without question and without having to return the broken dish.

ENROUTE TO NARVIK, NORWAY (BODEN, GALLIVARE AND KIRUNA)

BODEN Being both a rail junction and military town, it's not surprising that Boden offers an impressive military museum. The tourist office is 10 blocks from the train station. **Bjorknas Camping** is 17 blocks (600 meters) from the station. Open Jun 1-Aug 31; tent/35kr. The camp has hot water in the sinks, a day room and automatic washer.

GALLIVARE This is a main town on the rail line to Narvik, Norway. The tourist office is 200 meters from the train station (Jun-Aug M-Su, Sep-May M-F 9-5) The municipal **campground**, *Kvarnforsens*, is between the town and the River Vassara Alv. The distance is 1 km. from the station or about a 20-minute walk. Jun-Aug, tent/40kr. The restroom sinks have hot water and there is a sauna (fee) and automatic washer and dryer. For sightseeing, the Lappish Church (Lappkyrkan), open M-Su 9-8 or a museum.

KIRUNA Situated 140 km. north of the Arctic Circle, from May 28 to July 18, the sun never goes down below the horizon in Kiruna. Night turning into day attracts people to the best viewpoints--the top of Loussavaara or Kiirunavaara--to glimpse the northern lights and Aurora Borealis. But having come this far, be sure to take the journey to Narvik, Norway, which can be done in a one day roundtrip from Kiruna if desired. The area between Kiruna and Narvik is only accessible by train so motorists leave their cars in Kiruna and change to the train. The railway travels through magnificent mountain scenery and parallels Lake Torne-Trask for 66 km.. Once across the border into Norway, the mountainsides drop steeply down to clear blue fjords until the train finally reaches Narvik on the Atlantic Coast.

Gallivare

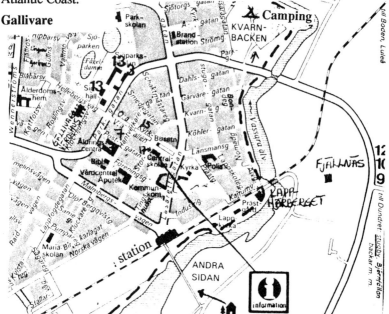

Swedish, Finnish and Lapp are all spoken in Kiruna, the Lapps having given up their nomadic way of life many years ago. The Lapps still maintain many of their customs, and some still follow the annual reindeer trek of the reindeer herds to the mountains in spring and summer for calving, and then back to their forest grazing areas in late fall and winter.

The train station is at the edge of downtown. **Kiruna Camping** is 1 km. from the station, part of Radhusbyn Ripan, a "village" of 90 vacation cabins. The central building in the village has a laundry, small store and sauna. Kiruna Camping is open Mar 1-Oct 31; tent/35kr.

Kiruna grew as a mining center and tours of the mine are offered daily in summer by the tourist office. There is also an outdoor folk museum (Hembygdsgarden I Jukkasjarvi), open Jun 1-Aug 28, 11-8, as well as some interesting artwork in the churches.

Trains leave **for Narvik** at 6:55am (ar. 10:18am), 11:35am (ar. ts 2:27pm), 4:35pm (ar. 7:30pm) and 6:40pm May 31-Aug 30 (ar. 9:40pm).

SWITZERLAND

Entering Switzerland from southern Europe is like coming home. Many Swiss speak English, the atmosphere is low-keyed, food is unit priced per 100 grams in the lavish supermarkets, and all the campgrounds have toilet paper. Of the four official languages of Switzerland, German is predominant with 73 percent of the population speaking it. French is spoken by 21 percent, Italian by 5 percent and Romansh by 1 percent.

THE BEST PLACES   The archetypal Swiss alpine village of **Zermatt** is all by itself at the base of the mighty Matterhorn. Much of its charm derives from never having allowed motorized transport to sully its pristine beauty. The drawback to Zermatt is the private railway fare that must be paid to get there. After having seen the village, there's not much to do unless you have the money to glacier ski or ride the lifts and do some hiking.

The **Interlaken** area has it all, though the town itself is not so much an attraction. Its charming medieval Swiss villages, lake cruises (included in Eurailpass), trails, uncrowded campgrounds and all the mountain lifts that money can buy will amply suit most people. Interlaken also makes a good base for day trips to Lucerne, Bern, and the Golden Pass. Even Basel and Zurich are not too far away for a quick visit.

Picturebook **Lucerne** pleases everyone just as it has been doing for eons. If you can only visit one town, make it Lucerne. **Berne** is the best of the larger cities to use as a base in Switzerland. The town is centrally located, making day trips to Interlaken, the Golden Pass, Lucerne, Basel and Zurich easily accomplished. These are the obvious places; to go off the beaten track head for **Chur and The Grisons.**

CURRENCY   Strong and getting stronger. The Swiss call their money francs just like the French, but one Swiss franc is worth about 4 times as much. One U.S. dollar is 1.5 francs. Each franc is divided into 100 rappen.

Banks give competitive rates and commonly don't charge a commission. Take advantage and get some currency for your next country.

WEATHER AND HIGH SEASON   Temperatures are never uncomfortably hot in summer, rather expect cool evenings. September is usually warmer than June. Being so close to southern Europe, should the weather turn bad, a few hours on the train will take you to sunny Italy. July and August are the most popular months for Swiss and European vacationers, with the first week in August the peak of high season. Swiss school vacations begin in mid-July and last through August.

The weather varies from one region to another more than you would think possible for such a small country. The Valais district (around Zermatt) and the Engadine have the least rainfall. Grapes, apricots and peaches grow here. Lugano in the Ticino district of southern Switzerland has relatively mild winters with sunshine and pleasant camping in May and early October. Vegetation in this area is reminiscent of the Mediterranean. The lakes of Lucerne and Thun (by Interlaken) have relatively warm weather starting in April because of the fohn wind which makes mountain areas highly uncomfortable, but becomes warm and dry by the time it reaches these two lakes. Within the lowland area which spreads between the Alps and Jura mountains, Lucerne, Basel, Zurich, Fribourg, Berne and all cities of this central plateau have fairly warm weather through October although rain can be expected. However if you're traveling outside of summer, keep in mind that Geneva is warmer and less rainy than Zurich or Lucerne.

CAMPING   Campgrounds are well kept by the immaculate Swiss and found in all touring areas. The Swiss Federation of Camping Clubs (FSCC) and Swiss Touring Club (TCS) are the main camping organizations. The latter has many excellent affiliated camps throughout the country. A map of Switzerland indicating the location of campgrounds is available free from the Swiss Tourist Office.

The campground fee is usually 3.50SF to 5SF per person, the tent fee 2-4SF. Hot showers are usually included, but some camps charge separately. Expect to pay a visitor's tax of 40SF to 1.60SF per person per night. The most popular campgrounds often charge a higher fee during high season; the person fee commonly increases .40SF and tent fee 2SF. Each camp defines high season differently, but generally it's July and August. Prices given in this book are for high season.

TRAINS   The Swiss Federal Railways (SBB) operate one of the best networks in Europe and their punctual trains go virtually everywhere. Reservations cannot be made for travel within Switzerland. Also a reservation is not compulsory for TEE or EuroCity trains for travel within Switzerland and to Italy. For local train travel within Switzerland on TEE or EuroCity trains, a reservation cannot be made but the trains can be used if a seat is available.

The best rail map is in the *Discover Switzerland* brochure that describes special Swiss train passes available from Swiss Tourist Offices abroad. Baggage can be checked through to another city for 7F by getting it to the train station at least an hour ahead to register it. Station luggage lockers and checkroom cost 2SF for 24 hours. The train information office in each city has a rack of free timetables for all the trains leaving that city. The official timetable, the 376-page *Amtliches Kursbuch*, is sold for about 7.50SF in train information offices, but the free schedules are all you need.

Any ticket office in Switzerland can issue a free family card. Ask for it when you buy your first ticket. The parent(s) pays full fare, children from 16-25 pay half fare, those under 16 ride free. The card is also accepted on mountain railroads and some lifts. Also applies to the Swiss Pass and Cards.

For tickets purchased in Switzerland, one-way tickets are valid for 2 days and round trip tickets are valid for 10 days with renewals possible. Reduction for round trip tickets is 25 percent. Unlimited stopovers are allowed on all tickets without having them stamped. Tickets purchased in the U.S. are valid for 6 months.   Rail tickets may be used on the corresponding lake steamer boat. Children under 6 travel free and those 6 to under 16 pay half. This is the definition of child for all train tickets, public transportation systems and amusements. Groups of 10 get discounts.

EURAIL BONUSES   (1) Free use of regular boat services on the lakes of Geneva, Lucerne, Thun (by Interlaken), Brienz (by Interlaken), Zurich, Neuchatel, Biel, Murten, on the Rhine River between Schaffhausen and Kreuzlingen and on the Aare River between Biel/Beinne and Solothurn. Ask at a tourist office in the region for the timetable.   When the steamship company or railway offers escorted tours via train or boat, a railpass holder can join these free of charge--inquire of the tourist office of city you are in for a brochure. If a private railway or lift is involved, the cost of these must be paid. (2) A 50 percent reduction on boat services on Lake Constance between Romanshorn and Friedrichshafen, and Rorschach and Lindau.   (3) 10 percent discount on the Europabus between St. Moritz and Munich.

SCENIC MOUNTAIN RAILROADS AND LIFTS   Narrow gauge railways have been constructed in mountain areas with steep gradients. Many of these are private and are not covered by Eurailpasses. The cost on these railroads is often fairly low from about 4SF to 13SF. They offer a chance to see spectacular mountains and waterfalls closeup.

A number of narrow gauge mountain railways are included in the Eurailpasses.   The **Golden Pass** between Zweisimmen and Montreux, and the 13-km. spur between Zweisimmen and Lenk are spectacular journeys. This is on the direct rail line between Geneva and Interlaken. On certain departures, vistadome cars are used. This trip can be taken as a day trip from Geneva, Berne or Interlaken.   See Interlaken for more information. **Lucerne to Interlaken** is 74 km. of beautiful mountains and lakes. See Lucerne and Interlaken. **Aigle to Champery** is a 25-kilometer spur leading to the ski resort of Champery from the main rail route between Geneva and Brig. Trains depart Aigle at 7:30am, 8:29am, 10:29am, 11:06am, 12:06pm, 1:06pm, 2:06pm, 3:29pm, 4:06pm, 5:06pm, 6:06pm, 7:06pm and 9:06pm. Trains return at 8:48am and 48 minutes past each hour until 8:48pm. The trip is one hour. The **Grisons** have several lines: (1) Between Chur, Thusis, Filisur and St. Moritz,   (2) Chur to **Arosa**,   (3) Chur to Disentis, (4) Landquart, Klosters, Davos and Filisur and (5) St. Moritz to Tirano. See Chur for more information.

Another group of lifts are the chairs, cablecars and rack (cogwheel) railways provided for skiers.   These range from expensive to exhorbitant. They are used by hikers to easily reach the trail head and tourists.

SCENIC ROUTES ON REGULAR RAIL LINES   Besides the scenic narrow gauge mountain trains, all regular routes over the alps to Italy are especially worthwhile. Also, the route from Brig to Martigny to Montreux traverses the alps at great height and provides access to many of the famous ski resorts, such as Zermatt, Crans, Verbier, Chamonix, and Champery.

SPECIAL TICKETS   The Swiss Railways offer the following special tickets.   The **Swiss Pass** gives unlimited travel on trains, postal motor coaches (buses) and lake steamers (boats), and discounts 25 percent on most cog-wheel railways, private railways and aerial cablecars.   The latter discount is important as prime tourist destinations in the alps are reachable only via these rather expensive cog-wheel and private railways. Please note that the unlimited travel rail network is more extensive than that available with the Eurailpass. For instance, Eurailpass is only valid as far as Interlaken, whereas the Holiday Card is valid as far as Grindelwald, Wengen and Stechelberg, and then gives a 20 to 30 percent discount on connecting transportation to the higher altitudes. Eurailpass is valid to Visp, the gateway to Zermatt; the Holiday Card is valid all the way to Zermatt. The Holiday Card includes city bus systems for 24 cities. The only city you're likely to visit not covered is Interlaken. The Card for second class is $105 for 4 days, $125 for 8 days, $155 for 15 days and $210 for 1 month. Children pay half. The pass can be purchased from a Swiss Tourist Office abroad by sending name, passport number and check, or at the train information office at Zurich or Geneva Airports. To compare, a point-to-point ticket from Basel to Berne to Interlaken to Grindelwald is 35F.

Regional Holiday Season Tickets are bought at any rail station in the region in which they are valid. The regions are Montreux/Vevey (92F); Bernese Oberland, includes Interlaken and Zermatt (110F); Lake Lucerne (112F or 82F for 7 days); Grisons (86F); Alpes Vaudoises/Portes du Soleil (56F); Walensee (38F); Locarno /Ascona (46F); and Lugano (60F). The first 7 mentioned sell tickets good for 15 days; on your choice of 5 of those days you get unlimited rail, boat, and bus travel on designated lines and for the other 10 days you pay half fare. Plus, for 15 days you get 25 or 50 percent off on adjoining lines as lifts and cog-wheel trains. For regions Locarno /Ascona and Lugano the ticket is valid 7 days, all for unlimited travel.

The Half Fare Travel Card costs $45 for one month $65 for 12 months. It allows purchase of tickets on railways, steamers, postal buses AND private railways like Zermatt-Gornergrat and the Jungfraujoch for 50 percent off. Cards may be purchased abroad from a Swiss Tourist Office or at Swiss train stations. The **Swiss Card** gives a free round trip ticket from any Swiss border point to any Swiss city plus the same half fare privilege as for the Half Fare Card and costs $65 for 1 month second class. For instance Geneva to St. Moritz via Zurich is regularly $65 one way.

POSTAL BUSES The Postal service operates a system of bus routes through the most scenic areas. Rates are similar to the train but routes are seldom duplicated; tickets and point of departure at the post office.

TOURIST INFORMATION Called Office du Tourisme, Associazone per il Turismo or Verkehrsverein in this tri-lingual country.

FOOD The quality of processed Swiss foodstuffs is very high. Food is priced differently than in surrounding countries because Switzerland is not in the Common Market so does not follow the market's agricultural policies and price supports. Swiss agricultural output is very substantial for a country which is half mountainous and whose crops must be carefully pursued in a small amount of cultivable land. Eighty percent of agricultural output consists of dairy products. Flocks and herds make good use of the mountainous parts by being taken into the Alps during the summer for grazing. Accordingly, fresh milk, cheese, butter, ice cream, powdered milk and milk chocolate are high quality.

Migros and Co-op Markets have good prices, especially on their house brands of chocolate and weekly specials. Supermarkets and public markets are the cheapest places to buy food in this rather expensive country.

Groceries have a "use by" date and are unit priced per 100 grams or per liter. A specially processed form of milk can be found in unrefrigerated counters and is marked UP. If unopened, this milk can be kept for several months without refrigeration. *Magermilch* is skim milk, *milchdrink* is two percent, *tafelbutter* is table butter, *kochbutter* is unpasteurized.

Fondue and *raclette* are two national main courses featuring cheese which is common to French speaking parts of Switzerland. Served in cold weather, raclette consists of chunks of cheese melted on a stick over a fire and then scraped onto potatoes on a plate. Swiss tourist offices abroad have a free pamphlet, *Guide Fromage Suisse*, which illustrates the varieties of cheese, lists free guided cheese factory tours, and mentions restaurants where cheese specialties are served.

Swiss restaurants are expensive. The saving grace of campers is the country-wide chain of M Restaurants (actually cafterias) that are found in **Migros** (MEE-gros) Markets (supermarkets). Not all Migros Markets feature a cafeteria, so it's best to inquire at the Tourist Office for a location. M Restaurants are very attractive cafeterias with good food and reasonable prices and the best value in Switzerland. Apple juice (*apfelsaft*), grape juice (*traubensaft*), either red (*rot*) or white (*weiss*), and milk are available in M Restaurants and in Swiss restaurants in general.

HIKING   Switzerland is well organized with regularly maintained and regulation-signed trails traversing the country. The Swiss Tourist Office distributes an excellent 68-page booklet, *On Foot Through Switzerland*, which describes with diagrams 42 hikes including six cross country ones, and includes a route map. Official sectional maps are published by the Swiss Topographical Service and can be ordered in advance from the Tourist Office. They're called *Landeskarte Carte Nationale* series and have a scale of 1:50,000 (3/4 mile per inch).

Trails are maintained by the Swiss Footpath Protection Association (Schweizerische Arbeitsgemeinschaft fur Wanderweg), except the Jura Ridge Trail which is looked after by the Swiss Jura Association. You have 42,000 miles of trails from which to choose. Signing is standardized. The basic sign is yellow with black lettering on a white signpost. Location and altitude are written on the post. A yellow sign points to the nearest fork, farm village, mountain hut or trail junction. Secondary lettering beneath indicates a more distant destination of the trail. According to regulations, this point should be within 6 hours walking time. Sometimes a sign will carry directions for several trails, in which case a black line separates the information. Yellow secondary signs are placed along the trail to indicate where the path continues if it is unclear. Also, small yellow diamond, rectangular or arrow-shaped markings are on rocks and trees along the route.

All trails in the central lowlands are marked by all yellow signs. This area between the truncated Jura Mountains and higher Alps is filled with meadows, lakes, forests and small hills, but also farms, villages and commercial and industrial cities. The region is the economic heart of Switzerland where most Swiss live. Trails pass through some towns and villages, but in most cases skirt them. Meals can be bought at village inns and campgrounds. The basic central lowlands trail starts at Romanshorn on Lake Constance (Bodensee--shared by Switzerland, Austria and Germany), passes through Zurich, Berne, Fribourg and Lausanne and ends in Geneva. Any section may be done without hiking the entire distance.

Half of Switzerland is taken up by the Alps, and signs for these mountain trails are specially marked with a white tip on a yellow sign with a red strip in the middle. A hiker should be prepared for sudden rain and cold in the mountains before venturing very far on this type of trail. Boots or shoes with lug soles and waterproof jacket should be worn on mountain paths if you're going for more than a hour's walk from a hut. Small white directional markers with a red middle stripe in diamond, arrow or rectangular shape help show the way.

In a separate category is the Jura Ridge Trail that follows the Jura mountains, a low mountain range flanking the central lowlands, in northern Switzerland. Signs are yellow with half red and half white tip. The trail begins in Zurich and ends at Lake Geneva.

Hiking is so well developed in Switzerland that food can be reliably obtained along the way. In some cases, such as the central lowlands trail, you needn't even camp but can stay in guesthouses and inns on the outskirts of small towns along the route. Even on mountain trails, the route is punctuated with mountain huts which provide a night's lodging for about $7 and/or prepared meals. A picnic lunch can be bought at a hut to see you through the following day until another is reached. There are climber's huts throughout the Alps which are maintained by the Swiss Alpine Club (Schweizer Alpen Club or Club Alpin Suisse). No food is available. Most mountain huts are staffed with a married couple who provide beds, dormitory style, and cook food. You can eat in a hut without staying there, however avoid camping on grass being grown for hay. Guidebooks describing routes, meals, inns and campgrounds are available for some trails. Ask at the tourist office in the locale of the trail when you get there.

PRONUNCIATION OF PLACE NAMES Appenzell (AHP-uhn-tsel), Davos (dah-VOHS), Lake Maggiore (mahd-JOH-ra), Lausanane (loh-ZAN), Leysin (LAY-zann), Montreux (mon-TRUH), St. Moritz (san mah-RITS), Ticino (tee-CHEE-no), Valais (va-LEH).

LE POTPOURRI Swiss post offices are excellent and easy to use. Most are near the train station and open 7:30-12 and 2-6 weekdays, and 7:30-11 am on Saturday. All letters go air mail and cost 1.20F for less than 10 grams. Shops are open 8-6:60 weekdays but some close earlier on Saturday and remain closed until Monday afternoon. The lakes of Lucerne, Lugano and Maggiore sometimes have problems and closed beaches are so marked. The lakes of Geneva and Zurich are clean.

BASEL

Switzerland's second largest city, Basel is situated on the Rhine River at the confluence of the frontiers of France, Germany and Switzerland. Each year, Basel hosts the important International Art Fair of 20th Century Art starting in mid-June and running 5 days. 1989 dates are June 14-19.

TRAIN STATION Basel Station has two parts. **SNCF station** serves trains to and from France, while **SBB station** handles other international services and local trains to Germany and the Swiss interior. If you are going into France, allow time to clear customs at the station before boarding. Allow an extra hour if you don't already have a visa and must purchase one. If your train is passing through Basel from France, you may have to debark at SNCF station, go through customs and board in SBB station. SBB station is the largest and most important station.   It has a tourist office (M-F 8:30am-7pm, Sa 8:30-12:30 & 1:30-6, Apr-Sep also Su 2-6pm.), post office, exchange office (daily 6am-11:15pm), luggage checking (5:30am-midnight), and reservations office (8am-7:30pm). Take tram 1 or 7 from SBB station to reach downtown.

Basel Bahnhof D.N.B. (Basel Badischer Bahnhof) is a minor German station across the river.   Coming from Germany, the train stops there first before continuing to SBB station.

CITY TRANSPORTATION   Trams and buses are operated by Basler Verkehrs-Betriebe. A one day pass costs 5SF.   Tickets are sold from machines at the stops.   Single tickets cost according to zone.   The yellow zone is .80SF, white zone is 1.40SF and blue zone 2SF.   Check the map on the ticket machines to determine which ticket to buy.   Children 6 to 15 inclusive pay .80SF regardless of zone.   Each ticket carries unlimited transfer privileges within a certain time period as follows: 30 minutes on the .80SF ticket, one hour on the 1.40SF ticket and 1-1/2 hours on the 2SF ticket.   Ticket books, containing 11 tickets for the price of 10, cost 8SF for .80 tickets, 14SF for 1.40SF tickets and 20SF for 2SF tickets. Operate the automatic ticket vending machines by pressing the button corresponding to ticket price, depositing the correct change (no return) and removing the ticket.   If you make a mistake, press button *Irrtumtaste* to release the money.

CAMPGROUNDS   **Camp Waldhort Basel** is located in Reinach, 6 km. south of Basel.   Open Mar 15-Oct 18; adult/5SF, tent/3SF.   Take tram 11 from Aeschenplatz, a 3-minute walk from SBB station.   Get off at stop *Landhof* and then a 500-meter walk.   The last tram leaves at midnight.   Fare is 2SF.   The camp has very good restrooms with hot water in individual sink cubicles in the restrooms.   Dishwashing sinks have hot water and there are automatic washers, store, and snack bar.   It's also possible to commute from Freiburg, Germany, or Mulhouse, France.

FOOD   The public market on Marktplatz next to the Rathaus (city hall) in the vicinity of Mittlere Rhein bridge is open M-Sa 7am-noon.

SIGHTSEEING   The museum of fine arts, **Kunstmuseum, is the finest in Switzerland and a top European museum.**   Tu-Su 10-5; adult/2SF, free on Sat, Sun and Wednesday afternoon.   It's located on St. Alban-Graben, a 6-block walk from SBB station, or take tram 2 from SBB station to the third stop.   The first floor shows the largest collection of Hans Holbein's works, and other European masters.   Elsewhere is an excellent contemporary section with Braque, Klee, Leger, Chagall, Picasso, Arp, Mondrian and all the important artists well represented.

The Basel **zoo** is renowned for success in breeding endangered species in captivity.   Animals roam separated by moats.   Open daily 8-6; adult/8SF.   It's an 8-minute walk from SBB station.   For a nice walk, follow Oberer Rheinweg along the right bank.   Other attractions include a Museum of Natural History and Anthropology, Kirschgarten Palace--18th century private mansion with period furniture, and Munster Cathedral--a landmark of Basel made of red sandstone in Romanesque and Gothic style with a tiled roof and twin towers.

TRAIN SCHEDULES   Trains from Belgium, Holland, Scandinavia and Western Germany stop in Basel before continuing south to Italy. A train departs **for Italy** at 8 minutes past even-numbered hours from 8:08am to 6:08pm. Trains go **north into Germany** at 17 minutes past the hour from 7:17am to 6:17pm. There are also other trains.

To Berne and Interlaken, trains leave on the hour from 7am to 9pm and then 9:50pm. (Last train to Berne is 11pm.) To Berne is 30 minutes, Interlaken, 1-1/2 hours.

To Lucerne, trains leave at 52 minutes past the hour and at 8 minutes past even-numbered hours. The last train back to Lucerne is 11pm. The trip is one hour.

To Zurich, trains leave at 27 and 58 minutes past the hour to 8:58pm and then at 9:58, 10:58 and 11:34pm. One-hour trip.

BERNE (BERN)

A capital city of red roofs and arcaded sandstone buildings, Berne makes a good choice of a Swiss city to visit. The excellent, uncrowded campground and good train connections make Berne a fine base for day trips to other towns.

Berne - Tram Route to Camping Eicholz

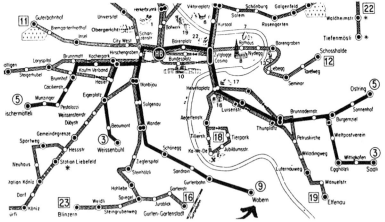

TRAIN STATION   The large station is downtown and faces Bahnhofplatz. The bus terminal is above the train station. Exchange is open daily 6:10am-10pm. One bank has a branch inside the station, open M-F 7am-7pm, Sa 7am-4pm. Luggage storage hours are 6am to midnight. The tourist office is open May-Oct 31 M-Sa 8am-8:30pm, Su 9am-8:30pm. Reservations office is open 7:30am-7:450pm; train information, daily 7:30am-8:30pm. The postoffice (hauptpost) nearby is open M-F 7:30am-6:30pm, Sa 7:30-11am. In the Station cafeteria, half a chicken plus fries and vegetables costs 8.50SF. Tables and chairs are provided or food can be purchased "to go" and will be packed in foil-lined bags and covered disposable containers.

CITY TRANSPORTATION   City trams cost .80SF to 1SF per ride. Purchase single tickets from the automat at the stops. To use the machine, study the colored map. The stop at which you are standing is marked with a red spot in the yellow area. Locate your destination and press the appropriate fare-selection button (yellow, blue or red). Insert exact amount of money (no returns) and remove the ticket.

A Day Ticket *(24-Stunden-Karte)* valid 24 hours costs 4SF. A Tourist Card *(Touristenkarten)* is valid 1, 2 or 3 days and costs 3SF, 5SF or 7SF respectively. Both tickets can be purchased at the SVB counter in the subway of the train station.

To open a bus or tram door, press the illuminated red button beside the door. When getting off, press the button near the door and the door will open automatically at the next stop. Most trams operate starting at 5:30-6am and start their last trip about 11:15-11:45pm.

CAMPGROUNDS   Camping Eicholz on the Aare River in the Wabern district is 3 km. southeast of downtown. Open May 1-Sept 30; adult/3.80SF, student/3SF, tent/1.50SF, hot shower/.20SF, room in bare cabin for 1 night/10SF. From the square in front of the train station at tram stop with "Wabern" on the sign, take tram 9 (yellow sign), direction Wabern. Trams run daily 6am to 11:45pm. (Trams return from 5:46am to 11:31pm.) Fare is 1SF. Get off at the last stop, Wabern. Walk back one block past the Co-op grocery store and post office to Eichholzstr. Turn right and follow signs to the campground, a 10-minute downhill walk. The camp has exclusive use of one section of a public park within a lovely residential area. The camp is especially nice for backpackers as cars are prohibited from the beautiful lawn of the camping area. (Tents have to be moved once a week to preserve the lawn.) The office, open 8-noon and 2-10, gives a good, free map of Berne. Restrooms have cold water in the sinks, but dishwashing and laundry sinks have hot water. Three outdoor nooks equipped with two-burner coin-operated gas stove and sink are available. Nearby are tables and chairs. Use of a freezer is free. Ask at the office to use the washing machine inside a special room; cost is 5SF including centrifuge and soap. There are clothes lines for drying. No store on the site, but a bakery *(boulangerie)* and grocery store *(epicerie)* are three blocks away. The restaurant at the camp has counter service, outdoor tables under cover, and closes at 10pm, but the restaurant kitchen closes earlier. Menu items are standards like two weiners *(wienerli)* with roll *(mutschli)* and mustard *(senf)*, chicken, milk, fries and salad. Two wading pools (one with slide), a small sandy beach area and cold water shower are in the park area. A trail beside the Aare River leads to downtown Berne from camp in about 40 minutes. The trail also leads to a footbridge crossing to the zoo *(tierpark)* across the river from camp.

Camping Eymatt on the road to Wohlen is 5 km. northwest of the city center. Open all year; adult/4SF, tent/4.20SF. Take postal bus Bern-Hinterkappelen from the bus station above the train station. The postal bus leaves once an hour and the fare is 6SF. Get off at bus stop "Eymatt."

FOOD   The public market is Tuesday and Saturday morning on Bundesplatz in front of the Houses of Parliament, 3 blocks from the station. A meat and dairy products market is held on the first Saturday of each month on Munstergasse, about 6 blocks further east. **Migros Market** on Marktgasse, open M 2-6:30, Tu-W 8-6:30, Th 8am-9pm, F 8-6:30 & Sa 8-4, is a very large supermarket that has everything including a tank with live trout. Its M Restaurant (cafeteria) upstairs opens at 6:30am and has modern decor and all sit-down tables and chairs. It's a quick and efficient self-service operation with various food stations, rather than one long line. Of the two stations for hot plates, one serves the daily special exclusively while the other has a grill and cooks hamburgers and fries to order, but heats up

418

previously cooked chicken. Hamburger and fries cost 5.50SF, a half chicken and fries 6.30SF. A salad bar displaying a selection of salads, some meat and hard-boiled eggs is priced at 1.50SF per 100 grams. (Be careful as price mounts quickly; the daily special is the best value.) At the drink station, milk, chocolate milk, and carbonated apple juice cost 1.50SF per glass. Selections from the dessert table laden with different puddings, fresh fruit, fruit salad, custards, cakes and ice cream are priced at 1.20SF per 100 grams.

SIGHTSEEING   Besides exploring the old town which centers on Marktgasse and visiting the bear pits at Barengraben which have drawn travelers since the 15th century (open 7-6, bring carrots to feed them), Berne offers the following attractions.

The **Kunstmuseum**, Hodlerstr. 12, has the most extensive collection of Klee's works in the world (he was born here) including 40 paintings, 150 gouaches and watercolors and 2,500 drawings.   The museum's Rupf Foundation shows mostly cubist works of Picasso, Braque, Gris and Leger. Open Tu-Su 10-5, Tuesday to 9pm.   During special exhibitions the fee is 3SF; at other times it is lower.   Good 9x12 reproductions sell for 6SF. Restrooms are on the main floor to the right of the entrance, and first floor up. The museum is 5 blocks from the station.

Naturhistorisches Museum (Natural History Museum) is at Bernastr. 15. It's one of the best of its kind in Europe. Open M-Sa 9-12 & 2-5, Su 10-12 & 2-5.   The museum is a 20-minute walk by trail from Camping Eicholz. Adult/1SF, student/.50SF. The modern, air-conditioned building, has a check room and lots of seating in the foyer. Restrooms are on the left beyond the ticket seller and on first, second and third floors at the top of the stairs.   The museum shows nicely done dioramas of stuffed animals in natural settings.   Ground floor: Aftican species including Aardvark, rhinoceros, pigmy hippopotamus. First floor: fish, lizards, birds, wall board display showing dung of various species, rows of nests with eggs and feathers, stuffed animals such as bats and shrews, mole in cross-section of earth showing his habitat, stuffed llamas, camels, hedgehogs, armadillo, anteater and other kinds of animals not often found in zoos. Also skull, antler and teeth collection, whale skeleton suspended from ceiling, model of a whale heart and display of stomach contents of whale.   Second floor: birds, reptiles, beautiful python skeleton, shells, insects, room devoted to honeybees showing assorted hives and large model of a bee. Top floor: rocks, crystals, fossils, prehistoric room.

Parlamensgebaude (Parliament) is on Bundesplatz.   To learn the fascinating workings of Swiss democracy, take a free guided 45-minute tour at 9, 10, 11am, 2, 3, or 4 pm daily, except no 4pm tour Sunday. No tours when parliament is in session during Mar, Jun, Sep and Dec. The famous **Clock Tower** at Theaterplatz performs at 4 minutes before each hour the same as it has been doing since 1530: crowing rooster, jester, carousel, etc.

The **Zoo** (Tierpark Dahlholzli) is across the river from Camping Eicholz, a 10-minute walk.   Follow the riverside trail north to the footbridge. Bring bread to feed deer. Free entrance. Just inside zoo grounds are pony rides and donkey cart rides for .50SF, half-franc coins required. Nearby are baby goats, guinea pigs and play eqipment.   Entry to zoo birdhouse is 1.50SF; restrooms are in birdhouse.

DAY TRIPS Lucerne, Basel, Interlaken, and the Golden Pass rail trip between Spiez and Montreux (see Interlaken) are all possible day trips from Berne.

MURTEN, a compact medieval walled town 30 km. west of Berne, makes a good train excursion. Take the train to Kerzers (direction Neuchatel) and then change for Murten. Trains depart for Kerzers at 6:07am, 7:17am, 8:20am and 20 minutes past each hour until 8:20pm. The trip is 19 minutes. At Kerzers you have 6 minutes to change to the train for Murten. Departures are at 45 minutes past the hour from 7:45am to 8:45pm. The ride to Murten is 10 minutes. To return to Berne, trains for Kerzers leave at 5 minutes past the hour to 9:05pm and then 10:24pm. Trains depart Kerzers for Berne at 20 minutes past the hour until 9:20pm, then 10:39pm.

FRIBOURG is another good excursion. Visit this ancient town during its market days, Wednesday and Saturday, when local costumes are worn. Trains leave Berne (direction Lausanne) at 6:16am and 16 minutes past the hour until 10:16pm. Additional trains leave at 38 minutes past even-numbered hours from 6:38am to 8:38pm and then 9:32pm and 11:20pm. The trip is 21 minutes. From the station, walk across Place de la Gare, the plaza in front of the station, and then take the important street that runs diagonally towards the left, Av. de la Gare. In 4 blocks you will reach the tourist office. Using their free folder outlining a walking tour is the best introduction to the town. There are no convenient campgrounds in Fribourg.

From Fribourg, it's a 30-minutes train ride to medieval Murten. Trains leave Fribourg at 42 minutes past the hour until 9:42pm. To return to Berne, trains leave Fribourg at 22 minutes past the hour until 11:22pm.

To Amsterdam, leave at 8:51am (change at Basel to EuroCity, change at Duisburg, ar. 6:14pm), 10:51am (change at Basel to EuroCity, ar. 7:59pm) and 8:51pm (ar. 9:38am).

To Basel, leave at 51 minutes past the hour from 6:51am to 9:51pm, and at 26 minutes past odd-numbered hours from 7:26am to 7:26pm. 70-minute trip.

To Brig, leave at 20 minutes past the hour. The trip is one hour and 40 minutes. Change at Brig for Zermatt and Chamonix.

To Geneva, leave at 16 minutes past the hour from 6:16am to 10:16pm and then 11:20pm, or at 38 minutes past even-numbered hours from 8:38am to 8:38pm. The trip is 1-3/4 hours.

To Interlaken, leave at 28 minutes past the hour from 7:28am to 11:38pm. The trip is 54 minutes.

To Lucerne, leave at 7:31am, 8:31am, 10:31am, 12:31pm, 2:31pm, 4:31pm, 5:31pm, 6:31pm, 8:31pm and 9:50pm. Trip time is one hour 10 minutes.

To Munich, leave at 8:17am (change at Zurich, ar. 2:04pm), 10:47am (change at Zurich to EuroCity, ar. 5:04pm), 1:47pm (change at Zurich, ar. 8:09pm) and 5:17pm (change at Zurich to EuroCity, ar. 11:04pm).

To Paris Gare de Lyon, leave at 6:58am TGV (ar. 11:25am), 11:16am (change at Lausanne to TGV, ar. 4:28pm) and 4:16pm (change at Lausanne to TGV, ar. 9:32pm).

To Zurich, leave at 47 minutes past the hour from 7:47am to 11:47pm. Trains leave at 17 minutes past even-numbered hours from 8:17am to 6:17pm.

INTERLAKEN AND THE BERNESE OBERLAND

Berne, Brig and Lucerne are rail gateway cities to Interlaken and the magnificent Bernese Oberland. Its magnet is the ascent of the Jungfraujoch (pronounced YUNG-fraw-yuk), which at 11,333 feet makes it the highest mountain station in Europe. The mountain itself is 13,642 feet. Other lifts in the area don't go as high, are less expensive yet still give a good view of the fabulous mountains. Numerous excellent campgrounds are near the villages and well-marked trails traverse the area.

Eurailpass is valid only as far as Interlaken. After that the private cogwheel railways and lifts get you. (Actually there is a lot of breathtaking mountain scenery on some routes included in Eurailpasses without paying the king's ransom on private mountain routes. In the Grisons (see Chur), many narrow gauge railways are covered by Eurailpass. From Interlaken, the Golden Pass via cogwheel railway can be seen as a day trip, and Eurailpasses are valid. Between Brig and Martigny on the regular highspeed train route loom awesome mountains.)

If you decide to go for the big one--the ascent up the **Jungfraujoch**, keep these points in mind. People with any kind of health problem should avoid the trip as oxygen is rather thin at that altitude and they may feel weak and dizzy. Even some people who are in good health but merely have cold feet may feel sick at the top. Everyone should take it slow and allow their body to adjust. Also, save your money if the weather isn't clear. Conversely, those intending to take the trip should do so on the first clear and sunny day, not knowing what tomorrow may bring.

To keep costs minimal in this expensive area means forgetting closeup views of the mountains and avoiding entrance fees into caves and museums. So what does that leave? Select a camp in the Interlaken area which can be reached by boat or on foot, and spend a day cruising on the lakes, perhaps stopping at medieval Spiez, or taking a hike along the shoreline. If you aren't going to Chamonix to see the Alps, the cogwheel railway to Grindelwald, in the midst of the three powerful mountains, might be considered.

Visitor's Card   Anyone who spends the night in the area is issued a Visitor's Card by the campground which entitles the person to certain reductions. The most useful ones are 25 percent off admission to the Alpine Garden at Schynige Platte, small discounts on admission to Thun Castle (20 percent), Spiez Castle (.50SF) and the Open Air Museum at Ballenberg (1SF), and discounts on sports facilities. No big deal though.

Walking Pass   Available at the tourist offices or train stations, this is a brochure listing 12 hikes ranging from 2 to 5 hours in length. Anyone completing 5 of them receives a bronze walking shoe pin souvenir. The hikes involve a lift up and then a hike down to a lower lift or village.

BERNESE OBERLAND SEASON TICKET   This ticket costs 102SF. It's valid for 15 days, out of which you receive unlimited travel for 5 of those days and half price travel for 10 days on certain lines. In addition, on those lines not covered by the pass, a discount of 25 to 50 percent is given. First off, it only discounts 25 percent the highest portion of the Jungfrau trip and the trip to Schilthorn. "Free" lines are those from Interlaken Ost as far as Murren, Stechelberg, Kleine Scheidegg and First. Included are almost all villages, the exception being Gimmelwald with a 50 percent reduction.

SAMPLE PRICES OF PRIVATE RAILWAYS AND LIFTS   These are included in the season ticket. Prices are one way. On lifts such as chairs and cablecars where people are likely to be walking down, the round trip price is usually not much greater than the cost of a one-way ticket. In other cases, the round trip ticket will be exactly twice the one way fare.

Interlaken Ost -	Kleine Scheidegg	20.30
Interlaken Ost -	Grindelwald	6.40
Interlaken Ost -	Mannlichen	21.40
Interlaken Ost -	Lauterbrunnen	4.20
Grindelwald -	First	18.40
Brienz -	Rothorn Kulm	21.00
Lauterbrunnen -	Mannlichen	14.60

Groups of 5 or More   Any group of 5 or more receives a 20 percent reduction on lifts and mountain railways. The ticket must be purchased at least 2 hours in advance of departure from the departing station. For instance, the regular price of the Jungfraujoch trip from Interlaken Ost is reduced to 84SF via Lauterbrunnen or 90.20SF via Lauterbrunnen and Grindelwald. (Regular fare is 107.60SF for either route.) There are no restrictions on departure times. The group discount does not apply to the excursion ticket described below.

EXCURSION TICKET JUNGFRAUJOCH   This ticket is a 25 percent discount off the regular price of the journey between Kleine Scheidegg and Jungfraujoch on the trains that depart Kleine Scheidegg at 8:02am, 9:02am and 3:02pm. The return trip can be made anytime. Puchase the ticket at any ticket office, but it must be used within 10 days of purchase. The regular roundtrip fare from Kleine Scheidegg to Jungfraujoch is 67SF. The excursion fare is 51SF.

The roundtrip excursion fare from Grindelwald is 79.20SF (85.80SF if via Lauterbrunnen); from Interlaken Ost (via Grindelwald or Lauterbrunnen), 91.60SF; from Lauterbrunnen, 80.20SF. To connect with the early trains from Kleine Scheidegg, you must leave Interlaken Ost at 6:35am or 7:37am or Lauterbrunnen at 6:58am or 8am. Though stopovers are permitted on the excursion ticket during its 10-day validity period, no extra is saved by buying the ticket from Interlaken Ost. The best approach is to purchase each segment individually, and not buy the expensive portion from Kleine Scheidegg to the top until you're satisfied the weather will be good.   If making this a roundtrip from Interlaken Ost, ascend via Lauterbrunnen and descend via Grindelwald to view the entire area.

JUNGFRAU TRIP   Bring warm clothing and sunglasses. Trains leave Interlaken Ost in the valley and climb mountains passing by Wilderswil, Lautenbrunnen, Wengen and Wengenalp until finally reaching the top station of the Wengernalp Railway, Kleine Scheidegg at 6,673 feet. This is also a good starting point for trails through alpine meadows that don't necessarily involve too much uphill trekking. At Kleine Scheidegg, transfer to the Jungfrau Railway which reaches Eigergletscher and enters a four-mile tunnel to eventually emerge at the mountaintop.   An ice skating rink, restaurant, souvenir stands and an unsurpassed view of the glaciers and highest mountains will greet you.

OTHER LIFTS: Schilthorn Cableway (9,748 feet) is the longest cableway in the alps and ends at the top of Schilthorn mountain, site of Piz Gloria, revolving restaurant. The coach is suspended from the cable. The roundtrip fare from Lauterbrunnen to Schilthorn is 52SF. **Schynige Platte** (6,454 feet) is a spendid vantage point giving a wide view of the Bernese Alps, and site of an alpine botanical garden with over 500 different plants. **First** (7,113 feet) is a wonderful viewing station reached by chairlift from Grindelwald.

EURAIL BONUS: LAKES BRIENZ AND THUNER EXCURSIONS

Large, comfortable ferry boats sailing on Lakes Brienz and Thuner are included in Eurailpass. Tables and chairs for picnics abound on the boats, but be sure to bring along water as that in the restrooms is not for drinking. Food is sold on board but at high prices. The lakes are connected by the River Aare. From Interlaken Ost Station, boats depart for Lake Brienz. From Interlaken West, boats depart for Lake Thuner. Take the underpass from the station.

A wonderful arrival to Interlaken is to get off the train at the other end of the lake, change to the ferry and cruise into Interlaken. If you are arriving from Bern, get off at Thun and change to the ferry which is directly beside the train station. From Brig, get off at Spiez and walk downhill about 10 minutes to the dock; or take the bus. From Lucerne, get off in Brienz.

Thunersee Interlaken West and Thun are the easiest points to change from train to boat as the train station and boat dock are next to each other. Local trains run frequently on the Spiez side of the lake, connecting the small towns to Interlaken. Sightseeing priorities would be (1) a cruise on the lake, (2) the old section of Thun, (3) the village of Spiez and (4) the Beatenbucht caves.

The town of **Thun** (pronounced thoon) is at the opposite end of the lake from Interlaken West. Its old town on the right bank across the river from the train station is delightful, and rates Michelin two stars. Walk on Hauptgasse, the picturesque main street. At the end of it, covered stairs lead to the castle (Schloss Thun). Trains leave Thun for Interlaken West and Ost at 7:08am, 7:20am and then at 12 and 20 minutes past each hour until 10:12pm and then 10:52pm.

To reach the dock from **Spiez** train station is an easy 10-minute walk downhill, but to transfer in the other direction requires climbing uphill or a bus. The bus leaves the dock for the train station at 8:40am, 9:40am, 10:42am, 11:46am, 12:40pm, 2:20pm, 3:20pm, 4:03pm, 4:45pm, 5:05pm, 5:47pm, 6:05pm and 6:18pm. The bus leaves the train station for the dock at 8:29am, 9:15am, 10:25am, 11:25am, 12:25pm, 2:10pm, 3:02pm, 3:45pm, 4:30pm, 4:52pm, 5:10pm, 5:54pm and 7:08pm. Trains leave Spiez for Interlaken West and Ost at 8:01am and 1 and 11 minutes past each hour until 7:11pm and then 1 minute past the hour until 11:01pm and then 11:22pm.

If you get off at **Neuhaus**, **Camping Manor Farm** is about a 10-minute walk from the dock. Coming from Interlaken West, Neuhaus is the second stop. Adult/4.40SF, tent/6SF and tax/1.10SF. The excellent camp has hot water in the sinks, automatic washer, store and restaurant. At Neuhaus are peddle boats for rent and a bathing beach. Boats leave Interlaken West for Neuhaus at 12:03pm, 1:44pm, 2:47pm 3:47pm and 4:47pm. Boats leave Neuhaus for Interlaken West at 11:33am, 3:12pm, 4:02pm and M-F & Su, Jul-Aug at 6:11pm. Frequent buses from Interlaken West are also available.

At **Beatushohlen**, the third stop from Interlaken West, a 35-minute uphill climb on a shady path from the dock will bring you to St. Beatus Caves. (daily 9-5.) The attendant at Beatushohlen dock is willing to keep your pack in his office until you return. A cafe, picnic tables and restroom are at the Caves, but the water in the restroom is not potable. Admission with mandatory guided tour is adult/6SF and student/5SF.

Brienzersee At Brienz is the **Ballenberg** Swiss Open-Air Museum showing 13 original farmhouses. Demonstrations by artisans are given daily. A bus goes to the park for 5.20SF roundtrip. Daily 9:30-5:30; 8SF, student/4SF. The best natural site is the Giessbach Falls at Giessbach.

INTERLAKEN   Train Stations   Interlaken Ost (east) is the main station. Those going to Grindelwald or Lauterbrunnen or taking any private mountain railway should get off here. All mountain railways depart from Interlaken Ost not Interlaken West station. Trains from Lucerne stop only at Interlaken Ost. Trains from Bern and Brig, stop first at Interlaken West and then continue to Interlaken Ost. Interlaken West Station is downtown in Interlaken and has a tourist office. The stations are connected by both trains and buses. A ferry dock is immediately beside both stations.

Campgrounds   Interlaken and the small towns of the Bernese Oberland are saturated with good campgrounds. Nine camps are accessible from Interlaken by bus or foot. Both stations have information on bus departures. A visitor's tax of .80-1.60SF is charged at each campground. Prices listed below are for high season, in most camps July and August. Prices drop about a franc off-season. The campgrounds on Lakes Thuner and Brienz require a walk on level ground to reach them from the ferry dock. Those in the valleys at higher altitudes than Interlaken invariably involve an uphill trek in at least one direction, though a lift may be available for a price.

Interlaken

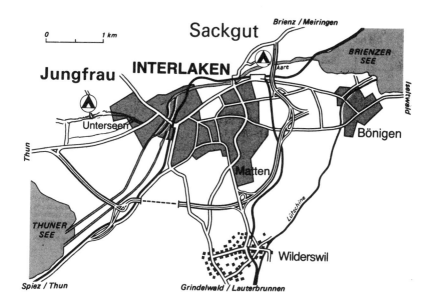

From **Interlaken West Station**, the closest camp is **Camping Jungfrau** in Unterseen, one kilometer from the station and easily walked in 15 minutes. From in front of the station with your back towards the river, turn left and walk to the main intersection, Bahnhofstrasse. Turn left on Bahnhofstrasse, cross the river and continue walking. You will reach the intersection Hauptstrasse. Continue walking in the same direction, but the street is now called, Scheidgasse. At the intersection with Beatenbergstrasse, turn left onto Muhleholzstrasse. The camp is ahead on the left. Fees are adult/4.50SF, tent/4SF and tax/1.10SF. The camp has excellent facilities including hot water in handwashing, laundry and dishwashing sinks, automatic washing machine, store, cafe and lounge. Within the next two blocks are **Lazy Ranch Camping** (adult/4SF, tent/5SF, tax/1.10SF) and **Hobby Camping** (adult/4SF, tent/4SF, tax/1.10SF). A few minutes beyond these camps is Camping Manor Farm. Jungfrau and Manor Farm are the highest rated campgrounds.

From **Interlaken Ost Station, Camping TCS Tiefenau** (Sackgut) in the Tiefenau district is closest at 500 meters, about a 10-minute walk. The campground is visible across the Aare River from the station. To find the bridge across the river, walk back towards Interlaken West for one block. Fees are adult/4SF, tent/3SF and tax/1.10SF. The attractive camp has hot water in the dishwashing and laundry sinks, automatic washing machine and snack bar. The next closest camp, **Camping TCS Bonigen** (Seeblick) is on Lake Brienz, 500 meters from the ferry dock at Bonigen and one km. from Interlaken Ost Station.

Day Trips   Visiting **Thun** and **Spiez** and cruising the Thunersee will give the visitor a glimpse of traditional Swiss villages. For viewing the Alps closely for free, the Golden Pass route to Montreux or the equally scenic route to Lucerne can be made as day trips, courtesy of Eurailpasses.

The Golden Pass in the high alps between Spiez and Montreux is another good trip that can be conveniently made from Interlaken. This also makes a fine route to take for those going to Geneva or Chamonix. The most scenic portion is between Zweisimmen and Montreux for which you change to a smaller train. Depart Interlaken Ost at 8:25am, Interlaken West at 8:30am and arrive in Zweisimmen at 9:39am. Here is where the change is made to a narrow gauge train for the trip over the pass. A Panoramic Express vistadome train leaves Zweisimmen at 9:50am, passes through spectacular alpine scenery stopping at Gstaad, Rougemont and Chateau d'Oex before arriving in Montreux at 11:44am. The next departure from Interlaken is the Golden Pass train which leaves Ost at 9:25am, West at 9:30am and arrives in Zweisimmen at 10:39am. If it's a Saturday or Sunday and you have a first class Eurailpass, change to the Superpanoramic Express vistadome train which leaves at 10:41am (ar. Montreux 12:15pm). Others can board the regular train leaving at 10:50am (ar. Montreux 12:40pm). A second Panoramic Express leaves Interlaken Ost at 1:25pm, West at 1:30pm (ar. Montreux 5:02pm).

For the return trip if you have a first class Eurailpass and it's Saturday or Sunday, the best departure is the 2pm all first class Superpanoramic Express with vistadome. This train arrives in Spiez at 4:51pm, where you must change for Interlaken. Otherwise, the best departure is the same Panoramic Express. It leaves Montreux at 2:20pm and arrives Interlaken at 5:35pm. Other departures are 3pm (change at Spiez), 4:20pm Oberland Express (ar. Interlaken 7:35pm), 5pm (ar. 8:23pm), 6:20pm (change at Spiez), and 7pm (change at Spiez, and arrive Interlaken 10:23pm).

Day Trip to Lucerne The narrow gauge train to Lucerne passes through spectacular alpine scenery after skirting Lake Brienz outside Interlaken. Passage is included in Eurailpasses. Trains leave only from Interlaken Ost station. Departures are at 6:32am, 7:35am, 8:41am, 9:33am, 10:41am, 11:35am, 12:41pm, 1:35pm, 2:41pm, 3:35pm, 4:41pm, 5:35pm 6:41pm, 7:35pm and 8:35pm. The trip is two hours. Be sure to start early enough to give ample time to see Lucerne. Lucerne's picturesque old quarter is a 5-minute walk from Lucerne station and can be seen in half a day. See Lucerne for the return train schedule. As far as lake cruising, the Thunersee has more interesting villages than Lake Lucerne.

To Bern leave Interlaken Ost at 7:39am and 39 minutes past each hour until 9:39pm. Stops at Interlaken West 5 minutes later; trip is 2 hours to Bern.

To Spiez, Brig and south to Italy, take any of the above trains for Bern, but get off at Spiez at 1 minute past the hour. From Spiez, trainsleave for Brig at 54 minutes past the hour.

To Lucerne, trains leave Interlaken Ost only at 8:41am, 10:41am, 12:41pm, 2:41pm, 4:41pm and 6:41pm. Arrival is 2 hours later.

To Zermatt and Chamonix, take the train to Brig and change there, or go via the Golden Pass route to Montreux and change for Martigny. Montreux to Martigny is on a major rail line and trains leave Montreux at 14 and 52 minutes past each hour up to 9:52pm. To Martigny is 25 minutes. The Golden Pass route is more scenic.

GRINDELWALD (GREEN-duh-vault) The village grew on a slope of the mountain and is a major hiking center in summer. The valley floor is below Grindelwald at Grindelwald-Grund. A lift links Grindelwald-Grund with Grindelwald train station for 2.80SF one way or slightly more roundtrip (but most people walk down). A post office and a luggage checking office (2F) are across the tracks in front of the train station. An information kiosk is outside the station, but the **tourist office** is one block uphill on the right side of the single main street of tiny Grindelewald. The tourist office will load you up with free literature including a free map of Grindelwald which shows the route to the campgrounds, the Visitor's Card and information on hikes and lifts (Sep-Jun M-F 9-12 & 2-6, Sa 9-noon & 2-5, Jul & Aug M-Sa 8-12 & 2-6). In front of the tourist office is a shady park with benches, playground, drinking fountain and free lifesize chess board. Across the street is a small Co-op supermarket, where a liter of milk costs 1.75SF and 500 grams bread, 2SF. Shops close from noon to 1:30pm.

Campgrounds The cheapest and closest camp in the area is **Camping Sand** (adult/3.50SF, tent/1SF and tax/1.50SF each person). Facilities are minimal and poorer than most other Swiss camps, but you will find conventional toilets, sinks with cold water, and outdoor laundry sinks. The smell of new mown hay and the sound of two rushing streams that bisect the camp accompany your arrival. Don't be discouraged by the uninhabited stationary trailers awaiting the ski season at the front of the camp. Keep your chin up and march beyond the trailers and the restrooms to the grassy area at the edge of camp. The impressive setting is beneath the north face of the Eiger Mountain, separated by a fence from a lush rolling pastureland. The friendly owner, Christian Bohren-Gerber, is not at the office but comes around in the morning to collect. We had the camp to ourselves in early July. After July 10, more people start coming.

To reach Camping Sand, with your back to the train station and facing the main street, walk to the right and then turn sharply right and walk downhill. Keep walking downhill staying on the same road, cross the river at the bottom, and then follow the signs. The pleasant walk downhill from 1034 meters altitude at the station to 951 meters at the campground is 15 minutes. To get there more quickly, take the Grindelwald-Grund lift from

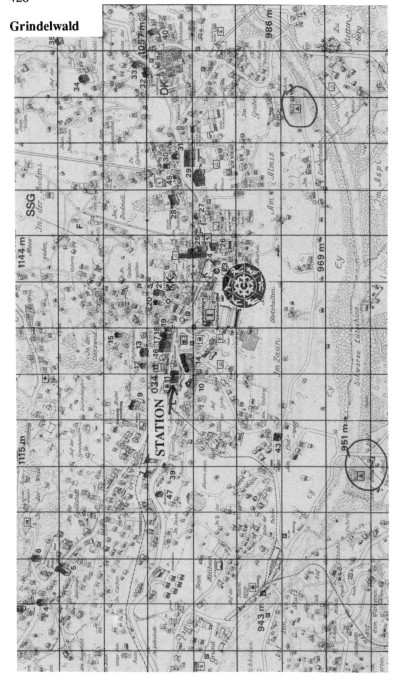

Grindelwald Station to Grindelwald-Grund. Buy a round trip ticket so you can ride back up. At the bottom, walk back along the road in the direction the lift brought you. The river should be on your right. Walk on level ground for about 5 minutes until the road crosses the river. Cross the river and then follow the signs. To return from camp to the lift, turn left after crossing the river and walk straight ahead. A one way ticket is 3.60SF.

Camping Gletscherdorf is only a slightly father walk and has better facilities (adult/4SF, tent/2SF and tax/1.50SF each person, except for July and August when the fee is 2SF extra a night). The camp has hot water in handwashing, laundry and dishwashing sinks. The view from here, as from everywhere, is spectacular. To reach the campground, follow the directions as for Camping Sand, but turn left (about two-thirds of the distance to the river) at the Glacier Hotel and keep going until reaching camp. Do not take the Grindelwald-Grund lift for this campground. If you are at the tourist office or have already walked any distance uphill on the main street, then keep going and turn right on the street, Fussweg Dorf, and walk downhill for about 10 minutes. When the road meets the river, do not cross but turn right.

Chairlift First The chair leaves from the uphill end of Grindelwald and ascends 7,200 feet in four stages. Total time aloft is 30 minutes. Roundtrip ticket Grindelwald to First is 30SF, one way is 19SF. Many well-signed trails of all levels of difficulty begin at the top. This chair is a good alternative to the Jungfraujoch trip. The top station is 2,168 meters as opposed to 3,970 meters for Jungfraujoch. Don't miss last lift back.

Cablecar Mannlichen Take it from Grindelwald-Grund station. The route via Zweilutschinen and Wengen costs 39.40SF roundtrip.

LAUTERBRUNNEN The village (2,640 feet) is in a valley on the rail route from Interlaken Ost to Jungfraujoch. Interlaken Ost to Lauterbrunnen costs 4.20SF. The tourist office is at the train station. **Camping TCS Lauterbrunnen** (Schutzenbach) is 600 meters from Lauterbrunnen Station, in the direction of the waterfalls, Trummel-bach (adult/4SF, tent/3SF, tax/1SF). Excellent facilities with hot water in the sinks, individual sink cubicles, automatic washer, store and dormitories.

THE RAIL LINE GENEVA TO ITALY
(Montreux, Martigny, Sion, Sierre, Zermatt, Brig)

An important rail line begins in Paris, goes to Geneva, travels beside Lake Leman and enters the Alps outside Montreux. Its major stops in the Alps are Martigny (change for Chamonix), Sion, Sierre, Visp (change for Zermatt) and Brig. Brig is the major rail junction in the alps, where lines from Bern and Geneva join before entering the Simplon tunnel to emerge in Italy. For mountain scenery, the distance between Montreux and Brig is unsurpassed. For lake views, the portion between Geneva and Montreux is rewarding.

GENEVA Center of French-speaking Switzerland and an international crossroads of Europe, Geneva is home base for such international organizations as the Red Cross, sections of the United Nations, and European branches of major corporations. It also provides excellent train connections to most parts of Europe.

428

Lake Geneva and Campgrounds on the Lake

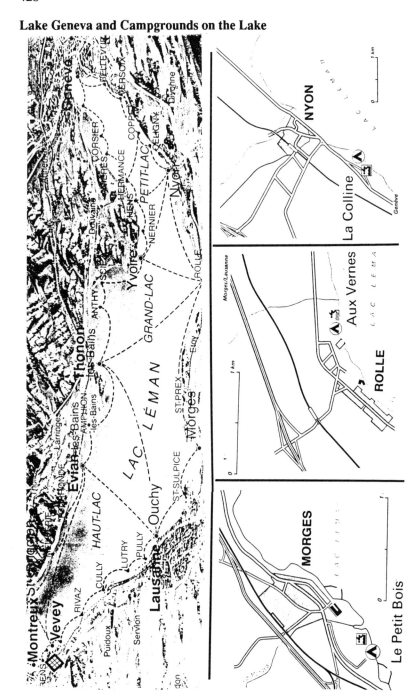

The main **train station** is **Gare de Cornavin**, which is across the river from the main shopping area. Tourist office, exchange office, post office, luggage check and TPG bus information office are inside. Outside is Place Cornavin, the terminal for buses and trams. All main line trains leave from this city. The small rail line going to Chamonix in France leaves from smaller **Eaux Vives Station** in the northeastern part of the city. Outside the station, take bus 5 or 6 and get off after crossing the river. Then look for signs to tram 12 which leaves from the Bel Air stop.

Eaux Vives Station handles trains for a part of France, particularly the Haute Savoie. Trains for Chamonix and Evian leave from this station. No trains connect the two stations. Instead you must take a bus. The woman in the exchange window at the station speaks English, exchanges money and sells bus tickets. A single ticket is 1.50SF or a card for 6 rides is 8SF. To reach the bus stop, go out the station door and turn left. At the end of the block, turn right onto Rue du Savoie. At the end of the block, turn right without crossing the street and the stop for tram 12 is partially down the street. Sit on the righthand side of the bus. The bus travels through downtown Geneva. Get off at the busy Bel Air stop, near the river. The name is on the bus stop sign. Once off the bus, follow the arrow to bus 5 or 6, which is half a block distant. Then change to bus 5 or 6 and get off at Cornavin Station.

City Transportation Bus maps and ticket vending machines are at each stop, but you need exact change. A single ticket is 1.50SF and includes free transfers in any direction for one hour. A child's ticket (6-16) is .80SF. A 6-trip card costs 8SF. The card must be punched in the machine before getting on board. Families can ask for a free *Carte Famille*, which entitles children under 16 to ride free, those 16-25 at half price, parents pay full price (1 parent must be along).

The small boats (*mouettes*) which cross the lake stop at various points in the city (1.50SF per crossing). Other trips are charged by distance. Eurailpass is only valid on the large boats belonging to the CGN. A timetable for the **CGN ferries** can be obtained from the Tourist Office. The CGN boats stop at docks: Mont-Blanc, Jardin Anglais, Paquis and Eaux-Vives. Mont-Blanc, on Quai du Mont-Blanc, is on the same side of the lake as Cornavin Station, a 7-minute walk straight ahead on Rue du Mont Blanc in the direction of the lake. Jardin Anglais is across the river from the station. Eaux-Vives is a 20-minute walk from Eaux-Vives Station.

There are various **CGN cruises.** (1) A one hour cruise leaves the Mont Blanc dock at 9:45am, 1:30 and 2:45pm. From the Jardin Anglais dock, a cruise leaves at 12:20pm. (2) A lower lake cruise departs Mont Blanc dock at 9am and Jul-Aug 3:45pm, and from Jardin Anglais dock at 10:30am and 2:30pm. (3) A complete tour of the lake departs Mont Blanc at 9am. This is an all day tour with a stop of your choice at Lausanne, Montreux or the Castle of Chillon. (4) An all day tour of Evian and Lausanne leaves Mont Blanc dock at 9am. (5) An evening cruise with dancing and music leaves Mont Blanc on Thursday and Saturday at 8:30pm, returning at 11:30pm. Eurailpass covers passage, not food or drink.

Campgrounds The best strategy to save time and bus fare is to stay at a camp within walking distance of a train station that is on the main rail route between Geneva and Lausanne. As even Lausanne is only a 30-minute ride, the train takes less time than a local bus would to a closer campground.

The Swiss Touring Club operates campgrounds at Nyon, Rolle and Morges; all are on the water and within a 10 to 20-minute walk of the train station. The towns of Nyon and Morges rate a Michelin star for their lovely situation and historical aspects, such as the ramparts of Nyon. Fast trains in the direction of Lausanne stop at Nyon and Morges; local trains stop at Rolle. Do not board just any train to Lausanne without checking the departure poster on the tracks to make sure it stops at the town you want; TGV's and express trains don't. All trains leave from Cornavin Station. Morges is the larger camp with more facilities. The other two are smaller.

Trains from Gare Cornavin (direction Lausanne) that stop at **Nyon** (in 15 minutes) and then **Morges** (in 28 minutes) leave at 5:07am, 5:42am, 6:42am, 6:50am, 7:18am, 7:50am, 8:28am and at 28 and 50 minutes past each hour until 10:28pm and then 11:02pm and 11:45pm. Trains return from Morges at 2 and 41 minutes past the hour, and from Nyon at 18 and 56 minutes past the hour. CGN boats stop at all towns along the lake.

Camping La Petit Bois is on Lac Leman in the town of Morges. Morges is closer to Lausanne than Geneva, but the train ride is less than 30 minutes. Apr 16-Oct 11; adult/4.80SF, tent/2SF (Jul-Aug 5SF), tax/.60SF. The camp is on the outskirts of town near the yacht harbor and town swimming pool. Excellent facilities including hot water in handwashing, dishwashing and laundry sinks, automatic washing machine, store, cafe and dayroom. Besides the train, a CGN boat leaves once a day for Geneva (Mont Blanc dock).

Camping La Colline is on Lac Leman, a little over 1 km. south of the small town of **Nyon.** Open Apr 16-Oct 4; adult/3.60SF, tent/2SF (Jul-Aug 3SF), tax/.60SF. Facilities include cold water in bathroom sinks, hot water in dishwashing sinks, automatic washing machine, store and dayroom. A CNG boat for Geneva leaves at 1:05pm (ar. 2:05pm); 2:30pm daily Jul-Aug, M-F May-Jun & Sep (ar. 3:40pm); 4:35pm (ar. 5:55pm); 7:46pm daily Jul-Aug, M-F May-Jun & Sep (ar. 9:05pm); 7:44pm (ar. 8:50pm). A boat leaves Geneva from Mont-Blanc at 9:15am and Eaux-Vives at 9:20am (ar. 10:20am); from Jardin Anglais at 10:30am (ar. 11:50am); from Mont-Blanc at 2:15pm (ar. 3:33pm); and 3:45pm from Mont Blanc, daily Jul-Aug, M-F May-Jun & Aug (ar. 5:01pm).

Camping Aux Vernes, at the tiny town of **Rolle**, is on Lac Leman near the village swimming pool. Open Apr 16-Oct4; adult/3.40SF (Jul-Aug 4SF), tent/2SF (Jul-Aug 3SF), tax/60SF. Facilities include cold water in bathroom sinks, hot water in dishwashing sinks, store and snack bar. A CNG boat leaves for Geneva at 12:17pm (ar. 2:05pm); and 7pm daily Jul-Aug, M-F May-Jun & Sep (ar. 9:05pm).

Camping de L'Abarc, is 6 km. from Geneva at 151 route de Vernier, in **Vernier.** Open Jul-Aug only to youth under 25 years old. Take bus 6 from Cornavin Station. Adult/3SF, tent/3SF.

Camping Pointe a la Bise is 6 km. from Geneva **at Vesenaz** on Lac Leman. Take bus 8, Veyrier, (1.50SF) in front of Cornavin train station to Rond Point de Rive and change to bus E (fare 2.50SF). Last departure is 11:35pm. Apr 16-Oct 10; adult/4.20SF, tent/2.10SF (June 15-Aug 31 tent/4SF). Swiss Touring Club camp; store, cafe, individual sink cubicles, hot water in dishwashing and laundry sinks, automatic washer, dayroom.

Camping Sylvabelle, 10 chemin de Conches, is 3 km. from downtown Geneva in the district of Conches. Mar-Oct; adult/4SF, tent/3SF.

Take bus 8, Veyrier, (1.50SF) in front of Cornavin train station. Last bus 11:45pm. Other campgrounds are much better.

MARTIGNY Martigny is the transfer point from the Swiss Federal Railways to a private railway that goes to the border, where a SNCF train can be taken to Chamonix. The fare from Martigny to the border is a worthwhile 11.40SF. A campground is within walking distance of the train station in Martigny. Train schedules are listed under Chamonix in the French chapter.

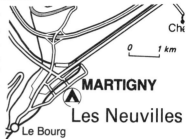

SION Sion is a 2-star Michelin town. Overlooking the 2,000 year old village is the fortress/church, built continually between the 11th and 15th centuries. Highly rated **Camping Les Iles** is 4 km. from the train station and reached by bus. Fees are adult/3.80SF (Jul-Aug 4.40SF), tent/2SF (Jul-Aug 4SF), and tax/.60SF. All facilities including hot water in all sinks, automatic washing machine, store, snack bar and dayroom.

SIERRE *We took a beautiful hike...it was well worth it. Take the train to Sierre and then a bus to Chandolin. It is about 15SF for the bus up a mountain but the scenery is well worth it. When at Chandolin, take the hike to BellaTola, about four hours up and three back. A hut with food and lodging is half way up. At the top is an incredible view of the Alps with snow and glaciers* (Lee Diamond). The bus ride from Sierre to Chandolin takes 1 hour and 10 minutes and departs 5 times daily.

    Camping Sierre-Ouest (Siders-West) is open Apr-Oct 15. The camp is west of town, 1 km. from the train station. Walk on the main street, turn left and walk through town until Hotel Atlantic. Turn left onto a little road along a narrow river and walk to the campsite. Also, bus 3 leaves every half hour from the station. Individual sink compartments, store.

VISP The private railway to Zermatt leaves from Visp. Visp is on the rail line between Brig and Martigny. The tourist office is two blocks from the train station. **Camping Muhleye** is a 15-minute walk from the station. May 30-Sep 30, adult/3.50SF, tent/1SF, tax/.30SF. Simple facilities with private sink cubicles and hot water in the dishwashing sinks.

ZERMATT Gateway to the famed Matterhorn, the delightful village of Zermatt (pronounced tzair-MAHT) nestles below the towering peak in an alpine valley. The village's charm has been maintained by its steadfast policy of forbidding cars and any motorized vehicle within the village. A popular ski resort in winter, glacier skiing and hiking through meadows and forests happily occupy its guests during summer. Zermatt is reached via the town of Visp. Visp is on the rail line between Brig and Martigny. Eurailpasses are not valid for the 28 km. of the private, narrow gauge railway between Visp and Zermatt.

    The tourist office is near the train station and sells an aerial map showing trails. **Camping Matterhorn**, operated by Lehner Richard, is open June 1 to October 1. Fee is adult/6.50SF including tent and tax. From the train station, walk north (away from the town) for three minutes.

432

BRIG Brig is the main rail junction for trains entering Italy. **Camping Geschina** is a little over one km. from the train station.

LUCERNE (LUZERN)

Lucerne has long enjoyed the reputation of being Switzerland's picturebook city. Its delightful medieval old quarter is everything a traditional Swiss city should be. Though the museums may be more outstanding in Basel, Zurich and Bern, if only a day can be spent in Switzerland, Lucerne makes a good choice. For a spectacularly scenic arrival, departure or day trip, take the train that goes between Interlaken Ost and Lucerne (see train schedules).

TRAIN STATION The station is downtown and faces Lake Lucerne across Bahnhofplatz. Inside are exchange office and post office. The tourist office is next door at Frankenstrasse 1; exit west of the train station.

CITY TRANSPORTATION The bus terminal is in Bahnhofplatz in front of the station. Tickets are purchased from the machines at the stops. From the map on the machine, figure the fare for the journey. Press the button for that amount. Insert exact change (no return) and retrieve ticket from slot. Press the error button if you've made a mistake and your money will be returned. Fares are .80SF for 2 zones, 1SF for 3-6 zones and 1.50SF for 7 and over zones. One day tickets are sold from the VBL transport office in the subway near the train station, but Lucerne is basically a walking town so don't bother. **Yellow-orange buses are free** city buses that connect the pedestrian shopping area with the rest of the city. Blue and white buses are regular city buses and charge fares. **Regular boat service** on Lake Lucerne is included in Eurailpasses. Brunnen and Fluelen at the opposite end of the lake are stops on the main rail route to Italy through the St. Gotthard tunnel.

CAMPGROUND Camping Lido Lucerne is at Lido (Bruelmoos) near the beach on the opposite side of Lake Lucerne from the station. The distance is about 2 km.. Open Mar 15-Oct 31; adult/4SF, tent/1.50SF, tax/.80SF. Many people walk to camp as the pleasant walk over the bridge and along the lake takes only 35 minutes. From the station, walk forward to Seebrucke bridge and follow the main street around the lake. Or take the boat or bus. Bus 2 from the station travels across Seebrucke bridge and follows the lakeshore to camp, a 10-minute ride. Get off at the Swiss Transport Museum and then walk 1 block farther. The camp can be seen within a fence on the left. The Lido swimming beach, ferry dock and parking area are on the right.

Lucerne

The camp can also be reached by boat, free with Eurailpasses. SGV (Schiffahrt Vierwaldstattersee) boats leave from the dock across from the station. The journey to the Verkehrshaus/Lido stop takes 10 minutes and is the first stop after leaving the Bahnhof dock. On the Luzern-Brunnen-Fluelen line, departure times are 9am, 9:30am, 10:20am, 11:25am, noon, 1:20pm, 2:20pm, 3:20pm, 5:20pm and 7:30pm. On the Luzern-Stansstad-Alpnachstad route, boats leave at 9:15am, 10:05am, 10:20am, 11:25am, 11:45am, 1pm, 2:15pm, 3:15pm, 3:20pm, 4:15pm and 5:15pm. Boats return from camp at 11:10am, 12:18, 12:34pm, 1:17pm, 1:38pm, 2:50pm, 4:10pm, 4:42pm, 5:44pm, 6:15pm, 6:27pm 7:32pm, 7:45pm and 8:30pm (runs daily in Jul-Aug only).

The campground is flat, grassy and guests pitch their tent wherever they find room. Facilities include individual sink cubicles with cold water, hot water in dishwashing and laundry sinks, automatic washers and dryers, store, dayroom with tables and chairs and a snack bar from which a rotisseried chicken may be ordered in the morning to be picked up hot off the spit with french fries for dinner. In July and August the campground is often filled to capacity.

For a less crowded campground in July and August, consider staying at the campground in the town of Zug (see Zug). Another possibility is to take the boat to a small town on the lake and stay there. The Vitznau campground is rather high (adult/5SF, site/8SF) but **Camping Sportzentrum**, between the small towns of Buochs and Ennetburgen costs less and is easily walked from the dock of Buochs. Look for it behind the tiny yacht harbor. Adult/4.80SF, site/4SF, tax .60SF, including hot water, excellent restrooms.

FOOD   The market is at Unter der Egg on the north shore of the Reuss River. Unter der Egg is near Reuss bridge, beside City Hall. A Migros Market is on Hertensteinstrasse 46, the street behind Hotel Schweizerhof.

SIGHTSEEING   Lucerne's picturesque old quarter is delightful. You can't miss the roofed Chapel Bridge (Kapell-Brucke) with its Gothic, wooden, octagonal water tower constructed in 1333. Each roof section is a painting which was donated by the different leading families of Lucerne at the time. The Town Hall, Kornmarkt, was built in 1602-1606. Its roof is characterized as Swiss hip roof. All around are the winding streets of the old quarter. In the distance can be seen nine defence towers which comprise Musegg Wall, 14th century fortifications. Schirmer Tower, sixth from the river, and some surrounding ramparts are open to the public. Spreuer Bridge, fifth from the lake, dates from 1408 and is similar to Chapel Bridge.

The motor launches that tour Lake Lucerne, free with Eurailpasses, reach the trailheads in the area. (Lifts are available for a price, but the view isn't any more spectacular than what can be obtained with Eurailpasses on the Golden Pass train route between Spiez and Montreux--see Interlaken.) Mt. Pilatus is an observation platform 7,000 feet high. A trail begins at Hergiswil that goes by way of the Brunni Hotel to the platform. The trail takes about 5 hours to the top. Hergiswil can be reached either by boat or train (see day trip). The private railway, not included in Eurailpass, starts from Alpnachstad and reaches the top in 40 minutes.

For trails in the **Rigi Mountain Ridge**, take a boat (direction Fluelen) and get off at Weggis, Vitznau or Gersau. The boat leaves Bahnhofquai at

6:50am, 9am, 9:30am, 10:20am, 11:25am, 1:20pm and 2:20pm. (Boats also leave from the Lido.) From any of the three towns, a trail begins that climbs to Rigi Mountain ridge in about three hours hiking time. The towns are at 440 meters and the ridge is 1440 meters. (From Vitznau, a private mountain railway goes there in 35 minutes. From Weggis, a cablecar goes to Rigi-Kaltbad.) On top many good trails begin through meadows and forests.

DAY TRIP TO ENGLEBERG   The narrow gauge railway from Lucerne to Hergiswil, Stansstad, Stans, Wolfrenschiessen and Engelberg is included in Eurailpasses. At Engleberg is an abbey, and a series of lifts that ascend Mt. Titlis (3,020 meters or 10,000 ft.). On Sundays, there is an express run to Engelberg at 7:55am and 8:55am. Otherwise, trains leave at 8:55am, 9:25am, 10:15am, 11:09am, 12:09pm, 1:09pm, 2:09pm, 3:09pm, 4:09pm, 4:55pm, 5:25pm, 6:09pm, 7:09pm, 8:15pm and 9:09pm. The last return from Engleberg is 7:50pm. Camping Eienwaldli is 1.2 km. from the station. Open all year, adult/4SF, tent/2.50SF, tax/1.40SF, 4-star camp, automatic washer, store, restaurant.

To **Amsterdam**, trains leave at 8:56am (change at Basel to EuroCity, change at Duisburg, ar. 6:14pm) and 10:56am (change at Basel to EuroCity, ar. 7:59pm). For non EuroCity trains, go to Basel and take a German InterCity train north, changing at Mannheim and/or Cologne as necessary.

To **Basel**, leave at 56 minutes past the hour from 7:56am to 9:46pm and 10:52pm. The trip is one hour and 12 minutes.

To **Berne**, leave at 7:13am, 8:13am and at 13 minutes past odd-numbered hours until 7:13pm and then 8:55pm and 9:55pm. 1-1/2 hours.

To **Brussels,** leave at 6:46am (change at Basel, ar. 2:34pm) and 11:46am (change at Basel, ar. 7:34pm).

To **Chur**, trains (direction Romanshorn) for Phaffikon leave at 9:05am, 11:05am, 1:05pm and 3:05pm. In 71 minutes, change at Phaffikon. (The 3:05pm departure arrives 3 minutes before the connecting train leaves at 4:18pm.) Trains depart Phaffikon for Chur at 9:40am, 11:40am, 1:40pm, 3:40pm and 4:18pm (change at Sargans this train only). To Chur is 1 hours.

To **Florence**, leave at 7:20am (ar. 3:20pm), 8:12am (change at Goschenen to EuroCity to Milan, change at Milan to Rapido, ar. 3:46pm), 9:19am (change at Milan to Rapido, ar. 4:46pm), 11:19am (change at Milan to Rapido, ar. 6:46pm), 1:19pm EuroCity (change at Milan to Rapido, ar. 8:46pm.

To **Frankfurt** (change for Wiesbaden and Rudesheim), trains leave at 56 minutes past each hour for Basel. At Basel either take a direct train to Frankfurt or take a German Intercity to Mannheim and then change for Frankfurt.

To **Geneva**, leave at 13 minutes past odd-numbered hours from 7:13am to 7:13pm.

To **Interlaken** Ost, a very scenic trip, leave at 6:06am, 7:22am, 8:02am, 8:12am, 8:58am, 9:22am, 10:12am, 11:22am, 12:09pm, 1:22pm, 2:12pm, 3:22pm, 4:12pm, 5:22pm, 6:12pm, 7:12pm and 8:12pm. Two Hours. The train ends at Interlaken Ost and does not go to Interlaken West.

To **Paris** Gare de l'Est, trains leave at 6:46am (change at Basel to EuroCity, ar. 12:59pm), 10:56am (change at Basel, ar. 6:05pm), 2:56pm not Saturday (change at Basel to EuroCity, ar. 9:16pm), and 9:46pm (change at Basel, ar. 6:48am).

To **Zurich**, leave at 10 minutes past the hour from 6:10am to 10:10pm. The trip is 50 minutes.

ZURICH

Switzerland's largest city and financial center, Zurich has an interesting old section and the excellent Swiss National Museum. Both Basel and Lucerne can easily be visited on day trips from Zurich.

TRAIN STATION   Hauptbahnhof is the main one.   Exchange (6:30am-11:15pm), reservation office towards the rear of the station (daily 8am-10pm), luggage check (closes midnight).   Tourist office (M-F 8am-10pm, SaSu 8-8:30) is outside the entrance to the left (other side of post office).
   The shopping area starts immediately across Bahnhofplatz in front of the station.   Buses and trams leave from Bahnhofplatz.   Tram 11 travels the main street, Bahnhofstrasse to Schifflande Bahnhofstrasse the pier on Zurich-See (Lake Zurich) from which ferries depart, free with Eurailpasses. Pick up a copy of *Zurich Excursions* from the tourist office or train information for its suggested rail excursions which can be duplicated with a Eurailpass or joined upon payment of non-railpass covered charges.

CITY TRANSPORTATION   *Tageskarte*, a 24-hour pass, costs 5SF. Buses and trams are 1.50SF for a 1 to 5 stop ride and 2SF for a 6 or more stop ride to the city limits.   Ticket books are also sold.   Purchase and cancel tickets in the machines at the stops.   Each suburb has a local train station and these trains are included in Eurailpasses.   Some international trains stop at suburban Enge Station, connected to Hauptbahnhof by train or tram 7.

CAMPGROUNDS   **Camping Seebucht** is 3 km. from downtown at See-Strasse 559 on the west side of Lake Zurich in the suburb of Wollishofen. May 1-Sept 30; adult/4SF, tent/2SF.   Take tram 11 from the station for four stops to Burckliplatz, next to the lake.   Change to bus 61 or 65 to bus stop *Stadtgrenze platz* near the camp entrance.   Buses (2SF)Fleave every 20 minutes; last departure 11:30pm.   Another way to get there is to take a local train to suburban Wollishofen station and then walk 15 minutes.   The camp is an attractive parklike area; hot water in restroom sinks, automatic washer, clothesline, store and snack bar serving breakfast and light snacks.   The camp is small and heavily used in summer, but walkers aren't turned away.
   Camping Sihlwald is about 15 km. from Zurich.   May 1-Sept 30; adult/3.50SF, tent/3SF.   Take tram 8 to Bahnhof Selnau, and then a train to Station Sihlwald.   Cross the river and go about 200 meters upstream along the road.   The campground has excellent restrooms with individual sink cubicles with hot water, hot water in dishwashing and laundry sinks, automatic washer, store, cafe and dayroom.

FOOD   The market is Tuesday and Friday, 6-11am, at Stadthausanlage on the lakeshore near Burckliplatz, where you take buses 61 or 65 to Camping Seebucht.   Another market, same days and hours, is further out at Helvetiaplatz, across the Sihl River.   Jelmoli (pronounced yell-mo-lee) department store on Bahnhofstrasse has a basement supermarket and third floor restaurant that serves a smorgasbord breakfast for about 12SF of nine kinds of bread, 5 kinds of meats, butter, cereal and eggs.   Migros Markets are at Lowenstrasse and Silhlbrucke-strasse, on Limmatplatz east of the river, Kreuzplatz on the east side of the lake, and at Folkenstrasse and Lowenstrasse.

SIGHTSEEING   The top priority **Swiss National Museum, Landesmuseum**, is located conveniently behind the train station.   After exiting, turn left and walk to the corner of the station building.   Turn left again and the museum is across the street.   Presented is a large group of Swiss art and chronologically organized exhibits on the country's cultural development begining with prehistoric times.   Open T-Su 10-5, free.

436

The **Rietberg Museum** is in Rieterpark at Gablerstrasse 15 near See-strasse. It's a 5-minute walk from Bahnhof Zurich-Enge, or take tram 6 or 7 from the main station. Shown is a private collection of non-European art from India, Africa, South America, East Asia, China and Japan. Open Tu-Su 10-5 & Wed evening 5-9pm. Free.

The fine arts museum, **Kunsthaus**, at Heimplatz 1, shows a group of 13th to 20th century paintings and sculpture, plus graphic art. The modern section is particularly large and important, and includes 100 works by the sculptor, Giacometti. Open Tu-F 10-9, SaSU 10-5, M 2-5. Adult/2SF, student/1SF, free Fri 5-9pm. Restrooms are on ground and "first" floors. The museum is a 15-minute walk from the station.

The **old quarter** of Zurich is off Limmat-Quai, the main street across the river from the station. Grossmunster on Zwingliplatz is the most important Romanesque Cathedral in Switzerland. Here is where Zwingli first began to talk of reformation in 1519. Though construction began in the 13th century, the modern bronze reliefs on the portal were done by Otto Munch. Giacometti created the chruch windows in 1932. Haus zum Rechberg, Hirschgraben 40, is a beautiful, rococo patrician house. Guildhouses from the 15th to 18th centuries include Zur Meisen (rococo), Munsterhof 20; Zur Waag (15th century gabled), Musterhof 8; Zur Ruden (now a restaurant), Limmatquai 42; and Zur Saffran (Baroque), a restaurant at Limmatquai 54.

To Amsterdam, trains leave at 9am (change at Duisburg, ar. 6:14pm), 11am (ar. 7:59pm), 1pm (change at Basel to EuroCity, change at Duisburg, ar. 10:14pm) and 11:37pm (change at Basel, ar. 9:38am).
To Barcelona Sants Station, leave at 8:03am (change at Geneva to EuroCity, ar. 9:26pm) and 6:03pm (change at Geneva & at the border-Port Bou, ar. 9:29am).
To Basel, leave on the hour and at 37 minutes past the hour 8am to 10:37pm and 11:37pm. The 6:37pm and 8:37pm are EuroCity trains. The trip is 56 minutes.
To Bern, leave at 3 minutes past the hour 7:03am to 11:03pm. 70 minutes.
To Frankfurt (change for Wiesbaden and Rudesheim), leave at 7am EuroCity (ar. 11:15am), 8am (change at Basel, ar. 12:15pm), 9am (change at Mannheim, at 1:15pm), 10am (change at Basel to EuroCity, ar. 2:15pm), 11am (change at Mannheim, ar. 3:15pm), noon (ar. 4:15pm), 1pm (change at Basel to EuroCity, change at Mannheim, ar. 5:15pm), 2pm (change at Basel to EuroCity, ar. 6:15pm), 3pm (change at Basel, ar. 7:15pm) and 4pm (chg. at Basel to EuroCity & at Mannheim, ar. 8:15pm).
To Geneva, leave at 3 minutes past the hour 7:03am to 9:03pm. 56 minutes.
To Lucerne, leave at one minute past the hour from 7:01am to 10:01pm and 11:11pm. Trip is 49 minutes.
To Munich, leave at 7:07am EuroCity (ar. 11:24am), 9:39am (ar. 2:04pm), 12:39pm EuroCity (ar. 5:04pm), 3:39pm (ar. 8:09pm) and 6:39pm EuroCity (ar. 11:04pm).
To Paris Gare de l'Est, leave at 7am EuroCity (ar. 12:59pm), 11:37am (change at Basel, ar. 6:05pm), 3pm EuroCity not Sa (ar. 9:16pm) and 10:37pm (ar. 6:48am).
To Salzburg, leave at 7:23am (change at Feldkirch, ar. 1:36pm), 9:34am EuroCity (ar. 3:36pm), 11:34am EuroCity (ar. 5:36pm), 1:34pm EuroCity (ar. 7:35pm).
To Venice, leave at 7:07am (is rapido in Italy, ar. 3pm), 8:07am EuroCity (change at Milan to Rapido, ar. 3:50pm), 10:07am EuroCity (change at Milan to Rapido, ar. 5:50pm) and 11:07am (change at Milan, ar. 7pm).
To Vienna, leave at 7:23am (change at Feldkirch, ar. 5pm), 9:34am EuroCity (ar. 5pm), 11:34 EuroCity (ar. 9pm) and 9:34pm (ar. 8:35am).
To Zug (direction Lucerne), trains leave at one minute past the hour from 7:01am to 11:11pm. Trip is 27 minutes.

ZUG Situated on the main rail line 27 minutes from Zurich and 20 minutes from Lucerne, Zug makes a good base for touring. The charming town itself has an interesting old quarter showing remnants oftowers and other fortifications. **Camping Innere Lorzenallmend** is on the Zuger See (lake), a little under 2 km. from the station. Most people walk, but there is a bus. Open May 1-October 4; adult/4.40SF, tent/4SF. The camp is directly on the lake, has excellent restrooms, hot water in all sinks, automatic washer, store and snack bar.

   To Lucerne, trains leave at 7:12am, 7:30am and on the half hour to 10:30pm and then 11:40pm and 12:22pm.

   To Zurich, trains leave at 6:05am, 6:32am, 6:55am, 7:05am, 7:32am, 7:53am, 8:32am and 32 minutes past the hour to 10:32pm and then 11:15pm.

   To Italy, Zug is on the direct route from Zurich that goes by way of the St. Gotthard tunnel. Trains for Milan leave at 7:35am (ar. 11:25am, ar. Genoa 1:42pm--change for Sestri Levante), 8:35am EuroCity (ar. 12:35pm), 10:35am EuroCity (ar. 2:35pm), 11:35am (ar. 3:35pm, ar. Genoa 5:42pm--change for Sestri Levante), 3:26pm (ar. 7:25pm) and 4:35pm EuroCity (ar. 8:30pm).

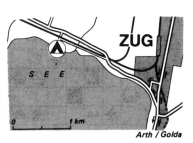

Arth / Goldu

CHUR (THE GRISONS)

Chur is the capital of the Grisons. Many scenic narrow gauge railways in this area are included in Eurailpasses. Because the area is away from the main rail and road routes, fewer vacationers come here. The tourist office is outside the train station. Camping is available in Chur, or camps closer to the trains stations are in the small villages of Thusis and charming Arosa.

   Camping Obere Au is by the Rhein River a little over 2 km. from the train station. Open all year; adult/4.60SF, tent/3SF, tax.65SF. Walk, or take bus 2 (fare 1SF) which originates at the station and ride to the last stop, Sportanlage Obere Au, an athletic complex. Then continue toward the river, a 5-minute walk. Buses leave the station M-Sa 6:48am-6:40pm, Su 9:35am-5:30pm. Service is about every 15 minutes. Buses return from Sportanlage Obere Au M-Sa 7:05am-6:53pm, Su 9:50am-5:45pm. The camp has very good restrooms with private sink compartments having hot water, hot water in dishwashing and laundry sinks, automatic washer, store and dayroom.

THUSIS If you take the train to Thusis, the fine campground there is only a 500-meter walk from the station. A scenic narrow gauge railway which is included in Eurailpasses goes between Chur, Reichenau, Thusis, Tiefencastel, Filisur, Bergun, Bever, Samedan, Celerina and St. Moritz. Departures from Chur are at 6:45am, 8:03am, 8:57am, 9:43am, 10:57am, 11:43am, 11:17am, 12:57pm, 1:43pm, 2:57pm, 3:43pm, 4:57pm, 5:17pm, 5:43pm, 6:57pm, 7:57pm and 8:47pm Friday only. From Chur to Thusis only, trains also leave at 10:17pm and 11:17pm. The distance to Thusis is 30 minutes, to St. Moritz, 2 hours.

   Camping Rheinau is on the river 500 meters from the station. From the station, walk forward to the river, turn left and walk along the river to camp. Open May 1-Sept 30; adult/3.80SF, tent/3SF, tax.30SF, includes hot water. Excellent facilities including individual sink cubicles with hot water, hot water in dishwashing and laundry sinks, automatic washer and store.

AROSA There is also a campground within walking distance in delightful Arosa, or this would make an excellent day trip from Chur. Arosa is so far off the beaten path that it's never crowded with tourists. The 26 km. to Arosa is covered by narrow gauge railway, free with Eurailpasses. The scenic trip takes 62 minutes. Trains leave Chur at 6:31am, 8:15am, 8:50am and at 50 minutes past each hour until 10:50pm. Trains return to Chur at 6am, 6:45am, 8am and on each hour until 9pm.

The campground in Arosa is open Jun 15-Oct 15, charges adult/5SF, tent/2SF including tax, has hot water in restroom and dishwashing sinks. Walk from the station. In Arosa an easy "squirrel path" (*Eichhornliweg*) through the woods leads to rural Maran.

CHUR TO DISENTIS Another scenic railway included in Eurailpasses is the narrow gauge train to Disentis. This is the first leg of the scenic route from Chur to Zermatt. The remainder is not covered by Eurailpasses. Trains leave Chur at 8:07am, 8:52am (Glacier Express, reservation required), 9:47am, 10:48am (Glacier Express, reservation required), 11:47am, 12:25pm (Glacier Express, reservation required), 12:47pm, 2:47pm and 4:47pm. The train stops at Reichenau, Ilanz and Trun and arrives at Disentis 1-1/2 hours later.

LANDQUART-KLOSTERS-DAVOS-FILISUR This scenic narrow gauge rail line is included in Eurailpass. Trains leave Filisur for the 70-km. trip at 8:09am and 9 minutes past the hour until 4:09pm and then 5:09pm Jun 20-Oct 18, 6:09pm, and 7:09pm F & Su only. Trip is 2 hours.

ST. MORITZ-BERNINA-TIRANO AND ON TO MILAN This scenic narrow gauge line free with Eurailpass is 61 km. and takes 2.5 hours. Trains leave St. Moritz at 7:35am, 9:03am, 10:40am, 11:35am, 1:40pm, 2:40pm, 3:40pm and 4:43pm. From Tirano, a 3-hour regular train ride carries passengers 156 km. to Milan. Trains leave Tirano for Milan at 7:02am, 9:02am, 11:38am, 1:34am, 2:18pm, 3:21pm, 5:02pm Sunday only, 6:43pm and 8:32pm.

TICINO - LUGANO

What? Palm trees in Switzerland? Once over St. Gotthard pass, the canton of Ticino (pronounced tee-CHEE-no) emerges. This is where southern Europe begins. Its warm climate makes Lugano (pronounced lu-GAH-no) the best best for a stop in Switzerland during May or October when the northern parts of Switzerland may be too cool to camp. The largest town in Ticino, Lugano combines a beautiful lakeside situation, Swiss solidity, Italian effervescence and a charming old quarter with cobbled streets replete with worn stone grooves from cart wheels. A funicular (cogwheel railway) connects Stazione FFS with downtown. Fare is .50SF. Bus 9 from the station follows the route, Paradise, city center, La Santa and Viganello. Bus 10 takes the same route in reverse. **Trains** go south to Italy and north further into Switzerland about twice an hour on this busy route.

No campgrounds are in Lugano, but several are in nearby towns. Five are at **Agno**, the fourth town on the train line from Lugano to Ponte Tresa. Trains leave every 20 minutes for the 15-minute ride; last trains about 11pm. The campgrounds are about a 5 to 10-minute walk in the direction of the lake from Agno station. They charge about adult/5SF, tent 3-5SF. **Maroggia**, between Lugano and Mendrisio on the Gotthard train line has several convenient campgrounds.

FRENCH

Good day	Bonjour	(bohn-**zhoor**)
Good envening	Bonsoir	(bohn-**swah**)
Goodbye	Au revoir	(aw-ruh-**vwar**)
Yes, no	Oui*, Non*	(we), (nor'n)
Please	S'il vous plait*	(seel-voo-**play**)
Thank you	Merci*	(mayr-**see**)
How much?	Combien?	(kawn-be-**ahn**)
Where is?	Ou est?	(oo-a) as in you-hay
I would like	Je voudrais	(zjhuh-voo-**dray**)
Do you go to?	Allez-vous vers?	(allay-voo-ver)
Camping	Camping	(kahn-peeng)
Toilet	Toilette	(twah-**leht**)
Market	Marche	(mar-**shay**)

What is this called?   Comment appelez vous cerci?
(ko-mahn tah-play-voo sessee?)

Is it within walking distance?   Est-il possible d'y aller a pied?
(eel po-**seebl** dah-**lay** ah pee-a?)

Thank you, that was a very good meal.*   Merci, c'etait tres bon.*
append monsieur, madame or mademoiselle   (mayr-**see**, say-**tay** tray bawng)

1	un	(uhn)	6	six	(sees)	11	onze	(awnz)
2	deux	(duh)	7	sept	(set)	12	douze	(dooze)
3	trois	(twah)	8	huit	(weet)	13	treize	(trehz)
4	quatre	(caht)	9	neuf	(nuff)	14	quatorze	(kah-**torz**)
5	cinq	(sank)	10	dix	(dees)	15	quinze	(cans)

100 grams cent gramme   (sahnt grahm)

service compris	service included
l'eau du robinet	tap water
eau potable (oh potahbl)	tap water
lait (leh)	milk
pain (pang)	bread
pain complet (pang kawn-pleh)	whole grain bread
beurre (burr)	butter
oeuf (urf)	egg
potage	soup
crudites	raw marinated vegetables
chauds	hot
froids	cold
assiette de charcuterie	assorted coldcuts
salade	salad
laitue	lettuce
tomate	tomato
poisson	fish
quenelle	fish mousse (superb!)
anguille	eel
fruits de mer	seafood
poulet	chicken
coq au vin	chicken in wine sauce
boeuf	beef

bifteck	steak	haricots verts	green beans
hache	hamburger	choucroute	sauerkraut
pot-au-feu	beef stew	riz	rice
veau	veal	en croute	in pastry crust
porc	porc	fromage du pays	local cheese
jambon	ham	fromage du chevre	goat cheese
saucisse	sausage	glace (glass)	ice cream
foie	liver	creme chantilly	whipped cream
legumes	vegetables	fraises	strawberries
petit pois	peas	framboise	raspberry
champignon	mushrooms	pomme	apple
pommes frites	french fries	peche	peach
pommes de terre	potatoes		

GERMAN

W is pronounced as V. Many German words are pronounced much the
same as our English, such as butter, fisch, glas, tee and kaffee.

Good day	Guten tag	(**goo**-ten-tawk)
Goodbye	Auf wiedersehn	(owff-**vee**-dayr-zayn)
Yes, no	Ja, nein	(yah, nine)
Please	Bitte	(**bit**-tuh)
Thank you	Danke schon	(**dawhn**-keh shen)
How much?	Wieviel kostet?	(vee-**feel kaw**-stet)
Where is?	Wo ist?	(voh eest)
I would like	Iche mochte	(ik mersh-tah)
Do you go to?	Gehen sie nach?	(gay-en-see nark)
Toilet	Toilette	(**toy**-letteh)
What is this called?	Wie Heisst das?	(vee highst dahss?)

1	eins	(eintz)	6	sechs	(zecks)	11	elf	(elf)
2	zwei	(tzvai)	7	sieben	(zeeben)	12	zwolf	(tzverlf)
3	drei	(dry)	8	acht	(ahkht)	13	dreizehn	(dry-tsayn)
4	vier	(fear)	9	neun	(noyn)	14	vierzehn	(fewnf-tsayn)
5	funf	(fewnf)	10	zehn	(tsayn)	15	funfzehn	(fewnf-tsayn)

wasser (vahs-ser)	water	schweinefleisch	pork
brot	bread	schweinebraten	roast pork
schwarzbrot	rye bread	schinken	ham
suppe	soup	wurst	sausage
vorgerichte	appetizers	lever	liver
salat	salad	aufschnitt	cold cuts
kopsalat	lettuce salad	aal	eel
gemischter	mixed salad	thun fisch	tuna fish
gurkensalat	cucumber salad	gemuse	vegetables
huhn	chicken	erbsen	peas
brathuhn	roast chicken	pilze	mushrooms
rindfleisch	beef	kohl	cabbage
rinderbraten	roast beef	kartoffeln	potatoes
Deutsches beefsteak	hamburger steak	grune bohnen	green beans
kalbfleisch	veal		

GREEK

Hello (how do you do)	(pooze ees thay)	1	(ay nuh)
Good day (how do you do)	(ka-li-mer-a) (ka	2	(dee oh)
Yes, no	(nay, oh he)	3	(tree oh)
Please	(pah-ra kah-**loh**)	4	(tess er-ruh)
Thank you	(eff-hahr-ee-**stow**)	5	(pen tay)
How much?	(po-so)	6	(ex he)
Where is?	(poo eeneh)	7	(ep tuh)
Toilet	(meros)	8	(ok toe)
Market	(ah **gor**-rah)	9	(enn tay uh)
What is this called?	(poss leh-yeh-teh ah-u-to)	10	(decks)

I am having a wonderful time. (ta pare now or ray ah)

water	(nee-**roh**)	sinagrid	bream (fish)
mezedakia, meze	appetizers	barbouni	mullet
	olives cheese, sausage	arni	lamb
melitzanossalata	eggplant salad	kotopoulo	chicken
lathera	marinated vegetables	moussaka	casserole
avgolemeno	egg and lemon soup	pastitsi	casserole
fassolada	bean soup	dolmas	stuffed grape leaves
marides	smelt	youvarlakia	casserole
kalimari	baby squid		

ITALIAN

Good day	Buon giorno	(bwahn **jor**-noh)
Goodbye	Ciao	(chow)
Goodbye	Arrivederla	(ah-ree-va-dair-lah)
Yes, no	Si, no	(see, no)
Please	Per favore	(payr fah-**vor**-ay)
Excuse me	Permiso	(payr-**me**-sew)
Thank you	Grazie	(**gzahts**-zee)
How much?	Quanto	(**kwan**-toh)
Where is?	Dov'e	(doh-vay)
Do you go to?	Dov'e vay	(doh-vay var-ee)
Market	Mercado	(mayr-**cot**-toe)
Toilet	Gabinetto	(gah-be-**net**-toe)
What is this called?	Come si chiama questo?	
	(kol-may see kee-all-may koo-**ayss**-toe)	

I am having a wonderful time. Mi diverto molto.
(me dee-vair-toh mohl-toh)

aqua (**ah**-quah)	water	burro	butter
l'aqua naturale	tap water	zuppa, brodo	soup
(**ah**-kwa nah-toor-**all**-av)		antipasto, struzzichini	appetizers
latte	milk	insalata	salad
pane	bread	pollo	chicken

carni di manzo	beef	melanzana	eggplant
vitello	veal	funghi	mushrooms
vitello cotolett	veal cutlet	patate	potatoes
vitello al forno	roast veal	fagiolini	green beans
carne di maiale	pork	pomodori	tomatoes
prosciutto	ham	riso, risotto	rice
salsiccia	sausage		
fegato	liver	formaggio della regione	local cheese
legume, verdura	vegetables	formaggio di capra	goat cheese
carcioti	artichokes	gelato	ice cream
piselli	peas	panna montata	whipped cream

SPANISH

Good day	Buenos dias	(bway-nose dee-ahs)
Goodbye	Adios	(ah-dee-ohs)
Yes, no	Si, no	(see, noh)
Please	Por favor	(pore-fah-bore)
Thank you	Gracias	(grah-thee-ahs)
How much?	Cuanto?	(kwahn-toe)
Where is?	Donde esta'	(dohn-day es-tah)
I would like	Quiero	(kee-yer-oh)
Do you go to?	Va usted a'	(var oos-ted ah)
Toilet	Retrete	(ray-tray-tay)
What is this called?	Como se llama esto?	(ko-mo say-yah-ma ayss-toe)
I am having a good time.	Me estoy divirtiendo mucho.	
		(may ess-toy dee-ver-tee-end-do moo-choh)

aqua (ah-quah)	water		
la aqua del grifo	tap water	legumbres	vegetables
leche (lay-chay)	milk	alcachofas	artichokes
pan	bread	guisantes	peas
mantequilla		barenjena	eggplant
(mawn-tay-key-ya)	butter	patatas	potatoes
sopa	soup	judias verdes	green beans
entremeses	appetizers	arroz	rice
hot	calientes		
cold	frios	queso	cheese
atun	tuna	queso de cabra	goat cheese
pollo	chicken	helado (a-lah-doh)	ice cream
carne de vaca	beef	nata	whipped cream
filete	steak		
albondigas	meatballs		
ternera	veal		
chuletas	veal cutlets		
cerdo	pork		
jamon	ham		
salchicha	sausage		
higado	liver		

DANISH

J is pronounced as a Y. In Danish, Norwegian and Swedish, the definite article is placed after the noun: en mann means a man, but the man is mannen.

Good day	God dag	(go th-day)	1	en	(een)
Goodbye	Farvel	(fahr-vel)	2	to	(toe)
Yes, no	Ja, nej	(ya, nigh)	3	tre	(tray)
Please	Vaer saa god	(vayr saw go)	4	fire	(fee-rah)
Thank you	Tak	(tahk)	5	fem	(fem)

6	seks	(secks)	11	elve	(el-vuh)
7	syv	(sue)	12	tolv	(tahlv)
8	otte	(oh-tuh)	13	tretten	(trett-un)
9	ni	(nee)	14	fjorten	(fyawr-tun)
10	tj	(tee)	15	femten	(fem-tun)

vand	water	kylling, hons	chicken
maelk	milk	svinekotelet	pork chop
franskbrod	white bread	kalvesteg	roast veal
rugbrod	rye bread	kodbuller	meatballs
smor	butter	stegt	fried
aeg	egg	ovnstegt	roasted
		kartofler	potatoes
sild	herring	kartoffelmos	mashed potatoes
cod	torsk	Franske kartofler	french fries
helleflynder	halibut		

FINNISH

Good morning	Hyvaa huomenta	(who-vahh who-men-teh)
Good evening	Hyvaa iltaa	(who-vahh ill-tah
Yes, no	Kylla, ei	(cool-lah, a)
Please	Ole	
Thank you	Kiitos	(key-eat-ohs)
Sir, Mr.	Herra	(hair-rah)
Mrs.	Rouva	(row-vah)
Miss	Neiti	(nay-tee)
Excuse me	Anteeksi	(awn-tek-see)
Goodbye	Nakemiin	(knack-eh-me-een)
I don't understand	En puhu suomea·	(en poo-hoo swo-may)

NORWEGIAN

Good day	God day	(goo dog)
Goodbye	Adjo	(ah-yer)
Yes, no	Ja, nei	(yah, nay)

Please	Var do god	(vair suh goo-duh)
Thank you	Mange takk	(mahng-un tahk)

1	en	(ayn)	6	seks	(secks)	11	elleve	(all-vuh)
2	to	(toh)	7	syv	(soo-eva)	12	tolv	(tahl)
3	tre	(tree)	8	otte	(ah-tuh)	13	tretten	(tret-uhn)
4	fire	(free-ruh)	9	ni	(nee)	14	fjorten	(fyawr-tun)
5	fem	(fem)	10	ti	(tee)	15	femten	(fem-tun)

vann	water	rostbiff	roast beef
melk	milk	svinekotelett	pork chop
franskbrod	white bread	lammestek	roast lamb
rugbrod	rye bread	erter	peas
smor	butter	sopp	mushrooms
egg	egg	poteter	potatoes
sild	herring	potetpure	mashed potatoes
al	eel	kokte	boiled potatoes
torsk	cod	bonner	green beans
halibut	kveite	tomater	tomatoes
kylling, hons	chicken	ris	rice
kjottboller	meatballs		

SWEDISH

Good day	God dag	(goo dah)
Goodbye	Adjo	(ah-**yer**)
Yes, no	Ja, nej	(yah, nay)
Please	Var snalloch	(var snell
Thank you	Tack sa mycket	(tahk sah micket)
How much?	Hur mycket kostar?	(hur micket **ko**-star)
Where is?	Var ar	(var air)
I would like	Jag vill ha	(yog vil ha)
Toilet	Toaletten	(too-ah-**lah**-ten)
To your health!	Skal!	(skol!)

I am having a good time. Jag har trevligt. (yog hahr tray-uh-vleekt)

vatten	water	kyckling, hons	chicken
mjolk	milk	kottbullar	tiny meatballs
vitt brod	white bread	kottfars	hamburger
knackebrod	Swedish bread	flaskkotlett	pork chops
smor	butter	bruna boner med flesk	
agg	egg		brown beans with pork
		rodbetor	beets
stromming	fresh herring	arter	peas
stekt stromming	fried smelt	svamp	mushrooms
flundra	flounder	kokt	boiled potatoes
torsk	cod	brutna bonor	green beans
al	eel	ris	rice

QUESTIONNAIRE

Dear European Traveler,

      To try to better serve future European travelers, we would greatly appreciate your opinion as to what types of information you would like more of and what could be omitted. We also are interested in learning about you and your trip.

What is your age_____, sex_____, and occupation_____

How many days were you in Europe?_____ Which months? _____

Who did you travel with? (circle) Alone   Spouse   Friend   Family

Excluding air and train fare, what did your trip cost? $_____ for ___ people.

What rail pass did you purchase? _____

Please rank the following topics in order of value to you with a 1 indicating greatest value.

Campground directions	Sightseeing
Campground information	Day trips
Campground prices	Food
Train schedules	Point-to-point rail prices
Hiking	Free activities
Small villages	What to pack
Boat schedules	Maps
Planning an itinerary	Other_____
Other_____	Other_____

What would you like more of and what new information would you suggest be included in the next edition?

What was your favorite city, town or resort? _____

Why? _____

What would you have left out if you knew before your trip what you know now?

What would you have done differently?

How did you learn of this book? _____

Please mail to Lenore Baken, Ariel Publications, 14417 SE 19th Place, Bellevue, WA 98007. **Thank you.**